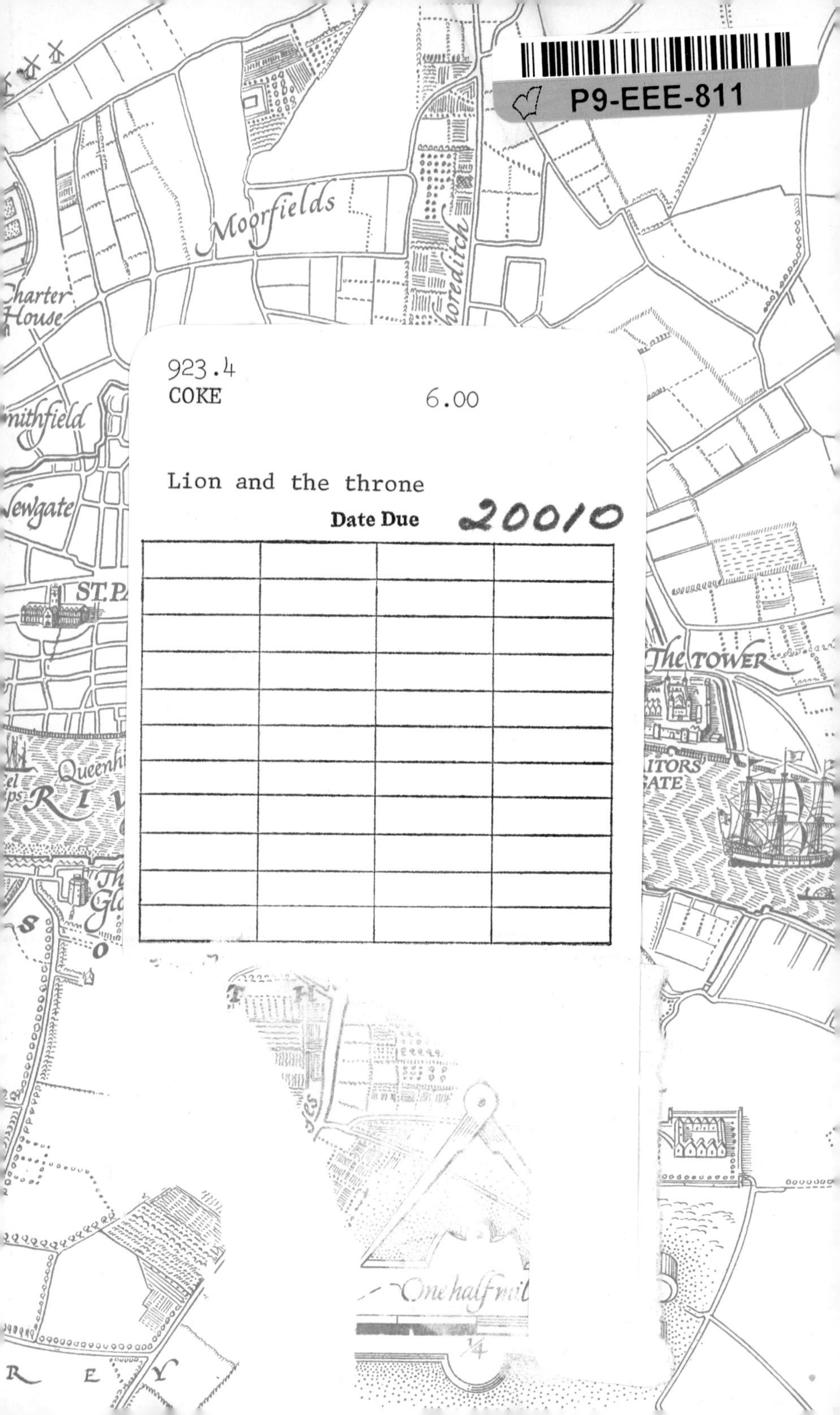
P9-EEE-811
Moorfields
The TOWER
923.4
COKE
6.00
Lion and the throne
Date Due
20010

Books by

CATHERINE DRINKER BOWEN

FRIENDS AND FIDDLERS

BELOVED FRIEND

The Story of Tchaikowsky and Nadejda von Meck

(IN COLLABORATION WITH B. VON MECK)

FREE ARTIST

The Story of Anton and Nicholas Rubenstein

YANKEE FROM OLYMPUS

Justice Holmes and His Family

JOHN ADAMS AND THE AMERICAN REVOLUTION

THE WRITING OF BIOGRAPHY

THE LION AND THE THRONE

The Life and Times of Sir Edward Coke

The Lion and the Throne

Edward Coke as Attorney General, aged forty-one

Portrait attributed to Cornelius Jansen. Reprinted with the kind permission of the Earl of Leicester and Country Life.

THE LION *and* THE THRONE

The Life and Times of Sir Edward Coke

(1552–1634)

CATHERINE DRINKER BOWEN

AN ATLANTIC MONTHLY PRESS BOOK

Boston · LITTLE, BROWN AND COMPANY · *Toronto*

LIBRARY OF CONGRESS CATALOG CARD NO. 56–10656

FIRST EDITION

ATLANTIC–LITTLE, BROWN BOOKS
ARE PUBLISHED BY
LITTLE, BROWN AND COMPANY
IN ASSOCIATION WITH
THE ATLANTIC MONTHLY PRESS

Published simultaneously in Canada
by Little, Brown & Company (Canada) Limited

PRINTED IN THE UNITED STATES OF AMERICA

FOR

HAROLD OBER

PREFACE

SIR Edward Coke — Lord Coke, his contemporaries called him — was Queen Elizabeth's Attorney General and Chief Justice under James, first Stuart King of England. I have written his biography as the last of three, following those of Justice Oliver Wendell Holmes of the United States Supreme Court and John Adams, our second President. Coke's name presented itself quite naturally as a rounding out, carrying the story of our form of free government back to England, where it had its inception.

Reading the pronouncements of Justice Holmes, his brief history of the common law, we glimpse this English background of our Constitution. Reading John Adams on the *Canon and Feudal Law* we see it plainly. Adams, seeking to break with England, found his inspiration in English books on law and government, books written in London, Sussex, Hampshire. To the Continental Congress in Philadelphia, to the Boston Sons of Liberty, John Adams quoted Locke, Harrington, Sir Edward Coke, calling England to bear witness against England.

Coke's life covered a long span, a wide arc of time; with him the Middle Ages ended and today began. Coke was English law personified. The volumes that he wrote — *Reports* and *Institutes, Commentary upon Littleton* — remained for nearly three centuries the backlog of legal studies in England and America. Such a career is looked on as quiet, philosophic. Coke's life was no more retired than a buccaneer's. He was a handsome country gentleman who married — in succession — two beautiful young wives, endowed with land, estate and the pound sterling. Coke was above all a fighter, a born advocate who loved to feel the courtroom floor beneath his feet. Raucous, witty, ruthless, he made puns on the prisoners' names, cracked broad jokes in Latin, and, at the trials of the Earl of Essex, Sir Walter Ralegh and the Gunpowder plotters, lashed out in bitter, shocking invective.

The world remembers this harshness, forgetting that Elizabeth's Attorney General moved within the framework of a time when judges and commissioners for trial showed themselves equally biased and, considering the position, even more merciless than the prosecutor. Coke's later life lifted him into a category altogether different. From Elizabeth's Attorney General to James's Chief Justice is a natural transition. But from state prosecutor to wholehearted Commons man, defender of free speech and parliamentary privilege, is almost a transmutation. As Judge and leader of the Commons, Coke risked his life for the very principles he seems at first to have betrayed, principles which today we take for granted: a prisoner's right to public trial and the writ of habeas corpus, a man's right not to be jailed without cause shown, his right against self-crimination in a court of law. When Coke was seventy, James I imprisoned him for these same championships, locked him in the Tower of London until it appeared more politic to set him free, "because he had become an oracle amongst the people." In 1628, at the age of seventy-six, Coke was prime champion of the Petition of Right, which served as model for our Revolutionary forefathers and which has been called one of the three great documents of English liberty. Through Coke we see the Commons gather strength, begin to cast their votes as they wish, not as they are told, devise that potent instrument — familiar in our halls of Congress — the committee of the whole.

Sir Edward Coke never set foot on American soil. Yet no United States citizen can read his story without a sense of immediate recognition. In these parliamentary struggles, knights, citizens and burgesses fought not for themselves alone but for states as yet unformed: Pennsylvania, Virginia, California. In Westminster courtroom battles over procedure, jurisdiction, "right reason and the common law," constitutional government found its way to birth. When the time came we changed the face of this English constitution; amid the sound of guns we repudiated what we hated, adapted what we liked. Yet the heritage endured.

CONTENTS

PART II

The Judgeship

PART I

Parliament Man and Attorney General 1552-1606

CHAPTER ONE

1593. The Scene.

> London oweth its greatness, under God's divine Providence, to the well-conditioned river of Thames.
>
> THOMAS FULLER, *Worthies of England*

THE tide runs in from the North Sea, flowing westward toward London, past Tilbury and Gravesend, past Greenwich Palace and the docks of Deptford, where high-pooped ships, scarred from long voyages, crowd in for repairs. Against the city wall to the northward, the Tower rises; the river laps at its ramparts, swells and pushes through the long teeth of Traitors' Gate. On London Bridge a hundred windowpanes reflect the light, while far below the tide boils through the arches. Even a Queen's barge must wait till ebb to shoot the Bridge, and men have been drowned for their impatience. The high, clumsy foreign carracks cannot pass at all; they circle and shift on the Tower side or lie at anchor, waiting to unload their cargoes. But the royal swans sail through in flocks, arching their wings as if they owned the river. Where the Bridge touches Southwark banks a massive gateway is crowned with towers, round, crenelated. Here in times of danger and rebellion, traitors' heads are set out on long poles for the populace to see.

And now the houses crowd and jumble within the city walls, spilling down to the waterside. On Ludgate Hill, Paul's Church looms high and bulky; its broken tower lacks a steeple. West of Paul's beyond the City limits the long garden of the Temple law school reaches to the river. Wharves and water gates are busy with people boarding ferries for the north-south crossing (there are no bridges west of London Bridge), or stepping into private craft to be rowed upstream to Westminster, a mile's journey. The Strand being what it is — slippery cobbles or muddy country track — the Thames is London's highway. Peers and dignitaries whose mansions line the water beyond the west wall of the city — these have their private barges, stylish affairs with crests lacquered on the bow and three sets of oarsmen at the least. Lesser citizens hire a wherry and waterman for the trip or simply pay a penny for a seat in the pinnaces which sail from London to Westminster. At Charing Cross, halfway in the journey, the river makes a deep bend toward the south. Here the Queen's palace of Whitehall fronts the water and though it is set back, with gardens toward St. James's Park, the tide has a way of oozing through the stones and flooding the Queen's kitchen until the fires go out and the beef appears at table somewhat raw.

Past Whitehall and Scotland Yard the Abbey comes in sight, the tower of St. Margaret's and the busy cluster of roof and turret, gable, shop, dwelling house and tavern which make up the city of Westminster. It is more town than city, actually, grouped close about the ancient Palace of Westminster, which houses the government and the law courts and which is itself a vast huddle of buildings, grown, through the centuries, any which way at the water's edge. There is the Painted Chamber, supposed to have been the bedroom of Edward the Confessor. It is said he died looking on these painted walls, but no one knows if it is really true. The Painted Chamber is sometimes used for Parliament on opening day, when Lords and Commons meet in the Queen's presence to receive her greetings and instructions before they part to do business in their separate Houses. The Commons Chamber is nearby in St. Stephen's Chapel, an upper-floor establishment where some five hundred members crowd like cards in a pack, sitting face to face in the choir stalls as if they were going to sing. But they make no complaint; the chapel is their own and as such they cherish it. Edward VI gave it to them, the Commons have sat here only forty years. Before that they assembled where they could — at the Monastery of Blackfriars in London or in the Chapter House of the nearby Abbey.

The Painted Chamber and the Commons Chamber, the Court of Requests where the Masters sit to hear poor men's petitions . . . the Prince's Chambers, where ancient kings withdrew to robe themselves for ceremony. And joining it, door to door, the House of Lords, built long ago by Henry III on the foundations of a still earlier building and known also as the Parliament Chamber, though this has become a grave misnomer, seeing that the Commons, an intrinsic part of Parliament, meet elsewhere. But old names cling and old customs; the English prefer adaptation to demolishment. The Lords have chosen to sit upstairs where the light is better, using their ground floor, once a king's kitchen, as a cellar to store coals (a handy place to lay a train of gunpowder, as Guy Fawkes will discover). The Star Chamber, too, is in the Palace precincts, an unpretentious building with five gables, fronting directly on the river and noticeably shabby. The stone doorway is crumbling and, inside, the golden stars are faded on the painted, ancient ceiling.

These chambers and chapels and courts are all of them connected by passageway, inner court or cellar to that central structure which towers over them and which is the original reason for their existence — Westminster Great Hall. It is the biggest hall in England and the oldest. The Conqueror's son put it up to show what a powerful rich king he was. It measured two hundred and fifty feet from end to end and seventy feet across, with a ceiling so high it could scarcely be seen in the gloom, besides which it was so cold that when men entered they put on their hats and coats instead of taking them off. William Rufus was killed in the forest before he could finish his project. But his Great Hall keeps its name, it is the "New" palace, even after Richard II rebuilds it and leaves his white hart couchant as a sign around the molding. Kings make use of the Hall for feasts and parliaments and even royal tennis courts and lose their balls high up among the hammer beams, where wooden angels fly face down above the dusty air.

In this place of gloom and echo, the law courts meet in term time as they have met since the thirteenth century.* The Hall is not partitioned but looms wide open from end to end. On the right hand by the arched entrance door is the court of Common Pleas, where civil suits are heard — cases of land or contract between man and man. "The pillow whereon the attorney doth rest his head," Edward Coke calls this court; and indeed it is in Common Pleas that lawyers find their living. At the upper, far end of the Hall, the court of King's Bench sits to settle pleas of

* Chapter Note.

the Crown — breaches of the King's peace, treason, murders, felonies. Here the Attorney General holds forth, whose name is terrible to offenders. Across the Hall in the southeast corner is the Court of Chancery, where the Lord Chancellor presides, flanked by his Master of Rolls and Masters of Chancery.

So filled and taken up is this old Hall with courts that its name has become a synonym for law. If a man is in trouble, people say that "Westminster Hall" will absolve him or "Westminster Hall" will prove his guilt. Anyone may come in and watch these legal shows. In term time* the Hall is a moving, jostling, noisy throng — jailers with their prisoners, attorneys, barristers and clients, solicitors hanging in the shadows looking for business, vendors of books, of paper, ink and food, the general public and an eternal army of law clerks carrying rolls of parchment to and from the cellar (known locally as Hell), where the legal records are kept. Among lawyers it is a matter of conjecture if Westminster Hall smells worse in summer when it is hot or in winter when it is cold and the public brings its rheums and agues and breathes them out behind closed doors. The Lord Chancellor comes to court with a nosegay of herbs in hand, marjoram or verbena to ward off infection.

The House of Commons is almost next door. Between the Court of Chancery and King's Bench, a broad flight of stone steps with a door at the top leads directly to the Commons lobby. When the House sits, there is a continual coming and going of lawyers between courtrooms and Commons, to the discomfiture of the Speaker, whose business it is to keep members in the House, not lose them to the pursuit of private affairs. But a lawyer whose case comes up is a mouse that smells the cheese; nothing can hold him. The lobby door opens, the voice of the Court Crier echoes from the Hall . . . *Oyez! Oyez!*. . . . The barristers are out and down the steps. In his book the Speaker notes their names for a fine and a remonstrance.

* There were four court terms a year, known (as today) by the church festivals which fall nearest them:

Michaelmas:	October 9 to November 28.
Hilary:	January 23 to February 21.
Easter:	from 18 days after Easter to Monday after Ascension Day.
Trinity:	from Wednesday after Trinity Sunday till Wednesday fortnight after.

This winter of 1593, Edward Coke of Norfolk counted himself fortunate in that the Queen had named him Speaker of her Commons for the ensuing session, called for February nineteenth. Coke was forty-one. The appointment would interfere, of course, with his law practice, which no lawyer likes to see disturbed after building it up, with infinite pains, to something like security and competence. The Speaker's pay was negligible, a hundred pounds for seven or eight weeks of backbreaking labor. If a session lasted over two legal terms, the Queen might pay what she called *double hire* to Speakers who were practicing lawyers; if especially pleased she might "reward" with something extra. On the other hand there were perquisites — fees from the boroughs for proposing private bills (five pounds for each bill before the first public reading), gratuities from city aldermen and corporations whose interests the Speaker had furthered — a purse of gold, six yards of Venetian velvet. *Free gifts,* these were called, and it was all quite open and acknowledged in the ledgers. Official salaries being what they were, Elizabeth's officers of state, from the Lord Treasurer down, lived on perquisites or starved; the Crown simply had not the money to support the whole vast government machinery. Everyone was aware of it and came to Westminster Hall with his hand in his pocket, prepared to pay his share of expenses.

Edward Coke walked gingerly on the edges of this system, being by nature no courtier and disliking the entanglements of gratitude, whether to one's Queen or one's constituents. His present election to the Commons (he sat as Knight from Norfolk) had been, he said, "free and spontaneous, *nullo contradicente,* without solicitation or seeking on my part." Happily, he could afford this attitude of independence. In the fifteen years since his admission to the bar, Coke had had marked success in his profession, besides which he had managed to marry a wife with thirty thousand pounds of dowry. He had served as Recorder, or legal adviser and magistrate, for Coventry, Norwich, and finally for London itself. No doubt it was Coke's ability to win cases which had prompted Elizabeth, in June of 1592, to name him as Solicitor General, second in command to Attorney General Sir Thomas Egerton. Royalty, like everyone else, prefers to have the best lawyers on its side. Coke held the office only six months, resigning when he was named Speaker. But as no one was appointed in his stead, there was the pleasant supposition that the Solicitorship would wait for him until Parliament rose in the spring.

Apart from his success as advocate, Coke had a growing reputation as a scholar. His lectures at the schools of law were well attended and though it was agreed his performance was more learned than scintillating — still, a name for wit is a doubtful asset to a man just entering public life. Coke, who could be funny if he chose, preferred, on the lecture platform, to hammer away at Littleton's *Tenures* or the *Statute of Uses*, which had been the subject of his last set of summer readings at the Inns of Court. Coke was a ravenous searcher after old parchment when it concerned the law and the origins of government. In charter and forgotten treaty, in the precedents of ancient law courts and Norman *parlements* were to be found, he said, the seeds and principles of English liberty. It was not too much, therefore, to rise by candlelight, seek out such law students as could be entrapped and read aloud to them — in Latin, of course — from Magna Carta. Latin, with law French, was the language of the courts. As a young man, Coke had won his first case by catching the opposing lawyer in a mistake of translation. It was a libel suit and the lawyer had carelessly referred to the statute of *Scandalum Magnatum* not in the ancient original but a faulty English translation. The story pointed an excellent moral for students who tended to look on classical scholarship as something apart from the realities of life and of legal business.

A lawyer with this double set of interests was well suited to be Speaker of the Commons. His experience in practical advocacy and the courts would enable him to face with equanimity a large body of vociferous talkers; his scholarship would add authority. Coke's insight as historian should gain, on the other hand, new depth and perspective from the vantage point of the Chair. The Speaker was responsible for procedure. And none knew better than Coke that in Parliament as in the law courts, procedure was vitally important to the liberties of the electorate. When a bill came to the vote, how were the voices counted? Should the Noes keep their seats during the count, and had the Speaker himself a vote? Small matters, but they could make the difference between freedom and tyranny, between an independent Commons and a Commons controlled by faction or by clique. In the previous Parliament (1589), Coke, sitting as Burgess from Aldeburgh in Suffolk, had noted these things, noted also how the Speaker's attitude and bearing affected every corner of the House. He had acquired a rare and helpful little book, still in manuscript. *Modus Tenendi Parliamentum*, it was called; *The Manner of Holding Parliaments*. It would be convenient to have at hand during sessions. And though Coke considered it more ancient than it later proved to be, its rules were clear and explicit. In such matters men prefer the authority of print. Coke himself confessed to the scholar's adage of *non lego non credo* — if I don't read it I don't believe it.

The Speaker was one of three officials who were paid by the Crown (the others were the Clerk and the Sergeant-at-Arms, who carried the mace). Yet the Commons considered that the Speaker belonged to them; he was their voice. It was for him to withstand any encroachment by the Lords' Chamber, for him to uphold the jealously guarded rights — freedom of speech, freedom from arrest — which were known as *the privileges of the House*. The Speaker was, in short, the servant of both Crown and Commons and ran the double risk of him who serves two masters. But a double prize might also be gained. A man who kept his wits about him, and his courage, carried with him in the end the friendship and confidence of Queen and Commons both.

Coke had already been out to Hampton Court to receive the Queen's notification and kiss the royal hand. There remained the formality of public election by the Commons and the more exciting ceremony of the oration before Lords and Queen, when the Speaker declares himself unworthy until his sovereign shall give public assent and encouragement. Neither event constituted actual hazard; the Commons' vote had already been ascertained in a private canvass by the leaders of the House. The ceremony of the Queen's *enabling*, as it was called, was a question of writing one's speech and getting it by heart so as not to stumble on the great day. Before and after speaking, three low congees must be made to the throne, a performance which had been badly fumbled by more than one encumbent — what with clasping the scroll in the left hand, a hat in the right, and the imminent danger of banging one's head against the bar of Parliament at the low point of obeisance.

But whether Parliament was formally opened, this year, in the Painted Chamber or the House of Lords, the fact was that Commoners would stand throughout the ceremony and Lords would sit; Commoners' hats would be in their hands while the Lords' heads remained covered. The Commons, moreover, were not permitted to move forward beyond the wooden bar of Parliament that stretched from wall to wall at the far end from the throne. By tradition they were mere *invités*, summoned by the Queen as she sat with her Great Council of Lords Spiritual (the Bishops), Lords Temporal (the peers) and Honorable Judges. Considering that Commoners must vote the tax money for which Parliament was called in the first place, considering also that Commoners outnumbered Lords fivefold, there was a touch of irony in these arrangements and the Commoners were beginning to feel it. They had even a suspicion that the Lords conspired to make it worse and humiliate them in various small ways. On opening day it was Elizabeth's custom to come down from Whitehall about noon, proceed to the Abbey for a preliminary service, then cross the square to Westminster Palace in all the pageantry of flags, trumpets, cheering crowds, and assume her place on the throne before Lords and Bishops. Not until then did she send Black Rod, her messenger, to fetch the Commons, who waited in their own Chamber.

But Black Rod had a way of being slow or he did not start soon enough. By the time the Commons, crowding through the long passages of Westminster Palace, reached the Lords' Chamber and pushed through the door to a narrow space allotted behind the bar, the Lord Chancellor's opening speech was apt to be half finished. The Commons resented it. They were jealous of slights put upon them by the Upper House, and though time was — centuries of time — when they dared not say so, they had begun to dare it now. In the past hundred years the House had not only doubled in numbers but the quality of membership had altered. Professional men, lawyers, royal officials, ambitious younger sons of peers sought seats, even contested them. It was a momentous change and was to have momentous consequences. In pre-Tudor days it had been looked on as a calamity to be sent to Parliament. To leave one's farm or shop or tavern and ride halfway across England, merely to vote a tax against one's community — what was gained but tired buttocks and an empty purse? Country communities could scarcely find cash to pay the parliamentary wages of their constituents: four shillings a day for knights, two shillings for burgesses, let alone provide an animal for the member to ride to London. Frequently, a man was elected simply because he owned a horse and was robust enough to endure a long journey over bad roads in winter weather. Boroughs bargained desperately with their electees, paid them in corn or red herring. Two knights from Oxfordshire fled the country on hearing of their election. Torrington in Devon managed to secure by charter perpetual exemption from representation in all Parliaments henceforth.

Queen Elizabeth was sparing of Parliaments. Since her accession (1558) she had called only eight, careful each time to explain the necessity. "What," her shrewd Secretary of State, Sir Thomas Smith, had written, "can a commonwealth desire more than peace, liberty, quietness, little taking of their money, few parliaments?" But that had been thirty years ago, before the great victory over Spain in '88, before Drake's voyages and Ralegh's — before England, in short, had begun to feel her strength. In this last decade of the century there was a restlessness among the people, a reaching out, an impatience with the old Queen's authority. Commoners were loyal to Elizabeth. Yet plain men had begun to see that with proper management and stiff backbones, something could be got out of Parliaments as well as something everlastingly poured in.

The trick was to withhold the subsidy, the tax vote, until the Commons' own demands had been met — no easy maneuver against a Queen who combined the Tudor flair for politics with her own devious habits of delay, caprice and a wily instinct for gaining a whole victory by a half retreat. England had been afraid of Henry VIII; it was afraid of his daughter. Yet father and daughter, when they planned some daring policy for England, liked to see it accomplished in the name of law and the legislature. Before Henry tore England finally from the papal authority, his famous Reformation Parliament was kept sitting, off and on, for the unprecedented space of seven years — creating statutes to dissolve the monasteries, statutes to punish rebellious priests and pardon submissive priests, statutes to *Abolish diversity in Opinions*. . . .

Elizabeth was, if possible, a more skillful politician than her father. Perhaps she had need to be. She saw to it that a number of her own men — members of her Privy Council * — were elected to

* Chapter Note.

each new Commons. These sat in front benches by the Speaker, ready to rise on occasion and make known the royal will, ready also to keep their mistress discreetly informed. The traditional right of secrecy was one of the Commons' most cherished illusions. No sooner did they rise at noon than somebody from the front benches made a path, it would seem, to the royal presence. Elizabeth had a genuine, abiding love for England. When she told her people she would give her life for them, they knew she meant it. She had also an instinctive understanding of English needs and English hearts, being herself, by birth and inclination, wholly insular. Such Spaniards and Frenchmen as were found about her court, she tolerated for her own skillful purposes of diplomacy. Elizabeth had never crossed the Channel, never left England. She knew her country from the shires, where in summer she went on progress, to the Tower, where as a girl she had suffered bitterest imprisonment.

But love is one thing and statecraft is another. Elizabeth respected her Commons — but she had no intention of letting them encroach on her prerogative. To initiate legislation was the business of Crown and Privy Council. The Commons' role was a supporting one, and if the Lower House had got hold of some other notion, they must be set right. Elizabeth never failed to be in London throughout parliamentary sessions. Her curiosity concerning bills proposed and speeches rendered was equaled only by her impatience to have the thing over and done before the Commons slipped out of hand as they had shown signs of doing in late years. "What," she had demanded of one Speaker toward the end of a particularly stubborn session, "has passed in the Commons?"

"If it please your Majesty, seven weeks," John Popham replied smoothly. The Commons heard of it and took pride in their Speaker. It was not easy to parry Majesty with a quip.

Such were the factions, such the scene and such the royal philosophy when Coke took upon himself the Speakership in 1593.

CHAPTER TWO

Thursday, February 22, 1593. Queen Elizabeth opens her Eighth Parliament.

> This Court is aptly resembled to a clock which hath within it many wheels and many motions; all as well the lesser as the greater must move; but after their proper manner, place and motion; if the motion of the lesser be hindered, it will hinder the motion of the greater.
>
> COKE, "The High Court of Parliament" (*Fourth Institute*)

YOUR Majesty's most loving subjects, the Knights, Citizens and Burgesses of the House of Commons, have nominated me, your Grace's poor servant and subject, to be their Speaker. . . ."

Edward Coke stood beyond the bar of Parliament and addressed his sovereign on her throne, according to the ancient custom. Between him and Majesty there stretched the length of the Lords' Chamber, filled, this February afternoon, with a most brilliant assemblage — peers, judges, bishops and archbishops, cousins of the blood royal and members of the Queen's Household, sitting each in his place according to his degree. Robes of velvet trailed the checkered floor; fur-lined hoods hung down behind, velvet caps sat snug on chilly noble ears. A winter light came pale through the south windows, a heavy arras stirred against the walls with the eternal draft of palaces.

Behind their rail, Coke's colleagues milled and jostled round him, as many as could squeeze in the narrow space between bar and door. They wore their ordinary dress of doublet, long hose and swirling, hip-length cloak. Four hundred and sixty-two had been elected to this Commons; the Lords' Chamber could not hold half that number. New members or unimportant small shop-keeping burgesses gave place to citizen representatives from London, grandees like Ralegh or Sir John Fortescue, whose house kept seventy servants; brilliant young leaders of the Commons such as Francis Bacon and Sir Robert Cecil the hunchback, who had lately been knighted and whose father, Lord Treasurer Burghley, sat with the peers.

The Commons knew well enough why this Parliament had been called. It was to vote money, the fat taxation which could not be commanded; the Crown could only recite the realm's necessity and hope for the best. On Monday last, Lord Keeper Puckering had delivered, in the Queen's name, a most eloquent description of the need for national defense — armies to be mustered, navies built. Such matters could not be financed by private loans nor from the Queen's private resources. Her Majesty, said Puckering, had even sold a part of her crown to pay for her subjects' defense! Because an Invincible Armada had been routed five years ago, did Parliament imagine the malice and power of Spain diluted? On the contrary, defeat served to whet the enemy's ambition. If England could not be conquered by pitched battle from the Channel, King Philip would attempt it by land and sea together, through strategy, a seeping in of conspirators through Scotland, Ireland and Spanish bases in the Low Countries. Her Majesty had reason to know that Philip was building ships — not clumsy, like his last armada, but swift, more like the French frigates. There was no time to lose.

Behind their rail the Commons heard and reserved judgment; the Crown, on these occasions, knew how to make a case. Members desired to know more. If the threat were so imminent, why had not war been declared upon Spain? Taxes, even though voted, were hard to collect. Open war would make collection easier. . . . The Commons recalled that the Lord Keeper's tone had sharpened, toward the end. It was her Majesty's pleasure the session be spent wholly for the cause described. No new laws and statutes need be made; enough of these existed already. Nor were members to delight themselves "in long orations, full of verbosity and of vain ostentation, the good hours lost through idle speeches." In other words, let the Commons get on with the subsidy and back to their homes and their businesses, as good subjects should. Old Parliament men had heard this kind of talk before; there were those who murmured under it.

This afternoon the Commons heard a humbler voice. Their Speaker could not protest the royal dicta and the House was aware of it; the "disabling" oration was by tradition a mere convention, a flowery supplication. Officially, Coke would not even be Speaker until Majesty "enabled" him. With that accomplished, there might be opportunity for a politic word or two if the Speaker was skillful and took quick advantage. Coke's voice emerged full and vigorous, though sweetened, at the moment, with an unnatural unction. "Yet this their nomination is only as yet a nomination and no election, until your Majesty giveth allowance and approbation. For as in the heavens a star is but *opacum corpus* until it have received light from the sun, so stand I *corpus opacum*, a mute body, until your Highness's bright shining wisdom hath looked upon me and allowed me. . . ."

On his square footstool, Coke stood out above the crowd, a noticeably handsome man, tall, big-boned, inclined to spareness. His face was oval and a trifle long; between mustache and pointed short beard the lower lip showed full and red. Dark hair, cut even with the ears, had as yet no trace of gray but had begun to recede at the temples, accentuating the height of his forehead. Coke's eyebrows were heavy and smooth, his complexion somewhat swarthy; there were few lines to his face. His eyes, large, dark, and brilliant, bore the watchful look of a man ambitious and self-contained. He wore the heavy Speaker's robe with style; for one with a scholar's reputation, Coke was remarkably well turned out. The ruff at his neck was wide, meticulously fluted and starched uncomfortably high; when he lifted his hand the gown fell back to show a sleeve fashionably puffed and quilted. On his left thumb he wore a heavy golden ring.

Remote and dazzling upon her throne, Elizabeth waited. Although the room was small, majesty removed her. Over her head a canopy glittered; the lion pranced and the dragon, holding the shield of England. A little behind the throne, at the left, Sir Robert Cecil's father sat in his box — old Lord Treasurer Burghley, the man whom Elizabeth trusted above anyone in England. His gray beard, cut square, flowed over his ruff; a gold chain of office hung about his shoulders. Under the wide black cap his calm shrewd eyes surveyed the chamber. Of those who held office under the Queen, there were few who were not beholden to Burghley. Through his hands went preferment, plan and treasure. Coke himself already owed to Burghley much of his opportunity.

For fifty years, Burghley had served Elizabeth — as Princess and Queen; he had weathered faction, plot and treason since the time of young Edward VI. He was deeply, strongly Protestant. Yet when Catholic Mary Tudor became Queen in '53, Burghley had not gone into exile with the others, to live in Strasbourg or Geneva, translate the Bible and pray for the death of a Spanish-hearted Queen. Instead, he had stayed in London, making himself of service as best he could, sitting in Mary's Parliament of '55 and even traveling officially to Brussels to bring home a cardinal, in the vain hope of reconciliation with Rome. He was possessed of a patience inexhaustible, amounting to genius. "It's commonly a good blade that bends well," he said. No rival, no palace favorite had been able to displace him, though more than one had tried. A Leicester, a Hatton, a Ralegh might come and go; Burghley remained. England's enemies spoke of him with respect. He had an intricate system of foreign intelligence which amounted to an army and for which he paid from his own purse; he was said to know the number of sailors on every Spanish warship. Italian agents, French diplomats, referred sourly to England as "Burghley's Commonwealth." The old gentleman suffered from gout; he was the only man to whom Elizabeth offered a chair in the presence chamber. "My Lord," she told him, "we make use of you not for your legs but for your head."

Even a Speaker not easily intimidated might look on this as no easy audience. In the exact center of the chamber, red-cushioned seats* — woolsacks — formed a square where sat the Honorable Judges . . . old Chief Justice Anderson of Common Pleas with his lined and rugged face, his coif set slightly crooked . . . Chief Justice Popham of King's Bench, heavy-shouldered, corpulent, numbered among the hanging judges, merciless to whores and cutpurses. . . . Lord Keeper Puckering had left the Chancellor's woolsack to stand beside the Queen, it being his business, on these occasions, to serve as her official mouth — unless, as sometimes hap-

* Chapter Note.

pened, Elizabeth chose to rise from her throne and make one of her brief, extraordinary addresses, scolding or commending according to her mood. There was no telling, today, what she would do. Even in Paul's Church she had been known to disagree loudly with the preacher in mid-sentence, calling roughly to him from her place.

A lesser hazard lay directly in Coke's line of vision, where the Masters in Chancery presented four eloquent, gowned backs. Should the Speaker slip in his quoting of the law civil or common, they would pounce like hawks. One of them was old Lambarde the antiquary, who had written the famous treatise on *Justices of the Peace;* Coke used it in his law courses. Behind the Masters, four clerks knelt on the floor, leaning their tablets on the woolsacks to write. Their long robes dragged across the marble.

"How great a charge this is," Coke was saying, "to be the mouth of such a body as your whole Commons represent, to utter what is spoken, *grandia regni,* my small experience, being a poor professor of the law, can tell."

Edward Coke was well aware that a lawyer, in this company of earls and archbishops, stood socially where a barber might stand in a company of physicians. *Scant-born gentlemen,* the aristocracy called them. (One Speaker, in his oration, apologized because his bearing was "lawyer-like and of the common fashion.") Yet lawyers were coming up in the world, and to the old nobility their rise was more than a little disturbing. Among the Commons were sixty practicing barristers; nearly half the House had a legal education, whether or not they chose to use it. Lord Keeper* Sir John Puckering was himself a lawyer and immensely rich; the Queen did not disdain his hospitality when she went on progress. Yet Puckering was a man of obscure birth; the Queen had knighted him for her convenience. "Heavy, lawyer-like and ungenteel," men said of Puckering. Fifty years ago it was not thus; old Lord Hunsdon could recall a day when blood counted in the government of England.

"But how unable I am to do this office," Coke continued, "my present speech doth tell, that of a number of this House I am most

* Lord Keeper of the Great Seal is the same office as Lord Chancellor. But when Elizabeth chose to appoint a man of common birth, she called him Lord Keeper, rather than the more distinguished title of Lord Chancellor.

unfit. For amongst them are many grave, many learned, many deep wise men, and those of ripe judgments. But I am an untimely fruit, not yet ripe, but a bud, scarcely blossomed. So as I fear me your Majesty will say, *Neglecta frugi eliguntur folia:* amongst so many fair fruit, ye have plucked a shaken leaf."

The picture of Edward Coke, at forty-odd, as a shaking leaf, a bud scarce blossomed, must have diverted the assemblage; this was not a self-effacing man. Yet the Lower House contained many who outranked him; this Commons would not be easy to control. The Queen's great captains, Ralegh and Sir Francis Drake, who sat for Plymouth, were more accustomed to give orders than to receive them; at sea their meals were served to the sound of trumpets, like a king's. Sir Edward Stafford, member for Winchester, had been ambassador to France. Sir Henry Unton put his birth so high that he had challenged the Duke of Guise himself to a duel for speaking "lightly and over-boldly" of Queen Elizabeth. Old Sir Francis Knollys had sat in Parliaments — he said — since 1534 and knew more rules of procedure than were written in the *Modus Tenendi.* Peter Wentworth the Puritan was sure to make trouble. An angry patriot, for the past twenty years Wentworth had been in and out of the Tower, his brother Paul with him, for talking too much. Moreover, this Commons included at least five Serjeants-at-Law, bearers of a legal rank which Coke coveted and would not attain for thirteen years. A mere barrister must show deference to the Serjeant's coif.

Coke's disabling oration was nearly done. Actually, it had been brief. "If I may be so bold," Coke finished, "as to remember a speech (which I cannot forget) used in the last Parliament in your Majesty's own mouth, 'Many come hither *ad consulendum, qui nesciunt quid sit consulendum*' [Many come hither to consult, who are ignorant of the matters under consultation] — a just reprehension to many as to myself also. But howsoever I know myself the meanest, and inferior unto all that ever were before me in this place, yet in faithfulness of service and dutifulness of love, I think not myself inferior to any that ever were before me. And amidst my many imperfections, yet this is my comfort; I never knew any in this place, but if your Majesty gave them favor, God, who called them to the place, gave them also the blessing to discharge it."

Coke bowed and stepped from his footstool. Lord Keeper Puckering, after consultation with the Queen, came forward and addressed Coke down the length of the chamber. Her Majesty, he said, had thought well of her Solicitor General since first she heard of him. Yet this his "modest, wise and well composed speech" had given her further cause of approval. And whereas Mr. Speaker thought himself *corpus opacum,* her Majesty now *enlightened* him, and not only enabled him, but much thanked the Lower House and commended their discretion in making so good a choice.

With these words, the Commons saw their Speaker allowed, approved, commended, invested. What followed was more serious and would concern them all. "Proceed in your office!" Puckering commanded. Coke stepped again upon his platform, to reply gravely, now, concerning the reasons for this Parliament, the danger from foreign foes and the unexampled peace the realm had enjoyed during the present glorious reign, during which no enemy had been able to set foot on English shores. Out of the statutes, he could prove, Coke said, how kings of England had maintained for three hundred years sovereignty in their dominion even over the Pope.

Such a sentiment, to a Protestant Commons, was good news and, to the Queen, gratifying. Twenty-four years ago, Pius V had excommunicated Elizabeth. Many in the House (Coke included) were old enough to remember that May morning when the Pope's Bull was found tacked to the Bishop of London's door, addressed to "Elizabeth, pretended Queen of England." A person excommunicated was outside the laws, outlawed, as it were, in his own realm. Anciently the thing had been accomplished with solemn ceremony and a tolling of bells. The Bull of 1570 absolved Elizabeth's subjects from obedience to her laws, making them, in effect, citizens of Rome rather than of England, splitting the kingdom into deadly faction and causing deep distress to Catholics who were loyal Englishmen. . . . The Commons were charmed, therefore, to hear this learned Speaker — a man of their own election — turn back three hundred years to prove "our own supremacy excluding the Pope." Without pausing for Majesty's permission, Coke swept, after his fashion, into the statutes aforesaid, beginning with Henry III and reciting chronologically up to Edward VI. Even for those members who understood not one word in ten, the Latin had a magic, sonorous authority.

Concerning the whole body of the English laws, in truth these were so great and many, Coke went on, that already they deserved to be called *elephantinae leges*. For Parliament to make more might indeed seem superfluous, as the Lord Keeper had indicated. Yet the Devil still walked abroad; evil was on the increase. (Here Coke quoted Cicero.) Sharp ordinances must be provided and "all care used for her Majesty's preservation." This was point two, and the Commons did not miss its significance — a hint that it was the business of Parliament to provide laws for the realm. Coke's pleasantries, his careful jocosity had not disguised his meaning. *Her Majesty's preservation:* when the Commons desired to frame statutes against English Catholics or even English noncomformists, they invariably said it was done for "her Majesty's safety," implying that extremists on both sides were ready to murder her in her bed. Since the Commons planned, this session, to pass a law confining all Catholics to a boundary within five miles of their homes, and another law designed to force "seditious sectaries" (nonconformists) into exile, it was as well to hint it tactfully, before business started. The Queen, whose distaste for Puritans was strong, disapproved drastic regulations in religion — not liking, she said, to open windows into men's souls.

Coke prepared, next, to recite the three great petitions to the throne. "Now am I to make unto your Majesty," he said, "three petitions in the name of your Commons: first, that they may have free speech, as of right and by custom they have used, freedom from arrest, and all their ancient and just privileges and liberties allowed them. Secondly, I humbly beseech that if any speech shall fall from me or behavior be found in me, not decent and unfit, that it may not be imputed blame upon the Commons but laid upon me, and pardoned in me. Thirdly, that as often as your Majesty's service and the good of the commonwealth shall require, I may have access to your Majesty." *

Of these famous petitions, the first was looked on as most important — freedom of speech. Their "ancient right," the Commons liked to call it, though actually they had no record of such

* Chapter Note.

a petition as a matter of right previous to Elizabeth's first year. But in seven former Parliaments of Elizabeth, the Commons had urged, through their Speaker, this "ancient" right — and in seven Parliaments the Queen had given grudging, hortatory reply. She gave it now. Her Majesty, proclaimed Puckering, after consultation with the throne, granted "liberal but not licentious speech, liberty therefore but with due limitation. God forbid that any man be afraid to answer Yes or No to bills according to his liking, with freedom to state briefly his reasons." Such, the Queen declared, was the true meaning of "liberty of the House." But should members construe this as freedom to frame a new form of religion and a government of their own devising, let such idle heads look to their peril and their safety, for no king worth his state would suffer such absurdities. . . . Concerning access to her Majesty's person, that also was freely granted — provided it be upon urgent causes and at times convenient. Freedom from arrest was allowed — but let no man employ it as cover for ill doings.

The crowded Commoners listened warily, braced by custom against the royal admonishing hand. Among those who stood behind the rail were five at least whose plans, already formed and written, were in full opposition to this princely exhortation. Yet liberty has its definitions and degrees. Across the Channel, no Third Estate could present such petitions to their sovereign, let alone expect to see them granted, "freedom of speech" being a phrase strange to Spanish tongues, to Italians, Frenchmen. The Commons were aware of it and could take pride even in partial failure. If the right had been grudgingly given, still, it was their right and they dared to urge it. "By these degrees came the house of commons to raise that head which since hath been so high and formidable to their Princes that they have looked pale upon those assemblies." Sixty years later, an Englishman would write it; in the Lords' Chamber were young men who would hear, before they died, of Harrington's mythical Commonwealth of Oceana, conceived within the pages of a book. Oceana, so dangerously like to England yet so dangerously free . . . where ballots were truly secret, where the land was divided equably and the sustenance of many could not be devoured by the few . . . a government, in short, of laws and not of men.

By petition refused or grudgingly granted, by the thoughts of men's minds, the hopes of their spirits, the books that derived from their pens. *By these degrees:* it was a tradition of the island that liberty came slowly, if it was to last.

In the Lords' Chamber, light was gone, the clock in the tower had struck five. It was time to make an end. "And now, Mr. Speaker," Puckering concluded agreeably, "that I may end as I began, with yourself, her Majesty trusteth that you will not commit any thing for which her Majesty should need to grant you such a pardon as you require. And in mine own opinion, your whole carriage of life hath been such hitherto, that I may say unto you, *Noveris intactum vitia servare vigorem* [May you have skill to keep your spirit from corruption]."

At last it was over. In the Queen's name this Parliament had been officially opened, in the Queen's name it was adjourned—"*usque in diem Sabbati prox' futur'*," the Clerk recorded, in his Latin shorthand. As the Queen rose, every man dropped to his knee. With the long train of her mantle held aloft by two noblemen, Elizabeth walked through the door behind the throne and was gone. The Commons, filing out, made their way from upper court and darkening gallery to their own St. Stephen's Chapel, where they took seats. One bill was read, according to custom, and Coke adjourned them. Next Saturday, Lords and Commons would meet in their separate chambers to initiate the practical business of the session.

Outside, the winter dark closed down over Westminster. The ride to London was long in the February cold; local taverns were crowded. Few members could afford, like Puckering, to keep a house near the Palace for convenience in Parliament time. The day had been arduous, the Commons on their feet almost since two o'clock. Their Speaker's role had not been easy. To recite the statutes from Henry III was a telling stroke; it was gratifying to know the Queen had heard it through, nor had she objected to Coke's bit about the need for further legislation. . . . Tomorrow could be a day of rest; by eight on Saturday morning the Speaker must be in his Chair.

Four hundred Commoners scattered . . . to Holborn, Walbrook,

Queenhithe, the wards and fields and liberties of London, tracing their several ways to supper and to bed. Westward the Queen's great barge, at rest by Whitehall water gate, swung with the evening tide.

CHAPTER THREE

The Commons meet in St. Stephen's. Speaker Coke at work.

> The Speaker is their mouth, and trusted by them, and so necessary as the House of Commons cannot sit without him.
>
> COKE, "The High Court of Parliament" (*Fourth Institute*)

BEFORE Coke again set foot inside the Commons Chamber, four members were in prison — Peter Wentworth in the Tower, the others in the Fleet. It was Thursday, February 22, when the Queen had adjourned Parliament. By Saturday night the thing was accomplished — an awesome beginning and for the Speaker most inauspicious.

Wentworth was primarily to blame. On Saturday morning, he and Sir Henry Bromley (son of a former Lord Chancellor) delivered a petition to the Lords, asking them to join in a bill entailing the succession to the Crown — a proposition not only hopeless but foolhardy. Next to the now abandoned subject of her marriage, the succession was the most combustible question a man dared put before Elizabeth. And she would hear of it; no bill passed without the Queen's consent. Since the beginning, Elizabeth had refused to name a successor, having learned the bitter lesson that around any such incumbent factions formed, new loyalties burgeoned and new ambitions, endangering the civil peace. As a young woman she had seen her Hatfield dooryard crowded with courtiers — Spaniards, Englishmen — who had hurried from her dying sister, Queen Mary Tudor, to ride north and prostrate themselves before the rising sun. It was an experience not calculated to soften the heart. Earlier still, as a girl of twenty, Elizabeth had been imprisoned under suspicion of plotting for the throne — taken downriver on Palm Sunday and landed ignominiously at the Traitors' Stairs. She had not expected to emerge alive from the Tower. "Does the Lady Jane's scaffold still stand?" she had asked fearfully. She was hardly on the throne before another Mary (Queen of Scots) began the years of perilous, persistent plotting to displace her. In 1587, Elizabeth signed, with heavy reluctance, the order for Mary's execution; it had required Burghley and the Parliament together to persuade her to the act. Before this was achieved, Elizabeth's own life had been many times endangered.

Every man in Parliament was familiar with these things, aware also that Elizabeth's likeliest successor was James VI of Scotland, Mary Stuart's son, but a Protestant. Catholic hearts cherished other ambitions, looking to that daughter of Philip II who had been Mary Tudor's husband; Isabella of Spain traced her line to John of Gaunt. A fantastic claim — but fantastic things had happened; Peter Wentworth the Puritan saw it as his mission to prevent them. He came to London fully prepared, his petition in his pocket: Elizabeth must name a Protestant successor.

The Queen had had enough of it; this was not Wentworth's first offense. She moved swiftly. That same afternoon of February 24, Wentworth and his three colleagues — Bromley, Stephens, Walshe — were called before the Privy Council, examined and sent to prison. Coke missed the entire performance. On Saturday morning when the Commons met, the Speaker's Chair had been empty; after prayers a messenger brought Coke's apology. He had "been last night and was also this present forenoon so extremely pained with a wind in his stomach and looseness of body, that he could not without his further great peril and danger adventure into the air at this time, which otherwise he would most willingly have done." Coke, in all likelihood, had caught one of the diarrheas — London called them fluxes — which plagued a dirty city. By Monday, happily, he was recovered and in the Chair.

Concerning the Wentworth affair, Coke found members divided. On opening day, the Commons had proudly claimed from the Queen their "ancient privilege" of free speech. Yet here were four members in prison already, for talking too much. Actually, the

privilege covered speech only inside of Parliament; Wentworth's talking had been done outside, in secret meetings along the Strand. Even so, considering the subject he had chosen to discuss, Wentworth had known the risk. Certain cynical members, old Parliament men, went so far as to remark that things might move more smoothly this session, with no Wentworths to launch their passionate factional harangues. Any convinced Puritan, once he got to his feet, could talk the Chamber clock around.

Nevertheless, the matter came very close to Coke. These privileges, these ancient rights were the Speaker's especial care; with his own mouth Coke had petitioned for them. It was his concern to keep watch, therefore, nip rebellion early, before news of it could reach Whitehall. The Commons preferred to see their Speaker rather than their Queen move for the punishment of overimpudent members. In the schedule which lay ahead, the succession question was not the only incendiary matter which might pop up. Including the subsidy, twenty-seven bills were under consideration, ranging from private bills such as *An Act to give liberty to the Lord Harrowden for selling certain of his lands,* to *An Act for the Restraint of new buildings in London.* The city was congested; crime had reached alarming proportions and the streets swarmed with beggars, large numbers of whom were crippled soldiers from the wars. Country burgesses expressed themselves shocked at the sight; a bill had been devised *For the Necessary relief of soldiers and mariners.* There was a bill *For the naturalizing of certain Englishmen's children borne beyond the seas;* there was one *For the bringing in of fresh water to the town of Stonehouse in Devon;* there were numerous acts to control fraudulent marketing, such as a bill *To regulate the breadth of plunket azures and blues* (kinds of cloth), and one *Against deceitful making of cordage.*

It was the Speaker's responsibility to push these measures through the House as fast as possible, leaving room for really important matters, which to the Queen meant the subsidy, and to the Commons, the two religious bills — one *For the restraining of Popish Recusants to some certain place of abode;* the other, against Puritan extremists, an extension of an earlier *Act to retain the Queen's Majesty's subjects in their due obedience.* Neither bill would pass without prolonged and possibly violent debate; if no more members reached the wrong side of the Tower door it would be, as any Speaker could prophesy, short of a miracle. There was no such thing as a quorum, the House voted when ready. The Speaker decided the order of reading bills — which came first and which could wait. When he wished to push a measure through, Coke was not above timing it for early in the morning when attendance was scattered, or toward noon when members were hungry for their dinners and elderly spines drooped. "To make the question when the House is desirous to rise," a diarist put it.

Bills had three readings; the Clerk stood up and intoned each, if it took ten minutes or (as with the subsidy) two hours. After first reading, members could ask to see the bill in the presence of the Clerk or buy a copy from the "writer-out" at a penny for ten lines. After second reading the bill was engrossed (written in legal form by a professional copyist) and debated until Coke decided it was time for the question. If the House said Yes, it was ready, Coke stood up with his hat off, holding the bill high so all could see it. The vote was oral, members simply shouted all at once, Aye! or No! When he doubted which cry was louder, Coke called for a division and the Noes sat still, the Ayes walked to the lobby to be counted by the teller.

It was a procedure which left room for infinite strategy. The Chamber was small and crowded, the floor space only sixty by twenty-eight feet. Four tiers of benches, rising on three sides, left not nearly room enough for everybody. During important debates, members pushed in, standing where they could or even perched on ladders leading to the highest tier. When Coke called for a division, the Ayes, walking out the lobby door, lost their seats to members who had been standing. Weaker souls, who cared more for comfort than for principle, promptly voted No so as to retain their places. Coke did not hesitate to use the strategy for bills he wished to see defeated. Parliamentary diarists remarked Coke's ruthless skill in handling these maneuvers. "The Speaker perceiving the Privy Councilors of the House desirous to have the bill expedited, did over-reach the House in the subtile putting of the Question. . . . Beguiled with the Question propounded by the Speaker . . . The subtlety in propounding the question thus gained the casting away of the bill."

Peter Wentworth had complained that members behaved like

sheep, sitting pat until they saw who went out and who stayed in and then casting their lot with the most important people. "It is common policy in this House to mark the best sort of the same and either to sit or arise with them." And indeed it is hard to blame these malleable ones; there was about this crowded, brilliant assemblage something genuinely terrifying. Many "timorous burgesses," as Coke called them, were known to remain mute throughout the session. Gentlemen farmers, skillful with hawk and hound, might be princes in their counties, but they were not used to meeting face to face a Ralegh, magnificent in velvet and diamonds, a Francis Knollys, a Fortescue, grandees who came direct from the mystery of the royal presence. Even Sir Robert Cecil at times showed awe, unless perhaps his modesty was maneuver. "I speak against my will," he said one day, "and to answer speeches unpremeditated upon the sudden, it is hard for me. . . ." "For myself I am but young," began Oliver St. John the soldier; "it is and hath been the manner of this House to allow a mixture in speaking, and after the grave, honorable and wisest, then to hear the meanest also." It was not permitted to read from script, though notes could be used. "I will be bold to look in my tables," old Fleetwood had said; "I see other men do it." Sheer terror sometimes overcame a speaker, as one Zacharias Locke, who rose, got a few words out, "but for very fear shook, so that he could not proceed, but stood still a while and at length sate down." Yet humble men at times spoke out with surprising bravery, so that Privy Councilors had need of increasing skill to achieve their mistress's royal ends (which in older days was gained by command rather than persuasion). The Speaker, by that same token, had need of such authority as time and heaven had bestowed upon him.

Concerning the division trick, Sir Walter Ralegh confessed openly, with his usual careless arrogance, that he had often held a neighbor by the sleeve when he desired him to vote No. "It was a small matter," he said. Sir Robert Cecil did not agree. Were members dogs, he retorted angrily, to be led "in a string"? Cecil and Ralegh seldom agreed; they were the leaders of two different factions, Ralegh for war with Spain, Cecil for peace. Cecil, at the moment, had decidedly the upper hand. Ralegh was in the Queen's bad graces, having spent six months in prison for getting a lady-in-waiting with child and then aggravating the offense by marrying her secretly. The Queen kept strict watch over the young women of her court; moreover she was fiercely jealous of her favorites. "S. W. R.," a courtier had written gleefully, "now must fall as low as he was high, at the which manie will rejoice. All is alarm and confusion at this discovery of the discoverer, and not indeed of a new continent but of a new incontinent." Ralegh's lady, Elizabeth Throckmorton, went also to the Tower. The two had been released only at Christmas and were still forbidden the court — though it was remarked the Queen had not demoted Sir Walter from his favored position as Captain of her Guard.

It was over such stormy petrels that Coke, six days a week for seven weeks, presided. Old Burghley's son, Sir Robert Cecil, sat just below the Speaker to the left, close enough to lean and whisper — to direct, admonish, urge the Queen's interest, no matter if the House looked angrily upon him or if members rose, as members did, to protest. "This earwig of the Court," contemporaries called Cecil; "his father's own son, whose little crooked person carries a headpiece of vast content." At thirty, Sir Robert Cecil led the Commons as his father (at seventy-three) led the Lords. From the cradle, Burghley had trained this son for statesmanship, sending him to France to learn the ways of courts, pressing him into service wherever he could. And contrary to custom in such cases, the son had not rebelled. This was already the fifth Parliament he had sat in, besides serving four years as the Queen's principal secretary (though without formal title: Elizabeth preferred to keep her younger servants in a salutary suspense).

Cecil's little crooked body was only five feet two; the Queen had given him the nickname of her Pygmy, which, he wrote, "yet seem I only not to mislike because she gives it." The deformity of his hump caused him much bitterness. An observant cousin, Francis Bacon, attributed to it the rapid, extraordinary Cecilian rise to fame; a man deformed was spurred perpetually to raise himself above the world's scorn. The power of these Cecils was astonishing. No less than nineteen of their cousins and connections sat with the Commons, including Robert's older brother Sir Thomas Cecil, old Burghley's heir and early paternal anxiety ("a spending sot, meet to keep a tennis court"). It was a constellation. Coke could not cast his eye down the Chamber without lighting on a Cecil satellite — and most of them men to be reckoned with, like the three Bacons — Nathaniel, lame Anthony and the youngest brother, Francis, who sat for the powerful county of Middlesex.

At thirty-two, Francis Bacon was recognized as a brilliant intellect who carried a vast advantage of birth and connections. His father, Sir Nicholas Bacon, had been Lord Keeper. Lord Treasurer Burghley was his uncle, Sir Robert Cecil his first cousin, and the powerful young Earl of Essex his patron and friend. Bacon had a smooth, insinuating manner which Coke, for all his striving, would never achieve; there was a siren note to Bacon's voice, a magical persuasion. He seemed born with an affinity for authority and was agile at twisting his mood to suit the royal purpose. "Till I think you think otherwise I am bold to think it," he had written to Elizabeth when no more than a youth (and would so write again). It was open knowledge that he had been Coke's rival for the post of Solicitor General last year and would probably put in for the Attorney-Generalship when it fell vacant. Considering Bacon's total inexperience in advocacy, his candidacy was not looked on too seriously. Should the Queen name him over Coke, it would be by virtue of the younger man's powerful friends at court. Between the two there was instinctive antagonism. Their outlooks on life and on the law were antipathetic, the differences the more marked because their interests were close, their careers parallel; they were to aspire to the same offices, the same honors and the same wife. They could not meet in Westminster corridors without bristling, and such words as they exchanged were sharp enough to be noted and set down for posterity.

Coke, who had lived in London for twenty years, was by now well acquainted with Bacons, Cecils, Hobys, Nevilles, Gawdys, Careys, Trelawneys, in all their ramifications of cousinship and political faction. As for the London citizens who sat on the front row right, Coke knew them intimately from his months as City Recorder, knew also that all of these members were ready to urge — and passionately — their several interests, and that it was the Speaker's business to keep peace among them, a not unexacting assignment. Coke had no deputy. Saturdays as well as weekdays he sat in his Chair from eight in the morning until he went downstairs to dinner; Tudor England ate its heavy meal at midday. Afternoons were devoted to committee meetings, and though technically the Speaker could not be on committee, he was often present by invitation and on occasion even took the chair. It was Coke's habit to rise at three in the morning (he went to bed at nine). Sometimes, arriving at Westminster before daylight, he found committees already sitting, huddled in their cloaks and arguing dazedly by candlelight.

There was no library, no room where members could retreat to refresh themselves or smoke a newfangled pipe à la Ralegh, unless they climbed to the Sergeant-at-Arms's cold attic over the lobby or went out to the taverns that clung like barnacles along the front of Westminster Hall. (The oldest of these was known as Heaven.) Committees met where they could — in the Exchequer Chamber, the Court of Wards or in London's Guildhall or some chamber of the law schools. Country members protested, though feebly, this crowded schedule; those lighter spirits who had got themselves elected primarily "to learn and see fashions" simply absented themselves, paid their fines to the Clerk and accepted humbly Coke's "admonishment." It was actually the Speaker and front-row members who bore the brunt of work — the five Privy Councilors, the London citizens, the Serjeants-at-Law who were on nearly every committee. Distinguished lawyer members were often paid to argue for bills. Parliament had begun, centuries ago, as a law court, the *curia regis*. Its title was still the High Court of Parliament. Why should not a barrister accept a fee to argue a case here as in the lesser courtrooms of Westminster?

Hopeful, anxious, daring or stubborn by turn, the Commons crowded day by day into their chapel, an ancient building intended for usages far different. St. Stephen's had once been a king's pride; Henry III had conceived it to rival the Sainte Chapelle in Paris. It was a century in building and when it was done (1365) it was all gold and crimson and heavenly blue, a jewel of bright painted glass and delicate stone tracery. When the Commons acquired it in 1547, they simply moved in, adopting, in thrifty English fashion, what they found — placed the Speaker's Chair on the topmost altar step, the table with the mace where the lectern had been, and sat themselves down, face to face in the choir stalls. As the Commons grew, new tiers of seats were added; between the cross benches at the rear was the bar or rail, like the Lords' rail where Coke had stood on opening day. Behind that in turn, a vaulted door led through the old chapel screen to an antechapel, now a lobby (called by members "the outer room") and noisy with petitioners, supplicants, or lawyers waiting their turn at the bar.

The Commons themselves did not think it strange to use this holy place for meeting. Roman churches had always served for lay purposes. Beside the great pillars in Paul's Church, lawyers met their clients by assignment: the wide aisle served as highway to the street beyond. At one time an ordinance had been posted to forbid donkeys being driven through, or men "shooting with handguns at doves hidden in eaves." A defiantly Protestant Commons may even have felt a joyful pride in dispossessing Rome of so glorious a monument as St. Stephen's. Down from her place had come the gentle gold-crowned Virgin. Around the walls, tapestries or wainscoting hid "idolatrous popish" paintings — beautiful stiff medieval saints, smiling shepherds and little boys playing pipes for Christian lambs to gambol. (The Age of Reason was far away, the age of tolerance yet farther.)

There were no desks. Members wrote with tablet on knee; if a man went to sleep he fell off the bench unless his neighbor's shoulder held him. There were no cupboards for documents and books and no place to hang one's hat. St. Stephen's lacked fireplace and fire; members wore their outdoor clothes and kept warm by mutually generated heat and ruthless shutting out of ventilation. Yet the effect of this crowding proved wonderfully dramatic. Rising to speak, men found themselves face to face with their opponents across a narrow space; nothing separated them but the table with the mace. It followed that swords and spurs must be left outside, and "no reviling or nipping wordes must be used; nevertheless with much doulce and gentle termes they make their reasons the one against the other." So, at least, Sir Thomas Smith had written in 1565.*

* Chapter Note.

CHAPTER FOUR

The Commons at work (continued). The "great bargain," and privileges of the House.

When we have raised the King's supply we may go home like fools, as we came.

A COMMONS MEMBER IN 1666

ON the twenty-second of March, 1593, the subsidy bill came to the vote and "in respect of the greatness of the sum, passed the House of Commons with very great difficulty." Technically, it offered "a treble subsidy and six Fifteenths and Tenths," * amounting, in all, to about £400,000, the largest grant a Commons had ever considered. Debate was heated, ranging into politics, religion and the Queen's prerogative. One man at least — Francis Bacon — all but ruined himself by what he said. That the money was to go for war with Spain had already been established by Lord Keeper Puckering on opening day. But with Elizabeth it went against the grain to declare war. Certain members aimed to force her to it. Ralegh began, in his light voice with the Devon burr: Let a preamble to the subsidy specify "lawful and open war" with Spain. The present situation of war-and-no-war impeded sea fighting. Gentlemen volunteers would come forward in plenty, once the word "piracy" was altered to "lawful seizure of enemy prizes."

The use of a preamble as bargaining point was fairly new; for centuries, preambles had included nothing more than flattery and

* Chapter Note.

humble prayer. ("Petition" was, indeed, the ancient name for a bill.) Members now suggested certain preliminary conditions to their money grant, a haybag dangled before the hungry monarchical nose. Aside from the subsidy bill, there was none among twenty-seven proposed measures which would serve the purpose; Elizabeth would veto them rather than yield. *La Royne s'advisera* — the Queen will think it over — was the traditional phrase of refusal. On closing day in the Lords' Chamber, the title of every bill would be read aloud by the Clerk while the Queen followed closely, paper in hand. Her formal assent came always in French, an ancient custom left over from Norman days, very surprising to foreign visitors. To public bills she said, *La Royne le veult* — the Queen allows it; to private bills, *Soit fait comme il est désiré* — let it be done as desired. For the Commons, the connotation of these various forms was of deep and vital importance (as Coke would one day testify when a Stuart King misused them, seeking to debase a great public measure to the status of a mere private petition.)

The subsidy involved an elaborate ceremony of its own; on closing day the Speaker must carry the bill bodily to the Lords' Chamber and deliver it on a silver tray to the Clerk, who in turn would bear it to the throne and lay it on a table flanked with lighted candles. By tradition the Queen would thank her Commons personally for their "free gift of money." She had been known to rise and spread arms and hands in a melting, gracious curtsy of acceptance.

Meanwhile, in the Commons, the bare word "subsidy" invoked a storm of talk. Sir Thomas Cecil suggested the Cinque Ports be taxed — Dover, Sandwich, Hastings. . . . Did not citizens transfer their households to the Ports, thus evading taxes? The House voted Sir Thomas down. It was now that Francis Bacon began the arguments which were to prove so hazardous to his future. How, he inquired, was this great tax to be collected? Six years was the time usually allowed for garnering a subsidy, and if the Commons proposed to vote the unprecedented sum of three subsidies, he for one could not agree to any plan of payment under six years. Poor men plainly could not pay; they must sell their brass pots and gentlemen their plate. These were hard times — famine times in counties where harvest had been meager; such heavy demands would cause general discontent. Furthermore, should the Commons create so burdensome a precedent, they would lose their ancient tradition of being "not subject, base or taxable." Future sovereigns would seize advantage, looking for sums equal or larger.

"Discontent," in the year 1593, was a dangerous word, carrying implications of active rebellion. In treason trials, a defendant with the reputation of a "discontented man" was lost before the jury retired. Francis Bacon, experienced since boyhood in palace intrigue, should have known his words would reach the Queen. . . . ("Sir Nicholas Bacon's youngest son, of Gray's Inn, declares the Queen's demands will cause discontent among the people. . . . He desires six years for collection. . . . Moreover he refuses to parley with the Lords concerning the bill, though the Lords request it.") Ralegh disagreed vigorously with Bacon; it was wrong to say the tax would cause discontent. And let the House note, added Sir Walter, that he took this position not to please the Queen but because he knew — as Sir Francis Drake knew — the urgency and the danger. Six years for collection? In six years the Spaniard would have a tow-rope to England!

Coke was vigilant and sharp of eye. There was no doubt of his authority, the record is full of it; sometimes he was too severe for the Commons' pleasure. "Mr. Speaker perceiving some men to whisper together, said, that it was not the manner of the House that any should whisper or talk secretly, for here only publick speeches are to be used." Members left their places and attempted to slide unseen from the Chamber, overlooking the Poor Box at the door. "A poor Burgess refused to pay his said Contribution of five shillings, would pay only two shillings sixpence; whereupon the Speaker would have Committed him for disobeying the Order of the said House, but most of the members of the same were against it, and so he escaped." (There was a new clock against the wall, very convenient, the charge to be collected at twelvepence the member.) More serious was the repeated maneuver of the oral vote and the division, wherein members felt they were being shunted about like pawns in a game. During the subsidy debate it came to a head in angry questions to the Speaker. Why should the Ayes have to go to the lobby and the Noes keep their seats? Why could not the Noes go out, for a change?

Coke did not hesitate. "The inventor that will have a new law," he said, "is to go out and bring it in; and they that are for the law in possession must keep the House, for they sit to continue it." This sounded reasonable. The Commons submitted; perhaps their Speaker bolstered it with some ancient rule of procedure; he seemed to have convenient precedents always at his tongue's end. His enemies said he made them up, and in Latin, too. It had been his habit, Coke told the House, since first he practiced law, "to observe strange learning," especially legal rules pertaining to procedure. When he was named Speaker, he began immediately to search after such ancient law as concerned the privileges of the House, judging it would come often into question. He prayed his colleagues to hear him plainly when such questions arose. "Let me not be ill thought of if I be rude in what I say, for it is my fault I cannot speak so mildly as some; but my manner is, that which I speak, I speak sharply and somewhat roundly."

Directness from Edward Coke was as inevitable as patience from old Burghley or deviousness from Francis Bacon. The very set of Coke's head revealed him, the level glance of his eye, the movements of his body, abrupt and quick; upon his shoulder sat the falcon, not the dove. The House, making its rules as it went along, needed decisiveness in the Chair. It was well to have a presiding officer whom few dared answer and who, if unwary members so ventured, countered firmly with some rule of English law.

During one such argument over procedure, a diversion occurred. On Saturday, toward closing time, a total stranger was discovered sitting by the ladder near the lobby door. When asked by astonished members how long he had been there, he replied innocently, "All the forenoon." Dragged indignantly to the bar, "and there being examined by Mr. Speaker: answered his name to be *John Legg*, and that he was Servant to the Earl of Northumberland; and pleading simplicity and ignorance for his excuse, and alledging that he had some business to do with Mr. Doctor Herbert, Master of the Requests, from the Earl his Master, and that therefore he entered into the said House, not thinking any harm nor knowing the danger thereof."

Coke sent him off under guard, bidding the Sergeant-at-Arms keep him closely over the week end. John Legg vanished — but the House was not as when he came. A cooling off was noticeable, a diminution of ardor. Who knew what tales might be carried by this unbidden stranger, and was he really the Earl's servant? On Monday when the House reconvened, Sir Henry Knyvet moved it be made a formal offense for any man to carry reports out of the Chamber. Sir Henry Unton agreed; he "thought this House much injured, that names be given up and noted to the Queen, of parties speaking against the subsidy."

Cecil, by now quite desperate with delay over the subsidy, expressed himself in reckless metaphor. Let "the sentence which hath had so many parentheses now be brought to a period, and the Bear's whelp that hath so many times been licked over, now be made somewhat!" Mr. Wroth, member for Liverpool, broke in with the startling suggestion that before they voted on the subsidy, the Queen be petitioned for the release of all imprisoned members. Might not constituents, otherwise, complain of a tax levied without their voices? The House was much deprived by these absences, "because an instrument, taking away some of its strings, cannot give its pleasant sound."

This was bargaining with a vengeance, no matter how poetically phrased. By now there were not four Commons prisoners but five — James Morrice, Burgess from Colchester, being the latest. A distinguished barrister with a government position — Attorney of the Court of Wards — Morrice had been so foolhardy as to propose a bill abolishing the oath *ex officio* by which Anglican bishops disciplined their lower clergy, forcing them to answer on oath questions which might incriminate them. The general public (the Puritan public especially) hated the oath. Most lay lawyers were against it; Lord Burghley himself had protested the Archbishop's stringent use of it.

But Elizabeth, supreme governor "in spiritual as in temporal causes," would bear no meddling with her bishops; Parliament had already petitioned (1584) against the oath *ex officio* and been refused. The Queen heard of Morrice's petition (it was never revealed who told her) and sent for Coke, bidding him bring the bill to the palace. Morrice was taken to the Tower. Coke in much perturbation made his way to Whitehall, then returned to his colleagues, bearing angry regal messages. "It is in me and my power," the Queen had said, "to call Parliaments. It is in my power to end and determine the same, it is in my power to assent and dissent to anything done in Parliaments." She wondered any could be of "so high commandment," to attempt a thing expressly forbidden; the Commons must not meddle with causes ecclesiastical. "And upon my allegiance," Coke finished, "I am commanded, if any such bill be exhibited, not to read it." The thing was hopeless, as Mr. Wroth of Liverpool no doubt knew when he offered a petition for release of Morrice, together with Peter Wentworth and the others. Five Privy Councilors, from their places in the front benches, signified negation; to press the Queen in this matter "would but hinder them whose good we seek."

When on March twenty-second the subsidy bill came to the vote, it was the preamble rather than the amount which stuck in certain craws. Presented to the House by the committee which had composed it, the preamble was read aloud. Every tooth had been drawn, it was a mere mumbling of the usual flattery. Plainly, the committee had lost its courage. Never, said the preamble, had England been blessed with such a Queen; the Commons would be happy to give their life's blood as it were — with the proviso that so extraordinary a grant be "not drawn a precedent for the times to come." Nothing was said about declaring war on Spain, or indeed about any war "impulsive and offensive." On the contrary, her Majesty was thanked for limiting all conflict, over the decades of her reign, to "only a defensive war for our quiet and prosperous preservation." (The fine hand of the Cecils was evident.) The entire amount must be paid in by November of 1596. But no taxpayer, examined concerning the amount of his income, need swear upon corporal oath (by touching the Bible.) Actually, had the corporal oath been required, the collectors would have got more prisoners for the jails than money for the treasury. Catholics could not swear on a Protestant Bible; Puritans had a dozen reasons for not swearing on sacred relics of any description. At best, collection would be for the government a heartbreaking task, with lamentations pouring in from every town and county — of double charges, unfair rating, everything a man could devise to cut down his share. Aliens had a trick of assigning lands over to their children; if caught they paid double for evasion.

The Commons, when they had heard the preamble, asked time to consider. The front row, at this, shook its composite head.

Coke took the hint. "*But the Speaker perceiving the Privy Councilors of the House desirous to have the bill expedited, did overreach the House in the subtile putting of the Question.*" The thing was done, accomplished. The Queen had her money. Ralegh could only hope for ships of war and captains to command them; the Cecils on their part continued blandly, skillfully to work for peace.

Yet Speaker Coke's business with the Parliament was not more than half completed. There remained a dozen bills on the agenda, important laws of trade such as the bill *Against Alien Strangers retailing their goods in London*, various private bills and the two great religious acts which had been debated, off and on, since the second week of session. Religion touched every facet of politics and trade; religion had run through the subsidy debate like a binding thread. . . . Why, after all, was the Spaniard coming with his warships, if not to change England's religion and set a Catholic king on the throne? In Rome and Madrid, the subjection of this stubborn small island, so shockingly Protestant since Mary Tudor's death — and since '88, so shockingly arrogant — was looked on as more than a conquest. It had become a crusade. "The Enterprise," good Catholics called it, and from Valladolid to Dublin the word passed, carrying overtones of courage, loyalty to the "true faith," and, for those wholly dedicated, the promise of a martyr's crown. In the Jesuit college at Rome, English initiates were taught to rehearse in imagination all possible scenes of torture, interrogation on the rack and the hideous death of a traitor, which they faced if they returned to England as missionaries. Since 1580 these Jesuits had filtered into Dover, the best educated young men of their time, brave and stubborn in their faith. Nobody knew how many "massing priests" circulated in London and the shires. The problem was to catch them; a hundred hands reached out to save and hide. Previous to 1535, every Englishman, after all, had been Catholic born. The ancient faith refused to die. England remained half Catholic in spirit if not in open practice. Since the Pope's Bull against Elizabeth (1570), a man could not be a true Roman Catholic without denying his Queen, his country and his country's laws. Those who could not in conscience take Elizabeth's Oath of Supremacy were known as *recusants*.

Increasingly severe laws had been passed against recusants by previous Parliaments. The English Catholic, already in hopeless case, was thrown by the Act of 1593 into near despair. Its official title was *An Act against Popish Recusants*, but common parlance called it the Five Mile Act. The preamble declared its purpose: "For the better discovering dangerous conspiracies by sundry wicked and seditious persons terming themselves Catholics, and being indeed spies and intelligencers, hiding their most detestable and devilish purposes under a false pretext of religion and conscience." Jails, the bill declared, were too good for recusants; many of them lived better in jail than in their houses. Therefore let them be fenced in at home, confined to an area within five miles of their domiciles, the penalty for disobedience being banishment from the realm. Furthermore, anyone suspected of being a "Jesuit seminary, or massing priest," and refusing to confess it, was liable to indefinite imprisonment "until he shall make direct and true answer to the said questions whereupon he shall be examined."

As first introduced, the bill was even more severe, and the Commons rejected it. The Messrs. Sandys and Dalton desired Puritan recusants as well as Catholics to be included. (The more extreme separatists refused, like Catholics, to take the Oath of Supremacy.) This motion, however, was quashed by Coke, who reminded the House that the act was entitled "Against *Popish* Recusants," not Puritans or sectaries. On Saturday, March 28, the bill passed the House. The second religious bill — against nonconformists — made twice the trouble, barely scraping through. Among English separatists, Brownists and Barrowists (named after their respective originators) were the most powerful. Thousands were newly sprung up. Established Churchmen looked on them as born shouters, fanatically convinced that their particular form of worship alone was righteous; theirs only, the sacred song to which God's ear was tuned. Imprisonment could not silence them nor martrydom discourage; they denounced the Elizabethan prayer book as "old rotten liturgy, rotten stuff to be called prayer." In 1588, the country had been roused by a series of separatist pamphlets, secretly printed, signed "Martin Marprelate" and directed against the Anglican bishops. Raucous pieces, filled with coarse humor and immensely popular, they descended on London in clouds of paper, denouncing all bishops as swinish rabble, "petty popes, proud, presumptuous, paltry, profane, pestilent and pernicious."

Such violence provoked a reaction; in the swing of it Parliament proposed its bill. Irreconcilables must go to prison — or "abjure the realm."

Sir Walter Ralegh, surprisingly, came out for toleration though he did not, of course, use the word, toleration as a political or religious program being as yet unknown. (In Europe as in England, a nation with more than one religion was looked on as critically weakened.) There existed, said Ralegh, at least twenty thousand of these Brownists; no doubt they deserved to be "rooted out of England." Once exiled, however, who was to maintain their wives and children? There was danger that innocent men would be caught in this net. How were the disloyal to be distinguished from the loyal? Laws that punished the fact, he could approve. But laws which punished a man's intention he considered hard. Were juries henceforth to be "judges of men's intentions, judges of what another means?" And on such judgment, were they to take life and send into banishment?

Ralegh's was not the only objection. The bill went into committee. In returning it, Sir Thomas Heneage, the Queen's Vice Chamberlain, advised that further care be taken to avoid "peril of entrapping honest and loyal subjects." On Saturday morning, April seventh, the Privy Council members of the House sent the committee for the bill up to the Sergeant's attic, bidding them stay there (and freeze) till they had reached agreement. Six hours later they reappeared. "We were," a member testified, "content to yield to anything so we might rise. I assure you Sir, a great many of us caught such a faintness there, with so long fasting, having neither meat in our bellies nor wit in our heads that we shall not (I doubt me) be able to make a wise speech there while we live."

By noon on Tuesday, April tenth, all business was concluded. The Queen came late down the river to Westminster. The clock on the Commons' wall said after five; westward the sun's rim touched the Abbey roof. The palace corridors were dim as Coke made his way to the Lords' Chamber, bearing the subsidy bill on its silver salver. On each side of him walked a Privy Councilor, robed and hatted. The door of the Lords' Chamber was shut. At the traditional knock it opened and Coke walked in, his colleagues crowding after him, striving for places at the rail. Coke delivered his burden to the Clerk, then stepped on the footstool and made his three low congees to the throne. "Most High and Mighty Prince!" he said. "The High Court of Parliament is the greatest and most ancient court within this your realm. For before the Conquest in the high places of the West Saxons we read of a Parliament holden, and since the Conquest they have been holden by all your noble predecessors, Kings of England. . . ."

Having got his teeth into history, Coke did not let go until he had explained to his Queen the meaning of *aldermen, knights, burgesses,* the *Convocationhouse of Bishops* and the significance of the royal writ of parliamentary summons. Had he been talking to law students in Fleet Street instead of a monarch and her statesmen, he could not have been more explicit. "*This sweet Council of ours,*" he said, suddenly changing his tone, "I would compare to that sweet Commonwealth of the little bees . . . who have but one governour whom they all serve. They forage abroad, sucking honey from every flower to bring to their King." It was unfortunate that two centuries must pass before the king bee's true sex was discovered; Coke missed a glorious opportunity. Nevertheless he stayed stubbornly in position and milked the ancient metaphor dry. Drones and doorbees must be expelled the hive, and where the spider draweth poison, there the bee must learn not to suck. . . . The new laws which the Parliament had passed, the old laws they had restated, were brought now to her Majesty that life might be breathed into them, especially those laws "to suppress the obstinate recusant and the dangerous sectary, both very pernicious to your government."

It was dark when Coke finished. Beyond a table where the subsidy lay, the Queen sat in candlelight, dim, remote. Through her Lord Keeper she thanked the Commons for "this offer of three subsidies" and accepted in all kindness. Nevertheless, said Puckering, her Majesty considered that more time than necessary had been spent by this Parliament. She misliked it that irreverence had been shown toward her Privy Councilors who sat in the Lower House. These ministers, appointed by herself, were — let the Commons remember — a permanent Council of State, "not to be accounted as common knights or burgesses of the House that are *Councilors but during the Parliament.*"

Ralegh was no Privy Councilor, nor Francis Bacon. Yet both had spoken against Sir Robert Cecil. Like bearded schoolboys they received the royal lash. . . . Elizabeth raised a hand, signifying she was about to speak with her own mouth. The Commoners fell on their knees and the Queen motioned them to rise. "The subsidy you give me I accept thankfully," she said, "if you give me your good will with it. But if the necessity of the time and your preservations did not require it, I would refuse it. But let me tell you, the sum is not so much, but that it is needful for a prince to have so much always lying in her coffers for your defence in time of need, and not be driven to get it when she should use it." For the Commons it was as well they had not bargained too openly, preamble or no preamble. Quite evidently their simple phrase "to be not drawn a precedent for the times to come" had raised the royal temperature. The Queen had more to say, concerning the Spaniard, war, peace, and a subject's duty. Seating herself, at the end, she told Attorney General Egerton to read aloud the titles of all acts; it was after seven and she could not see. The ancient words rang through the Chamber . . . *La Royne le veult. . . . Soit fait comme il est désiré. . . .* Nothing was refused, nothing vetoed. "May God," said the Clerk in French, "grant your Majesty health, happiness and long life."

"Amen!" said Commons, Lords and Bishops. Amen and Amen.

Appraising his own part in a stormy seven weeks' Parliament, Coke could say that he had not lost his head and had kept the legislative wheels turning, which was about all a chairman could accomplish at best. Did not such assemblies invariably rise dissatisfied? Taxes were overlarge or ill-proportioned; acts were looked on as too lenient or too severe according to the personal bias of members. Any statute must be a compromise — or remain unenforceable. The business of James Morrice had been truly melancholy. Coke disapproved the oath *ex officio* and trial by inquisition. Yet if the Cecils could not save a man from the Queen's anger (and Robert Cecil had confessed openly that Morrice was "a learned man whom he loved"), then Edward Coke most certainly could not have attempted it. Morrice, however, had been included in the Queen's General Pardon on closing day. Wentworth remained in the Tower.

Such slight applause as Coke might permit himself concerned no doubt his moments as instructor of a House which, ignorant of its strength, was apt to blunder by overmeekness or overboldness. Yet where, outside of Parliament, could a simple country burgess learn the traditions of the lower Chamber and the privileges he had a right to claim? Not in school or university, certainly. Parliament issued no record of debate, of division or the count of voices. Small wonder that a Ralegh could bully his neighbors out of their votes! There had been a morning when Coke asked leave to tell the House its story — how, anciently, meeting with the Lords, the Commons had not liberty to speak their minds, and so "the House was divided and came to sit asunder." On the king's demanding by what right this move was made, a Commons member replied that each lord (sitting by birth, not election) represented only himself and his land. Whereas the Commons, though by birth and fortune inferior, "every one of them represented a thousand of men."

Yet each one represents a thousand. The statement lay at the heart and root of the Lower House, of its rights and one might justly say, of its pride. The Queen herself did not forget it, even in her most hortatory moments. "The body of this realm," she called the Commons. Not the Third Estate, as in France, but the body of the realm. A day might come when a sovereign of England would choose to overlook this balance and apportionment, so hard won in history. It was well the Commons should be reminded. In his notebook Coke had set down the qualities a Parliament man should have — "properties of the elephant." First, that he possess no gall or envy. Secondly, that he be "constant, inflexible and not to be bowed, or turned from the right, either for fear, reward or favour." Thirdly, he must be of ripe memory, so that, recalling perils past (as they are written in the rolls), he may prevent dangers to come.

There was something yet to add. . . . The elephant goes before, breaking paths that men may follow. *Philanthropos, homini erranti*. . . . Ah, that was it! "Benevolent, he shows wandering men the way."

CHAPTER FIVE

Education of Edward Coke. Burghwood, Norwich and Cambridge.

Norfolk County, the most fruitful nursery of lawyers. On the east and north sides, the German ocean, abounding with fish, beats with a strong tide upon its coast.

CAMDEN'S *Britannia*

EDWARD COKE was a Norfolk man. *Kuke,* his country neighbors called him. He was born in Mileham parish, some twenty-five miles west of Norwich city and a like distance southward from the marshes of Holkham and the North Sea. It is a country harsh, exposed, three quarters of it bounded by open ocean, swept by the Atlantic tides that come down unimpeded from Greenland and the Pole. The twisted trees shrink landward, the sheep huddle under brittle winter hedges. No shire of England has so many windmills or so many churches; the square squat towers are built of Norfolk flint stone and built to last, and most of them were old when Coke was born.

Coke's father could trace his name through five respectable Norfolk generations, commencing with a Roger Cooke of Crostwick. Robert Coke was a barrister, well educated, with a practice in London as well as Norfolk. There were nine children, one of whom died in infancy; Edward Coke grew up with seven sisters. His mother, born Winifred Knightley, was the daughter of a Norwich attorney, descended from the Knightleys of Fawsley, an ancient Northamptonshire family. Edward Coke was born on the first of February, 1552. There is a legend about his birth — that his mother sat downstairs on that cold St. Bridget's Day, warming herself by the fire, when suddenly her body was gripped with a very climax of pain. Before she could get decently upstairs to bed, the boy was born. (Coke told the story himself to his friend Sir Henry Spelman the antiquary, led him through the house and pointed to the spot upon the hearth where the child had fallen.) People seemed to think it characteristic, the strong man-child leaping into the world without warning, giving out his feeble cry of rage and protest.

Robert Coke had rented Burghwood but when his son was born he bought the manor with its sandy, rolling acres, pasture for sheep and the small meager cattle of the region. The boy grew up among country sights and sounds and superstitions. Time was told by the sun or stars. . . . *Charles' wain is over the chimney*. All nature's mysteries had a meaning. Cocks were the enemies of witches, crows could change their sex at will, the magpie was a thief since Noah's time — the only bird that refused to enter the Ark at God's command and therefore to be harried and hunted forever. The unicorn existed, the basilisk and the cockatrice were real as the barnacle-goose of Norfolk, which everybody knew was descended from a shellfish attached to a tree.

Burghwood and the surrounding region was farmed after the ancient fashion, in long narrow strips which followed the contour of the land. After spring planting it was the business of neighboring boys to run along the furrows, shooting with arrow or slingshot at crows which hovered over the seed. For lack of feed, cattle could not be kept through winter; from Christmas to Easter the Cokes lived on salted meat and fish, with such game as could be brought down. In autumn, farmers and landed gentlemen, their artillery strapped to their backs, took horse and with their sons (all things being lucky) behind them on the saddle rode down below Norwich to the marshes where roamed the bustard, mottled black and brown birds as big as three ducks and excellent eating. Young Coke saw a world all water and reeds and rippling cloudy reflection. Bittern and mallard and kingfisher darted and dived, and the gentlemen were divided on the question of dyking and whether the government did well in bringing over Hollanders to drain and fill. (In the western marshes by King's Lynn, Norfolkmen rose against these strangers who ruined the countryside for hunting and took from the poor their rightful food.)

Besides Burghwood and his ancestral patrimony of Sparham and Stiveskey, Robert Coke owned manors at Reepham and Happisburgh — he called it Hazeburg — on the east coast where the cliffs began. It was necessary to visit these holdings occasionally with his bailiff, see that the buildings were in repair and that the tenants were not cheating with the rents. Robert Coke's neighbors knew him for miles around, many had known his father. When he rode by with his son he was greeted as Squire; men touched their caps, prayed him to dismount and eat or drink with them. The Cokes themselves no doubt kept country hospitality; the family connection was large and neighborly: Barshams and Knightleys, Woodhouses, Gawdys, Clippesbys.

Edward Coke learned to read at home, learned also at an early age his Latin accidence. When he was nine, his father died suddenly in London. The boy went off to school at Norwich, living in town (the Free Grammar School did not take boarders) and running each day through dark winter streets as the last bell rang for prayers. The school stood in the Cathedral Close; in pre-Reformation days it had been the carnery of Christ Church priory. Its crypt was filled with paupers' bones and in the vaulted upstairs chapel that was Coke's schoolroom, monks had sung Masses for departed souls.

The scholars numbered a hundred, ninety from the country round, ten from Norwich. In a city of twenty thousand, with only two small private schools as rivals, this meant the Grammar School students were a picked lot. If a boy proved stupid or lazy he was quickly dropped and another, as the records have it, "set in his room." Young aristocrats were tutored at home or taken into some great household such as Lord Burghley's, where Francis Bacon was reared, then sent abroad to Italy or France to learn court manners and court ways. At the Free Grammar School, Coke's mates were the sons of prosperous burghers and landowners, merchants, lawyers, Church of England priests or important guildsmen. There was no advancing in trade — and certainly in the professions — without a knowledge of Latin. Merchants and bailiffs wrote their accounts in the language; Coke had seen his father's estate books so inscribed. Even master mariners must plot their voyages in Latin, and the Constable of the Army his tactics and campaigns. For lawyers the language was of course indispensable, with pleadings written in Latin and court reports in law French — a mixture of three languages. The Free School *Ordinances* had been conceived and written by certain practical-minded citizens assembled in Norwich Guildhall — "Lawes and Statutes for the better educãon and bringing upp of the youth within the Gram̃er Schoole of the Cittie of Norwiche as well in good maners as in godly Lytterature, to the glory of God and profight of the com̃on welth." A Latin and a Greek lexicon were chained to Master Hawe's desk, and in the curriculum, Homer is listed along with Caesar, Sallust, Virgil, Ovid, Cicero, Juvenal, Valerian. There was emphasis on "oratory" and the proper recitation of poems and Ciceronian prose; such English grammar as Coke absorbed he learned from the Latin. When he reached fifth form, his rhetoric books included no English at all . . . Erasmus's *De Copia Verborum,* Linacre's *De Figuris.*

Part of the system was to have the big boys teach the smaller — almost a necessity, with a hundred scholars and only one master. Edward Coke, at fourteen, stood in his vaulted schoolroom and heard the stumbled Latin declensions of small Norfolk Aldriches, Pickerings, Leeds, Townsends. There was a special catechism, written in English by the great John Colet, who had founded St. Paul's School in London:

Fere God (it began)
Love God
Fallynge down dispaire not
Wasshe clene
Be no slogarde
Awake quyckly
Teche that thou hast lerned lovyngly.

Teach lovingly. . . . All his life, Coke would follow this precept.

The school lay almost under the walls of Norwich Cathedral. On Sundays the boys walked two by two in the wide western door and up a nave so long the end was all in shadow. The sermon would be required of the scholars next day, written out in Latin as far as remembered. Instruction was slanted carefully away from

Rome — the New Testament in English to avoid the papal tinge of the Latin Vulgate, the Psalter sung metrically after the Genevan fashion. The Bishop of Norwich himself, John Parkhurst, was a returned Marian exile, one of the scores who had fled England during Mary Tudor's reign, then come home zealous to establish "the true religion." They were serious men, the exiles, with narrow notions of religion and sometimes broad notions of education, like one Norwich rector, who went so far as to declare there should be grammar schools for girls as well as boys — a notion patently ridiculous, so that nothing came of it.

Norfolk's Protestantism was a natural inheritance. The old port of Yarmouth lay across the water from Antwerp and Amsterdam; for nearly a century, Netherlanders and Flemish had sailed across to find refuge from persecution, bringing their religion with them. When Norfolk felt the heavy hand of Mary Tudor, its people in turn sailed east to Holland. It was a Norwich citizen, Matthew Parker, whom Elizabeth chose as her first Archbishop of Canterbury, a man gentle and saintly. When Parker returned to Norwich on episcopal visitation, the boys of the Grammar School saw him, heard him preach.

There is no overestimating the effect of this burning missionary Protestantism on the youth of Edward Coke. Morning and evening the boy knelt with his fellows on the stone schoolroom floor and chanted the Lord's Prayer and the Creed, with some final devotion in English from the recently established Book of Common Prayer. The reiterated words, English and Protestant where, since time immemorial, they had been Latin and Catholic, reached very deep. Coke lived — and died (his daughter was to testify) — a Church of England man, "a deare lover of its Liturgie, constant to it in his life and at his death." Throughout Coke's writings there runs a strong religious note, half Latin, half Norfolk Anglican: "Be chearful and *servite Domino in timore*. . . . Honor God and the Common Laws of England . . . *Favente Deo et auspice Christo*."

The town which spread and grew about Christ Church Cathedral, Coke learned to love and to think of as his. "This famous and free city of Norwich," he wrote proudly in the *Institutes*. Its freedoms he took for granted, its representative council and assembly, the stormy seasonal elections which rocked the county and caused concern as far away as London and Westminster. Actually these freedoms were a phenomenon; Norwich led all English boroughs in political experiment, breaking early from feudality and the usual servile dependence upon local lords and landowners, boasting a fourteenth-century constitution of its own, with a major and sheriffs "elected by the commonalty" instead of appointed by king or duke. Norwich was rich, and (Coke later said) "as large within the walls as London," its twelve gates forever filled with travelers entering and departing. Men in armor, servants and archers wearing the Duke of Norfolk's livery, men with crossbows strapped to their backs and game flung over their saddles . . . sheep being driven to market, pushing and jostling, the herd dogs yapping at their heels. Guildsmen in furred gowns, craftsmen with their tools . . . mud on the roads in spring, dust on the roads in summer when Coke rode home to Burghwood; and in November, fog rolling in from the sea by Yarmouth.

Between town, Grammar School and Cathedral there was close and friendly connection. At Christmas, when Norwich installed its mayor, the ceremony began by the Mayor's visiting the Cathedral, with his aldermen, for prayers. The Grammar School figured large on this occasion, presenting two comedies for which the boys rehearsed all autumn. Any scholar not included in the cast had to write six original Latin verses, sign them and pin them to the Cathedral door, where Mayor and aldermen stopped to read them before entering church. Hero of the day was the Speech-boy, chosen from among the brightest scholars to sit on horseback before the Cathedral and greet the Mayor and aldermen (gorgeous in scarlet and silver trappings) with a Latin oration, while Master Hawe stood by with the prompt book. Afterward, everyone went to the square to watch the whifflers dance in costume around the well; Norwich treated the Free Scholars from house to house and parents lamented because boys drank too much and were "thrown into feavers." The wine was thereupon severely rationed for next year; everybody knew the rules would not hold but set them down piously nonetheless.

Such English history as Coke learned, he picked up perforce outside of school, not in it. To England, "the classics" meant the Greek and Roman classics, which were, with the Bible, all of history and all of literature. (Coke, as a man, read Chaucer and liked to quote the *Tales,* but that was later, when England had begun to feel her national identity.) Yet history hovered over the spires and cobblestones of Norwich. To the southward as Coke emerged from school, there rose on its hill the square white keep of Norwich Castle, called *Blancheflower*, hoary, mysterious, bearing on its walls the arms of Roger Bigod, Earl of Norfolk. North of the Madder Market, another Duke of Norfolk, Thomas Howard, lived in his lovely palace with gardens sloping to the river, a palace always building, never finished, boasting the only covered bowling alley in England, where — the Duke told Queen Elizabeth — he felt himself "great as any king in Scotland." (It was an unfortunate remark; the Howards were Catholics, and the Duke was later to lose his head for his ambitions; he had plotted in 1570 to marry Mary Stuart and put her in Elizabeth's place.)

Over by Yarmouth was another castle, belonging to the Norfolk family of Paston and giving evidence of history more ancient still. Here the Romans had maintained a fort; helmets of the Legion were found buried in the moat. The Romans, as every schoolboy knew, had been driven out of England by Angles and the Angles in turn by Danes, who murdered King Edmund the Martyr, patron saint of Norwich. Norfolk had been East Anglia long before it bore the name of England. And then came William the Conqueror, and in due time on England's quarterings appeared the lily of France. Coke saw it carved above church doors that were nearly as old as the Conqueror's time, rubbed now and weathered until lilies and lions could scarcely be distinguished from the three squat towers of Norwich's own armorial shield. No city had so many churches, one for every week in the year, it was said. Rich men, grown great on Norfolk wool, had built them for pride rather than devotion, a visible testimony to their wealth and position. There were not people to fill them nor priests to order them, so that windows gaped, walls crumbled. But on Sundays the bells rang anyway, a clashing symphony of voices that called and clanged across the countryside.

Beyond the walls to the northeastward was the hill called Mousehold Heath, gorse-covered and golden in spring, where boys could run and climb and play at tilting — and, turning, see the city spread before their eyes, the long Cathedral roof and spire rising over all. On Mousehold, Kett the Rebel had camped with his peasant army, three years before Coke was born. Sixteen thousand hungry, desperate men, risen against the gentry who had taken their land . . . men fighting on Bishops Bridge with spear and pitchfork, battling at the gates until they captured the city and held it six long summer weeks, when the Earl of Warwick came against them under his hated banner of the Ragged Staff, and beat them and hanged Kett in chains from Norwich Keep. Coke knew the story, and how his father's friends had fled their homes to hide in the woods for fear of the rebels' cry, "Kill the gentlemen!" Burghwood itself must have set a night watch by the gates. Yet sympathy for Kett was slow in dying; young Coke heard of men who lost their ears for speaking in the rebels' favor.

There was a wide moat round Norwich Castle, called the Ditch. Here, Protestant martyrs had perished in Queen Mary Tudor's time. Simon Miller . . . Elizabeth Cooper . . . Richard Crashfield . . . Thomas Carman . . . Cicely Ormes . . . Rowland Taylor. Coke's father had known the names, his Norwich aunts and uncles had seen the smoke rise, if indeed they were not actual witness to the scene. The city remembered other, earlier burnings . . . Little Bilney, much beloved, who went to Cambridge University and came back persistent to preach the new doctrines, then recanted for fear of the fire but went out and preached again and died for it in the Lollards Pit beyond Norwich walls, crying "*Credo, credo!*" as the flames blew from his face.

When Edward Coke first came to Grammar School, reaction against Mary Tudor (dead three years) was at its height. For those who desired revenge, the city's threescore churches offered ample opportunity. Certain harsher spirits went about the Lord's business with hammer and torch until the savagery of their rioting reached Elizabeth's ears and she took measures to curb this smashing of stained glass, this battering down of old stone saints. Decent Protestants were shocked by such violence and would sometimes secretly (for fear of being called *papist*) bury their beautiful painted Virgins rather than see them hacked to pieces. Norwich Cathedral moved its communion table to the center of the church; there were to be no more altars toward the east, no carrying of candles on Paschal Eve, of ashes on Ash Wednesday and on Good Friday no more creeping to the Cross.

Yet custom dies hard and though their world was changing, in remote parishes the bells still rang on Thomas Becket's Day, and on

All Hallows Eve men sang forbidden Masses for the dead. In the country there remained thousands of Catholics who lived quietly, bothered no one and whom no one bothered. Norfolk possessed, second to Canterbury, the most famous shrine in England — at Walsingham, just north of Mileham where the Cokes lived. The starry galaxy itself had anciently pointed the way to Our Lady of Walsingham; kings walked barefoot to that altar, defaced now and broken. Yet at Burghwood, when Coke went home in summer, he saw the yeomen cross themselves if Walsingham shrine were mentioned, and do it before the Squire,* too.

At fifteen, Coke was ready for the university and the world which lay beyond — that great world where waited strangers, manhood, ambition and the law. His days henceforth would be spent far from country parishes. Yet the imprint of his Norfolk boyhood remained. Sixty years of London could not erase it, nor the robes of a Lord Chief Justice; there was about him always the stubborn intransigence of the country-bred; the wind might blow but it could not blow him down. Sights and sounds went into his making . . . drums on Norwich square, calling for the Queen's recruits . . . by the Town Close a gibbet erected and a boy of sixteen hanged for murder, parents taking their young to see him, a warning and an ensample . . . the fog, the bitter North Sea gale, the sandy thin home pastures and the shimmering reaches of Marshland and the Broads . . . Norwich city, which lay so close to Amsterdam and so far, so very far from Spain. (The Bishop of Rome was wicked, all popes forever had been Satan's kin, God was a word for which men shed blood and committed high treason — of all sins most deadly, Judas's crime.) In Norwich Cathedral were gaping pedestals where saints had been. Yet on Sundays the nave reached eastward as if eternity had no special creed, and on the undersides of choir seats were little carven figures, fat monks and grinning demons centuries old, fashioned by hands that surely were not wicked (though Romish) but patient, pious, humorous. On weekday mornings the cathedral bell rang loud and near above the schoolhouse roof, and at night called far off through sleep and mist and rain, the very tongue of God.

Coke knew these things and was nourished by them, and showed

* In 1563 there was a new Squire at Burghwood; Coke's mother married again. Her husband was Robert Bosanne, a Norfolk man.

pleasure all his life when he returned to Mileham parish. "Norfolk, my dear and native country," he called it in his *Institutes.*

In the autumn of 1567, Coke rode down across the Norfolk border to enter Trinity College. The University was only sixty miles away and the transition a natural one; Norfolk had long been a feeding ground for Cambridge. The Bacons of Stiffkey went there, the Townsends of Brampton and a pleasant succession of boys from Norwich Grammar School — Aldriches, Pickerings, Leeds, Goldes; the school prided itself on the connection. Boys from the east of England usually went to Cambridge, westerners to Oxford. The renowned Dr. Caius of Caius College was a Norwich man; as also Dr. Perne, Master of Peterhouse. A Duke of Norfolk had been High Steward of Cambridge in the 1540's, the great days of Roger Ascham and John Cheke and Dr. Redman, when little St. John's College had bred, it was boasted, more learned men in one year than the great University of Louvain in many. But the Duke, with his conservative Howard tendencies, was not happy in his office and had been heard to say regretfully that "it was merry in England before the new learning came up."

Beyond any place in England, Cambridge had fostered the new learning. The University was in fact a Protestant stronghold. Erasmus had taught there, and Thomas Cranmer, who met death at the stake. (Cranmer the Martyr, Cambridge liked to call him.) If Mary Tudor had favored Oxford, Elizabeth favored Cambridge, surrounding herself with advisers who were Cambridge bred; in youth she had been tutored by the brilliant and kindly Roger Ascham. Lord Burghley was Chancellor of the University, much concerned over religious quarrels which threatened to swamp all scholarship and indeed all decency. The trouble could be traced (as so often) to one man: Thomas Cartwright the Puritan, fellow of Trinity and soon to be named Lady Margaret Professor of Divinity. Eloquent, dramatic, Cartwright contrived to keep the colleges in a turmoil over the stricter points of Calvinism — the ringing of ritual bells, the wearing of the square black scholar's cap which had, said Cartwright, a monkish look. (From Geneva the good Beza, Calvin's successor, insisted that it turned innocent students into "priests of Baal.") Above all, the chorister's surplice was an abomination — "habit of the stage, relic of the Amorite, imitation of Antichrist."

Students walked into chapel sans surplice and were fined, whipped, admonished or, when they grew violent, expelled. There had been ugly riots like the ones at Norwich, with property wrecked, friend set against friend. To ignore it was impossible. If a man did not take sides his name became a byword, like Dr. Perne of Peterhouse, who, long before Cartwright's coming, had set his sail in the dangerous middle, changing his religion when England changed sovereigns — four times in twelve years. In Mary Tudor's time, Perne's tolerance had saved more than one overconscientious don from prison. But tolerance was a synonym for moral weakness and the jests at Perne's expense were many. "A Papist a Protestant a Papist a Protestant but still Andrew Perne," men said; and the University wits translated the Latin verb *perno*, *pernare* as "I turn, I rat, I change often." When somebody had a coat turned for thrift's sake, it was said to be *Perned*. On the other hand the great Dr. Caius of Caius College was suspected of celebrating Mass in his rooms; a junior sophister had seen the pix and canopy hidden in a chest. Besides being Professor at Cambridge, Caius was President of the Royal College of Physicians in London, greatly revered by his fellows. Yet so angry was the persecution that Caius would not have lasted at Cambridge another year had he not been so rich; he was a munificent donor to the college that bore his name. (In the end his rooms were ransacked, the holy symbols found and burned publicly at night in the college yard. Caius died shortly afterward — from grief at the incident, men said.)

Cartwright's extremism only made matters worse. The burning of relics — indeed, the entire Vestiarian controversy — was everywhere a prelude to rebellion against church government itself. Cartwright, quite obviously, must be checked. In 1567 (Coke's first year) Elizabeth and Burghley appointed a new Master of Trinity, John Whitgift (later to be Archbishop of Canterbury), a man whose life would touch Coke's at many points. Whitgift was a born disciplinarian. With intellectual whip and thong he pursued the adversary up the very pulpit steps. Yet, even backed by the prestige of government, it required four years and a new university constitution to rid Cambridge of Thomas Cartwright. Edward Coke was caught at the heaviest point of strife. The colleges degenerated (scholars everywhere deplored it). In such an atmosphere only the most perfunctory and conventional teaching was possible. If Coke learned anything at Trinity, it was how to use his tongue. From the rostrum of Great St. Mary's in the town, students launched their "disputations" as they had done for centuries. Doctors, robed in scarlet, held examinations while the public crowded in to listen. The traditional scene was set, the church bell tolled its invitation. "*Domine Doctor, incipias!*" intoned the Proctor — "Sir Doctor, begin!" — and the ancient show proceeded.

The truth was that at both universities, during these decades, the original fires of the Reformation burned low. England, and indeed the world, was on the verge of scientific revolution. Before the century ended, English mariners would redefine the boundaries of land and sea, unfix the western limits and lay out new continents across the world. (In 1613, Galileo charted his heaven, in 1615, Harvey discovered the circulation of the blood.) Yet Cambridge and Oxford remained islands of classicism and the ancient theoretic authority. Coke's teachers were in no way concerned with the solid observable world about them but rather with searching of Scripture, the solving of such puzzles as the Flood. To cover the earth had required eight oceans at least; where was all this water found? Whence did it flow and whither sink when at God's command it dried so neatly? Cambridge had its Caius, it was true, who in his London College dissected — by royal permission — human corpses. (The bodies of hanged criminals were used, and if they came alive on the table, the physicians were held responsible for expenses of reimprisonment and a second hanging.)

But to the University such practices, besides being atheistical, were the business of mechanics, artisans, surgeons who worked with their hands — not scholars whose concern should be with the intellect alone. For scholars it was enough to know that the body was regulated by the four humors — blood, phlegm, choler and black bile or melancholy — and that life derived from the heavenly bodies, whose influence spontaneously generated the seed of plant and insect. It followed that certain vegetables, like the turnip (a root lately imported) must be eschewed because, moon-born, its properties, overmoist and overhot, augmented the seed of man, provoking carnal lust.

The mathematical sciences were suspect; their figures and symbols savored of necromancy and godlessness. The elementary rules of arithmetic sufficed for any student, and the first book of Euclid; in geography the authorities were Pliny, Strabo and the pagan writers of the first century. One's cosmic theory rested comfortably upon the word of Ptolemy and Plato's lost Atlantis. As for astronomy, why count the stars when they were already fixed at 1002? Absurd and impious, to augment the number! Far better, where the firmament was concerned, to take as authority the blessed Scripture, which contained all secrets of heaven and earth. Copernicus had said the earth revolved about the sun. Yet what was one man's word against revelation itself? Besides which, Copernicus' book was written at Rome, dedicated to the Pope and no doubt inimical to Gospel truth. A spate of such volumes flowed from the English presses: Eden's *Art of Navigation*, Dee's *Pathway to Knowledge*. Dr. Cuningham's *Cosmographical Glass* included a map of Norwich. Dr. Recorde's book, *The Castle of Knowledge*, was especially liked, with its explication of the sphere, its opening dialogue which told how Copernicus had taken his ideas from "Aristarchus Samius." Few readers had heard of Aristarchus; yet the name, being classical, was comfortably authoritative.

Such notions were troublesome altogether; parents sent their sons to the University to have their minds settled, not upended. If the earth forever moved and turned, where then, asked Dr. Recorde in his book, was quietness to be found? People agreed that it was fortunate the matter had little significance except for master mariners, who must learn to sail as Magellan had sailed, beneath the globe, entirely upside down. In the universities these things were neither taught nor needed as they were in London, Norwich, Portsmouth, where practical men must contrive ways to direct their vessels across strange oceans, guns to fire straight and sails to take ships into the wind. The sailors of Norfolk knew more geography than any university don. Cambridge turned her academic face from the world of touch and sound and visible report. (Francis Bacon, disgusted, left Trinity College before his term was up.)

Yet Edward Coke by his nature loved tradition and did not fear its stultifying influence. To a boy from Norwich Grammar School, Trinity Great Gate led not to prison but Thule, the ultimate place that pointed to the star. In all ancient disciplines was glory — especially that medieval discipline called *logic*, which for centuries had been the first, best mental exercise, ground-base of university education. By logic — Coke believed it readily* — man's mind was raised above the brute's; by logic alone could search be directed toward the essence of things natural and occult. A man might be a barrister without a university education; Coke's father had gone from Norfolk straight to the law schools of London. His son was to have better preparation. The argument *a divisione*, the syllogism modal or indirect — these were tools to the discomfiture of the adversary. Coke's young mind slid into logic like a ship from the ways, followed the charted course and felt thereby no constriction. Boundaries and rules for Edward Coke did not mean imprisonment.

He came to the University at fifteen and stayed three years and a half; when he left, the down was soft on his cheek though he called himself a man. He was moreover the head of his family, his mother having died in 1569, his second college year. Cambridge has no record of his degree, but at Holkham there is a paper in Coke's handwriting which says he was "at Trinity College, Cam., and afterwards proceeded Master of Arts." That Coke left without graduation is not unusual; no more than forty per cent of students stayed the full period of their bachelorship. Yet it is possible to love one's college though one has gained there little that the world outside could not teach; Coke kept a warm affection for Cambridge. One day he would be proud to serve as the University's High Steward and "Governour of the Possessions of Trinity College under their common seal" . . . "That famous university of Cambridge, *alma mea mater*," he wrote when he was old.

* "How necessary it is that our student should (as Littleton did) come to the study of the common law from one of the universities, where he may learn the liberall arts, and especially logick, for that teacheth a man not only by just argument to conclude the matter in question, but to discerne betweene truth and falsehood, and to use a good method in his study, and probably to speake to any legal question." *First Institute*.

CHAPTER SIX

1571-1594. The Inner Temple and the Law.

> After the making of Magna Charta, divers learned men in the laws, that I may use the words of the record, kept schooles of the law in the city of London, and taught such as resorted to them, the laws of the realme.
>
> COKE, Preface, *First Institute*

THE long gardens of the Inner Temple reached below Fleet Street to the Thames — gardens so old that princes of York and Lancaster had plucked here (so Shakespeare says) their chosen emblems of the white rose and the red. Above the gardens stood the ancient Round Church that gave the place its name, built by Knights Templar before the year 1200, round-domed, after the Holy Sepulcher in Jerusalem. Next door was Middle Temple, equally renowned, over whose western wall rose the roofs and turrets of Essex House, beyond which lay Arundel House and the great mansions that lined the river to Whitehall Palace. Actually, the Temple was more fraternity than law school, a delightful fellowship to which a man, once initiated, belonged for the rest of his life — an institution peculiarly national which gave its name to that section lying between London and the town of Westminster, a mile away. Temple Stairs, leading to the waterside, had been a public embarkation point since Edward III was King, and through the city gate at Temple Bar, travelers passed to western suburbs.

Northward, the Temple gave directly on to Fleet Street, a few minutes' walk from Ludgate Hill, Paul's Church, the Mermaid Tavern. Across Fleet Street and spreading over Holborn were the sister

Inns of Court, not so old but quite as important and even larger as to grounds and buildings: Lincoln's Inn, where Robert Coke had studied (and died in chambers there); Gray's Inn, to which Francis Bacon and his father, the Lord Keeper, belonged. There was a little rhyme about them:

> Grayes Inne for walks,
> Lincoln's Inne for a wall,
> The Inner Temple for a garden,
> And the Middle for a Hall.

Young fledgling barristers were often identified, in court, by their membership. In Star Chamber records of the 1590's, side by side with "Kuke, the Queen's Atturny," is "Bacon, of Grayes Inne." (The principal house in each school had once been some nobleman's town house or inn.) Lincoln's Inn, Gray's Inn, the Inner Temple, Middle Temple: each of these four Houses of Court, as Coke called them, was fed by two or more smaller schools called Inns of Chancery, where students had a year's preparation before entering the larger institutions.

It was a little kingdom of the law, comprising some fifteen hundred students who moved freely in the city, bound by few rules, independent yet in close comradeship, taught voluntarily, without pay, by the best legal minds of England. Judges came from the bench, barristers from court or chambers, Parliament men from committee room to dine in hall, to lecture, preside over moot courts and finally to examine for the bar. The entire establishment had grown up centuries ago, nobody knew just when or how, unchartered, unendowed, a great guild of apprentices in English law. On the Continent, the law (which meant Roman law) had been codified centuries ago by the Emperor Justinian in his *Institutes* and *Digest*. And this Corpus Juris Civilis — body of the civil law — remained as it had been in the year 540, the boundary and definition for legal rights and obligations, a frame of authority to which all dispute might be referred. Those who mastered it were called *civilians,* Doctors of the Civil Law. Oxford and Cambridge gave civilian degrees, which did not admit to practice at the bar, but qualified the holder as counselor in the ecclesiastical courts, Admiralty and certain prerogative courts which still used the Roman system.

The English law — the native, island law — had never been codified but was, like England's constitution, a thing of custom and long acceptance, of statute law as found in the Parliament Rolls, reports of proceedings in the courts as set down in the Year Books and in such individual manuscript reports as existed; of maxim and legal rule as interpreted in the treatises of former judges — Glanville, Bracton, Britton, Fleta, Fortescue, Sir Thomas Littleton. The books were few and expensive; it followed that training was for the most part oral, by word of mouth and rule of thumb. Above all, this training was practical. The student got to his feet and argued mock cases before practicing lawyers. In term time he went down to Westminster and followed procedure from the opening of a case to its close, learned to make out a writ and shape in Latin the elaborate preliminary pleadings of the day, discovered which among conflicting jealous courts had jurisdiction over which type of cause, saw the judges of equity in action, learned under what condition a client might seek relief in Chancery — in short, absorbed by eye and ear the thousand technicalities and formalities with which the courts were then (far more than now) beset, ignorance of which could cause an attorney to lose his suit before it was fairly begun.

These matters constituted a craft, or in the current word, a "mystery," like the mystery of workers in gold or iron or tin. That Oxford and Cambridge did not undertake such training was natural. They had no course in English history, why should they have one in English law? No single book existed which set out for students the native law in its long continuity from Saxon days. Coke himself, in his *Institutes of the Laws of England,* was to write the first one, "to break the ice herein," he said. The Inner Temple's legal library was no more than a few shelves of volumes, chained to a bar, in charge of the Chief Butler. Not until a century after Coke's death did Oxford establish, in 1758, the first Professorship of English Law, setting Blackstone to his memorable course of Lectures.

On the twenty-first of January, 1571, ten days before his nineteenth birthday, Edward Coke, fresh from Cambridge, walked up Chancery Lane, turned into Clifford's Inn and signed his name in the book. A year later, his preparation finished, he crossed Fleet

Street and became one of the great fellowship of the Inner Temple. The hierarchy was rigid. A student moved slowly from rank to rank — and in the dining hall, from table to table: two years in Clerks' Commons, two in Masters' Commons, Utter Barrister in eight years, and in sixteen, Reader and Bencher, enthroned on the raised platform among the Ancients. Five or ten years after that, a fortunate few were called by the Queen to the degree of Serjeant-at-Law, from which the judges were chosen. Only Serjeants could plead at the bar of Common Pleas (though barristers and clerks could assist). The degrees were more than merely academic; they placed a lawyer in the courts. A real barrier of iron or wood separated judges from lawyers and litigants, so that a pleader stood actually at the bar or "ouster the bar." *Apprenticius ad Barros,** the ancient records have it, and later, Utter Barrister. Solicitor was not a degree at all; the Lord Keeper and even the Queen inveighed repeatedly against "common and prowling solicitors who set dissension between man and man, lurking to prey upon the courts."

The first book put into Coke's hands was old Judge Littleton's *Treatise on Tenures*, written in the previous century and concerned wholly with the land laws — fee tail and fee simple, homage, socage, tenancy by dower and tenancy by the *courtesie of England*. Benchers and barristers were unanimous in the book's praise. Yet even in translation from its original law French, the small crowded black-letter pages were bewildering, with their strange, heavy jargon: *plea pleadant* and *count countant*. "Terms and words of art," Coke called them, "a diffuse dark labyrinth." Ordinary words had, too, in law their special, artful meanings, such as *reason*, *inconvenience*, *possession* — which last, to be legal, must be "continual, calm and peaceable." Judge Littleton searched their etymology, "fetched words from their originals." Land, it became evident, had in law an importance equal to the men who lived on it, and concerning the land's inheritance and division, nothing was left to chance. The law explored and reached, devised boundary and definition until no crack, no hole remained for the adversary to slip through . . . or so it appeared until the student took his notebook to Westminster and witnessed what a clever attorney could do with a very small crack indeed. Two words ruled the court of Common Pleas. "These two great pronouns, *meum* and *tuum*," Coke called

* Chapter Note.

them. With *mine* and *thine* the common pleas were most of all concerned; *meum* and *tuum* put money into barristers' pockets.

From his first day at the Temple, the student plunged, headfirst, into full legal vocabulary. There was no leading by the hand, no smoothing of the way. Wrestling at the first, Coke said, with as difficult terms and matter as in many years after he will meet, the young student is at the first discouraged. "Some doth object against the lawes of England that they are darke and hard to be understood." In default of understanding, the student memorized terms, rules and maxims, trusting blindly that at some future day and hour — perhaps at court, perhaps in some other book — he would stumble upon a clue. "And albeit, the reader shall not at any one day (do what he can) reach to the meaning . . . yet let him no way discourage himself but proceed; for on some other day, in some other place, that doubt will be cleared." Let the student "read no more at any one time than he is able with a delight to bear away."

"True it is," Coke wrote later, "that I have been ever desirous to know much." Yet desire was not enough. To master the common law a man must be dogged, stubborn as an Anabaptist chanting the Psalms while he rode to gallows hill. It was like hawking with no game in sight, like running a race and no goal given. Let a man stop to take breath, and he fell back. "Therefore," Coke was to say, "I allow not to the student any discontinuance at all (for he shall lose more in a month than he shall recover in many). . . . Knowledge of the law is like a deep well, out of which each man draweth according to the strength of his understanding. He that reacheth deepest, he seeth the amiable and admirable secrets of the law."

Fortunately, when a man had got through Littleton's *Tenures* into pleas of the Crown, the face of things began to clear. The criminal law was simpler; it lacked the cautious give-and-take of trading, inheritance and the laws of real property. The ancient penal terms were almost self-explanatory, with their harsh Saxon tinge. A thief caught *handhabbend* (goods in hand) or *backberend* (bundle on back) was presumed guilty. Much that was terrible in law was also familiar: the hue and cry, the tumbril, stocks, gallows. The legal age of discretion Judge Littleton gave as fourteen years. Had any reached the age of discretion without seeing a man hanged, or whipped, or stooping in the market pillory with bloody slashes where his ears had been? Every crime within the common law had its prescribed remedy or punishment. And in this calendar of judgments, penalties were dreadfully fitted to their crimes.

On the Continent, the English law was looked on as brutal. Frenchmen, visiting in England, expressed themselves as shocked at the numbers hanged each year, which, covering the forty counties, by calculation reached near to eight hundred. It was an awful thing to see a poor man sentenced to the gallows for stealing a sheep. "What a lamentable case it is," Coke would one day write, "to see so many Christian men and women strangled on that cursed tree of the gallows, insomuch as if in a large field a man might see together all the Christians, that but in one year, throughout England, come to that untimely and ignominious death, if there were any spark of grace or charity in him, it would make his heart to bleed for pity or compassion. And true it is, that we have found by wofull experience, that it is not frequent and often punishment that doth prevent like offences, for the frequency of the punishment makes it so familiar as it is not feared."

There were in England at least fifty offenses which carried a death penalty.* Judges, helpless to change the law, leaned over backward to obtain acquittals. The royal pardon was lavish, escapes from jail were numerous, even from such bastions as the Tower of London. But prescribed penalties are one thing; trials are another. Because a penalty is oversevere does not mean the trial has been unfair. Coke was immensely proud of the English trial at common law. It was, he pointed out, public, not secret, by a jury of twelve; while on the Continent, men were tried by inquisition and interrogation on oath, the jury being a Norman or Saxon creation, unknown to Rome and Rome's civil law. In England, even a traitor was allowed to stand before the public and speak in his own defense. Moreover, he might challenge his jury — "challenge the array for unindifference," Coke called it — to the number of thirty-six. Across the Channel, a defendant was given no chance to speak thus publicly, let alone challenge jurors. Often as not he found himself hustled into the castle dungeon of some great lord, where he languished indefinitely or was done to death and his friends none the wiser. Englishmen for three hundred years had

* Chapter Note.

been protected from such treatment. Any second-term Templar could recite the pertinent chapter of Magna Carta: "*Nullus liber homo*" . . . "No freeman shall be taken or imprisoned or be disseised of his freehold or liberties but by lawful judgment of his peers or by the law of the land." "Upon this chapter," Coke wrote, "as out of a roote, many fruitful branches of the law of England have sprung."

"A Freeman may have *habeas corpus* out of the king, upon which writ the gaoler must return by whom he was committed and the cause of his imprisonment." So the great Bracton had said in Henry III's time, and so Edward Coke believed. There were no bounds to his conviction. Coke quoted recklessly and to his purpose from the *Dooms of Canutus*, through Glanville, Bracton and the later discredited *Mirrour of Justices*, down to the great Edmund Plowden, who taught at Middle Temple. "If the ancient laws of this noble island had not excelled all others," Coke wrote, "it could not be but some of the several conquerors and governors thereof, that is to say, the Romans, Saxons, Danes or Normans, and especially the Romans, who (as they justly may) do boast of their Civil Laws, would (as every of them might) have altered or changed the same."

Exactly when this pride of law was planted in Edward Coke, none can say; it is not illogical to suppose that it grew and was nourished in his student days at the Temple.* Coke came there in the early 1570's, the very seed-time of his country's expansion, when the national spirit prepared to show itself in most extraordinary flowering . . . a Sidney, a Shakespeare, a Drake, a Ralegh. The law too had its heroes. The company at the Temple was little short of dazzling. During term time, when the courts were sitting, barristers came to live in chambers, leaving their wives conveniently in the country. These great ones walked and talked in the garden or stood in clusters by the gate, their green bags slung across their shoulders. Lord Keeper Sir Nicholas Bacon came to dine and drink a grace cup, a knight urbane and infinitely witty, heaving his huge bulk to the platform where the benchers sat at dinner. Sir Thomas Bromley, the Queen's Solicitor General, very much the gentleman with his courteous manners and aristocratic air; Mr. Justice Manwood, beloved wherever he went; Serjeant Gawdy the Norfolk-

* See Chapter Note on the English "Reception" of the civil law.

man; Serjeant Edmund Anderson, who had the honor of being Double Reader and had given two sets of lectures; Chief Justice Dyer of Common Pleas, whose court reports, in manuscript, were circulated, borrowed, copied, queried until the pages scarcely held together. Edmund Plowden, nearing sixty, acknowledged as the best legal mind in England, strolled across the lawns from Middle Temple. His reports, just published, opened a new vista in court reporting. "Exquisite and elaborate commentaries," Coke called them, "learnedly and curiously polished, and, with all the professors of the Law of high account." Because Plowden was a Catholic, the Queen could not make him a serjeant; in his reports he called himself "*un apprentice de la comen ley*." He was outspoken as to his religion, in consequence of which the Middle Temple was, contemporaries complained, "pestered with papists." Plowden possessed, aside from his legal attainments, an integrity and simple dignity which won him wide respect; the authorities let him go his way.

An aura surrounded the Temple and the Inns of Court; through the centuries they had developed a cachet. England's Third University, people called them. Here a gentleman's son might acquire, in a year's residence after Oxford or Cambridge, enough law to settle disputes of tenants on the family estates, or to act as Justice of the Peace in his home county. Gradually, if somewhat paradoxically, these highly practical guilds of *apprentici ad legem* had acquired a reputation for teaching not only law but social graces — how to hold one's own in a part song after dinner, how to dance, drink, bow, make a knee before one's betters. Noblemen and courtiers were to be found here, and even those great adventurers, Drake and Ralegh. The Earl of Leicester in his time had had chambers at Brick Court in the Temple; when Coke was a student, Lord Howard of Effingham, the Queen's Chamberlain, chose to call himself an Inner Templar. Queen Elizabeth came down the river with her ladies to dine and watch the Christmas masques and pageants.

Within these halls and along these pleasances and walks, great names of the past were remembered. . . . Sir John Fortescue, who wrote *In Praise of English Law* to teach his royal exiled pupil, Prince Edward, the excellence of what lay at home (a book "worthy," said Coke, "of being written in letters of gold") . . . Judge Thomas Littleton, whose arms, three cocks crowing, adorned the Inner Temple Hall . . . Lord Chancellor Sir Thomas More, who as a student had filled his rooms with strange whimsical pets, an ape, a fox, a ferret and a weasel. Open country was near; there was excellent hunting in the Surrey fields across the river and landward behind Holborn, where houses were scattered and remote. The amount of student brawling was scandalous. Chief Justice Popham, tall and burly, as a student had been one of the Roaring Boys — *swingebucklers*, Shakespeare called them — who issued from Temple Gate by night to cut purses by way of entertainment. Rules forbade carrying weapons into hall beyond dagger and knife, to eat with. But swords and bludgeons found their way into chambers, and so did doubtful ladies, against whom bans proved equally futile.

Each school had its symbol. For the Middle Temple, the Lamb; for the Inner Temple, Pegasus, the winged horse. Pegasus flew across door lintels, spread embossed bright wings over the windows of the Hall. Pegasus, forever flying to the left, adorned the gilt badge that swung its chain above the porter's stomach. Actually, Pegasus was a dashing interpretation of the Old Templars' insignia — a knight in chain mail holding a wounded man before him on a horse, symbolic of charity and love. During the Christmas revels of 1561, somebody, no one remembered who, had taken a paint brush, eliminated the riders and set wings in place of humility. The Inns were not famous for humility, or for charity either, though beggars seeped in continually from Fleet Street, claiming the ancient rights of sanctuary; and parentless babies were found in baskets by Temple Gate, to the vast annoyance of Authority, which reared the children and presented them with the surname of "Temple."

Here then for seven years Coke lived, until the place was part of him — Pegasus, the Round Church, where Knights Templar lay in stone, cross-legged above the floor; the garden, where red and white roses bloomed and fell as they had bloomed and fallen for centuries. Beyond the river wall was heard the bargeman's cheerful shout. At evening, snatches of song drifted shoreward, the sound of lutes from little pleasure boats that slipped downstream. Northward, a narrow avenue — Ram Alley — led to Fleet Street bookshops, in particular the *Hand and Star*, where Richard Tottel sold his beautiful slim editions of the old Year Books as they came in black-letter from his press. Tottel was Upper Warden of the powerful Stationers' Company; there was nothing he did not know and was not ready to impart concerning books and printing. On his shelves were occasionally to be found old fifteenth-century rolls and parchments, humble petitions of poor men in Chancery asking relief *for the love of God and that peerless Princess his mother,* or *for his sake who died on the Rood Tree a Good Friday.*

To Edward Coke it must have seemed all knowledge lay at his elbow . . . jumbled at first and incoherent, but, as the years passed, unfolding until he held it almost in his hand. At some time in his seventh and last Temple year, Coke acquired considerable local fame as spokesman for fellow students who wished to put in a complaint (perennial since colleges began) about their food at commons. Coke went into the business heart and soul, drew up in Latin a legal declaration that the cook, having failed in the performance of his office, had forfeited his engagement. This Coke presented to the benchers and asking their favor stood up and argued his case, "stating it so exactly," says a chronicler, "that all the House admired him and his pleading it, so that the whole Bench took notice of him."

In Temple annals the affair was known henceforth as "The Cook's case." Nothing more is heard of Edward Coke until that day of April 20, 1578, when he was called "to the Outer Barre." The usual time of apprenticeship was eight years; Coke got off with seven (counting the first year at Clifford's Inn). It has been assumed he was so favored because of especial brilliance. Actually, the rules were flexible and if a student showed himself prepared, the benchers could call him when they pleased. Coke's sponsors on that great day were Father Alvey (Chaplain and Master of the Temple), two barristers and Sir Thomas Bromley, the Queen's Solicitor General. With his hand on the Temple Bible, Coke swore "to do no falsehood in the Court, increase no fees but be contented with the old fees accustomed, delay no man for lucre or malice, but use myself in the office of an Attorney within the Court according to my learning and discretion, so help me God, Amen."

Legend has it that Coke, at twenty-six, was launched from the Temple with no possessions beyond a horse, a rapier, ten pounds, a ring set with three rose diamonds and the motto "O prepare." He was scarcely out of law school (1578) when he found himself — quite possibly from sheer luck and proximity to the scene — involved in a case which brought him recognition and made his name known to Westminster Hall. It was a libel suit, a type of case common in the day; Coke tells of ten such suits in which he had an early interest. Men seemed to dote upon insulting their country neighbors and then waging battle anew in the courts. Everyone came to listen and look; it was a diversion second only to cockfighting. From the scribbled pages of Coke's commonplace book, loud voices call across the centuries: "Mr. Brittenridge is a perjured old knave. . . . B's wife is a whore. . . . Thou art a thief, for thou hast stolen my apples out of my orchard. . . . Davis's daughter dwelt in Cheapside and there was a grocer did get her with child, I know her well." . . . Sometimes the actionable words, in their strong country dialect, had to be explained to London judges. "If a man says of a counsellor in the north," runs one report, " 'Thou art a daffa-down-dilly' — an action lies, the words signifying that he is an ambidexter [a lawyer who takes money from both sides]." People were forever slanging at each other, in high places and low; Queen Elizabeth's favorite godson, the witty Sir John Harington, made a note in his diary to "write a damnable storie and put it in goodlie verse aboute Lorde A.; he hathe done me some ill turnes."

Putting damnable stories into goodly verse was a hazardous occupation when the lawyers had wind of it. Coke's first case was one of those libel suits which, though it contained no actual domestic scandal, got itself talked about. Great names were involved, and that most touchy of current subjects, religion. Lord Henry Cromwell, the plaintiff, was a baron of the realm whose estates lay almost next door to Burghwood Manor in Norfolk. The defendant, an obscure country parson named Denny, Vicar of North Elmham Church on Cromwell's land, had had the temerity to talk back to his noble patron. The occasion concerned two Puritans whom the Earl, a zealous nonconformist, had invited on successive Sundays to preach at North Elmham. (A recognized Puritan tactic was to persuade large landholders, like Cromwell, to displace, as often as possible, Established Churchmen in their benefices.) The Vicar, staunchly

Church of England, was outraged. On the two Sundays in question he placed himself below the pulpit and in full hearing of the congregation forbade the preachers to go up, informing them, quite justifiably, that they "had no license to preach." But the Puritans went up anyway and had their say, which included remarks highly derogatory to the Established liturgy, "affirming," Coke says, "the Book of Common Prayer to be superstitious and impious."

To a Church of England man this was more than heresy; it was close to treason. And besides, it was impudent, a poaching on other men's territory. Had not the Book of Common Prayer been established, the Vicar asked indignantly, "by the Queen and the whole Parliament in the first year of this reign?" Lord Cromwell, in the presence of witnesses, shouted back, using the second person (fit only for servants and children):

"Thou art a false varlet and I like not of thee!"

To this the Vicar replied with equal heat, "It is no marvel that you like not of me, for you like of those that maintain sedition against the Queen!"

"Sedition" was a word about which the grandson of Thomas Cromwell* might well be tender; its use, the nobleman decided, was actionable at law. Thirsting for his Vicar's blood (including costs and damages), Cromwell had his lawyer draw up a complaint under the ancient act of *Scandalum Magnatum*. The Vicar, when the writ was served, ran straight to the nearest lawyer, who happened to be Edward Coke of the adjacent parish, fresh from London and no doubt bursting with confidence in his ability as recently exemplified in "The Cook's Case."

The suit reached Westminster Hall in Trinity Term of 1578. To Coke's dismay his plea was immediately thrown out of court as "insufficient." All would have been lost had not Coke, brooding over the papers, discovered a mistake in the written declaration of opposing counsel — only one word, but it sufficed.† The original act of *Scandalum Magnatum* had been, since its passage in 1378, translated from Latin into law French, then into English. Cromwell's lawyer, instead of referring to the original statute, had been content with a third-hand English version which rendered the French word *messoinges* (lies) as "messages." Translating this back

* Minister to Henry VIII and beheaded for treason in 1540.
† Chapter Note.

into Latin, Coke's opponent wrote *nuncia* (Latin for *messages*), "whereas," Coke told the court triumphantly, "it should have been *mendacia* [lies]."

The move proved instantly successful and the case was thrown out of court. But the litigious Earl would not give up. He brought a new suit. This time, Coke questioned if the matter were actionable at all and was tempted to ask for a demurrer — bait and ruin of the inexperienced. But the judges, among whom were Chief Justice Wray and Thomas Gawdy the Norfolkman and Inner Templar, advised strongly against it. Coke, falling back on the facts, won his case by pleading special justification — admitted, in short, that his client had said the offending words, but was justified.

Coke reported the case with many a flourish, including an apt, three-line quotation from Virgil on sedition, probably interposed later on when Coke had time to think of it. The report ends with advice to young lawyers, pertinent today as when Coke wrote it: Never, if it can be avoided, "hazard the matter upon a demurrer," but plead the facts when the facts will serve your client.

During these years of his early apprenticeship in the law, Coke did a vast amount of traveling, roaming over the shires on horseback, to Coventry, where he was official town counselor or Recorder; to London and Essex and then north again to his own "dear native city," when Norwich in turn elected him Recorder, and Lord Chancellor Bromley named him Justice of the Peace for Norfolk. In 1582, when he was thirty, Coke married his first wife, Bridget Paston, seventeen years old, bearer of a distinguished Norfolk name — and a dowry of thirty thousand pounds. The young couple went to live at Huntingfield in Suffolk, on an estate of Bridget's mother. In term time, Coke rode to London, his saddlebags stuffed with papers, a doe or fat buck thrown over the horse behind a servant as present for Sir Thomas Bromley or some Inner Temple friend. That the young barrister prospered, there is no doubt. In the sixteen years between his call to the bar in 1578 and his being named Attorney General in 1594, Coke acquired much property — lands and houses to the amount of ten thousand pounds, starting off with Tittleshall Austens in Norfolk, bought from a yeoman for five pounds.

Wherever he went in the courts, Coke carried his notebook with him, beginning early, after the manner of born historians and writers, to set down what he saw and heard. His *Institutes*, none of which appeared in print before 1628, refer to cases in Westminster Hall as early as 1572 — "And so it was cleerly holden *Pasch. 14 Eliz.* in the court of common pleas, which I my self heard." Beyond Plowden's Reports and Judge Dyer's (1585), no court reports existed. The Year Books had stopped in 1535. Judges must write down their decisions if they did not wish to forget them and the reasons behind them. To take down a case on paper, in court, is notoriously demanding in any century. Other men of Coke's time accomplished it and their notes were published. Yet no one else was so persistent. Coke's notes, taken for his private, immediate use over a period of forty-odd years, made up, in the end, thirteen printed *Parts*, nearly six hundred cases. For three centuries the legal world relied on them, referring to them, quite simply, as *The Reports*, while all other reports were known by the names of their authors: *Dyer's Reports*, *Moore's Reports*, etc.

Edward Coke, then, *aetat* thirty . . . thirty-five . . . thirty-nine, sat scribbling as the lawyers talked, until his hand must have ached and those large bright eyes, already nearsighted, burned and watered. ("He was of wonderful painstaking, as appeares by his writings, short-sighted but never used spectacles to his dyeing day.") Coke included what he chose and omitted what he chose. No forms had been set for court reporting. If a writer wished to leave out the names of counsel or even the decision itself, who was to stop him? Term after legal term, year after year, Coke's notebooks accumulated, a peculiar treasury not alone of law but of social history . . . a vast scribble of law French, English, Latin . . . of rules and maxims delivered from the bench . . . arguments by counsel, decorated with quotations from Cicero, Virgil, Deuteronomy, the Psalms, interspersed with Coke's own notions of what was permissible by precedent or suitable by circumstance. Included were matters not part of any law reports before or since — Judge Dyer was "a man of handsome countenance, a patron and encourager of men learned in the laws and expert clerks." If Coke omitted to tell who won a suit, he did not forget to make running comment on the argument. "As much was said on the plaintiff's side as the wit of man could think or invent." When politics entered the courtroom, Coke ranged himself without hesitation on his chosen side.

Enclosure, for instance, was, next to religion, the most controversial political question of the day. Coke made it plain he was on the side of the small farmer who ploughed and reaped as against the new sheepherding landlord who seized all available land and converted it to pasture. Parliament, Coke reported in Tyrringham's case (1584), had made excellent statutes to keep up the price of corn — yet these were ineffectual so long as men were permitted to convert arable land to pasture by the hundred and the thousand acres. Populous towns were decreased for the "maintenance only of two or three herdsmen, who keep beasts, in lieu of great numbers of strong and able men. The common law prefers arable land before all others," wrote Coke the Norfolkman, and cited his statute (*4 Hen. VII, cap. 19*) to prove it.

Shelley's case opened in 1579 as a simple suit of trespass in King's Bench, with Coke as counsel — one of six for the defendant. Henry Shelley was accused by Nicholas Wolf (a tenant of the Shelley family) of letting cattle into his grounds and thereby destroying grass to the value of one hundred marks. By the time the case was ended, two years later, it had become a bitter family dispute between Henry and Richard Shelley as to who actually owned, by inheritance, the land in question. Sudden death came into it, a posthumous child, a grandfather's bequest "to the heirs male and the heirs male of the heirs male." All the judges of England were called in conference, including Barons of Exchequer and Lord Chancellor Bromley. Coke must have worn down goose quills by the dozen. Printed, his report covers thirty-seven pages, most of them incomprehensible to lawyers as well as laymen, yet bearing on every page the author's high excitement and satisfaction. Whether Henry Shelley, "a gentleman of good and ancient family," won or lost has been forgotten. The suit is famous for establishing a precedent concerning the inheritance of land. Known forever as the *Rule in Shelley's Case*, it was to embellish the bar examinations of three centuries and two nations: "What, Sir, is the Rule in Shelley's Case?" *

As Coke gathered experience, his name no longer appeared as junior counsel under Plowden and that robust Middle Templar, John

* Answer: Where a transfer of real estate provides that the property shall be owned successively by a number of people, John Doe has rights of property for his lifetime. When he dies, his heirs receive full rights. The effect is: John Doe has full rights for himself and can cut off his heirs by selling the property or leaving it to others.

Popham, but alone, against such masters of the trade as Thomas Egerton, whose persistent legal antagonist Coke was one day to be. In addition to his commonplace book, Coke kept, in Latin, a little private register. His *Vade Mecum*, he was to call it, his testament, "from whence at one view he took a prospect of his life past, having noted therein, most remarkables." Here Coke set down his father's death and burial in 1561, his own entrance into Cambridge and the Inner Temple, his admission to the bar and election as Reader of Lyon's Inn, his marriage to Bridget Paston, the sons and daughters born at Huntingfield, adding the saint's day and position of the moon as it was fortunate or unlucky:

Edward, 7 November. *Luna in Libra.*
Anne, 1 March, 1584. *Luna adtunc in Cancere . . .*

Children made their appearance with gratifying regularity: Edward, Anne, Elizabeth, Robert (named after Coke's father), Arthur, John, Henry. Seven in eight years, and more to come. They were christened in the little church at Huntingfield, where Coke and Bridget Paston had been married. All but one child, Elizabeth, survived the dangerous hazard of infancy. Hospitality was lavish, with godparents and cousins traveling from Norfolk and from Essex. Knightleys came from Fawsley in Northamptonshire. There were Gawdys and Townsends, Clippesbys, Heveninghams, Wingfields, Pastons, with each name listed carefully in the little book. Horses were bedded in stable or field, guests in the big four-posters above stairs. Servants, masters and mistresses fed upon venison pasty or lark pies according to their station and degree.

The manor house of Huntingfield was enchanting, with a legend for every turret. The ill-starred family De la Pole, of the blood royal, had lived here, and that daring nobleman, Charles Brandon, Duke of Suffolk. There were tales of clandestine marriages, of a young abandoned bride whose ghost still wept by midnight at a certain casement window. A splendid gallery ran the length of the house, the Great Hall was built around six massive oaks which supported the roof as they grew. On their branches, yeomen and foresters, coming in for dinner, hung nets and crossbows, hunting poles, calivers, saddles and belts. Queen Elizabeth (it was said) had stopped here one morning in her youth when her cousin Hunsdon owned the place. Two fields from the house stood a great oak tree, in whose broad low branches Elizabeth had perched with her crossbow, shooting as the park deer were driven by.*

So passed the striving, busy years. Edward Coke, still in his thirties, ambitious to make his way, reached toward public office and, before long, achieved it. 1586, Recorder of Coventry and Norwich and Justice of the Peace for Norfolk . . . Member of Parliament for Aldeburgh . . . 1590, Bencher of the Inner Temple . . . 1591, Recorder of London . . . 1592, Reader of the Inner Temple and Solicitor General, "by the grace," wrote Coke, "*serenissimae nostrae Reginae, Elizabethae*" . . . 1593, representative to Parliament for Norfolk county, Speaker of the House in Elizabeth's Eighth Parliament. A stormy session, brief, only seven weeks, yet long enough to see five members carried to prison for questioning the Queen's prerogative. . . . But the subsidy was voted at last, engrossed and ready for presentation. Throughout these early years, one man beyond all others remained ready to help and advise — William Cecil, Lord Treasurer Burghley. "When I remember," Coke wrote, "what comfort I have received by your Lordship's preferment and commendation of me to her Majesty's service, vouchsafing to direct me in all things that might turn to my good, and what care and pains your Lordship took for my instruction in the last Parliament and (omitting many others) what exceeding favour your Lordship extended to me lately . . . all that I can yield is a dutiful and faithful heart."

April, 1593. A new post vacant in the government, an honorable post, extremely lucrative: Attorney General to the Queen. More than one man would seek it; powerful courtiers had the Queen's ear. Whose voice would reach her and what man she would choose were questions that belonged to the immediate future.

* Chapter Note.

CHAPTER SEVEN

1593-1594. Francis Bacon fights for the Attorney-Generalship. "The Bacon and the Cook." The Queen's Prosecutor at Work.

Anthony Bacon to his mother, Lady Bacon

18 July, 1593

Our most honorable and kind friend the Earl of Essex was here yesterday three hours, and hath most friendly and freely promised to set up, as they say, his whole rest of favour and credit for my brother's preferment before Mr. Cooke. . . . His Lordship told me likewise that he hath already moved the Queen for my brother.

"TO set up a rest" meant to build a platform from which to shoot one's heavy cannon. ("The Spaniard hath set up his rest for England," Robert Cecil said in Parliament.) For this particular campaign Robert Devereux, Second Earl of Essex, would need his heaviest artillery. Coke, already Solicitor General, not only stood next in line for the Attorney-Generalship, suitable in age (he was forty-one to Bacon's thirty-two), but had a record of fifteen years' practical experience in the courts. Not one of the eight common-law judges, six Barons of Exchequer and the entire Chancery but had watched Edward Coke argue cases and, likely enough, dined with him afterward at Westminster. Coke's recent Speakership of the Commons (February-April, 1593) had given him further prestige and put him in the public eye. As for Lord Keeper Puckering, who had introduced Speaker Coke on opening day, quite obviously that great man was ready to oppose all rivals to his protégé's advance. Francis Bacon, moreover, in this same Parliament had angered the Queen by questioning her triple subsidy and brief collection period. "In the King my father's time," Elizabeth remarked, "a less offence than that would have made a man be banished his presence for ever."

Coke, then, entered the lists as logical candidate; Bacon, with the black mark of royal disfavor against him — a man who, though his lectures at Gray's Inn were well spoken of, had never had a client nor argued a case in the courts — "never yet entered into the place of battle," his opponents said. Toward advocacy as a profession, Bacon seemed to cherish a distaste second only to the hatred he bore his rival, Edward Coke. But Bacon was poor, he must make a living and had expected to be settled long ago in some financially rewarding government place. Had not the Queen shown favor since he was twelve, when his father, the Lord Keeper, first brought him to the palace? Every courtier knew the story — how her Majesty had put a question to the boy and he answered so quickly and cleverly that the Queen had laughed and kissed him, calling him "her young Lord Keeper."

Of such trifles might a man's career be built. With Bacon it rankled to recall that his father had been given royal office at twenty-seven, while he himself, at thirty-two, as yet had nothing. Conscious of his extraordinary powers (how could such a man be otherwise?) he lived tormented by ambition, impatient, fearful of poverty and the obscurity that poverty promises. His health was uncertain, his face already showed lines. "His countenance," wrote a near contemporary, "had indented with age before he was old; his presence grave and comely; of a high-flying and lively wit, striving in some things to be rather admir'd than understood. He had a delicate, lively hazel eye; Dr. Harvey tolde me it was like the eye of a viper."

Restless, secretive, the Baconian eye darted down the hierarchy of officialdom — and fixed upon Essex. That impetuous nobleman, in the high tide of youth, beauty and royal favor (he was twenty-seven) was genuinely devoted to Bacon, whose genius he perceived and whose crafty, considered judgment he sought as balance for his own rash impulsiveness. Bacon had spent hours and days upon the Earl's business. ("It was in a sort my vocation," he wrote later. "I did nothing but devise and ruminate of anything that might concern his Lordship's honour, fortune or service.") There was no reason why this advice and rumination should not pay off. The Earl was generous and liked to reward his followers.

More was involved, however, than friendship. Essex, already leader of a growing faction in Parliament and crown circles, looked to increase his influence by placing his own men in key positions near the Queen; while Elizabeth, herself an old hand at intrigue and perfectly aware of the situation, sought at once to please her favorite yet prevent his power from swelling to dangerous size. In pre-Tudor days, fiery noblemen of the Essex type had more than once gained control over king and court and country. It was Elizabeth's business to see that it did not happen again.

But Essex, when he had his teeth in a situation, never let go until he worried it to rags. Throughout the summer of 1593 he continued his suit. On the Queen's protesting that Bacon was too young to be Attorney General, the Earl replied that between Bacon and Coke "was such a difference in the worthinesse of the persons, as, if Mr. Cooke's head and beard were grown grey with age it would not counterpoise his other disadvantages." As Essex grew ever more insistent, the Queen grew more wary. Elizabeth was past mistress at the art of putting off. Why this haste, why this hurry? Lord Burghley was away at his county seat; they must wait upon his return. She was of opinion he preferred Mr. Bacon for the second place (Solicitor General). "She did in this," wrote Essex, "as she useth in all; went from a denial to a delay, and said when the Council all were here she would think of it." Francis Bacon in person, the Queen refused to see; he had been forbidden the court because of his speech against the subsidy. But Essex she kept by her. The spectacle of that proud young Earl on his knees, suing for favor, was not unpleasant. "To-day," wrote Essex in October, "I found the Queen stiff in her opinion that she would have her own way. Whereupon I grew more earnest than ever I did before, insomuch that she told me that she would be advised by those that had more judgment in these things than myself." The Queen acknowledged that Bacon had "a great wit and an excellent gift of speech and much other good learning. But in law she rather thought that he could make show to the uttermost of his knowledge, than that he was deep."

In January of '94, Bacon made a move to correct this bad impression, arguing his first case in King's Bench with an éclat which caused his Uncle Burghley to send congratulations and ask for notes of his pleading to show the Queen. In February, Bacon took a second case, speaking this time before a whole garland of judges, including Lord Keeper Puckering and Burghley. A young fellow-barrister of Gray's Inn wrote to Anthony Bacon about it. Francis, it seems, had not been content with arguing the facts but "spangled his speech with unusual words, somewhat obscure and as it were presuming upon the judges' capacities." No man in England could spangle his speech with such stars as Francis Bacon; yet judges are not fond of oratory from the floor, and the bench had seemed uneasy. Bacon's performance, however, had been impressive; people talked about it. "All is as well as words can make it," finished the young Gray's Inn man, "and if it please her Majesty to add deeds, *the Bacon* may be too hard for *the Cook*."

Throughout this battle royal, Edward Coke kept silent. Or if he did not, if he too wrote letters, suing through the Cecils as Bacon sued through Essex, through Greville — any who might help — the record is lost. Coke was never the courtier. When he won a seat in Parliament or received new honor he was quick to urge that it had been accomplished without solicitation on his part. His manner was abrupt at times to rudeness; his faults bordered rather on brutality than subservience. Whereas Francis Bacon, quivering with sensitivity and the quick perception of other men's feelings, approached life in a series of almost fantastically convoluted, self-made entanglement and plot. Bacon seemed incapable, at the moment, of trusting anyone, even the Cecils, though he had himself been reared in Burghley's household. "Pray spare not my competitors to the great ones," he urged Essex. But let the Earl beware of Sir Robert Cecil, a man who played both sides and whose face could turn two ways — like a boatman rowing up the Thames, who, wrote Bacon, "looketh toward London Bridge when he pulleth toward Westminster." And had not Robert Cecil, going secretly to the Queen, perhaps undone the advantage of Essex's own insinuations against the Huddler (Coke)? The Earl had best be watchful. . . . Destroy this letter! . . . "I pray you, Sir, let not my jargon privilege my letter from burning, because it is not such but the light showeth through."

It was wonderful and awful, considering the transcendent genius of the man who composed these plots and careful warnings — not mentioning names, referring to Coke always as the Huddler. At times the light was far from showing through. Bacon's own mother could not unravel his twisted sentences, though she was a learned old lady with an easy command of Latin and Greek. "Construe the interpretation. I do not understand his enigmatical folded writing," she complained to her older son, Anthony Bacon. Anthony, himself a courtier since boyhood, knew at first hand the shifts and turnings of such a career. One of his letters quotes from Roger Ascham on the arts necessary to a courtier:

> To laugh, to lie, to flatter, to face;
> Four ways in court to win men grace.
> If thou be thrall to none of these,
> Away, good Peek Goose! Hence, John Cheese!

In her son's behalf, old Lady Bacon wrote to her brother-in-law, Burghley, who she was convinced need but lift a hand and the Queen would grant his request. Burghley knew better. For years he had walked his world besieged by sycophants and placemen. Had he not, in every plea and suit, considered the state's welfare equally with the Queen's pleasure, he would long since have lost his own high office. His reply to Lady Bacon was kind, and wearily cautious: "Good Madam, for your sons, I think them so well qualified in learning and virtues, as, if they had a supply of more health they wanted nothing. For my goodwill to them, though I am of less power to do my friends good than the world thinketh, yet they shall not want the intention to do them good."

The Earl of Essex to Francis Bacon

28 March, 1594

Sir, I have received your letter, and I have had opportunity to deal freely with the Queen. . . . I find her very reserved, yet not passionate against you till I grew passionate for you. She said that none thought you fit for the place but my lord Treasurer [Burghley] and myself; marry, "the others must some of them say so before us for fear or for flattery." . . . She said she neither was persuaded nor would hear of it till Easter, when she might advise with her Council who were now all absent; and therefore in passion bade me go to bed, if I would talk of nothing else. Wherefore in passion I went away. . . . Upon Friday morning I will be here again and follow on the same course, stirring a discontentment in her, &c.

And so wish you all happiness, and rest
Your most assured friend,

Essex

Twelve days later, the thing was decided. Burghley returned to court, and on April 10, 1594, Elizabeth signed letters patent advancing Thomas Egerton to the vacant office of Master of the Rolls,* Sir Robert Cecil to the First Secretaryship which she had so long delayed — and granting the Attorney-Generalship to Edward Coke.

Bacon was in anguish, convinced that the whole world pointed him out in scorn. "No man ever received a more exquisite disgrace," he wrote. "I have been like a piece of stuff bespoken in the shop . . . like a child following a bird." His health, he told Essex, was "almost overthrown." Dangerously in debt from fourteen months of maneuver and vain hope, he implored Essex now to sue the Queen in his name for the vacated Solicitor-Generalship. Second place was better than none. (Had Bacon so aimed in the beginning, it was the general opinion he might have won.) But on Essex's approaching her, Elizabeth at once refused — as she refused the jewel Bacon sent. Peremptorily she informed her favorite that if he "continued in this manner, she would seek all England for a Solicitor rather than take Francis Bacon." ("Though the Earl showed great affection," wrote old Lady Bacon, "yet he marred all with violent courses.")

Essex retreated moodily, after his fashion, choosing to look on the Queen's refusal as a personal rebuff, diminishing to his prestige. Promise of office for one's friends was a very real kind of credit; one could borrow money on it, live on it and live well. The

* Highest office in the Chancery Court next to Lord Chancellor. The Master of Rolls had charge of all patents, grants, etc., made out under the Great Seal. These were kept in the Rolls Office in Chancery Lane (where the Public Record Office is now).

Queen (Essex was sure) desired to put him down, and it was this — not Bacon's unworthiness — which impelled her to so humiliating a decision. "Master Bacon," Essex said, "you are ill because you have chosen me for your mean and dependence. I die if I do not somewhat towards your fortune; you shall not deny to accept a piece of land which I will bestow upon you."

Bacon accepted the land and sold it. Yet never, in Elizabeth's lifetime, would he receive permanent office, though he did not cease to try. One small sop the Queen threw him — the reversion of a clerkship in the Star Chamber when it should fall vacant, worth about £1600 a year. Like another man's ground, said Bacon ruefully, "buttailing upon his house, which might mend his prospect but not fill his barn." He tried to sell this promised plum; failing, he borrowed money on it. Three years later, he offered it to Egerton (now Lord Keeper), if Egerton would obtain for him the Mastership of the Rolls.

The Lord Keeper refused.

In April of 1594, the Queen's new Attorney General was sworn, and commenced his duties. The Queen sent for him. There is a little story about their meeting; Coke gives it in his *Third Institute:* "And I well remember when the lord treasurer Burghley told Queen Elizabeth, Madame, here is your attorney generall (I being sent for) *qui pro Domina Regina sequitur* [who prosecutes for his mistress the Queen], she said she would have the forme of the records altered, for it should be *attornatus generalis qui pro domina* VERITATE *sequitur* [who prosecutes for his mistress the truth]."

No less characteristic was the message Coke received from his one-time Master of Trinity College, John Whitgift, now Archbishop of Canterbury and Primate of England. From his palace at Lambeth, hearing of Coke's promotion, Whitgift sent a Greek Testament. His old pupil, he wrote, "had now studied common law enough; let him hereafter study the law of God."

It was serene and hortatory, but the Archbishop chose an unpropitious moment. Religion had been made into a crime, the laws of man subverted the laws of God. For twelve years, Coke was to act as Attorney General, first for Queen Elizabeth, then for King James I. For twelve years, to track down "papist traitors" would be his especial charge — not a pretty business nor one which endears. But Attorney Generals do not choose their cases. The Queen's prosecutor has but one client, exigent, demanding, without mercy and without soul — that great, expedient corporation, the State.

The King of Spain, Elizabeth told a French ambassador blandly, had fifteen times attempted her life. Should a sixteenth attempt be successful, anarchy would ensue and English papists combine with France and Spain to put a Catholic on the throne of England. It was no idle fear. Within the decade, a Prince of Orange, a King of France had met death by assassination. The faith of princes was scarcely less uncertain than their lives. Henry of Navarre had changed his religion in order to be King of France. ("Paris is worth a Mass," he said.)

In the minds of young Jesuit missioners, a holy ambition flared. "There is," wrote Henry Walpole in 1591, "a great hope and inclination to the Catholic faith of late in England, in court, camp and country." The champion of champions still lived on. Philip of Spain, once Mary Tudor's husband, sat now in his black velvet wheelchair in the Escorial, tormented with stone, gout, asthma and hurling anathema at his sister-in-law Isabella (Elizabeth) of England. *Scorpio,* Burghley called him in cipher. His mind undimmed, his plans forever forming, shifting, as his armadas ranged the seas, Philip, at sixty-seven, had by no means put away ambition toward the English crown he had come so near to wearing; his daughter, the Infanta, by blood assuredly had claim. From the Rising in the North of 1569, when Coke had been a student at Cambridge, down through the Babington plot that sent Mary Stuart to the block and the Lopez affair that was soon to astonish London, every attempt on Elizabeth's life could be traced to Catholicism and Spain. Decade by decade and bitterness on bitterness the thing had piled up until heaven itself — let alone the Queen's Attorney — would have been troubled to disentangle right from wrong.

Men confused piety with deceit, the celebration of the Mass with secret poisonings. In the Parliament House itself a traitor had been caught: Dr. Parry, a Kentish Burgess who confessed a plan to pistol the Queen as she rode in the fields by Greenwich. Then there was the young Warwickshire gentleman who informed his friends that he was going to London to kill the Queen and "set her head on a pole because she is a sarpent and a viper," and who set off cheerfully and quite alone on his mission and ended, of course, in the Tower. The danger was real, the plots existed. Because a man is crazy (or dedicated) does not mean his pistol will shoot crooked. London went in throngs to see these poor wretches executed, shouted "Death to traitors!" and watched the terrible sentence carried through — the hanging, the cutting down alive, the castrating and disemboweling. At every scaffold, future martyrs were born. Young Henry Walpole of Norfolk, standing close during the quartering of Father Campion, was spattered with blood and swore then and there to dedicate his life to the Catholic cause.

Elizabeth hated this butchery of priests, and there were those at her Council Table who questioned its efficacy. Spain boasted that Inquisition methods were successful and had wiped out the Lutheran heresy within her borders. In England, severity seemed to have perverse effect and the Catholic faithful to multiply under the rod. Lord Burghley preferred that priests be hanged only, and "the manner of drawing and quartering be forborne." Errors of "zeal rather than of malice" should be gently dealt with. Sir Thomas Smith also disapproved the rigor of the new penal laws; violence was not the way to advance religion.

But cruelty, once accepted as a policy, cannot easily be dispensed with, nor can penalties be readily mitigated after the public has grown used to seeing them enforced. Parents took their children to executions. The dying men made long, passionate speeches to the Crown, and if a prisoner "repented" and vowed he "died in Christ," it was considered edifying. In such a climate, men did not stop to distinguish criminal from saint. Every suspect was a would-be assassin, even those gentle missioners, the Fathers Campion and Southwell, who on the scaffold had protested that they wished no harm to Queen or country but desired only to further the cause of true religion.

No sooner was Coke named Attorney General than a pamphlet appeared in London, entitled *A Conference about the next succession to the Crown of England*, and nominating the Infanta of Spain. The very boldness of the maneuver was shocking, and the author had dedicated it to Essex, pointing suspicion where it might be most effectual. The pamphlet was signed *R. Doleman*, pen name for the cleverest, strongest Jesuit of them all, Robert Parsons of Somerset, living somewhere on the Continent, in close touch with Spain and Rome, believed to be the brains behind all Catholic attempts on England — a man "whose doublings and turnings are such as would trouble a right good hound to trace him." From his secret presses rolled a stream of *Discourses*, *Treatises on the English Persecution*, *Response to Elizabeth* . . . persuasive, dangerous, appearing anywhere and everywhere, even on the pews of St. Mary's Church at Oxford when the parishioners came to Sunday service. A skilled politician, Parsons knew the cause could not succeed unless the home ground was well prepared. Spain was deceived if she thought "to get the upper hand in England without having a party *within the realm.*" Nor would such a party form itself — that too, said Parsons, was "a great illusion." It must be shaped and instigated from without; from without must come money and men to hold it together.

To prevent the creation of such a party was the Attorney General's especial business. Ownership of Parson's *Conference on the Succession* was declared high treason; Coke searched out copies where he could. London was gripped with a kind of panic, though the Queen, as usual, seemed less affected than most. Refusing, she said "to mistrust the love of her subjects," she made herself easy of access and rode the streets lightly guarded, horrifying her escorts by singling out humble persons in the throng and giving them her hand to kiss. To count heads was useless; for the Attorney General it was enough to know that a foreign power had agents in England's midst and they must be hunted down. For the first fifteen months, Coke acted alone, as both Attorney and Solicitor General; the Queen had yet to appoint a second in command. But he had powerful backing. Lord Burghley's men were at his call; informers and pursuivants are never hard to come by when the purse is open. Essex also employed his private spies, with the Bacon brothers, Anthony and Francis, acting as interrogators of suspects or translators of captured foreign cipher.

To read the *State Papers Domestic* one would think government, in the 1590's, had been busy at little else. Coke's name appears again and again, as signature to depositions of witnesses, in letters to Burghley about penalties to be imposed, or certifying the confessions of suspects to be examined in the Tower, the Gate House, the Marshalsea, the Clink. An official nomenclature had developed for kinds and degrees of recusants. The "schismatics" were Catholics by conviction who attended Protestant church to escape ruinous fines for nonattendance; the "old Mary priests" were Fathers left over from Queen Mary Tudor's day, tolerated because they kept quiet and did not proselytize. Elderly and easy-going, these Mary priests disliked the vigorous young Jesuit missionaries, with their Continental education and arrogant ways. Jesuits, besides, were apt to be gentlemen born, extraordinarily attractive in person, accomplished courtiers in conversation and address — Father Gerard and the four Walpole brothers of Norfolk could talk falconry with any peer's son, wear a sword as casually as Ralegh and ride as gracefully as Essex. Many were brilliant scholars who had left Oxford or Cambridge because they would not take the Oath of Supremacy necessary to a University degree. It was said they were making converts by the score, and not poor converts either, but rich ones who in their country manors could shelter these young fathers and contribute bountifully to the cause.

It was a most painful dissension in the body politic. Neighbor spied on neighbor, men hunted recusants for prize money as they would have hunted owls or wolves. Catholics were the conservatives of the time, upholders of the past and of "the old religion," landholders of inherited title whose servants shared their ancient loyalties. In the confiscation of recusant property lay a mine of enrichment for officialdom. The temptation was strong. At one sitting of the Hampshire Assizes, four hundred recusants were brought in; at a sitting in Lancashire, six hundred. Jails overflowed, local Justices of the Peace were at their wits' end. The Bishop of Winchester petitioned that among the lustier offenders, two hundred be sent into Flanders "to labor for the army."

Dishonest officials — the Justice Shallows and their henchmen — made the most of it where they could, pocketing fines, forging passports for recusants to come and go. In the Star Chamber, Coke informed against "one Enster, a minister, for forging six passports and against Egles, the Clerk of a Justice of the Peace, for forging 73; which was confessed by them. They were sentenced to be whopte in Wiltshire and fined each £5 and imprisonment." The government tried hard to stop all such trafficking. In Star Chamber Coke brought information against five Lancashiremen who had gone into papist-catching as a business, counterfeiting warrants under the Lord Admiral's seal and reaping a harvest of "papists, seminaries, *agnes dei* and crucifixes, receiving money and thus having collected divers sums and deceived the Queen's people." Wearing on their breasts the Queen's Arms like pursuivants, the five, under the leadership of one Johnson, had terrified a priest into "confessing" that he had burned a child in an oven — after which Johnson pocketed five pounds to keep quiet about it. The men even forged warrants for their own maintenance in the town of Lancaster. When a plucky mayor refused to give them lodging, Johnson, in the law French of the reporter, "*done luy blowe del eare*."

The judges made short work of the case. Four of the culprits were sentenced to stand on the pillory "and lose their ears if they have any," be branded on the forehead with the letter F, "for Fraymaker or Fighter," and perpetual service in the galleys. The fifth man had an easier sentence, "inasmuch as he wrote the forged names through fear of a stab from Johnson." Lord Burghley, as sentence was being pronounced, interrupted with a grimly practical suggestion. "Inasmuch," he said, "as such burnings in the ears and hands die out in a short time, the prisoners should be scarified on the balls of the cheeks with the letter F by a surgeon, and some powder put there to color it, so that it should never vanish."

"But the others," the report ends, "made no reply to this."

All traitors did not bear the Roman stigma. Coke was at times concerned with recusants of another color. "Puritan" was a word used indiscriminately, in the 1590's, for nonconformists, whether Presbyterians, Brownists, Barrowists, Enthusiasts, Antinomians, Anabaptists or Norfolk's imported Family of Love. And though these were not "Spaniards" but mere rioting Englishmen, they were dangerous enough. Any one of them seemed equipped (like Lord Cromwell's two Puritans at North Elmham Parish) to mount a pulpit without license or official preparation and preach violently against the Episcopal Establishment. Country people flocked to hear them, flocked also to those meetings called "prophesyings," where revelation twisted itself readily into temporal forecast and discussion concerning the most acceptable Protestant successor to the Crown.

There seemed no end to self-styled prophets. One William Hacket — possessed, he said, by the soul of John the Baptist — ran through London with his followers, crying "Repent, England, repent!" — which might have been overlooked had not Hacket stuck bodkins through the Queen's picture and insisted she must be "unthroned." In prison, Hacket "confessed" and revealed the names of his associates, all of whom, at their examination, refused to remove their hats because they were "of higher dignity" than the Bishops and the Lord Keeper who sat to question them.

Nor were Martin Marprelate's libels (1588) forgotten. It had taken the government five years to discover the presses and round up conspirators enough to make a show and example. The chief instigator turned out to be a Welshman named John Penry, who possessed the infernal talent of being funny in print on religious subjects. Puritans still quoted his pieces. Archbishop Whitgift hated the sight of Penry and those ardent dissenters, Barrow and Greenwood. Separately or together the three were interrogated, commencing with the High Commission, the supreme ecclesiastical disciplinary court which tried heresy cases without a jury. Whitgift presided. When, he asked, had Barrow last been to church?

"That," said Barrow, "is nothing to you."

"Of what occupation are you?" asked the Archbishop.

"A Christian," Barrow said.

"So are we all," said Whitgift.

"I deny that!" Barrow retorted. He would not, Barrow added, answer truthfully any questions concerning religion, nor would he swear an oath or give bond. "The Lord knoweth," he told the Archbishop, "I am ignorant. I have no learning to boast of. But this I know, that *you* are void of all true learning and godliness" — after which he called the Archbishop a monster, resembling the beast from Revelation "with horns like a lamb that spoke like a dragon, which compelled people on earth to worship the image of the beast or be killed."

It was courageous, considering the circumstances. But it sounded mad. These Independents had drifted into a jargon all their own, violent, colorful, borrowed largely from Revelation and Jeremiah — and extremely irritating to those outside the fraternity. It was too much for Whitgift, who cried out from the bench, "Away with him! Clap him up close, close! I will make him tell another tale yet. I have not done with him!"

The men gave their judges no chance, they seemed to ask for martyrdom. They had none of the Jesuit finesse and certainly none of the Jesuit learning which so roused Coke's curiosity later on. The High Commission let Barrow and Greenwood go for the moment, then rearraigned them under the statute of *23 Elizabeth* (1581) making it a felony to "devise and write, print or set forth any manner of book, rhyme, ballad, letter, or writing containing any false, seditious, or slanderous matters to the defamation of the Queen's Majesty, or to the encouraging, stirring or moving of any insurrection or rebellion." Tried again at the Sessions Hall (Old Bailey) with a jury, Barrow and Greenwood swore they had no "malicious intent." They were found guilty and executed at Tyburn. John Penry too had his trial at common law in the court of Queen's Bench. He was convicted of treason, then taken across the river into Surrey and hanged, to the satisfaction of the orthodox.

CHAPTER EIGHT

1594-1597. The Lopez conspiracy. Father Gerard. The Bloody Question and the doctrine of equivocation.

> As these learned English fugitives [Jesuits] studied to advance the Infanta of Spain to the Scepter of England by writing; so others of their number secretly attempted the same by the sword, sending privily certaine murderers to kill Queen Elizabeth: and some Spaniards attempted it by poyson, using the help of Roderigo Lopez, a Portugal, for a long time a man of noted fidelity.
>
> William Camden, *Annales*

DR. Roderigo Lopez was the Queen's physician. He had lived in England for years, owned a handsome house in Holborn not far from Coke's, was a member of the College of Physicians and was consulted by most of the nobility. Some said the Doctor owed less to expertness and learning than to his sympathetic manner and an "ability to make great account of himself." It was told around town that Lord Burghley had ordered him to return a fee after failing to cure a servant's "swelled shin-bone." But such slanders are part of every fashionable practice; Lopez was content with his position. Francis Bacon described him as "very observant," of a "pleasing and appliable behaviour."

He was accused of conspiring to murder Elizabeth, "stir up a rebellion and a war within the realm and overthrow the commonwealth." It was Essex who found him out. The young Earl, in his running rivalry with the Cecils, looked continually for means to enlarge his foreign intelligence so as to surpass Burghley's. But while Burghley used his spies to maintain the peace (and said so), Essex, whose hope of glory lay in arms, not treaties, desired open war with Spain and to this end produced, when he could, proof of Spanish perfidy. Each captured suspect fed the Essex fire, at once heating popular hatred toward the enemy and lighting up the Earl's own patriotic efforts. Actually, Dr. Lopez dipped his fingers somewhere in the Spanish pie; he confessed to accepting a jewel from Philip II — which he promptly gave to Elizabeth — and said he had "listened" to a bribe of fifty thousand crowns. Yet it is extremely doubtful if Lopez ever plotted harm to the Queen. He might have lived out his life quite peacefully had it not occurred to Essex that so accomplished a linguist, with friends all over Europe, would be a perfect instrument for foreign correspondence. Essex made an offer; Lopez not only refused but, to the Earl's vast annoyance, told the Queen about it. Essex next intercepted some suspicious-looking letters, on the strength of which he obtained from Privy Council permission to search the Doctor's papers. Robert Cecil went with him. They found nothing. The Queen, angry, told Essex that he was "a rash and temerarious youth to enter into a matter against the poor man which he could not prove." The Earl retired to his rooms and sulked for forty-eight hours, then emerged and laid his nose again to the scent. "I will make this conspiracy as clear as the noonday," he said.

In a week's time, Dr. Lopez was in the Tower and with him half a dozen Spanish and Irish suspects. From now on, accounts conflict and every tale is different. Yet from the moment these men entered prison, the world accepted their guilt. (In times of civil danger any foreign victim serves the purpose.) Coke, Essex, the Privy Council went down-river to interrogate the conspirators. For one suspect, the State Papers have six succeeding examinations by Coke, witnessed by the Tower Lieutenant or members of Privy Council. Known as "preparing for the trial," this was regular procedure—formal interrogation and answer, written out, signed, witnessed, then repeated later to see if the answers matched. Inevitably, contradictions cropped up as new conspirators were caught. Men swore and forswore, confessed and "retractated." The English common law forbade torture — a fact of which English legal writers, including Coke, were very proud. "There is no law to warrant tortures in this land," he wrote in the *Third Institute*, "nor can they be justified by any prescription being so lately brought in." Quoting Chief Justice Fortescue, Virgil, Luke and John — torture, Coke concluded, is against Magna Carta, *Capitus 39*. "And accordingly all the said ancient authors are against any paine or torment to be put or inflicted upon the prisoner before attainder, nor after attainder, but according to the judgement. And there is no one opinion in our books, or judicial record (that we have seen and remember), for the maintenance of tortures or torments."

Elizabeth's famous Secretary, Sir Thomas Smith, had gone even further, declaring torture to be contrary to the very nature of Englishmen. "Torment or question, which is used by order of the civill lawe and custome of other countries, to put a malefactor to excessive paine, to make him confesse of him selfe, or of his felowes or complices, is not used in England, it is taken for servile. The nature of our nation is free, stoute, haulte, prodigall of life and bloud; but contumelie, beatings, servitude, and servile torment and punishment it will not abide."

Considering the high tone taken, and considering Edward Coke's persistent care for legal precision in writing, it is extraordinary that neither man saw fit to mention the frequent torture of suspects that took place during their respective tenures of office. It was true that in England torture was not used as penalty after conviction but only before trial, to induce confession; true also that warrants of torture came never from the common-law judges but from the Queen or Privy Council — in short, from that mystic authority known as the *prerogative*, where all blame could rest. Coke said repeatedly that in England the prerogative was limited by common law. (Under two Stuart kings, he was to risk his life to prove it.) Yet in Elizabeth's day, no common-law judge seems to have questioned the royal warrant. Coke, Bacon, Burghley, Robert Cecil — every man in government, when so commanded, signed the Queen's warrant for torture. "Obstinate fellows," who before trial would not talk, were put to the manacles, the rack, or an instrument known as Skevington's Irons. Some were shut into the cell-box called *Little Ease* or in the Tower hole below high water mark, referred to officially as "the low dungeon with the rats."

This distinction between law and the prerogative, accepted without question before the Stuarts' time (1603), would be obliterated only by revolution.* But if judges and attorney generals found justification, Tower prisoners could take small comfort in nice juristic lines between law and prerogative; the rack was no more endurable because the Queen and not her judges had ordered it. The truth is that government, unless prevented by the people at large, in all times and climes employs such methods as it finds convenient. "Cruel and unusual punishments," once used, will be used again, and by a kind of tacit conspiracy, accepted. Elizabeth's warrants for torture, far from being destroyed as shameful, were filed methodically with other records and remain to tell the truth. Nor was the rack used solely for traitors and prisoners of state; particularly heinous robberies or murders were "solved" by evidence so obtained. Strong men who could look on the scaffold without flinching broke down under torture. Henry Walpole, racked by Topcliffe until he could not write, gave the names of his friends and declared himself ready to change his religion and conform. (It did not save his life.) Yet men under duress stood up valiantly for their rights; more than one prisoner is reported as demanding "to see the warrant for my racking."

Dr. Roderigo Lopez was not tortured, nor, probably, were his accomplices, though Louis Tinoco, a bragging, impudent liar, was "shown the manacles." Experienced examiners knew that to some minds a glimpse of the rack could be as efficacious as the first turn of the screw. "The brake," people called it with a kind of rough jocosity, "the Duke of Exeter's daughter." Yet a populace which went to public executions as to a circus hated this Tower torturing. The government took care to repudiate, at public trial, any accusation of its employment. Richard Topcliffe, the notorious Tower questioner, was especially loathed. His name had become a byword — *Topcliffian customs* — by which he felt himself aggrieved, "for only doing my duty," he said plaintively.

Lopez's trial was held in the Guildhall before a special commission, headed by the Earl of Essex. Coke conducted the prosecution. Perhaps the clearest story rests in his own *Heads of the indictment.* Set down briefly for his convenience, the notes lack that professional courtroom oratory, at once brutal and self-righteous,

* After the Commonwealth (1649) there is no instance of torture in England. France forbade it by decree in 1780, Russia by ukase in 1801, the German states not until later in the nineteenth century.

which in treason cases disfigured speeches from bench as from bar. There are eight headings, each carefully dated and purporting to give the main facts of guilt — a jewel accepted from the King of Spain, "1 Oct. 1591"; conferences with Andrada, de Gama and Tinoco, "for poisoning the Queen"; a repeated statement by Lopez that "when he had performed the same, he would go to Antwerp and thence to Constantinople, where he would dwell."

Little in the written evidence or indeed in this performance at the Guildhall would today convict a man of capital crime — unless public feeling demanded it. Lopez was a foreigner and, according to Francis Bacon, a converted Jew. By the time he reached the courtroom he had no chance, the thing was decided. "Perjured and murdering traitor!" Coke exclaimed. "Worse than Judas himself!" Robert Cecil, writing late that same afternoon to Windebank, Clerk of the Signet, remarked with satisfaction that "a most substantial jury have found the doctor guilty in the highest degree of all treasons and judgement has been passed against him with the applause of the world. Though the villain said he had belied himself only to save himself from racking, which the Lord knows is most untrue."

For three months, the Queen left Lopez's death warrant unsigned, possibly from compassion, for she had liked the old Doctor, but more likely, persuaded that he might reveal further guilty names. It was now that Francis Bacon maneuvered himself into the affair, traveling to the Tower to interview the condemned and to prepare his *True report of the Detestable Treasons intended by Dr. Lopez* — a form of propaganda at which Bacon was especially skillful. "Our Tower employment," he called it, writing to the Lord Keeper. The government, after important convictions, put out such statements to justify and inform; they were usually translated and sent to France and the Low Countries.

Early in June, 1594, the Queen signed Lopez's death warrant. With his confederates, the Doctor was dragged up Holborn Hill and out the long road to Tyburn. A great crowd followed. From the scaffold, Lopez cried out that he had only meant "to deceive the Spaniard and wipe him of his money." The mob, bloodthirsty, delighted, could not have enough of him. He was first up the ladder, and trying, against the noise and catcalls, to make a dying speech, swore that he "loved the Queen as he loved Jesus Christ" — which, says Camden, "from a man of the Jewish profession, was heard not without laughter." Young Tinoco, when his turn came, was cut down alive and rushed on the executioner, struggling with him while the mob, breaking through the gates, made a ring to watch. Knocked down finally by a blow on the head, Tinoco was held on the scaffold while the rest of the fearful sentence was carried out.

Elizabeth refused to deprive the Doctor's family of his property by the usual attaint of blood that was part of a traitor's penalty. The affair created infinite talk. It was said the Queen continued to wear at her belt the jewel Lopez gave her. Marlowe, Dekker, Middleton referred to the Doctor in their plays; Shakespeare is thought to have used him in his studies of Shylock.

Yet on the calendar of the Queen's Attorney General, Lopez was one among many. A month after the Doctor's execution, three more conspirators were caught — English gentlemen, by name Yorke, Williams and Young, who had been living in Brussels with the Catholic exiles and confessed a plan to "kill the Queen and raise rebellion in Wales." Once again it was Essex who brought information and conducted much of the pretrial questioning. The prisoners accused each other of wildly dramatic crimes. Williams had taken eighteen hundred pounds' worth of plate from Winchester Cathedral and coined it into money at chambers in Gray's Inn. Young was "cunning in poisoning." Yorke had called Lord Burghley a bloodsucker and sworn to "lay a coal of fire upon the stairs in a privy place and put poison upon it, so that as many as came up the stairs would fall down dead." They were fools who tried to kill the Queen, Yorke added, for "she was always mewed up in her chamber." Better "to kill the Lord Treasurer's horse, for he would take it so grievously if the old jade were dead that he would die too." (Everyone knew about Burghley's old horse, of which he was so proud.) In the end, all three swore on the Sacrament, in Coke's presence, that they had been sent from Brussels to kill both the Queen and Burghley. All three were executed at Tyburn.

Fantastic as the accusations seem, and the "proofs," it is to be noted that these single traitors, these ineffectual would-be assassins were considered, every one, as part of a larger plan. Their orders came from abroad, from France, Spain, the Low Countries. Williams and Yorke testified there was in Brussels a Council of State for England, composed of well-known exiled English gentlemen — Williams gave their names — which met every morning to debate on plans for the "Catholization of England." Suspects confessed they had "listened to Robert Parsons the Jesuit expound the doctrine that it was laudable and permissible to kill a heretic prince." Some came with plans to fire the Queen's ships, or confessed they "adhered to the King of Spain, robbed and spoiled divers English ships at sea." "John Annias," runs one of Coke's examinations, "undertook the burning of the Queen's ships, had a pension from Spain; L—— undertook to kill Her Majesty. . . . The others are obstinate and seducing priests and Jesuits, and have long remained in Spain."

The fact of their willing exile raised indignation. Could a true Englishman prefer to live in enemy country, let alone use enemy country as a base from which to attack his native land? "Who sent you?" It was the first, most frequent question. The stones of Newgate gave it back, and the Tower bastions. *Who sent you?* Every Catholic exile used, of necessity, an alias, forged passports to come and go. "One John Patrick, an alleged Englishman." The words were scornful, suggestive of perjury. There is an injured note to some of the reports — "how these men plot to kill our Queen, whereas our Queen has never been privy to any practice against the King of Spain's life." *Our Queen,* meanwhile, was busy putting out her own pirate ships, which did extremely well; the *Swiftsure,* the *Crane,* the *Malescourge,* slipping past enemy beacons, running under the walls and guns of Spain and returning laden with gold which bore no English imprint. An order to Sir John Hawkins for "a voyage to the southward" names six ships — ending, significantly enough, with the *Foresight* — "for which her Majesty is to have a third part of any booty taken from her enemies."

A war-and-no-war, men called it, grumbling. On shore the Spaniard-hunt was expensive, time-consuming. After a notorious case like the Lopez conspiracy, whole nests of suspects were netted. The seaport watches were strengthened, directives sent out *For the apprehension of suspicious persons coming into England from beyond sea.* Special officers saw to it that no one landed until examined as to why he came. "If the cause does not appear clear," runs the order, "they are to be committed to prison or kept on board until their examinations have been sent to the [Privy] Council. Every Irishman shall present himself to the Lord Mayor to be examined how he lives and why he remains in England. No one who has served for the King of Spain is to be allowed to come into the realm. If any one has done so without leave, he is to be attached, imprisoned, and punished as an enemy, and whoever detects any such person shall have a good reward, and not be made known to the offender."

In 1596, Spain captured Calais from the French, which meant the enemy was entrenched within twenty-two miles of the English coast. War-and-no-war, the chase went on. The accounts have a quality of fantasy, picaresque, incredible — "Thomas Hygate, seminary priest, broke from Wisbeach Castle, rode with his man waiting on him, a hawk on his fist and a lackey running by him. . . . Brewster, a priest, was hid in a chimney. . . . Topcliffe came near to taking one Pixter, a priest, took his girdle, hangers [holding-loops on a sword-belt] rapier and cloak but he made his escape and went beyond sea. . . . In Mrs. Rigsby's house in Old Street behind Golden Lane there is a vault under the stairs going up to a chamber where two or three may be hid, and a place on top of the stairs where they can take up the boards to go down to the vault. . . . In Wolfes, in a little gallery, there is a place for an altar and other massing stuff . . . at Mapledurham there is a vault under a table with a grate of iron for a light into the garden and has rosemary growing against the grate."

Hawk on fist and lackey running; rosemary growing against the grate "as by a cellar window." These things were true, they happened and gave their color to the times. Edward Coke, by virtue of his office, was marked by them as the huntsman is marked by his cry. When danger threatens, the pack runs together: Coke, Burghley, Popham, Anderson, Francis Bacon, John Whitgift, Egerton. Attorney, judge, bishop, Lord Keeper, their nose was to the scent. ". . . found guilty of all treasons," wrote Robert Cecil, "with the applause of all the world."

Coke examined dozens, perhaps scores of Catholic suspects. One of the most celebrated was John Gerard the Jesuit, son of a Derbyshire gentleman who had been imprisoned for trying to rescue Mary Stuart. When Coke encountered him, he was a tall, strong, swarthy man of thirty-three, with dark hair, square-cut beard and a formidable reputation with the authorities. Already he had escaped from three English prisons and seemed to pass back and forth across the Channel at pleasure, to the vast embarrassment of port officials. Suave, knowledgeable, he had a kind of naïve snobbishness. His very humility was arrogant and he was perfectly honest except when he came up against Protestants. Money poured into his pockets for the cause. "They gave without my asking and looked on it as a favour when I accepted," he wrote often. (Actually, he was to die in his bed at a ripe age, "unworthy," he said, "the crown of martyrdom.")

On a spring day of 1597 — April 14 — Coke, with William Waad, clerk of the Privy Council, and Solicitor General Thomas Fleming, went down to the Tower to question Father Gerard. Fleming had been appointed late in '95. He was slow and reliable, the perfect second in command. Coke liked him and said he had a "sociable, placable nature and disposition." Even Francis Bacon had no word of disparagement. Bacon was part of this Tower mission, the Queen having finally named him among her "counsel learned in the law," which meant merely that he could act for the Crown in a legal capacity. Coke noted with satisfaction that Bacon was only named, not sworn.

The three lawyers were prepared to meet a skillful antagonist, a scholar from Oxford, Rheims and Rome who could match anyone's Latin or logic. Gerard had been too much for Topcliffe when that gentleman put to him the dreaded "bloody question," devised by Burghley: "Should the Pope send an army to England, for whom would you fight, Rome or England, the Pope or the Queen?"

"I am a loyal Catholic," the Jesuit had replied. "And I am a loyal subject of the Queen. If this were to happen — and I do not think it at all likely — I would behave as a loyal Catholic and a loyal subject."

Topcliffe, at this, had lost his temper, unbuckled his sword and flung it threateningly on the table. Gerard merely looked at it in distaste and was led, loaded with irons, back to his cell. The old Dean of Westminster, Dr. Goodman, had been equally routed on undertaking to prove, by the best Cambridge logic, that Gerard was a heretic. The Jesuit had trapped the Dean into a syllogism, then turned it back on him, explaining blandly that the Dean's logic was false, because it "descended from the general to the particular and contained four terms."

What could be done with such a man? The story leaked out, with other tales about Gerard. How, when first captured, he had argued religion through the night with the Bishop of London's chaplain, and had all but converted him. How, in Marshalsea prison, Gerard contrived secretly to celebrate Mass for the other Catholic prisoners. How he got out on bail, escaped to France, and, returning, made his way through Norfolk by pretending to be a gentleman out looking for a lost hawk. ("Did you not hear his bell tinkle?" Gerard asked.) He could play at dice and cards and did not hesitate to do so when disguise seemed necessary. Under his cloak and courtier's dress he carried a gilt dagger and rapier, and under that a hair shirt, badge of the Jesuit.

Sir Richard Berkeley, Lieutenant of the Tower, lived in a little house within the walls. Here the examiners waited — Coke, Fleming, Bacon, Berkeley and William Waad. Led from the Salt Tower up hill and across the Yard, Gerard entered the room wearing his priest's robe. Coke, seated behind a table, was, as always, methodical. His questions, written out in legal form, asked nothing about religion or creed and were confined to matters political. Gerard denied everything. If he had corresponded with Jesuits abroad, the letters were concerned, he said, only with the financial assistance of Catholics living on the Continent. Where, he was asked, did the man live in England who received and forwarded these letters?

"I do not know," said Gerard, "and if I did, I could not and would not tell you."

Coke next inquired the whereabouts of Father Henry Garnett, a famous Catholic missioner who bore, in the Jesuit order, the title Superior of the English Province. "You say," Coke began, "you have no wish to obstruct the government. Tell us, then, where Father Garnett is. He is an enemy of the state and you are bound to report on all such men." *

Father Garnett was no enemy, Gerard replied. On the contrary, given opportunity, he would lay down his life for Queen and country. "But I do not know where he lives. And if I did, I could not and would not tell you."

It was a form of answer well known to the examiners — the fa-

* Gerard's *Autobiography* is written in Latin — intended, probably, for his friends in the Jesuit order. Though the questions and answers, translated into modern English, read strangely here, they are quoted verbatim.

mous Jesuit *equivocation.* Taught at Rome as a justified doctrine and device, it effectively blocked examination. Sir Richard Berkeley produced a warrant for Gerard's torture, which the prisoner promptly asked to see, "to make sure it was properly made out and signed."

It was.* His jailers led Gerard away. For three days the examiners waited in the Lieutenant's house, sending from time to time to know if the prisoner had answered the questions. He had not. On the third morning, Waad went to the torture chamber, told Gerard he came straight from the Queen and Sir Robert Cecil, both of whom had sworn on their honor that Father Henry Garnett was a danger to the state and must be delivered up. Gerard merely shook his head. He was taken back to his cell. Four weeks later, when he had recovered from the torture, he was again led to the Lieutenant's house and confronted by the same men, with the exception of Bacon. By some means, Gerard had had a letter from Father Garnett, telling him to expect immediate trial and execution — "a gift which cannot," Gerard wrote later, "be had for mere willing or striving and which my great unworthiness prevented." He seemed calm, indifferent, wholly prepared, and as usual answered readily, up to a point. "Yes," he replied to Coke's question; he had "endeavored to seduce people from the faith approved by English law, over to the Pope's allegiance." No, he had not plotted against the government.

This, Coke retorted, was a paradox; it was impossible. "How could a man try to convert England and yet keep out of politics?" And what means had Gerard used to achieve his purpose? "Name the Catholics you know," Coke said shortly. "Do you know X, and Y?"

"I do not," Gerard replied. "And if I did, I could not mention their names."

Such equivocation, Coke interrupted angrily, not only countenanced lying but undermined all social intercourse between men.

* Referring to the fact that Gerard had been receiving intelligence from abroad, the warrant directed the Lieutenant of the Tower to see that the prisoner be "put to the manacles and such other torture as is used in that place." The manacles were iron bracelets which clamped round the wrists, and by which a man was hung to staples driven into a pillar. Steps were withdrawn from under his feet and he was questioned, hanging, until he fainted. Gerard, by his own account, fainted nine times the first day.

He had met it before, in Father Southwell's trial, a "most wicked and horrible doctrine" which would barbarously supplant all justice and make perjury lawful.

Gerard disagreed. Equivocation, he said, differed from lying. Intent was not to deceive but simply to withhold truth which the questioned party was in no way bound to reveal. "What," asked Gerard, "would this board of examiners do if attacked by thieves who asked where their money was hidden?" In England, he went on, it was the custom of the accused to answer "Not guilty," until witnesses were produced against him, or a verdict returned by the jury. No one condemned such practices as lying. Nevertheless, Gerard added, a witness examined concerning temporal matters had no right to use equivocation or to deny crime "if he be guilty and lawfully interrogated."

On Coke's asking what the prisoner considered lawful interrogation, Gerard said he meant interrogation concerning "action in some way harmful to the State." Had not our Lord himself used equivocation when he told his Apostles he was not going up to Jerusalem for the feast, knowing all the time that he intended to go? And again, when he told the Twelve that none knew the Day of Judgment, not even the Son of Man? Here Waad broke in and the six men were suddenly involved in theological argument, an exercise seemingly irresistible to Elizabethans, at which a Jesuit could outdistance anybody except another Jesuit. Gerard was pleasantly sure he had won. "My examiners," he wrote, "had practically no answer to make. But the Attorney General wrote down every word and said he would use it against me before very long when I came up for trial."

The Attorney General did indeed write down every word. Next day he sent it to Burghley, with a note pointing out the hopelessness of such examinations. Against the Jesuitical equivocation no weapon existed. "What desperate and damnable doctrine this is," Coke exclaimed, "that taketh away the use of an oath that God hath appointed to be a mean to decide controversies!" A horrible abuse of the oath, Coke said, twisted thus to a man's self-justification. "Strange opinion of these boy priests and devilish good Fathers!" He had, Coke went on, asked Gerard to write out his extraordinary defense of equivocation. Such "damnable and blasphemous heresies" should not be laid at a man's door without his consent and signature. "But he denied [refused] the same, not because it is untrue but because he would not publish it. Then being requested to subscribe [sign] the same, he denied the same also."

It was like putting on trial a fish, a bird, a salamander. A man no sooner had his finger on something than it slipped away, flew off and was gone. To the legal mind, even perjury is hardly more baffling than silence. A silent defendant can be neither saved nor damned; he has set himself outside the law's protection. The court is blocked, the wheels stop. *Fidelis testis:* the truthful witness stands at the heart of legal procedure. Not without reason (Coke would have said) did the common law punish a man who refused to be tried. In the Star Chamber, silence was taken for confession of guilt.*

At the outset of Gerard's examination, Coke had told him the questions would follow the phrasing and form to be used in the actual prosecution. The Jesuit's answers made it plain not only that death was to him a matter indifferent and martyrdom a glory, but that he intended to make the trial into a farce. *I did and I did not. . . . I do not know, and if I did I would not tell you.* Devious, un-English performance, smelling of Spain, Rome, of a dark subtlety nourished beyond the Alps! ("Suffer not thy sons to pass the Alps," Burghley had written, "for they shall learn nothing there but pride, blasphemy and atheism.") Coke's transcript of this Tower examination, enclosed in his letter to Burghley, found its way to Oxford and was the subject of a lecture by the Master of University College. "What nattily sophisticated men are these Jesuits!" said the Master. "They do their best, with shocking evasion, to bury the truth in a cloud of darkness."

Only a cloud of darkness could save them. Puritans also, fleeing before Pilate, had their shifts and stratagems. Among the Queen's College Manuscripts is a nonconformist paper entitled "Forms for Answering Interrogatories," devised for use under the oath *ex officio* — "How to answer some facts and deny the rest . . . '*I did not to my memory do. . . . I do not know that I did or said any such thing. . . . I am upon oath and not you, and I pray you to forbear. Leave me to my conscience.*' "

Leave me to my conscience: it is the eternal invocation of men

* Chapter Note.

taken prisoner for their religion. Yet courts, Coke would have said, cannot decide by conscience; to do so would expose the accused to the caprice of every judge upon the bench. In times of national strife the hearts of judges are no less hot than the hearts of those they sit to judge. Law, form, due procedure; these are the only hope of men standing in the dock. England had as yet no rules of evidence. Anything was accepted — hearsay, opinion, garbled recitation of gossip two years old. And on the presentation of evidence the prisoner's fate depends; what is allowed, what overruled. "Strike it from the record!" No prisoner of Coke's day heard these words in his defense. Three centuries must pass before the law — and custom — evolved them, and the public could demand the protection therefrom accorded. The law changes slowly; Coke worked within the existing frame.

"True it is that we have found by wofull experience that it is not frequent and often punishment that doth prevent like offences. Violent courses are like to hot waters that may do good in an extremity, but the use of them doth spoil the stomach, and it will require them stronger and stronger, and by little and little they will lessen their operation."

So wrote Coke the judge, from the fullness of experience. *My Lord Coke*, they called him then, *Chief Justice of England*. But in the year 1597, Attorney General Coke had other notions, other duties. The forces gathered, the winds blew dark. The Queen's prosecutor heard the enemy behind the hill — and followed after.

CHAPTER NINE

1597-1598. The House in Castle Yard. Star Chamber. Death of Bridget Coke.

CASTLE Yard ran down from Holborn into Cursitor Street. It was a pleasant neighborhood beyond the city wall, far enough from Fleet Street so that houses were thinning and there was room for an herb garden, a plum tree or two. *Faringdon Without*, the neighborhood was called. Coke's house was big and comfortable, built on the site of the old Castle Inn. During term time, Bridget Coke came in from the country with her daughter Anne, aged twelve, and the baby Clement. Edward, the eldest son, was already at Cambridge; the four younger boys stayed on at Huntingfield in Suffolk, boarding with a clergyman until they were ready for Westminster School. London airs were almost lethal for the young. Periodic plague and summer fevers kept the average life span at eight years; people left their children in the country when they could.

Castle Yard was not five minutes' walk from the Inner Temple. Had Coke contrived to set up housekeeping in Westminster Hall, he could not have surrounded himself more closely with his kind. Fetter Lane lay to the right, Chancery Lane and the Rolls Office to the left. On quiet mornings, Coke could hear from his chamber the short hoarse blast of the porter's horn, calling the Temple students to breakfast. Lincoln's Inn, where Coke's father had had chambers, was only a step away; a block to the eastward rose the spire of old St. Andrew's, where Robert Coke was buried. His son had set a marble slab above the tomb, bearing the children's names, a flower-like list of sisters with Coke at the head: "Edward, Winifred, Dorothy, Elizabeth, Ursula, Anne, Margaret, Ethelreda." Here, on Sundays, the family came to worship, young Anne walking with them, prim in farthingale and ruff. Coke's aunt and uncle, a Mr. and Mrs. George Knightley, lived in the household; poor relations, it would seem, who made themselves useful about the place.

A retinue of servants waited upon the family — housemaids, cooks, scullery maids, grooms, a steward, a courier, a falconer. The Queen's Attorney General could not walk the streets unattended. At night it would have been dangerous, in daytime his position demanded it. A man's rank was known by his attendants. If an Earl of Essex rode the streets with fifty followers, the Queen's Attorney General must have three or four. The amount of food consumed by the household was extraordinary. Each week the steward submitted his accounts and each week his mistress wrote across the bottom, "Discharged by me, Bridget Coke." Beef was bought three hundred pounds at a time and with it gray salt by the peck, "to powder the beef withal." Fish came from Norfolk, flounder, mackerel, sturgeon, skate. Roasted blackbirds and sparrows were devoured by the dozen, suckling pigs, rabbits and quail, pheasant and snipe and woodcock. "Eleven swyne," wrote the steward, "for the provision of the house." The cooks were lavish with spices — mustard seed, saffron, Jordan almonds, "leaf gold to gild pastry withal, whyte wyne to boyle capons withal." Presents came, of "hartichokes . . . a great borre ready dressed." The Temple Steward sent up an "oringadowe pye and an apple tart." The Countess of Derby sent a buck and so did Sir Robert Cecil; their men were bountifully tipped at the door. The Queen sent a buck, a quart of strawberries. "Mr. Collins, Gentleman Usher to the Queen, sent two loaves of her Majesty's bread. . . . The Queen's gardener sent apples. . . ."

Northward across Holborn Road lay almost open country, with small game plentiful. It was possible for Coke to ride out on fine afternoons, his favorite hawk upon his wrist, his falconer and huntsman riding with him. Cattle wandered in the pastures; there were orchards and sheepfolds and the whole was crisscrossed with a jumble of muddy paths and thoroughfares bearing names like Cow Lane, Chicken Lane, Cock Lane, until one came to the gray walls of

St. Bartholomew's, below which the city spread southeast, ward upon ward, to Cheapside, Cornhill and the Tower.

Holborn Road was, after the Strand, the principal highway east-west through London. It led up from Newgate and the Old Bailey, out the west wall to Tyburn, some three miles beyond. *The heavy hill*, men called it. "To ride a cart up the heavy hill" was a way of saying you were going to be hanged. From his window, Coke could see the hurdle pass and hear, at dawn, wheels rumble as the cart rolled over the stone bridge above Fleet Ditch . . . drunken shouts from the crowd that followed. A country dance tune called "Put on the Smock a Monday" was a favorite melody (no one knew why) for the dying lamentations of criminals. The sound of it came through a man's dreams. In chambers under the roof, old servants, half awake, heard it and crossed themselves before they remembered. Protestantism was new, as such things are counted. It was no easy matter to forgo the ancient comforts, the final absolution and Mass for departed souls. Hell yawned and against its sulphurs the Protestant conscience had small insurance. It was of utmost importance that a man "die in Christ, a confessed believer." In what frame of mind one's relatives left the world was of greater importance than why they left it, though the why be cholera or a decimating summer flux. Old books of instruction were read — *De Arte Moriendi*, *The Booke of the Craft of Dying*. Family letters reveled in pious repetitions of last words. Small children, gasping out their life with whooping cough or fever, managed, it would seem, something appropriate. "In the midst of life we are in death," was true as written each minute of the day. At night the awful prayer went up, rhymed by young voices like a charm against evil: "If I should die before I wake, I pray the Lord my soul to take."

As though disease and dirt were not quick enough, at the Fleet end of the two streets, just east of Castle Yard, gallows stood. The city was used to such sights. In Stow's *Survey of London*, the great annalist remarks casually that a man was hanged "almost on my porch." There had been a plague year in the early 1590's, and plague years did not end neatly with the calendar. It seemed as if all the beggars of Middlesex converged upon London. They died in the streets and alleys; around St. Bartholomew's the carts carried them away. Coke had been forced to curtail his summer readings at the Temple and take his family to the country. Nine benchers and forty Templars had escorted him beyond the city gate as far as Romford. Nobody knew how or why a plague year was started, but everyone had his theory. The alien strangers brought it from the Low Countries; those who were enthusiastically Puritan said it came from Italy, that source of popery, culture and forbidden delight. Harvests were thin; in certain districts, famine threatened and with it disorder. It was rumored that in the west "the poor were up and only waited for a drum."

In the Star Chamber, Coke brought information against forestallers, engrossers, regrators who cornered local grain markets, taking advantage of scarcity to push up prices. Norfolkmen attacked pack trains carrying grain to the coast and "riotously unloaded vessels in port." In Wiltshire, men fell upon the carts of grain dealers hauling across country. Rich and poor alike, the offenders were led to court. A member of the famous Sidney family, brought from Norfolk to answer charges of engrossing corn, was imprisoned and swore that he was innocent. He had "relieved four hundred poor men weekly at his door last year and sold his corn in the market at twelve shillings eightpence under the price of the market." From the Gatehouse he wrote that he was terrified his case "would be taken by the Attorney General to Star Chamber where the offense is punished with fyne and pillery, a horrible disgrace to the honorable name of the Sidneys." His friends advised him to bribe his way out of trouble but he refused, not from conscience, apparently, but from parsimony, though he had rather die, he said, than be brought to open trial. Star Chamber judges made no allowance for noble blood and were entirely capable of standing a Sidney in the pillory as they stood humbler men, "an empty corne sacke in his hande, a paper on his heade, to paye five pound to the Queene, ten to the party Constable and all his Costes."

As Attorney General, Coke did much business in Star Chamber, though capital cases were not tried here. "This Court may inflict punishment," Coke wrote, "by pillory, papers, whipping, losse of ears, tacking of eares, *stigmata* in the face, &c. (For it extendeth not to any offence that concerns the life of man or obtruncation of any member, the ears only excepted, and those rarely and in most hainous and detestable offences.)" Star Chamber existed to try cases for which the common law provided no remedy, principally "routs and riots" which local county courts had failed to settle. Procedure, as in all courts of equity, was by systematic interrogation on oath, without a jury — inquisitory, not accusatory.* Yet there were few complaints, the Star Chamber had not received its bad name. That was to come later, under the Stuarts. In Elizabeth's day it was still, as Sir Thomas Smith said, "the poor man's court, in which he might have right without paying money." Old Lambarde the antiquary called it "this most noble and praiseworthy Court, the beams of whose bright justice do blaze and spread themselves as far as the realm is long or wide." In suits between man and man, the Star Chamber did its best to obtain fairness and justice. "Better to acquit twenty that are guilty than condemn one innocent," the judge said when Coke was present. Only if the Queen was involved, and "matters of state," did judges seem to go mad and trial become a mockery — and high treason was not tried in Star Chamber.

Powerful nobles — the few who were left — had a healthy awe of this court. A Percy, a Neville might bribe or intimidate justices of the peace across a whole county. But when Star Chamber called, he obeyed. "A sea most proper for whale-fishing," a contemporary called the court; "little boats might cast out nets for smelts." Actually, Star Chamber was apt to favor poor men. "His punishment would have been far greater but for his base birth, being a peasant and a boy." So reads a decision. Three gentlemen were brought in, one morning, with a vintner. They had been picked up the previous night for getting drunk at the Mermaid Tavern and raging about Fleet Street with drawn rapiers, insulting the watch and "uttering seditious words in Paul's Churchyard." The court acquitted the vintner. He was poor and wine-selling his business. But *gentlemen* should know better — and were fined two hundred pounds apiece.

Star Chamber fines were known to be ruinous. "The greater the man, the greater the punishment, as an example to others," the Lord Chief Baron of Exchequer remarked, giving sentence on Lord Dudley of Staffordshire. That bearer — or borrower — of a distinguished name had assembled some six hundred armed men, stormed into a neighbor's pens and driven off three hundred head of cattle which did not belong to him. Such a riot was disturbingly

* "It may perhaps be doubted whether systematic and deliberate interrogation were less fair to a man on his trial than the running fire of cross examination by the judges [in common-law practice] restrained by no rules of evidence, which the prisoner had to stand in all ordinary criminal cases down to the Restoration (1661)." Sir Frederick Pollock, *The Expansion of the Common Law*.

reminiscent of bad old pre-Tudor days, when armed nobles terrorized entire neighborhoods and thought themselves as good as kings. The Star Chamber pronounced itself scandalized. Lord Burghley alone demurred at the size of the fine. He knew Dudley well, the man hadn't the money. What was the sense of these huge mulcts which must be pardoned or compounded later? "Then let him pay with his body!" the Lord Baron retorted, and the case was closed.

The court was housed in a long, five-gabled building across New Palace Court from Westminster Hall, directly facing the river. "It is called the Star Chamber," Coke wrote, "in respect the roof of the court is garnished with golden stars. In all records in Latin it is *camera stellata.* Some have imagined that it should be called the star-chamber because *crimina stellionat'* are there handled; others of this Saxon word *steeran,* to steer or rule as doth the pilot, because this court doth steer and govern the ship of the commonwealth. Others, because it is full of windows; but the true cause of the name is because, as is aforesaid, the roof is starred . . . the most honourable court (our parliament excepted) that is in the Christian world. . . . The right institution and ancient orders thereof being observed, this court doth keep all England in quiet." In term time the judges met twice a week, on Wednesdays and Fridays. *Star-days,* people called them. The panel usually numbered from five to fifteen; its true name was "The Privy Council sitting in the Star Chamber." Besides the Lords of Privy Council, the Archbishops sat, both Chief Justices and such judges as were required. Star Chamber was, of course, a prerogative court, outgrowth of a day when the whole government of England had consisted of "the King, sitting with his Council." To attest it, a chair was kept empty among the judges, blazoned with the Queen's arms, the Seal and Mace laid before it.

In full session the court looked like a little Parliament, composed, Coke said, of "the Grandees of the Realm." People took pride in it, crowding to watch; by three in the morning there was a line at the door. "It was a glorious sight upon a Star-day," writes Rushworth, "when the Knights of the Garter appear with their stars on their garments and the Judges in their Scarlet; and in that posture they have sate sometimes from nine in the morning till five in the afternoon, before every one had done speaking their minds in the Cause that was before them." Judgment was delivered seriatim, as in a jury, with the least important man speaking first and so on up to the Lord Keeper.

On Star-days when the weather was fine, Coke came from the city by barge, landing at the Water Gate and walking up the steps along the causeway. He liked to plead here. The court was a superb theater for lawyers who knew their business. Lord Keeper Egerton as presiding officer was punctual, quick, and impatient enough to keep matters moving. As the Westminster clock struck nine, Egerton walked from the Inner Chamber to take his place, the Seal and Mace carried before him, the Lords following in their robes, the two Chief Justices in scarlet. Only Egerton wore his hat, the others were bareheaded. The Lord High Admiral walked with them, hero of the great year '88, and Essex, his young head thrust a little forward after his habit. Spectators bobbed as the procession passed. Egerton alone was an awesome sight, tall, and so handsome that people came to court just to look at him. Having been Attorney General himself, he knew every legal trick and was notoriously strict with lawyers who pleaded before him. Longwindedness he looked on as more than an annoyance, it was a misdemeanor. Not a barrister in London but knew of the unfortunate attorney who had appeared in Chancery with a brief one hundred and twenty pages long. Egerton, remarking angrily that the matter could have been covered in sixteen pages, ordered the man to cut a hole through his manuscript, stick his head in it and be led around Westminster Hall while the courts were sitting, after which he was fined and "Fleeted" (put in Fleet Prison) for wasting the court's time. Nor could the Lord Keeper abide the sight of hungry solicitors hanging around the courts, looking for business. There was no warrant for them in law, he said from the Star Chamber bench; they were "caterpillers del common weale." When lawyers were stupid, he told them so. "You are not well advised. You forget your place. You must go to school to learn more wit. . . . And to be plain, it is a lie."

Coke's unimpeded eloquence in the face of such threat was surprising. In Star Chamber he said what he pleased and took his time about it. When he wished to quote the ancients he quoted in full and if a lawyer mistook his Latin syntax, Coke put him right. "And the Attorney General brought the law books," wrote the reporter, "and showed and read the cases themselves in the books." Once, when Egerton had unadvisedly called a defendant to York

House for questioning, previous to the hearing, "I find," Coke said wryly, "that God doth assist the judge in his judgement but not in his chamber." And concerning "a treasonable book" which libeled Queen Elizabeth, "I say to this libeller, as it was said of Diogenes that hurled down the chair and cushions that were set for Aristotle — the greater pride is in him that hurleth down."

One day in Easter term there was called as witness a quack physician named Wood, who had been having a rogue's holiday at the expense of the Countess of Shrewsbury, dosing her with "oil of stag's blood for the gout, quintessence of cream and liquor of pear" — and contriving, during his ministrations, to drink up twelve gallons of the Countess's best Canary under pretense of "drawing the spirits of wine." Wood was a clever talker, the panel disagreed and the case dragged. The question was, How much did "Doctor" Wood actually know of physic? Coke went over the papers, "and proved Wood to be no scholler for that he wrote false ortography, for *process*, 'prossus,' whereas every scholer knoweth process to come of *procedendo*." The court was satisfied. When Coke quoted Bracton to the effect that no man "acquainted with the practice of poisoning" was acceptable as witness, Wood himself was put on trial.

The reporter, John Hawarde, was young, an Inner Temple student and, obviously, Coke's admirer. "The Queen's Atturney," he wrote, "read a sage speech and was greatly commended by Lord Buckhurst for his fealty and trouble in finding the offenders, which was very good service to the Queen and the realm; and by the Lord Keeper commended likewise." Francis Bacon did not fare so well, making — says the reporter — a rambling speech of lavish praise toward the Queen, of whose plans he was, he claimed, the happy confidant. "Bacon, Counsel at Large to the Queen, made a long oration, and to no purpose, of the divine and princely regard of the Queen Her sacred Majesty, with whose intent towards him he was so blessed as to be privy, and all not to the purpose."

Coke at this time was Treasurer of the Inner Temple, much involved with the students, talking with them, sitting as judge at evening moot courts and, when he could find time, reading to them from Bracton or Magna Carta. In court — even, apparently, in the august Star Chamber — Coke had a habit of turning, where he stood before the bench, and throwing his voice down the room to reach the law students sitting against the wall with their commonplace books. There was a case in Star Chamber of a man who had accepted money to act as substitute in the army — *press money*, it was called — and then decamped without serving. This, Coke told the court, was a felony by the statute of *3 Henry VII*, "which is not repealed but continues in force. And therefore [adds the young reporter] *the Attorney advises students of the law to read the Statutes at large, and not to trust to the Abridgments.*"

Because Star Chamber covered cases for which the common law provided no remedy, the judges were hard put to invent punishments. There was a grim suitableness to Lord Egerton's devices. A man who beat his grandfather was sentenced to be whipped "before the old man's portrait," the old man being unable to leave his bed and enjoy the spectacle in public. When two rascals broke into Fleet Street lodgings and cruelly beat a woman and her maid, Egerton ordered a pillory set up before the house and the culprits flogged there, "gagged with the same gags, each with his own gag, that they had used to the said Mrs. Whitingham and her maid."

Revenge was still a recognized part of punishment. (Time had been when the victim's relatives drew the murderer to the place of execution.) A lawsuit was a fight, a combat, the only difference being that in olden days men fought with swords — ordeal by battle — whereas now they fought with words. The principle of humiliation in punishment was strong. Men were ordered to stand bound in the market place and make confession, or to ride through town with their face to the horse's tail, a placard round their neck to advertise their misdeeds. Old Burghley in particular was never at loss for penalties which were beautifully suited to the crime, but contained an element of fantasy that caused them to be voted down by the panel. Students at an Inn of Court were victimized by smooth-talking scoundrels who induced them to give bond for large sums of money. This, Burghley insisted, was due to the neglect of careless parents. Let playwrights be ordered to make a comedy round the situation, using actual names. Embarrassed fathers would take a lesson therefrom "to look over their sons and certify their manner of living."

On occasion, Egerton returned suits to local county courts, declaring they did not belong in Star Chamber, though often enough the court took care of cases when local grand juries would not find — small riots in the shires where men fought with "pickle-prongs," and, in Hawarde's law French, "pitched le partye over the hedge." Judges were exhaustively painstaking. Hawarde complained of a case where "155 interrogations were made on the one side and on the other 125, with 77 witnesses examined," many of whom seized the opportunity to make long sermons about "doctrine and religion, the which Counsel should know was not the business of Star Chamber." Old Lord Burghley, worn out, remarked lugubriously that he had measured one bill with a yardstick; it was "9 foot long and contained 5 skins [of parchment]."

A large part of Star Chamber operations was purely administrative. Coke was ordered by the court to make a census of all gentlemen living in London or Westminster "and inform against them," that they might be ordered back to their country manors and country hospitality — which meant they were to go home and feed the poor of their parishes. Elizabeth had strict laws against gentlemen residing in London purely for pleasure. They must have excuse of crown employment or take their families out of town. Every June, as Trinity term ended, the eight common-law judges were summoned to Star Chamber for instruction, before riding into the shires on circuit. Let them see to it that justices of the peace performed their duties honestly, "not maintaining unjust causes or discouraging, encouraging or instructing jurors." Every man must pursue a fugitive when the hue and cry was up, yet none might make his house into a jail to hold people "but only for their examination."

The Attorney General stood in his robes and listened, while overhead the painted stars, a trifle chipped in this bright noonday light, wheeled on their faded blue.* Coke himself had been J.P. in Norfolk and knew whereof the Lord Keeper spoke. The home ties still were strong. At Godwick, near the old Burghwood place, Coke had built a handsome house, and every June when term was over and the Long Vacation began, the family undertook migration, traveling to Norfolk sometimes thirty strong. (The bill for one meal at Norwich included food for twenty-five servants.) The steward's accounts have a cheerful, domestic note. . . . June, 1597, Bridget Coke sends four housemaids ahead from London, armed with two

* Chapter Note.

pounds of frankincense "to air the house at Godwick" . . . then goes off herself. Coke spends a week in chambers at the Temple, dining four nights in the Hall with the students, twice at York House with Lord Keeper Egerton. The Queen sends raspberries, "Mr. Dr. Drewry" sends "two great salmon trout," which Coke promptly forwards to Egerton.

On July fourteenth, Coke followed his wife, riding fast and covering the ninety miles in two days. Humble neighbors welcomed him. "Goodwife Clover, Goodwife Church, ould Frank's wife, ould Benet Wigge" brought honey, green gooseberries. The Squire in turn extended hospitality, a neighborly feast of swans and mallard ducks, green geese and "fourteen rabbits." The summer proved wet and windy. Coke worried over his wheat. It would rot in the fields, he wrote to Lord Burghley, "unless God of his mercy do send a more seasonable time to ripen, and [harvest] corn and other commodities." Bridget Coke's uncle, Clement Paston, sent an invitation from the Paston family seat at Oxnead, asking a neighbor for a buck so that he might "entertain Mr. Attorney Coke and his wife as is fitting for such personages."

In September, Coke rode to Norwich to cast a vote for his cousins Gawdy and Townshend as Knights of the Shire. The Queen had called a Parliament for autumn; the holiday was over. "My mistris and her company," writes the courier, Robert Mathew, "take their journey to Norwich, and soe to Huntingfield, and soe back to London." En route, the courier buys beer for young Clement, gives Mistress Anne two shillings to play at cards with her cousin Gawdy, and one shilling "to bestow on the prisoners at Norwich Castle."

But wherever Coke stopped or stayed, it would seem that he dropped in at town hall or shire house, keeping in touch with the borough fathers, mending his political fences. Twelve miles from Huntingfield, where the Coke sons lived, was Dunwich, a thriving fishing port which was forever in trouble with pirates — the notorious Dunkirkers across the Channel. Ships brought men who had been maimed by the Turks, their tongues ripped out, a hand cut off. Would his worship suggest proper alms for these unfortunates? Twelvepence each, perhaps? Dunwich enjoyed fierce and complicated embroilments with neighboring towns, Southwold in particular. The matter was referred to "the upright censure and judgement of Mr. Edward Cooke, the Attorney General." The town clerk set down careful evidence of gratitude. "Wyne sent to Mr. Attorney's children at Thorington," and again, "Wyne and sugar bestowed upon Mr. Attorney's sonnes and his friends, 23 shillings sixpence."

The Earl of Essex was High Steward of Suffolk. As such, he could expect to control many votes; he had built up a powerful faction in opposition to the Cecils. The boroughs of Dunwich and Aldeburgh each returned two members to Parliament; Aldeburgh had sent Coke as Burgess in '89. Coke was not running for election this year, but he had no intention of letting the Earl control all four borough seats. The Dunwich records for September 15, 1597, announce that Essex had asked to have the "nominating and appointing" of both Aldeburgh representatives—to which the fathers give "pleased and willing consent" for *one* burgess but not for two: "the choosing of the other being given to Mr. Edw. Cooke the Attorney General, in respect of his former and continual favour and friendship in many ways."

With a pair of Norfolk knights and one Suffolk burgess promised, Coke returned to London. He had no seat in Parliament, but the Attorney General must attend the Upper House as legal adviser to the peers, a not unexacting assignment. Coke would be in and out of the Commons during all the session. On his arrival in Castle Yard, the Queen sent pears, the Countess of Cumberland a doe, a gammon of bacon and cucumbers.

Serenity and success for Mr. Attorney, in this happy autumn. A good life, within doors and without. The rich and great send tribute, clients are turned away in half dozens—while word comes that one's rival, Francis Bacon, is deep in debt and at pains to dodge his creditors on the streets. One's wife, still handsome at thirty-two and as usual "expecting," makes all things calm and charming, ministering to her master's wants as a wife should, and showing herself pleased at the doing.

In January, while Parliament was sitting, a seventh son was born to Bridget and Edward Coke. The youngest child was barely twelve months old. In fifteen years, Bridget Coke had given her husband ten children. Eight remained: Edward, Anne, Robert, Arthur, John, Henry, Clement, Bridget. That their mother had come safely through so many births may have been due to her country accouchements; infection was far less prevalent than in town. Coke, moreover, disliked doctors and would not take physic. Perhaps his wife was spared the frightful "remedies," the lancing and bleeding, the potions of frogs' eyes and crushed spiders' legs, the filthy ministrations of midwives. Six sons, Mr. Attorney boasted, in the year 1598. Six healthy male creatures to bear his name, inherit his lands.

The seventh son brought disaster. Thomas, they named him; he was christened and died. Six months later, obscurely, with no recorded outcry, Bridget Coke was dead. In Star Chamber reports a brief note appears: "Kuke, the Queen's Atturney, was absent by reason of the death of his wife, Monday, 26 June."

Bridget Coke was gone, quietly, obscurely, a young woman serene, beloved of this harsh masterful joking husband whom she loved in turn. Coke carried her body to Tittleshall in Norfolk, buried it in the old church by the altar steps and put a monument in the wall. She kneels, poor young Bridget, in farthingale and ruff, veil flowing down her back. Her children kneel below her in a row, their hands pointed in prayer. Coke had an inscription carved above her figure: "Many daughters have done virtuously, but thou surpassest them all."

A stilted sentiment, as becomes a marble tomb. On the day she died, Coke wrote a sentence in his little private book, in Latin. "Most beloved and most excellent wife, she well and happily lived, and as the true handmaiden of the Lord, she fell asleep in the Lord, and now lives and reigns in Heaven." Seventy-three years later, Anne Coke Sadleir died, after preparing the inscription for her tombstone: "Here lies the body of Anne, eldest daughter of Sir Edward Coke *by his first and best wyfe, Bridgett Paston.*"

CHAPTER TEN

1597-1599. Coke and Lady Hatton.

Lord Burghley to his son, Robert Cecil

Use great providence and circumspection in choosing thy wife. For from thence will spring all thy future good and evil. And it is an action of life, like unto a stratagem of war, wherein a man can err but once. If thy estate be good, match near at home and at leisure, if weak, far off and quickly. Enquire diligently of her disposition and how her parents have been inclined in their youth. Let her not be poor, how generous soever. For a man can buy nothing in the market with gentility.

ACROSS Holborn Road from Castle Yard, just west of Scropes Inn and occupying an entire long block from the Fleet Ditch to Fetter Lane, was one of the most romantic houses of London. Ely House, it was called, because it had once been the seat of the Bishops of Ely. Here, among gardens laid out in boxwood, among orchards, paved courts and arching splendid gateways lived the Lady Elizabeth Hatton, young, beautiful, high-spirited, fond of society and richer in land than in ready cash. She had given her elderly husband, Sir William Hatton, one child, a daughter. In March of 1597 Sir William died and left behind him not only Ely House but Corfe Castle on the Isle of Purbeck and Holdenby in Northamptonshire, a house of great magnificence. To these properties, more showy than fruitful, his young widow fell heir. Every acre was hampered with debts, bonds, leases, wardships — impossible for any but a land-lawyer to comprehend. Years later, Lady Hatton was to say bitterly that "her bridegroom, Cooke," had comprehended only too well, by stratagem achieving, before they were married three years, complete control — a complaint to be taken, like most of Lady Hatton's stories, with three grains of salt. It is natural to be more vivid than accurate where one's wrongs are concerned.

There is no telling when Coke first met Lady Hatton nor how long he had known her before Bridget Coke died. Certainly, he was on terms of friendship and close confidence with Lady Hatton's family. For she was a Cecil, fourth daughter of Lord Burghley's eldest son. Sir Thomas Cecil was her father, Sir Robert Cecil her uncle, and the Lord Treasurer her loving and harassed grandfather.

Sometime in the year 1597, Bridget Coke's steward entered in his accounts the present of "one fatte buck" for which Lady Hatton's man received ten shillings at the door — a tip larger than even the Queen's messengers received. Lady Hatton was not a neighbor to ignore. There was an aura about her, she was the stuff from which legend is made. All London knew the story of Ely House, where she lived — how, in the great banqueting hall (seventy-two feet long and thirty feet high), royal Harry had feasted with his first Queen Catherine, on cocks and capons, swans, larks and pullets, "24 beefes and 100 fat Muttons." Serjeants-at-Law for more than a century had celebrated here their feasts of investiture, while minstrels played from the gallery. The Bishop's chapel was a gem of lacy stone and high rose window, and as for Ely House strawberries in their season, playwrights made use of them to lighten their dialogue:

> Gloucester: My Lord of Ely! . . . When I was last in Holborn
> I saw good strawberries in your garden there.

It was common knowledge that Queen Elizabeth had forced Bishop Cox (whom she disliked) to vacate this ancient Episcopal palace and "rent" it to her Lord Chancellor and favorite, Sir Christopher Hatton, "the dancing Chancellor" — handsomest man ever to hold that high position. For the annual payment of one red rose, Sir Christopher had lived modestly at first, in the Gate House, permitting the ousted Bishop to walk in the garden and gather, yearly, twenty bushels of roses. And then ambition grew and Sir Christopher borrowed from the Queen to buy the place — palace and chapel, fields, gatehouses and orchards. The Queen demanded her money and Hatton fell sick (of chagrin, it was said). Elizabeth came to see him, soothed him, fed him with a spoon — and let him die with the debt unforgiven.

Those who sided with the Bishop continued to call the palace Ely House, to others it was Hatton House. In 1596, Lady Hatton's name appeared in the records when Archbishop Whitgift granted to her husband and herself and "4 others he may name," indulgence to eat flesh upon forbidden days, "on the payment of 13 s. 4 d. to the poor box of the parish wherein they reside." Forbidden flesh, forbidden fruits; the lady was not one to be balked of her desires. The walls of Hatton House were high but the gates were wide and welcoming. *Bleeding Heart Yard*, the place would be called when Lady Hatton died, because she made, it was said, a pact with the devil. One night he claimed his bargain and carried her off in a clap of thunder, so that next morning nothing was to be found save her bleeding heart in the pump yard by the steps. . . .

From first to last, Lady Hatton got herself talked about. She was clever as well as rich, knew how to dress her beauty to advantage, loved dancing, hawking, masqueing, the society of the court. She was invited everywhere, not only by virtue of her husband's connections — he had been nephew and heir to Sir Christopher Hatton — but because she was herself a Cecil. The year that her husband died (1597), Lady Hatton's father had a suit in Exchequer over some land in Northamptonshire. The Crown being plaintiff, the Queen's Attorney could not argue for the defendant. Yet something Coke said and did won the case for Sir Thomas. Among the usual piled-up mass of legal points in Coke's *Reports*, victory is vague but discernible.

Plainly, the Attorney General was on good terms with Lady Hatton's father and in the way of doing him favors. Sir Thomas Cecil was careless, easygoing, not good at managing his money, traits distressing to Lord Burghley, whose heir he was, and to his shrewd brother, Sir Robert the hunchback, Elizabeth's Principal Secretary. Coke had been on intimate footing with the Cecils for years. It is even possible that Sir Thomas, after his son-in-law's death, discussed with Coke his daughter's future. Coke was still a married man and Lady Hatton, the greatest catch in town, was besieged right and left. It was the business of her father and uncle to see that she allied herself not with some penniless courtier who might take her fancy but with a man whose fortune equaled her own and who would know how to look after her property. The young widow had refused offers, it was said, from a Pembroke and a Greville. Francis Bacon also aspired, having in mind, he told Essex, to "attempt a fortune *in genere oeconomico.*" Bacon had come into the public eye through a little book he had lately published. Entitled *Essays* (a new word in literature), it was dedicated to his brother Anthony and contained ten pieces, wry, brief and lively. People liked them. "They come home to men's business and bosoms," Bacon said. *Of Negotiating* might have been written by Machiavelli himself. "If you would worke any man, you must either know his nature and fashions and so lead him, or his ends and so persuade him, or his weakness and disadvantages and so awe him, or those that have interest in him and so govern him."

This shrewd counsel got nowhere at all with the Cecils. To the notion of their cousin Bacon as son-in-law, the family was cold. They knew too much about him, and while there was no doubting his mental attainments, Bacon's worldly prospects were not good. The Queen had never received him back into full favor, he was deeply in debt. If, as seemed obvious, Bacon needed a rich wife, let him find her outside the family. The Earl of Essex, at Bacon's suggestion, intervened as matchmaker, writing to Sir Thomas and Lady Cecil warm letters in his friend's praise. Were the lady his to dispose of, he "had rather match her with Mr. Bacon than with men of far greater titles. . . . If she were my sister or daughter, I protest I would as confidently resolve myself to farther it. And though my love to him be exceedingly great, yet is my judgement nothing partial, for he that knows him so well as I do, cannot but be so affected."

Lady Hatton, however, remained a widow and fashionable London continued to lay wagers as to her future. Rowland White wrote to Sir Robert Sidney; John Chamberlain exchanged details with that hungry news-savorer, Dudley Carleton, at Ostend. By June of 1598, Coke was himself a widower and Lady Hatton had worn her weeds full fifteen months. They must have become her dramatically, with her slim young figure, her animation and graceful, worldly air. St. Andrew's Church lay nearby and very likely the young widow walked there on fine Sundays with her father, white coif close about her cheeks, the long veil, fastened to her headdress, swaying as she moved, hands demure about her prayer book on its golden chain.

Mr. Attorney General, too, was in the habit of attending service at St. Andrew's, only a step from Castle Yard. Coke was forty-six to Lady Hatton's twenty, but he was still a handsome man, tall and straight. His hair and mustache kept their color — he was one of those men who refuse to turn gray — and he was richly, even fastidiously dressed. His manners were rough and direct, almost countrified at times, but this in itself is not unattractive to women. A forceful, masterful man and one who, quite patently, pursued his ends without benefit of intermediary, employing neither the arts of *Negotiating* nor the pleading pens of earls.

On August 4, 1598, old Burghley died. William Cecil, aged seventy-eight, founder of the family fortunes, the Queen's great minister whom she called her *Spirit* and whom alone in this decline of her age and reign she trusted wholly. Burghley's two sons had looked for his death, expected it. Yet when it came it must have seemed the foundation had been swept from their house. The half brothers were left with vast properties to manage and keep up: Burghley House in Northamptonshire, a pile of turreted stone big enough to shelter an army; Theobalds in Hertfordshire, even more magnificent, which a King of England would shortly covet (and acquire); a London palace that went to Sir Robert. Ely House, moreover, was under a debt of £42,000 to the Crown, and though the Queen had not mentioned it since Sir Christopher Hatton's death (1591) there was no telling when she might remember and demand payment.

Without his father, Sir Robert Cecil stood very much alone. Against the Essex faction, the rapidly growing Essex strength, there was no organized support, no "cabinet." Everything that Sir Robert had built up — his faction, fortune, future — lay in the Queen's hand and favor. Not favor as Essex knew it, personal, intense, but favor such as stemmed from Mr. Secretary Cecil's usefulness, his value to the state and to the daily business of government. His enemies said that Sir Robert's place and influence had come to him through his father. With his father's death all this might vanish or fade slowly through royal evasion and that subtile, seemingly innocent neglect which Elizabeth knew how to employ. (Francis Bacon's father had been Lord Keeper, yet it had not availed the son.) Sir Robert's young wife, whom he adored, had died in childbirth; it was noted that his hair had lately turned gray though he was not past thirty-five. With his tiny stature, crooked back and white, quiet face, what chance had he, for all his cleverness, against the generous young warrior Earl, either in court or country? Essex's popularity was extraordinary. In the streets the people ran to cheer him.

For the brothers Cecil it was a time to take stock, count enemies, rally friends and supporters. Among the latter, Attorney General Coke stood out. There had never been a doubt on which side his loyalties lay. In Parliament and out he was heart and soul a Cecil man. Hungry hands reached for plums that might slip from the Cecil fingers. Elizabeth had told old Burghley she did not wish to live longer then she had him with her. Though he had brought up his son Robert, she said, "as near as might be like unto himself, yet he [Burghley] was to her in all things, and would be, Alpha and Omega. No prince in Europe had such a councillor as she had of him." The Queen, it was well known, liked handsome men about the palace and the court. Her Pygmy, she called Sir Robert, her *Pygmy* and her *Spirit*. If comparison came to Mr. Secretary's mind, it was not reassuring.

When Elizabeth heard that Burghley was dead, she wept. In his sickness she had visited him. The chamber door was low and the steward prayed her to stoop. "For your master's sake I will stoop," the Queen replied, "but not for the King of Spain's." On August twenty-ninth, she gave her Lord Treasurer a magnificent funeral at Westminster Abbey. The mourners, five hundred strong, moved to solemn music through the streets. Edward Coke walked with them. It was at the funeral that he approached the Cecils and asked for Lady Hatton's hand in marriage.

Historians have pictured Lady Hatton as a reluctant bride, a beautiful young woman constrained by her elders to marry a man more than twice her age. Yet if future conduct is a gauge, the bride was far too high-spirited to be pushed into marriage against her will. When Lady Hatton was inconvenienced, the noise she made reached easily to Whitehall Palace, and concerning this match there was no outcry. Long afterward, Lady Hatton complained to the Privy Council that she had been "hastened into marriage" without decent settlement of her property. But the statement, given in anger and bitter quarreling, is not altogether to be trusted.

For Coke the marriage meant disaster. It was the mistake of his life. Beyond propinquity and his admiration for the Cecils, he had nothing in common with this gay willful lady, absorbed in dress and society. They were as ill-mated as two people can be. Neither husband nor wife was to have another peaceful domestic moment. Their mutual surprise at this catastrophe argues, in both, a strange naïveté. Lady Hatton's first husband had been elderly; she said later that she never knew discontent until Sir William Hatton died. Coke's fifteen years of connubial felicity had apparently convinced him that domestic peace was the rule; a man need only lead a young wife into his house and peace came with her, riding on her shoulder like a dove. From a worldly point of view the match for Coke was excellent, alliance with the Cecils being the best thing that could happen to a rising government man. Perhaps it did not stop at expediency and Coke fell in love with his beautiful neighbor. The widowers of happy marriages are notoriously addle-headed. Whatever the reasons, Edward Coke, determined, forceful, whose path had heretofore run true, in the summer of 1598 took temporary leave of his senses, first in his choice of a wife and then, as will be seen, in the manner of his wedding.

*John Chamberlain to Dudley Carleton**

London
22 November, 1598

The seventh of this moneth, the Quenes atturney married the Lady Hatton to the great admiration of all men that after so many large and likely offers she shold decline to a man of his qualitie, and the world will not beleve that it was without a misterie.

By "admiration," the writer meant surprise, by "qualitie," he meant birth. And by "misterie," he hinted that the Lady Elizabeth had got herself into trouble and needed a husband's name more quickly than might be convenient. The position of pretty young widows is vulnerable and Lady Hatton had been widowed twenty months. The affair had proceeded, indeed, with almost reckless haste. In July, 1598, Mr. Attorney buried his wife. In August he proposed to Lady Hatton, in November he married her. The wedding was held at the town house of the bride's father,

* Chamberlain was a London gentleman who, from 1597 to 1616, exchanged a series of newsletters with his friend Dudley Carleton the diplomatist (later Viscount Dorchester).

Sir Thomas Cecil (now Lord Burghley), and it broke the law on three separate counts: no banns were published or special license procured; the ceremony took place in a private house, whereas the law said it must be "in the parish church where the couple resided"; marriages were required to be celebrated between eight and twelve o'clock in the forenoon. Coke was married at night.

At this flouting of the law ecclesiastical, Archbishop Whitgift was angry. His old pupil had behaved with arrogance. It was true that Coke had been extremely distracted, at the time, by a shocking new treason case. One Edward Squire, former stableboy of the Queen, had confessed an attempt to kill her Majesty by rubbing poison on the pommel of her saddle. The trial was set for November ninth, two days after Coke's wedding. All day on the seventh, Coke was at Westminster, took the evening off as it were to be married and was back at work by 7:30 next morning. Yet even the Queen's business could not excuse such casual disregard of life's sacred ceremonies. Great persons should set an example to the lower orders. The Archbishop haled the wedding party into his court at Lambeth, including Coke's father-in-law and the unfortunate Henry Bathwell, Rector of Okeover, who had conducted the ceremony. All of them were subject, they learned, to the "greater excommunication," accompanied by fine and imprisonment. To this wrathy whirlwind, Coke bowed his head and made "humble submission," pleading — for the first and last time in his life — that he did not know the law.

Coming from the Queen's principal prosecutor, this was hard for Whitgift to swallow. Only a year ago, in Parliament, the bride's father had headed a large and vigorous committee for the reform of abuses against the marriage laws. The Queen herself had been interested and sent down messages concerning a certain "horrible and incestuous marriage discovered in the House of Commons." On the strength of the Committee report, a bill had been voted through the Commons. Surely, Mr. Attorney General, who by virtue of his office was continually in and out of the House, knew of these things? Coke's head remained bowed.

The Archbishop relented and let them off. But he took occasion to issue a circular letter to his Bishops, reviewing (without proper names) several improperly celebrated unions that lately had taken place. His clergy were commanded "to have a vigilant care for the avoiding of all future scandals and offences."

Coke and his lady went home to Ely House, then walked down Shoe Lane to St. Andrew's Church and were properly married. London relished the episode. That "most severe and learned Mr. Attorney" had forgot the law and had been chastised for it like any schoolboy. Those who knew the bride prophesied that she would benefit from a husband who could rule her. As for Mr. Attorney, he had bargained for wealth, youth, beauty — then let him pay for it. Lady Hatton kept her own name, from pride, people said; plain Mistress Coke would not become her. There was a story which persisted; John Aubrey gives it in his *Lives:* "Coke's second wife, Elizabeth, the relickt of Sir William Hatton, was with Child when he married her: laying his hand on her belly (when he came to bed) and finding a Child to stirre, What, sayd he, Flesh in the Pott. Yea, quoth she, or else I would not have married a Cooke."

When Elizabethans wished to spread gossip they did it thoroughly, lips fat against the pipes of slander. For the name, there was no reason Lady Hatton should not keep her own; other titled women did so. In point of birth (though not of fame) Coke's family, actually, was quite as good as his bride's. Cecils, Hattons and Cokes were equally *parvenu.* All three had achieved position not through blood or ancestry but by the laborious and adventitious shaping of their own careers. Lord Burghley had made his own fortune, coming up from obscurity to what contemporaries called "a rich man on London Bridge." No sooner was Burghley risen in the world than, like Sir Christopher Hatton, he suddenly took thought on his lineage and with the aid of heralds discovered a Norman ancestry. (Nobody actually believed in the new-spangled quarterings which Elizabeth's obscurely born statesmen secured at vast expense, yet it was the fashion and must be indulged.)

The Queen's Attorney, however, was still plain Edward Coke. (His wife spelled it always, *Cooke.*) The world continued to talk about Lady Hatton. In the *Calendar of State Papers* is a sheet dated April 30, 1599 — five months after the marriage — and marked *Affidavit of Mary Berham.* Who Mary Berham was and why she gave affidavit has passed into darkness. But what she said was startling. "It is no marvel Mr. Attorney wept sitting with the Judges, for he has gone up and down ever since his marriage like a dead man discomforted. Also Mr. Attorney has been sick lately and no marvel, for Denis, servant to the Countess of Warwick makes it his common talke that Lady Hatton was forward with child before she was married and that the child was by one of her servants who was sent away with a piece of money. . . . And the Lady Hatton has never lived in good name and it will kill Mr. Attorney to be so cozened as to assure £1000 a year to a bastard."

Rumor ran above stairs as below. On the twenty-third of August, 1599 — more than nine full months after Coke's marriage — John Chamberlain wrote again to his friend Dudley Carleton at Ostend: "The Lady Hatton is brought abed of a daughter, which stoppes the mouth of the old slaunder, and about ten days since it was christened with great solemnitie, the Quene (by her deputie the Lady of Oxford) and the countesse dowager of Darbie being godmothers, and the Lord Treasurer Godfather."

Obviously the child was Coke's; anybody with ten fingers could prove it. Queen Elizabeth, moreover, was strict in such matters and would never have acted as godmother to a child of doubtful parentage. Coke had bought a country house at Stoke Poges, a few miles north of Windsor. Here the christening was held, an affair so stylish it would have astounded Coke's Norfolk cousins. Frances, the child was called. The Queen sent a gilt bowl with a cover, weighing, says the record, "41 and a half oz."

On the surface, highly gratifying. The royal seal lay on this marriage, and the royal favor. At Stoke House the goose hung high. Ancient beeches spread their shade above the lawns, while to the tune of lute and viol, guests strolled, eating and drinking from tables spread on terraces above a little curving stream. The gardens were laid out in the new Italian style, with flower beds set formally and pleasing statues rising here and there against the hedges. A thousand acres of woodland stretched within the manor confines. Indoors and out there was profusion, a vigorous prodigality characteristic of the age. Diamonded window panes, glowing with color, gave back the light. Paneled walls were dark and rich, a score of tall brick chimneys stood against the sky. Over a great stone fireplace in the hall, the Hatton arms showed brilliant quarterings.

Riches and fame, a beautiful young wife. Health, strength and work to do. What more could man desire? Yet mortal blessings, counted by digits, can fall strangely short of the heart's own secret tally. ". . . *Mr. Attorney wept sitting with the Judges, for he has gone up and down since his marriage like a dead man discomforted.*"

CHAPTER ELEVEN

February, 1601. The Essex Rebellion. Coke prepares for the trial.

> Peruse over all our books, records, and histories, and you shall finde a principle in law, a rule in reason and a trial in experience, that treason doth ever produce fatal and final destruction to the offender.
>
> COKE, *Third Institute*

REBELLION does not come by sudden chance. The hen must sit before the egg is hatched, the citadel does not fall until it is weakened within — and the greatest lord of England, unless he has a history behind him, does not run through London with two hundred swordsmen, crying out to the citizens that he is betrayed.

Long before that fatal February Sunday, trouble was indicated. Essex's jealousy had become proverbial. At twenty-one he had fought a duel with a courtier who wore the Queen's gold favor on his arm; it required official intervention to keep him from fighting Sir Walter Ralegh. Dispatched to France at the head of four thousand soldiers, he went hawking in hostile country, challenged the enemy commander to single combat, knighted twenty-one of his followers (an exercise usually reserved for ruling princes) — behaved, in short, more like one of King Arthur's champions than a soldier sent abroad on the serious business of war.

Years could not change him. Openhanded, adored by the populace, at thirty-four as at twenty he dashed about on errands of glory, a brave anachronism, handsome emanation as it were from the Middle Ages. The story is well known — how the aging Queen loved

Essex, boxed his ears for his rudeness and told him to go and be hanged . . . then forgave and heaped new honors on him for the world to see. As success at court became a habit, Essex developed a dangerous tendency to sulk when thwarted. Returning from the Azores expedition (1597) and learning that Admiral Lord Howard had been made Earl of Nottingham, Essex refused to attend Parliament and see the old hero of '88 take precedence over him. "Conquer yourself!" Egerton advised in all friendship. Essex's reply was proud and bitter. "He is entirely given over to arms and the war," wrote the French ambassador that same winter. "He is on bad terms with the Lord Treasurer Burghley, his son [Robert Cecil] and the Admiral, and cannot accommodate himself to them nor even to the Queen. He is entirely his own Councillor. I believe that, so far as an Englishman can, he covets glory."

Essex's conduct in Ulster was the beginning of the end. At his own urgent pleading he had been named Lord Deputy of Ireland and leader of an army of nearly eighteen thousand, to conquer the rebel Tyrone. In April, 1599, he made a brilliant departure from London, cheered and acclaimed by the populace. While he was away, Shakespeare's *Henry V* was performed for the first time. The chorus of the last act was expressive of the country's goodwill:

> Were now the general of our gracious empress—
> As in good time he may—from Ireland coming,
> Bringing rebellion broachéd on his sword,
> How many would the peaceful city quit
> To welcome him!

The General, meanwhile, had conquered nothing at all; in three months his army had unaccountably dwindled to four thousand men. As though the fault were in no way his, he wrote home complaining. He must have more soldiers immediately! From England he had received "nothing but discomforts and soul's wounds"; and while he was fighting, "a Cobham or a Ralegh" made use of his absence. When news reached Dublin that Robert Cecil had been granted the lucrative post of Master of Wards (once held by Burghley), Essex, beside himself, told Southampton he had a mind to bring the army back to England and use it for his own purposes. He was dissuaded; this would mean civil war. Elizabeth ordered him to follow up the enemy and attack. Instead, Essex met Tyrone privately, and made a truce. In a letter of passionate indignation, the Queen repudiated what Essex had done. The Earl, convinced that his enemies at court were conspiring to turn the Queen against him, rushed home to plead his cause and his wrongs.

It was too much for Elizabeth. Generals do not abandon their armies in rebel country to stride beswordcd into the royal bedchamber before breakfast and show their private temper. "By God's Son I am no Queen!" Elizabeth exclaimed. "That *man* is above me!" She placed the Earl under Egerton's custody at York House in the Strand and left him there all winter, though free custody* was, she hinted, too easy and he should be publicly censured in Star Chamber. The public reaction was strong and remained stubborn in the Earl's favor. No one beyond the Privy Council knew of Essex's behavior in Ireland, his threats to use the army for his own purposes. Why then was the Queen's great General kept in confinement? What had he done to deserve it? Rumors flew about the city. . . . His Lordship was not even allowed to see his wife or newborn son. Could the Queen be frightened? "The Earle's greatnesse," wrote a contemporary, "was now judged to depend as much on her Majesties feare of him, as her love to him." Resentment became open. Sermons were preached in Essex's favor, prayers for his welfare pronounced from the pulpit. Pamphlets were published vindicating him, and on the palace walls, writings appeared overnight, scurrilous, impudent.

Elizabeth set the date for a Star Chamber hearing. Essex's friends begged him off. Star Chamber fines were ruinous and the Earl already greatly impoverished; Essex, moreover, had committed no riot or affray. Let him be judged privately at York House by a special commission of peers and justiciars, with the Lord Keeper Egerton presiding, an audience invited from all walks of life, to go out afterward and publish the Earl's submission and humble apology. . . .

The hearing took place in June of 1600. For Edward Coke it must have seemed the strangest courtroom scene of his experience. Bareheaded, Essex walked in, dropped on his knees before the Council table, acknowledged his sin and wept tears of contrition

* A prisoner in free custody could come and go according to the custodian's judgment, as opposed to close custody, which meant strict confinement to the cell, sometimes in chains.

until half the room wept with him. There was a magic to this young warrior nobleman, a dazzling effect of openness and spontaneity that could melt the flintiest heart. Four prosecutors came forward: Serjeant Yelverton, Coke, Solicitor General Fleming — and to the general surprise, Francis Bacon. No one understood why Bacon was part of the prosecution. Certainly he had no official position requiring such action, and he was widely known as the Earl's close friend, counselor and protégé.

For eleven hours, the four lawyers in turn had at the culprit. It was noted throughout that only one of them, Coke, dared use the word "disloyal." The others harped on disobedience . . . faulty judgment . . . indiscretion. What, Coke demanded abruptly of the judges, was to be said of a general who abandoned his army in hostile country and fled home in pursuit of private ends? Dishonorable! Coke said it bluntly, brutally. This was dishonorable conduct. If none had asked in what spirit it was done, then he would ask it, now: "*Quo animo?*"

The Earl's bearing, at this, faltered and he began to argue, justify himself. "And so he entered," wrote William Camden, who was present, "into a kind of answer to the Attorney General's speech from point to point in order." Sympathy was not with Coke. He had overreached himself, dared to challenge Essex's conduct to his face — an act of presumption from a commoner to this great lord whom even the Privy Council accused of nothing worse than indiscretion. "I hear," wrote a Londoner three days later, "the Atty. Gen. would in his speech have proved wilful contempt to have been disloyalty. Her Maj. is not resolved what she will do; she is much satisfied to see him held worthy of more punishment than has been inflicted."

The Queen, after some weeks, let the Earl go in freedom to his house, though she refused to see him. He grazed in the fields like Nebuchadnezzar, Essex wrote despairingly. Time was a perpetual night, the world a sepulcher till he might kiss her fair correcting hand. If her Majesty would not receive him publicly, then let him come in secret. He had a plan, no man should know. . . . In November of 1600, Elizabeth made a gesture that was like the fall of a sword. Since his imprisonment, the Earl's credit was ruined and he depended for his living largely on the sweet-wines monopoly. The lease fell in and Elizabeth left it in her own hands. From now on,

Essex was a person demented. "His soule," wrote Harington, who visited him, "seemeth tossede to and fro like the waves of a troubled sea. His speeches of the queene becomethe no man who hath *mens sana in corpore sano*. He uttered strange wordes borderinge on suche strange desygnes, that made me hasten forthe and leave his presence. Thank heaven! I am safe at home." *

Things moved rapidly toward disaster. Below Essex House the Water Gate was thronged each night with boats, empty, knocking with the tide while their masters sat late within. "Military men," Camden reported. "Bold fellowes, men of crackt credit, malecontented persons and such as sawcily used their tongues against all men." The Temple gardens lay just over the wall. Coke, leaving his chambers to walk up to Hatton House, could see the crowds pass in and out; anyone could see them. The Earl's wicket gate was locked, now, to all who had not the password. What was it this mad lord, this firebrand of discontent, planned to do? On Sundays, as the Christmas season approached, not one sermon but two were preached in his private chapel by Puritans who ranted that a king might be deposed, "providing the cause were just." Catholics too went through the wicket gate: Francis Tresham, Sir Christopher Blount, Sir John Davis. . . .

On Thursday, February fifth, the tragedy of *Richard II* was performed at the Globe Theatre, a story of rebellion, the deposing of a king and the triumphant setting of another in his place. Discontented men forever sang the song of Richard II. ("Know ye not," Elizabeth said bitterly to old Lambarde the antiquary, "that I am Richard Second?") A new book about that unhappy monarch had appeared not long ago, with a flowery dedication to Essex. Had it not been for Francis Bacon's wit, the author might have had harsh treatment. "He should be indicted, not for treason," Bacon told the Queen, "but for felony. He stole many of his sentences and conceits out of Tacitus." The Southwark actors had not wished to play *Richard II*. Old works, they protested, lose money. Forty shillings from Essex's friends persuaded them.

The Privy Council, aware of these manifestations, sent for Essex; they had questions to ask. He refused to come. He was sick, he

* Sir John Harington, the Queen's godson, served in Ireland with Essex and had been one of the men whom Essex brought home with him in the fall of 1599.

said, and could not leave his apartment. No sooner was the messenger gone than the Earl received an anonymous note, warning that he was in danger and had best provide for himself. Essex sent out runners over the city; all night they spread the alarm. . . . *There was a plot to murder him. . . . Cobham, Ralegh and Cecil were behind it, also "certain Jesuits to the number of four."* Early Sunday morning a crowd collected in the courtyard of Essex House, among them the Earls of Southampton, Worcester, Sussex, Rutland, Bedford; the Lords Sandys and Monteagle, Sir Christopher Blount (Essex's stepfather) and "three hundred gentlemen of prime note." The Queen, to find the reason, sent Lord Keeper Egerton, Chief Justice Popham and two Privy Councilors. All four men were known to be favorably disposed toward Essex; one was his uncle, Sir William Knollys. They were let in the wicket gate but told to leave their attendants outside.

Essex led them through the crowd to his library at the back of the house. (His book chamber, he called it.) Telling them to be patient for half an hour, he locked them in and left them guarded. Then he drew his sword and rushed into the streets, followed by his friends to the number of several hundred. "For the Queen, for the Queen!" he shouted. "A plot is laid for my life!" Citizens ran from their houses, straggled along behind, more from curiosity than any fighting spirit. (Actually, they were bewildered. Had the Queen ordered Essex to make a triumphant armed foray through the city?) Essex turned on them, shouted that the crown of England was sold to the Infanta of Spain. . . . Ralegh planned to murder him! . . . "Come you naked to me?" he said. "Get arms, weapons!"

Behind Ludgate the guard, on Essex's insistence, let him pass. At Paul's Cross the Earl had thought to find a great congregation, listening as usual to the Sunday morning sermon. Essex knew the city loved him. Had they not always acclaimed him when he rode by? A few words, telling of his danger, and the crowd would surely turn and follow. His purpose, he said afterward, was to reach the Queen at Whitehall, force access (so long denied), throw himself on his knees, beg for favor and revenge against his enemies — and prevail as he had always prevailed when the Queen heard his voice.

The palace lay to the westward, up river; the Earl's original plan had been to go there direct from Essex House. But the guard before the Palace had been doubled. To get through, Essex would need the city's help. Of twenty-four London aldermen, twenty-one, Essex's friends assured him, were on his side. Their several bodies of armed men would be at his service; Sheriff Smith could muster a thousand. Yet when he came to Smith's house in Fenchurch Street, it was empty; the Sheriff had slipped out the back door, "to consult with the Lord Mayor," he said. On Gracechurch corner stood Sir Thomas Cecil (Lord Burghley) with a herald who blew his trumpet and proclaimed Essex a traitor to her Majesty the Queen. There was a fanfare of sound, the loud words rolled and lingered. It was supremely effective. (Robert Cecil was responsible.) Essex, standing, braved it out. Enemies had bribed this fellow to shout the foul words. "A herald," the Earl said contemptuously, "will do anything for two shillings." Besides, he knew this man, who bore a brand for felony.

But when the herald turned to go, the streets were bare. Citizens were not trusting to chance. This foray through town, this wild affray was then no mere prank of an impulsive favorite. Whatever might lie behind, if the Queen chose to call it treason, substantial men had no further wish to be party to it. ("By reason of their wealth," says Camden, "they were fearful withall; poverty soonest plungeth the English into rebellion.") In growing despair, Essex turned back toward the Temple. Sweat poured from his face though the air was raw. Those who saw him said he looked in torment — "extremely appalled and almost molten with sweat by the perplexity and horror of his mind." He was stopped near Ludgate by a company of soldiers and citizens got together by the Bishop of London. Three men were killed. Lord Sandys was shot in the leg, Sir Christopher Blount severely wounded. A bullet went through Essex's hat. With fifty of his followers the Earl made his way to the water at Queenhithe and reached his house by boat, only to discover the hostages were gone: Egerton, Popham and the two Privy Councilors. (Sir Ferdinando Gorges had let them out to save his own skin.) Running to his room, Essex broke open an iron casket and burned some papers, declaring they "should tell no tales to hurt his friends." Then he barricaded his house, prepared to die rather than surrender.

The Queen was at midday dinner when they brought the first news, a wild, false rumor — the city risen, Essex with an army approaching the palace gates. "He that has placed me in this seat will preserve me in it," Elizabeth said, and went on with her dinner. By midnight, Essex was in prison and his friends captured: the Earls of Southampton and Rutland; the Lords Sandys, Monteagle, Cromwell; Sir Gilly Merrick, Sir Charles Danvers, Sir John Davis, Henry Cuffe, Sir Christopher Blount, Francis Tresham, Owen Salisbury. Desperate men; ruined men, now, scattered in prisons throughout the city. On the Lord Admiral's appearing before Essex House with a company of soldiers and a battering train from the Tower, Essex had changed his mind and surrendered.

Next day, Monday, the heralds were again on the streets, scarlet coated, trumpet at lip. . . . Crowds at the corners listening, and below the pulpit at Paul's Cross . . . "Hear ye, hear ye, loyal citizens! The Queen thanks you for your loves!"

"And so that dismal tumult, like the fit of Ephemera, or one-day's ague, ceased." A Londoner, Vincent Hussey, wrote it to a friend, two days after the affray. On the face of it truly an ephemera, hardly to be dignified by the name of rebellion. Three men killed, a few wounded. Yet great names were behind it; this was no rabble, no peasants' revolt. Had Essex, on leaving his house, turned westward to Whitehall instead of eastward to the city, he might have prevailed. It was true the guard had been doubled at Whitehall and a barricade of wagons placed over the wide street before the palace, true also that the people of Charing Cross and Westminster flocked to the Queen's defense with such weapons as they could find. But actually, the Lord Admiral had not appeared with his armed horsemen until three in the afternoon. "It is a blessed thing," wrote Hussey, "that the Earl failed in judgment and attempted London first, for had he gone straight to Court, he would have surprised it unprovided of defence, and full of his well wishers, before the world had notices of his treasons. The main point was the providence and celerity of the Secretary [Cecil], who forsaw before he was believed, and showed great dexterity and courage in ministering sudden remedies."

The city was tense, uneasy. Street corners bristled with pikes, the squares with soldiers. People kept to their houses. Each day new prisoners were taken — "15 knights and 8 gentlemen . . . 6 noblemen in the Tower, 5 knights and three others in the Fleet. 6 in the Lord Mayor's house, 3 in Ludgate. Also Lord Sussex committed on suspicion to Sir John Stanhope's house, the Earl of Bedford to an alderman of London . . ."

Coke listed the prisoners. By February tenth there were a hundred. Who knew how much further the discontentment reached, or when a second attempt might be launched and Essex's friends arrange his deliverance from the Tower? "The city of London," declared Thomas Wright, an imprisoned priest, "might with chain shot make their passage into the Tower in one night and release the Earls. And if the Earl of Essex were King it would be a glorious kingdom for he would not be so inhuman but would free us all." People waited anxiously. "This one day's work," Hussey wrote again, "may pave the beginning of many years' trouble . . . a grievous sickness to bring about alteration of the face of our State, like the effects of some terrible eclipse." It was the Attorney General's business to set up machinery for the trials. The noblemen would be judged in the Lord Steward's Court by a jury of their peers — twenty-four or twenty-five lords, all of whom had to be located and brought to Westminster. The gentlemen conspirators would appear before a special commission named for the purpose, the commoners be arraigned in King's Bench. "By the common voice they are already damned," wrote Hussey. "But some say that bye and bye it will be considered what a loss it would be to cut off so many brave men, though it were neither safe policy nor good pity to spare the principals."

It was term time, all the courts were sitting. On the thirteenth of February (four days after the Sunday attempt), Star Chamber held its customary grand session. The room was crowded, the doors would scarcely close on the people. If the audience came expecting the word "traitor," they were not disappointed. One after another the judges spoke out. "The traitorous earl," said Robert Cecil, "more monster than a man! The traitorous earl has been devising five or six years to be King of England." "Arch-traitor!" said Egerton, when his turn came. Three times, he repeated it. Last night — only last night, he said, a new plot had been hatched, spawn of this hideous rebellion. At the Queen's chamber door an armed man had been apprehended, waiting to slip in and murder her! A gentleman by birth, one Thomas Leigh, soldier and close friend of the Earl. Telling it, Egerton seemed overcome, and "in great grief stopped up his speech with tears, the people shouting for joy at her Majesty's most happy preservation."

So, at any rate, ran the report which Coke received. Yet to shout "Long live her Majesty" costs nothing. The audience was not convinced. Why should Essex or Essex's friends desire the Queen's death, let alone sit down to plot her murder? And why had Essex shouted to the citizens that Ralegh threatened his life? Surely, something was left untold! Today the Lords of Council had spoken their minds, condemning Essex out of hand. Yet it was the business of Star Chamber thus to speak out. "Instruct the people" was the customary phrase. Moreover, the Queen had not been heard from. Always, she had forgiven Essex; it was more than likely she would forgive him again. The Earl confessed to no treason and would plead *Not guilty*, standing, it was said, on a plea of self-defense: Ralegh, Cecil, Cobham, Grey had plotted his death; the journey through London had been merely in search of friends. Essex was to be tried by a commission of twenty-five peers and nine judges. He would have full opportunity to speak, tell his story in his own way. London intended to hear it and until then reserved its judgment.

The trial was set for February nineteenth. The militia of four counties were called up and surrounded the Queen's palace, which "is guarded," wrote Hussey, "like a camp, and troops of armed men march up and down as if the Spaniard were in the land." On February eighteenth, Tuesday, five of the conspirators, led by Sir Ferdinando Gorges, broke down and confessed to previous plottings. Long before that Sunday, they said — three months before — the thing had been planned. . . . The Earl of Southampton had lent Drury House, where the leaders might meet privately, without fear of detection. The project had been to capture first the Tower, then the Court, and, "without harm to the Queen," effect a change of government. Sir Christopher Blount confirmed Gorges's confession, "being too weak from his wound to set down all the truth before." Sir Charles Danvers, Sir John Davis, Sir Edward Littleton followed. The confessions agreed on every point.

That night the five declarations were sent round to the Attorney General, with a note from Cecil bidding him leave less important matters and "forthwith peruse them." This proof of premeditation did more than merely clinch the case; it seems to have shocked Coke genuinely. From now on he showed himself wholly partisan, as if the thing had gone beyond the personal guilt of Essex. In the body politic a foul disease had been uncovered; its brand lay deep, a shame to the nation. Already the news had traveled. Tyrone in Ireland, the French King in Paris, waited to see who now was first in the English nation, Earl or Queen. Hundreds had been drawn after Essex, running with greedy hands to profit from the Queen's humiliation, perhaps her death. The plotters denied all intention of harm to her Majesty. Yet they confessed that Essex had intended to call a Parliament, appoint a Speaker, name his own Privy Council. Would the Queen, meanwhile, be permitted to sit idly in her palace at Whitehall? In Coke's mind it was unlikely, to say the least.

On the margin of one of the confessions, Coke scrawled his indignation: "*O tempora, O mores!*" Actually, before the Essex affair was settled, the Queen's Attorney would prosecute in court seven men. Six of them would die, their "trials" would not be trials at all but public inquiries into guilt already established and proclaimed. Within this frame and system, Coke was to show himself in many guises — reasonable and dignified or raucous and brutal, yet evincing throughout one marked, consistent trait, a deep reverence for the throne, a vigorous urge to defend the legitimacy of the prince who, once crowned and anointed, signified the law and the nation.* Any subject, any man who took it upon himself to overset this prince and discredit this legitimacy discredited the law and the law's majesty which upheld the state. Since 1558 — close on half a century — the nation had rendered homage to Elizabeth as prince. In return she had made England feared in every quarter of the globe. And now in her declining years, an English nobleman whom above all subjects living she had enriched, honored and so often forgiven, attempted to set her down and put himself in her place.

To Edward Coke it was monstrous, hideous. He prepared his speech for the prosecution. Neither eloquence nor invective would be necessary. The facts were in his hand and could speak for them-

* Later, in Stuart times, Coke would say to his peril that the King was below the law, not above it.

selves. But at the very end, if things went as planned, he would quote Cicero against Catiline: "*O tempora, O mores! Hic tamen vivit?*" — and then add blunter words in English: "Robert, Earl of Essex, had thought to be King of England, his title, Robert the First. Let him rather be declared, of his race and blood, Robert the Last, attainted to posterity and all his generation."

CHAPTER TWELVE

Trial of Essex.

THE trial was held in the lofty gloom of Westminster Hall, swept clean, garnished and cleared as for a solemn festival. At the southwest end, the Court of Chancery had been blocked off by an arras and in front of it a court built, with a chair and canopy of state for the presiding officer. On each side were benches for the jury and below them the judges. Across the Hall in the southeast corner was the prisoners' box, with benches under it for the Attorney General and counsel.

Long before eight in the morning, the streets of Westminster filled with people. Had the judges attempted to come from London by land, they would have had trouble pushing through. King Street was thronged and round the square before the Hall, cookshops and dramshops spilled customers from their doors. The proprietors would be rich before night. The Water Gate had been blocked off to all but official boats and barges. Beyond a guarded area the river was dotted with small craft, laden with spectators hoping to see the noble prisoners brought from the Tower, see the two Earls land and walk, the bared axe carried after them, up the long causeway and past the Star Chamber to New Palace Yard. Henry, Earl of Southampton would stand trial with Essex today.

Westminster clock struck eight. Within the Hall, ranged straight across, stood forty of the Queen's Bodyguard, halberds up, their Captain, Sir Walter Ralegh, at their head. Under their breastplates they wore red velvet doublets and over their backs, short cloaks with the Queen's arms in red and gold. Essex had said — and shouted to the city — that Ralegh planned "to murder him in his bed." No doubt this would come up today. It was rumored that Ralegh, to clear himself of the imputation, had asked to be called as witness. Ralegh had reason to know the Earl well, having sailed on numerous voyages with him against the Spaniard. Essex was notoriously jealous of this Devon Captain who stood guard at the Queen's chamber door. More than once, as Ralegh's commanding officer, the Earl had overlooked, in official reports, Sir Walter's skilled or even heroic part in their mutual adventures. Ralegh forgave it, but this last year he had lost patience, declaring the Earl had become "a tyrant."

Sir Walter was known as perhaps the most independent-minded man in England. Unlike Essex, he had never made a step toward popularity. "There is none on the face of the earth," he said, "that I would be fasten'd unto." His manner was arrogant, ruthless; and it was generally said that he showed himself greedy of money, an oppressor of the poor on his estates. He made enemies as readily as Essex made friends — and remained perfectly indifferent to the reputation. Ralegh was forty-nine, Edward Coke's age. Today he stood impassive at command, a soldier who wore his armor as if it were a courtier's dress. His sword belt was studded with gems, a diamond sparkled at the hilt. The dark, bearded face was inscrutable, the dark glance careless, poised.

A proclamation echoed through the Hall and the Lord Steward entered, preceded by seven Sergeants-at-Arms, bearing maces. As the Lord Steward took his place, the maces were laid before him. Old John Popham came next, Chief Justice of King's Bench. With Lord Keeper Egerton, Popham had been six hours imprisoned at Essex House that Sunday, in danger of his life. Offered his liberty (without Essex's knowledge) the old man had refused; he would not desert the Lord Keeper. A notorious rake and brawler in his youth, Popham had become the especial terror of highwaymen, whom he hanged by the half dozens or deported — stocking Virginia, it was said, from the jails of England. Of late he had been very hard on the bawds of Southwark and threatened to clear them out to the sound of trumpets, as if they were bears or wolves. Immense under his robes he walked to the bench, his great shoulders stooped, the white coif close about his jowls. Chief Justice Anderson of Common Pleas followed, after him Judge Gawdy the Norfolkman, Coke's kinsman; then five other judges, including the Lord Chief Baron of

Exchequer. Their role was to add authority and advise the jury of peers concerning the law. (William Camden, who was a spectator, writes of the jury as "justicers," the professional judges as the "justicers' assistants" — an old distinction, come down from Magna Carta and before.)

When all were seated, a Sergeant-at-Arms made proclamation that the prisoners should be produced:

> Then the Constable of the Tower, Lord Thomas Howard, the Lieutenant of the Tower, Sir John Peyton, and the Gentleman Porter who carried the axe before the prisoners, came in, the prisoners following them, and made their appearance at the bar, the Gentleman Porter with the axe standing before them with the axe's edge from them; and so the Lieutenant delivered his precept unto the court. The two Earls meeting within the bar, kissed hands and embraced each other.

It was the courtly greeting of noblemen — English society still took its manners from the Continent — and under the circumstances, highly dramatic. Essex was dressed in black from head to foot. Those sitting near noted that his face was troubled at first, "somewhat unsettled," but that it soon cleared and he stood at ease, a little slouched as always, his head thrust slightly forward. Essex's beard and mustache were light, with a reddish tinge; his hair, dark and wavy, fell below his ears. He was a tall man, strongly built; beside him Southampton looked a boy, with his bright yellow hair and wide blue eyes. Southampton was twenty-eight to Essex's thirty-four.

The jury filed in, standing as their names were called:

> All Earls, Viscounts and Barons of the Realm of England, which were Peers of Robert Earl of Essex and Henry Earl of Southampton, and summoned to appear this day.

Essex of course knew each of the twenty-five. Several were his kinsmen — and several, his antagonists. The Earl of Nottingham (Lord Admiral) had defended Whitehall Palace on Sunday, then forced the final surrender at Essex House. Lord Cobham, Essex counted as a deadly enemy; Lord Grey de Wilton not two weeks since had attacked Southampton in the street and tried to kill him. Grey had been "Fleeted" for it. As Grey's name was called, spectators watched to see how the prisoners would take it. Essex "laughed upon Southampton and jogged him by the sleeve." Might he, Essex inquired of the Chief Justice, challenge one or two of the jurymen? No, Popham replied; the peers of England were not subject to exception nor were they compelled to take the oath. Coke stepped forward, citing, in support of Popham, a case from Henry VIII's time.

Essex knew the disadvantages of a nobleman's trial. In a jury of lords the verdict need not be unanimous; a majority could convict. With no challenge permitted and at least two sworn enemies sitting, it was for the prisoners no auspicious beginning. The system went unquestioned; great lords must accept the sacrifices and obligations of their position. Yet despite this initial setback, Essex today had had the first word. Having seized the offensive, quite patently he meant to keep it. Holding up his hand to be sworn, he remarked that he "had before this time done it often at her Majesty's command for a better purpose." The confidence of this was almost breathtaking and left no doubt what the Earl's plea would be. The Clerk began to read the indictments :

> . . . conspiracy to deprive and depose the Queen's Majesty from her royal state and dignity, and to procure her death and destruction; and also to cause a cruel slaughter of her Majesty's subjects, to alter the religion established and change the government of the Realm. And for the effecting thereof, the said Earls intended to go to her Majesty's house at Whitehall. . . .

As the Clerk's voice droned on, describing the tumult at Essex House, the crazy run through the city, Essex showed open contempt — "smiled several times and lifted up his eyes to Heaven." The two prisoners had not been told of the confessions of their confederates, delivered last night to the prosecution. Essex had no notion that proof of premeditation and criminal intent was in Coke's hands today. In criminal cases it was customary to keep the accused in the dark. Had Coke or the Chief Justice been challenged concerning the equity of this procedure, they would have replied indignantly that it was done "for the Queen's safety." If favor were shown to traitors, would not the realm be endangered, and all its loyal citizens?

Coke was familiar of course with the state trials of the sixteenth century. And from the Duke of Buckingham in 1522 to the Earl of Arundel in '89, only one of these noble or gently born suspects had gone free — Sir Nicholas Throckmorton, who in the year 1554 was indubitably implicated in Wyatt's Rebellion. On trial at the Guildhall, Throckmorton had confounded the lawyers, hypnotized the jury of twelve citizens and talked himself into an acquittal. The jurymen had been imprisoned; the eight who refused to retract, ruinously fined. Citizen panels were easily intimidated or bribed by the friends of powerful accused men; in some counties it was difficult to find twelve honest jurymen. Yet Throckmorton's acquittal had held. English judges, though they might punish a jury, would not upset a conviction. No felon — least of all a man accused of treason — was allowed counsel or the privilege of calling witnesses. (Only five years later, Parliament was to pass a law allowing the accused in certain felonies "the benefit of such witnesses as can be produced for his better clearing and justification" — a law conceived, said Coke, "for the better consciences of the jury and justices." And "to say the truth," Coke added, "we never read in any act of Parliament, ancient author, book case, or records, that in criminal cases the party accused should not have witnesses sworn for him; and therefore there is not so much as *scintilla juris* against it.") *

Yet "rules of evidence" was a phrase unknown to Edward Coke. The Crown was expected to call, as witness, anybody it considered good for its case. Chief Justice Popham himself planned to step down today and turn state's witness against Essex. (And why not? the audience would have asked. Had not Popham been imprisoned in Essex House, his life threatened?) Judges were prepared to lead criminal investigations, take an active part in the prosecution. As for the jury — in old times, jurors had been called as neighbors having direct local knowledge, witnesses not necessarily to the deed but to the fact of the crime.† The talkative, accusatory peers who constituted Essex's jury sat balanced as it were between this ancient concept and the later silent jury, which sat only to judge upon the facts as presented.

"Not guilty!" said Essex clearly, in answer to the Clerk's question. "I call God to witness," he went on solemnly, "that I

* Chapter Note.

† Because juries were anciently called, not to hear evidence and judge it but to give their *vere dictum* or true statement of the facts in their knowledge, a false verdict was looked on as perjury — a view which persisted long after the jury had changed its function.

bear a true heart to her Majesty and my country, and have done nothing but that which the law of nature commanded me to do in my own defence, and which any reasonable man would have done in the like case."

Reason, the law of nature? The prosecution listened. These were lawyers' words, scholars' words. Essex, patently, had been well rehearsed. Yelverton rose to open for the Crown. As Serjeant-at-Law he had precedence over Coke, though his speech was to be brief, a mere formality. He wore his parti-colored Serjeant's gown, half light green, half dark. He was short and fat and the gown voluminous, so that he seemed to float rather than walk to the bar, as if blown there. He wondered, said Yelverton, the two earls did not "blush to stand upon their trials without confession, when their intended treasons are in all men's judgments so palpable." How could the Earl of Essex's heart be so *beflinted* as to forget all the Queen's benefits! This was ambition like the crocodile's, "which is ever growing as long as he liveth." This was treason more manifest than Catiline's. "As Catiline entertained the most seditious persons about all Rome to join with him in his conspiracy, so the Earl of Essex entertained none but papists, recusants and atheists for his abettors in this his capital rebellion against the whole estate of England. . . . My hope is," Yelverton finished, "that God of his mercy will not suffer any hurt to the State, or prejudice to her Majesty's most royal person, whom I pray God long preserve from the hands of her enemies."

"Amen!" exclaimed the two Earls in unison. "And God confound their souls," they added piously, "who ever wished otherwise to her sacred person."

The Attorney General's name was called. Coke got up ("suddenly rising," the report says) and walked to the bar, his black woolen gown swinging. He bowed to the Lord Steward, addressed five words to him and turned to the jury. There was no oratory to what he said. Rather, these were the words of a Temple lecturer, a professor at the University expounding the law:

"May it please your Grace . . . In all good governments, men's judgments and censures are and ought to be directed by reason and precedent. The laws do best express the one, and true histories the other. The laws, that by long experience and practice of many successions of grave, learned and wise men, have grown to perfection, are grounded no doubt upon greater and more absolute reason than the singular and private opinion or conceit of the wisest man that liveth in the world can find out or attain unto. Therefore the law shall stand for reason."

It was not the first time nor the last that Mr. Attorney said it. "Right reason and the common law"—for centuries the words would be associated with Coke's name. The jury listened. As orator, Coke was sometimes ridiculous, sounding off into Latin or epithet. But as teacher he was supreme; to expound the law seemed part of his nature. "Now my Lords and Judges," he continued, "who are the fathers of the law, do know that by the law, the thought or imagination of the death of the Prince is treason. But because the thoughts are known only to God, it is not permitted to be so adjudged, till they appear by discovery either by word or writing, or some outward act."

There was an ancient principle of English equity which said that a man's secret thoughts could not be put on trial. Long before Coke's time, Chief Justice Brian had declared it: "The thought of man shall not be tried, for the devil himself knoweth not the heart of man." Yet in Essex's case there was little need for probe or research; the man had bared his intent to all the world. "He that raiseth a rebellion or insurrection in a settled Government," Coke went on, "doth, in construction of law, imagine the death and destruction of the Prince, and is therefore guilty of treason. For the law doth intend that where a man doth raise power and forces to reform anything in the government of the commonwealth, he doth usurp upon the Prince and take upon himself his authority, and therefore intendeth his deposition and death; for he that abuseth the government hateth the governor."

Sentence after sentence, Coke pounded it in. "If a man doth assemble force to redress his wrongs, he is guilty of treason. . . . All this I will fully prove to your Lordships by several cases and precedents. . . ."

Coke was off, now, into history, citing various attempts that had been adjudged treason, telling it simply, without legality, to peers who knew more of hawk and hound, of tilting and deerstalking than of law or history. "Again," Coke said when he had listed his cases, "he that doth for any purpose assemble power and continueth it notwithstanding the King doth command him upon his allegiance to dissolve it, without any question is guilty of high treason in levying war against the sovereign."

In this Sunday affray, little actual harm had been done. Three men killed fighting, half a dozen wounded when the Earl's advance had been stopped by the Bishop of London's guards . . . To send the Earl to a traitor's death for this seemed somehow barbarous. Yet if, in law, the attempt constituted treason, if like attempts in former ages had been so adjudged, then the jury's duty was plain. Such knowledge lifted the onus of conviction from their several consciences and put it squarely upon the law, where, as Coke well knew, in Christian societies it belonged.

"In declaring this case to your Lordships, I will follow this method. First . . ."

Coke's voice droned on. Occasionally he consulted his papers, holding them in the dim light, close to his face. . . . Mr. Attorney was verging upon tedium, no doubt about it. Yet in so highly charged an atmosphere, there was in this very tedium something reassuring; it removed the element of private revenge. Audience and prisoners had looked to hear invective, angry insult. Coke, so far, had not once used the word traitor, though there had been an epithet or two, echoing Serjeant Yelverton . . . *Catiline, popish, dissolute*. . . . But nobly born traitors were always called Catilines and popish, and as for dissolute, the Earl's private morals were no worse than other men's. The Attorney General had turned to the prisoners' box. "And by your favor, my Lord of Essex," he said, with palpable irony, "I will answer now your excuse that the *law of nature* compelled you to do this which in my judgment you have most traitorously attempted."

Here the Attorney General became slightly vague and went off into Latin, then settled down to a point-by-point account of the riot, beginning on the Saturday morning when Essex had been summoned to the Council table and refused to come. "Now the tale of the rebellion is thus," Coke said. "When her Majesty sent to have the Earl of Essex come before her for no other end or purpose but for his good admonishment, he refused to come; and having a guilty conscience and suspecting his treasons were laid open, or would be presently, he renewed his consultations with his friends, began at Drury-house three months before. And among other things they conferred together whether it were more advisable to take the Tower, to surprise the Court, or to try their friends in London. Wherefore they resolved, four days before they broke into open rebellion, that to surprise the Court first was best. And for this purpose they appointed Blunt to have the custody of the [palace] gates, Sir John Davis of the hall, Sir Charles Danvers of the Presence [chamber], and the Earl of Essex himself was to take charge of her Majesty's person."

To the audience — and the prisoners at the bar — this evidence of premeditation was news of the first water. The Attorney General's delivery was confident, consecutive; it was obvious he must possess written proof, ready at hand. . . . Coke went on, now, to tell of the Lord Keeper's imprisonment in Essex House, together with the Chief Justice and two Privy Councilors, of their lives threatened by the courtyard mob. Leaving the law for Essex's immediate story, Coke's tone changed; he became suddenly the advocate, colorful, oratorical. "This offence," he said, "was not of that suddenness that they make show of. For my Lord of Essex ever wore a black bag on his breast next his skin, containing the names of such as were of his numbers. A black bag, meet for so black a cause! This treason-bird hath been secretly long a-hatching, and was hatched in such a hollow tree, that only God's Providence discovered it before it was fully fledged to fly of itself."

Here was matter readily understood — words that hung in the memory, fit to travel from mouth to mouth through the countryside. "Doth not my Lord of Essex," Coke continued, "enjoy his titles of Hereford and Essex by the gift of Henry VIII and of her Majesty, to his father? Was he not made Master of the Horse at twenty-two years of age . . . one of her Majesty's Council . . . Earl Marshal of England . . . General of her Majesty's Forces in Ireland? And lastly, hath he not received divers gifts and sums of money, to his own use, of her Majesty's gracious and princely bounty, to the value of thirty thousand pounds? Yet all these benefits were as cleverly forgotten as if they had never been. . . . *O tempora, O mores! Hic tamen vivit?*"

Essex shook his head in vigorous protest, stepped forward and moved his body "with wondering and passionate gestures." . . . "My Lord the Earl," Coke continued, "did not any whit scruple to give order, before he went into the City, that if he and his complices should miscarry in London, then the Councilors which he caused to be imprisoned in his house should be slain. This was not all; for the Earl would call a Parliament and himself decide all matters which did not make for his purpose. A bloody Parliament that would have been, where my Lord of Essex, that stands now all in black, would have worn a bloody robe! But now in God's judgment, he of his earldom shall be *Robert the Last*, that of a kingdom thought to be *Robert the First*. . . ."

The words were out, shocking, violent. Coke turned to the judges. "Why should I stand upon further proofs? The treason is so evident that my Lord himself will not deny it."

Coke walked away. He had not taken his seat when the Earl was heard addressing the jury, his words easy, persuasive, as a man who confides in friends and equals. "Mr. Attorney," he said, "playeth the orator and abuseth your Lordships' ears with slanders against us. These are the fashions of orators in corrupt states, and such rhetoric is the trade and talent of those who value themselves upon their skill in pleading innocent men out of their lives, and who never think that they have sufficiently discharged their duty unless they aggravate all things against such as are charged by them."

The world has never been in love with lawyers. Among the jury was scarcely a nobleman who had not been plagued by suits in his day — suits brought by tenants or wards, suits about boundaries, fences, inheritance, enclosure of pasture land. Attorneys were low-born rascals at best, and coming up in the world alarmingly; Coke was said to be one of the richest men in England. . . . Robert the Last! . . . The word "traitor" would not have been more offensive. There was impudence here, an overstepping the decent boundaries of birth and place. This Mr. Attorney, had he met the Earl outside of court, would have been compelled by custom to stand hat in hand before him. Time was — law or no law — when a nobleman so bespoken would have stepped down and cut the fellow across the face. . . . "Corrupt states," Essex had said. There was no doubt of his meaning. It was the Cecils he aimed at and all those busy, well-rewarded government men of the "new aristocracy" whom Tudor monarchs set at their Council table in preference to noblemen of greater name and lineage. Mr. Attorney presumed far, today. . . .

"We beseech your Lordships," Essex was saying, "that it may please you to allow us first to answer generally to that wherewith we have been generally charged, and afterwards to every particular piece of evidence as it is delivered. For otherwise we shall soon confound our own memories and give liberty and advantage to our enemies, for lack of precise answer to each particular objection."

Coke rose to object. The Earl's request was a usual one, though seldom granted in treason trials. Popham, after conference with his brethren, declared the plea to be "very reasonable"; he trusted the Lord Steward would acquiesce. The Clerk stood to read aloud the testimony of the first witness. It was Widdrington's, a government man who by accident had been in Essex's courtyard early Sunday morning. "I beseech your Lordships," Essex interrupted, addressing the jury, "not to consider what may be only said by these gentlemen, but what shall be directly and plainly proved."

The Earl, quite obviously, possessed qualities other than the power to charm. Through the minds of counsel there may have passed the thought that Essex, had he not been born an Earl, would have made an excellent lawyer. . . . Widdrington's deposition was long. When it was done, Coke called the Chief Justice as witness. It was an awesome moment. Wrapped in the majesty of judicial scarlet, Popham stepped from the bench and stood waiting for the first question.

On Sunday morning, Coke began — when his Lordship first crossed the Earl's courtyard — had he overheard the words, "Kill them! Kill them!" directed at himself and the Lord Keeper?

Yes, Popham replied. There had been a man standing near . . . he could not remember his face but he had on a white satin doublet. This man had shouted, "Kill them!" Also, as he and Lord Keeper Egerton entered Essex House, followed by the Queen's Sergeant-at-Arms bearing the Seal, a voice had cried, "Cast the Great Seal out the window!" Others shouted, "Kill them!" Still others, "Nay, let us shop them up." *

Popham's testimony was detailed, careful, and by virtue of his position, impressive. He had done his best to persuade the Earl to carry his wrongs to the Council table; failing that, to confide in him or the Lord Keeper. They would see that Essex received justice and — were he truly in danger from private enemies — protection.

Popham sat down. Essex spoke at once. The Lord Chief Justice

* Slang for "imprison." Used especially for spies, informers.

and the Lord Keeper, too, were "ever his best friends." Why should he wish them harm? On the contrary, he had locked them up to keep them safe! He had meant no harm, no harm whatever. "And for any intent of treason to her Majesty or to the state, I am clear, and can say as much for all the rest there present."

"But, my Lord," Coke protested, "you had three hundred men in arms at your house. Why did you not dissolve them, being commanded upon your allegiance from the Queen to do it?"

Disperse them? repeated the Earl. It was too late, the men were roused, excited. . . . Coke stepped forward. According to the testimony of the Chief Justice, the facts were different. Southampton interrupted: Mr. Attorney spoke as if all this were gospel. Oaths of allegiance? What good were oaths of allegiance against men whose lives were threatened by their enemies? Had not his own life been threatened by Lord Grey in the street, on horseback?

Grey, at this, stood up in the jury box and gave Southampton the lie. In a second, the two were shouting at each other. . . . The Lord Steward interposed, after which Coke came forward to accuse Essex of an elaborate machination concerning certain forged letters, the originals of which lay in a casket belonging to the Earl's wife. Essex, furious, accused Coke of lying. "Thou swearest, but it is not on a book. . . . Well, Mr. Attorney, I thank God I have not so uncharitable a judge this day as you are."

COKE: My Lord, we shall prove anon what you are, and what your pride of heart and aspiring mind have brought you unto.

ESSEX: Ah! Mr. Attorney, lay your hand upon your heart and pray God to forgive us both.

It was nearing eleven o'clock. Dinner time, but today there would be no dinner for court or audience until after nightfall. The Sergeant-at-Arms called Sir Walter Ralegh as witness. The Captain left his post and strode forward. Falling on his knee before the bar, he asked the Lord Steward to swear him — "when vehemently the Lord of Essex cried out, 'Look what book it is he swears on!' And the book being decimo-sexto, or the least volume, was changed to a book in folio of the largest size."

It was an extraordinary scene, unlooked for, dramatic. Nor was Essex merely creating a diversion. Great superstitious reverence was attached to the oath. Time had been, indeed, when the act of swearing was considered more important than the matter sworn to. In the days of trial by ordeal, a perjured witness risked being struck down by heaven on the spot. Oaths originally were elaborate, ceremonious to a degree. Each detail must be correctly repeated after the judge, and if an oath-taker fumbled it was because God impeded the perjured tongue.

Essex was in deadly earnest. The audience waited. As Ralegh laid his hand on the Bible, Essex leaned to Southampton:

"*What booteth it to swear the fox?*"

The words, startling, pungent (and supremely impudent) rang through the Hall. Ralegh took no notice. His testimony was brief and concerned only the movements, on Sunday, of Sir Ferdinando Gorges, military governor of Plymouth — and Ralegh's kinsman. At Essex's bidding, Gorges had quit his post without permission from the Queen and traveled up to London. Ralegh told of meeting him on the river and bidding him leave town at once, "or otherwise he would be laid in the Fleet," to which Sir Ferdinando replied that Ralegh himself had best get quickly back to the Palace, "for he was like to have a bloody day of it."

"Whereupon," finished Ralegh to the court, "Sir Ferdinando shoved off the boat that I was in, and bade me make haste hence, which I did."

Essex did not know, as yet, that it was Sir Ferdinando who first betrayed the secret conferences at Drury House. As Ralegh left the witness box, Essex remarked shortly that Sir Walter's testimony conflicted with what Sir Ferdinando had told *him* — another way of saying that Ralegh lied. Sir Ferdinando's confession now was produced and read aloud by the Clerk. It was long, explicit, damning, and to the accused, doubtless a stunning blow. Perhaps Essex did not believe it, considered it fabricated by the prosecution. Perhaps he hoped, if once he could see Gorges, he could break his testimony. . . .

"I desire," Essex said peremptorily, "to have Sir Ferdinando Gorges face to face."

Gorges was led in from prison, "pale," wrote Camden, "with unsettled countenance." Essex addressed him in a kind of contemptuous compassion. "Good Sir Ferdinando, with all my heart I desire thee to speak freely. I see thou desirest to live. Yet I pray thee, speak like a man! Remember your reputation and that you are a gentleman."

Gorges, however, could not be turned from his story. He repeated it, including the statement that he had "advised the Earl to leave his enterprise and submit to her Majesty." Essex, suddenly changing his tactics, turned to the jury. "My lords," he said, "look upon Sir Ferdinando and see if he looks like himself! All the world shall see, by my death and his life, whose testimony is the truest!"

It was a trick the Earl used more than once against witnesses for the prosecution. Fear caused these men to betray him falsely! Fear of the rack, fear of death. . . . No! Coke retorted. Neither rack nor torture had been used on any witness. Sir Ferdinando was the only one of Essex's friends brought into court. The remainder of the testimony was written; the Clerk read it aloud. There were seven depositions, referred to severally as *confessions*, *examinations* or *declarations*, each signed by the examinate: Sir Charles Danvers, Sir John Davis, Lord Sandys, the Earl of Rutland, Lord Cromwell, Lord Monteagle and one Edward Bushell, said by the prosecution to be "very inward" with Essex, who quickly denied it. The man was only "his servant waiting on his table."

The declarations gave all the same story, though with interesting embellishments. Danvers, for instance, revealed how, when the Earl's company reached the palace, it was planned that he, Danvers, should "step between the Bodyguard and their halberds," which rested against the wall. "Upon a signal, the Earl would come into the court with his company. . . . They would have secured the Captain of the Guard [Ralegh] had he resisted, and then have sent to satisfy the City and call a Parliament." Many of the Bodyguard "had been my Lord's [Essex's] servants and of them they had no doubt."

The declarations took a long time, interspersed with quick, disagreeable suggestions from the Attorney General, hotly disputed by Essex. Was it not extraordinary, Coke remarked to the jury, how fact and confession agreed with each other, to make out this case? It was indeed extraordinary, Essex retorted drily. "The selfsame fear and the self-same examiner may make the several examinations agree all in one, were they never so distant." He heard himself, said Essex, accused of being at the same time papist, dissenter and atheist. How could one man attain to such variety of offenses?

He had intended no violence to the Queen; his act was to be judged therefore "by the intent in conscience."

COKE: Nay, our law judgeth the overt act.
ESSEX: Well, plead you law and we will plead conscience.

Southampton, when his turn came, bore himself more meekly. His bright hair fell to his shoulders, his blue eyes were hurt, helpless. When Coke bore down on him he answered plaintively, like a child that has been wrongly slapped by his nurse. No, he never saw the herald on Sunday nor heard Essex proclaimed traitor. He himself had been in the city on private business, unarmed except for the sword he always wore.

COKE: My Lord, it hath been confessed that you had a pistol when you were in the City.
SOUTHAMPTON: Mr. Attorney! It is the uncivilest thing in the world to interrupt a man who is speaking for his life.

Uncivil . . . with the mark of prison on his face, standing in the shadow of the axe? This young courtier, accomplished, brave, at whose house poets forgathered, this soldier who spoke French, Italian, and was forever at the play — here in the courtroom showed himself a very baby, bewildered, resentful. Coke waited. Strange, how these lords thought themselves even now in their own great halls, where men bespoke them always with civility, with deference! A criminal trial was no levee. Time was when the two Earls would have been tried by the ordeal of battle. Now they must undergo an ordeal of words, wherein the courtesies of the tiltyard had no part.
"But touching a pistol," Southampton went on, plaintively, "I carried none out with me. But being in the street, I saw one having a pistol and I desired it of him and had it. But it had no flint nor could it hurt a flea. From this kind of behavior can be gathered no thoughts of treason."

COKE: My Lord of Southampton, is this no treason, to force the Queen in her own house, to set guards at her gates, in her chamber and in all parts of the house, to the end that having her in your power you might do what you listed?
SOUTHAMPTON: Good Mr. Attorney, let me ask you what, in

your conscience, you think we would have done to her Majesty if we had gained the [Queen's] Court?

The young Earl could not have devised a question more unfortunate. Already it was the general conviction that Southampton had intended no harm; he had been led astray by Essex. (As a matter of fact the Queen would remit his sentence and after two years in prison he would go free.) But at Southampton's question it appeared the Attorney General had received a legacy or swallowed a sugar plum. "What," Coke repeated, "would you have done to her Majesty? . . . *How long, my lord, lived King Richard the Second after he was surprised in the same manner?*"

Southampton, it was plain, had cooked his goose; it was he who had arranged the performance of *Richard II* before the rebellion. Yet a prosecuting attorney can defeat himself by oversharpness, while an accused man, by a kind of innocent stupidity, sometimes works on the jury to his own advantage. The Attorney General saw it. "I protest upon my soul," Coke went on earnestly, "I do believe the Queen should not have lived long after she had been in your power." All such talk, Coke intimated, was rather surmise than evidence and the law. "But I know this for certain: to surprise the court or take the Tower by way of defence from private enemies, is plain treason."

The jury turned to the judges. Would their Lordships be pleased to deliver their opinions severally on this point? After conference, the judges declared that Essex's actions had amounted to actual rebellion; Southampton's following him into the city was also rebellion. All who adhered to Essex that day were traitors. Only those who joined him briefly, dispersing at the herald's proclamation, should not be so adjudged.

It was now well into the afternoon. The depositions had been read, the witnesses heard from, including those who sat on the judges' bench and in the jury. Essex launched into bitter accusation of his enemies, naming them abruptly — Cobham, Cecil, Ralegh — men who had "abused her Majesty's ears with false informations." Cobham especially had "carried himself in factious and dangerous courses. . . . *But*," said Essex, "*such a back-biter and informer I would have removed from the Queen even with the loss of my right hand!*"

Cobham, from the jury bench, jumped up to protest. The Lord Steward rapped for order. The matter was impertinent; the three gentlemen named were not on trial. Essex yielded, then added stubbornly, "My opinion of them is not mine alone, but is fortified by the opinions of others."

Throughout the trial, one well-known face and figure had so far been lacking. Sir Robert Cecil was nowhere to be seen. As a mere knight he ranked far below Essex and could not, of course, be included in a jury of the Earl's peers. Yet it seemed extraordinary that the Queen's Secretary should remain out of sight. His absence bade fair to confirm the Earl's slanders against him, as if he dared not show himself before the judges and the people.

Someone else, however, was present — and by the general opinion he had better have stayed away. Francis Bacon, the Earl's great friend, sat with the lawyers. As Queen's Counsel he had appeared against Essex at York House last June. Yet the possibility that today he had come, voluntarily, further to betray his friend was hard even for palace cynics to stomach.

When Essex had finished his long narrative and defense, Bacon rose and stepped to the bar. He did not address the jury but faced the Earl and spoke to him direct, with the authority given by long trust and intimacy. What he said was deadlier far than anything conjured up by Coke, Yelverton or the judges. How, Bacon demanded, could his Lordship stand here in self-defense, who should be standing in confession? In danger from private enemies, the Earl had said — in need of the City's help? These prudent, grave and wise peers who sat today in judgment were not so simple as to credit such a tale. Lived there in all history an evil-doer who had not a reason for what he did? "Cain, that first murderer, took up an excuse for his fact, shaming not to outface it with impudency." Perhaps the court remembered Pisistratus, who slashed himself with a knife and ran bleeding through the streets of Athens, calling on the citizens to defend him? "Even such," said Bacon, "was my Lord's confidence too, and his pretence the same — an all-hail and a kiss to the City. . . . You, my Lord, allege this matter to have been resolved on a sudden. No! You were three months in the deliberation."

Statement of the law was not needed to prove this treason, Bacon went on. Common sense could see it. My Lord protested that he came unarmed into the City, in doublet and hose. And how came the Duke of Guise to the Parisian barricadoes but in doublet and hose, with only eight gentlemen to keep him company? *Yet what had Guise intended?*

It was a cruel stroke. To Elizabeth the name of Guise was anathema. Deposer of kings, traitor not of ancient Athens but of today, of the very moment . . . Bacon turned to the jury. "My Lords," he said, "I have never yet seen in any case such favour shown to any prisoner; so many digressions, such delivering of evidence by fractions, and so silly a defense of such great and notorious treasons."

For the first time, Essex seemed to lose his composure. Mr. Bacon, he said, had pretended to be his friend, pretended to grieve at his misfortunes. A strange alteration! "I call forth," said Essex, "Mr. Bacon against Mr. Bacon!"

"I confess," Bacon replied quickly, "I loved my Lord of Essex as long as he continued a dutiful subject, and I have spent more hours to make him a good subject to her Majesty than ever I did about my own business."

It was true enough, though Bacon did not stop to explain that for ten years the Earl's "business" had been identified with his own ambitions. Essex interrupted, blurting out a criminal accusation against Sir Robert Cecil: Cecil had declared the Infanta's title to the English crown to be "as good as any others." Moreover it was Cecil and none but Cecil whom he meant when on Sunday he had shouted to the citizens that England had been sold to the Spaniard. . . .

A man stepped through the arras behind the judges, made his way round to the bar and fell on his knee before the Lord Steward. (Sir Robert Cecil, it was said later, seemed to have dropped by magic into the court.) Praying leave, Cecil walked to the prisoners' box. Those in front noted his pallor and how he shook with anger. "My Lord of Essex," he said, "the difference between you and me is great. For wit I give you the pre-eminence, you have it abundantly. For nobility also I give you place. I am not noble, yet a gentleman. I am no swordsman, there also you have the odds. But I have innocence, conscience, truth and honesty to defend me: and in this court I stand as an upright man and your Lordship as a delinquent. You have a wolf's heart in a sheep's garment. You have drawn noble persons into your net of rebellion, their bloods will cry vengeance against you. . . ."

ESSEX: Ah! Mr. Secretary, I thank God for my humiliation, that you, in the ruff of all your bravery, have come hither to make your oration against me this day.

Who first had spread this slander against him? Cecil demanded. Where had the Earl come by it? Essex shook his head, but Southampton spoke: "It was Sir William Knollys, the Queen's Comptroller." At Cecil's insistence, Knollys was sent for across the City. When he came he denied the charge against Cecil; he had heard no such words concerning the Infanta. Cecil spoke again, his face turned up to Essex standing above him. "The Secretary" (wrote an onlooker) "cried out at the top of his voice, the [jury of] peers showing in their faces more fear of this little man than of their conscience and their queen." "Out of your malice towards me," said Cecil, "your Lordship desires to make me odious, having no other true ground than the breach between us about the peace with Spain, which I labored for the profit and quiet of my country. But with you it hath ever been a maxim to prefer war before peace, in respect of the importance it gave your Lordship and such as followed you. Councilors of State have many conferences; I confess I have said that the King of Spain is a competitor of the Crown of England, and that the King of Scots is a competitor. *And my Lord of Essex I have said is a competitor*, for he would depose the Queen and call a Parliament and so be King himself. But as to any affection to advance the Spanish title to England, I am so far from it that my mind is astonished to think of it. And I pray God to consume me where I stand if I hate not the Spaniard as much as any man living!"

There was more, and it revealed to the audience state policies they never thought to know — factions, a party for war and a party for peace. When Cecil sat down it was nearing six o'clock, the winter dark had fallen. Along the walls, torches flickered. Behind lighted tapers the judges were shadowed, remote as priests before an altar. Coke spoke again, summing up the evidence. Was it treason, he asked, by force to offer to remove any of her Majesty's Privy Council? Yes, the judges answered. It was treason. And for a subject to make his passage to the presence of the Prince by force upon her Court or Council, was that treason likewise?

And it was likewise by them adjudged treason.

Southampton spoke again, briefly, Essex more at length and humbly, this time, as if pleading with the jury to believe him. His desire had never been for bloodshed, he was at fault in barricading his house against the Lord Admiral's forces. He begged her Majesty to free certain guiltless men who were with him yet had no knowledge of his intent. If he had lied today, then, "O Lord," cried Essex, "show some mark upon me in this place, for a testimony to all the world of thy just vengeance for my untruth! And thou, O God, which knowest the secrets of all hearts, knowest that I never sought the crown of England, nor ever wished to be of higher degree than a subject!"

It was over. The depositions all were heard, the prisoners had spoken in their own defense, the judges delivered advice — and more than advice — when so requested. The Attorney General had produced his depositions and had countered the Earl's eloquence with every weapon at his command, including the oral deposition of Chief Justice Popham, the Lord Keeper — Cecil — Grey — Cobham — the Lord Admiral in the jury box. Francis Bacon, owing to his long intimacy with Essex, had served more as witness than as prosecutor.

Nothing remained but the jury's verdict. There was little doubt what it would be. . . .

Then the Lord High Steward directed the Peers to go together, and ordered the Lieutenant of the Tower to withdraw the prisoners from the bar. They being removed, the Lords went together into a private place provided for them, fairly hung with tapestry, behind the canopy and chair of estate, where the Court of Chancery is kept.

They were out nearly an hour. (Afterward, it was said in the City that they had eaten and drunk and even taken tobacco, a palpable scandal. Any ordinary juryman — a commoner — who so much as sipped his beer was disqualified and liable to punishment.) Returning, the peers awaited the Lord Steward's question: "Whether is Robert Earl of Essex guilty of this treason whereupon he hath been indicted, as you take it upon your honor, or no?" As each juryman rose to answer, he bowed low, his arm across his breast.

"Guilty, my Lord, of high treason, upon my honour."

The roll was called again for Southampton. Twenty-five voices answered, Guilty! The two Earls were led to the bar. Lord Steward Buckhurst, rising, pronounced sentence. The axe, held high for all to see, turned its edge toward the prisoners. Accepting from a Sergeant-at-Arms the white wand of his office, the Lord Steward with both hands raised it above his head and broke it in two.

CHAPTER THIRTEEN

Essex confesses. Coke's glory, Bacon's chagrin. The end of a great reign.

Lord Burghley to his son, Robert Cecil

Seek not to be Essex, shun to be Rawleigh.

BECAUSE of Essex's noble blood, his sentence of hanging and quartering was commuted. On February twenty-fifth, six days after the trial, he was beheaded within the Tower grounds. Coke was not present at the execution. But Ralegh saw his enemy die and the people hated him for it, saying that he came to gloat. There were not many witnesses. The Privy Council gave out that the Earl had begged for privacy; the people's acclamations might tempt him from true Christian repentance — a statement received by the populace with skepticism. Why should a nobleman so beloved desire to die without the applause and sympathy of his friends?

So extreme was the Earl's self-abasement that in France they said he died "more like a silly minister than a stout warrior." Having borne himself with courage (some called it impudence) throughout his trial, Essex was not out of Westminster Hall when he hinted that before his death he might reveal somewhat of interest to the government. And reveal it he did, dragging in names the prosecution had never suggested — Sir Henry Neville, now in France as Ambassador; Lord Mountjoy, Deputy Governor of Ireland; and even Essex's own sister, the beautiful Lady Rich, who, said Essex, "did continually urge me on with telling me how all my friends and followers thought me a coward and that I had lost all my valour." The Queen could never be safe while he lived. He had lied at his trial, "imagined all falsehood," and looked on himself as "the greatest, the most vilest and most unthankful traitor that ever had been in the land."

The abjectness of this recital shocked even the Privy Councilors — among them Cecil — who witnessed it. On the morning of his execution, Essex was at pains to repeat the confessions. His conduct had been sinful, he had stiffly defended an unjust cause. He was fit to be spewed up by the commonwealth for the foulness of an enterprise which, "like a leprosy, spread far and wide . . . had infected many." Standing at the scaffold rail he again besought God's pardon, forgave the executioner who knelt at his feet. "Thou art the minister of true justice," he said. Phrase by phrase, after the chaplain, he recited the Creed, begging those nearest to pray with him against the terror of death. Then taking off his black velvet gown and satin doublet, in scarlet waistcoat he lay down "without muffle" and placed his cheek on the block, bidding the executioner strike when he should spread his arms sidewise. "Come Lord Jesus, come Lord Jesus," he said, "and receive my soul."

The arms flashed out. After one blow the Earl's body lay motionless, but the axe struck twice more before the executioner stooped, and lifting the head, proclaimed, after the ancient custom:

"God save the Queen!"

Nothing that Essex had said, nothing he did, could make the people hate him. If, on the scaffold, he failed to mention his wife and children or beg the Queen's mercy for them, as was expected — this was no selfishness but the measure of true repentance; the Earl's mind had been fixed not on earth but heaven. Besides, who knew if these Raleghs and Cecils brought from the scaffold true report? No friend of Essex had witnessed this death. "The Earl died a Christian." The populace repeated it. The executioner, coming from the Tower, would have been mobbed but for the Sheriff's protection. On Cecil's door was scrawled in chalk, "Here lieth the toad." Ballads appeared overnight, for sale on the streets. In taverns the people sang them, and far out over the countryside:

Sweet England's pride is gone,
  Welladay, welladay!
Brave honour graced him still,
  Gallantly, gallantly.
He ne'er did deed of ill,
  Well it is known.
But envy, that foul fiend,
  Whose malice ne'er did end,
Hath brought true virtue's friend
  Unto this thrall.

He always helped the poor,
  Which makes them sigh full sore.
His death they do deplore
  In every place. . . .

Five men died for Essex's ambition. Blount and Danvers, being nobly born, were beheaded on Tower Hill; Henry Cuffe and Sir Gilly Merrick were hanged at Tyburn. Coke tried them together, in one day, as was the custom. Much new evidence was produced — collusion in Ireland, a plot whereby "Essex was to be King of England; Tyrone, Viceroy of Ireland." In proof, Coke produced letters of Essex's, confessions of Thomas Leigh, Warren, Wood, Hetherington and others. The evidence was damning; Coke insisted on presenting it item by item, even though several of the prisoners declared themselves ready to confess in court without further proof. The scene held none of the high dignity of Essex's trial, but degenerated, as the hours passed, into a circus of crimination and recrimination, rough jokes between accused and prosecutor, patriotic speeches from the commissioners, the prisoners and from Coke on the floor. Henry Cuffe, who had been Essex's confidential secretary, braved it out, arguing with Coke, citing the classics. Before the day was done he even contrived, by clever quotation from Ovid,* to hint broadly that Mr. Attorney had been cuckolded by his young wife.

Coke in turn was outrageously jocular, told Latin jokes and made puns on Cuffe's name. ("I will give you a *cuff* that shall set you down.") Actually, Cuffe had the better of him more than once, trapped Coke into an elaborate syllogism and then demolished the structure as if judges and jury did not exist and the two were

* Chapter Note.

standing on an Oxford debating platform. Sir Robert Cecil, sitting with the commissioners, took occasion to animadvert on the "free and liberal confessions" of nobly born prisoners, in comparison with the defiance shown by Cuffe and "others of baser sort." (The Cecils never quite forgot their lack of noble blood.) Coke's loyalties rested on another plane. He was pleased to note, in this plot against the state, that no lawyer had been implicated. "To the honor of the City of London," he said, "not one Inns of Court man followed the Earl. Not one scholar of the law, not one!" ("Often repeating," says the reporter.) The Lord Keeper, Lord Chief Justice and two Councilors — Coke went on — shut up all day at Essex House, their lives threatened, had shown no moment's fear or capitulation. "To their honors I will speak it," Coke finished triumphantly, "that in some gown-men there rest as valiant minds, where the cause requires it, as in them that wear swords!"

Southampton and Sir Thomas Smith (Sheriff of London) remained in the Tower. Of the other conspirators, "the richer sort," says Camden, "were heavily fined (which very few of them payed), the rest were pardoned by the Queen." Mountjoy, Lord Deputy in Ireland, so dreaded a public trial that he contemplated escape into France, "fully resolved," he wrote, "not to put his neck under the file of the Queen's Attorney's tongue."

Perhaps it was the quickness, the resolution with which the prosecution, trials, executions had been carried out which made more bloodshed unnecessary. Elizabeth did not waver — though once, it is true, she remanded the order for Essex's execution, then canceled her remander. At the French court her resolution was much admired. Had their own King shown half her spirit in dealing with the Duke of Guise on the Day of Barricadoes, France would have been saved great trouble. "She only is a King!" exclaimed Henry IV. "She only knows how to rule."

But though foreign kings might applaud her resolution, Elizabeth's subjects remained sullen. They did not speak of Essex's execution but of his "murder," and when the Queen passed through the City she was not acclaimed as she had been. Among lawyers, none had a pen so facile as Francis Bacon's. Elizabeth commanded him to write a narrative that might appeal to plain men. Within a few weeks (April 21, 1601) the result was in print: *A Declaration of the Practices and Treasons attempted and committed by Robert Earl of Essex*. It was book-length and included everything — arguments at the trials, depositions of witnesses, post-trial confessions with which the public was not acquainted. For it (and his earlier services against Essex), Bacon received twelve hundred pounds. He needed the money, having actually been arrested on the street for debt. (He spent the night in a Fleet Street sponging house, rescued by his cousin Cecil in response to a pleading, humorous note.) Since then, Bacon's fortunes had mended a little, yet he had not found the requisite rich bride and still lacked official position with the government. "The Queen," he told a creditor, "hath done somewhat for me, though not in the proportion I had hoped."

Bacon's *Declaration* was logical, clear, dramatic and should have convinced, damning the name of Essex to eternity. Perversely, it had the effect of damning its author, who in the end was constrained to write an elaborate apology for the part he had taken against his friend. Nothing, it seemed, could blacken Essex's name or lay this noble ghost. (Twenty years later it would rise to plague Elizabeth's successor.) That the Earl had betrayed his friends was overlooked; the noble lord was a martyr to faction and to the ambitions of meaner men. Gallant soldier, knight beyond reproach. Generous to the poor! That was what the poor remembered.

Oddly enough, the public resentment did not include Edward Coke. His harshness throughout the trials was remarked. Yet Attorney Generals were not noted for mincing words and this one had displayed a certain rough picturesqueness of speech that was admired. *Elephants' whelps, eggs hatched in hollow trees* — anybody could understand such talk and besides it had relieved the tedium and tension, made a better show for the money. It was upon Ralegh the general anger turned — Ralegh, who had stood by Essex's scaffold "to feed his eyes with the Earl's torment." The Devon adventurer, thrice-privileged Captain standing in silver armor at the Queen's door . . . lord over estates in five Midland counties . . . forty thousand acres in Ireland, a palace on the Strand, monopolies from the Crown in cloth, tin, playing cards, wines. Ralegh took the Queen's bounty yet scattered no largesse, dispensed no patronage. Vice Admiral of Devon, Governor of Jersey, Lord Lieutenant of Cornwall and Warden of the Stanneries*

* Tin mines in Cornwall employing from ten to thirteen thousand men.

— titles and honors usually reserved for noblemen, not upstarts. His arrogance was "intolerable, without regard for any, as all the world knows. No man is more hated than him, none more cursed daily of the poor." So a Cornishman had written to Lord Treasurer Burghley twenty years ago, when Ralegh's star began to rise. There was about Sir Walter something mysterious, close; he kept his counsel and did not ask God's help or man's. Around him and his chosen friends hung the name and stain of atheism. His brother Carew, Christopher Marlowe, Ben Jonson, Thomas Harriot the mathematician who lived in Ralegh's household, actors, men of dubious reputation, banded it was said in a blasphemous society called the *School of Night*, whose members questioned Scriptural authority, "accidents that do happen in the air or the earth or the waters, referred by them to natural causes because they were unwilling to acknowledge that God had a hand in them." Members jested about Moses and the Commandments, taught young men to spell God backwards (a favorite device of necromancers). The Privy Council had dissolved the society and would have arrested one member — Marlowe — but he died in a tavern brawl before he was apprehended.

These things were recalled, now in the year 1601. Actually, Ralegh had not stood by Essex's scaffold to watch that final agony, though as Captain of the Guard he had walked there with other witnesses. "But being admonished," says Camden, "not to presse upon the Earl at his death, which is the part of ignoble beasts, he withdrew himself farther off, and beheld him out of the Armourie." * Not until seventeen years later, when Ralegh stood so tragically on his own scaffold, did he confess how he saw Essex die, and that he shed tears at the sight.

The truth was that with Essex's disappearance from the scene, Ralegh found himself in a shifting, anomalous position. Cecil had been his friend, if only for the reason that both were Essex's enemies. Now the Earl was dead, and in court and Parliament the Cecilian faction triumphed. The old alignments slipped and shuffled; in politics, friends are made and unmade in a day. Impossible, from a distance of centuries, to follow these quick loyalties and quicker abandonments. By their natures these two were antagonistic: Cecil the

* The Armory was high up in the White Tower. See Chapter Note for Ralegh's full statement.

cautious statesman, Ralegh the gentleman-adventurer, a poet, man of battles. (In Ireland, Sir Walter had once caused six hundred prisoners to be slain.) Cecil found it hard to credit Ralegh as a skilled mariner. *Jonah*, he called him, saying Sir Walter was forever losing her Majesty's ships or putting back because of storms. It was true that misfortune dogged Ralegh at sea. He had never been given command of an expedition nor made Privy Councilor at home. His schemes for colonization were looked on as chimerical. The adventure at Roanoke had failed and Ralegh sold his Virginia shares. Gold was the cargo Elizabeth desired brought back in her ships. Not tobacco, vegetable roots or feathered aborigines.

Yet the Queen knew Sir Walter's value and while she lived, Sir Walter was safe with all his wealth and place. To Elizabeth the arrogant wit, the dark poetic fancy were attractive. She was aware that Ralegh had his dangerous side, a kind of natural affinity for plots, never in them yet never out of them, gliding near to dubious situations, skirting disaster and keeping his own counsel about it. Elizabeth, whose playful names for those nearest her were sometimes very apt, called him *Water*.

In the streets, that year of Essex's death, a ballad was sung:

Little Cecil trips up and down,
He rules both Court and Crown,
With his Brother Burghley Clown,
In his great fox-furred gown;
With the long proclamation
He swore he saved the Town.
Is it not likely?

Ralegh doth time bestride,
He sits twixt wind and tide,
Yet up hill he cannot ride,
For all his bloody pride.
He seeks taxes in the tin,
He polls the poor to the skin,
Yet he swears 'tis no sin.
Lord for thy pity!

Coke's own fortunes rode high, in these last years of Elizabeth. The Queen was sixty-seven — a fact not to be mentioned in her hearing. She seemed in excellent health but there was an occasional melancholy about her, disturbing to those who knew her best. In the early autumn of 1601 she set out on progress, traveling through the green countryside with the usual crowds of retainers, receiving homage, making a knight or two, though as always she was sparing of this honor. Wherever she went, there was gaiety; "great chere, singing, dancing and playing wenches and such like." In Buckinghamshire she "made a step," wrote Chamberlain, "to Master Atturneyes at Stoke, where she was most sumptuously entertained and presented with jewells and other gifts to the value of a thousand or twelvehundred pound."

Elizabeth's visits were no easy honor. She might bring four hundred in her train and of course no provisions; the countryside must be scoured for food. Ambitious gentlemen almost impoverished themselves for the glory of her presence, built wings to their houses, gilded chambers fit for such a guest. Country sheriffs were known to fall sick with anxiety when a royal visit was announced. Coke, beforehand, sent off worried bulletins to Sir Robert Cecil. Lady Hatton's court experience proved of great help and comfort, Coke being hardly the man to select the perfect gift for a Queen. "This morning," he wrote to Cecil on August tenth, "my wife attended on her Majesty, and she will vouchsafe to take dinner at Stoke on Thursday next, when I shall expect your presence. For the gown and jewel, whatsoever you shall think fit I will assent unto, and rather to be above the sum your Honour mentioned than under, for I would give that which shall be acceptable, whatsoever it cost. I have written to my cousin Stanhope to take pains for me herein, and to do what you shall command him." And a few days later, dated "*Stoke, this present Saturday:* My wife her learned counsel hath very exactly considered of every part of the jewel. A friend of mine hath provided another of as good value. Which shall best like you shall be presented. I have sent this bearer to take direction for the gown. To me at this time trifles are of importance, as you best know."

Trifles, at such a moment, were indeed important; the Queen's visit marked the peak of Coke's worldly glory. He was still plain Mr. Attorney, not yet a Serjeant-at-Law and not a knight; in court he wore his thick black woolen gown — the "fusted gown of an Attorney General." Yet Majesty was to step across his threshold, eat his bread and smile, accepting gifts. . . . When the day came, trumpets from far off announced the royal approach; the dusty procession reached a full mile beyond Stoke gates. Knights on horseback, ladies whose long skirts swept below their stirrup; wagons and pack horses laden with gear — wardrobes of court dress, velvet and satin, gold-encrusted, bulky, musty with many foldings. Lady Hatton was in her element, moving easily through strictest etiquette or sparkling play, a woman who could wear diamonds at nine in the morning as other wives wear aprons. How she disposed of the ten children is something of a puzzle. By Sir William Hatton, she had herself a daughter; Coke's eight children ranged from the ages of seventeen to four; their mutual small daughter, Frances, was barely two. When Bridget was alive the children's names were often mentioned, traveling with their parents to Norwich in summer or visited at school in Suffolk. But now they seemed not to exist unless as pawns in some great ceremony. In 1601, Coke's eldest daughter, Anne, made a splendid marriage, "To Sir Thomas Sadlers sonne," * wrote Chamberlain, "with whom Master Atturney gave 3000 pounds and furnished the feast with all magnificence." The wedding was held at Burghley House in Covent Garden. The bride, aged fifteen, went with her husband to live in a walled country place called Standon Lordship, vast enough for a child to be lost in. (Coke himself would one day come there for refuge when deprived of place and honor by a Stuart king.)

To Francis Bacon the glitter of Coke's progress was as sand in the eyes. That this Norfolk farmer should ride so high and in the corridors of Westminster Hall brush past with a brutal indifference was unendurable. Bacon's resentment mounted until one day in Exchequer Court he let it out and the two quarreled loudly before a crowded bar. Sore and bruised, Bacon went home and wrote his cousin Cecil a detailed account of the affair; then, still unsatisfied, sent off a letter to Coke. Angry, eloquent and very characteristic, it remains as testimony:

MR. ATTORNEY,

I thought best, once for all, to let you know in plainness what I find of you, and what you shall find of me. You take to yourself a liberty to disgrace and disable my law, my experience, my discretion. . . . You are

* Anne's husband was Sir Ralph Sadleir, grandson and heir of that Sir Ralph Sadleir who had been Secretary to Henry VIII, trusted minister also of Elizabeth and before his death reputed the richest commoner of England.

great, and therefore have the more enviers which would be glad to have you paid at another's cost. Since the time I missed the Solicitor's place (the rather I think by your means) I cannot expect that you and I shall ever serve as Attorney and Solicitor together. . . . And if you had not been shortsighted in your own fortune (as I think) you might have had more use of me.

But that tide is passed. I write not this to show my friends what a brave letter I have written to Mr. Attorney; I have none of those humours. But that I have written is to a good end, that is to the more decent carriage of my mistress' service and to our particular better understanding one of another. This letter, if it shall be answered by you in deed and not in word, I suppose it will not be worse for us both. Else it is but a few lines lost, which for a much smaller matter I would have adventured. So this being but yourself, I for myself rest.

FR. BACON

The answer, if ever it existed, is gone. Bacon's position, at the moment, was insignificant; during the Queen's lifetime he would remain helpless, poor and angrily impatient. About Coke there must indeed have been the look of a man mounting upward, and no doubt a ruthlessness in his forward stride. "*You are great and therefore have the more enviers. . . .*" Yet domestically, Coke's affairs were proceeding far from smoothly. In the connubial chamber that overlooked Hatton Gardens, violent scenes took place, if Lady Hatton's word is to be believed — a breaking open of a wife's cabinet by the husband, the seizing of a note for four thousand pounds . . . Lady Hatton running home to her father's house in Covent Garden and refusing to return "for a whole year after, with a resolucon ever there to continew, had not the great Queen Eliza: Commanded my deare father and unckle [Robert Cecil] to reconcyle us, and promysed to see that her Attourney should use me well and p'forme all promyses her Mat'ie died in short tyme after."

Perhaps it is true and perhaps the fault lay all with Coke. Yet Lady Hatton's statement, given years later before the Privy Council, is so garbled with wrong dates, with blame beforehand for things that happened long after, with omissions and embroideries, that it is hard to credit. In all likelihood the pair quarreled fiercely, in all likelihood Lady Hatton did run home, to the vast embarrassment of her father and uncle. Coke was autocratic — perhaps brutal; his wife was arrogant and untruthful. From the beginning this had been an unmatched pair and London would hear more of their troubles — much more, until the newsletters hummed and even King James became involved.

This however was in the future. Whatever quarrels occurred in these early years of marriage were hushed, kept from the public knowledge. Certainly there was no breach between Coke and the Cecil family. Letters, subscribed *Ely House*, flowed from Coke to Mr. Secretary Cecil. . . . Her Majesty had graciously granted to her Attorney the manor of Swaffham in Norfolk, "near the place of my nativity." . . . By command, Coke was busy forwarding, from his wife's property of Corfe Castle, "the brass ordnance taken from the enemy in '88 and sent to Corfe by the Lord Admiral . . ."

Cecil in turn must have sent innumerable briefs and orders from his house in the Strand to the great walled mansion in Holborn. Coke's answers held a genial note, though he seems to have executed the orders immediately. "If I were not persuaded," he writes one day, "*quod bonum est benefacere in Sabbato*, I should think that I have broken the whole Sabbath yesterday in speeding of this business, and now do mean in satisfaction of nature's due to shrive on my bed." Obscure men, caught on the edge of treason, came to Ely House to beg off. One Swift, writes Coke to Cecil, "fell downe upon his knees and with crocodile teares bewail'd much." In his old age, Coke boasted that he had never known illness. Yet in these early notes to Cecil he more than once mentions some incapacity or "indisposition of body." Physicians, he writes in 1601, have ordered him to stay at home. Fever "hath painted my face with such a hue as is not fit for me yet to present myself. I am not idle nor careless of her Majesty's business, as your Honour at my next attendance shall perceive." There was mutual arranging of visits from Cecil's beloved son, William, to Stoke or Ely House. "Your niece," writes Coke, referring to Lady Hatton, "continues her suit that her cousin, 'your jewel,' may recreate himself these holidays at Stoke. I would have attended myself, but that my brother Sir Thomas Sadleir* is fallen very dangeriously sick and hath sent for me about the setting of an order in his house; which, by the laws of friendship, I cannot deny." Lady Hatton also writes to Robert Cecil, begging for his "sweet son's company at Stoke." The young man, she says, attends well to his book while in her house. In a day of reckless spelling, Lady Hatton's is notable. "It is unposybell,"

* Father-in-law to Coke's daughter Anne.

she writes. . . . Coke goes hawking and sends the bag to Burghley House: "These partridges, which according to their creation were a prey for my hawk this afternoon, should not have come *in tam minuto numero* [in so small a number] if the afternoon had not been extremely hot. A brace of them are thought to be old, all killed in the foot as myself can witness; so as the partridges nowadays have the same cause that in old time the partridges had to say *odimus accipitrem quia semper vivit in armis* [we hate the hawk because it lives always clothed in armor]."

There is something pleasant about these neighborly communications. If Coke indulged in Latin it was because the Cecils loved Latin as Coke loved it; old Burghley had carried Cicero in his pocket to read on coach trips. Other men wrote in testimony of Coke's friendship with Robert Cecil — Fulke Greville, courtier and great landowner in Warwickshire, writes to Cecil of "Mr. Attorney, your Lordship's dear and honest friend." Another, one "B. Langley," sends a note to Cecil in 1602, enclosing a bill to be signed by the Queen. "Mr. Attorney hath taken much pains in penning thereof, and yet would not take any fee, whereof I thought it my duty to inform you."

For Coke, the Cecils — Bacon too — these were crucial years. Their fortunes were bound up with Elizabeth. By her hand they had risen or failed to rise, without her they might fall. Yet Elizabeth's health and powers were declining, signs of it were slight but portentous. A Parliament had been called, and on opening day — October, 1601 — there was an ominous little scene. Standing in her heavy robes of state, Elizabeth swayed and would have fallen, had not — wrote a member — "some gentlemen suddenly cast themselves under that side that tottered and supported her. . . . As she went through the Commons" (it was further noted), "very few said *God save your Majesty*, as they were wont in all great Assemblies." Perhaps Essex's death had lessened Elizabeth's popularity. Perhaps, as Bacon suggested, the country was tired of a long reign, restless "in the declination of an old prince."

With Elizabeth the Tudor line would end. Yet even now she refused to name a successor. She knew it would be James, knew also that should she name him publicly, every heart and eye would turn from her to Edinburgh. *Video et taceo:* I see and am silent. It had been her motto since the beginning. Casting about, she saw the forces shift and change. The great Spanish enemy was gone. Philip II had died in agony,* without complaint, leaving a son of twenty, a frail pious Philip III. For England, peace with Spain was becoming almost a necessity. This war-and-no-war, these mutual sea piracies consumed more gold than they brought in. Domestic debts piled up. The City of London pressed for royal payment of a sixty-thousand-pound loan. Private citizens awaited settlement of their "Privy Seals" (loans secured by the Queen's promise), made in Lord Treasurer Burghley's lifetime. France owed the realm a tidy sum, unlikely of collection. There was trouble with Denmark over fishing rights and piracy. Ireland had been openly rebellious since 1586 and cost a fortune to patrol, with Tyrone in and out of hiding, the O'Sullivans and O'Driscolls conniving with Spain. Don Juan of Aguila prepared to enter Ireland with his army, carrying gold chains and swords of honor with which to reward victorious chieftains. Trouble flared along the Scottish border. Troops must be kept there, fortresses garrisoned against Franco-Scottish intrigue. The northern Catholic earls had not relinquished their hopes.

Parliament showed itself obstreperous. This was the famous "Parliament of the Monopolies," when the Commons moved to block the royal right of granting to private persons monopolies or patents such as Essex had enjoyed in wines, Ralegh in playing-cards. Restriction of trade was customarily conceived by the rich in terms of their own fortunes. Now the tables turned and the Commons banded firmly in defense of plain men's rights against the favored. Abuse had grown beyond all bounds. Poor men could not buy shoes; looms were stopped when patent holders sent spies to the counties and pursuivants to close down shops. . . .

The House was outspoken, passionate and greatly daring, though Francis Bacon (once bitten twice shy) protested any questioning of the Queen's prerogative, calling members to witness that he preferred humble petition to statute. The loud talk reached beyond St. Stephen's Chapel, beyond Westminster. Cecil scolded his colleagues: "Parliament matters are ordinary talk in the street.

* Philip II was carried off by a lingering nameless sickness, "with pain so intense," wrote an eyewitness, "that he could not even endure a cloth to touch the parts and lay slowly rotting to death for fifty-three dreadful days without a change of garment or the proper cleansing of his sores."

I have heard, myself, being in my coach, these words spoken aloud: '*God prosper those that further the overthrow of these monopolies! God send the prerogative touch not our liberties!*'"

Cecil's rebuke carried its own significance. Nine years ago (1593) when Coke presided as Speaker, protest had been confined to the Parliament House and did not reach the streets. Now the great Queen's power was waning with her life. Men looked toward another ruler, another reign. Throughout the nation there was apprehension. Could a new sovereign be crowned without wars, actual rebellion or that "alteration of religion" so feared by Protestants, so desired by Catholics? Rumor said that England might attempt to govern itself by estates, as in the Low Countries.

Fourteen possible if quite fantastic claimants to the throne were mentioned, among them four who must be reckoned with. "Competitors," Sir Robert Cecil called these: (1) The Infanta of Spain; (2) Lord Beauchamp (son of Catherine Grey—Lady Jane Grey's sister); (3) Lady Arabella Stuart; (4) James VI of Scotland. (A choice, in short, between the Suffolk and the Stuart lines.) James was the son of Mary Stuart, Queen of Scots and her husband Lord Darnley; Arabella, the daughter of Darnley's younger brother, Charles Stuart, Earl of Lennox. This thrice-damned heritage qualified neither of them; Arabella and James drew their claim by descent from Margaret, sister of Henry VIII. Some considered Arabella's the better title because she had been born in England, whereas James, born in Scotland, was excluded by law from inheriting English land.

Arabella was personally unprepossessing, incapable of rallying a faction. She lacked ambition, beyond a quite natural desire to escape the custody of her tyrannical aunt, old Bess of Hardwick (Lady Shrewsbury). Yet about her there ran perpetual dangerous surmise. The general feeling was against another female ruler. But suppose Arabella married a Catholic prince? Her name had become a focus for forlorn hopes. Both sides used her. It was even whispered that Sir Robert Cecil planned to marry Arabella and rule England himself! Actually, that astute and politic mind occupied itself, during the year 1602, in busy secret plans to bring James peacefully across the border when the time should come and get him crowned without a war.

James burned with impatience. Must the Queen endure, he wrote, "as long as the sunne and the moone?" Having governed for some twenty years "this wild unruly colt" of Scotland, he longed to exchange it "for Saint George's towardly riding horse." His impatience drew him into continual intrigue. He needed money and sent embassies to sound Elizabeth on the question of the succession or to urge that she augment his pension. (Cecil offered help from his own funds — said to be ten thousand pounds.) In the end, James was brought to a complete trust in Cecil's wisdom and advice. He would peacefully await his time, he wrote, rather than "by climbing of hedges and ditches for the pulling of unripe fruit to hazard the breaking of my neck." In short, he would cease dealing with France, Spain, the domestic Catholic earls and would, while holding out vague promises of a toleration, advertise to the Protestant world his faithfulness to their religion.

If Elizabeth knew of this secret correspondence and these careful plans, she gave no sign, unless weariness were a sign. When she missed familiar faces and asked where such a one was gone, she heard that he had ridden northward. "Now the wit of the fox is everywhere on foot," she said sadly to old Lambarde the antiquary, "so as hardly a faithful or virtuous man may be found." Even her favorite godson, Sir John Harington, at Christmas (1602) sent congratulatory verses to James, a lantern engraved with the appalling motto: "*Lord, remember me when thou comest in thy kingdom.*" Toward the end of January, 1603, Elizabeth caught cold. Her throat and gums swelled but she refused bloodletting or physic. At night she was restless and could not sleep. It was said that she grieved for Essex, for her old friend Lady Nottingham, the Lord Admiral's wife, who died in February. "They have yoked my neck," Elizabeth said. "I have none whom I may trust; my estate is turned upside down."

In March the Queen fell into a settled deep depression, refused food, refused to go to bed and sat crouched all day upon a heap of cushions. Her women were afraid of her. Sometimes she rose and with an old sword thrust savagely at the arras. "Her illness," the French Ambassador reported home, "was entirely due to a profound sorrow which had fallen on her secretly. She declared that she wished to die — nor would she name her successor." The Privy Council did its best to elicit some official utterance, and, failing, permitted rumors to leak out conveniently. . . . At mention of James's name, her Majesty had raised a hand and made the circle of a crown around her head. . . . she had murmured that only a king should succeed her — "the King of Scots, for he hath the best right, and in the name of God let him have it."

News of the Queen's condition spread; Cecil sent his brother, Lord Burghley, with troops to patrol the Scottish border. (Two years ago, Burghley had been appointed President of the Council of the North.) Eight armed galleons lay ready in the Thames, each carrying five hundred troops. There was a busy raking in of recusants. On March nineteenth, Robert Carey wrote from Richmond Palace to James at Holyrood. The Queen, he said, could not live more than three days. Horses were placed along the great north road, to race with the news when it should come. There must be no delay, no opportunity for "competitors" to seize the Tower, or for a mob to rally round some new impatient Essex. . . . A proclamation must be made ready. Francis Bacon drew one up, long and flowery; it was discarded for a briefer document of Cecil's. Yet beyond deep melancholy, the physicians could find nothing wrong with the Queen. Her body (they testified later) was "of firme and perfect constitution, likely to have lived many yeares." By Archbishop Whitgift's persuasion she was finally got to bed. Speechless, with signs she directed Whitgift to remain by her side and pray with her.

On March twenty-fourth, the last day of the official year (1603), shortly before three in the morning, Elizabeth turned on her side and laying her cheek on her right arm, "departed this life," said her chaplain, "easily, like a ripe apple from the tree."

So died the woman who had ruled England for close on a half a century. "She leaves the fame of past though never quite lost beauty," wrote an ambassador. "She was more than a man," said Robert Cecil, "and in troth, sometimes less than a woman." Cecil's father, who knew her better, went further. "The wisest woman that ever was, for she understood the interests and dispositions of all the princes in her time, and was so perfect in the knowledge of her own realm, that no councilor she had could tell her anything she did not know before."

Video et taceo: I see and am silent. . . . "Now if ever any person had either the gift or the style to win the hearts of people, it was this Queen."

CHAPTER FOURTEEN

A new King comes from Scotland. Coke and Bacon are knighted, Cecil becomes a Baron — and Sir Walter Ralegh is arrested for treason.

Upon Thursday it was treason to cry God save king James of England, and upon Friday, high treason not to cry so.
THOMAS DEKKER, *The Wonderfull Yeare* (1603)

EARLY on the morning of Elizabeth's death, Sir Robert Cecil, with a crowd of noblemen and "five trumpets," rode through London to proclaim the new ruler. "James the First, King of England, Scotland, France and Ireland, Defender of the Faith, lineally and lawfully descended from Margaret, daughter of the high and renowned Prince Henry the Seventh, his great grandfather; the said Lady Margaret being lawfully begotten of the body of Elizabeth, daughter of King Edward the Fourth." Cecil read the proclamation, sitting on his horse. It was "heard," wrote a diarist, "with great expectation and silent joye, no great shouting. I thinke the sorrow of her Majesties departure was so deep in many hearts they could not so suddenly showe any great joy. . . . At night they shewed by bonfires and ringing. No tumult, no contradiction, no disorder in the city; every man went about his busines as readilie, as peaceably, — as securely, as though there had bin no change, nor any newes ever heard of competitors. All long to see our newe king."

And on that same day, with talk of glory there was talk of

money, of certain practical realities faced by this new ruler. Elizabeth had died financially indebted to her people. The question was, would James pay the old debts? "Talke is," ran the same diary, "of the subsidies and fifteenes taxed in the Queenes time, how much indebted she died to the Commons. . . . They half despair of payment of their privy seales, they will not assure themselves of the loan." Should James release the Earl of Southampton and others from the Tower, could not these noblemen, themselves made rich by the Queen's bounty, help to pay the royal debts? Also there was the hazard of place to speculate upon. By law and custom the authority of all officers of the Crown expired "with the prince's breath." The entire hierarchy of government positions would very likely shift.

The Queen had died on Thursday morning. By Saturday night, March twenty-sixth, James received the news at Edinburgh; Robert Carey had ridden 395 miles. On April fifth the King left Holyrood, making a royal progress of his journey south, stopping at country houses, hunting and hawking in the bright spring weather and creating knights by the dozens as he came. So great was the general desire to love him that men overlooked, at first, the unkingly appearance, a tongue too large, lips that slobbered, the strong almost comic Scotch accent, rolling walk and weak legs. They saw a man in the prime of young maturity, "pale and very fair," with blue eyes, a small mouth above "a longish square-cut beard, well-made in body," dressed in rather odd-looking clothes, his manners easy, ready to talk and to be pleased. Even Catholics could look on him with hope and let themselves be happy at his coming. Born of Catholic parents and baptized in the ancient ceremony, was he not married to a princess whose inclinations were three quarters Catholic? Anne of Denmark, reared in the Lutheran faith, had a leaning toward Rome, though she was too easygoing to press the point.

Over the countryside, bells pealed, songs were sung, poetic welcomes declaimed. Schoolchildren threw flowers in the royal path. Sheriffs bearing white wands rode out from towns, mayors in scarlet, gold chains (when they had them) about their shoulders. Presents were showered. Godmanchester gave seventy ploughs and seventy teams to draw them, explaining it as the service of their ancient fief. With or without explanation, James was delighted.

After his own barren wild domain, this kingdom seemed rich as Babylon, rich as Guiana. One of his train, a bluff plain Scotsman, was heard to say, "This people will spoil a good king." (Afterward it was remembered as sadly prophetic.)

There was one disquieting incident; news of it went quickly through the counties. At Newark-on-Trent a thief was caught and confessed he had followed the King all the way from Berwick, cutting purses. Without trial, without a hearing, James had him hanged. Was this, then, the law in Scotland, and did James look to bring it across the border? Roman law which followed the prince's pleasure: *Quod principi placuit legis habet vigorem:* What pleases the prince has the force of law. "I heare," wrote Elizabeth's good-natured godson, Sir John Harington, "oure new King hath hanged one man before he was tried; 'tis strangely done: now if the winde bloweth thus, why may not a man be tried before he hath offended?"

James rode down through the pleasant April sunshine, the soft April rains. In London, Elizabeth lay in her leaden coffin, wrapped in serecloth. James had ordered her funeral to proceed without him. "They say," reported the Venetian ambassador, "he wishes to see her neither alive nor dead, for he can never expel from his memory the fact that his mother was put to death at the hands of the public executioner." On April twenty-eighth, the City watched Elizabeth borne in state to Westminster Abbey "on an open chariot," wrote a witness, "drawn by four horses trapped in black velvet, beset with the Arms of England and France, wherein lay the body of the dead Queen embalmed and enclosed in lead; and over that her image in her parliament robes, with a crown on her head and a sceptre in her hand, all very exquisitely framed to resemble life."

Coke walked in this slow procession, before him the judges of the courts, the Lord Mayor of London; by his side the Solicitor General. Coke's own position was secure. On April twenty-second his patent as Attorney General had been renewed under the Great Seal. With or without past benefits, there is no doubt that Coke genuinely mourned the Queen, loving her as those who served her not too intimately were able to love Elizabeth. In Coke's mind this had been a true sovereign, fearless, wise; while she lived, her Attorney General remained the open and vigorous champion of Majesty and the prerogative. As years advanced, Coke would speak of Elizabeth with increasing reverence. The fact that he had known her would add to his prestige as elder statesman, "one who served in the Queen's time."

Now he walked in her funeral while all through London the people waited, lining the streets, and when the coffin came in view, "fell a weeping," says Clapham, "and began to talk diversely, many seeming to marvel even at vain and ordinary things, as namely that living and dying a virgin she was born on the vigil of that feast, which was really kept in remembrance of the birth of our Lady the Virgin . . . that she departed the world at Richmond, where her grandfather, King Henry VII, whom she very much resembled, ended his life, and upon the selfsame day of the week whereon he deceased; that she had reigned so many years, as the greater part of them living had never known other prince. Some also there were that spoke fondly of predictions going before her death, and among others it was given out that an old lion in the Tower bearing her name, during the time of her sickness, pined away and died."

For one man at least, Elizabeth's death meant ruin. Sir Walter Ralegh strode behind her coffin, his helmet black-plumed, mourning band around his arm. Like everyone he expected drastic changes, though Cecil, acting swiftly, had forestalled actual chaos. James, quite naturally, would desire his old friends about him — new officers of the Bedchamber, a new Captain of the Guard. Ralegh looked for it. Moreover, he had already been rebuffed, if John Aubrey's story is true. Going north to meet the monarch (against Robert Cecil's advice), Sir Walter had introduced himself at Burghley House in Northamptonshire. Kneeling, he was greeted with a heavy royal pun: "On my soule, mon, I have heard rawly of thee!"

It was humiliating but by no means fatal. Already, James was noted for chiding his new English friends, watching closely to see how they received it and letting reward or punishment fall accordingly. Ralegh had received a check and knew it. But that his entire fortune, credit, honor — and very soon, his life — were in danger, he could not have suspected. He knew nothing of his enemies' machinations during the past year, nothing of Lord Henry Howard's letters, Essex's letters, which had so effectually poisoned James's mind by hints that Ralegh was ambitious, opposed to the succession, harbored plans of his own. James's shrewd Scotch heart was fertile to suspicion; to turn it against Sir Walter had not been difficult. First of all, Ralegh desired war with Spain. Ralegh's name was almost a symbol for war — and James loathed fighting. Secondly, Ralegh had been Essex's enemy, whom James chose now to speak of as "my martyr," confident that the "unfortunate Earl" had desired nothing so much as to help him to the throne. (That little black bag, meet for so black a cause, which Essex wore about his neck was said to have contained letters from James.)

Sir Robert Cecil, while he did nothing to accentuate the royal distrust, by all the records did nothing to dispel it, though at the moment, Cecil had large sums invested in Ralegh's profiteering ventures. The intrigues that formed around James's accession were mysterious, greedy, shameful — and in Ralegh's case, tragic. To solve the plots, explain their motivation, is impossible. One thing, however, is sure: James left Scotland convinced that Ralegh was a threat and Cecil the strongest, wisest man in England. His *little beagle*, James called Sir Robert. Cecil's sister-in-law, Lady Kildare, used another word. "That weasel!" she said. *Robert the Devil*, his enemies called him. Cecil, like James, was set against war with Spain, whereas Ralegh could not have enough of talking about it and had even prepared for James's edification a *Discourse touching a War with Spain and the protecting of the Netherlands.* On top of this, Ralegh, after the Burghley House rebuff, went again to see the King on his journey — at Beddington Park, where James was visiting Lady Ralegh's uncle — and offered to invade the Spanish dominions at his own expense of two thousand pounds! He had another discourse ready, *How War may be made against Spain and the Indies.*

It was typical of Sir Walter, yet an extraordinary indiscretion, considering the new monarch was so fearful of blood that he fell sick at the sight of a naked sword. His mother (so ran the general explanation), while carrying him, had seen her lover Rizzio murdered before her eyes. A pious King, fond of theological disputes in the Presbyterian manner, James instinctively disliked this magnificent Captain who was reputed godless. Besides, Sir Walter smoked tobacco, a matter for the royal loathing. (James's book, *A Counterblaste to Tobacco*, declared the devilish, unhealthy weed was brought to England by "a father generally hated.")

But Sir Walter, in this hopeful springtime of a reign, saw little reason why he should not win the royal confidence, bend the royal mind and purpose and win eventual favor. He had every intention to try. Official London made it plain it shared a like ambition. In crowds, Elizabeth's courtiers rushed north to greet the monarch, "as if," wrote Chamberlain jovially, "preferment were a goale to be got by footmanship." Francis Bacon looked on it as "a kind of sport, this continual posting of men of good quality toward the King." . . . Down through the counties came the monarch, stopping at Hinchinbrook to visit "Master Oliver Cromwell" (uncle of the future Protector), stopping at Sir Thomas Sadleir's, where Coke's daughter, Anne Coke Sadleir, made her curtsy in the Great Hall of Standon Lordship. At Theobalds, Lord Treasurer Burghley's country mansion, James met Elizabeth's household officers and held a conference concerning monopolies. It was decided to cancel, among others, Ralegh's monopolies on wines and tin and to advise Sir Walter that he resign as warden of the Cornwall mines and Governor of Jersey. Already, Ralegh had learned he was no longer Captain of the Guard; the King had named a Scotsman in his place.

As James drew near to London, so great were the throngs in the fields that people were in danger of being trampled. The Lord Mayor rode out with the keys of the City, the Sheriffs of London and Middlesex behind him, "in fair livery cloaks on gallant horses," twenty-four aldermen in scarlet gowns, five hundred citizens with "velvet coats and chains of gold." That day, James made eleven dozen knights. When he came to the Tower he stopped overnight, created Sir Robert Cecil, Lord Cecil, Baron of Essingdon.* Coke had already applied to Cecil for knighthood in a brief note, highly characteristic in its justification by historical precedent:

Edward Coke to Sir Robert Cecil

4 May, 1603

I perceive the least public grace from the King does the poor Attorney good, and I heard by some one near about him that he had a disposition to confer that favour upon me that King Edward 4 conferred upon Hussey his attorney, Henry the 7 upon Hubberd his attorney, Henry the 8 upon Hales his attorney, and the Queen my dear Mistress upon

* In 1604, Cecil became Viscount Cranborne; in 1605, Earl of Salisbury; in 1606, a Knight of the Garter. To avoid confusion, he will be referred to hereafter as Robert Cecil.

Gerrard her attorney. Besides, in ancient time, Speakers of the Parliament have been graced with knighthood. I thank God I am not ambitious, but as all my good fortunes have come either by your honourable father or by you, so I would account it the greater if it came by your honourable means.
P.S. When you have read this letter it is fit for the fire.

On May twenty-second, Coke was knighted in the palace at Greenwich with six others, among them his old friend the Speaker of the Parliament of 1601, Recorder John Croke of London. There was a grand banquet and when darkness fell, fireworks on the Thames, the sky all sprayed with arching light. "Sir Edward" went home to Stoke. His wife hastened north to meet Queen Anne and the royal children,* having petitioned to be in her Majesty's service, "to keep her jewels and help to make her ready." The young Queen loved dress; she brought a scanty wardrobe over the border and James wrote twice to Whitehall asking suitable jewels and attire for his Queen. Elizabeth had left no will, and whole rooms full of dresses. Court seamstresses altered them for Anne, who at first had declared she "would never wear cast clothes," but changed her mind when she saw — wrote the Venetian Ambassador — "6000 dresses, costly and gorgeous." It was remarked also that Anne showed especial favor to Mr. Attorney's wife and to her mother, Lady Cecil. Ten days later, Lady Hatton was again noted at Windsor with a dozen ladies, "exceeding rich and glorious in jewells." Forty thousand were at the King's court, and it was said in some alarm that coronation day would see more than a hundred thousand extra mouths to feed in London.

Even a hundred extra mouths made serious trouble almost anywhere in England; let the harvest fail and starvation threatened. Yet no practical problem dared intrude as the dazzling tally mounted — rewards, gifts of place and favor near the King. Sir Thomas Egerton became Baron Ellesmere. Very suitable, people said. But James, now that he was come into his kingdom (though still uncrowned) had been making knights by the basketful — at least six hundred in three months. There was about this royal advent something almost farcical. When Sully, the French Ambassador, appeared with his nobles in mourning for Elizabeth, James ordered them to change their dress. So "they all got into their most fantastic

* Henry, aged 9; Elizabeth, 7; Charles, 2.

costumes," wrote Scaramelli, "and went to Greenwich" Palace. Continental courtiers made unkind remarks: England, that had been ruled by *King Elizabeth*, now made obeisance to *la Reine Jacquette*. "A scabbard without a sword," they said of James in Spain. The monarch, himself unconscious of these strictures, issued from Hampton Court a summons surprising to the country: all who had forty pounds a year in land must come and be knighted or pay a fine. People were uneasy. Did not this lower the honor? And besides, what need for so many *milites* in time of peace? In all her reign, Elizabeth had made but six earls, eight or nine barons. As for knights, when one was involved with the law, some counties had scarcely enough to assemble a jury of his peers. "This almost prostituted title," Bacon called it with his usual felicitous wry precision. Nevertheless, for himself he would be pleased to have the title, he wrote his cousin Cecil. Three of these new knights sat at his table at Gray's Inn; moreover he was thinking of marriage. He had found an alderman's daughter, "an handsome maiden to my liking." He was loth to receive the title "merely gregarious in a troop." Could not his cousin arrange some occasion more suitable? After all, the coronation was at hand.

While so much glory and booty was in the making, Sir Walter Ralegh remained at his gray stone palace on the Strand. *Durham House*, the place was called, because it had belonged to the Bishops of Durham. Elizabeth (as with Ely House) had granted the lease to whom she chose — and in 1584 she chose Ralegh. He had lived there ever since, spending thousands of pounds on repairs. It was a house of peculiar charm, with walls and gardens reaching to the river and a study, high up, where Ralegh liked to sit late with his friends. John Aubrey described the room "in a little turret that looked over the Thames and had the prospect which is pleasant perhaps as any in the World, and which not only refreshes the eie-sight but cheeres the spirits and (to speake my mind) I beleeve enlarges an ingeniose man's thoughts."

But Tobias Matthew, Bishop of Durham, was not one to bear his wrongs in silence. Through Ralegh he had lost, in the old days, not only Durham House but the Episcopal See of Salisbury. To Elizabeth he could not, of course, protest. But James had not left the Scottish border when Tobias was at Berwick on his knees

— and rose with a promise that the church would have its London residence again. On the seventh of June (1603) Ralegh received a peremptory note, ordering him by royal warrant to vacate; Bishop Matthew would take possession of Durham House on the twenty-fourth of the month.

Of all the humiliations endured since Elizabeth's death, this was the bitterest. Ralegh could not believe it. He wrote immediate protest, addressing the letter to Lord Keeper Egerton, Chief Justice Popham, "and to my very good frinde his Majesties Aturney Generall." The Bishop's letter had been "very strange; the poorest artificer in London hath a quarter's warning given him by his landlord." He perceived, said Ralegh, the Bishop did not lack good friends. But he had made the place his home full twenty years; this spring he had stored it with provisions for forty persons and twenty horse. "To cast out my hay and oates into the streats at an hours warninge, and to remove my family and stuff in 14 days after, is such a severe expultion as hath not been offred to any man before this daye."

It was of no use. Ralegh was forced from Durham House; the Bishop moved in triumphantly. Nevertheless, Sir Walter clung doggedly to his position. If enemies — men close to the throne — intrigued against him, well, it had been done before, in the Queen's time, and he had prevailed. Dressed in his old magnificence he continued to frequent the court, his bearing easy as ever, eyes enigmatic beneath their heavy lids, thick beard curling upward. (To his rivals, Ralegh's beard had always been a point of irritation. It "turned up naturally" while theirs must be curled with irons.) Each move that Ralegh made, now, was watched, reported to the Privy Council. Sir Walter, for one who stood so high, had endured well-nigh unendurable humiliation. By every sign of his past nature he would strike back, either in open challenge to his enemies or by secret plans to overthrow them. Who then were his friends, with whom did he consort on these late evenings and why was he so "inward" with that dubious man of riches and wayward temper, Lord Cobham, Warden of the Cinque Ports? Weeks before Ralegh left Durham House, the royal spies were out. Boats leaving his water gate were counted, their occupants noted. Already, by Lord Howard's means, James suspected some dark alliance between Ralegh, Cobham and the Catholic Percy, Earl of Northumberland. "That diabolical triplicity," Lord Howard called the group.

In June a Catholic plot had been discovered, though not as yet made public. One William Watson was at the bottom of it — a secular priest who had been a Catholic agent at James's court in Scotland and had begged a toleration. (Actually, he thought he had succeeded, and so reported to Rome.)

Even before Elizabeth's death, Watson had been in custody, but set free, on James's accession, to act as decoy. Immediately he obliged, seeking out various "discontented men," some Catholic and some, oddly enough, strongly Puritan. Chief among them were Cobham and his brother George Brooke; Sir Edward Parham, a distinguished Catholic layman; and Sir Griffin Markham, notorious spendthrift and owner of the forest of Beskwood, a place so vast and wild that should Sir Griffin take refuge there, a thousand men — so Cecil informed — could not rout him out.

At Beskwood Park, shortly after James's arrival in London, there had been a meeting of souls. A plan was formed, absurd on the face of it and crazily similar to Essex's attempt. The King was to be "surprised" in his palace at Greenwich, the Tower guard overpowered and the King kept there as hostage until Catholic demands should be granted. Lord Grey de Wilton (Essex's great enemy) was, Sir Griffin told his confederates, already committed to the plan. Grey was rich and fervently Puritan. His bitter enemy, Southampton, had been pardoned by James. Grey resented it; his letters expressed dislike toward the crowd of Scotsmen in James's train — foreigners, rivals, upstarts.

Among these plotters, Ralegh had no observable connection, with one exception. Lord Cobham and Sir Walter had been close. Mutual visiting was noted, late meetings, midnight talks at Durham House — on the face of it, little for James to proceed upon. But it was enough. At Windsor Castle the blow fell. One morning in mid-July, Ralegh waited on the terrace, having expected to accompany the King out hunting. Cecil came to him. Would Sir Walter be pleased to go indoors? The Lords of Council had some questions to put.

Six days later, Ralegh was in the Tower, accused of high treason. The charge was conspiracy to kill the King, raise rebellion, alter the religion of the realm and set Arabella Stuart on the throne. Nine other suspects had been taken: Lord Grey de Wilton, Lord Cobham and his brother George Brooke, Sir Edward Parham, Sir

Griffin Markham, Brooksby, Copley and the two Catholic priests, Watson and Clarke, whose discovered activities had first brought exposure.

London was astonished. The thing had come suddenly, without warning. Moreover, the choice of confederates was bewildering. What, people asked, was Lord Grey de Wilton doing in this company of priests and atheists? "I hear muche (by pryvate means)," wrote Harington, "of strange plottes by Cobham, Grey, Raleighe and others." Of Ralegh almost anything could be suspected and the populace was ready to believe it. But that the Queen's old Captain, seafighter, explorer, privateer had turned spy for the Catholic enemy — this was puzzling indeed.

As the news spread, it began to be credited. The old dislike of Ralegh deepened to hatred. This swaggerer in silver armor who asked so easily, What is the soul? — this atheist who had "gloated" by a hero's scaffold was at last exposed, discovered, brought low. The friends of Essex had found their victim.

Ralegh stayed in the Tower four months, while Coke and his lawyers collected testimony and confessions from the prisoners, collating, "preparing" for the trial. Not alone Coke but the judges helped with investigation.* "Taking examination" of suspects was recognized procedure. Every word would count later against the prisoners — with the legal proviso that such evidence had not been extracted under duress. (Yet the royal prerogative, as we have seen, was a short way round Magna Carta, and the word "duress" has many definitions.) For the accused there existed, under the common law, no presumption of innocence: the Roman law, it was true, had its *presumptio juris tantum.* The common law looked on it rather as a *privilege* of proof. Every witness and every courtroom spectator would be aware that upon Ralegh, speaking in his own defense, rested this privilege of proof. If the accused were not "reasonably" guilty, then why (so ran the public question) would the Privy Council, Attorney General and judges bring him to open trial? If he were innocent, he would after examination have been set free.

* This pretrial examination by magistrates — judicial questioning — remained in use for two succeeding centuries. It was abolished by statute in 1848.

To Ralegh all this was common usage; he had been reared to accept it. His audience would enter the courtroom bearing pre-established notions of his guilt or innocence. And these preconceptions would be founded, as always, rather on bias than evidence. With Essex the bias had been love. What it was to be in his own case, Sir Walter would discover before he set foot inside the courtroom door.

Ralegh had been arrested in mid-July. On the twenty-fifth (St. James's Day) the King was crowned at Westminster. Shortly afterward, Cecil was congratulated upon not being obliged to speak to Majesty on his knees, as he had used to do with the Queen. "I wish to God," Cecil replied feelingly, "that I spoke still on my knees." The plague was raging in London, one of the worst visitations the city had ever experienced; report had it that two thousand a week were dying. Whole rows of doors were marked with the official placard: "Lord, have mercy on us." The King fled with his household. It was decided to hold the autumn term of court at Winchester, sixty miles down into Hampshire. Early in November, nine of the men accused with Ralegh made the trip under guard of fifty light-horse. On November tenth, Ralegh followed in his own coach with Sir William Waad, Clerk of the Privy Council, and Sir Richard Mansell, Vice-Admiral of the Fleet.

It was a terrible journey. The London streets were black with crowds which braved even the plague to curse at Ralegh. So great was the disorder that watches were set far into the suburbs. "It was hob or nob," wrote Waad to Cecil, if Ralegh "would escape alive through such multitudes of unruly people as did exclaim against him. If one hare-brained fellow amongst so great a multitude had begun to set upon him, as they were near to do it, no entreaty or means could have prevailed; the fury and tumult of the people was so great." At Wimbledon, a little group of Ralegh's friends waited to greet him. Everywhere else he met only fury and insult. "It is almost incredible," wrote Cecil's secretary, "with what bitter speaches and execrations Ralegh was exclaimed upon all the way he went through London, and the towns; which they say he neglected and scorned, as preceding from base and rascale people. They threwe tobacco pipes, stones and mire at him, as he was carried in the coach."

Ralegh was cold, contemptuous. "Dogs," he said, "do always bark at those they know not." The trip consumed five days. Sir Walter remembered every mile of this pleasant country through which they passed. It was the road to his own estate of Sherborne in Dorset, which Elizabeth had given him and where he had his bowling green and falcons, the groves that he had planted and the stone seat where he had sat in pleasant summer weather, gazing over the hills.

Winchester, when they came there, was crowded. The walled old town could scarcely hold the visitors — the Lords Commissioners appointed to try the case, each with his train of mounted servants; the four judges with their attendants, the Attorney General with his; the twelve knights of the jury and a general outpouring of spectators and hangers-on such as a famous trial attracts. Lady Arabella Stuart was lodged in town. She had come down with Lord Admiral Nottingham, who was no friend to Ralegh. From turret and roof top flags flew, the town had the air of a fête day or a fair. Up a steep narrow street to the castle Ralegh's coach labored; soldiers rode ahead to clear the way. When they reached the castle courtyard and Ralegh stepped from coach to prison, he could see in that brief moment's respite the gentle valley spread below, the chalk hills to the westward, brick barns rosy in the low November sun.

Down to the left was the Cathedral and College of Winchester. At the King's command, scholars and clerics had vacated their premises in favor of the distinguished visitors. The castle was old almost beyond computing, its great hall long and lofty. *Arthur's Hall*, this was called, from an immense round board which hung at the eastern end, inscribed with the names of knights long dead and said to be King Arthur's Round Table. Beneath the hall was Ralegh's cell, a place remote, cold enough to bring on his old ague after a night's imprisonment. Shortly before Sir Walter's arrival, seven of the conspirators had been tried in a court fitted up in the Bishop's palace. All but one had been condemned to death, news not calculated to make Ralegh sleep the sounder.

Only two days stood between Sir Walter and a knowledge of his fate. The cathedral clock gave out the hours; from a grassy ditch below his barred window, cattle lowed. At dawn there came a sound like a great beast's cry, strange and penetrating. It was a signal horn, blown for the city gates to open. Like the Temple horn at home that called to breakfast, but hoarser, more imperative. A sound ominous, that in days past had called to war.

CHAPTER FIFTEEN

Trial of Sir Walter Ralegh (Part I).

'Twas a dark kind of treason, and the veil is still upon it.
RUSHWORTH, *Historical Collections* (1659)

I thinke Sir Walter's hearte is well fixed in every honest thinge. He seemeth wondrously fitted, both by art and nature, to serve the state. In good troth I pitie him and doubte the dice be fairly thrown, if his life be the losing stake.
SIR JOHN HARINGTON (*written October, 1603, between Ralegh's arrest and trial*)

ON the seventeenth of November, 1603, Ralegh was taken down the hill for trial. When he came with his guard to the Bishop's palace, the old stone hall was crowded. People sat in the minstrels' gallery, leaned against the stone pillars until their legs must have ached. Some of them had been there since dawn; many had waited all night in the street before the doors. Lady Arabella Stuart — *Arbella*, everyone called her — sat with the old Earl of Nottingham. Before the day was out she would have her say; the indictment was full of her name. Poor Arbella — forever the center of plots she had not conceived! One look at her seemed enough to turn men's ambitions elsewhere. Lord Cobham had said that once he saw Arbella he "resolved never to hazard his estate for her." Yet she was herself to die a prisoner in the Tower. Here in the Bishop's palace, Cobham lay imprisoned beneath the courtroom or in some turret chamber. And Cobham was Ralegh's only accuser, the single witness on whom the prosecution must build its case.

A Special Commission of Oyer and Terminer had been appointed for the trial; it included seven laymen and four judges: Popham (Chief Justice of King's Bench), Justice Anderson of Common Pleas and the puisne judges, Gawdy and Warburton. The laymen were Mountjoy (Lord Deputy of Ireland), who had said he would flee England rather than come under the file of Coke's tongue; Sir William Waad (Clerk of the Privy Council), a zealous and unscrupulous trapper of recusants who had escorted Ralegh in the coach from London; the Earl of Suffolk, who had fought with Ralegh at Cadiz; Sir John Stanhope of the King's household. And lastly, to the eternal shame of the King, who had approved his appointment, sat Sir Walter's greatest enemy, the man that had poisoned James's mind against him: Lord Henry Howard, who four times changed his religion and in whom the truth did not dwell.

The jury of twelve knights had been brought down from Middlesex County. Such a panel was considered harsh and somewhat biased; King James himself remarked that he would not wish to be tried by a Middlesex jury. There was rumor that Sir Edward Darcy, Ralegh's friend and neighbor, had been named and removed overnight from the panel.* But there is no proof that the jury was packed, though the mere fact of Lord Henry Howard's presence as commissioner is suspicious. Ralegh declined to challenge a single juror. He "thought them all honest and Christian men and knew his own innocency." He had however one request. His memory was never good, sickness in prison had weakened him. Might he answer questions severally, as they came up, rather than all at once? Coke objected, as he had with Essex. The King's evidence, "ought not to be broken or dismembered, whereby it might lose much of its grace and vigor."

The judges conceded the point to Ralegh. Yet Coke's remark concerning the King's evidence came as no surprise in Winchester Hall. A threat to the sovereign was a threat to every English subject, dangerous moreover to a Protestant Reformation which even yet was not secure. The King's evidence (not the prisoner's) must serve as focal point. To bring out this evidence was the business of the Attorney General. Unfortunately for Ralegh, his four judges considered it their business too, as did the seven lay commissioners

* The manuscript of the original panel shows three erasures, elaborately scratched out and written over by new names.

who sat upon the dais with the judges. The majority of these men already knew the evidence by heart. Since the moment of Ralegh's arrest (and likely a month before) they had been searching it out, fitting part to part until confession matched confession. In Essex's case such "preparation" had been easy; hundreds saw his armed passage through London. With Ralegh the evidence was slim. Moreover, the court considered that it had here a knight far cleverer than Essex, one who by common parlance was an easy liar; in Coke's own words, "the father of wiles."

Ralegh's judges plainly were part of the prosecution, determined from the start to prove the prisoner guilty. Yet there could have been no question of collusion; Popham, old Judge Anderson, Gawdy, Warburton were neither venal nor corrupt. On the contrary, they were men of high character who sat to do their duty. And judicial duty, in the year 1603 (and for two centuries after) meant bringing forward every damaging fact of character and circumstance which could be gathered in the King's favor — hearsay evidence, gossip at third hand, the confession of confederates. In treason cases smoke was hot as fire and bare suspicion tantamount to the act overt. Those keeping company with traitors were *ipso facto* guilty; any evidence could pass.* Yet Coke, Chief Justice Popham, Robert Cecil, who sat with the commissioners, took pride in the English legal tradition, pride even in their system of trial at common law. Was not such trial by accusation rather than inquisition, as in France and Spain? Was it not, by general agreement, speedy, open, viewed by any citizen who cared to come? Above all, was not the accused permitted to speak in his own defense, holding, if he wished, a day-long altercation with judges, commissioners, Attorney General? "Sir Walter Ralegh," wrote Cecil to a Privy Councilor before the trial, "yet persists in denial of the main treason. Few men can conceive it comes from a clear heart. Always, he shall be left to the law, which is the right all men are born unto."

Cecil believed what he said. Moreover he was to be the only man in Winchester courtroom who stood out for Sir Walter in the matter of his legal rights and privileges.

Ralegh's indictment, read aloud by the Clerk, was short: Sir Walter had conspired to "kill the King, raise a rebellion with in-

* Chapter Note.

tent to change religion and subvert the government." The overt acts charged were listening to Spanish bribes, conferring with Lord Cobham concerning Arabella Stuart's claim, together with promises, plans, statements and conspiracies to that end.

Serjeant Heale opened for the Crown. He was brief, his speech is remembered only for a startlingly facetious peroration where he remarked that as for the Lady Arabella, upon his conscience she had no more title to the Crown than he had himself, "which, before God," he finished, "I utterly renounce." Even Raleigh smiled. It was the last time he would smile that day.

Coke followed and spoke at length. Foul treasons had been unearthed, though no torture was employed to find them, and no "rigorous usage." (The prosecution invariably took care to make this claim in treason trials and the audience took care to disbelieve it.) "This great and honorable assembly," Coke said, "doth look to hear this day what before hath been carried on the rack of scattering reports. . . ."

There was no telling who might be listening, hidden in some dark gallery. Arthur's Hall, up the hill, had a pipe in the wall behind the judges' dais, leading to a little chamber where kings had anciently sat concealed, their ear to all that passed. People knew about it, knew also that James was visiting at a nearby country house. Those who had witnessed Essex's trial recalled the sudden appearance of Cecil from the parted arras. . . .

Two conspiracies had been discovered, Coke reminded the jury; the *Bye Plot* and the *Main*,* they were called. The Bye was the Priests' Plot, hatched by Watson and Clarke; the Main was Ralegh's conspiracy. As Coke continued, it became plain he was describing, not Ralegh's plot at all, but the Bye, a business far more flagrant and more foolish. Ralegh broke in, addressing the jury: "I pray you, Gentlemen, remember that I am not charged with the *Bye*, which was the treason of the priests."

No, Coke said; Sir Walter was not so charged. Yet all these treasons, "like Sampson's foxes, were joined together at the tails, though their heads were severed." Coke went on to describe and define

*These names meant nothing more than Main Plot and By-plot or Secondary Plot. The fact that the Bye had been perpetrated, chronologically, before the Main, was only one of a dozen ambiguities drawn by the prosecution over a murky legal trail.

the law of treason, and was proceeding reasonably enough until, after a sugary panegyric on the character of James, he suddenly turned on Ralegh and demanded, "To whom, Sir Walter, did you bear malice? To the royal children?"

It was the first of Coke's attacks, unexpected, startling, brought on perhaps by Ralegh's quick positive denial of Coke's charge, perhaps by the realization that here was a prisoner equipped to defend himself with skill and passion. "Mr. Attorney," Ralegh answered, "I pray you, to whom or to what end speak you all this? I protest I do not understand what a word of this means, except it be to tell me news. What is the treason of Markham and the priests to me?"

COKE: I will then come close to you; I will prove you to be the most notorious traitor that ever came to the bar! You are indeed upon the Main, but you have followed them of the Bye in imitation; I will charge you with the words.

RALEGH: Your words cannot condemn me; my innocency is my defense. I pray you go to your proofs. Prove against me any one thing of the many that you have broken, and I will confess all the indictment, and that I am the most horrible traitor that ever lived, and worthy to be crucified with a thousand torments.

COKE: Nay, I will prove all. Thou art a monster! Thou hast an English face but a Spanish heart. . . . I look to have good words from you, and purpose not to give you worse than the matter press me unto. But if you provoke me, I will not spare you and I have warrant for it. . . . You would have stirred England and Scotland both. You incited the Lord Cobham. . . .

Cobham, rich, discontented and apparently somewhat of a fool, had been one of the "diabolical triplicity" which, according to Lord Henry Howard, met at Durham House to conspire the King's death and set Arbella in his place. Cobham planned to cross the Channel and obtain money for the support of Arbella's title — a bargain which included promise of a "toleration of the Popish religion in England." All this, said Coke, Lord Cobham had confessed: dealing with Aremberg, the Spanish agent; Aremberg's offer of 600,000 crowns. Ralegh, Coke urged, pretended the money was merely a Spanish offer "to forward the peace." Yet if the Spanish King had in mind such an offer, would he have chosen a recipient like Cobham, who was "neither politician nor swordsman?" No! It required a Ralegh to carry through these plans. "Such," said Coke, "was Sir Walter's secrecy and Machiavellian policy that he would confer with none but Cobham, 'because,' saith he, 'one witness can never condemn me.' It will be stood upon Sir Walter Ralegh today," Coke continued, "that we have but one witness. But I will show your Lordships that it is not necessary to have two witnesses."

On this point, so crucial to Ralegh, Coke was securely within the law. It was true that during the reign of Edward VI (1547-1552), statutes had been enacted, declaring for two witnesses. But on the accession of Mary Tudor, these statutes were repealed (1553), and since then, one witness was held sufficient in cases of felony tried under the common law. This was the legal view as known to every barrister who had argued in Westminster Hall. Nevertheless, the country at large clung stubbornly to the old two-witness rule. The Bible declared for it, and was not Holy Scripture corroborative of the common law?

Coke, in this first long offensive, did not stop upon the point. It would come up again and could more properly be dealt with by the judges. "In our case in hand," Coke proceeded, "we have more than two witnesses. For when a man, in his accusation of another, shall by the same accusation also condemn himself and make himself liable to the same punishment, this is by our law more forcible than many witnesses, equal to the inquest of twelve men.* For *the law presumes that a man will not accuse himself in order to accuse another.*"

Coke turned now to the jury and repeated the charge of setting up Arbella as "titular queen." On Ralegh's interrupting, Coke retorted angrily that he did not wonder to see Sir Walter "moved." "Nay," Ralegh replied, "you fall out with yourself. I have said nothing to you. I am in no case to be angry."

As the reporter's bare account* moves forward, it is hard to see why Ralegh's calm interpolations were to Coke so palpably infuriating. Was it something in Sir Walter's manner, the old easy arrogance, impossible of description, which for thirty years had earned a host of enemies? Whatever it was, it caused Coke to lose control again and again, spitting out words shameful, unworthy,

* Chapter Note.

never to be forgotten. After Ralegh's quiet rebuke, Coke reverted once again to the Bye plot, of which the prosecution well knew that Sir Walter was innocent, yet which, as the tale unfolded, seemed to implicate the prisoner by the very telling. As Coke talked, his anger mounted. "And now," he informed the jury, "you shall see the most horrible practices that ever came out of the bottomless pit of the lowest hell. . . ."

There followed the recitation of an involved, fantastic maneuver of Cobham's, turning on a forged letter "placed in a Spanish Bible," an answer forged and falsely dated.

RALEGH: What is that to me? Here is no treason of mine done. If my Lord Cobham be a traitor, what is that to me?

COKE: All that he did was by thy instigation, thou viper: For I *thou** thee, thou traitor! I will prove thee the rankest traitor in all England.

RALEGH: No no, Mr. Attorney, I am no traitor! Whether I live or die, I shall stand as true a subject as any the King hath. You may call me a traitor at your pleasure, yet it becomes not a man of quality and virtue to do so. But I take comfort in it, it is all you can do, for I do not yet hear that you charge me with any treason.

CHIEF JUSTICE POPHAM: Sir Walter Ralegh, Mr. Attorney speaks out of zeal of his duty for the service of the King, and you for your life. Be patient on both sides.

Coke now ordered the Clerk to read Cobham's confession from the Tower, dated July twentieth. It was almost a repetition of the formal indictment, but more impressive, coming direct from Cobham: "Confesseth: that he had conference with the Count Aremberg about procuring 500 or 600,000 crowns, and a passport to go into Spain to deal with the King, and to return by Jersey.† And that nothing should be done until he had spoken with Sir Walter Ralegh for distribution of the money to them which were discontented in England. Being shown a note under Ralegh's hand [Cobham], when he had perused the same, brake forth, saying, 'O

* If thou *thous't* him some thrice, it will not be amiss; . . .
Let there be gall enough in thy ink . . .
Toby to Aguecheek, said to derive from Coke's speech at the trial. *Twelfth Night*, Act III, Scene 2.

† The Channel island where Ralegh was then Governor.

traitor! O villain! I will now tell you all the truth!' And then said that he had never entered into these courses but by Ralegh's instigation, and that he [Ralegh] would never let him alone."

Coke directed the Clerk to repeat the last words — "Sir Walter would never let Cobham alone." As for the "note under Ralegh's hand," so disturbing to Cobham, it was to prove one of the deadliest facts toward Ralegh's conviction. Written in July, before Sir Walter's imprisonment, it was addressed to Cecil. Coke explained the occasion. At Windsor, when Ralegh first was questioned by the Privy Council, he had said he knew of no plots between Cobham and the Spanish agent. But later the same afternoon, Sir Walter, riding home to London, remembered an incident of early spring, after Cobham had spent an evening at Durham House. Cobham had left by the water gate, and Ralegh, looking out a turret window, saw the barge turn upstream, glide past Cobham's own stairs and stop at the house of La Rensi, a Spanish agent. As soon as Sir Walter returned from Windsor, he wrote out the story and sent it to Cecil.

To the jury, this action of Ralegh's was positively damning. Why should Sir Walter, this early in the game, have taken it on himself gratuitously to inform against his friends, unless as a guilty man he hoped by such betrayal to save his own skin? Cobham, when first arrested, had sworn to Ralegh's innocence of all plots and "conversations." Only when shown this letter, had Cobham broken down and accused Ralegh of treason.

Sir Walter, in rebuttal, asked to see Cobham's confession. While it was being carried to him, he addressed the court: "Gentlemen of the Jury, this is absolutely all the evidence that can be brought against me. This is that which must either condemn me or give me life, which must free me or send my wife and children to beg their bread about the streets. This is that which must prove whether I am a notorious traitor or a true subject to the King. . . ." Having read Cobham's confession, Sir Walter answered at once concerning his own July letter to Cecil. Yes, he had written it. But it revealed to Cecil nothing new. Long since, in the late Queen's time, said Ralegh, it was known that Cobham had dealings with agents from the Low Countries. Even Cecil's father, Lord Burghley, had been aware of it. Cobham, glimpsing this letter in the Tower, had jumped, added Ralegh, to wild unwarranted conclusions.

Were not Lord Cobham's bitter railings well known? The man's passions, indeed, had "such violence," said Ralegh, "that his best friends could never temper them."

The note was never produced in court. Apparently, it had vanished, or at least it made no part of the bundle of depositions at Coke's disposal. Chief Justice Popham now intervened. He himself had been in Cobham's Tower cell when Cobham saw this letter. The Lords of Council had brought it at the exact moment when Cobham was signing his first statement of innocence. (Actually, Cobham had balked at signing. Subscription was like taking an oath. And noblemen, Cobham protested, were not required to swear to documents, their bare word being considered sufficient.) At Popham's insistence however, Cobham took up a pen — and as he wrote his name the Lords walked in the door, bearing Ralegh's note "of betrayal." Cobham looked at it and burst into fury, calling out upon Sir Walter as a wretch and a traitor. "Hath he used me thus? Nay then, I will tell you all!" Cobham's face as he said it (testified Popham) was the face of a man speaking truth; his face and all his actions.

The testimony of a Chief Justice is not easy to disregard. Clearly, Popham believed in Cobham's word, which meant he disbelieved in Ralegh's. And upon this point — which man spoke truth, Ralegh or Cobham — the trial hung, and Ralegh's life. To the jury in Winchester courtroom, Ralegh's word was if anything less reliable than Cobham's. Both were liars, opportunists. Sir Walter by all reports was much the cleverer and stronger. Did it not follow he was also the more guilty?

It was now Ralegh's turn to speak in full. He had two lines to pursue: (1) show that Cobham's word was not to be trusted; (2) convince the jury that his own circumstances made the alleged plots ridiculous, his past history being incompatible with such ill-timed and evil machinations. He began with the second argument, and what he said covers three printed pages; it is instinct with poetry and dignity, and, throughout, magnificently reasonable. By nature his voice was low; in Parliament men had complained they could not hear him when he spoke. Why, he asked now, if he desired to plot with Spain, would he have chosen this time of all times, when England was strengthened by a union with Scotland, the Irish rebels quieted, the Low Countries at peace with England, Denmark's friendship assured by the royal marriage — and on the English throne, "instead of a Lady whom time had surprised, we had now an active King, a lawful successor to the Crown who was able to attend to his own business?"

Elizabeth, the old Queen! *A Lady whom time had surprised.* No man had said it half so well. The phrase would be repeated, would become famous. "I was not such a madman," Ralegh was saying, "as to make myself in this time a Robin Hood, a Wat Tyler, a Kett, or a Jack Cade. I knew also the state of Spain well, his weakness and poorness and humbleness at this time. I knew that he was discouraged and dishonoured. I knew that six times we had repulsed his forces, thrice in Ireland, thrice at sea, and once at Cadiz on his own coast. Thrice had I served against him myself at sea, wherein for my country's sake I expended of my own properties, four thousand pound. I knew that where beforetime he was wont to have forty great sails at the least in his ports, now he hath not past six or seven; and for sending to his Indies he was driven to hire strange vessels — a thing contrary to the institutions of his proud ancestors, who straitly forbad, in case of any necessity, that the Kings of Spain should make their case known to strangers. I knew . . ."

It was a saga, as Ralegh told it; it was the story of England's glory unrolling. Men who had forgotten Drake, forgotten Hawkins, remembered them now and for one quick moment remembered also the days before '88, when England, a small and feeble island, had lived in terror of the Spaniard. Ralegh had never lost his broad Devon accent. It was impressive, here in the courtroom; it breathed of the sailor, not the courtier.

"What pawn had we to give the King of Spain?" Ralegh went on, passionately. "What did we offer him?" He turned to Coke. "And to show I was not *Spanish*, as you term me, I had written at this time a Treatise to the King's Majesty of the present state of Spain, and reasons against the peace. . . ."

The jury listened. ("Never," wrote a spectator, "any man spoke so well in times past nor would do in the world to come.") Yet as Ralegh left his own history and came to Cobham's dubious character — his second argument —what he said seemed less convincing. Sir Walter acknowledged an intimacy with Cobham, an "inwardness," he called it. But their frequent meetings had been concerned only with private business; Cobham had wished advice about his estate. Moreover, Ralegh argued, if he himself desired a treasonable confederate, why would he have chosen Cobham, one of the richest noblemen of England? Discontented earls, such as Bothwell and Westmoreland, were easily available — "men of better understanding than Cobham, ready to beg their bread."

Poverty or riches, the condition of a man's estate, played a large part in treason trials. Rich men seldom make revolutions. As had been said of the Essex affair, "Poverty soonest plungeth the English into rebellion." Essex's final act of violence had come when the Queen took away his monopoly of sweet wines and he felt himself nearing destitution. Ralegh finished speaking, and Cobham's second Examination was read by the Clerk: When he had been about to return from Spain with the 600,000 crowns, Cobham had feared to stop at Jersey and confer according to plan. At Jersey he would have been wholly in Ralegh's power, and Ralegh "might well have delivered him and all the money to the King."

Was Ralegh, then, doubly nefarious, mistrusted even by his accomplices, ready to play his cards both ways and betray his own confederate for credit with the King? Even if Cobham lied, these plots and counterplots were shocking, disturbing. They could not be all invention. . . . Had Cobham, Sir Walter asked quickly, put his signature to this second statement in the Tower? No, Coke replied. A declaration given in the presence of Privy Councilors needed no subscription to be valid.

RALEGH: Surely, Mr. Attorney, you would not allow a bare scroll to have credit with a jury?

COKE: Sir Walter, you say the Lord Cobham's accusing you was upon heat and passion. This is manifestly otherwise; for after that the Lord Cobham had twice called for the letter and twice paused a good while upon it and saw that his dealing with Count Aremberg was made known, then he thought himself discovered and after said, 'O wretch and traitor, Ralegh!' As to improbability, is it probable that my Lord Cobham would turn the weapon against his own bosom and overthrow himself in estate, in honour and in all his fortunes, out of malice to accuse you? . . . If he feared that you would betray him, there must of necessity be a trust between you. No man can betray another but he that is trusted, to my understanding. . . . You seek to wash away all that is said, by affirming the evidence against you to be but a bare accusation, without circumstances or reason to confirm it. That I will fully satisfy. For as my Lord Cobham's confession stands upon many circumstances, and concerns many others, I will, by other means, prove every circumstance thereof to be true.

RALEGH: But, my Lords, I claim to have my accuser brought here face to face to speak. And though I know not how to make my best defence by law, yet since I was a prisoner, I have learned that by the law and statutes of this realm in case of treason, a man ought to be convicted by the testimony of two witnesses if they be living. I will not take it upon me to defend the matter upon the statute *25th Edward III,* though that requires an overt act. . . .

Ralegh referred, of course, to the great statute of 1351, upon which, for six hundred years, subsequent statutes were based* and which defined treason as "compassing or imagining the king's death, levying war against the king, and adhering to the king's enemies." Not the killing of a king but the compassing or imagining his death — *intent to kill him:* this was treason. For centuries therefore the question was to arise: Whether mere words, when plainly evident of intent to kill the king (or to subvert the state), could be construed as an overt act? In times of national emergency, courts invariably have so construed them. In times of peace and national security, the overt act takes narrower construction, and courts require deeds as well as words before they will convict of treason.† On this vital question, Coke as Chief Justice was himself to alter, on occasion, his own interpretation, giving, under Stuart kings, far greater latitude to the accused than he gave to Ralegh or even to Essex — and not only in the matter of the act overt but the rule concerning two witnesses.

Sir Walter went on to cite the statutes of Edward VI (1547, 1548) concerning two witnesses. "Mr. Attorney," he said, "if you proceed to condemn me by bare inference, without an oath,

* In the United States as well as the British Commonwealth.
† Chapter Note.

without a subscription, without witnesses, upon a paper accusation, you try me by the Spanish inquisition. If my accuser were dead or abroad, it were something. But he liveth and is in this very house!"

Ralegh turned to the Commissioners. "Consider, my Lords, it is no rare case for a man to be falsely accused, aye, and falsely condemned, too! And my Lords the Judges — remember, I beseech you, what one of yourselves said in times past. I mean Fortescue, a reverend Chief Justice of this kingdom, touching the remorse of his conscience for proceeding upon such slender proof. '*So long as he lived* [he said] *he should never purge his conscience of that deed.*' And my Lords, remember too the story of Susannah; she was falsely accused. . . . I may be told that the statutes I before named be repealed, for I know the diversity of religion in the Princes of those days caused many changes. Yet the equity and reason of those laws remains. They are still kept to illustrate how the common law was then taken and ought to be expounded. By the Law of God therefore, the life of man is of such price and value that no person, whatever his offence is, ought to die unless he be condemned on the testimony of two or three witnesses."

It was a long speech and there was more, referring not only to Deuteronomy but to St. Paul. How the judges were to receive it would presently be seen, but to the audience it was supremely effectual. Ralegh, in calling on the Law of God, appealed not alone to religious faith but to the national conception of LAW as apart from *the laws* — a distinction sharp in English minds: *the laws* were made by men and could be found in statute book or in judicial maxim and decision. LAW was deeper, higher, derived from God. LAW antedated *the laws* and would exist if every man-made statute were expunged. It was a native conception, part of the common inheritance. Sir Walter had presented the law as plain citizens knew it in their minds and held it in their hearts, no matter what construction had been put upon it by legalists now or in Queen Mary Tudor's time.

"If then," Ralegh finished, "by the statute law, by the civil law and by God's word it be required that there be two witnesses at the least, bear with me if I desire one. Prove me guilty of these things by one witness only, and I will confess the indictment. If I have done these things I deserve not to live, whether they be treasons by the law or no. Why then, I beseech you, my Lords, let Cobham be sent for! Let him be charged upon his soul, upon his allegiance to the King. And if he then maintain his accusation to my face, I will confess myself guilty."

CHAPTER SIXTEEN

Trial of Sir Walter Ralegh (Part II).

> Sir Walter answered with that temper, wit, learning, courage and judgment, that, save it went with the hazard of his life, it was the happiest day he ever spent. And so well he shifted all advantages that were taken against him, that were not *fama malum gravius quam res*, and an ill name, half-hanged in the opinion of all men, he had been acquitted.
>
> CARLETON TO CHAMBERLAIN, *Nov. 27, 1603*

IT was now midday, the trial was half over. Through high windows, light drifted down; on stone floors the rushes were pulled around chilly feet. Ralegh had argued brilliantly from the statutes but his judges were quick with refutation. The laws quoted did not apply, later statutes had repealed them. "I marvel, Sir Walter," Judge Warburton said, "that you being of such experience and wit, should stand on this point; for many horse-stealers should escape if they may not be condemned without witnesses. By law, a man may be condemned upon presumption and circumstances, without any witness to the main fact. As, if the King (whom God defend!) should be slain in his chamber, and one is shown to come forth of the chamber with his sword drawn and bloody, were not this evidence both in law and opinion without further inquisition?"

RALEGH: Yet by your favour, my Lord, the trial of fact at the common law is by jury and witnesses.

POPHAM: No! The trial at the common law is by *examination.* If three conspire a treason and they all confess it, here is never a witness, and yet they may all be condemned of treason.

RALEGH: I know not, my Lord, how you conceive the law; but if you affirm it, it must be a law to all posterity.

POPHAM: Nay, we do not conceive the law. We know the law.

RALEGH: Notwithstanding, my Lords, let me have thus much for my life. For though the law may be as your Lordships have stated it, yet is it a strict and rigorous interpretation of the law. Now the King of England at his coronation swears to observe the equity and not the rigour of the law. And if ever we had a just and good King, it is his Majesty; and such doth he wish his ministers and judges to be. Though, therefore, by the rigour and severity of the law, this may be sufficient evidence, without producing the witness, yet your Lordships, as Ministers of the King, are bound to administer the law in equity.

POPHAM: Equity must proceed from the King. You can only have justice from us.

Popham was confident in what he said. To him as to every lawyer in the hall, Sir Walter's trial had proceeded according to law. Should the King, after Ralegh's condemnation, pardon him, it would be done by virtue of his Majesty's prerogative. That was what Ralegh implied by "equity," and to the judges it was confusion deliberately created. The spectators reacted otherwise; to them these fancy distinctions meant nothing. Sir Walter had shown himself not only eloquent but reasonable; he seemed to know more law than the judges. Many in the hall had sat at Essex's trial, an occasion when the Attorney General made much of overt acts, stating that conviction in England was by the act overt, never on bare words alone. Yet where here was an overt act? The jury waited.

To Coke, Ralegh's arguments were mere casuistry. Laymen who talked law were irritating and Sir Walter, in this respect, was worse than Essex. Ralegh had lived in rooms at the Temple when Coke was a student; yet it did not follow Sir Walter had studied the law.These swordsmen and sailors who skimmed the cream of knowledge — these swashbuckling poetical lords and Queen's favorites with their persuasive tongues — spouted law as the devil quotes Scripture.

"The Crown," Coke said, "shall never stand one year on the head of the King if a traitor may not be condemned by circumstances. . . . *Scientia sceleris est mera ignorantia* [the wisdom of a scoundrel is pure ignorance]. You, Sir Walter, have read the letter of the law but understand it not."

It was the old contention, the old debate between lawyers and laymen: Which shall prevail, law or justice? To Ralegh's audience the words were not synonymous. Yet in the centuries-old calendar of criminal courts, no crime had been more difficult to construe than treason. Sir Walter's judges could cite a whole array of recent statutes, passed to strengthen Queen Elizabeth's position and to give to the Crown all advantage in the struggle against Spain, France, Rome, and against such domestic extremists as cherished ambition to alter the government and religion of England. When statutes, being new, were doubtful of application, the Crown was always favored, not the suspect. Sir Walter's judges saw no reason to take a new position.

Ralegh's own words were now produced, as taken down in the Tower on August thirteenth: "He confesseth the Lord Cobham offered him 10,000 crowns of the [Spanish] money for furthering the peace between England and Spain, and that he should have it within three days; but said, 'When I see the money I will make you an answer,' for [Ralegh] thought it one of [Cobham's] idle conceits and therefore made no account thereof."

To the jury, this was a serious acknowledgment: Ralegh had actually listened to an offer from Spain. That he had not accepted the money — had never even seen it — they promptly forgot. Men who listened to bribes were tainted men, dangerous, vulnerable. . . . Ralegh's "confession" (which in truth confessed nothing) upset this jury of Middlesex knights who knew little of the tangled politics of faction, the bargains by which courtiers lived and moved and the shifting of loyalties with each wind that blew from Europe. (Cecil himself was later to accept a pension from Spain.) Ralegh saw that he had lost ground and urged again that Cobham be produced in court. "Were the case but for a small copyhold, you would have witnesses or good proof to lead the jury to the verdict. And I am here for my life!" Once more the Chief Justice refused: "Sir Walter, you plead hard for yourself, but the laws plead as hard for the King." Cecil interposed. Might he hear the opinion of all the Judges on this point?

The judges all answered that in respect it might be a mean to cover many treasons and might be prejudicial to the King, therefore by law it was not sufferable.

As the afternoon wore on, spectators showed themselves restless; the temper of the hall was seen to alter. ("Sir Walter behaved himself so worthily, so wisely, so temperately, that in half a day the mind of all the company was changed from the extremest hate to the greatest pity.") Ralegh had employed no histrionics but bore himself with simplicity, abusing no one beyond his own accuser, Cobham, and keeping his argument to the law and the state of the realm. Coke, on the other hand, digressed into any field that seemed fruitful. One of the indicted priests, Watson, had quoted in the Tower words spoken by some nobleman (unnamed), suggesting annihilation of James and his family. Coke let the words roll from his tongue, managing, during the recital, to repeat them three times: "Now let us destroy the King and all his cubs, not leaving one!"

RALEGH: O barbarous! Do you bring the words of these hellish spiders against me? If they, like unnatural villains, used those words, shall I be charged with them?

COKE: Thou art thyself a spider of hell, for thou dost confess the King to be a most sweet and gracious Prince, yet thou hast conspired against him.

The matter of a treasonable book was next. In Ralegh's library a manuscript had been found, written by a lawyer in the 1580's to justify Queen Elizabeth's proceedings against Mary Queen of Scots. By inference it argued against James's title to the English crown. Ralegh acknowledged possession but said he had borrowed the book years ago from Lord Treasurer Burghley. "I marvel," Ralegh said, "that it should now be urged as a matter so treasonable in me to have such books, when it is well known there comes out nothing in these times but I have it and might as freely have it as another. And as my Lord Cecil hath said of his library, I think a man might find in my house all the libels that have been made against the late Queen."

COKE: You were no Councillor of State, Sir Walter, and I hope never shall be.

CECIL: Sir Walter Ralegh was truly no *sworn* Councillor of State. Yet he hath been often called to consultations.

Coke now produced, with something of a flourish, his only oral witness of the trial, an English sailor, a pilot named Dyer, who put his hand on the Bible and testified that last July, in Lisbon, he had heard "a Portugal gentleman say that King James would never be crowned, for Don Cobham and Don Ralegh would cut his throat first."

Nobody was impressed; such a fellow could palpably be bought for a few pounds. The sailor retreated. Ralegh spoke contemptuously: "This is the saying of some wild Jesuit or beggarly priest. But what proof is it against me?"

COKE: It must perforce arise out of some preceding intelligence and shows that your treason had wings.

Again it was the old tactic of the treason trial, wherein the prosecution quotes damaging statements made by anybody at all, and then, by hinting association, or merely by constant repetition of the words, hypnotizes a jury into laying on the prisoner the initial responsibility for what was said. Robert Cecil, at this point, rose to remark that two innocent names had been implicated. Count Aremberg, the Ambassador,* should not be blamed for "what others said to him or presumed of him, but of how far he consented or approved." (Ralegh, hearing this, must truly have despaired; he was himself being tried on nothing beyond "what others said to him or presumed.") Among the auditory, Cecil went on, was a noble lady whose name should be cleared, seeing the indictment charged a plot to set her on the throne. All eyes turned to the box where sat Arbella with the Earl of Nottingham. The old Earl rose. "The Lady," he said, "doth here protest upon her salvation that she never dealt in any of these things."

That, apparently, disposed of Arbella, a lady habitually dragged into public notice and then summarily dismissed. Coke, however, had reserved his two best points of evidence. He now produced

* Count Aremberg was, actually, Minister of the Archduke Albert and his wife, the Infanta Isabel, daughter to Philip II. Known currently as *the Archdukes*, they ruled together over the Low Countries (still, of course, Spanish territory). James, eager for peace with Spain, had already begun negotiations. Any official implication of Aremberg would therefore be extremely embarrassing to governmental plans.

the first one: a confession by Cobham, under date of October 13, saying that Ralegh had sent a letter to the Tower, bidding Cobham not to be dismayed because "one witness could not condemn him." If they both kept silence, both were safe. The man who carried it was Kemys, a soldier and sea captain who had accompanied Ralegh to Guiana in 1595.

RALEGH: I deny the writing of any such letter! For Kemys, I never sent him on any such message. This poor man hath been a close prisoner these eighteen weeks and hath been threatened with the rack to make him confess, but I dare stand upon it he will not say it now.

Instant clamor broke among the commissioners; the lords all spoke at once. There had been no torturing of any prisoner. The King had given order that "no rigor should be used."

RALEGH: Was not the keeper of the rack sent for and he threatened with it?

SIR WILLIAM WAAD, from the commissioners' bench: When Mr. Solicitor [Fleming] and myself examined Kemys, we told him he deserved the rack but did not threaten him with it.

COMMISSIONERS: That was more than we knew.

The matter was dropped, but not until Kemys's own confession had been read, wherein he swore he had delivered the letter to Cobham. This time it was Ralegh's word against his own servant, a man known to be both faithful and brave. To the jury it looked as if Mr. Attorney had trapped Sir Walter into a lie. For the last time, Ralegh begged to have Cobham brought into court. "It is you, then, Mr. Attorney, that should press his testimony, and I ought to fear his producing, if all that be true which you have alleged." Cecil supported Sir Walter. Could not the proceedings be delayed while the judges sent to ascertain the King's pleasure in this matter?

But the judges resolved that the proceedings must go on and receive an end. . . . Whereupon Sir Walter Ralegh addressed himself to the Jury and used a speech to this effect. . . .

What Sir Walter said now included little of law or logic. It was a simple, eloquent appeal: "You, Gentlemen of the jury: for all that is said to the contrary, you see my only accuser is the Lord Cobham, who with tears hath lamented his false accusing me, and repented of it as if it had been an horrible murder. I will not expect anything of you but what reason, religion and conscience ask for every man. . . . Remember what St. Augustine saith, 'So judge as if you were about to be judged yourselves, for in the end there is but one Judge and one Tribunal for all men.' . . . Now if you yourselves would like to be hazarded in your lives, disabled in your posterities — your lands, goods and all you have confiscated — your wives, children and servants left crying to the world; if you should be content all this should befall you upon a trial by suspicions and presumptions — upon an accusation not subscribed by your accuser, without the open testimony of a single witness — then so judge me as you would yourselves be judged!"

Serjeant Phillips, ordered by Popham to sum up for the Crown, repeated the charges briefly, adding that Cobham had confessed to all of them. "Now the question is," Phillips said, "whether Sir Walter Ralegh be guilty as inciting or procuring the Lord Cobham to this treason. If the Lord Cobham say truth, Sir Walter Ralegh is guilty. If Sir Walter Ralegh say true, then he is free; so which of them says true is the whole question. Sir Walter Ralegh hath no proof for his acquittal, though he hath as much wit as man can have. But he uses only his bare denial. But the denial of a criminal is not sufficient to clear him, neither is the evidence on oath of a defendant in his own cause allowed to clear him in any Court of law or equity, much less therefore in matters of treason."

Now the business, [wrote the reporter] seemed to be at an end. Then said Sir Walter Ralegh, "Mr. Attorney, have you done?"

COKE: Yes, if you have no more to say.

RALEGH: If you have done, then I have somewhat more to say.

COKE: Nay, I will have the last word for the King.

RALEGH: Nay, I will have the last word for my life.

COKE: Go to, I will lay thee upon thy back for the confidentest traitor that ever came to the bar!

CECIL: Be not so impatient, good Mr. Attorney. Give him leave to speak.

COKE: I am the King's sworn servant and must speak. If I may not be patiently heard, you discourage the King's Counsel and encourage traitors.

Was it now the spectators hissed? (A spectator, writing afterward, said the auditory hissed at Coke, not specifying the moment.)

Mr. Attorney, [says the reporter] sat down in a chafe and would speak no more until the Commissioners urged and entreated him. After much ado, he went on and made a long repetition of the evidence for the direction of the jury. And at the repeating of some things, Sir Walter Ralegh interrupted him and said he did him wrong.

It was here that Coke lost all control, speaking words which are held forever to his shame. Nor were they phrases a man can whisper. Coke stood directly in front of Ralegh. Sir Edward was a big man and, at fifty-two, still in the prime of strength and vigor; his full dark robes made him seem even larger. Long afterward, it was said he shook his fist at Ralegh, though no eyewitness mentioned it. Nevertheless, Coke's voice must have filled the hall: "Thou art the most vile and execrable traitor," he shouted, "that ever lived!"

RALEGH: You speak indiscreetly, uncivilly and barbarously.

COKE: Thou art an odious fellow! Thy name is hateful to all the realm of England for thy pride.

RALEGH: It will go near to prove a measuring cast between you and me, Mr. Attorney.

COKE: Well, I will now lay you open for the greatest traitor that ever was. This, my Lords, is he that hath set forth so gloriously his services against the Spaniard, and hath ever so detested him! This is he that hath written a book against the peace [with Spain]. I will make it appear to the world that there never lived a viler viper on the face of the earth than thou! I will show you wholly Spanish, and that you offered yourself a pensioner to Spain for intelligence. Then let all that have heard you this day judge what you are, and what a traitor's heart you bear, whatever you pretended.

During this terrible exchange, Coke carried in his hand a scroll. It was his final evidence, a surprise card he had withheld, a last damning word against Ralegh, given by Cobham only yesterday from his prison cell. Coke's first words would indicate he held the paper up so all could view it. "See, my Lords, what it hath pleased

God to work in the heart of my Lord Cobham, even since his coming hither to Winchester! He could not sleep quietly till he had revealed the truth to the Lords, and therefore voluntarily wrote the whole matter to them, but yesterday. And to discover you, Ralegh, and all your Machiavelian tricks, hear what the Lord Cobham hath written under his own hand, which I will read with a loud voice, though I be not able to speak this s'ennight after."

Turning to the audience, Coke began to read Cobham's words, "commenting," says the reporter, "as he went along":

"Sir Walter Ralegh, four nights before my coming from the Tower, caused a letter, inclosed in an apple, to be thrown in at my chamber window, desiring me to set down under my hand and send to him an acknowledgment that I had wronged him, and renouncing what I had formerly accused him of. His first letter I made no answer to; the next day he wrote me another, praying me, for God's sake, if I pitied him, his wife and children, that I would answer him in the points he set down, informing me that the Judges had met at Mr. Attorney's house, and putting me in hope that the proceedings against me would be stayed. Upon this I wrote him a letter as he desired. I since have thought how he went about only to clear himself by betraying me. Whereupon I have resolved to set down the truth, and under my hand to retract what he cunningly got from me, craving humble pardon of his Majesty and your Lordships for my double dealing. . . ."

"The truth"—as Cobham saw it in this last retraction—was Ralegh's bargain with Aremberg for a flat yearly pension of 1500 pounds in return for spying service, "to tell and advertise what was intended by England against Spain, the Low Countries or the Indies." To the jury this was new and shocking. Bribes had been mentioned, but nothing so damning as a continuous, yearly payment. As instance—Cobham wrote further—Sir Walter, returning one night from the palace at Greenwich, revealed "what was agreed upon betwixt the King and the Low Countrymen, that I should impart it to Count Aremberg. . . . And Sir Walter in his last letter advised me not to be overtaken by confessing to any preacher as the Earl of Essex had. . . ."

Here Coke broke off his reading, and turning to Ralegh, spoke in passion: "O damnable athetist! He counsels not to confess to preachers, as the Earl of Essex did! That noble Earl died indeed for his offence, but he died the child of God, and God honored him at his death. Thou, Ralegh, wast by when he died. *Et lupus et turpes instant morientibus ursae!*"

Wolves and bears press close upon the dying. The Latin, rolling out, was like a curse; it was anathema, incantation, and, considering Coke's own part in Essex's trial, was least excusable. This was not law but rabble-rousing. It was the stones and mire hurled once more at Ralegh. Whatever the jury thought of it, they could not disregard the new evidence — a letter written at Winchester not twenty-four hours past. Tomorrow or next day, Cobham himself would stand trial in this very hall. Impossible that a man with death so close upon him would lie thus to the Lords. What had he to gain thereby? Was any favor, Popham inquired of the commissioners, "promised or offered" to Cobham for the writing of this letter? No, Cecil replied; to his knowledge there was none. "I dare say not," Ralegh interposed drily. "But my Lord Cobham received a letter from his wife that there was no way to save his life but to accuse me."

This, to the jury, was beside the point. "The Lord Cobham's confession," wrote the reporter, "seemed to give great satisfaction and cleared all the former evidence, which stood very doubtful." Coke's triumph was plain. For him, the trial was over. The withholding of this evidence until the end had been wise, he could tell himself — especially in dealing with a man of Ralegh's skill. Now it was too late for denial. No trick of Sir Walter's, no appeal of eloquence could counteract this final accusation of his enemy. Ralegh, said the reporter, stood "much amazed."

"Now, Ralegh," Coke said, "if thou hast the grace, humble thyself to the King and confess thy treasons."

But Coke (though for the last time) underestimated his adversary. Sir Walter too had reserved a surprise.

By-and-by, [wrote the reporter] Sir Walter Ralegh seemed to gather his spirits again, and said: "I pray you hear me a word. You have heard tale of a strange man. . . . Before my Lord Cobham's coming from the Tower, I was advised by some of my friends to get a confession from him. Therefore I wrote to him thus, 'You or I must go to trial. If I first, then your accusation is the only evidence against me!' Therefore it was not ill of me to beg of him to say the truth. But his first letter was not to my contenting. I wrote a second, and then he wrote me a very good letter."

Ralegh thrust a hand in his breast and produced a folded small sheet. "It is true," he said, "I got a poor fellow in the Tower to cast up an apple with the letter in it, at Lord Cobham's window; which I am loath to mention lest Mr. Lieutenant of the Tower might be blamed, though I protest Sir George Harvey is not to blame for what passed. No keeper in the world could so provide but it might happen. But I sent him his letter again, because I heard it was likely now he should be first tried. But the Lord Cobham sent me the letter a second time, saying it was not unfit I should have such a letter."

Ralegh held up the paper. "And here you may see it, and I pray you read it."

The Clerk came forward to take the note. The jury watched. In the history of trials, had evidence ever been so given and retracted, so sworn and forsworn? No matter what this new note of Cobham's might say, Ralegh, in producing it, confessed what he had earlier denied — communication with Cobham in the Tower. "But what say you," Popham interposed, "to the pension of 1500 pounds a year?"

He could not deny it, Ralegh replied, though it was never his purpose to accept it. "It was my fault I did conceal it, and this fault of concealing, I acknowledge. But for attempting or conspiring any treason against the King or the State, I still deny it to the death and it can never be proved against me."

"I perceive," Popham said gravely, "you are not so clear a man as you have protested all this while, for you should have discovered this matter to the King."

The Clerk, during this exchange, stood waiting, Cobham's letter in his hand. "Hear now, I pray you," Ralegh said, "what Cobham hath written to me."

Mr. Attorney would not have this letter read, saying that it was unfairly obtained from Lord Cobham. And upon Lord Cecil's advising to hear it, he said, "My Lord Cecil, mar not a good cause!"

Cecil: Mr. Attorney, you are more peremptory than honest. You must not come here to show me what to do.

Ralegh: I pray my Lord Cecil particularly to read the letter, as he knoweth my Lord Cobham's hand.

Then was read the letter of the Lord Cobham to Sir Walter Ralegh, to this effect: "Now that the arraignment draws near, not knowing which should be first, I or you, to clear my conscience, satisfy the world with truth and free myself from the cry of blood, I protest upon my soul and before God and his angels, I never had conference with you in any treason, nor was ever moved by you to the things I heretofore accused you of. And for any thing I know, you are as innocent and as clear from any treasons against the King as is any subject living. Therefore I wash my hands and pronounce with Daniel, *Purus sum a sanguine hujus.** And so God deal with me and have mercy on my soul, as this is true!"

It was impressive; this was a day when men did not lightly call upon God's name. Ralegh followed it quickly. "My Masters of the Jury," he said, "this is a confession made under oath, and the deepest protestations a Christian man can make." Yet the jury was weary with these retractations and denials of retractations; they came too late. Cobham's confession of yesterday, as read aloud by Coke, invalidated this earlier statement, eloquent though it had been. Too much lay counter to it — notes tied to apples, servants bearing secret letters, connivance and what looked like deliberate falsehood in court. "The acknowledging," wrote the reporter, "of this 1500 pounds a year pension made the rest of the Lord Cobham's accusation the better credited. . . ." Chief Justice Popham addressed Ralegh direct. "In my conscience I am persuaded that Cobham accused you truly. I observed his manner of speaking. I protest before the living God I am persuaded he spoke nothing but the truth."

The prosecution rested its case. Coke's three points had been stated, embellished, gone over until twelve knights of Middlesex knew them by heart: (1) Ralegh's July letter to Cecil, informing of Cobham's midnight visit to La Rensi; (2) Ralegh's letter to Cobham in the Tower, reminding Cobham that two witnesses were necessary for conviction and urging that as long as Cobham kept silence, they both were safe; (3) Cobham's confession of November 16, given from his cell in Winchester. The first two points were hearsay, the letters never seen by the jury, never produced in court. Yet testimony which the judges accepted, the jury accepted also. As for Point 2, the fact that Ralegh denied the

* "I am innocent of this blood."

writing of such a letter seemed only to enhance his guilt; Kemys had confessed to delivery of it. That Cobham had three times retracted his testimony proved only that he was, like all traitors, untrustworthy and should be destroyed. The Attorney General had trapped Sir Walter into a lie concerning communication with Cobham in the Tower. And though Magna Carta said that no man should be forced to testify against himself, in the jury's mind Coke's harsh questioning was no derogation of this law. On the contrary, the prisoner had been given every opportunity to reply and clear himself of guilt.

The day was done, the light was gone. Winchester gates were shut and barred. On its hillside the ancient Hall of Arthur loomed in shadow; lanterns swung behind the tall grilled gates that led to the cells and dungeon far below. . . .

The Jury were willed to go together; who departed and stayed not a quarter of an hour, when they returned, bringing in their verdict, GUILTY OF TREASON.

Ralegh was led to the bar. Chief Justice Popham stood up, bareheaded. In his hand he held the black cap that signified a death sentence. "Sir Walter Ralegh," he said, "I am sorry to see this fallen upon you this day. You have always been taken for a wise man. And I cannot but marvel to see that a man of your wit, as this day you have approved it, could be entangled with so many treasons. I grieve to find that a man of your quality would have sold yourself for a spy to the enemy of your country for 1500 pounds a year. This covetousness is like a canker, that eats the iron place where it lives. . . ."

There was more; to Ralegh it must have been well nigh unendurable. "O God!" he had written to his wife from the Tower, "I cannot live to think how I am derided, the scorns I shall receive, the cruel words of lawyers, the infamous taunts and despites, to be made a wonder and a spectacle! O death, destroy the memory of these and lay me up in dark forgetfulness!"

Of all these cruel taunts, Popham's solemn pronouncement was the worst. Coke had raved but Ralegh could answer him. Now, for Ralegh, denial and affirmation were forever blocked. What the Chief Justice said, the world (or so thought Ralegh) would take as truth.

"It now comes to my mind," * Popham continued, "why you may not have your accuser brought face to face: for such an one is easily brought to retract when he seeth there is no hope of his own life. . . . It now only remaineth to pronounce the judgment, which I would to God you had not to receive this day of me. I never saw the like trial, and I hope I shall never see the like again."

Raising both hands with the deliberation of an aged man, Popham set the black cap on his head. "Sir Walter Ralegh," he said, "since you have been found guilty of these horrible treasons, the judgment of this court is, That you shall be had from hence to the place whence you came, there to remain until the day of execution. And from thence you shall be drawn upon a hurdle through the open streets to the place of execution, there to be hanged and cut down alive, and your body shall be opened, your heart and bowels plucked out, and your privy members cut off and thrown into the fire before your eyes. Then your head to be stricken off from your body, and your body shall be divided into four quarters, to be disposed of at the King's pleasure.

"And God have mercy upon your soul."

* Chapter Note.

CHAPTER SEVENTEEN

"All riddle and mystery."

THE warrant for Ralegh's execution was dated December thirteenth, almost a month away. The Lords Cobham and Grey were yet to be tried. Few doubted the outcome, yet the general talk and temper showed a violent shift. Sir Walter's trial had made plain that of all these plots and counterplots, nothing whatever had resulted. Were nine men, then, to suffer death for mere talk and midnight visitings? King James at nearby Wilton House received immediate report. Two of his courtiers (sent to the trial as royal reporters) told of Sir Walter's extraordinary bearing, the brilliance of his argument, the lack of that arrogance so long associated with him. Whereas, said one, when he first saw Sir Walter, he was so led with the common hatred that he would have gone a thousand miles to see him hanged; yet ere he parted, he would have gone a thousand to have saved his life. "In one word," remarked Sir Dudley Carleton, who witnessed the trial, "never was man so hated and so popular in so short a time."

Sir Robert Cecil remained at Wilton House with the King. Yet what Cecil thought, few could discover. Heart and soul a servant of the state, this was a man wholly discreet; one of those "who have no windows in their breast." Michael Hicks, his secretary, wrote that Cecil wept when sentence was pronounced. Certainly, he had been the only man who ventured support to Ralegh in the courtroom. Yet Cecil's narrative of the trial, dispatched immediately to the English Ambassadors at Paris and The Hague, was noncommittal, composed for ambassadorial convenience in answering foreign questions. For himself, wrote Cecil, he had been influenced by Ralegh's early letter to Cobham, urging silence because one witness could not overthrow them. Concerning Count Aremberg, there was no doubt of his involvement. Yet it would not do to implicate him at this moment, when King James was pressing for peace with Spain. . . .

Other letters went off, neither discreet nor careful but angry, detailed, vehement. "Some circumstances there were to give presumption but no proof at all," wrote one. "The main evidence was Cobham's accusation, which, all things considered, was no more to be weighed than the barking of a dog. I would not for much have been of the jury to have found him guilty." For the Attorney General, there was no denying his brutality to the accused — though quite obviously this had not influenced the jury against a verdict of guilty. Coke had lost his temper to the extent that Cecil twice reproved him sharply. The audience had hissed and Coke "sat down in a chafe"; it had required urging to get him back on his feet. Yet one story had it that Coke was himself shocked by the verdict. When the jury retired, the Attorney General went out (it was said) for a breath of air. Fifteen minutes later, a messenger found him walking in the garden behind the castle, and repeated to him the verdict. "Surely thou art mistaken!" Coke replied, astonished. "I myself accused him but of misprision of treason."*

James heard the reports and waited, saying little. He was advised to hold back Sir Walter's execution. Perhaps Cobham and Grey, at their trials, would implicate Ralegh further; or there might be, on the scaffold, last-minute confessions. The present temper of the people made it hardly politic to put Sir Walter to death. A new monarch must feel his way. . . .

Lord Cobham was tried on Friday, November twenty-sixth. "Never," wrote Carleton, "was seen so poor and abject a spirit. He heard his indictment with much fear and trembling . . . exclaimed upon Ralegh as one who had stirred him up to discontent and thereby overthrown his fortunes. . . . Being asked of his two letters to different purposes, the one excusing, the other condemning Ralegh, he said the last was true, but the other was drawn from

* "When one knoweth of any treason or felony and concealeth it," Coke later wrote, "this is misprision; in case of misprision of treason the offender is to be imprisoned during his life, to forfeit all his goods, debts and duties for ever, and the profits of his lands during his life." Coke adds that "by the common law, concealment of high treason was treason."

him by device in the Tower, by young Harvey, the Lieutenant's son, whom Ralegh had corrupted and carried intelligence betwixt them (for which he is there committed and is likely to be arraigned at the King's Bench)."

People recalled Ralegh's testimony on this point—how he had "got a poor fellow to . . . cast up an apple with the letter in it, at Lord Cobham's window." The "poor fellow," it now appeared, was none other than the Lieutenant's son. Sir Walter had lied to protect his friends, whereas Cobham revealed all and any "truths" in hopes of his own life. In this conflict of moralities the public judgment did not waver; it preferred Ralegh's bold evasions. "Having thus accused all his friends," finished Carleton, "and so little excused himself, the Peers were not long in deliberation what to judge; and after sentence of condemnation given, [Cobham] begged a great while for life and favour, alleging his confession as a meritorious act."

Lord Grey, on the day following, showed different mettle, defending himself "with great assurances and alacrity . . . from eight in the morning till eight at night. . . . There was great compassion had of this gallant young Lord, so clear and fiery a spirit. . . . Yet the Lord Steward condemned his manner much, terming it Lucifer's pride . . . and the Judges liked him as little, because he disputed with them against their laws. We cannot yet judge what will become of him or the rest, for all are not like to go one way. . . . They say the priests shall lead the dance tomorrow. . . ."

The prophecy was correct. Next day—November twenty-ninth—Watson and Clarke were hanged in the prison courtyard. "They died boldly," wrote Carleton. "But Clarke," reported another, "would have told tales how they were misled, and how the people were blinded with colored shows: and was most miserably tortured, to the great discontent of the people who now think that matters were not so heinous as were made shew of." The victim's heads were set on the Castle tower, their quarters on Winchester gates. A week later, Cobham's brother, George Brooke, was beheaded, showing himself resolute and asking the executioner to tell him what to do, as he "was never beheaded before." When the executioner held up the streaming head, crying out "God save King James," not a voice but the Sheriff's (it was noted) seconded him. Ralegh had begged that Cobham might die before he did — not for revenge but in hopes of a last dying retractation. Concerning the date, Sir Walter had his wish: Cobham, Grey and Sir Griffin Markham the Catholic (former Lord of Beskwood Forest), were scheduled for execution on Friday, December tenth.

Whatever scene Sir Walter had envisioned at Cobham's scaffold, it could not have equaled the reality. Ralegh saw it all; his cell, high up, overlooked the courtyard and the crowds. Sir Griffin was led out first. It was a dark day, pouring rain. Markham's friends had misled him with hopes of a reprieve, reports that James was disposed to leniency. He left his cell therefore unprepared to die and looked about him in horror, like a man stunned. Yet when a friend, standing near, offered a napkin to cover his face, Markham refused it, saying he could look on death without blushing. Bidding farewell to those who loved him, he began to pray, as was the custom.

The Sheriff, meanwhile, was seen to leave the scaffold. After what seemed an unconscionably long time, he returned and, to the mystification of the crowd, told Markham that since he seemed ill prepared for death, he might have two hours' reprieve, locked into Arthur's Hall to meditate upon the hereafter. He was taken away.

Lord Grey came next, escorted "by a troop of the young courtiers and supported on both sides by two of his best friends, and had such gaiety and cheer in his countenance that he seemed a dapper young bridegroom." Again the prayers, the farewells — again the Sheriff's reprieve to walk in Arthur's Hall. Cobham was last. If at his trial he had cringed, pleading for life, he walked bravely now, made his prayers in a resounding tone, begged pardon of the King and the world for his offenses and declared, "upon the hope of his soul's resurrection, that what he had said of Sir Walter Ralegh was true."

At this moment the headsman was halted by the Sheriff; it had been ordered that Cobham be confronted by some of the other prisoners. Lord Grey and Markham were led back to the scaffold, "looking strange one upon the other, like men beheaded and met again in the other world." With the three actors "being together on the stage as use is at the end of the play," wrote Carleton, the Sheriff made a short speech, inquiring if their condemnation were just and lawful. All three assented miserably. "Then," said the Sheriff in a loud voice, "see the mercy of your Prince, who of himself hath sent hither a countermand and given you your lives!"

A great shout went up from the crowd, echoing "from the Castle into the town and there began afresh." All eyes turned to the window where Ralegh stood, "with hammers working in his head to beat out the meaning of this stratagem." James, it seems, had worked out the hideous farce alone, with no advising, though in the end the plan nearly miscarried. The Scotsman bearing the reprieves arrived so late he could not get through to the scaffold and was "thrust out among the boys." Only a calling and shoving caught the Sheriff's attention in time.

For Ralegh the scene was not repeated. Simply, he was told that James had "given him his life," commuted his punishment to imprisonment. A week later he was taken to London. Cobham and Grey were also put in the Tower.* Of the others, Markham, Brooksby, Copley were banished the realm. Sir Walter, directly after conviction, had written to the Lord Commissioners and to the King, pleading mercy. Before leaving Winchester he bade his wife, Lady Elizabeth, recover if possible "those letters wherein I sued for my life. God knoweth that it was for you and yours that I desired it; but it is true that I disdaine myself for begging it."

The King with all his train moved toward London. It was nearly January; danger from the plague should be gone. London counted thirty thousand dead. By night, lamps flickered beside doors splashed with long red crosses; in the streets the smell of burning feathers lingered, consumed against infection. Coke and the judges remained at Winchester to finish term business. The visitors who had come for the trials went home; once more the old town lay quiet upon its hill.

Yet the matter was by no means done but lingered in men's minds, a troubled, ever deepening legend. Some believed that Sir Walter knew all about Lord Cobham's treasons and invited him to Jersey with purpose to "betray him and the plot, and make his peace with the King." It was a known trick of politicians, this tempting of dissatisfied men into treasons and then informing on them.

* Lord Grey, his spirit broken, died after eleven years of imprisonment. Cobham, released in 1615 because of his health, died two years later, alone and in miserable poverty.

Those who hated Cecil hinted that he himself had engineered the whole thing for reasons of state, to weaken a party, rid the King's court of a faction and thereby strengthen his own credit. "It was as necessary for Cecil there should be treasons as for the state they should be prevented."

There was to be no end to the stories; for centuries the world would tell new tales of Ralegh's trial. One historian, writing in 1650, even stated that "some of his jury were afterwards so far touched in conscience as to demand of Ralegh pardon on their knees." Gawdy the Norfolkman — who had sat as judge — was reported to say on his deathbed that "the justice of England was never so depraved and injured as in the condemnation of Sir Walter Ralegh." Sir Walter himself told the story to the Privy Council. It was received with caution and recollection that during the trial, Judge Gawdy's one recorded remark had been directed against the prisoner, not for him.

The plain fact was that the people could not seem to stomach the performance as they had seen it and felt called upon, as time passed, to invent deathbed repentances, juries on their knees and an Attorney General surprised at his own most vehement and brutal victory. Yet this victory had been obtained under a system accepted and applauded throughout England for centuries. If, in the past, innocent men had suffered, it was the fortunes of war; the realm must be preserved. Now the clouds parted and men saw injustice where formerly they had seen only danger to the state and a hard necessity for immediate destruction of all traitors.

In quick succession, England had experienced two famous trials, dramatic enough to reach the public conscience: Essex, beloved of the people, who the world well knew was guilty; Ralegh, who after a noble self-defense was condemned to death on nothing more than presumption and surmise. Ralegh's judges had enunciated harsh principles, said to derive from the English common law. Did it not follow that the laws were monstrous, designed less to safeguard than to entrap?

To say that from Ralegh's trial dated a change in the laws would be to say too much. Yet from that day there entered it is said the possibility of change — a groping after procedure which might give to the unfriended single prisoner fair chance against the solid power of the state. For such a demonstration, Ralegh was the perfect candidate. His had been a political trial, a settling of order at the beginning of a new reign, a new regime. Ralegh was not martyred for a cause. He was no Ridley, whose pyre would "light a candle never to be put out." In the dock at Winchester, Sir Walter stood fighting for his own life.

Yet the life of a Ralegh would serve as vivid symbol of what other men might lose. When they carried Sir Walter to the Tower he was fifty-one; the noblest part of his career still lay ahead. He could not bring himself to believe that his imprisonment would last. For twelve years he was to maneuver, write letters, win friends in prison and out (including James's eldest son, Prince Henry). Sir George Harvey gave Ralegh the freedom of a little garden for his chemical experiments, invited him to dine, let him walk on a high wall overlooking the Thames, permitted Lady Ralegh and their son to live in his prison apartment, together with various of their servants. Sir William Waad, when he became Lieutenant, complained to the Privy Council that Sir Walter "doth show himself upon the wall to the view of the people who gaze upon him and he stareth on them." Nor did the King impoverish Ralegh as he impoverished the others. How James came to his decisions in this case was not revealed, though Queen Anne is said to have interceded. Of nine men concerned, James spared all but three lives, and for this he received extravagant praise — domestically at least; he had made a "most noble, princely gesture." In France the royal "generosity" was looked upon with skepticism. Who, asked Henry IV, had paid for Ralegh's reprieve? Was it Spanish gold, obtained by Cecil's influence? Or had it come, perhaps, from Sir Walter's own estate?

The questions were not answered. Sir Walter walked upon the Tower battlements and watched the ships sail eastward with the tide. The riddle and the mystery remained.

CHAPTER EIGHTEEN

1604. King James and the country.

O Lord, make thow his Council wise,
That they may give him good advise.
Blesse the Commons, and all those
That seeke the ruine of his foes.
And may he dye a thowsand shames
That with his heart loves not King *James!*
Shirburn Ballads

JAMES and his court returned from Winchester. With his coming the city took heart and seized once more upon a life that had been as if suspended. Counting Westminster, Lambeth and the suburbs, almost a sixth of London's population had been carried off by plague in this one year. Yet now there was a quick resurgence; fear had fled though infection lingered. Visitors from the counties poured in to see the King or perhaps to profit from the proximity of those who saw him. Tradesmen disposed of leftover wares. Herders drove their cattle to the Southwark butchers. At the shambles in St. Nicholas parish the blood of new-killed beasts ran richly in the gutters. Even the city birth rate showed a rapid recovery. Across the river, flags flew again from Bear Garden and Globe Theatre, though audiences grumbled. The playwrights having fled the plague to sit idle in the country, there was nothing to produce but old comedies.

Taverns that had been closed by order reopened without order. Shops took down their boards. Signs, new-gilded, bright with color, caught the eye like banners. On Goldsmiths Street, foreign visitors expressed themselves dazzled by the rich wares shown, the gilt tower and fountain on the corner, the mirrors ornamented with pearls and velvet, "the hippocamp and eagle stone, very curious and rare." Trade was brisk, visitors careless with their money. A fashion of crazy betting sprang up overnight. Ramsy, the King's watchmaker, put out clocks to be paid for "when King James shall be crowned in the Pope's chair." One of Ben Jonson's characters gave odds on the performance of a journey to Rome by himself, his cat and his dog. On Sundays, apprentices played at football in the streets with fresh bladders saved from hog killing. The light new caroches of the rich rolled noisy on the cobbles, their coachmen cursing at the litter of tumbled straw, old bedding, rags and quilts thrown out from infected chambers of the dead. Sir William Waad complained to Cecil that the prisoners' cages by the city gates were filled with sick who lay and died therein, contaminating the air. Dogs were said to be carriers; five hundred had been killed by order in Westminster alone. But in the dark alleys of Shoreditch, Cripplegate, St. Sepulchre's, where lived the poor, black rats swarmed beneath the filthy rushes, ran behind rickety eaves, emerging to spin their drunken dance of death, and none suspected them as cause of the infection. "Ha' ye any rats," sang the catcher cheerfully:

> Ha' ye any rats, mice, polecats or weasels?
> Or ha' ye any old sows, sick of the measles?
> I can kill them and I can kill moles,
> And I can kill vermin that creepeth up and
> creepeth down and peepeth into holes.

From St. Stephen's Day to Twelfth Night the usual revels were held, with street music, plays and dancing. The City got ready for the coming celebration of March. The King's triumphal entry from London into Westminster had been delayed by reason of the sickness. Seven great arches were to be set up, with allegorical figures of Wisdom, Unanimity, Peace. Odes would be read, songs sung in chorus. Dekker, Jonson, Middleton, Drayton were hard at work. William Shakespeare was to walk in the procession with the King's actors and had been presented, like the others, with four and a half yards of red cloth to make a suit. The merchant companies rehearsed their parts, prepared fresh banners and ensigns, striving to outdo each other. The black feathers of mourning for Elizabeth were discarded. Gentlemen, riding to the King's court, flaunted red and yellow ribbons, symbolic of the royal arms, "the ruddy lion rampant in gold." Spanish high-crowned hats with tassels became the rage, the stiff Dutch bloomers and red stockings which the King affected — though word had it his Majesty cared nothing for fashion, having rejected a hat of Spanish block, refused also the customary fat satin roses for his shoes, demanding of the courtier who brought them, "if he would make of him a ruff-footed dove?" So little did the monarch heed appearances that when a gentleman groom brought the royal hat for hunting and placed it on his head, James seldom touched it but let it sit there, square upon his brow.

In everything James said or did, the nation showed unflagging interest. There was about this sovereign nothing unexpected or capricious. He lived by rote, ate and drank the same dishes. A courtier was heard to say that were he asleep seven years and wakened, he could tell where the King each day had been and every dish eaten at his table. James drank often, not so much from greed as from habit, and seldom more than four spoonsful at a time. Though he chose strong wines — canary, Frontignan, high-country brew and Scottish ale, he was never overtaken. He drank while hunting and, as he was all day on horseback, his courtiers were sometimes fearful they would lose their balance if they matched him drink for drink. There was no denying the monarch's good disposition, so long as he was not crossed. "The swetest pleasantest & best nature that ever I know," wrote Wilbraham, who was not inclined to flattery. James's connubial life was extolled as exemplary. The large brown eyes, "ever rowling after any stranger," did not linger on the young beauties attending Queen Anne, nor had the royal attraction toward graceful young gentlemen as yet aroused suspicion. "Jo. Grant told me," wrote Manningham in his diary, "that the King useth in walking amongst his nobles often tymes to leane upon their shoulders in a special favour, and in disgrace to neglect some in that kindeness." The Stuart legs were weak and needed support — a trait inherited, unfortunately, by Prince Charles. His father wished to put the little boy in iron braces, but Lady Carey, to whom his bringing up had been entrusted, held out stoutly against it, resisted also the King's wish to have the string cut beneath the Prince's tongue, to cure an impediment of speech. There had been, at first, much jockeying and vying for this royal guardianship — until the Prince's weaknesses were known, when suitors for the office fell off fast. No credit was to be gained in the rearing of so unhopeful a piece of royalty.

James, at thirty-seven, was not unpleasing in person, though even the most egregious flatterer would have boggled at the word "handsome." His beard was thin. When he drank, his thick tongue slobbered "very uncomely, as if eating his drink, which came out into the cup on each side of his mouth. . . ." "His skin," wrote the same observer, "was soft as taffeta sarsnet, because he never wash'd his hands, only rubbed his finger ends lightly with the wet end of a napkin." Courtiers, when adjectives failed, seized upon the word "wise." James was fluent in Latin, and what other King of England had published so many books? There were a dozen sonnets written in schoolboy days, *Meditations* on the Scriptures, a *Daemonologie*, filled with learned lore about witches, and the recent *Counterblaste to Tobacco.* When James forgot to be a king he wrote racily, especially about things he hated, like tobacco and Puritans: "What is betwixt the pride of a glorious Nebuchadnezzar and the preposterous humilitie of the proud Puritanes . . . crying, *Wee are all but vile wormes,* and yet will be judged or controlled by none? Surely there is more pride under such a ones blacke bonnet, than under Alexander the great his Diademe" . . . "This filthie smoke, sucked up by the Nose . . . to imitate the wilde, godless and slavish Indians who use it as a stinking Antidote against the pockes, making so one canker or vermine to eate out another. Here in England it is refined, and will not deigne to cure here any other than cleanly and gentlemanly diseases. O omnipotent power of Tobacco! And if it could by the smoke thereof chace out devils, as the smoke of Tobias' fish did (which I am sure could smel no stronglier) it would serve for a precious Relicke, both for the superstitious Priests, and the insolent Puritanes, to cast out devils withall."

James took especial pride in his book *Basilikon Doron* [*Kingly Monument*], which was one of those parental homilies fashionable at the time, addressed to Prince "Henry, my dearest sonne and naturall successor." It was sugary with moralism except when

James lost himself in description of something he had actually felt and smarted under. Having learned in Scotland (at no small cost) that thrones are precarious — "Joves thunderclaps," he wrote, "light sorer upon the stately oakes than on the low and supple willow tree; the highest bench is sliddriest to sit upon."

Unfortunately it did not occur to James that kings, like willows, might profitably bend; he had merely been stating a fact. *Basilikon*, together with the *Trew Law of Free Monarchies* (1598), contained James's convinced views of kingship — positive, complacent, pious and ominously divergent from the philosophy of government entertained by Coke or indeed any who took their starting point from the common law of England. There were Kings, James stated, before there was law. A king was created by God as his "little God to sit on his Throne and rule over other men." It followed that subjects must never rebel, not though oppressed by a Nero, "that monster and idolatrous persecutor." God would punish the tyrant as he had punished Pharoah. Subjects were born to endure "without resistance but by sobbes and teares to God."

The nation chose to ignore these royal dicta. There had been no opportunity to test them, Parliament had not met. It was more agreeable to remark upon that most noticeable of kingly characteristics, a manly appetite for hunting the stag, the buck and the hare. James would not stay in London but moved from one to another of his country seats and hunting boxes: Woodstock, Newmarket, Oatlands, Royston, pursuing game with crossbow, dog and falcon. The court moved so often that it was, wrote Cecil, more a *camp volant* than a royal residence. And if my Lord Howard, added Cecil, could help him to a good river hawk and send her immediately, he would "not stick to give gold, so she fly high" . . . "I thinke," wrote the Earl of Worcester from Royston, "I have not had 2 hours of 24 of rest but Sundays, for in the morning we are on horseback by 8 and so continue in full career from the death of one hare to another until 4 at night; then, for the most part, we are 5 miles from home; by that time I find at my lodging some times one, most commonly 2 packets of letters, all which must be answered before I sleep, for here is none of the Council but my self, no, not a clerke of the Council nor privy signet, so that an ordinary warrant for post horse must pass my own hand, my own secretary being sick at London."

Only when the rain came in torrents were the courtiers spared, and then the King sat at the game called *maw*, snapping his cards impatiently, waiting for the sun. The country neighborhood was disturbed by these royal visits. Food must be found not only for King and court but for a veritable army of hangers-on, followers who set up tents at the lodge gates when housing failed. "A reasonable pretty jest is spoken," wrote Lascelles to the Earl of Shrewsbury, "that happened at Royston: There was one of the King's speciall hounds, called Jowler, missing one day: The King was much displeased; notwithstanding went a hunting. The next day, when they were on the field, Jowler came in amongst the rest of the hounds; the King was very glad, and looking on him, spied a paper about his neck, and in the paper was written, 'Good Mr. Jowler, we pray you speake to the King (for he hears you every day, and so doth he not us) that it will please his Majestie to go back to London, for else the country wilbe undone; all our provision is spent already and we are not able to entertain him longer.' . . . It was," finished Lascelles, "taken for a jest and so passed over, for his Majestie intends to lie there yet a fortnight."

For he hears you, Mr. Jowler, every day, and so doth he not us. . . . It was true. This friendly, talkative King, with his hounds, his easy manner and careless clothes, kept himself remote from his subjects. He hated a throng and when crowds pressed to see him, he shuddered at their reaching hands and swore his favorite oath — "God's wounds!"— so that the people heard him. Elizabeth, for all her mystery and magnificence, had been far easier of access, had loved to show herself. "The wisest princes are the most gaudy." The city of Norwich remembered, after a visit, how Elizabeth had paused at the gates to look back, tall on her palfrey, "shaking her riding rod and saying, Farewell Norwich, with the water standing in her eyes."

James seemed to feel no obligation to be seen, to establish a connection with the people. His open chariot, lined in crimson velvet, plumes blowing from the roof, passed swiftly through the towns. Courtiers, riding beside him, learned to close ranks, shutting out the crowds. James dreaded the ceremony of "touching for the King's evil," traditional since Norman days. At the urging of advisers, he met the throngs of dirty, scabbed sick in a room of his palace. But he grumbled openly at such "silly superstition." Laying his hands upon a sick man, he burst out in broad Scots, "God gie ye better health and more sense!"

This first of the English Stuarts never relinquished his Scottish dialect, wrote "whilk" for which and "syne" for since. England showed a profound distaste for the Scotsmen who followed his court. *Foreigners!* they were called. Uncouth creatures, without manners, without grace; and worst of all without money. In this glorious new harvest, should foreigners receive the plums? "Bonny Scot," sang the countryside sourly:

> . . . we all witness can,
> That England hath made thee a gentleman.
> Thy shoes on thy feet, when thou camest from plough,
> Were made of the hide of an old Scots cow;
> But now they are turned to a rare Spanish leather,
> And decked with roses altogether.
>
> Thy sword at thy arse was a great black blade
> With a great basket hilt of iron made;
> But now a long rapier doth hang by thy side,
> And huffingly doth this bonny Scot ride.
> Bonny Scot, we all witness can
> That England made thee a gentleman.

The verses were endless and flexible, to be amplified as occasion presented. James himself grew tired of his onetime countrymen who had been born apparently with but one gesture — the outstretched hand. Yet his Majesty continued to make new knights, a transaction profitable to himself but increasingly distasteful to the holders of old titles. Judge Gawdy's nephew wrote that Norfolk sheep-reaves and yeomen had been knighted and the sons of London peddlers, "amongst the rest Thimblethorpe the attorney that was called *nimblechappes*, full of the pox, was knighted for seven pounds ten shillings." There were new jokes every day. *Clenches*, they were called, not very funny but somehow comforting to those who had the short end of the stick: A Suffolk mercer followed the court, sleeping in tent or stable until he was "most wonderfully lousy and yet paying well for it, he was made a lousy knight." . . . Two friends out walking, spied some one in the distance and wondered who or what he was. "A gentleman," said the first. "No, no," said the second: "I think he is *but a knight*."

There was a rough masculine jocularity, now, to the gossip from court, as if the presence of a king had revivified a royal entourage which in Elizabeth's time had been careful to take its pleasures — especially its amours — in secret. Queen Elizabeth could swear like a guardsman; her conversation had a strong earthy flavor. Yet certain topics had been forbidden. They were not forbidden now. James enjoyed a quick answer, "with mirth and good conceits," he said. Lord Admiral Nottingham, hero of the Armada fight, nearing seventy but still handsome ("there was not a goodlier man for person in Europe"), danced with a young lady in waiting — James's cousin — married her at court and next morning fairly leaped to the King's chamber to boast of his exploits as a bridegroom. "All is well liked and the K. pleased," wrote Cecil. "But the next day," reported a second courtier, "the Lord Admiral was sick of the ague."

Yet amid the good times and easy rejoicing, a certain uneasiness began to show. Why did James remain in the country hunting? The plague could no longer be excuse. The Archbishop of York complained to Sir Robert Cecil of his Majesty's "immoderate exercise of hunting, and a wastening of the realm's treasure." To Cecil, such comment was "impertinent." Loyal subjects should find it a joy to behold a King "of so hale a constitution, promising long life and blessed with so plentifull a posterity, with no fears for the succession." Both letters came to the royal eye, as Cecil knew they would. "His Majesty," it was reported, "was merry as he read."

So much for exchange with an Archbishop. What Cecil said to his trusted friends carried a different ring. "Our Sovereign spends £100,000 yearly on his house, which was wont to be £50,000," he wrote to the Earl of Worcester. Elizabeth's godson, the witty and adventurous Sir John Harington, had retired from court and lived now on his country estate, chafing a little under the retirement. "Good Knight, reste content," Cecil wrote, "and give heed to one that hath sorrowed in the bright lustre of a courte and gone heavily even to the beste seeming fair grounde. 'Tis a great task to prove ones honesty and yet not spoil ones fortune. You have tasted a little hereof in our blessed Queen's time. I wishe I waited now in her presence-chamber with ease at my foode and rest in my bed. I am pushed from the shore of comfort and know not where the winds and waves of a court will bear me. . . ."

It was a weary note of prophecy. Upon Cecil, at forty-one, there fell now the burden of the realm. He was always overworked and frequently ill. With his tiny figure and crooked back he was no hero to the multitude, who looked on his habitual reserve as craftiness and could not forgive him for the death of Essex. "Backed like a lute-case," they chanted as he rode by:

> Backed like a lute-case,
> Bellied like a drum,
> Like Jack Anapes on horseback
> Sits little Robin Thumbe.

Word had it that Cecil depended much on Sir Edward Coke; "the Cecills are very inward with Mr. Atturney." These two knew the state as Elizabeth had left it — as she had, indeed, with her father and grandfather, created it. Coke and Cecil moreover were fervently Protestant; "of the old English temper," the French Ambassador remarked, "that is to say, enemies of France, not too friendly towards Spain." Both men were skilled parliamentarians. The government would have need of such; James had called a Parliament for March. On the front bench of St. Stephen's Chapel, Elizabeth had been careful to place at least eight from her Privy Council, men of prestige who kept order, reported if anything went wrong. Now there would be but two or three Privy Councilors in the entire Commons, and those of indifferent ability. Cecil, a lord, was exiled to the Upper House. Coke, as Attorney General, would be in and out of both Houses, but he would have no vote.

Elizabeth's great bishops were dying off when most needed; there was serious dissension within Protestant ranks. Archbishop Whitgift succumbed to a palsy shortly before the New Year — a prelate after the old style who had kept great state in his house, with five dozen man-servants martially trained and war horses in his stable. Dr. Thomas Cartwright, whom Coke had known at Cambridge, died at sixty, possessed still of the old fire and eloquence, yet so afflicted that he had been forced to study on his knees. It was necessary to reconcile growing Protestant differences; the Church was an integral part of government. The King called a conference at Hampton Court. Next to hunting the stag, James loved theological disputation; he remained buoyantly certain that if men would only meet and talk together, discord could be resolved. (He even suggested to the Pope a general conference of Protestants and Catholics, designed toward a unity in Christendom. His Holiness was not interested.)

It was James's hope that at Hampton Court, surpliced Bishop and irreconcilable Dissenter, under the leaven of the royal presence, would somehow fuse and be as one — or at least the Puritans might be persuaded to cease their loud complaining. James could not have been more mistaken. The Dissenter, Reynolds, staring at eight Bishops, gorgeous in their robes, demanded rudely why they wore these "Turkey gowns"? At first mention of the word "Presbyterian," James himself lost temper, having suffered much in Scotland from that faction. If Presbyters would not conform themselves, he would "harry them out of the land or do worse." Sir John Harington rode over from Kelston to see the fun and wrote to his wife about it. "The King talked muche Latin and disputed . . . he bid the petitioners away with their snivelling: moreover he wished those who would take away the surplice, might want linen for their own breech. The Bishops seemed much pleased and said his Majestie spoke by the power of inspiration. I wist not what they mean, but the spirit was rather foule-mouthed."

After four days the conference broke up. The Puritans departed angrier than they had come, nourishing seeds of bitter dissatisfaction. One important matter had been agreed on. The Bible was to be newly translated, "as little altered as the original will permit." Forty-seven scholars were assigned to the work, divided into six companies which would meet at intervals to compare. The public showed interest in every detail of the plan, pleased when their local ministers had a part. Dr. Layfield, parson of St. Clement Dane's, "being skilled in architecture, was much relied on for the fabric of the tabernacle and temple."

Parliament was to meet on the nineteenth of March (1604). On the twelfth, James came in from the country with Queen Anne and Prince Henry, a handsome boy of twelve. They lodged in the Tower. The Lieutenant led them on a little tour — jewels, mint, armory and ancient chapel. James's eye remained glassy, his spirit dim, until they reached the lion pit by the gates. Here the King sprang to life, inquired from whence came these noble creatures? Surely, England never bred such beasts! Edward Alleyne, Master of the Bear Garden, present for the occasion, said no, but England bred another beast of great courage. Between mastiff and lion in a pitched fight he would not put all his money on the lion.

Alleyne was ordered to fetch three of his best mastiffs from Southwark. James, Queen Anne, Prince Henry and four or five nobles watched as one by one the dogs were lowered and dragged across the pit, fought for their lives, bit the biggest lion in the belly until he roared and ramped. When two dogs lay dead the lions tired suddenly and slunk into their cave. The third mastiff, badly hurt, was saved. Prince Henry commanded Alleyne to keep him at the Garden "and make much of him, since he that had fought with the King of beasts should never after fight with any inferior creature."

It would be long before James enjoyed himself again in such royal fashion. Before him lay the ordeal of crowds, official greeting, a Parliament stubborn and factious. On March fifteenth, his triumphal entry began, with the City in a transport of delight, music all the way from London Bridge to Westminster Abbey and the conduits running claret wine. First in procession came the royal servants: Gentleman Ushers, Pursuivants at Arms, Clerks of the Privy Seal and Signet. Then the City Aldermen in scarlet gowns, their gold chains flashing. Sir Edward Coke, splendid in court dress, rode between his Solicitor General and Sir Francis Bacon. The Lords Chief Justices followed with the Masters in Chancery, behind them the King's trumpeters, who at each archway let fly in unison their high clear joyful blast.

James rode a white Spanish jennet. Over his head a canopy, held by eight knights, bobbed when the knights lost step. At Cornhill the first archway rose like a little castle, "so goodly, top and top many stories," the official narrator wrote with pardonable civic pride. Here the pageant commenced: odes, poems, songs, presentations designed to last until the monarch, bone-weary, saw the sun go down. At the first official stop, three hundred children from Christ's Hospital were ready with a poem. A block farther, there was a Latin Oration Gratulatory which lasted half an hour at the least. It closed not merely with the customary salutation to *Rex Angliae, Scotiae, et Hiberniae,* but with a phrase even more pleasing—words which James himself had sponsored, new and strange to English tongues: REX BRITANNIAE, King of all Britain!

At Paul's Church, one of Master Mulcaster's boys from the

Free School had his Latin speech by heart. "Sing, sing!" cried the chorus:

> And make Heav'n ring.
> Earth hath not such a King,
> O! this is he!

The Companies of Trade were glorious with banners and streamers. Mercers and Stationers, Vintners, Haberdashers, Goldsmiths marched rank on rank. The Merchant Strangers (described vaguely as Italians and Dutch) took a handsome part, with rich gifts to King and Queen. Figures dressed for allegory stepped forward, recited their flowery odes and retreated. St. Andrew and St. George, "in compleat armour" . . . Peace, Plenty, Gladness . . . Fame, in a sky-blue robe, embroidered with tongues and eyes, wings at her back, a trumpet in her hand . . . Vigilance, "her buskins ribanded." Justice, veiled and crowned with stars. Envy, "unhandsomely attired all in black, her hair of the same color filletted about with snakes and herself feeding on the heads of adders." Promptitude carried in her hands a squirrel, "as being the creature most full of life and quickness." The figure called *Genius Loci* turned out to be Master Alleyne of the Bear Garden, now part of the Prince's entourage. At every archway there was singing:

> Rumour, thou dost lose thine aims;
> This is not Jove but one as great, KING JAMES!

When the words did not make sense, the music did. To the populace everything was delightful; bells pealed all in tune; there was glory, holiday and sweet singing. By sundown even the newest apprentice boy could stagger home, happily drunk at the King's expense and confident for once that he would escape a beating.

CHAPTER NINETEEN

The Gunpowder Plot.

When these things shall be related to posterity, they will be reputed matters feigned, not done.

Coke, *opening the prosecution of Guy Fawkes*

They fall a-working in the vault. Dark the place, in the depth of earth; dark the time, in the dead of night; dark the design. O, how easy is any work, when high merit is conceived the wages thereof!

Thomas Fuller, *Church History of Britain*

JAMES had not been six months on the throne when his policy of leniency to Catholics ceased — a reaction caused partly by the plots of the priests Watson and Clarke and the notoriety of Ralegh's trial, partly by a startling increase in the activity of English Catholics, who boasted ten thousand new converts since the coronation. It was brought to the King's notice that this was no mere problem of doctrine or even of religious conscience (as James liked to think) but a question of sovereignty itself. Should Catholics increase as rapidly in the next few years, the "Pope's subjects" in England might outnumber loyal Englishmen.

In February, 1604, James issued a royal proclamation ordering all Romish priests to make their way, cross in hand, to the nearest port of embarkation and "abjure the realm." In May, Spanish commissioners arrived to discuss a treaty. Peace with Spain, James's dear ambition, meant for English Catholics an end to all secret help from Philip — no more invasion plans, no secret monies slipping across the Channel from the Archduke. Guy

Fawkes, crossing to Flanders, had the news firsthand from Don Velasco, High Constable of Castile. The agreement as drawn contained no mention of a toleration or any bargain concerning treatment of the English faithful. Don Velasco was to act as Commissioner for the signing. He would be happy, when he came to London, to put in his personal word of persuasion to King James. Beyond this, English Catholics must accept their fate as they found it.

In August, Don Velasco landed at Dover, bringing two hundred and thirty-four retainers and enough ice to keep his wine cool during final negotiations. For a Castilian grandee, life on this fog-bound island would be punishment; the English had no manners. (One heard they devoured raw fat to line their stomachs against the damp.) England, after all, was "but a hand's breadth of ground compared with the worlds possessed by his Catholic Majesty." On the night the treaty was signed, James gave a banquet and ball for Don Velasco, with all the gold plate in his treasury on display. Outside Whitehall Palace, bareback riders entertained the people. Tumblers danced on a rope and when the ball was over, fifty halberdiers with torches lighted the Spaniards homeward in their coach. James was delighted, all signs propitious. Even the lioness in the Tower whelped, a thing unheard of in northern latitudes. Queen Anne, much pleased at the turn things were taking, told Don Velasco of her wish that Prince Henry might marry the Infanta, Philip's eldest daughter. The Constable replied charmingly that his master would be most agreeable to the suggestion. Let Prince Henry proceed at once to Spain "to be educated as a Catholic."

This was too much even for James, who demanded if there were no end to the arrogance of Catholic princes? Yet it was gratifying to have concluded so difficult a negotiation, now at the opening of his reign. Sir Robert Cecil had had much to do with its success. The treaty was no sooner signed than he was rewarded with a viscountcy, and shortly afterward created Earl of Salisbury. Spanish pensions fell as rain in seedtime: for Cecil, a thousand pounds a year to keep King Philip informed should England alter her peaceful plans. The Earls of Dorset, Devonshire, Northhampton had like remuneration. Only one man refused — the Earl of Suffolk, knighted at sea in '88 for his services against the Armada.

In his Tower chamber, Ralegh heard it, who had been condemned for the mere listening to a Spanish bribe. Once more,

Spaniards walked openly on London streets as they had in Queen Mary Tudor's time. The people cursed them; a "Spanish peace" went sharp against the native grain. Castilian pockets were picked, one courtier lost a hat with jeweled buckle, snatched from his head as he leaned from a coach window. Count Aremberg returned as Minister. He was very lame and had an impediment in his speech. "The Archduke," said James, "has sent me an Ambassador who can neither walk nor talk. He hath demanded an audience of me in a garden because he cannot come upstairs."

Judges received instructions to enforce the laws against recusants. Two seminary priests were executed in Manchester for high treason. An old gentleman, Mr. Pound, protested by petition to James and was prosecuted in Star Chamber — Coke officiating — and punished with pillory, fine and imprisonment. Word went round that the Attorney General intended no mercy to papists: Sir Everard Digby wrote of "Mr. Attorney whose drift (as I have heard) is to prove that only being a Catholic is to be a traitor." In November the King called in the larger recusancy fines, remitted during the first months of his reign. English Catholics were to be scourged — they saw in it dread and anger — not with whips but with scorpions. On the eleventh of December, 1604, the Gunpowder conspirators assembled in London and went to work in earnest.

They were an extraordinary group: Catesby, Fawkes, Percy, Grant, Keyes, Wright, Winter. Seven gentlemen of fiery spirit and remarkable personal attractiveness, accomplished swordsmen, hawkers and hunters with estate and ancestry behind them, all young but Percy and every one a passionate religionist. Their plot was nothing less than a design to blow up the Parliament House on opening day, with King, Queen, Prince Henry, Lords and as many Commoners as happened to stand behind the bar. The motive — desperation, revenge, the fanatic hope of setting up a Catholic government in England and thereby recovering at once their fortunes and their religion.

Each of the seven men possessed a history of activity in the cause. Five had been "swaggerers in the Essex action," as their enemies later described it, buying pardon at cost of their estates; Robert Catesby forfeited the very manor house in which he lived. Guy Fawkes had served as soldier of fortune in the Archduke's army; in Europe he was known as *Guido*. Wright and Winter had traveled on various Catholic missions to Madrid; Thomas Percy carried messages to Edinburgh from his cousin the Earl of Northumberland, telling James (1602) it "were pity to lose so good a kingdom for not tolerating a Mass in a corner." Percy swore that James responded with promise of a toleration. But James, once safely crowned in London, denied it — denied indeed, every reminder of his twenty-year flirtation with Rome. "Na na," he said cheerfully, "we'll not need the Papists now."

It was Catesby who conceived the plan. Gunpowder attempts were not new; they had been tried on the Continent. King James's father, Lord Darnley, had been murdered in Scotland by explosion of gunpowder placed in a room beneath his bedchamber. Fawkes, from his military experience in Flanders, knew how to gauge the amount of ammunition needed. Directly abutting on the Parliament House — the Lords' Chamber — was a small house with a cellar from whence a mine might be dug and powder placed near the Chamber. Thomas Percy rented the dwelling without raising suspicion; as Gentleman Pensioner to the King he could say he needed a Westminster office. Fawkes, whose face was not known in London, assumed the name of John Johnson, Percy's servant, and took possession of the keys. Meeting at a priest's house behind Clement's Inn, the seven men made solemn promises of secrecy, kneeling, their hands on a missal, then partook of the Mass and received the Sacrament in confirmation of their vow.

Providing themselves with tools, a quantity of baked meats, hard eggs and pasties, the conspirators entered the rented house under cover of darkness. All day they dug and at night carried the earth and rubble to a little building in the garden. Fawkes stood sentinel. Shot and pistol were at hand; each man resolved to die rather than be taken. The gentlemen were amateurs with pick and shovel, the wall was nine feet thick. By the beginning of February they were only halfway through. Catesby and Percy, being tall, suffered from cramps in their legs. The work was halted by a variety of hazards. A bell tolled, the sound seemed to come from the wall itself. Fawkes was sent for; he listened, crossed himself, went out for holy water and sprinkled the stones. The tolling ceased until the first shovel touched earth, when the bell struck again. For several days it rang, muffled, awful, then was heard no more.

The men were digging toward the river. Water began to flow in, hindering the work and threatening to ruin the powder. At this point the conspirators received their first — perhaps their only — stroke of luck. The Lords' Chamber was on a second floor. Directly beneath it lay a vault which once had served as kitchen, a far better position for the powder than the cellar toward which the plotters were digging. A rushing, roaring noise was heard in this overhead kitchen; the men seized their weapons, certain they were discovered. But Fawkes, hurrying in, said it was only the noise of coals being moved; the proprietor was preparing to vacate the premises. By prompt action, Fawkes was able to rent the vault, saying that his master, Mr. Percy, needed it for coals and wood. This meant an end of digging. That night, the conspirators began to carry in the powder, twenty barrels, ferried across the river in hampers from Catesby's house at Lambeth. When it was placed, they laid stones and crowbars over it; the weight, said Fawkes, would make the explosion bigger. The whole was then hidden with a covering of faggots, billets of wood, empty bottles and such paraphernalia as is found in the cellars of occupied houses.

These preparations had consumed some five months. It was now May of 1605. When all was ready, Fawkes marked the door on the inside so they might know if it were opened in their absence. Parliament was to meet October third; it would not do for the conspirators to be seen about London. Fawkes crossed immediately to Flanders to seek the aid of prominent Catholic exiles: Sir William Stanley, Hugh Owen, Baldwin and others. Sir Edward Baynham, one of Catesby's friends, was sworn to secrecy and sent to Rome; after the explosion, some one must tell the Pope at first hand what had happened. In September, Fawkes returned, reporting his mission unsuccessful. Peace with Spain had blocked all help from the Continent.

The day approached. For the second time since the plot's conception came an announcement that Parliament was unexpectedly prorogued; it would not meet until November fifth. The conspirators were alarmed; there was a sinister note to these repeated delays. Was it possible the King's ministers suspected? Prorogation was a solemn ceremony, carried out by commissioners appointed. This time, the ceremony took place in the Lords' Chamber, directly over the vault. Thomas Winter, a retainer of one of the commissioners (Lord Monteagle) went upstairs as observer. He saw the Lords — Cecil, Suffolk and the rest — walk and talk as lightheartedly as if gunpowder had never been invented, much less stored in quantities beneath their feet.

This was reassuring; the conspirators took new heart. Catesby left London to raise troops in the midland counties, together with horses, arms, powder. The explosion would be only the beginning; a military force must be ready to follow it up. Catesby was a man of extraordinary charm, twenty-six years old, handsome, with a winning generosity of manner that held men to him in love and loyalty. He managed to enroll three hundred gentlemen volunteers, never revealing the plot but giving out that he was recruiting troops to fight in Flanders for the Catholic cause. A friend, Stephen Littleton, was given command of a company. Catesby invited them to Dunchurch in Warwickshire "for a hunting party in November." From here, when news came of the explosion, the plan was to lead the little army to nearby Coventry, where the Princess Elizabeth lived. Should Prince Henry have been killed by the powder and Prince Charles be unavailable, the Princess could be proclaimed Queen. This done, the conspirators were happily though vaguely confident that "some friends would appear," armed and ready to take their part.

The raising of even a small army, however, required funds. It became necessary — though patently dangerous — to bring new allies into the secret. Catesby selected three gentlemen of great fortunes who were either openly or secretly Catholic: Sir Everard Digby, Ambrose Rookwood and Francis Tresham. On first hearing the plot, Digby and Rookwood were horrified. What of the Catholic Lords in Parliament? Must these perish too, and was it not "a matter of conscience to take away so much blood?" The Church, Catesby replied, had said there were times when the innocent must suffer with the guilty. Their particular friends would be saved "by tricks put upon them." Tresham, the third new partner, was a cousin of Catesby and Winter, "a wild and unstay'd man," by general report, who seems not to have known a lie from the truth, but who had lately come into his inheritance and promised the conspirators two thousand pounds. Actually, he was to be the plot's undoing.

Twelve men were now in the secret: the seven original conspirators; three rich recruits, Robert Winter, Christopher Wright's brother John (a noted swordsman) and Catesby's servant, Bates, sworn into the plot because he knew too much. Somewhere along the way, Winter's brother-in-law, John Grant, had been included; also Robert Keyes, who lived as tutor in the house of Lord Mordaunt of Bedfordshire.

It was now autumn. Ten fresh barrels were brought to the cellar in case the old powder had been spoiled by damp. The new recruits remained doubtful, fearful. Tresham objected vigorously to the idea of blowing up his two brothers-in-law, the Lords Stourton and Monteagle. Robert Keyes could not bear to see his patron, Lord Mordaunt, killed. And Lord Montague, though not related to any of the plotters, was a valiant Catholic champion who had stood up in James's first Parliament and protested the bill against recusants. Must he die also? To these objections Catesby replied that the peers mentioned would not be present on opening day. He had himself spoken to Lord Montague. . . . And yet, added Catesby, "were they dear unto me as mine own son they should be blown up rather than the project should fail." Tresham remained moody, restless. Why not defer everything until the closing day of Parliament rather than opening day? At the moment, his money was unavailable. Why should they not all cross comfortably into Flanders and wait?

On the twenty-sixth of October, Tresham's brother-in-law, Lord Monteagle, ordered a supper prepared at his house in Hoxton, a suburb to the northeast of London. Though a Catholic and an ardent Essex supporter, Monteagle was by no means one of the conspirators. On the contrary he enjoyed high favor at court, having made his submission early in the reign, even writing James privately that he desired to turn Protestant. It was a Saturday when Monteagle's household gathered at Hoxton, just ten days before Parliament was due to open. As the peer sat at table, one of his pages brought a letter — handed to him, he said, in the street by a stranger. Monteagle, opening it, saw that it had neither signature nor date. He gave it to one of his gentlemen, bidding him read it aloud:

My Lord: Out of the love I bear to some of your friends, I have a care of your preservation. Therefore I would advise you as you tender your life, to devise some excuse to shift of your attendance at this Parliament; for God and man hath concurred to punish the wickedness of this time. And think not slightly of this advertisement but retire yourself into your country where you may expect the event in safety, for though there be no appearance of any stir, yet I say they shall receive a terrible blow this Parliament and yet they shall not see who hurts them. This counsel is not to be contemned because it may do you no good and can do you no harm, for the danger is past as soon as you have burnt the letter; and I hope God will give you grace to make good use of it, to whose holy protection I commend you.

It was mysterious, it said everything and nothing, it might be a hoax. Monteagle took the letter to Cecil at Whitehall. The King was at Royston, hunting; it was decided to make no move until his return. On Sunday, James read the letter. "I remember," he said, "that my father died by gunpowder." Yet he agreed with Cecil that nothing should be done for the moment. If this were a trick, the government must not appear to be frightened. If it were an actual conspiracy, then let the plotters draw the net tighter about themselves and bigger fish be caught. Parliament was to open on Tuesday, November 5. It was Monday the fourth before James dispatched his Lord Chamberlain to search the Parliament House. This would look natural enough, it being the Lord Chamberlain's business to make ready the Chamber. Lord Monteagle went along. Under pretext of hunting for missing tapestries, they searched first the Upper Chamber, then walked down to the cellar. At their knock, the door was opened by a tall man of soldierly bearing who said he was Johnson, servant to Mr. Thomas Percy, one of his Majesty's gentlemen pensioners, who had stored here a quantity of coals and faggots for winter use.

The two Councilors expressed themselves satisfied and retreated. At the name of Percy, however, Monteagle became suspicious. Thomas Percy was his cousin, the two lived on intimate terms, yet Percy had never mentioned owning a house in Westminster. All this coal and wood was enough for a full winter's use. The auburn-bearded servant, moreover, looked "a very tall and desperate fellow." Monteagle and Suffolk hurried to the palace and told the King what they had found. To avoid suspicion, James did not send the same two men back to Westminster but ordered a magistrate, Sir Thomas Knyvet, to make immediate search of houses and cellars in the neighborhood, under pretext of looking for tapestries missing since Queen Elizabeth's time.

It was close to midnight when Knyvet and his men reached the vault. At that moment, Fawkes approached, carrying a dark lantern with the light showing through. He was ordered to stand. Under the wood and coal, Knyvet found the powder and when Fawkes was searched, his pockets held bits of slow-match,* touchwood and a watch. They bound him hand and foot. Yes, Fawkes said bluntly. He had aimed to destroy the King and the Parliament. Had he been surprised in the cellar rather than outside the door he would "have blown up Sir Thomas Knyvet, the House and himself." Guards took him to Cecil's apartment at Whitehall. The King summoned such Councilors as slept at the palace; Fawkes was brought to the royal bedroom and questioned. He answered calmly, stuck to his story of being John Johnson, servant to Percy, declared again that had he not been taken he would have blown up King, Lords, Bishops and whoever was in the Upper House. What, he was asked, had he intended concerning the Queen's Majesty and her royal issue? He could not have helped them, Fawkes said; they must have perished with the rest. Who was in this conspiracy with him? He accused no one, Fawkes replied. James asked how a man could conspire against so many innocent souls. "A dangerous disease," said Fawkes, "required a desperate remedy." Moreover it had been his intent — Fawkes indicated the Scottish guard by the door — "to have blown *them* back again to Scotland."

A little before dawn, Fawkes was taken to the Tower.

Early that morning, London had the news. An attempt had been made to blow up the Parliament . . . Powder found under the floor in hogsheads . . . A man called Johnson caught at midnight with a dark lantern and matches, seven feet tall, red bearded, a hair shirt next to his skin. A Jesuit perhaps, his face unknown to any of the Council . . . A most blessed escape, due it was said (as the day wore on) to his Majesty's prescience and foresight when shown a mysterious letter. . . . A piece of the divine mercy manifested through England's new King . . .

That night the skies over London were red. So many bonfires had

* Slow-match was fuse; touchwood meant kindling. The watch also was damning; scarcely anyone carried a watch.

not been seen on one occasion. Bells pealed, shadowed figures leaped and capered before the flames. It was a wild ominous wintry rejoicing, spiced with an old and bitter anger. Who was behind this plot? Why had Beaumont, the French Ambassador, left England the very day before Fawkes was taken? Spanish gold! Peace or no peace, the man with the dark lantern was in King Philip's pay — one of the new foreigners who swaggered through the Strand in jeweled hats and high Castilian feathers. Don Velasco's man, or Aremberg's. Whoever he was, by the general opinion he should be torn to pieces, without benefit of trial. Had such a plot been discovered in Madrid, the perpetrators, if they were English, would have been set as living torches in some public arena. It was ironical, certainly, to see in front of the Spanish Ambassador's door the largest bonfire of all, built prudently at his Excellency's order, to show his happiness that Protestant lives were spared. . . .

Meanwhile, in his Tower chamber the man called John Johnson held out stoutly against his examiners: Coke, Cecil, Popham, Bacon, Waad, the Earl of Northampton, Lord Admiral Nottingham. The prisoner refused all names. "You would have me discover my friends?" he said. He had been captured on Tuesday. On Thursday he confessed that the conspiracy had been conceived eighteen months before and that the plotters intended to set Princess Elizabeth on the throne and marry her to an English Catholic. But still he gave no names. "This tough piece," they called him. "Dogged as if he were possessed," wrote Waad to Cecil after two days. "What foreign aid did you look for?" Coke asked him. "Was Edward Neville, titular Earl of Westmoreland, involved, and the titular Lord Dacre? How many of the nobility have you seen at Mass? After the act was done, would you have taken the Tower? What persons in the Tower were to partake of the Mass with you?"

On the ninth of November, Fawkes was told that his friends had all been killed or captured in Staffordshire the day before. "Then of what use to reveal their names?" Fawkes inquired reasonably. Some hours later he gave his real name and the names of the conspirators — always excepting the Jesuits and priests. His confession was signed with only one word, set down in faint uncertain letters . . . "*Guido* . . ." He fainted, Catholics said indignantly. Fainted before he could write his full name, exhausted from torture on the rack.

Actually, it was the manacles that Fawkes had suffered. James, accustomed to torture as part of the Scottish law, had shown no hesitancy. He sent a list of questions to the Tower, directing that should Fawkes refuse to answer, "the gentler tortures are to be first used unto him, *et sic per gradus ad ima tenditur* [and thus gradually extended to the most severe]. And so God speede youre goode worke!" The words, to later generations monstrous, met no disapproval in Privy Council; anger and fear can shift any balance. The Inquisition dungeons of Madrid — it was common knowledge — harbored a score of Englishmen whose only fault was Protestantism. And which of those poor wretches had been granted public trial, the opportunity to clear himself or even to see his friends?*

Coke had told the truth when he said that Fawkes's friends were captured. They had shown extraordinary foolhardiness, lingering in London an entire week after they knew they were betrayed, stubbornly determined to discover, before leaving town, which of their number had written the note of warning to Monteagle. Francis Tresham denied it with oaths and protestations. Only the sight of guards around Whitehall on the morning of the fifth had caused the last of the conspirators to take horse and ride swiftly northward to join the little army at Dunchurch. They arrived at midnight, gave the alarm and the crowd dispersed. Even now, Catesby did not despair. He rode westward with his friends, breaking open stables for fresh horses, knocking on doors, beseeching the country people to follow him. "For God and the country!" he cried. Yeomen and landlords turned away. "We are for God and the King," they said. In the end the conspirators all were taken, some by the hue and cry over the countryside, some by the Sheriff's posse, storming a house in which they were barricaded. The brothers Wright were killed, Thomas Winter and Rookwood badly hurt by arrows from a crossbow. Catesby and Percy, braced back to back against the assault, were hit by two bullets from one musket. Catesby fell, crawled to the Virgin's picture, took it in his arms and died. Percy lived only a few days.

* As instance, when Sir Robert Cecil's great-nephew, Lord Roos, was making the grand tour, his tutor, John Nolle, was taken in the streets of Rome by Inquisition officers and imprisoned. Thirty years later Nolle died in prison. During that time, only one friend saw him or was allowed communication. His offense had been the translation in English of Du Pleissis' book *The Visibility of the Church.*

Those who remained were taken to the Tower. Francis Tresham was not among them. He had not left London with the others but stayed on alone, discouraged with the enterprise and hoping to escape suspicion. But on the fifteenth of November, after questioning by the commissioners, he was committed to the Tower, where he at once fell very ill. *Poisoned!* said the Catholics. No, countered Sir Robert Cecil. Merely an old illness, "a natural sickness such as he hath long been subject to. . . . If any die in prison of sickness," Cecil added grimly, "they say he is starved or tortured to death; if any man kill himself, he is made away by us" — a species of Catholic fabrication which, said Cecil, hindered examination seriously, causing the government to resort to plot and subterfuge, contrived meetings of prisoners who talked without knowing they were observed. . . .

Neither Cecil nor Coke were grateful for the advice that poured in as to pretrial procedure. The Scottish Chancellor, Lord Dumfermline, recommended that the prisoners be kept apart from one another, in darkness, and "examined by torchlight with slow tortures applied at intervals, as being most effectual." Cecil wrote back without enthusiasm. He would not slacken in his duty, he said. From Paris, Dudley Carleton reported that people did not believe this Gunpowder Plot; France looked on it "as a fable." Even at home, doubts were expressed as to how much damage thirty-six hogsheads of gunpowder could actually do. A certain Lord Wilmot declared he had seen a like quantity of powder fired on a Dublin wharf; because the vault below Parliament House had been narrow, the wood and stones heavy on the powder, the explosion would have wrecked the building and "wrought dire effects upon the City itself."

The more distinguished (and richer) of the Tower prisoners bombarded Cecil with appeals, letters, bargains for their freedom. Sir Everard Digby would undertake to secure the Pope's promise not to excommunicate King James, providing his Majesty would promise to deal mildly with Catholics in future. Lord Northumberland swore innocency. His cousin Thomas Percy, he said, had stolen four thousand pounds from him for this conspiracy, not to speak of horses and armor. He prayed leniency. Lady Griffin Markham, herself a Catholic, offered information against the Jesuits in return for the freedom of her husband, condemned at

Winchester with Cobham. Ben Jonson told Cecil he was sure "five hundred were enweaved"; he would be happy to help in the pursuit. Ralegh was suspected, the Privy Council called Lady Ralegh for questioning. *The rebels*, people called the plotters now; *the insurgents*. It was thought the number had increased. Suffolk ports were guarded to prevent escapes. Lists were drawn of recusants indicted during the past year; the total came to nearly two thousand. King James was unhappy, disliking the notion that such a plot could be conceived in his glorious new reign. Had he not been received into the kingdom with joy, music, flowers, gifts, all the way from Berwick-upon-Tweed?* He wished it shown, if possible, that this Powder plot had its inception in Elizabeth's reign, not his own. The facts bore it out — the long correspondence between Catholics at home and Catholics in exile, as Hugh Owen in Flanders, Baldwin, Sir William Stanley, Father Parsons and the rest.

Christmas approached and people asked why the trials were so long delayed. Surely, the government did not lack evidence? The heads of Catesby and Percy, already set on spikes above the city, were in themselves a kind of awful evidence.† All the prisoners had confessed when confronted with each other's testimony, though at first they denied everything. Their solemn vows of secrecy, taken on the Sacrament, left them no other course, they said. But the government aimed higher and wider than the mere destruction of eight wild young religionists. Somewhere were master minds; neither Coke nor Cecil doubted they were Jesuit. The Fathers Gerard, Greenway, Garnett, were known to be living in England. "An old priest," Coke said, "may easily be found out. But these young priests in feathers and fashions infect all with whom they converse." If the Jesuits could be captured, exposed and the trials rightly conducted — this recusant trouble, these plots and rebellions

* James loved to dwell on this. "Shall it ever be blotted out of my mind," he told Parliament (1604), "how at my first entry into this Kingdom, the people of all sorts rid and ran, nay rather flew to meet me? their eyes flaming nothing but sparkles of affection, their mouths and tongues uttering nothing but sounds of joy, their hands, feet and all the rest of their members in their gestures discovering a passionate longing and earnestness to meet and embrace their new Sovereign."

† The Salisbury Papers contain a bill to the government "for iron work for the setting up of the heads of the two traitors, Thomas Percy and Robert Catesby, 23 shillings sixpence, which was expended by the smith that made the iron work."

could be ended once for all. Harm had been done by James's early leniency; it should be canceled out. The thousands of new Catholic converts must be forced back into obscurity and silence.

Yet the prisoners, who seemed ready to confess every detail concerning the mining and powder, continued to shut up tight when the word "priest" was mentioned. Thomas Winter's servant, Bates, finally acknowledged he had told Father Greenway of the plot in the Catholic confessional. Tresham too admitted it, implicating Garnett as well. But Tresham was mortally ill. Before his death in the Tower he dictated to his clerk, Vavasour, a flat denial. No priest had been told of the conspiracy, either in the confessional or out of it. "The King is in terror," the Venetian Ambassador wrote home. "He does not appear nor does he take his meals in public as usual. He lives in the innermost rooms, with only Scotchmen about him."

Sir William Waad was beside himself. What should he do with Tresham's body? he demanded of Cecil. The man's relatives claimed it for honorable burial, notwithstanding it was so rotted with disease it could hardly be approached. (This was not the first enemy of the state to be described as giving off, after death, a scandalous odor of the French pox.) Catholics heard that the body was decapitated, the head taken to Northampton to be set over the town gates near the family estate. Without a trial! they said indignantly. Without so much as formal indictment, this poor body punished. "O pitifull and tragicall intendment!" wrote Garnett's friend, the Catholic Lady Vaux.

At last, toward the end of January (1606) the government reported the capture of LittleJohn, the famous carpenter who had built so many Catholic hiding places. Father Oldcorne's servant was taken with him. Shortly afterward, the searchers had word that Oldcorne himself was hidden at Hindlip House.

Meanwhile, on January twenty-first, Parliament convened, thereby — from the government point of view — at once magnifying the problem. With every move concerning the plotters, Parliament must be taken into account. The conduct of the trials would have immediate effect on legislation. Those with ambition to push anti-Catholic laws through both Houses saw this as the time of times, Catholic peers being vulnerable because of possible implication in the plot, the Lower House favorably disposed by what they chose to look on as the common danger. There must be no delay; Coke and Cecil, skilled parliamentarians, knew how rapidly the temper of such assemblies can shift. In July of 1604, King and Parliament had parted in mutual anger and suspicion after a stubborn battle concerning privileges, religion, matters of revenue and the royal plan of union with Scotland. ("By what laws," Bacon demanded, "shall this 'Britain' be governed?") In the end, James had come down to Westminster and scolded the Commons like an old Scottish uncle. In Edinburgh, he said indignantly, parliaments had heard him "not only as a king but as a counselor. Contrary, here, nothing but curiosity from morning to evening to find fault with my propositions. There, all things warranted that came from me. Here, all things suspected!"

The Gunpowder Plot acted as instantaneous leaven, a quick dissolver of differences. Between James and his Commons a love feast was immediately in progress. On the famous Fifth of November the King came to Westminster and addressed both Houses in a jovial, fatherly talk before proroguing them until January. One thing at least he thanked God for, he said. Had this horrible attempt succeeded—"this roaring thundering sin of fire and brimstone, it should never have been spoken nor written in ages succeeding that I had died ingloriously in an ale house, a stews or such vile place. But mine end should have been with the most honourable and best company . . . and fittest place for a King to be in!" In France, it was remarked that gunpowder attempts can be convenient to princes. When Parliament met in January, the Earl of Shrewsbury wrote from London to Sir Thomas Edmondes, Ambassador at Paris: "The Commons of the Lower House, where yourself was wont to be placed amongst the mutineers, are much more temperate than they were at the first session, and now spend all their spirits and endeavors in devising laws tending to his Majesty's safety, and suppressing of the dangerous members of this state. I heard not of any one transcendent speech uttered amongst them as yet."

The Earl did not exaggerate. On its second meeting, the Lower House proposed a bill to make November Fifth a day of sacred thanksgiving forever, followed by a bill requiring all persons passing overseas to take the Oath of Supremacy. Two thousand young men, the Speaker said, had left England last year to fight for the Archduke in Flanders or to aid the Catholic cause in other ways. Next came a bill "for the better preserving his Majesty from danger" (always a convenient phrase for drawing the lines together). After that, a bill "for the more expedient execution of the laws against recusants."

All this in the first four days of sitting. Eight conspirators were to be tried by special commission on January twenty-seventh, a Monday. The Lower House arranged an adjournment for the day. Before they rose a petition was proposed, requesting his Majesty, after the trial, to stay judgment until Parliament might devise some "extraordinary punishment," harsher than was usually accorded to traitors. "A more sharp death," the words were. Scripture, said a member, held examples of extraordinary punishments for extraordinary acts. In Henry VIII's time, poisoners had been boiled alive by act of Parliament. Surely, this Powder Plot was worse than poisoning, worse than any treason attempted in the realm, even though nothing, by God's grace, had come of it!

The bill was defeated. Yet its very proposal gave indication of the ferocity with which the plotters were looked on — indication also of the time-honored propensity of legislators to proclaim their loyalty and save their skins by flaying alive the nearest vulnerable neighbor.

CHAPTER TWENTY

Trial and death of the conspirators. Father Garnett. "Two religions cannot stand together."

THE public came to Westminster Hall looking for a spectacle. There was little doubt of the outcome. But it remained to be seen if Attorney General Coke would lash out as he had at Essex and Ralegh or content himself with recital of the facts, which in themselves carried drama enough, without expletive or suggestion. Catholics who dared to mingle in the throng could pray only that the prisoners might bear themselves with dignity, confess their religion in courage and hold fast to the end.

Eight prisoners stood in the dock. They had been brought from the Tower by barge and held in Star Chamber until the court was seated: Fawkes, Keyes, Bates, Grant, Thomas and Robert Winter, Ambrose Rookwood and Sir Everard Digby, who was to be tried separately at the end of the day. King James was said to be somewhere within hearing — behind the judges' dais, very likely, whence Sir Robert Cecil had issued suddenly during the trial of Essex. The commission for tiral consisted of six earls (Cecil among them) and three judges: Sir John Popham (Chief Justice of King's Bench), Sir Thomas Fleming of Exchequer and Sir Peter Warburton of Common Pleas. The Commons arrived in force, hurrying down the broad stairs from St. Stephen's to a private tier of seats set up by the Fleet Warden, who took occasion to reap a tidy sum for places. The Commons looked on this affair as very much their business. The King, indeed, had delayed the date of trial so as to coincide with their assembly.

English Catholics understood the calamity that had befallen them

— trapped suddenly in awful representation by a handful of wild young gentlemen who had imagined that with forty barrels of gunpowder they could change a world. Of these eight conspirators, not one had looked for personal advancement; there had been no previous naming of Sir Everard Digby as Lord Treasurer of England, Guy Fawkes as Captain of the palace Guard. Their intent, mad and murderous though it was, had aimed at something quite nearly selfless — or at any rate they so persuaded themselves. Catesby's sword and Digby's (the story circulated) were engraved with Christ's death and passion.* No drop of blood had been shed beyond the plotters' own. Yet the noise of this conspiracy — English Catholics knew it in dread and sorrow — would retard their cause by years if not by centuries, making a toleration impossible.

To Coke, ready with his evidence, the picture was very different. English Catholics? For how many years the phrase had been a contradiction in terms! Incredible, that he must expose this fallacy once again in a public courtroom: *a man is not English who gives first allegiance elsewhere.* It was a conflict of loyalties which had troubled the realm since the time of Henry VIII. And now in a hopeful new century it had caught and all but trapped King James. Surely this was the climacteric, the end? All violence has its peak and the Powder Plot had been so extreme as to be well-nigh incredible. Coke, wrapped in his dark woolen robe, waited on the lawyers' bench. In five years, this was the third great treason trial in which he had been prosecutor. The opening ritual was impressive: the slow procession of lords commissioners and judges, the solemn seating and congees, the delivery of mace and white wand. But it took up time. The reading of the indictment alone consumed a good half hour, with its sonorous legal repetitions.

> . . . traitorously amongst themselves did conclude and agree with gunpowder, as it were with one blast, suddenly, traitorously and barbarously to blow up and tear in pieces . . . most barbarously and more than beastly to destroy and swallow up . . . And secretly, did dig and make the said mine, with a traitorous intent to bestow and place a great quantity of gunpowder in the mine aforesaid, so as aforesaid traitorously to

* The declaration of Cradock, the cutler who did the work, can be seen in the Public Record Office.

be made for the traitorous accomplishing of their traitorous purposes aforesaid. . . .

If proof consisted of a repetition of adjectives, the trial need go no further: the word "traitorous" pounded through the chamber. But when the Clerk had done his reading and asked each prisoner how he pleaded, all but Digby replied, *Not guilty*, and in the ancient phrasing, "put himself upon God and his country." Chief Justice Popham inquired of Fawkes how he in particular could so plead, having been actually taken in the cellar with the powder and never before denying the fact? Because of certain conferences mentioned, Fawkes said, of which he knew nothing and in which he had not taken part.

Actually, it was these conferences in which the government was most of all interested — earlier meetings in Spain, Rome, Brussels, undertaken by Thomas Winter, Catesby, Fawkes. The mining in the cellar, the desperate wild hazard by young men foolish and fanatic was but one more manifestation of a plan far grander which had shown itself in various guises: the Duke of Norfolk's plot in 1570, Dr. Lopez's plot, Squire's plot, the Bye, the Main; Essex, Ralegh, Cobham, the priests Watson and Clarke. Coke's intention was to expose this long relationship, publish it to the world once and forever. "The eye of all Christendom," Coke said as he began, "is bent upon the carriage and event of this great cause." And if Ralegh's trial had been hindered by Cobham's retractations (as also by Sir Walter's extraordinary eloquence in the dock), no such "hindrance" was looked for today. Every prisoner had confessed. The confessions agreed, there had been no retractions beyond Tresham's deathbed statement — Coke called it Tresham's *equivocation* — concerning the innocence of Father Garnett.

There was however a new problem, not a little embarrassing to the prosecution. Spain could no longer act as public whipping boy. England was at peace. There must be no talk of "Spanish hearts," of connivance by midnight with an Aremberg or the creatures of Madrid and the Archdukes. Coke, who hated Spain with every drop of his uncompromising Norfolk blood, met this point at the outset with a blunt dismissal, as if he had learned it by rote. No foreign prince was on trial today, he said; only Englishmen. A King of Spain, it was true, had listened to certain plans of invasion proposed by

Thomas Winter. But the two nations had then been at war, and "whilst kingdoms stand in hostility, hostile actions are holden honourable and just."

With this point settled and perhaps an hour of his time already gone, Coke made no effort to present his eight cases separately but simply lumped them together, laid the plot's initial conception flat on the doorstep of the Jesuit order, where the indictment had said it belonged — and loosed his blast. His denunciation, hot and passionate, in essence was not so much Protestant as political. Patently, he wished to distinguish Catholic religious faith from Catholic international policy and to prove that in England, men were never executed for religion alone — only for their attempts against the state. "In Queen Mary's time," said Coke, "there were cruelly put to death about three hundred persons for religion, but in all her late Majesty's [Elizabeth's] time, not thirty priests nor above five receivers and harborers of them, and for religion not any one!"

There is no doubt that Coke believed it, and that every Catholic in the audience called it a lie. Actually, the distinction between religion and politics was impossible, a fact which for Catholics was infinitely tragic. Time had been, Coke said, when Roman bishops themselves were martyrs. "But now the Popes are become temporal princes, they seek supremacy upon earth. . . . Heresy, say the Jesuits, is a leprosy, an hereditary disease, and of leprous parents come leprous children, so that sons also must be driven from the succession. With a goose-quill the Jesuits think to remove the crown from the head of any king christened; with the wings of their light-feathered distinctions they imagine to mount above the clouds!"

Books containing Jesuit doctrines had been found in Tresham's rooms at the Temple. Thomas Winter's friend in Spain, Father Cresswell, had written a like tract, called *Philopater*. In rolling Latin, Coke quoted from these and other Jesuit works, then lapsed suddenly into plain vernacular. Did his auditory know that gunpowder had been invented "by a friar, one of the Romish rabble?" (Here the Attorney General stood on solid ground. Roger Bacon, dead in 1294, was indeed a Franciscan monk whose share in the invention of gunpowder has not been disproved.) Moreover, Coke went on, "there never was any Protestant minister in any treason and murder yet attempted within this realm!" Coke did not pause to prove his point but swept on, making use of any and all ammunition that came to hand. "And here," wrote Hawarde the reporter, "Mr. Atturney told a prettie tale of a fable of a Catte." Putting on a priest's habit — Coke said — a cat shaved his head and addressed the mice "formally and fatherlike; 'O brothers I am no more a cat — *non sum quod fui sed tonsum, frater!* See my habit and shaven crown!' To which the mice replied, 'Talk what you can, you have still a cat's heart within you. You do not watch and pray, but you watch to *prey!*' "

There was a raucous note to Coke's speeches as prosecutor, which the judges in former trials had deplored. "A levity," they called it. Edward Coke was an advocate. And it is the advocate's nature, once he sniffs the courtroom air, to use any and everything the jury can comprehend, from Scripture to bad puns. Judges and commissioners, whatever they thought of Coke's performance, did not interrupt but let the strong voice roll on. This was a trial upon which the government had seized as a forum to expose "false doctrines" — not the first such occasion in history nor the last. Coke was effectual, he reached the crowd. And reaching the crowd, today, was of grave importance to the state; not a judge or commissioner present but would have agreed. Continuing, Coke spent little time upon the actual Powder Plot. His audience knew it by heart and besides, the indictment had given it in detail. What the prosecution stressed was the confessed aim of the conspirators: "to breed a confusion fit to beget new alterations" — Thomas Winter's words, from his signed declaration. And because it was in Parliament (said the plotters) that unjust laws had been made against Catholics, they had chosen the Parliament House as "fittest place to revenge and do justice in. Gunpowder law!" said Coke. "Fit for justices of hell, executed by 'Justice' Faux, a man like enough to do according to his name!" And the means for accomplishing these designs? "Most cruel and damnable, by mining and by thirty-six barrels of powder, having crows of iron, stones and wood laid upon the barrels to have made the breach the greater . . . Lord!" said Coke, "what a wind, what a fire, what a motion and commotion of earth and air would there have been! *Horret animus*, I tremble even to think of it! O barbarous and more than Scythian or Thracian cruelty!" This powder treason of the Jesuits, like Ralegh's treason and the treason of the priests Watson and Clarke, had one aim and end. "I say not that we have any proofs that these of the Powder Plot were acquainted with Ralegh, or Ralegh with them. But as before was spoken of the Jesuits and priests, they all were joined in the ends like Samson's foxes in the tails, howsoever severed in their heads."

Orators, once they light on a telling simile, never spare it; this was the fourth time that Coke had brought up Samson's foxes. He now ordered the Clerk to produce the prisoners' confessions, show them to the defendants for verification, then read them aloud "openly and distinctly," as affording truer proof of guilt than anything that could be said from the floor. But first, said Coke, he thought well to review the punishment provided for high treason. The law did not give such penalty capriciously; behind each part of it lay ancient symbolic meaning.

The recital which followed was to be quoted and repeated for centuries, as long as the traitors' penalty remained in use. Coke began by explaining that King James, with "admirable clemency and moderation," would not "exceed the usual punishment of law nor invent any new torture or torment." Though this treason had exceeded all others, his Majesty was "graciously pleased to afford as well an ordinary course of trial as an ordinary punishment, much inferior to their offence."

It would seem plain, from this preface, that Coke addressed his recital not so much to audience or jury as to the Parliament benches, where sat, as Coke well knew, those who had urged and might urge tomorrow "a more sharp death" for the plotters. Suggestions had poured into the Commons: Let the traitors "be quick wrapped up alive in lead, with their arms spread abroad, and set upon the highest pinnacle in every city and port town in England, and let them there starve to death." A pair of gallows should be built in every churchyard "and all Papists and wilful recusants be hanged there. Too much pity ever overthrows town and city, which pity good Queen Elizabeth never used as it is feared King James will do so too."

Coke's symbolic explanation, as given in court, was shocking enough to quiet the most vengeful Puritan on the Parliament benches. "After a traitor hath had his just trial," Coke began, "and is convicted and attainted, he shall have his judgment: To be drawn to the place of execution from his prison, as being not worthy any more to tread upon the face of earth whereof he was made. Also, for that he hath been retrograde to nature, therefore is he drawn backward at a horse-tail. And whereas God hath made the head of man the highest and most supreme part, as being his chief grace and ornament, he must be drawn with his head declining downward and lying so near the ground as may be, being thought unfit to take benefit of the common air. For which cause also he shall be strangled, being hanged up by the neck between heaven and earth as deemed unworthy of both or either; as likewise, that the eyes of men may behold and their hearts contemn him. Then is he to be cut down alive, and to have his privy parts cut off and burnt before his face as being unworthily begotten and unfit to leave any generation after him. His bowels and inlay'd parts taken out and burnt, who inwardly had conceived and harbored such horrible treason. After, to have his head cut off, which had imagined the mischief. And lastly, his body to be quartered and the quarters set up in some high and eminent place, to the view and detestation of men, and to become a prey for the fowls of the air.

"And this," finished Coke in a last burst of Old Testament savagery (which may well have saved the prisoners from even worse torments) "is a reward due to traitors whose hearts be hardened. For it is a physic of state and government to let out our corrupt blood from the heart." *

The prisoners' declarations followed, read aloud by the Clerk. They were long and full and, after what had gone before, seemed doubly damning, pieced together as was customary, to give the prosecution's argument in the best light. The defendants, wrote Hawarde, "said little for themselves, but what they did was out of their love to their friend Catesby and the good of the Catholic cause." The jury brought in seven convictions. Sir Everard Digby pleaded guilty and was condemned on his own confession — of all the conspirators, the only one reported as daring to state in open courtroom that the Powder Plot stemmed from communal despair at the King's "broken promises."

On January thirtieth, four days after the trial, Bates, John Grant, Robert Winter and Sir Everard Digby were drawn on single sledges to a scaffold set up in St. Paul's Churchyard. The streets were lined with a shouting, jeering populace. At alternate door-

* Chapter Note.

ways stood a sentry, halberd up. The condemned men died bravely. Bates alone "seemed sorry for his offence and asked forgiveness of God and the whole kingdom." Next day, a Friday, Guy Fawkes, Thomas Winter, Ambrose Rookwood and Robert Keyes were taken on the same slow journey — this time through the length of the City and suburbs of Westminster. A high scaffold had been erected in Old Palace Yard, directly facing the Parliament House, under which the mine had been dug. Thomas Winter, first to go, told the crowd he died a true Catholic, made his Latin prayers and crossed himself as the hangman swung him off. Ambrose Rookwood, standing at the edge of the platform, confessed his sin in seeking to shed blood, begged forgiveness of the whole state and had nearly won the crowd to sympathy when he suddenly "marred all," says the witness, "by praying God to make King James a Catholic." The hangman, thrusting him off the ladder, cut him down almost immediately and drew him to the block. Thomas Keyes, having stood to witness all this and knowing his turn was next, said a few abrupt words to the crowd, sprang up the ladder and off with such a leap that he broke the rope. Amid roars from the crowd he fell alive to the ground — "and after," says the reporter, "was drawn to the block and there quickly divided into four parts. . . . Last came the great devil of all, Fawkes, *alias* Johnson, who should have put fire to the powder. His body being weak with torture and sickness, he was scarce able to go up the ladder, but yet with much ado, by the help of the hangman, went high enough to break his neck with the fall; who made no long speech, but seeming to be sorry for his offence, asked a kind of forgiveness of the King and the state for his bloody intent; and with his crosses and idle ceremonies, made his end upon the gallows and the block."

The bloodshed and horror of these eight executions by no means closed the problem for the government. Immediately, official bulletins went out, describing the behavior of the condemned men on the scaffold, insisting upon their "fears and prayers for forgiveness," their "gratitude" for his Majesty's "mercy" in not meting out "worse punishment." In reality, nothing could conceal the fact that of fourteen Powder plotters, eleven had died in public acknowledgment of their religion, using the sign of the cross on breast and forehead and praying only that their attempt had not harmed the

Catholic cause. No Jesuit had been captured, though proclamations offering reward for the persons of Garnett, Gerard, Greenway were posted in London and "all the market towns." At the trial, the indictment had opened with these three names, accusing them of initial responsibility for the plot:

> Henry Garnett, Clerk, of the profession of Jesuits: Greenway (alias Tesmond) and John Gerard . . . falsely and traitorously persuaded the said Guy Fawkes, &c . . .

It had been Coke's care to prove the truth of this indictment, together with the primary guilt of English Jesuits on the Continent and at home. Yet here it was the end of January and not a Jesuit had been brought to court. Father Gerard was probably in Flanders. Father Greenway had been seized in London while reading a proclamation containing his description, walked quietly with his captor — and at the first empty alleyway, shook himself free and fled. Sir William Stanley, Hugh Owen, the Fathers Parsons, Cresswell and the rest were eating their dinners comfortably in Brussels, Rome, Madrid. People had begun to ask if Jesuits, after all, had been concerned with this plot. And if so, why did not the Attorney General produce one?

The authorities, meanwhile, were still searching Hindlip House, where LittleJohn, the Catholic carpenter, had been captured a week before the trial. Finally, Garnett was caught with his humbler friend, Father Oldcorne, the household chaplain. For twelve days the two had crouched in a secret compartment behind the chimney. They emerged looking like ghosts; the man who found them ran away in terror. Garnett's legs were swollen, he could scarcely stand. They had been fed, they said, by soup poured down a reed through the wall. Garnett, a genial, easy-tempered man who loved his wine second only to his religion, declared the two had been "very merry and content within and heard the searchers every day most curious over us. If we had had but one half-day liberty to come forth, we had so eased the place from books and furniture that we could have abidden a quarter of a year."

The prisoners were taken by easy stages to London — "passing well used," Garnett told a friend, dining with their hosts on the way, drinking the King's health in what Garnett described as "a reasonable glass." On Candlemas Eve (February second) they dined at Worcester in the house of Sir Henry Bromley the magistrate. With the wine there was brought in a fat wax candle, taken at Hindlip and decorated with pictures of Jesus and Mary. Garnett rose, took the candle in his hands, walked down the table and gave it to Father Oldcorne, remarking that he was happy to have carried, after all, a holy candle on Candlemas Day.

Garnett was head of the Jesuit order in England; he was known as the English Provincial. People seemed to like him at sight. "Very judicious," they said of him, "a nice, understanding man." He showed none of the proud impatience of Father Gerard. The authorities had done all they could to make Garnett odious, yet when he passed through London after his capture there was no violence. The Jesuit himself seemed diverted by the stir that he created: "A great multitude surrounded me. One said, 'There goes a Provincial'; another, 'There goeth a young Pope.' "

Toward this important prisoner, Coke by no means shared the prevailing easy temper. For two months he journeyed to the Tower at intervals, interrogating the Jesuit in his cell. Garnett showed no defiance. He merely assented, everlastingly assented, then backed and filled, retracted and slipped sideways. He seemed to have unlimited friends, sent letters out of prison written invisibly in lemon juice or sack and when the notes were intercepted, complained that his jailers had dealt dishonestly with him.

What the government must now obtain was full acknowledgment of Jesuit implication in the plot. Bates's admission was not enough. To convict a priest on information obtained under seal of the confessional would be to outrage the entire Catholic Continental world. Catesby had acknowledged, though vaguely, certain lay conferences with the priests. Tresham had stated definitely that he had talked with Greenway — and then, dying, denied it.

Garnett, confident, admitted nothing: no Jesuit had known of the Powder Plot either before or after November fifth. Altogether, nearly five hundred depositions had been taken; none of them served the purpose. This Jesuit in his mild way matched even Father Gerard in the art of equivocation — a word which turned Coke's lawyer's soul to dust. In the end the government resorted to its own equivocation — told Garnett that Father Greenway had been captured in London and had confessed everything, then moved

Garnett and Oldcorne to adjoining cells with a door that could be opened. Agents, conveniently placed, took down what they heard.

The results were immediate, though Garnett at first denied having talked with Oldcorne at all. But when the transcript was read back to him, he acknowledged that he had concealed the truth and that "it was a sin unless equivocation saved him." Sir Robert Cecil, remarking on this sudden capitulation, said it had been achieved by pampering and flattering, "seeing that we dare not proceed against them by such meanes as they do in other countries to get out the truth." *Such means* meant, of course, torture. Cecil too seems to have shared the proud illusion that torture was not used in England, though all London knew that Fawkes was so crippled from the rack he could not climb his own scaffold, knew also that Father Oldcorne's servant, LittleJohn, had killed himself in his cell rather than face a second day of hanging by his thumbs.

Garnett came to his trial on March twenty-eighth at the Guildhall, a place much smaller than Westminster but filled with color and gold leaf, hung about with banners of the companies of trade. The Jesuit pleaded *Not guilty*. Upon Garnett's challenging one of the panel — a London merchant — the juryman stepped down. In Coke's green bag or somewhere about his lawyer's person was a note from Cecil, received that morning, reminding him to make plain that this plot had had its inception in Queen Elizabeth's time, "before his Majesty's face was seen or he had done anything in government." Cecil went into some detail. Coke must be sure to mention the Catholic exiles in Flanders and their complicity. "Remember to lay Hugh Owen as foul in this as you can." And, Cecil added tactfully, he troubled Coke with the suggestions only because he had been "so directed" by the King.

Actually, there was nothing more dishonest in these instructions than was (or is) common practice in state trials for treason. James had urged no points for which the government did not possess what it considered full evidence. Coke, rising when his turn came, directed the jury to look on this trial "as but a latter act of that heavy and woeful tragedy, the Powder Treason." He had heard complaints of the long delay between Garnett's capture and trial. It was even said about town that "no Jesuits or churchmen were privy to this treason and that king-killing and queen-killing was no doctrine of theirs, but only a fiction and policy of state to make the Popish religion despised and in disgrace!"

It was this point which concerned Coke most of all; three quarters of his speech was in rebuttal of it. Garnett, said Coke, had been no actual executor in the plot but "author and procurer," an agent for papal ambitions. The prisoner himself was "a grave and learned person. I will force myself," Coke added surprisingly, "to deal mildly with him." Taking his audience back to 1570, Coke reviewed the papal bull excommunicating Elizabeth, described the arrival of the first Jesuits in the '70's, "purposely to make a party in England for the Catholic cause." Yet not until '85 did Parliament pass an act prohibiting the coming of any Romish priest to England. Despite this law Garnett himself landed two years later, "breaking through the brassy wall of treason, being the year 1586 when the great navy of Spain was collecting, which the Pope blessed and christened by the name of 'The Invincible Armada.' "

It was a disquisition on English history and the Protestant Reformation which Coke was well equipped to tell, having lived it, been part of it since his boyhood in Norwich Free School. He had seen the stone saints lying broken before their cathedral pedestals, had said Genevan prayers in English with the carnery floor cold beneath his knees in the morning dark. Coke had been a scholar at Cambridge when the papal bull arrived; he remembered ugly riots, a burning of books and relics. . . . *The Invincible Armada!* Not three months after the defeat, Coke had heard Elizabeth pronounce the words in Parliament with all the ringing scorn of triumph; he would never be able to repeat the phrase without emotion. From that day and time, Coke added, "in this land there never passed four years without a most pestilent and pernicious treason, tending to the subversion of the whole state." Coke again described the attempts, from Dr. Lopez in '93, Williams, Yorke, Squire, down to "Sir Walter Ralegh and others." With each incident, Coke gave contemporary Continental policy which had served to incite or aggravate the affair: Pope Clement's breve of 1601 which bade English Catholics, should "that miserable woman die," place no heretic upon the throne. But "all the letters and bulls and their calves also," said Coke, "were overthrown and subdued by those four noble and magnanimous lions, firmly and individually united" in the person and lineage of his Majesty King James the First.

Coke must have talked four hours at the least, ranging over times and deeds with which the prisoner in the dock could not possibly have been implicated. Yet for the prosecution, no word was beside the point. It was in the tradition of political trials past and future. The direction and meaning were plain, the bias unescapable; Coke was a man of his time and place. "In the year 1603," he said, arriving finally at the matter in hand, "her Majesty, that morning star, lost her natural light." At that moment the Powder plotters began their wicked machinations, "before they had seen his Majesty's face."

It was Cecil's instructions to the letter. From here the story proceeded as at Fawkes's trial, but better rehearsed, more consecutive and very easy to follow. Had Coke used a map and pointer he could not indeed have made himself clearer as to times, places, names, the plot's development. Much was made of the assumed names under which Garnett moved about the country, "alias Wally, Darcy, Roberts, Farmer, Phillips. . . . And has any true man," Coke demanded, "commonly been observed that hath so many false appellations?" Once again Coke endeavored to demolish the Jesuit defense of equivocation, "by which," he said indignantly, "it is maintained lawful and justifiable to express one part of a man's mind and retain another. God help us! For then shall all conversation, all trading, all trials by juries be useless and mischievous. The law and sanction of Nature hath as it were married the heart and tongue; when there is discord between them two, the speech that proceeds from them is conceived in adultery, a breed of bastard children, offending against chastity." And yet this man of deception and evasion, Henry Garnett, was "by country an Englishman, by birth a gentleman, by education a scholar of Winchester and then of Oxford, afterwards a corrector of the common law print with Mr. Tottell the printer, and now is to be corrected by the law. . . . He is a doctor of Jesuits, that is, a doctor of five DD's — Dissimulation, Deposing of princes, Disposing of kingdoms, Daunting and Deterring of subjects, and Destruction. . . . And I never," added Coke the Cantabrigian with his usual shameless partiality, "knew any priest of Cambridge to be arraigned in court."

Garnett's prison confessions were read aloud, also a transcript of the "secret" conversations with Oldcorne, ruthlessly edited by Coke after the practice of the time, with marginal notes directing the Clerk to omit such sentences as were favorable to the accused.* The two agents who had overheard the conversations were called as witnesses, Mr. Forset and Mr. Locherson. Next, the Clerk read confessions of the treasons Coke had earlier described, beginning in 1593: Annias, Cullen, Squire, Yorke, Williams. And each statement — as in the first trial — led inevitably to "Ralegh's treason, the Bye, the Main, the Powder Plot."

After all this, for Garnett to attempt a defense seemed not only pitiful but useless. Yet speak he did, logically, at length and quite evidently from careful preparation — though less in defense of himself (he acknowledged he had deceived the Council) than in justification of Church doctrine. If the prosecution had used the courtroom as a forum, the Jesuit was not far behind. "Take your time," Cecil told him from the commissioners' bench. "No man shall interrupt you. Good Mr. Garnett, whatever you have to say, say on in God's name and you shall be heard."

Equivocation, said Garnett, was defensible only when a man was "unlawfully interrogated. Our Church condemns all lying." But if a man be asked "what he thinketh," it is right to equivocate. No magistrate may require a man's secret thoughts. The Pope's authority over temporal kings and princes (so much deplored by the Attorney General) was a doctrine held in many Christian nations and "endured by so many Christian princes without fear or suspicion." The Church's policy concerning the deposing of heretic kings applied only to such sovereigns as had already suffered papal excommunication, among whom King James was not numbered. "And whereas Mr. Attorney hath said that there hath never been any plot, but books have been published by Catholics to stir them up and make them ready for plots and rebellions, I utterly deny any knowledge of any such matters. . . . Mr. Attorney hath charged that I was acquainted with the coming of the Spanish Armada in 1588. I utterly deny it, and I think the Spaniard was then so confident in himself that he never labored for any help in England. . . . I always abhorred this wicked attempt. I would to God I had never heard of the Powder Treason. I do protest," Garnett added when he

* See Chapter Note for Garnett's declaration as edited by Coke.

had done, "that Catholics in general do bear loyal hearts to his Majesty. And it was a particular crime of mine that when I knew of the action I did not disclose it."

There followed long, stubborn arguments between Garnett and the Earl of Northampton (Ralegh's great enemy) on the commissioners' bench. Sir Robert Cecil spoke more to the point. "All your defence, Mr. Garnett, is but simple negation. Give me but one argument besides your bare negative, that you were not consenting to the Powder Treason."

"Whereat," says the reporter, "Garnett was mute."

Searching questions were put concerning the Catholic confessional. "Mr. Garnett," asked the old Lord Admiral, "if one confessed this day to you that tomorrow he meant to kill the King with a dagger, must you conceal it?"

"I must conceal it."

Coke took immediate exception. "By the common law of this land, howsoever it were by the law of Popery (which is flatly against the common law), this being *crimen laesae Majestatis*, any person, whether confessor or not, was bound to discover a treason against the King so soon as it came to his knowledge."

On this point — concealing a plot against life revealed in the confessional — whole treatises were to be written. Legally, Coke was correct; English law makes no provision for the excuse of the confessional. The Jesuit was silent. The jury withdrew; it was nearly seven at night. In fifteen minutes they returned, bringing a verdict of *Guilty*. Popham gave judgment, Garnett begged the King's mercy. He was taken back to the Tower.

It was the end of the Gunpowder trials. But though Fawkes and his plotters had been condemned in court with little sympathy, Garnett received compassion from many sides. He had lied. Yet who, caught in such a trap, would tell the truth? It was evident at sight that he was by nature easygoing, he had been caught in this plot like a dove in a snare. Cecil in a few words had revealed the real cause of judgment. "Alas, Mr. Garnett!" he had exclaimed. "Why should we be troubled all this day with you, were it not to make the cause appear as it deserveth?"

To make the cause appear as it deserveth. The stark admission, torn from the King's First Secretary in a moment of irritation, expressed the aim of governments everywhere in trials for treason. To Continental minds, Garnett's trial seemed but a flaunting of "evidence," not to serve justice but as occasion for the strengthening of English political plans. Indignant letters flowed out from ambassadors in London. Coke's speech had been altogether too free with names and dates and places. "The Attorney General," Guistinian reported to his Doge, "went into the question of the Jesuits' operations in England and was compelled to trace the threads back to their endeavors at Rome and in Spain and Flanders to hinder the King's accession to the throne. Although this took place before the peace, still the mere recital of it was highly distasteful to the Ambassadors of those powers on account of the bad impression produced on the populace, which crowded the hall, and especially because his Majesty left the Court with signs of great anger, and to his intimates burst out into expressions of resentment at the methods adopted, under cloak of religion, for the disturbance and overthrow of Sovereigns and their states."

Father Garnett, meanwhile, waited in prison, continually visited by members of Privy Council and Anglican divines for purposes of interrogation. His execution, set for May first, was postponed three days "for fear of disorder among the prentices and others." (May Day at best was unruly.) A high scaffold was erected west of St. Paul's. Even here, the condemned man found himself beset by Deans: the Dean of Winchester, the Dean of St. Paul's, reinforced — at James's suggestion — by Sir Henry Montague, Recorder of London, who was to put final questions in the hearing of the populace. Garnett begged off from speechmaking; he was weak and tired, he said. But Deans and Recorder were inexorable. Equivocation? said Garnett when the word came up. No; today he would not use equivocation. He was sorry he had dissembled with the Privy Council, "sorry that I did not declare the truth until it was proved against me, but I did not think they had such sure proofs against me till they showed them to me. I beseech all men that Catholics may not fare the worse for my sake, and I exhort all Catholics to take care not to mix themselves with seditious or traitorous designs against the King."

Crossing himself, the condemned man began to pray in Latin. The ladder was drawn away. "By the express command of the King," wrote the reporter, "he remained hanging from the gallows until he was quite dead."

There were two more executions. Father Oldcorne was tried and hanged at Worcester and with him Stephen Littleton, whose house, Holbeach, had sheltered the plotters. Eleven men had suffered a traitor's death; four were killed during capture; one was a suicide, one died in prison from natural causes. This was the toll; it was not large. Yet the effect upon the country was deep. About the deaths of Garnett and Oldcorne, legends sprang up immediately. Oldcorne's heart and bowels, cast into the fire, kindled a flame that burned for sixteen days — the number of his missionary years in England. On the spot where Garnett died a well of oil burst up, and at Hindlip House, a strange new grass grew in the form of an imperial crown. A devout young Catholic student, standing near the quartering block at Garnett's execution, found in his hands a piece of bloody straw, blown from the executioner's basket. He took it home, put it in a bottle and when next he looked at it — lo! one of the husks held a picture of Garnett's head, "a star and cross on the forehead, a cherubim hovering, and a glory surrounding the whole."

London ran in crowds to see this heavenly testimony. The government, disturbed, commissioned the Archbishop of Canterbury to hold public inquiry. There were depositions, speeches; one Hugh Griffith attested that the picture might be Garnett or "it might be any man with a beard." Francis Bowen the painter swore (like a true artist) that any skilled draughtsman could have done a better limning. But the story spread. "This inspirited straw," wrote Thomas Fuller, "was copied out and at Rome printed in pomp with many superstitious compartments about it (as a coronet, a cross and nails) and gave the groundwork to Garnet's beatification by the Pope some months after."

For every Guy Fawkes tale told by Protestants, the Catholics had refutation. The country wavered between hate and pity. The suspected Catholic lords were yet to be tried and censured; the King gave orders it should be done in Star Chamber, not the common-law courts. The Lords Mordaunt and Stourton were heavily fined. Lord Monteagle, who had received the famous letter (and thereby, said James, saved the royal family) was granted a yearly pension for life. But Henry Percy, ninth Earl of Northumberland, was brought to Star Chamber "for contempt and misprision of treason" and scolded fiercely by Coke as if he had been a Guido Fawkes rather than one of the greatest noblemen of England, eighth heir presumptive to the throne. Even in this most august of courts, Coke's tongue ran free. "From the Pope were brought two bulls, they never bellowed." This great earl had tried to shift responsibility to his cousin, Thomas Percy, "an old trick of a traitor, to rail upon his accuser!"

Northumberland was fined thirty thousand pounds and sent to the Tower.* Before judgment was given, each lord and bishop, *coram consilio*, had his say as was the custom. Robert Cecil remarked, characteristically, that "the cause of this combustion was the Papists seeking to restore their religion." It was Lord Zouche (Ben Jonson's friend) who in five brief words came to the heart of the matter. "Two religions," he said, "cannot stand together."

Trials, plots, executions, rebellions — the whole could not have been explained more succinctly. *Two religions cannot stand together:* all Christendom shared the conviction. Because of it, Fawkes had died, Garnett, Catesby and the rest. And because of it, much blood would yet be shed in England.

With the trials over and done, a river of print commenced to flow from government sources. *A Discourse on the Gunpowder Plot* was ascribed to James, though some said it read more like Francis Bacon's composition, with its presentation of the Lopez and Essex treasons molded to suit the case. Robert Cecil admitted that the object of Garnett's trial had been not so much to convict the Jesuit as "to make a public and visible anatomy of Popish doctrine and practise." Thomas Fuller undertook by a grim Protestant logic to refute some "falsehoods concerning Garnett's death:

AS, NAMELY,	WHEREAS,
(1.) That he manifested much alacrity of mind, in the cheerfulness of his looks at his death.	(1.) He betrayed much servile fear and consternation of spirit, much beneath the erected resolution of a martyr.

* Like other huge fines in Star Chamber, awarded *in terrorem*, Northumberland's fine was later reduced to a third the amount. He was not released from the Tower until 1621.

(2.) His zealous and fervent prayers much moved the people.	(2.) His prayers were faint, cold, and perplexed, oft interrupted with his listening to and answering of others.
(3.) The people hindered the hangman from cutting the rope, and quartering him while alive.	(3.) That favour, by special order from his Majesty, was mercifully indulged unto him.
(4.) The people so clawed the executioner, that he hardly escaped with life.	(4.) No violence was done unto him, able many years after to give a cast of his office, if need required.
(5.) When he held up Garnett's head to the people, there was a panic silence, none saying, "God save the king."	(5.) Acclamations in that kind were as loud and general, as heretofore on the same occasion.

But nothing could still the rumors nor stop the argument. On the Continent, Catholic apologists took it up: Bellarmine, L'Heureux the Jesuit. King James wrote an answer to Bellarmine, then engaged a distinguished scholar, Isaac Casaubon, to refute the Jesuit's arguments further. Bishop Andrews and Dr. Abbot produced pamphlets. In Spain, Father John Gerard wrote his *Narrative of the Gunpowder Plot*, acknowledging the guilt of the eight conspirators but protesting his own innocence and the innocence of Catholics at large. Seventy years later, when England was engulfed in the cruel scandal known as *The Popish Plot*, these Gunpowder pamphlets and papers served to whip the flame. Again, when the Catholic Relief Bill of 1829 was pending, *Gunpowder Plot* flew as flag and banner for the opposition, a "proof" that Roman Catholic tenets and English Protestant government were incompatible. Jardine in his book *The Gunpowder Plot* (1885) made new and careful analysis of the evidence on both sides. Twelve years later, a second Father John Gerard (a Jesuit like his namesake) published a book, *What Was Gunpowder Plot?* accusing Robert Cecil and the government of having invented the entire conspiracy, including the letter of betrayal to Monteagle and the cellar scene of Fawkes's capture. Was not the government testimony, asked Gerard, a mass of inconsistencies? One witness swore that Fawkes was captured in the cellar; another that he was taken at the door, booted and spurred for escape on horseback, while Fawkes himself testified he was caught in his lodgings. And why did Lord Monteagle, when handed, at supper, the mysterious letter of warning, give it to his retainer, Ward, to read aloud? Ward was a friend of Winter's and would naturally warn the conspirators immediately. Surely there was something contrived about all this? Was it not odd that the government, once in receipt of the letter, waited eight full days before searching the cellar to uncover so dangerous a plot? Immediately, Gerard's questions were answered point for point by the historian Gardiner: *What Gunpowder Plot Was* (1897).

The whole truth will never be known. No one doubts there was a conspiracy to blow up the Parliament House and that Father Garnett was aware of it before the conspirators were caught. But that Father John Gerard was innocent, none can question after reading his book. There is no slightest evidence that the Pope had knowledge of the plot, or indeed, any Catholics on the Continent, no matter how they may have wished to see a Catholic on the English throne. But the government surely knew of the conspiracy long before Monteagle received his mysterious letter; it is more than possible the letter actually was contrived between Francis Tresham and some member of the Privy Council. Treason at best is a murky affair and the Gunpowder Plot, for all the print expended on its solution, remains almost too strange for posterity to credit, as Sir Edward Coke himself remarked in the courtroom.

The government made it a business to keep memory alive. On every Fifth of November, Westminster Hall was emptied while the judges walked to the Abbey to hear a Gunpowder Sermon and give thanks "for the happy deliverance of King James I and the three estates of the realm from the most traitorous and bloody intended massacre by gunpowder." Fifty-five years later, the Gunpowder service was made part of the established liturgy and remained in the Book of Common Prayer until the year 1859. "Lord," said England on its knees, "who didst this day discover the snares of death that were laid . . . by Popish treachery in a most barbarous and savage manner beyond the examples of former ages . . . scatter our enemies that delight in blood. Infatuate and defeat their counsels, asswage their malice and confound their devices. Strengthen the hands of our gracious King . . . to cut off such workers of iniquity as turn religion into rebellion and faith into faction. . . ."

Far away in the American colonies, Puritans kept the day with sermons in the morning, fireworks at night. Yet as years passed and emotions faded,* the names of the conspirators were forgotten all save one, and the business assumed that slightly comic aspect which sometimes attaches to large domestic violence when the danger is past. On Hallowe'en, children wore Guy Fawkes masks, carried hooded lanterns, jumped roaring from cellar doors. The ballad makers reaped a little fortune:

Our King he went to the Parliament
to meet his Noble Peers-a;
But if he had knowne
where he should have been blowne,
He durst not have gone for his Eares-a.

Then "Powder I smell," quoth our gracious King
(now our King was an excellent smeller);
And lowder and lowder,
quoth the King, "I smell powder",
And downe he run into the Cellar.

Then the Noble-men that there stood by
and heard the words of the King-a,
"By my Soul, if the Fire
had come a little nigher,
'Twould have made us all flye without wing-a."

Soe many Barrells of Gunpowder,
the like was never seen-a,
That eke if the match
had chanc'd for to catch,
Good Lord, where should we all have been-a?

* "The keeping of this day," wrote Fuller in 1655, "begins already to wax weak and decay. God forbid that our thankfulness for this great deliverance, formerly so solemnly observed, should here after be like the squibs which the apprentices in London make on this day; and which give a great flash and crack at the first but soon after go out in a stink."

PART II
The Judgeship

CHAPTER TWENTY-ONE

*Lord Coke takes his oath as Chief Justice of Common Pleas. His charge to the Grand Jury at Norwich.**

> And it is certaine that the authority of justices of assises itinerant through the whole realme, and the institution of justices of peace in every county being duely performed, are the most excellent meanes for the preservation of the king's peace, and quiet of the realme, of any other in the Christian world.
>
> COKE, *First Institute*

IN midsummer of 1606, Coke rode home to Norwich. It was a route well known, every mile familiar, past Hatfield, where Elizabeth's old brick palace slept behind its sycamores and where Robert Cecil's great country house so soon would rise, "a most pleasant and delicious vineyard"; around by thin poor fields of Cambridgeshire and over a border to greener pastures, to the windmills and round towers of Norfolk, to a glimpse, far off as one approached the city, of the hoary Castle of Blancheflower, high and glittering on its mound.

Every landmark was familiar, the same yet not the same. To a man whose own stature has altered, can any landscape keep its old proportions? Beneath the velvet facing of Coke's broadcloth coat rested the wide gold shoulder collar of a judge. *The SS collar*, it was called, from the letters ornamenting it, though no one knew or remembered what the letters meant; Coke said "Sapience and Sci-

* Chapter Note.

ence." * Whatever they signified, between golden links the figure of a spiked portcullis stood out, sharp-toothed like Traitors' Gate. Kuke of Norfolk was my Lord Coke now, Chief Justice of the Common Pleas, returning home in pomp and dignity to conduct the Norwich Assizes. Trumpeters rode ahead, pikemen behind; the official train numbered fifty or more: clerks in livery, sumpters with pack mules carrying Coke's judicial wardrobe — gowns of violet silk, of scarlet silk and black, faced with changeable taffeta for summer (in winter furred with miniver); long hoods of scarlet velvet, satin lined; a square black velvet hat to wear over the close white cap or coif that was a Serjeant's ancient insignia. The Order of the Coif was the most venerable in England, antedating even the Garter; the coif itself was said to have originated just after 1207, when ecclesiastics, forbidden to act as advocates in the secular courts, adopted a close-fitting cap to hide their tonsures. Englishmen liked to spell it *quoif* and by Coke's day the word carried almost magical significance, symbolic of the whole power of the law. The coif must not be doffed to any man — "not in the King's presence," wrote the great Judge Fortescue (1450), "though he be in talk with his Majesty's Highness."

A man could not be named a judge until he had first been created Serjeant-at-Law. The word "created" was itself significant. (Only peers and princes are created; knights are made.) Sixteen or twenty years' practice in the court was a prerequisite. "Judges call them Brothers," said Cowell in his law dictionary, "and hear them with great respect." Serjeants alone could practice in the court of Common Pleas; they had precedence over all other lawyers. Even the King's Attorney General waited — in plain black wool — until the King's Serjeant, sumptuous in violet silk, had finished his oration. "The Serjeant," Coke wrote, "is called by the King's writ directed to him in the plural number, *vobis*, a special mark of dignity. The manner of his creation is most ancient, as the solemnity of his call. . . . his hood, robes, coif and other significant ornaments, the great and sumptuous feast he makes, the rings of gold he gives, his attendants and other great and honorable ceremonies." Coke, as it happened, became Serjeant and Judge all at once. Chief Justice Gawdy of Common Pleas had been ill and absent

* Science to Coke meant *scientia*, knowledge. What today we call *science* was "natural philosophy."

for the whole of winter term. Some time in the late spring he died. There was little question of his successor. For thirteen years, Coke had been Attorney General; his services in the Gunpowder prosecutions alone would have qualified him for promotion. At the close of Garnett's trial, Sir Robert Cecil had risen to tell the court that he "never heard such a mass of matter better contracted nor made more intelligible to the jury." Rumor said that Coke might be made a baron; the wonder was that so distinguished a barrister had never been created Serjeant. Perhaps James and Elizabeth (or the Cecils), knowing that Serjeant was first step toward a judgeship, preferred to keep Mr. Attorney on the floor of advocacy, where he made himself so useful.

Coke, forewarned as to what lay in store, characteristically sent off to Cecil a careful little program outlining the ritual of his own investment: "I am bold to inform you what course I must take. First, I must be made Serjeant, which may be on Saturday next, and the Chief Justice on Monday. There must be a writ (for which my Lord Chancellor will have warrant) returnable on Saturday to call me to be a Serjeant, and a warrant for the patent of the office of Chief Justice of the Common Pleas. Hereof I presume to inform you, lest if other should complain, blame might be imputed on me."

Mysteriously, this letter is dated February 2, 1606, though Coke was not made a judge until summer. When the day came, it was old Sir John Popham, Chief Justice of King's Bench, who laid across Coke's shoulders the striped, particolored robes of a Serjeant. "And presently," wrote a colleague, "after his writ read and count made, Coke was created Chief Justice and sat the same day, and afterwards rose and put off his parti-robes and put on his robes of a Judge; and the second day after, went to Westminster with all the society of the Inner Temple attending upon him." This must have been the day when Coke feasted his friends; he was not one to skimp on hospitality, and the great banqueting hall of Hatton House had been for a century the scene of Serjeants' feasts. We know that Coke distributed rings, each of officially prescribed weight, engraved with its motto or "posie" —*fidei symbolo*, the age-old feudal pledge of fealty to the king. Lord Chancellor Hatton's scutcheon carried the motto, *Virtus tutissima cassis*. Inscribed below the Hatton arms, the words often met Coke's eye at home; Lady Hatton liked to see the Hatton quarterings on wall or windowpane of her houses. Coke must have borrowed from it as well as from Cicero; the motto on his serjeants' rings, to be quoted often in ensuing centuries, was *Lex est tutissima cassis*, the law is the safest shield. Coke delighted to enlarge on it. "The law," he wrote, "is the surest sanctuary that a man can take, and the strongest fortresse to protect the weakest of all; *lex est tutissima cassis*."

The Lord Chancellor* administered the Judge's oath — solemn words yet practical, conceived, old Lambarde had said, "not only to set God before the eyes [of judges] but to strengthen their minds and arm their courages against the force of human affections, which otherwise might allure and draw them out of the way":

"Well and truly ye shall serve the King and his people. And ye shall take no fee or livery of none but the King, nor gift or reward of none that hath a do before you except it shall be meat or drink of small value, as long as the plea hangs before you. And ye shall do equal law and execution of Right to all the King's subjects rich and poor, without having regard to any person. Ye shall counsel our Sovereign Lord the King in his need. And ye shall not delay any person of common right for the letters of the King or of any person nor for any other cause. . . . So help you God."

Ye shall not delay any person of common right for the letters of the King . . . Ten years later, in a time of conflict, Coke would remember the phrase and quote it (at grave danger to himself) in a letter to King James: "We hold it our duties to inform your Majesty that our oath is in these express words . . ."

But amidst all the ceremony and ritual experienced on that day of early summer, 1606, perhaps the most poignant, for Coke, had come when he was rung out of the society of the Inner Temple. As a Brother of the Coif, he could not live in his old chambers but must move to Serjeants' Inn. Only a few steps eastward through a door in the wall, and yet for Edward Coke a long journey, surely, and a brief farewell. For nearly thirty years, Coke had kept these chambers, looking down the Temple gardens to the river. He had slept there many nights, rising early, as was his custom, to study or to teach, sometimes subscribing his letters, "From the solitary Temple." The chambers had been his refuge in distress, his retreat in contentment. He would come back and walk in the gardens, an

* Sir Thomas Egerton, Lord Keeper, became Lord Ellesmere on July 19, 1603, and a week later received the title of Lord Chancellor.

honored and a welcome guest. There was a wall and high brick gate, put up in 1589, the year Coke first sat in Parliament as Burgess. Light struck against the twelve celestial signs adorning the pillared gate, bright painted in azure, red and gold. The roses blew along their beds, on the river the bargeman's horn sounded. From the ancient Round Church a bell tolled, ringing out Edward Coke forever, by custom and consent. . . .

Norfolk was in the Midlands circuit; Chief Justice Coke had half a dozen shires to cover in as many weeks. The twelve common-law judges left Westminster to cover the circuits twice a year, winter and summer. The ride to Norwich was one that he loved and had taken each year when he could. His manor near Mileham — Godwick Hall — was kept ready by his bailiffs. Richard Constable, Robert Mather, John Pepys, Gentlemen: their names are on the estate books. Journeying northward through the country, Coke saw the grain bursting into head; lambs, half-grown, nosed the hedges; everywhere was the smell of haying. By general tradition, midsummer bred a restlessness in the counties. "In the warm time," one of Elizabeth's Secretaries had noted, "the people for the most part be more unruly." "Cuckoo time and the hot weather," said Henry VIII's Archbishop, "mad brains be most busy." This holding of General Assizes after Trinity term was salutary, a wholesome seasonal reminder of the law.

Some miles south of Norwich, at Wymondham or Attleborough, the Sheriffs waited with their train. Norfolk boasted two such high officials; one was John Shovell, whose father had been made citizen of Norwich sixty years before. Coke had known these people all his life; he had been close to local business and local politics when he was scarcely out of law school. Now the fathers came to do him honor. Some were his kinsfolk; a man could not ride far in Norfolk without hearing or seeing the name of Paston. To Coke it must have brought — in spite of fame and Lady Hatton — a quickening sense of home.

For the county, Coke's appointment as Chief Justice was gratifying — a man indigenous as the marsh hawk, Norfolk born and reared, who could on occasion slip into county dialect, say "tree" for three and "trew" for through — a man who owned much land and came home each summer to farm it. Coke could argue strip ploughing as against enclosure; he had been on the committee to draft Elizabeth's great Poor Law in Parliament, he was familiar with local problems: flooded fens, dishonest clerks of market, false concealers who cheated poor yeomen under pretense of searching out land titles for King James ("Harpies and hellions," Coke called them disdainfully in his *Institutes.*) This common-law judge was Protestant to the bone, yet no fanatic Puritan or sectary but sober-minded, essentially practical and though reputedly somewhat harsh in court with evil-doers, in lay life a good landlord, considerate and protective to his tenants. Local constables, apprised of his Lordship's coming, looked to it that the parish pillories stood in good repair as the judicial troupe clattered by. "And every one that hath a leet or market," Coke said, "ought to have a pillory or tumbril to punish offenders, as brewers, bakers, forestallers" who sold their corn before the bell rang, contrary to law.

In the vast pyramidal structure of English government, spreading down from sovereign and Privy Council to local justices of the peace, the circuit judges served as link between high and low, between London and the farthest parishes of Yorkshire, Northumberland, Wales. Coke's duties at the assizes would be more than judicial in merely legal sense; they would be paternal, protective. He must look about him, search out abuses from subject to King and from neighbor to neighbor, see to the health of the county and how the harvest was coming, note dissatisfactions, disorders, the too rapid spread of alehouses, which Parliament was eternally trying (and failing) to suppress by statute. The last Parliament had listened to angry talk concerning abuses perpetrated by the King's purveyors, petty officials who were empowered to take not only timber for ships and saltpeter for gunpowder but hay, oats, straw for the royal stables. James had a shooting box at Thetford in Norfolk; complaints had risen that his purveyors exceeded their authority, popping up where they had no business. "Like Pharaoh's plague of frogs," somebody remarked, "that skipped in every man's dish."

What Parliamentary statute had failed to effect might still be achieved locally, on the spot, by a judge with sufficient authority and a talent to make himself heard, touch the county imagination and win its support. Coke's charge to the Grand Jury, on opening day, must be directed not alone to calendared causes but to general conditions in the county and a wide review of the realm, for the benefit of those whose lives were bounded by farm-hold ditch or village lane. Norfolk had at least fifty justices of the peace, whose duty it was to attend the assizes, together with all coroners and high constables of hundreds. These must be ready with their prisoners for jail delivery, produce the records and be prepared to receive from the London judges instructions for the coming half-year, as the judges themselves had received instruction from the Lord Chancellor before setting out on circuit. In the hands of the justices of the peace there lay, as Coke had said, "the quiet of the realm and the institution of the King's peace." It was Coke's business therefore to lay searching eye upon these officials. If the last Quarter Session court had not concluded its cases, those that held over must be pushed through.

Few justices of the peace were lawyers, yet the list of offenses under their jurisdiction was wide as the ingenuity of man. "For keeping of dove-houses without license, for baking of horse-bread, for eating flesh on fast-days, for homicide by misadventure . . ." Justices of the peace must appoint surveyors to keep up bridges and highways; justices must bring in taxes for hospital and almshouse, fix wages in the different trades, bind apprentices, hear oaths of allegiance, punish poachers and robbers of orchards, grant licenses to beggars and strolling players, see that artificers, mechanics, servants did not exceed their legal wage. Carpenters who refused to work for twelvepence a day, householders who had not followed the hue and cry, thereby making the town liable for heavy fine — these were to be found and dealt with. The sins of incontinence were numbered as sands of the sea, the fathers of bastards eternally clever at hiding, "having fled long before" — the phrase runs through the records like a refrain. Every so often, high constables must make systematic search throughout their district for what Coke referred to as "vagabonds, idle wanderers, night-walkers, draw-latches and Roberdsmen, the followers of Robin Hoode." As Attorney General, Coke in 1599 had drawn up a set of eighteen articles which at each assizes were to be put to the high constables — officers who in Coke's view should be landholders, "for if poor men should be chosen to this office, who live by the labour of their hands, they would rather suffer felons and other malefactors to escape, and neglect the execution of their office in other points, than leave their labour, by which they, their wives and children live."

Any judge worth his salt enjoyed the circuits, with their practical, down-to-earth problems. "Besides knowing the gentry and people and manners of England, which is best attained in that way," wrote the great Lord Chancellor Hyde, "there is a very good and necessary part of learning in the law which is not so easily got any other way as in riding these circuits; which as it seems to have much of drudgery, so is accompanied with much pleasure and profit."

It was a program that would hold for centuries, spreading to the colonies and retaining, at home, its solemnity of ritual. (At Cambridge Assizes today, the judge's coming is heralded by blast of trumpets.) When Edward Coke reached Norwich gates he was met by the Mayor in scarlet and a troop of important guildsmen. The civic banner fluttered red and white, the armorial towers of Norwich painted on one side and on the other, Justice, blindfolded, with the naked sword and scales. Joshua Culley, the grocer, was Mayor now; he lived over Fye Bridge, not many blocks below the Erpingham Gate through which Coke once had run to school. It was Culley's business to escort Chief Justice Coke to the Guildhall and then home. Norwich had grown and changed since Coke's early days — and yet it was the same. Green as an orchard, with the feel of country about it even at its busiest. Market carts still blocked the narrow passages; under the horses' feet, cobbles were slippery with hay; at noon and evening the bell of Christ Church spoke with its old authority. The Free School boys were taught arithmetic now; along with their Latin accidence they chanted sums — an unscholarly sort of occupation yet much approved by the practical-minded board of burgesses who made the rules. Norwich displayed a spate of new buildings in this first decade of the century. Round Dutch gables were coming into style, especially favored by Norfolk with its Flemish connections. Down the hill, southeast of the Cathedral, was a venerable part of the city called Conisford, where Coke had his own house, a dwelling built to face the narrow, pleasant street. Behind it on the river, work-boats drifted by, laden deep, sliding out of sight beneath an arched stone bridge.

Norwich had its Shire House, "over against the Castle wall," where court sessions were held four times or more a year. But in county towns an easy custom prevailed of holding court wherever convenient; in church, if the parish had no hall large enough. Assize week brought throngs to Norwich, for business or for fun. From all points of the county they came, from Yarmouth, Thetford, Swaffham, King's Lynn. The juries alone numbered at least a hundred men — a grand jury of twenty-four, and from each hundred a petty jury of twelve. When such a crowd was looked for, the Castle Hall was preferred to the cramped quarters of the Shire House. Court opened at eight in the morning. By seven, streams of people converged upon the Castle mound. Justices of the peace with round badges swinging from neck chains . . . constables in striped tunics . . . beadles in blue coats, scarlet-lined, the shield of office on their breast, their long staves tapping as they moved. Important citizens in black gowns edged with red, their wives waddling after them on cork-soled pattens, built high against the mud and dust. . . . Young men swaggering in tight doublets, old men in russet gowns with long hanging sleeves that made them look like Noah. Country girls, their cross-laced bodices well filled. Housewives in narrow neat ruffs and cambric aprons — a busy, noisy crowd, coming from eastward across the river Wensum or round by the Cattle Market, where crook-horned Norfolk beasts, fat with summer, lowed from their pens.

Inside, the great stone hall was bright with color as a fair, with scarcely a suggestion of the somber black that was later to be associated with such scenes. Law clerks wore short, particolored tunics. Attorneys in buff and green, with long pen-holders at their belts, conferred with filacer and prothonotary. Below the judges' dais was a green baize-covered table, where legal parchment was laid out in narrow skins, one end rolled neatly. Prominently placed and awaiting the Judge's entrance were the town fathers. The two Sheriffs in mulberry velvet — *murray*, they called it — glowed like ripe berries in autumn. Mayor Culley of Norwich wore his gold-plated shoulder chain and civic gown of scarlet; over it a mantle of changeable lilac silk, its edges faced with lambskin to the hem; his aldermen too wore scarlet, with velvet tippets. On the dais, chairs were set not only for the Chief Justice of the Common Pleas but for two representatives of the ecclesiastical law, John Jegon, Bishop of Norwich, and his Chancellor. Jegon had been Coke's classmate at Cambridge nearly forty years ago. He was very rich and the county disliked him, partly because he was stingy and partly because, with his brother the Archdeacon, he insisted on conformity in a city notably diverse in its Protestant religious belief.

A crier stepped before the dais, struck his staff upon the floor and sang his nasal *Oyez* thrice. Preceded by two mace bearers in black stuff gowns, Coke walked in. His new silk robe, reaching almost to the floor, gleamed red as fire, making him at once awesome and amiable; he had words to say, intimate, cheerful, to his old friends before the day's business commenced.

". . . and though my speech be purposely directed to you of the Jury which are sworn, I think it not amiss first to begin with myself, and of myself to speak this much. There was a certain young Roman . . ."

The whole world loves to hear a tale, and Sir Edward Coke by his own admission spoke in parables when he could. *Similitudes*, he called them; "*comparisons* which do best confirm our understanding and fastest cleave unto the memory." At such times his pedanticism left him; there was no tedious "arguing by trialities." This young Roman, Coke went on pleasantly, as a reward for years spent "in reading and the study of good letters," was named by the Senate as a judge. He found himself dismayed at the appointment, for the reason that he possessed numerous friends, kinsfolk and patrons in government office, "whose hate or love," said Coke, "might unhappily produce some occasion wherein his sentence in the place of judgment might give distaste, procure enemies, lose friends and gain suspicion of hateful partiality. Judging amongst friends and kinsfolk, he should assuredly (as he thought) by some detractors be thereof suspected."

There was no doubt to whom this parable referred. All Norwich knew that Coke, when Bridget Paston died, had married the Lady Hatton, whose uncle was the King's most trusted officer of state, son of the great Lord Burghley. And was not Coke's father-in-law, Lord Thomas Cecil, President of the Council of the North? Our Roman citizen, continued Coke, consulted a faithful friend, who advised him to decline an office "in which so much danger rested." But when the Senate refused to alter its resolution, the young Roman consulted a second friend, a nobleman long employed in affairs of state, who at once advised acceptance. How, the nobleman asked, could it be dangerous to judge among friends? "For he that is a judge, ceaseth to be a friend! In judgment no acquaintance, no griefs, no friends, no remembrance of forepassed, present or hope of future friendship must direct the thoughts. All that on judgment's seat is done, must be because justice commands the doing. And therefore (said this noble gentleman) 'Be no longer loath to execute the honorable office of a judge. But in thy love to Rome's Commonwealth, dedicate thy labours to her public benefit.' "

The young man, convinced, accepted the judgeship. But he told no one, and, pretending that he was about to leave the country, invited his friends to a farewell banquet. "It is true," he told the assembled company, "that I purpose, as I must, to take leave of you all and to be a stranger to my dearest friends and nearest allies. Thus must I depart from you and yet continue amongst you. For I am appointed to be a Judge, and in the seat of Justice I must forget the remembrance of your former friendships and acquaintance. In the person of a Judge, with respect to keep my conscience clear, I must with equity and uprightness administer justice unto you all.

"And this," finished Coke, looking out upon his own dear friends and kinsfolk assembled in Norfolk's venerable Castle of Blancheflower, "this is my cause also! For by the love and favor of my gracious master, King James, I am, *sine precatione, vel precatio* — without price or request — freely called unto this great office and sent to be a Judge amongst my kinsfolk and familiar friends, even in the bosom of my native country. I must therefore, as the young Roman did, take leave of all former acquaintance, and do that which is just unto all estates and degrees, without partiality."

This gentle warning finished, Coke turned to the Grand Jury. "We, the Justices of Assizes and Gaol Delivery," he said, "must know ourselves and the place wherein we are. We must know and understand each cause before us brought." Let a judge take but one bribe, Coke added with especial emphasis, "but once execute a justice purchased, and all his words and actions forever after may justly be suspected, though never so uprightly done or spoke." Going on to tell the people the meaning of justice and the laws, Coke reverted to homely similes of land and wind and weather. "Methinks, that oftentimes, when I ride by the way, I see the effects of justice rightly resembled, when I behold a river with a silver current. Bounded in her equal course — with what just proportion she doth disperse her streams, without bewraying any little rage of intemperate violence! But if the passage of that stream be stopped, then how like a raging sea she overflows her banks! And then by unresisted force, the meadows, humble valleys, weak and low-grown shrubs are drowned up, enduring a recureless wrack; whilst hills and mountains stand safe from fear of harm."

Coke's audience knew the Norfolk saying, "Night rains make drowned fens." Not a marshland farmer but feared it. Yet with equable weather, marshlands grew rich pasturage and the county liked to boast about it. (One West Norfolk farmer told King James that where *he* lived, grass grew so fast that if you put a stick on the ground at night, next morning you could not see it. To which James retorted that he knew meadows in Scotland where, if you put a *horse* overnight, you would not see it next day!) If justice in her equal course were stopped — Coke went on, pointing his moral — it was the poor who would be drowned and overwhelmed, "whilst great and wealthy men, like hills and mountains, build their stations sure. Justice withheld, only the poorer sort are those who smart." There had been an incident, two years earlier, when Coke was Attorney General, concerning pirates along the Norfolk and Suffolk coasts who preyed on poor fishermen and mariners. Dunkirkers despoiled small ships, cut off the hands or fingers of sailors and sent them home disabled. An appeal had come to Coke and he had acted at once to procure a levy for protection, "to cheer the hearts of the weatherbeaten poor coast-men and daunt or discourage the enemy."

Coke swung next into religion and the state, repeating the story of treason as he had told it at the Gunpowder trials, explaining, condemning, telling his country the history of England as he saw it. "Elizabeth!" — Coke said the name and his prose took wing. "She lived renowned through all the corners of the world; she ruled in peace, beloved of all her subjects." Going on to tell the dangers he had seen England suffer and surmount, Coke "wanted words," he said; he "knew not what to speak" — and immediately, his phrases rose and moved in rhythm. Had certain "wild complotted actions taken place . . . then, this sea-environed island, the beauty and wonder of the world; this so famous and far-renowned Great Britain's monarchy, had at one blow endured recoverless ruin, being overwhelmed in a sea of blood! This so well-planted, pleasant, fruitful world, accounted Eden's Paradise, should have been by this time made a place disconsolate. Then, in our congregations, the songs of Sion had no more been sung. . . .

"Dear countrymen," said Coke, coming suddenly back to earth, "we have then enough, and need not the help of any Pope!" But there existed, apart from papists, a second kind of recusant, "not to be tolerated in any monarchical government — a certain brotherhood which can endure no Bishops."

It was a reminder highly pertinent. Since the days of Little Bilney, Norwich had been the nest and nurture ground of sectarian fanaticism. Anabaptists, Brownists, Independents, the Family of Love — angry congregations who would have no bishops — and, worse than that, no lawyers and no earthly laws. A Brownist in court was as obstructive as a Jesuit. Coke could remember one of them, standing in the Archbishop's court between his guards and calling the judge "a beast that spoke like a dragon." What could you do with men thirsting for martyrdom, who denied all worldly authority, declared they would obey none but a heavenly father and were led off to jail quoting Scripture in full voice? "The most part of Brownists," Coke told his Norfolk audience, "are simple and illiterate people, nothing so dangerous as the Popish recusants. And though their ignorance understands not what they do, yet do their endeavors strive to shake in sunder the whole frame of our imperial government."

From here, Coke left religion for a brief, brisk classification of various rascals who had recently been victimizing the county. "It was once my hap," he said, "to take a certain Clerk of the Market in these tricks. But I advanced him higher than his father's son — by so much as from the ground to the top of the pillory! If you of the jury will therefore have a care to find out these abuses, by God's grace they shall not go unpunished. For we have a *coif*, which signifies a helmet, whereby in the execution of justice we are defended against all oppositions, be they never so violent." As for the men known as *promoters* (professional informers to the courts), Coke had brought to Star Chamber more than one such, who lived upon bribes extracted from ignorant and frightened countrymen. "The office, I confess is necessary," he said now; "and yet it seldom happeneth that an honest man is employed therein. Yet there is some hope that by punishing their abuses they may at the last be made honest against their wills. In which employment, you of the jury shall do well to use a respective diligence. . . ." * Counterfeiters, monopolists of corn, vagrants — Coke had a warning for them all, including "a sort of idle-seeming gentlemen, whom if you do observe, you shall find them walking with a greyhound in a slip or a birding-piece upon their neck. And they, forsooth, will make a path over the statute law and into any man's grounds, lordships or liberties, pass and repass at their pleasure. As if it were lawful for every fellow to keep a greyhound and to hunt when and where he listeth! Or as if a birding-piece were no gun and so not included in the statute made against guns! But if you would find out these fellows and present them, they shall be taught to know themselves."

With a final blast at drunkards, "those who do desire to swim until themselves and their whole estate do sink in the slimy dregs" (words as ineffectual, in any company, as the warning against poachers with their fowling pieces), Coke's charge was done. "Dear countrymen," he said, "betwixt God and your conscience, therefore, make your peace!"

* "Viperous vermin," Coke calls the informer in his *Third Institute* "who under the reverend mantle of law and justice instituted for protection of the innocent, did vex and depauperize the subject, and commonly the poorer sort, for malice or private ends, and never for love of justice."

CHAPTER TWENTY-TWO

1607. Common law versus the prerogative. Fuller's Case. The onset of a long campaign.

MICHAELMAS term opened in October; the great doors of Westminster Hall let in their heterogeneous stream. Chief Justice Coke sat behind the bar of Common Pleas, receiving cases in their turn.

Only three steps from courtroom floor to bench, yet Edward Coke became, almost overnight, another man. "The most offensive of Attorney Generals," wrote Francis Bacon's biographer, "transformed into the most admired and venerated of Judges." When advocates turn judge, the world expects them to be worthy of the occasion; the bench would seem to lift the spirit as well as the body of a lawyer. But with Coke the breach is not merely noticeable, it is startling and from a distance of centuries, hard at first to credit. A sharp road cuts between the countries of this life; Coke's farewell at Norwich carried a symbolism deeper than he knew. Attorney General Coke, sharp driving tool of crown authority, put on the robes of judgeship and became to all appearances the champion of another cause. "There is a maxim," he told the Lower House: "*The common law hath admeasured the King's prerogative.* It is not I, Edward Coke, that speaks it but the records that speak it." "The King," he advised James, "cannot take any cause out of any of his courts and give judgment upon it himself." "No person," he wrote in the *Second Institute*, "ought in any ecclesiastical court to be examined upon the cogitation of his heart or what he thinketh."

Such pronouncements, had they come from England's Attorney General, would have been near to treason. As Elizabeth's servant moreover, Coke could hardly have shaped the words; his mind was turned another way. But spoken by Chief Justice Coke, the words were to come as natural evolvement, behind them the long affirmation of Coke's years as scholar, judge and Commons man. Times had changed, the scene was ready.

Leaving the Attorney-Generalship, Coke left an office which, above any in government, existed (as Bacon said) to guard the prerogative; the King's Attorney was the King's watchdog. On the draughty bench of Common Pleas — *the common bench*, lawyers called it — Coke sat now as judge, pledged by his oath to "well and truly serve the King and his people." Before three months were out, Chief Justice Coke attacked the same court of prerogative which as Elizabeth's Attorney General he had upheld.* Because the shift was sudden, historians have ascribed it to greed, a judge's jealousy lest his powers be infringed, his cases slip into another court. A judge's salary — even a Chief Justice's — was low, only a few hundred pounds a year (often enough not forthcoming), together with robes and travel money for spring and summer circuits. Judges — and indeed every clerk of court — depended for their living on certain fees connected with the volume of business that came in. For each writ of process that he sealed, Coke was paid by the party bringing suit. His prothonotaries had two shillings for every plea roll brought by a Serjeant-at-Law, and more if the plea ran over one roll of parchment. Judges could grow rich by the sale of offices. Of three prothonotaries in Common Pleas, Coke had the appointment of two, the King had the third — and appointment meant sale at no set price.

Long before he became a judge, Coke had protested this kind of barter; long after his judgeship he was to protest it again in Parliament. (He loathed office selling and in the first year of his Attorney Generalship had protested to Burghley by letter.) The custom had grown from the old medieval concept of office as a freehold which gave the owner such fees and perquisites as he could pick up. Throughout the sprawling labyrinth of Westminster Hall, below

* See Cawdry's Case (1591).

and above stairs, where court led into court, office into office, the system invited corruption — time-honored, everywhere accepted. The wonder is that Edward Coke, no hater of money, remained under such a system incorruptible.

Yet Coke was no saint. Fifty-four years old when he became a judge, before him lay nearly three decades; not the serene last years of a philosopher nearing his end, but days hot with struggle, tempest, domestic scandal, prison, triumph, near despair. Moreover, where "Romanism" was concerned he remained fanatically biased, pursuing plot and traitor where neither existed. "The soft spot in Coke's head," his enemies have called it. No saint indeed. Yet in the broad issues of law and government, once Coke fixed direction he held his course. Legally he was inconsistent and on occasion, did not hesitate to invent or bend precedent and maxim to his purpose, usually in Latin for better mystification. His detractors for three centuries have made much of it, and in truth it is not easy, even now, to pin Sir Edward Coke to theories beyond the theory that England is governed by the common law. If legal consistency is a virtue, Coke did not have it; in his reversal his greatness is contained and his life prior to 1607 seems but a preparation. "It is a wonder," noted a Recorder of London in 1684, "that Sir Edward Coke lord chief justice should differ from Mr. Attorney Cook, for we know his thoughts in Sir Walter Ralegh's time and his speeches in Charles I his time; they are as different from each other as the times were, and in this particular that gentleman hath had more followers than precedents; but the query is, What is law?"

Coke's change of direction was logical: Stuart England was not Tudor England; a man could with honesty uphold Elizabeth's prerogative and cry down James's. Not only had Elizabeth her country's welfare at heart, with skill and strength to sustain it, but the situation around her had been different. Tudor England suffered under continual threat from the Continental Catholic powers. "War-and-no-war," Ralegh had called it in 1593, begging for fighting ships against the Spaniard. To a growing nation, unity is above all essential, a strong central government, discipline throughout the realm. A succession of armadas, then as now, can blow away the very breath of civil liberties. Elizabeth, like her father before her, was careful not to let such questions come to full public issue; when they reared their heads, as with the brothers Wentworth, she put the talker in the Tower. Her Commons were too inexperienced for effective protest, her judges of common law had not yet seen the need for independent action.

James came to the throne, and for a brief year or two the issue and the antagonists seemed to remain the same; in the Gunpowder trials it was Rome, Spain, a foreign enemy that Coke, Attorney General, continued to fight. Yet by the year 1607, James had revealed himself to those with eyes to see. This good-natured prince, fond of theological disputation and the deer hunt, desired to rule England as he had ruled Scotland, above the state and above the law. Parliaments were a trial laid on recurrently, like God's plagues on Pharaoh. There were kings, James wrote blandly, "before any Parliaments were holden, or laws made" — a statement which to Coke's mind was un-English as the tasseled crown of Don Velasco's hat. Squarely behind James stood Lord Chancellor Ellesmere, served by Masters in Chancery, Clerks in Chancery and a battery of civilians learned in Roman law. At Ellesmere's side Archbishop Bancroft exercised the wide legal powers of the Anglican Established Church. "*Rex est lex loquens,*" said Ellesmere. "The King is the law speaking." "It is clear by the word of God in the Scripture," said Bancroft, "that judges are but delegates under the King." "The twelve Judges of the realm," said Francis Bacon, "are as the twelve lions under Solomon's Throne. They must be lions, but yet lions under the throne, being circumspect that they do not check or oppose any points of sovereignty." Edward Coke did not agree. "The King is under God and the law!" he said.

The pronouncements clashed, ringing discordant like bells of state whose voices would not mix. Each voice represented a theory of government. Bacon, later to be Chancery's greatest champion, as yet had scarcely entered the arena. Ellesmere and Coke as chief anatagonists were well matched, superficially similar. Both men despised disorder, remaining convinced that England should be ruled by "the better sort," which meant gentlemen with a substantial yearly income from land and manor. Both were strikingly handsome. If spectators came to Chancery for a sight of the old lord presiding whitehaired in his robes (Ellesmere was sixty-seven), Coke had an added attraction, the dramatic quality of the unexpected. To the end of his official life no one knew what Coke might say or do; the quality of outrageousness remained.

Coke's first point of attack was not Chancery (that would come later) but Archbishop Bancroft's disciplinary body, the Ecclesiastical High Commission. This was a group of men, led by Bishops and Privy Councilors, who in 1559 had been authorized by Act of Parliament to keep order within the Established Church, discipline the clergy and punish such lay offenses as were included in the ecclesiastical jurisdiction — at the time, a necessary and useful body. Toward the end of Elizabeth's reign, however, the Commission began to extend its powers; already in the 1590's there had been murmurs against it, mostly from Puritans and Nonconformists. Since James's accession the Commission had grown larger; it numbered nearly eighty and called itself a court — the *Court of High Commission* — encroaching, Coke noted with concern, on common-law jurisdiction.

Against this encroachment there was but one recourse. If cases already on trial by the High Commission could be proven to be lay cases rather than ecclesiastical, trial might be summarily stopped by a writ of prohibition.* The distinction between "lay" and "ecclesiastical" was not however easy to come at, the Church authority being wide and reaching far beyond theological or clerical matters. Since time immemorial — in the lawyers' phrase, "time out of mind" — the Church had regulated family affairs. Marriage and divorce, baptism, burial and the making of wills were under ecclesiastical jurisdiction. Church courts were empowered to punish perjury, defamation, drunkenness, breaches of faith, mistreatment of wives by husbands, incontinence and crimes of sexual behavior not covered by the common law. In his *Fourth Institute*, Coke described the hierarchy of Church government — Consistory Courts, Courts of Delegates and of Appeals; the Court of Convocation which sat in Parliament time; Courts of the Archbishops in Bow Street church and that great Court of Audience at Lambeth Palace, where Archbishop Whitgift once had haled an Attorney General for certain irregularities in his marriage to Lady Hatton.

Elizabeth, as head of the Established Church, quite naturally upheld this ecclesiastical jurisdiction, exercised once by Rome and

* Chapter Note.

transferred to Episcopal Canterbury only by long and bitter struggle. To Coke as to Elizabeth the transfer meant national independence, an English Church authority rather than a Roman one. Why should they not uphold it? When, in the House of Commons, James Morrice in 1593 opposed the High Commission and the oath *ex officio* which governed its procedure, Speaker Coke did not defend him.

But times and rulers change. Elizabeth had never called herself "a little God to rule over men," nor said, as James did: "General laws, made publicly in Parliament, may by the King's authority be suspended upon causes known only to him." Above the horizon a cloud loomed; Coke saw it darken England's sky. Archbishop Bancroft presented complaints to Star Chamber in the form of twenty-five elaborate articles of grievances against the common-law courts. Coke called them *Articuli Cleri*, after an old statute of 1300, and the name stuck. In 1607 a new law dictionary appeared in London, entitled *The Interpreter*, dedicated to Bancroft, much read and talked of. Under the word "king" was to be found the following: "He is above the law by his absolute power; he may alter or suspend any particular law that seemeth hurtful to the publick estate. Thus much in short because I have heard some to be of opinion that the laws be above the King." Dr. Cowell, the author, served as Professor of Civil Law at Oxford; there was little doubt as to what circumstances had fed his fire.

During the same year of 1607, the Commons asked Coke and the Chief Justice of King's Bench for an opinion concerning the legality of the oath *ex officio*, as administered in the ecclesiastical courts. Actually, all courts of Roman law procedure, including Chancery, operated by this oath. Without it, judges could not proceed to that examination of the defendant which was the hub of inquisitorial procedure. Nobody objected to the oath in any courts but the ecclesiastical — and for perfectly good reason. In Chancery as in Star Chamber, defendants were shown the bill of charges against them — factual charges to which they swore guilty or not guilty and then proceeded upon questioning under the oath. Such procedure was quick, efficient and far cheaper than the tedious process by jury at common law. In consequence, the prerogative courts of Roman law procedure were thronged with suitors who brought their cases voluntarily, to save time and money. In days long gone by, when suits had been settled by compurgation and oath-helpers, the inquisitorial oath had come as a great step forward; men welcomed a chance to defend themselves by their own answers under oath. As long as such inquisition concerned facts, it was equitable, by all odds the most practical way to get at truth.

But when case and questioning concerned matters not of fact but of opinion, religion, heresy, a man's private belief, the thing changed color and the oath *ex officio* became a trap to catch unwary or ingenuous men — "an unlawful process of poking about in the speculation of finding something chargeable." Even Lord Burghley had expostulated against the methods employed. "I think," he wrote to Archbishop Whitgift, "the inquisitors of Spain use not so many questions to comprehend and trap their prey. This kind of proceeding is rather a device to seek for offenders than to reform any. This is not the charitable instruction that I thought was intended . . . the parties are first subject to condemnation before they be taught their error."

Before Gunpowder Plot, it had been mostly Catholics who were caught by the oath *ex officio;* Jesuits, in desperation, resorted to their defense of "equivocation." Yet now, the prevalent heresy had turned Protestant and domestic; the nonconformist, the sectary was at bay and must defend himself. For every seminary missioner dead or silenced, a double dozen of Puritans came up to harry the authorities, hurling against the Established ritual the fire they once had thrown against the Pope. *Discard the Book of Common Prayer!* they cried. *Discard the surplice, the ring in marriage; in baptism the sign of the Cross. Let no altar face east, the great ordinance is not the Sacrament but preaching!* Puritans stamped into church on Sundays, tore surplice from the minister's back, bread and wine from altar rails, broke up services and defied the ecclesiastical courts which tried to punish them.

A hard assignment for Archbishop Bancroft, who must keep order within his vast Establishment. Puritans had increased alarmingly in the House of Commons — men of ability, trained in law and parliamentary practice. A ringing Biblical vocabulary accompanied them and their clients to court, spilling out in torrential harsh variation. Judges were "Babylonish . . . members of the House of Rimmon . . . Satan's minions . . . petty anti-Christs, paltry popes." Andrew Melville the Scotsman, brought before Privy Council, seized Bancroft by the white sleeves of his rochet and cried out, "Romish rags, a mark of the beast!" King James was only too familiar with the phraseology. In Scotland he had suffered perpetual bombardment from the Kirk; the word *Presbyter* was enough to make him raise his fist or turn his back. James began to couple Puritans and Papists in one sentence. "I shall make them conform themselves," he had been heard to say of the Puritans, "or I will harry them out of the land." His royal *Proclamation concerning Conformity* declared there was "no cause why the Service of God, the Book of Common Prayer or the Church discipline by law established, should be changed."

To the farthest borders of Northumberland, Wales, Ireland, the question reached, encroaching on the daily life of plain men, unlettered and poor. In 1607, Parliament was sitting; the Commons requested Coke's opinion concerning the oath *ex officio*. Coke's reply seems startling, considering his past loyalty to monarchism and the Church of England: "No man ecclesiastical or temporal shall be examined upon secret thoughts of his heart or of his secret opinion. And the defendant must have, as in Star Chamber and Chancery, the bill [of charges] delivered unto him, or otherwise he need not answer to it. Laymen for the most part are not lettered, wherefore they may easily be inveigled and intrapped and principally in heresy and errors of faith."

During these months, when Coke and Parliament together challenged Archbishop Bancroft, there ran in the courts a notorious suit, very pertinent to the point at issue. *Fuller's Case*, it was called, after the barrister who defended it. Nicholas Fuller, a Parliament man (member for London) had been much employed by Puritans in their troubles with the ecclesiastical discipline. Voluble, active, indiscreet, Fuller was given to protesting subsidy bills in Parliament and saying unkind things about the Scots. "Nick Fuller," they called him in the Lower House. At the moment he had in tow no less than twenty Puritan clients, most of whom were trying to escape fines for nonconformity. Two of these — Lad, a Norfolkman, and Mansell, a preacher — had been imprisoned for contempt because at their trial before the High Commission they refused the oath *ex officio*. Fuller, in defense of his clients, overreached himself and insulted the bishops in open court. High Commission procedure, said he, was "popish, under jurisdiction not of Christ but anti-Christ"; the oath *ex officio* led "to the damnation of their souls that take it"; he had heard said that bishops embezzled the fines of poor nonconformist preachers instead of paying them properly into Exchequer.

Fuller, upon this, found himself in custody for contempt. ("Nicholas Fuller," it was said, "pleaded so boldly for the enlargement of his clients that he procured his own confinement.") The two clients were forgotten; to this day, no one knows what became of Lad and Mansell. But for nearly nineteen months, Fuller's Case rocked back and forth between King's Bench and High Commission — directed largely by Fuller himself from the White Tavern in Southwark, where Archbishop Bancroft had locked him in. King's Bench defended its prohibition on grounds that a barrister's conduct in court was a lay matter, to be tried at common law. Archbishop Bancroft declared otherwise. In the end, after two arraignments, Fuller was convicted, fined two hundred pounds and put in Fleet Prison. The charge was slander, schism, heresy, impious error, and the holding of pernicious opinions.

Coke, technically, had not been concerned beyond acting as mediator between King's Bench and Archbishop Bancroft. Yet for the common law it was a notable defeat, the case having been badly managed not only by Fuller, who talked too much in court, but by Judges Fenner and Croke of King's Bench, who issued their prohibition during the summer vacation when the other judges were away. Putting Fuller in jail only heightened popular feeling and emphasized the point at issue: Was the High Commission a court of record, with power to imprison and to fine? Bancroft, Ellesmere and James said *Yes;* the common law said *No.* London visitors wrote home to their counties about Nicholas Fuller and his case, Parliament discussed it. The Lower House took Fuller's side. King James showed agitation. By Elizabeth's Act of Supremacy (1559) James was monarch over Church as well as state; who impugned ecclesiastical authority impugned the sovereign. "I pray you," he wrote to Sir Robert Cecil, 'forget not Fuller's matter. I prophecy unto you that when soever the ecclesiastical dignity together with the King's government thereof shall be turned into contempt and vanish in this kingdom, the kings hereof shall not longer prosper in their government and the monarchy shall fall to ruin."

Dr. Cowell had been right; it was high time for an authoritative definition of the word "king." Lord Chancellor Ellesmere was ready to add a definition of his own. When the public conscience got out of order, the Lord Chancellor must set it in line by public rebuke delivered from Star Chamber or such official platform as was available. During Fuller's troubles a magnificent forum presented itself. Calvin's Case came to court in a blaze of fame and dignity. It was a test case to determine if a man born in Scotland after James's accession could call himself an English subject and inherit English lands — in a sense, James's own suit, brought largely at his instigation. Parliament had defeated the royal plan of union with Scotland; James hoped to salvage at least the rights of citizenship for his onetime countrymen. Fourteen judges, drawn from all three courts, tried Calvin's Case in Exchequer Chamber; each judge, during several days of trial, gave an oral opinion before a crowded courtroom. Ellesmere spoke last; the gist of his oration centered upon neither Calvin nor Scotland. It was a heavy salvo directed at loose talkers who during the past months had expressed themselves too vividly concerning the oath *ex officio*, bishops in general and the royal prerogative in particular. Certain new-risen philosophers, said Ellesmere scornfully, looked upon the common law as above the monarch, even daring to declare that "kings have no more power than the people from whom they take their temporal jurisdiction!" Such persons called upon the law of nature, asking "if kings or people did first make laws?" Near treason! said Ellesmere warmly. "The monarch is the law. *Rex est lex loquens*, the king is the law speaking."

In his place nearby, Coke must have heard it with gloom and revulsion. "Our constitution," Ellesmere went on indignantly, "is to be obeyed and reverenced," not bandied by persons walking in Paul's aisle or sitting in ordinaries "drowned with drink, blown away with a whiff of tobacco!" Such "busy questionists" cited Plato and Aristotle on the framing of states and commonwealths. In Ellesmere's opinion, Plato and Aristotle were men "lacking knowledge of God, born in popular states, mislikers of monarchies" and no more fit to give laws "than Sir Thomas More's *Utopia* and such pamphlets as we have at every mart."

It was a typical expression of a point of view. And the Lord Chancellor, without referring openly to the court of Common Pleas, had employed the oratorical trick of classifying thoughtful, purposeful men all in one lump with popular demagogues — and, by the use of More's name, with "popery" too. Ellesmere added a three-column definition of the English common law that must have well-nigh curdled Coke's blood. Pronouncing the word *moreover* like an ejaculation, he fired a parting shot: "Moreover! Had Calvin's Case proven difficult, his Majesty himself should have decided it — the most religious, learned and judicious king that ever this kingdom or island had!"

Such a statement, made officially in an English courtroom — and by the Lord Chancellor himself — was a slap in the face of Edward Coke and all who held his ideas on government. "It is not customary," the great Chief Justice Fortescue once had said, "for the kings of England to sit in court or pronounce judgment themselves." Every English lawyer knew it, a maxim bred in the bone. Against it the Chief Justice of Common Pleas had but one official recourse: to withdraw suits from prerogative courts whenever and however he could, narrow down the Roman law jurisdiction and starve it to bones. By siege or by assault, Coke's weapons were slight. Mere legal quibbles, some called them — prohibitions, for instance. Yet giants still were vulnerable if pebbles could be found.

During the year following Fuller's imprisonment and Ellesmere's oration, prohibitions flowed out from Common Pleas under Coke's seal. Fuller's friends meanwhile distributed pamphlets, designed to get him out of jail, eloquent with Fuller's previous courtroom arguments, many of which were clever and some of which were sound. Coke, defending his own position, even borrowed certain of the phrases — unless, indeed, Coke had inspired it in the first place. In an icy January of 1608, Fuller, having "kist the rod and made his submission," was freed, romping out of jail "very frolick," wrote a Londoner, "and so joyfull that he would not lose so much time as to go about (by London Bridge) but would needs passe over the river on foot.* His owne weaknes and want of judgement hath ben his greatest enemie."

* The Thames froze solid that winter. Chamberlain's letter is dated January 8. Fuller apparently walked from Fleet Prison to the Surrey side where he lived.

Archbishop Bancroft watched the prohibitions roll from Common Pleas in term time and was alarmed. He appealed to James, advised him of the danger. Let his Majesty summon Coke and his brethren, tell them they overstepped.

Chamberlain to Carleton

London, 8 November, 1608

The King hath had two or three conferences of late with the Judges about prohibitions, as well touching the Clergie and high commission as the courts of Yorke and Wales, which prohibitions he would faine cut off, and stretch his prerogative to the uttermost. The judges stand well yet to theyre tackling: but *finis coronat opus* [the end crowns the work]. . . .

The Privy Council met customarily on Sunday mornings at Whitehall Palace. (It had been a Sunday when Essex gave his last fatal refusal to attend.) On Sunday, November 6, 1608, common-law judges and ecclesiastics were summoned to Whitehall. The two sides, said James, might give their reasons and cite authorities; he would act as arbitrator to decide if the disputed prohibitions were valid. It was a role James fancied, being quick at disputation; next to running down a deer he loved to track the argument to its undefended lair. Actually, decision on this Sunday morning would hang not upon individual suits prohibited but on a final interpretation of Elizabeth's original patent authorizing the Court of High Commission — several long skins of parchment, to Bancroft perfectly explicit and clear. Coke thought differently. Could the patent be proven faulty, High Commission was ruined. Bancroft was prepared to defend it, Coke to destroy it.

Yet as the meeting progressed, no valid arguments were pro-

John Chamberlain's letters to Carleton, to Secretary Winwood and to Carleton's sister Alice are a bonanza for the biographer. Chamberlain, a bachelor, lived in the heart of London, close to St. Paul's; it was his delight to stroll in the famous middle aisle and pick up news, then go home and write it to Sir Dudley Carleton at The Hague. He knew everybody and went everywhere; he was humorous, racy, witty yet not unkind. A true newsman, Chamberlain relished detail, being, as he said, "never cloyed with particulars." His long communications are forerunners of the professional newsletters later to appear, with blanks for private additions. Politically, Chamberlain was antiprerogative, though he had no special admiration for Coke or the lawyers, preferring easier, less controversial company.

duced. Opponents stood sullen, merely denying each other's statements. James, impatient, demanded if the patent were too long a document — the judges too busy to read it? — and adjourned the meeting until the following Sunday, when "he hoped both sides would be better prepared. All the courts were under one King, one God, one country; he had excellent expectation of them all." But Coke, before the churchmen could reach the door, burst out with a long, disagreeable speech, repeating, among other insults, Nicholas Fuller's charge that commissioners had embezzled their fines. Archbishop Bancroft retorted indignantly. James interrupted, warned the two, "Take heed of heat in this business!" adding that he intended to make note of those who disregarded his wishes.

Next Sunday, Bishops and Judges reconvened. James sat in his chair, the disputants remained standing before him. Sir Julius Caesar, a Doctor of Roman Law, took notes. The King opened the meeting by remarking shortly that he had come neither to hear nor to make orations. Coke, as spokesman for the judges, this time was well prepared. ("Questions short," wrote Caesar; "deliberations long, conclusions pithy.") Ecclesiastical courts, said Coke, had undoubted authority to proceed, so long as no temporal matters were involved. But let a temporal issue enter the case, and it must be transferred to the common-law courts — even in causes of clearly ecclesiastical nature. Drawing on statutes of Edward II, III, VI, Coke acknowledged that civil lawyers construed these statutes otherwise. . . .

The King broke in. Common-law judges, he said, were like papists who quoted Scripture and then put upon it their own interpretation, to be received unquestioned. Just so, "judges allege statutes, reserving the exposition thereof to themselves." At this point some one, probably Bancroft, brought up the touchy matter of James's own powers. Coke's *Report* gives the statement unidentified:

"In cases where there is not express authority in law, the King may himself decide it in his royal person; the Judges are but delegates of the King, and the King may take what causes he shall please from the determination of the Judges and may determine them himself. And the Archbishop said: that this was clear in divinity, that such authority belongs to the King by the Word of

God in the Scripture. To which it was answered by me: that the King in his own person cannot adjudge any case, either criminal—as treason, felony, &c., or betwixt party and party; but this ought to be determined and adjudged in some court of justice, according to the Law and Custom of England. . . . And it was greatly marvelled [Coke adds in comment] that the Archbishop durst inform the King that such absolute power and authority, as is aforesaid, belonged to the King by the Word of God."

The sovereign, Coke told James, might sit in Star Chamber, "and this appears in our books." But only to consult with the judges, not *in judicio*.

(In Star Chamber was a chair of state, emblazoned with the royal arms. For thirty years Coke had seen it empty; Elizabeth never claimed her right to sit. There were powers a wise sovereign did not put to public test.) "And it appears by Act of Parliament," Coke went on, addressing the King, "that neither by the Great Seal nor by the Little Seal, justice shall be delayed; *ergo*, the King cannot take any cause out of any courts and give judgment upon it himself. . . ."

Here the record becomes confused and it is difficult—as always in Coke's *Reports*—to separate what was said at the moment from what may have been added later. It is unlikely that James would have endured without interruption so long and violent a speech. From Sir Julius Caesar and various newsletters, it appears that at some point James broke in, told Coke he "spoke foolishly." Himself, the King, as supreme head of justice, would defend to the death his prerogative of calling judges before him to decide disputes of jurisdiction. Moreover, he would "ever protect the common law."

"The common law," Coke interjected, "protecteth the King."

"A traitorous speech!" James shouted. "The King protecteth the law, and not the law the King! The King maketh judges and bishops. If the judges interpret the laws themselves and suffer none else to interpret, they may easily make, of the laws, shipmen's hose!"

At this point James shook his fist and Sir Julius Caesar, after one brief sentence, stopped taking notes. Coke's *Report* picks up the story. "Then the King said that he thought the Law was founded upon Reason, and that he and others had Reason as well as the Judges. To which it was answered by me, that true it was that God had endowed his Majesty with excellent science and great endowments of Nature. But his Majesty was not learned in the Laws of his Realm of England; and Causes which concern the Life, or Inheritance, or Goods, or Fortunes of his Subjects are not to be decided by natural Reason but by the artificial Reason and Judgment of Law, which requires long Study and Experience before that a man can attain to the cognizance of it; and that the Law was the golden Metwand and Measure to try Causes of the Subjects, which protected his Majesty in safety and Peace: With which the King was greatly offended, and said that then he should be under the Law, which was treason to affirm (as he said). To which I said, that Bracton saith, *Quod Rex non debet esse sub homine, sed sub Deo et Lege* — that the King should not be under man, but under God and the Laws."

Sir Rafe Boswell to Dr. Milborne

. . . the Lord Coke humbly prayed the king to have respect to the Common Lawes of his land &c. He prayed his Majesty to consider that the Ecclesiastical Jurisdiction was forren. After which his Majesty fell into that high indignation as the like was never knowne in him, looking and speaking fiercely with bended fist, offering to strike him, &c. Which the Lo. Cooke perceaving fell flatt on all fower; humbly beseeching his Majestie to take compassion on him and to pardon him if he thought zeale had gone beyond his dutie and allegiance. His Majestie not herewith contented, continued his indignation. Whereuppon the Lo. Treasurer [Robert Cecil] * the Lo. Cooke's unckle by marriage, kneeled down before his Majestie and prayed him to be favourable. To whom his Majestie replied saying, *What hast thou to doe to intreate for him?* He answered, *In regard he hath married my neerest kinswoman*, &c."

There is another account of this Sunday meeting, written within a fortnight by one John Hercy to the Earl of Shrewsbury and postmarked *Westminster Hall at 10 in the forenoon:* "The Lord Cooke amongst other offensive speech should say to his Majestie that his Highnes was defended by his lawes. At which his Majestie was very much offended, & told him he spake foolishly and said that he was not defended by his lawes but by God; and so

* Robert Cecil had been created Lord Treasurer — his father's office — in May preceding.

gave the Lord Cooke in other words a very sharp reprehension both for that & other things." Nothing is said here about Coke's falling on all fours, though the writer adds that if Cecil, "most humbly on his knee," had not interposed "to pacify his Majesty," it would have gone hard with Coke. Whatever happened, it was a tremendous scene: a king's fist raised against a judge, the small pale hunchback throwing himself between. "*My little great Lord,*" they called Cecil now; he carried more power and more care than any man in England, and after his father's example he remained faithful to his friends.

Very likely, Coke did fall on his face. It was that or a cell in the Tower. The Chief Justice of Common Pleas knelt, and rose, and went out into November city streets. King James, having disposed of these vexing questions, as it seemed in one brief forenoon, turned his face again to Royston where the red deer ran.

Next morning a new prohibition, under Coke's seal, went out to High Commission from the Court of Common Pleas.

CHAPTER TWENTY-THREE

Parliament steps in. Bonham's Case.

> The division between the clergy and the temporal law is full of great peril to the State, as much as the discontent of the common people against the gentry. But God defend and continue His peace.
>
> *Journal of Sir Roger Wilbraham*

THERE was peril to the state, but as yet no more than the peril of confusion. Armed rebellion — the Long Parliament of 1641 — civil war and regicide: not James but James's son would suffer these. Oliver Cromwell, nine years old, ran in the fields of Hinchinbrook, learning to handle crossbow and caliver. The Commons of 1609 contained no Pym or Prynne or Eliot, ready to dispossess a King; no Robert Kett cried, "Kill the gentry!" The country gentry indeed, with their brothers the lawyers, were busy discovering just what it was they wanted and how they desired to be governed. Chipping and whittling at the power of royal officials, the Commons before long would much reduce the influence of those Privy Councilors who sat in the front row. Yet no man among them wished to do away with the royal prerogative, though on one point all were clear: private property must be preserved, safeguarded against crown encroachment. None were revolutionists. All were monarchists, Coke included. The Commons distrusted James but they did not hate kingship. "A King," said John Selden, the legal scholar, "is a thing men have made for their own sakes, for quietness' sake." "It was a wonder to hear," said Edward Coke, "that the liberty of the subject should be thought incompatible with the regality of the King." "If false glasses did not stand between us and the King," said John Eliot in Parliament, "our privileges and his prerogative might both have been enjoyed."

Yet by 1609, Parliament as well as Coke had become restive. England had as yet no bill of rights; against crown encroachment the subject's only guarantee lay in those procedural rules of law court and assembly that had been developed over the centuries. Coke knew it, as did those of his colleagues who were scholars and could lay their hands on precedent. A man who is by inclination a rebel looks ahead and invents a system, complete with slogan, precept, rule. ("If you do not like your laws," Voltaire would one day tell his countrymen, "destroy them and make new ones.") The suggestion would have angered Edward Coke, to whom law could not be "made" but must grow from ancient roots. Legally, the word *innovation* was, to Coke, despicable; it meant a flouting of time-tested rule and custom. Coke searched for England's freedom not in the future but the past, and found it and desired his countrymen to rest upon it and retain it.

But in the common-law courts of 1609, Chief Justice Coke was very much alone. Four Brethren sat with him: Foster, Walmesley, Warburton, Daniel. James had added a fifth judge for decision when the vote split two and two. Foster, an Inner Templar from the north of England, was Coke's junior by seventeen years. Thomas Walmesley, aged seventy, had been Judge since 1589; he came from Lancashire and enjoyed a fortune from speculation in land. William Daniel's name had appeared in Coke's *Reports* as early as 1591; he was of Gray's Inn; Burghley had recommended him to the Queen as "very honest, learned and discreet." Sir Peter Warburton, a Lincoln's Inn man of about sixty years, had sat in Common Pleas since 1600; beyond that, little is known except that he had been married three times. Two of these men were shortly to be replaced by Justices Winch and Nichols, the latter a "patient man, very honest . . . even," it was said, "to the rejection of gratuities after judgment given"—in itself a telling commentary on the current system of office holding. Winch had been Chief Justice of Ireland; Bacon admired him as a person of some brilliance.

Men characterized as "honest, patient, discreet," may be excellent judges and administrators, but among Coke's Brethren in

Common Pleas something more was needed as defense against such antagonists as Lord Chancellor Ellesmere, Archbishop Bancroft and Sir Francis Bacon. Coke must look for help beyond his own court, in Parliament, where new laws originated. As Judge of Common Pleas, Coke's business was not to change the law but to adjudicate between John Doe and Richard Roe in whatever private dispute they might present. Judicial choice lay between suitors, not between principles. "General propositions," Justice Oliver Wendell Holmes was to say, "do not decide concrete cases." Only accidentally might a case come up that was pertinent to the larger point at issue. Because of Coke's years and experience, because too of a dramatic quality in what he said and did, he was listened to, sometimes beyond his just deserts. Already the word "oracle" followed his name: "oracle of the law." Yet Coke's pronouncements from the bench changed no law and altered no constitution. Rather they may be looked on as great dissents expressed in the ordinary run of judicial duties, forerunners of future legislation. Concerning Parliament as ally, it is significant that Coke's courtroom lay physically so near the Commons. Only a flight of stairs, a sharp turn leftward separated him from close friends and sympathizers — Fuller, Whitelocke, Sandys, Wentworth — eager to join forces against prerogative encroachment.

For Coke it was a natural alliance. Himself half medievalist, he still regarded Parliament as a court: the High Court of Parliament, last appeal above King's Bench. And now that he was Judge, Sir Edward Coke continued to report on his own cases in the same magnificent confusion of detail and startling omission. "Coke, C. J., presiding," he wrote. Because suits in Common Pleas were concerned with private law (as King's Bench with public law) it followed that some of Coke's noblest judicial statements grew out of cases that were piddling, almost farcical. A Bonham's Case for the false imprisonment of a physician whose name, save for Coke's pronouncement, would long ago have been forgotten. An Edwards's Case for libel, brought by High Commission because of letters sent to a bishop's grandson, "lewd ungodly and uncharitable," hinting in dog-Latin ("*siphilam lichenen mentegram,*") that the Bishop had suffered from unmentionable diseases and flaunting that last worst insult, the drawing of a horn. "And we require you upon your oath," High Commission commanded the defendant, "to set down whether you meant not that he was a cuckold and what other meaning you had, to the dislike of the dignity and calling of Bishops." Upon this ludicrous foundation Coke built a noble statement, sending against the High Commission a prohibition in words that roll and echo down the years: "The Ecclesiastical judge cannot examine any man upon his oath, upon the intention and thought of his heart. *Cogitationis poenam nemo emeret* [no man may be punished for his thoughts]. For it hath been said in the Proverb, THOUGHT IS FREE."

Day after day from eight to noon, "*meum* and *tuum*, those great pronouns," sounded in Common Pleas like a refrain. Mine and thine. Property rights to be protected: John Doe against Richard Roe for loss of a sheep, Black Acre feuding with White Acre for possession of a ploughed strip. "Enter into the land," says Justice Coke in the ancient phraseology. "Enter into the land and God give you joy." England trembled on the edge of change, ready to abandon feudal customs, put off the old man and put on the new. Stuart ineptitude would hasten the change. Coke fought stubbornly and almost alone, not yet quite sure of the ultimate boundary between Crown and Parliament. The Commons, ready in their minds to espouse Coke's cause, held back, still loyal to a King who claimed supremacy in government yet who patently was not to be trusted with the general welfare.

James, after four years' rule, was desperately in need of funds. Kings of England were supposed to "live of their own estate": that is, to cover personal and palace expenditures from their hereditary revenue. Only the national defense, foreign war or state emergencies justified a call on Parliament. Yet James, during the past year, had overreached his income by £81,000, with a total debt of £1,300,000 (a sum worth today at least fifteen times the amount). Elizabeth for all her grandeur had practiced thrift; James gave money away in fistfulls. Stories circulated: the King, walking through the long gallery at Whitehall with Sir Henry Rich, "a young ingenious knight"; porters passing with three hundred pounds, bound for the Privy Purse. "Would that I had such a sum!" sighs the knight, and his Majesty tells the porters to take their moneybags to Sir Henry's lodgings. . . . Lord Hay, the Scottish favorite, with his new vanity of "ante-suppers": guests, on entering, saw the board piled with choice viands — fish from Russia, so big no dish in England could hold them; dried sweetmeats and comfits to the value of ten shillings the pound. And all removed as soon as viewed, given to servants or beggars at the gate, replaced in the dining hall by a second serving of the same.

James called on Parliament for money — and the Commons balked. As Treasurer of England, Robert Cecil proposed a scheme. After providing for the present debt and unusual naval expenses, let Parliament vote a perpetual yearly revenue of £200,000 for crown use. In return, besides the redress of grievance, his Majesty would consider giving up certain hereditary revenues or tenures — such as the right to wardship and purveyance. The largest part of crown monies was derived from impositions — taxes taken at English ports on goods going out or coming in. Parliament already had tried to query the King's right to impositions and got nowhere with it. Cecil, questioned now from the floor, turned immediately cautious. He would have to consult with the Lords, he said.

Actually, Cecil's scheme was excellent. The *Great Royal Contract,* he called it; he had put his heart in it. The Commons however were in suspicious mood. They refused to credit Cecil's figures. The royal tenures, they said bluntly, were not worth the stated £200,000. And what surety had they that the money, once voted, would not find its way into the pocket of a Hay, a Carr, a Henry Rich? The question was not only rude but sharply indicative. England had no "budget" and Parliament no shadow of right to query the disposal of monies once granted. Under Elizabeth, no member would have dared; the Queen might use her subsidies to buy jeweled sword hilts for Essex if she chose. But times had changed. The Treasury, a speaker ventured roughly, was a "royal cistern, wherein his Majesty's largesse to the Scots caused a continued and remediless leak; for his part he would never give consent to take money from a poor frieze jerkin to trap a courtier's horse withal." Furthermore, judges reported royal meddling with the common law. His Majesty, sitting at dinner, had praised Cowell's law dictionary, with its arbitrary definition of kingship, its nefarious hint that taxation was part of the royal prerogative. Just who carried this tale to the Lower House is not known; very likely it was Coke. Whoever the messenger, the effect was inflammatory. James thought best to retreat. He suppressed the dictionary by proclamation. No one might buy or read it — "The author being only a civilian writing a dictionary, disputes on the mysteries of this our monarchy, mistaking the true state of Parliament and speaking irreverently of the Common Law."

This was mollifying. To cap it, James met Lords and Commons formally at Whitehall and spoke from the throne. "I am not ignorant," he said, "that I have been thought to be an enemy to all prohibitions, and an utter stayer of them. Anent the common law, some had a conceit I disliked it, and that I would have wished the civil law to have been put in place of the common law for government of this people." Yet he had "the least cause of any man," said James in the pleasant, fatherly tone that he liked to affect, "to dislike the common law." To do so would be "to neglect his own crown, for no law could be more favorable and advantageous for a King and extend further his prerogative."

Extend his prerogative? The Commons heard it in disbelief. How clever, this smooth twisting of the argument, this air of wounded royal acquiescence! A century earlier, the Commons might have been fooled. But in this Chamber sat more than a hundred Inns of Court men who told themselves they knew the law — and knew also the sentiment of the country behind them. Of course, James went on, he approved of prohibitions, provided they were issued by King's Bench or Chancery. "For other benches" (a plain thrust at Coke) "I am not yet so well resolved of their jurisdiction in that point. . . . To the courts of common law I gave admonitions that they should not be so forward and prodigal in multiplying their prohibitions, and that none should be granted by any one particular judge, or in time of vacation. Two several times dealt I with this cause, once in the middest of winter and again in the middest of the next following summer; at every of which times I spent three whole days in that labour. . . . In faith," James added plaintively, "you never had a more pain-full king —"

Pain-full? Those in the room who had served Elizabeth saw irony in the word. The royal deeds belied the royal words. Three days in town away from hunting and the King felt himself overworked, on the edge of fever. Leaving prohibitions and the common law, James swung into a topic closely related yet more congenial:

"The state of monarchy is the supremest thing upon earth. For Kings are not only God's lieutenants upon earth and sit upon God's throne, but even by God himself they are called Gods . . . for that they exercise a manner or resemblance of divine power upon earth. For if you will consider the attributes to God, you shall see how they agree in the person of a King. God hath power to create or destroy, make or unmake at his pleasure, to give life or send death, to judge all and to be judged nor accountable to none. Kings make and unmake their subjects; they have power of raising and casting down; of life and of death . . . and make of their subjects like men at the chess; a pawn to take a Bishop or a Knight, and to cry up or down any of their subjects as they do their money. . . ."

To judge all and to be judged by none. An ominous statement. The Commons left the Palace, returned to Westminster to thrash out their part of the Great Contract. A *petition,* they called it; *Petition of Grievances.* James could take small comfort in the title; bills in Commons had always originated as petitions. "Most gracious Sovereign," the preamble began, "Your Majesty's loving subjects through the whole realm . . . perceive their common and ancient right and liberty to be much declined and infringed in these late years. . . ."

There were nine headings or grievances — prominent among them four matters with which Coke was closely concerned: Ecclesiastical Commissions, Writs of Prohibitions, Jurisdiction of Shires near Wales, Proclamations. Privy Council of late had been trying to govern the Welsh border shires by peremptory instruction. Suits at common law, said the petition, had been stopped by injunction in Chancery, "sometimes before, sometimes after judgment;" prohibitions issued from the Common Bench had been denied. Each grievance was set out in lengthy detail, full as a legal brief. Parliament wished to draw these matters under legislative jurisdiction: accomplish reform by parliamentary statute rather than by royal leniency or "grace." Under Elizabeth such attempts had been rewarded with a stay in the Tower. Yet today the few bold spirits did not stand alone; men felt at least a sense of solidarity.

It was a time and a moment to take inventory, review the lines of battle. Whoever might direct the fight in Parliament, in the law courts the primary responsibility was Coke's. While Robert Cecil lived, Coke had at least a single ally in Privy Council. The wonder was that James had not displaced Cecil with some young Scotsman like Robert Carr. Yet Cecil's health was delicate. He bore too great a burden, frequently fell ill. Beyond him there was not a man in

Privy Council who knew how to handle the Commons or who sensed the full danger of a break with Parliament. (Francis Bacon knew it, but Bacon was not yet a Privy Councilor.) Again and again, Cecil met the Lower House with attempted compromise. Men noted that his natural pallor had increased; he looked as if a breath would blow him down. As Chief Justice, Coke must be on hand to advise the Upper House — Lords, not Commons — though the latter frequently sought guidance and support. But it was to his own court, his own northwest corner of Westminster Hall that Coke now carried the fight. That vast chamber, where still among ceiling cobwebs the angels flew, face down in faintly seen benignity — that vast chamber which Attorney General Coke had seen cleared and garnished for an Essex trial, a Gunpowder trial — was now a working-place, busy, humdrum, matutinal. There were no screens round Common Pleas; with three law courts in session (counting Chancery), the Hall hummed like a hive. Throngs passed up and down the middle aisle between the courts: booksellers, stationers, scriveners, vendors of bread and hot meats. In winter Coke sat wrapped in miniver, the tabs of his velvet cap pulled down over the coif to warm his ears, his full robe tucked around his feet against the drafty floor. A mustiness lay upon this ancient place; old Ellesmere, mounting to the marble chair, clutched his sprigs of wormwood to ward off evil vapors.

All during the winter of 1609-1610, while Parliament was sitting, Coke sent out his prohibitions, battling Archbishop Bancroft, "in contempt," wrote Bancroft angrily, "of the command of the King." Repeatedly, Lord Chancellor Ellesmere called the judges to conference, sometimes in the King's presence, sometimes alone. They failed to shake Sir Edward; he never changed position: The High Commission "hath not properly cognizance over anything concerning *meum* and *tuum*, as legacies, tithes, and pensions. . . ." Magna Carta forbade fine and imprisonment by such a court. . . . "And if every man should be examined upon his oath, what opinion he holdeth concerning any point of religion, he is not bound to answer the same. For in time of danger, *Quo modo tutus erit* [How will he be safe]?"

In response to the royal demand, Coke sent the King a carefully prepared treatise, clear, unequivocal: "Actes of Parliament are to be interpreted by the judges of the laws of England and not by any canonist or ecclesiastical judge. And this is expressly proved by many authorities and judgments reported in our bookes of Lawe . . . so as . . . we hope the Lo. Archbishop (being now truly informed hereof) will herewith rest satisfied." The Archbishop was far from resting satisfied. Coke's final sentence, complacent, hortatory, was enough to heat the noble prelate's blood to apoplexy. Bonham's Case came to court; Coke seized occasion to declare the common law above Parliament as well as above the King: "When an Act of Parliament is against common right and reason, the common law will control it and adjudge such Act to be void."

It was the most controversial judicial dictum of Coke's life, due to be celebrated out of all proportion to its real significance — one of those public statements which, as history progresses, men seize upon and interpret according to their need. The facts of the case were these: Dr. Thomas Bonham had practiced medicine in London without a certificate from the Royal College of Physicians. The College censors arrested him and put him in the Fleet, whereupon Bonham brought action for false imprisonment. The censors' defense lay in their College statute of incorporation, empowering them to "regulate all London physicians and punish infractions with fine and imprisonment." So far, so good. But the statute, Coke noted, gave the college one half of each fine collected, thus making the censors at once judge and party to every case they brought to court. There was, said Coke, a maxim of the common law: No man ought to be judge in his own cause; "*Aliquis non debet esse judex in propria causa*." On this alone the statute of incorporation should be disallowed. "And it appears in our books," Coke added characteristically, "that in many cases *the common law will control acts of Parliament and some times adjudge them to be utterly void; For when an Act of Parliament is against common right and reason, or repugnant, or impossible to be performed, the common law will control it and adjudge such Act to be void*."

Actually, Coke based his decision on five points, not one. But it was the above clause which echoed down the centuries . . . 1765, and a Stamp Act passed in Parliament. New England protesting. "An Act against natural equity is void!" shouted James Otis of Massachusetts, and from Boston to Virginia trumpets blew. Massachusetts Assembly declared the Stamp Act invalid, "against Magna Charta and the natural rights of Englishmen, and therefore, according to the Lord Coke, null and void." Patrick Henry also cited Coke as authority for nullification. But how, a doubtful judge inquired of John Adams, can such nullity be proven? By the *jus gladii divinum* — the divine right of the sword? Never mind *jus gladii*, replied John Adams at once. "Tell the jury the nullity of acts of Parliament. . . . I am determined to die of that opinion." Coke would have been astonished at the uses to which Bonham's Case was put. *Lex est tutissima cassis;* the law is the safest shield. Coke's motto sounded in colonial law courts beside the name of Bonham, dead two centuries and more. . . . 1787: a federal convention to construct a United States Constitution, create a Supreme Court of judges that would pass on legislation and interpret it.

In England, Coke's doctrine met with differing response. "A foolish doctrine," Lord Campbell called it (1849), "alleged to have been laid down extra-judicially in Dr. Bonham's Case. . . . a conundrum that should have been laughed at." "What my Lord Coke says in Dr. Bonham's Case is far from any extravagancy," declared Chief Justice Holt (1688); "for it is a very reasonable and true saying," it being "impossible that one should be judge and party to a suit." Coke's contemporaries received his dictum with complacency if not indifference, though Lord Chancellor Ellesmere took occasion to grumble sarcastically at Coke's highhandedness. Dr. Bonham himself went happily free, sans fine and sans license. "No man should be judge in his own cause" — one need not be a lawyer to see it. Parliament, still busy with grievances versus the King's supply, showed no agitation, though Coke, their trusted ally, had declared the judges could abrogate a statute, pronounce it null and void. His dictum did not come as a surprise. Coke, during the course of Bonham's Case, was in daily communication with his friends of the Lower House; they knew where his thoughts lay.

Coke's own report of Bonham's Case, far from sounding the cosmic tocsin, gives off a local, intimate note that is somehow charming — and entirely overlooked by history. This is not the organ boom of a judge who consciously adjudicates for posterity; quite patently, Coke is thinking of the case at issue. Why, he asks indignantly, should the Royal College take upon itself to license a graduate of Cambridge University, as Dr. Bonham had the honor to be? "No comparison is to be made between that private College [of

Physicians] and the Universities of Cambridge and Oxford, no more than between the father and his children or between the fountain and the small rivers which descend from it. The University is Alma Mater, from whose breast those of that private college have suck'd all their science and knowledge." (Actually they sucked nothing of the kind, the firm classical breast of Alma Mater remaining closed to new methods such as anatomical dissection long after the Royal College, in William Harvey's person, uncovered the heart.) Considering the academic arguments that were to follow for centuries, Coke's report of Bonham's Case is brief indeed. It concludes with a sentence of great simplicity, expressing a judge's satisfaction in a job well done:

"And I acquainted Sir Thomas Fleming, Chief Justice of the King's Bench, with this judgment, and with the reasons and causes of it, and he well approved of the judgment which we had given: And this is the first judgment on the said branch concerning fine and imprisonment which has been given since the making of the said Charter and Acts of Parliament, and therefore I thought it worthy to be reported and published."

CHAPTER TWENTY-FOUR

Government by Proclamation. Parliament is dissolved. Coke takes the battle to Lambeth.

That wonderful Edward Coke was loose — masterful, masterless man.

F. W. Maitland, *English Law and the Renaissance*

ON the fourteenth of May, 1610, Henry IV of France was murdered, "stabbed about the short ribs by a priest or Jesuit, in Paris, being in his coach." Actually the assassin was not a Jesuit, having been refused admission to the Society years before. But James, when he heard the news, "turned whiter," wrote the French Ambassador, "than his shirt." At once he issued a proclamation forbidding recusants to come within ten miles of the palace and requiring every subject to take the new Oath of Allegiance (composed by Parliament after the Gunpowder Plot).

Robert Cecil, struggling with the Commons for the King's supply, turned this new regicide to what use he could. Papists, he told the Lower House, had devised a new heaven for the murderers of princes! King Henry's death upset the balance of Europe, "threatening a general alteration in Christendom." The young Prince of France desired King James's advice as to proceeding with a war in Europe; being under his mother's regency he was unresolved what to do. King James had already sent £6,000 and promised £30,000 more. The money must be found. And what of Prince Henry's glorious late investiture and creation as Prince of Wales? All London remembered the procession, the masques and music, the rich pageant.

Would any in the Commons have wished frugality on so joyful, so comforting an occasion? Yet his Majesty had incurred debts to pay for it. Today — said Cecil — was St. Barnabas's Day, the longest of the year, when the sun returns and alters his course. Could not the Commons follow suit and alter theirs? They had spent "almost five months in matters impertinent and extravagant discourses, whereof some square, some long, some short, but all circular — for we are there almost where we first begun."

It was a cold audience. The country at large did not welcome James's proclamation, requiring every subject of whatever religion to take the oath — an order "by divers found strange," noted John More, "because it is so general. . . . The best bond of all is love." Must Protestants too give evidence of allegiance? Parliament, when it composed the Oath of 1606, had aimed it at Catholics, Jesuits, potential Guy Fawkeses. James's proclamations, moreover, had increased alarmingly of late; in seven years this monarch had put out more such orders than Elizabeth had issued in thirty. Their content, too, was disturbing. Royal proclamations traditionally were limited to the reinforcement of old laws — reminders of a citizen's duty — proclamations to keep down rioting, preserve the peace, recruit for the militia, announce a fast-day for prayers against the enemy or gratitude for victory achieved. James's proclamations, it was complained, imposed fine and punishment, threatened men for actions against which no laws existed; he seemed to think the realm could be ruled by proclamation. It was arbitrary, un-English. If laws could be created simply by posting placards and sending heralds to read them aloud in market towns and on London street corners, then of what use Parliament?

As instance, recent royal proclamations forbade (1) the use of wheat in making starch, (2) the erection of new buildings in the City. These were perennial problems. Old Parliament men recalled Elizabeth's care concerning the unhealthy crowding of London; during poor crop years, grain was always restricted. In this session of 1610, the Lower House had already brought up both topics with a view to legislation. James's trumpeting heralds lifted the matter out of hand as if the Lower House were a schoolroom of children whittling toys. "There is a general fear conceived and spread amongst your Majesty's people," — so ran the Commons' Petition — "that Proclamations will by degrees grow up and increase to the strength and nature of laws. The people of this kingdom [possess] indubitable right not to be made subject to any punishment that shall extend to their lives, lands, bodies or goods, other than such as are ordained by the common laws of this land or the statutes made by their common consent in Parliament. . . ."

In July of 1610, the petition with its nine solemn counts was ready. A delegation brought it to the King at Whitehall. (Coke was away, riding circuit in the counties, but he would soon hear of it.) Francis Bacon acted as spokesman. Since James's accession it had been Bacon's care to soothe the extremer element in the Lower House and look after the royal interest. Standing before the throne, Sir Francis unrolled the petition, a parchment nearly four feet square. James laughed, calling out that it was large enough "to serve as a piece of tapestry." "Excellent Sovereign!" Bacon said. "Let not the sound of grievances, though it be sad, seem harsh to your princely ears. It is but *gemitus columbae*, the mourning of a dove, with that patience and humility of heart which appertaineth to loving and loyal subjects. . . ."

James received document and compliments with his usual good nature, promising royal consideration. Some weeks later the Commons had their reply. Proclamations could not, in truth, claim equal force with laws; this much James conceded. Yet on occasion, proclamations were necessary. In emergencies, a monarch could not wait on Parliament.

Emergencies, reasons of state . . . Eternal excuses of princes, oil for the wheels of absolutism. The nation faced a choice between a tightening of crown power (following the Continental trend) or a loosening of the central bonds, a shift of power to Parliament and people. Nobody stood up at Westminster and said so; in terms of wide political philosophy the Commons as yet were tongueless or confused. But every day saw a reaching out in practical ways; as instance, the Petition of Grievances.

In the matter of proclamations the Lower House had done all it could; beyond petition there was no way for Parliament to reach the throne. The Commons, frustrated, became obstreperous beyond anything seen before. "Very farouche and intractable," wrote John More. "Every day some quarrel springs up," the Venetian Ambassador reported home. Surprising scenes took place, impudencies that would not have been tolerated when Elizabeth was Queen — or when Coke presided in the Chair: "*Affirmed by Mr. Speaker*" (wrote a worried clerk) "that Sir E. Herbert put not off his hat to him but put out his tongue and popped his mouth with his finger in scorn." . . . "Henry the hardy," said a newsletter, referring to Yelverton, "was bold to bluster out." Sir Thomas Wentworth told the House confidently that God was angry with the King's treasury. A timid member, writing home, declared it was "a tickle thing for a privat man to be reporter of such speaches."

This was in July. Two months later, Coke returned from summer circuit and immediately was summoned by Privy Council to give opinion on the legality of royal proclamations. James was not present, being in the country to enjoy the fine fall weather. But the meeting proved dramatic and even more important than the famous Sunday encounter of 1608. "Upon Thursday, 20 Sept. *8 Regis Jacobi*," wrote Coke, "I was sent for to attend the Lord Chancellor [Ellesmere], Lord Treasurer [Cecil], Lord Privy Seal, and the Chancellor of the Duchy, there being present the Attorney [Hobart], the Solicitor [Francis Bacon] and the Recorder [of London] . . ."

The question, Coke affirmed at once, was of great importance; he had not heard of it "until this morning at nine of the clock, for the grievances were preferred and answer made when I was in my circuit." He would like time to confer with his Brethren and then to make "an advised answer according to law and reason." When Edward Coke sounded off on law and reason, Ellesmere knew what to expect. He broke in, reminded the company that where no precedent existed, it were better to leave decision to his Majesty; otherwise all royal authority would be gone and "the King would be no more than the Duke of Venice." A physician, the Lord Privy Seal put in, was not always bound to precedent but applied medicine according to the disease. Yet perhaps Lord Coke was right, and the King's prerogative should be confirmed by the judges' opinions. "The King," Coke said, "cannot change any part of the common law, nor create any offence by his proclamation, without Parliament, which was not an offence before."

Bacon interrupted. Did not the Lord Chief Justice recall how penalties had more than once been given in Star Chamber for infraction of the proclamation against building? The Lord Coke had himself given sentence "in divers cases of the said proclamation."

It was clever of Bacon, this reference to Coke's own decisions in

Star Chamber. But Coke was equal to it. "All indictments," he retorted, "conclude with the words, Against the law and custom of England, *Contra legem et consuetudinem Angliae;* or against laws and statutes, *Contra leges et statuta.* But I never heard an indictment to conclude, *Contra regiam proclamationem;* against the king's proclamation." The Lords gave in, granting Coke's request for time. What Coke did next was characteristic: he went to the records, the Close Rolls of Henry IV, Edward IV, Henry VIII, Fortescue's *De Laudibus,* Holinshed's *Chronicles*—traced out former proclamations that had been allowed or disallowed, including a proclamation of 1546, where "whorehouses, called the *Stews,* were suppressed by proclamation to the sound of trumpets." And if what Coke found in 1610 cannot be found today, if one or more of his "precedents" have the aspect of ghosts conjured up for the occasion —in Coke's own day the Lords of Privy Council accepted all he said.

"*It was resolved:* That the King by his proclamation cannot create any offence which was not an offence before, for then he may alter the law of the land by his proclamation in a high point; for if he may create an offence where none is, upon that ensues fine and imprisonment. Also the law of England is divided into three Parts: Common Law, Statute Law, and Custom; but the King's Proclamation is none of them.

"*Lastly,* if the offence be not punishable in the Star Chamber, the prohibition of it by Proclamation cannot make it punishable here." "After this resolution," Coke's *Report* concludes, "no proclamation imposing fine and punishment was afterwards made."

Coke and the Commons had gained their point. Their decision would stand. In a few words, Coke had set forth salient features of the constitution—"and at a time," wrote an English historian, "when a clear statement of the points at issue was greatly needed." Yet for Coke and his contemporaries, what was one victory, one grievance conceded out of so many? On all other counts, James remained immovable: prohibitions, reform of the High Commission, jurisdiction of the shires near Wales, and the royal taxes called *impositions.* Parliament asked for reform by legislation. James replied that in matters of the prerogative there could be no reform by legislation but only by the King's grace. The Great Contract seemed doomed; James was ready to dissolve Parliament. Cecil, nearly at his wit's end, urged royal patience. "His Highness," the King's Secretary replied to Cecil, "wisheth your lordship to call to mind that he hath now had patience with this assembly these seven years, and from them received some disgraces, censures and ignomies, than ever Prince did endure." "Your greatest error," James wrote to Cecil, "hath been that ye ever expected to draw honey out of gall, being a little blinded with the self-love of your own counsel in holding together of this Parliament, whereof all men were despaired as I have oft told you, but yourself alone."

Twelve days later James sent a message to Privy Council. "No house save the house of Hell could have treated him as the commons had been doing." If the Lower House continued to balk he would force a vote on supply. Cecil, at this, adjourned Parliament for five days (November 24 to 29), hoping that tempers might cool. During these exchanges the King remained, unfortunately, in the country. With him was his Scottish favorite, Sir Robert Carr, a young man notable for shrewdness, a fine appearance in the tiltyard and considerable insolence. James had heaped money on him, the latest gift being Ralegh's beloved manor of Sherborne in Dorset. Carr kept his own agents in the Lower House, ready to report statements derogatory to Scotsmen, proposals to "send them one and all back to their own country." Such talk, Carr persuaded James, must be punished, as also a speech comparing James to Joram, King of Judah, who began his reign by massacring his brothers.

James let the Christmas holidays pass, then could contain himself no longer. On February 9, 1611, he dissolved Parliament. Through the country ran a rumor, troubled, dark. In Europe, parliaments were falling into disuse; the French Estates on the brink of dissolution, the Spanish Cortes rendered impotent. Was England, with her proud tradition, to follow down this path?

With his friends of the Lower House gone home to their counties, Chief Justice Coke of Common Pleas found himself more than ever alone. His Brethren bore their share of the daily judicial load, but in larger matters of policy they attempted little. Yet Parliament was no sooner dissolved than two new prohibitions appeared against the High Commission, dated in Coke's handwriting and spelling battle — cases, said James, "of a nature extraordinary and showing more the perverseness of [Coke's] spirit than any other prohibitions." The Lord Coke's defense, James's Secretary wrote to Cecil, had best be something more than "a quibble of law. Or else his Majesty's resolution wilbe as God speaketh. . . . *My spirit shalbe no longer vexed with this man.*" Before the month was out, Coke went to Newmarket at the King's command and they talked alone. Whenever this occurred, the two got on well enough. What James could not endure, apparently, was Coke's defiance of him in public.

Archbishop Bancroft, meanwhile, had chosen this difficult moment to take sick and die, carried off by the stone at sixty-six. George Abbot, his successor, was a man notably stiff-backed, with Calvinist leanings, little experience in the broader pastoral duties, an expressed determination to control Church discipline. Shortly after his installation (April, 1611), bishops and ecclesiastical lawyers — the "civilians" — sent a petition to the King, signed with a long list of distinguished names. It complained that the Lord Coke had risen "to such height of opposition as were not the effect thereof continuallie before our eyes and eares, we should think such vyolent Coarses against your Majesty's often admonitions to be incredible." Enclosed was a list of "incorrect" prohibitions lately granted by Coke, the whole concluding with a prayer that his Majesty might "sett some certaine Limitts and bounds to both our Jurisdictions."

James sent the document to Coke, warning him that the matter touched not only the Court of Common Pleas but the Chief Justice personally. Let him be at pains to return answer satisfactory on both counts! Coke directed his reply to Archbishop Abbot. The result was a summons, addressed to Coke and his four Brethren, to come to Whitehall and defend their conduct before certain Lords of Privy Council. Coke obeyed. For three days he stood in the narrow Council Chamber, defending his conduct and the conduct of his court, while the Lords sat at the long table challenging his statements. On the second day Coke broke out, showed his indignation. This, patently, was no conference of equals seeking a way out of difficulty. The common-law judges were on trial here, before lords and bishops! "I think," said Coke, "this to be the first time that ever any judges of the realm have been questioned for delivering their opinions in matter of law according to their consciences in public and solemn arguments."

The Lord Coke's prohibitions, Archbishop Abbot retorted, had "become so flagrant there existed no crime so great as not to win protection in the Court of Common Pleas." Plainly, the Lord Coke was endeavoring, "all upon his own devise," to overthrow the ecclesiastical courts, which had existed "time out of mind." Coke denied it hotly. He was, he said, "a true son of the Church." Lord Chancellor Ellesmere interposed and the proceedings came to an end. In June, Ellesmere called another conference. It was no use, Ellesmere talked to the deaf. A month later, James came himself to Council Chamber, greeted the members of all three common-law courts — King's Bench, Exchequer, Common Pleas — and launched into a speech announcing that he had decided to reform the High Commission and "reduce it to certain spiritual causes." New letters patent would be drawn up, incorporating the changes.

It looked a clear victory for Coke and the common law. Cecil went so far as to say that "the principal feather was plucked from the High Commissioners, and nothing but stumps remaining." But royal capitulation had come too suddenly. Coke was wary. Late in August, word went round that the new patent was ready. It had passed the Seals and would be officially read — Coke's word is "published" — at some future date in the great chamber of Lambeth Palace. Coke did not read the patent that summer — did not, he was to testify, so much as lay eyes on it. For this extraordinary oversight he gives no reason. Perhaps he was in the country, riding circuit. More likely, he knew what the new patent or commission contained and desired to keep silence until the strategic moment. King's Bench judges read the commission that summer; all five were Coke's friends. Most certainly Sir Robert Cecil had read it, and Cecil kept close touch with Coke. On the other hand it is possible the new commission was never submitted to Common Pleas, as Coke later intimates with an indignation real or assumed. Either way, Coke surely must have known that James's promised reforms were not incorporated, the new commission being in all ways like the old. If there was a difference it lay only in the fact that the new commission's powers were more specifically defined, which, from a common-law point of view, meant that jurisdictional oversteppings could be more easily detected when prohibitions seemed in order.

Beyond this, nothing was altered, nothing bettered. Moreover, Coke's name appeared among the new commissioners; he was "commanded to sit." Name a man to a place of honor, give him a share and title and his opposition fades: it is the ancient strategy of power. Yet its effect must have appeared doubtful to Coke's friends. Was it likely that my Lord Coke would sit openly upon that very body whose powers he had been fighting for five years past?

The meeting at Lambeth Palace was called for a Thursday in October. Archbishop Abbot, to prevent obstruction, had his program carefully laid out. A list of cases were to be tried on the spot, thus testing and confirming the commissioners' new powers: in the Archbishop's own words, "causes of heresy, incest and enormous crimes." ("Enormous," thus applied, was a legal term; Coke had insisted that High Commission had jurisdiction only over "enormous" crimes.) Ninety-two members, the new commission included; a little Parliament in itself. Over the Thames they went, by ferry and by barge: bishops, deans, archdeacons; judges, Barons of Exchequer . . . Sir Julius Caesar, Dr. Cowell of law dictionary fame, with a host of civilians . . . Sir Francis Bacon, Solicitor General, with his chief, Attorney General Hobart . . . Robert, Lord Cecil, Earl of Salisbury, Treasurer of England and first Secretary of State. Sir Thomas Parry, Chancellor of the Duchy of Lancaster, preceded by a fine showing of blood and aristocracy: Edward, Lord Zouch; Henry, Earl of Southampton; Edward, Earl of Worcester; Thomas, Earl of Suffolk; Viscount Wallingford of the royal household . . . Over the Thames to Lambeth Pier, past the Lollards' Tower facing on the water, with the bishop's prison at the top, then round by an ancient red brick gatehouse to the cloisters, walks and stables of the palace.

Robed, surpliced, coifed, the procession came to the Archbishop's great chamber. Coke wore his golden collar of SS; his scarlet gown was topped with winter mantle of miniver. The dignitaries were directed to their places.

But Coke, as each man sat down, continued to stand, his Brethren with him. For Archbishop Abbot it was an embarrassing moment. What to do with a Chief Justice, fifty-nine years old, steeped in the dignity of experience, who would not sit down when he was told? There was a spare look to Coke's face now; the bones of cheek and forehead stood out; moustache and pointed beard, iron gray, hid the lips. With age Coke had not put on flesh but lost it; his tall figure held its shape under the great robes. Cecil, gowned and hatted in all the majesty of five feet two, waited with his usual pale intensity.

> And I was commanded to sit [runs Coke's *Report*] by force of the said Commission, which I refused for these causes:
>
> (1) For that I, nor any of my Brethren of the Common Pleas were acquainted with the [new] Commission, but the Judges of the King's Bench were.
>
> (2) That I did not know what was contained in the new Commission, and no Judge can execute any Commission with a good conscience without knowledge; and that always the gravity of the Judges hath been to know their Commission, for *Tantum sibi est permissum, quantum commissum.* [You are allowed only so much as your Commission permits.] And if the Commission be against law, they ought not to sit by virtue of it.
>
> (3) That there was not any necessity that I should sit, who understood nothing of it, so long as the other Judges were there, the advice of whom had been had in this new Commission.
>
> (4) That I have endeavored to inform my self of it, and have sent to the Rolls to have a copy of it, but it was not enrolled.
>
> (5) None can sit by force of any Commission, until he hath took the Oath of Supremacy, according to the statute of *I Eliz.* And for this, if they will read the Commission so that we may hear it and have a copy to advise upon it, then I will either sit or show cause to the contrary. . . .
>
> But the Lord Treasurer [Cecil] would for divers reasons persuade me to sit, which I utterly denied.

Archbishop Abbot found himself in serious trouble. Coke was playing for delay. If the new patent, a lengthy document, were read aloud by the Clerk as requested, would the Lord Coke continue to stand in that spectacular manner, then begin his eternal, rude objections? It would be safer to override him and proceed. In their seats there was a noticeable murmur and stirring among the judges of King's Bench and Exchequer. ("The Chief Justice, Chief Baron and some other of the Judges seemed to incline.")

The scene is vague and far away, one moment retreating, then flashing to sudden clarity. Coke's *Report* omits more than it tells. What, for instance, were Cecil's "divers reasons" for persuading Coke to sit? By every indication, Cecil, like his father Burghley before him, did not love the High Commission nor the oath *ex officio* that ruled it. Was the Lord Treasurer serious in his remonstrance with his old friend and kinsman, Coke — or were his "reasons" mere lip service to a King whose official servant he was sworn to be? Whatever ran through Cecil's mind, he took charge of events, "conferred in private," says Coke's *Report,* "with the Archbishop, who said to him, that he had appointed divers causes of heresy, incest and enormous crimes to be heard upon this Day, and for that he would proceed; but at last [the Archbishop] was content that the Commission should be solemnly read, and so it was, which contained three great skins of parchment, and contained divers points against the laws and statutes of England. And when this was read, all the Judges rejoiced that they did not sit by force of it. . . .

"Then the Lord Archbishop made an oration. . . . And after, came to the Chief Justice [of King's Bench] and to me, and promised us that we should have a copy of the Commission, and then I should observe the diversity between the old Commission and this; and all the time that the long Commission was in reading, the Oath in taking, and the [Archbishop's] oration made, I stood and would not sit, as I was requested by the Archbishop and the Lords, and so by my example did the rest of the Justices."

The scene was ended, and this time not in victory. High Commission continued active — and Coke continued to send out prohibitions against its authority. ("I will break the back of prohibitions," Archbishop Laud was to say, "or they shall break mine.") After the Lambeth encounter, there were no more meetings between Common Pleas and High Commission. The matter lay too deep for compromise.

Yet nothing Coke said or did was wasted. He had struck against abuse of power with what weapons he possessed. Stubborn, tireless, the Lord Coke stood and rudely spoke his mind. From now on, the bare sight of him in Westminster Hall was to plain men assurance of protection.

CHAPTER TWENTY-FIVE

Deaths of Robert Cecil and Prince Henry. Coke is removed from the Court of Common Pleas.

ROBERT CECIL, "the little great Lord," was ill. James sent his French physician, Mayerne, whose examination showed "a large abdominal tumor" — a symptom which, once noted, seems to have been disregarded. Mayerne wrote to Paris that Cecil suffered from an "hydropsical affliction complicated with scurvy." Though dangerous in so delicate and feeble a frame, the patient's "invincible courage" might bring him through.

During March and April, Cecil's illness "drowned all other newes," wrote Chamberlain. "Every mans care or curiositie ran that way, insomuch that it seemes he was never so well beloved as now when they thought him so neere lost. The King and Prince [Henry] were with him on Sonday and the Quene every second day the last weeke. You will not thincke what a number of competitors stoode (or were named) nor what manner of men for the place of secretarie." Since 1607, Cecil had served both as Treasurer and first Secretary of State. "The least Lord Treasurer in person that ever was, but greatest in offices," noted Wilbraham in his diary. "Haughty and terrible," a Venetian emissary described him. "Friend to his friends and ready to do them a service, though readier for revenge than for affection. A bitter foe to the Catholics. His wealth passes the bounds of all belief; he guides the Council as he likes; it may be said he is the Prince of this kingdom."

Toward the end of April, Cecil, growing no better, decided on a trip to Bath. Before leaving London he rallied sufficiently to go to Whitehall for long talks with the King. The treasury was bankrupt; Cecil's recent device of baroneticies for sale at £1,000 was but a drop in the bucket. Failure of the Great Contract, dissolution of Parliament, James's capricious largesse to his favorites — these weighed heavily on England's Treasurer; people said they had broken Cecil's health. He was irritable, flew into passions, then begged his servants' forgiveness. It was the pain in his body, he said. Accompanied by three physicians and three surgeons, the faithful Michael Hickes, and, wrote Chamberlain, "about three-score horse," the household set off for Bath, going first "to the Lady Hattons at Stoke," then on to Reading, stopping now and again to shift the poor racked body from lumbering coach to litter and "portative chair."

Among Coke's letters to Cecil, none remains to tell of this visit, or any word indeed of Coke's feelings and fears as he saw his greatest ally so near to dying. To the Cecils, father and son, Coke owed in large part his whole advancement. "That fountain, whereout hath flowed all my good hap," he once had written. With Robert Cecil he had served in Parliament since 1589; in religion and politics the two saw eye to eye. Who now among the weak ambitious men at court could guide King James? The execrable Robert Carr, now Viscount Rochester, insolent, favored, to all intents and purposes would rule the government. A mere courtier, base, flattering, whom Elizabeth would not have tolerated beyond her threshold.

At the door of Stoke House, Cecil took his leave, climbing wearily into his litter. Coke would never see him again. It was an old friendship — St. Stephen's Chapel in the Queen's time, with young Cecil sitting below the Speaker's Chair, ready with shrewd advice — old Lord Burghley at Greenwich Palace on that day when Coke was called to the Attorneyship: "Here Madam is your Attorney, *qui pro Domina Regina sequitur*." There were memories too, of easy, friendly things. Coke had sent a hunting dog to Robert Cecil, of the breed called *Norfolk tumbler*, "to play on Salisbury warren." Like a small greyhound the dog was, with a trick of falling down to simulate injury while stalking game. Sir Robert Cecil loved hawks and horses; the last ship to Virginia had carried his stallions, sent to breed with the American wild mares. Cecil's father and

Cecil's only son, William — his "jewel" — Coke had been close to all three. Lady Hatton too loved young William Cecil and had carried him often to Stoke as guest in the holidays from school and college.

Cecil knew that he was dying. He had not been long at Bath when his son William came to him; they took their farewell in tears. Queen Anne dispatched her messenger from London with a token. James sent a diamond with a fancy message: his affection, like the stone, was "endless, pure and perfect." Not quite perfect, Cecil might have amended wearily. James's *little beagle*, Elizabeth's *Pygmy* . . . If a man cannot be loved he can at least be useful. Packets of documents brought in from Royston or Newmarket, in hunting season, superscribed by the royal hand: "My little beagle, although I be now in the middest of my paradise of pleasure, yet will I not be forgetful of you and your fellows that are frying in the pains of purgatorie for my sarvice."

But as Cecil's end approached and the news spread from Bath, friends and followers seemed to melt away — "fell from him apace," wrote Chamberlain, "even some neere about him." A courtier's friends seldom outlast his good fortune; those who sought patronage now scurried home to see what fresh plums might be plucked at court — filched from a dying man who could no longer defend himself. Cecil saw it; a lifetime in palace circles had left him with few illusions. He would return to court, he told his doctors; "countermine his underminers and cast dust in their eyes." Back across Wiltshire went the pitiful cavalcade, coach, litter and portative chair, until Cecil grew faint and could go no farther. At Marlborough they stopped and Cecil was carried into the parsonage. Here, on Sunday, May twenty-fourth, he died, "betweene one and two in the afternoon, his memorie perfect to the last gaspe."

Robertus Diabolus, the proud and terrible hunchback, was gone. "Of whose death I took notice," wrote D'Ewes the parliamentarian — "by reason of all men's rejoicing." Like a pack of dogs at the kill, Cecil's enemies leaped upon his reputation. "I never knew so great a man so soone and so generally censured," noted Chamberlain. The body was carried to Hatfield for burial. A marble tomb, sculptured and ready, waited in the little chapel; Cecil himself had approved the model. The park and gardens of Hatfield House were like a small friendly kingdom. Five hundred mulberry trees newly planted, thirty thousand grape vines sent from France. Yet Cecil's humbler neighbors did not love the place; enclosure of Hatfield Wood had robbed their common pasture. There was more than ordinary envy in the talk. "Instead of funeral elegies, infamous libels," wrote D'Ewes. The foul disease of which his Lordship died "brake the lead he was wrapped in with noise and stench." Poison! said the whisperers; Carr had poisoned Cecil to get him out of the way:

> Here lies, thrown for the worms to eat,
> Little bossive Robin that was so great:
> Not Robin Goodfellow nor Robin Hood,
> But Robin th'encloser of Hatfield Wood;
> Who seem'd as sent from ugly fate
> To spoil the Prince and rob the state;
> Owning a mind for dismal ends,
> As traps for foes and tricks for friends.
> Now in Hatfield lies the fox,
> Who stank while he lived, and died of the pox.

It was nothing new for a courtier's enemies to announce that he had been taken off by pox or poison. Nevertheless, here was a depth of malice from which Cecil's father had not suffered, or perhaps the court of James was natural breeding ground for such reaction. Sir Simonds D'Ewes undertook to explain it in terms of Cecil as chief contriver of Essex's death. "I cannot but conceive that the first ground of the people's hatred arose from their love formerly borne to Robert, Earl of Essex, of whose death and destruction no man doubted but that [Cecil's] subtle head, actuated by his father's principles, had been the contriver and finisher."

Cecil's funeral was held on the ninth of June, 1612. Coke walked behind the coffin. No great crowd came to Hatfield; the ceremony was quiet, simple. Cecil had left only two hundred pounds to pay for it, with provision that an equal amount be distributed among the poor. Scandalous! people said; obsequies so plain were unfitting for the greatest lord of England. A half dozen earls, dark in mourning gowns, walked in the procession — Suffolk, Worcester, Pembroke; William, Lord Cranborne (Cecil's son); Exeter, who was Lady Hatton's father.

Somewhere among them walked Sir Francis Bacon, Cecil's nearest cousin, intimate with him since childhood, reared in the same household, schooled by the same tutor. Nothing brings out old feuds like the funeral of a near relative. Questions rise under the tongue, bitter, unanswerable. For Bacon, the family of Cecil had caused genuine suffering. Always their wealth had shamed his poverty. When he sued for intercession with a Queen and then a King, the Cecils had replied with fair words — and failed him. Now, father and son both were dead, powerless, enclosed from air while he, at fifty-one, survived. In the bare fact was triumph. Time and opportunity remained. Let the world see and judge between a Bacon and a Cecil, who was the greater man! What need so long a coffin for a body so small and crooked? Had any other, thus deformed in person, achieved in England a station as high? And did such ugliness act upon its host as brake or spur? Before the year was out, Bacon would answer the questions in print. *Of Deformity*, the essay was to be called.

Edward Coke was talked of as the next Lord Treasurer. Should this occur, a place would be open in Common Pleas. Lord Chancellor Ellesmere was old and tired; the marble chair would soon be empty. Whichever way the cards fell, Cecil's death must cause a shifting; perhaps immediately, perhaps at the new year. Already, Bacon had written to King James, "Now that [Cecil] is gone, I will be ready as a chessman to be wherever your Majesty's royal hand shall set me."

Almost in the same breath with which it cursed Cecil's memory, the country was called on to mourn Prince Henry, who died the following autumn, "in the rage of a malicious extraordinary burning fever." Strong, fairhaired, the Prince delighted in riding and in games. Many thought the fever came after profuse sweating at tennis: his Highness played too eagerly. "Putrid fever," reported the learned Dr. Atkins, "the seat whereof is under the liver in the first passages." "Some said that a French physician killed him," wrote Roger Coke; "others that he was poisoned, again others thought that he was bewitched." A Prince who hated Rochester and admired Ralegh possessed a dangerous enemy and a doubtful friend; to the last, Sir Walter held Prince Henry's admiration. "Who but my father," the Prince had asked, "would keep such a bird in a cage?"

Dr. Mayerne, close to the truth,* suggested the fever had its

* Today, physicians are agreed that Prince Henry died of typhoid fever.

onset at Richmond Palace in the summer, when the Prince went out each night to swim in the river—a reckless habit on a full stomach. "But he could not be prevailed on to discontinue the practise and took likewise great delight in walking by the Thames in moon-light to hear the sound and echo of the trumpets; both the situation and season exposing him too much to the evening dews." "This ordinarie ague," Chamberlain called it, "that hath raigned and raged allmost all over England since the later end of sommer."

Poor young Henry! It is pitiful to read of him, weakening day by day, rallying, dressing to go out, then fainting dead away. There was a pain in his forehead, he said; "a giddy lumpish heaviness, the pain of which obliged him to stroke up his brow and forehead with his hand before he put on his hat, bleeding likewise at the nose often and in great quantity, by which he found great relief." As he grew worse the doctors shaved off his hair, put warm dead pigeons to his forehead, "which he bore with admirable patience but without benefit." A cock, "cloven by the back," was applied to his head. "With no successe," wrote Chamberlain. In his sleep he tossed and sang, and waking, called for Sir David Murray, whom he loved and trusted: "'*David, David, David:*' Who coming to the Prince to know his pleasure, his Highness answered with a sigh, 'I would say somewhat, but I cannot utter it.'"

On the seventh day after the Prince took to his bed, a lunar rainbow appeared, hanging in the sky directly over St. James's Palace—an ominous sign, presaging the death of princes and the desolation of kingdoms. Queen Anne sent to the Tower for Ralegh's help; Sir Walter was known to be skillful with herbs. Ralegh had his own garden in the Tower yard, with a little henhouse which he had converted to a chemist's workshop. It was said he "spent his time all day in distillations." The French Ambassador's wife, Madame Beaumont, had asked for Ralegh's Balsam of Guiana; his Great Cordial or Elixir had been administered to old Chief Justice Popham in his last illness, his pellets to the dying dowager Countess of Rutland. ("Sir Walter Ralegh," wrote Chamberlain, "is slaundered to have given her certain pilles that dispatcht her.") But a magic that had killed one person might cure another; and if a boy was dying, what harm to try? Anne's royal messenger carried Ralegh's elixir to the palace. Members of Privy Council, waiting in the bedchamber, hesitated; with the medicine had come a letter, expressing tender concern for the

Prince but adding mysteriously that the mixture "would certainly cure him or any other of a fever, *except in case of poison.*" But the Prince's gentlemen, after tasting, passed the elixir to the Prince, who drank it, opened his eyes and spoke, then sank into a final coma. *Too late!* said Ralegh; his Highness should have had the medicine at once, when it arrived.

James was in the country when his son died. Paternal solicitude constrained him, said his courtiers; a visit would be too much for the royal sensibility. And besides, the disease was said to be contagious. Actually, James not only feared the sight of death and illness, but he was envious of the heir apparent — something noticed long ago by those in a position to see it. "A reasonable jealousy of the rising sun," the Venetian Ambassador had reported when Prince Henry was only twelve; "nor is the King pleased," wrote another, "to see his son so beloved and of such promise that his subjects place all their hopes in him." After Henry was created Prince of Wales, it was noted that his levees were much better attended than his father's. "Will he bury me alive?" James asked petulantly. Princess Elizabeth, officially pledged in marriage to Frederick, Elector Palatinate, was shortly to leave England forever. Charles, the remaining son, at twelve did not carry the hope and promise of his brother. The boy stammered, his legs gave way a little if he ran. "When I am King," Prince Henry had said one day, not too kindly, "I shall make Charles an Archbishop; the long gown will hide his legs."

The mourning for Prince Henry was genuine — a young man dying before he could offend. No one sorrowed with better reason than Ralegh, gray-haired now, who paced his Tower wall beside the Thames. After nine years' imprisonment, Ralegh's vitality was remarkable. He busied himself with a dozen projects, chief among them a tremendous *History*. "Beginning with the Creation," the preface announced with characteristic assurance, "I have proceeded with the history of our world." Prince Henry was said to have seen the manuscript; Ralegh, indeed, had written it for the Prince. Sir Walter, noted Chamberlain on November twelfth, "hath lost his greatest hope, and was growne into speciall confidence with the Prince, insomuch that [the Prince] had moved the King divers times for him; and had, lastly a graunt that Ralegh should be delivered out of the Tower before Christmas."

Prince Henry was buried in Westminster Abbey. Coke walked with the other judges in the procession. To all who had built their hope upon the Prince's patronage, his death meant disaster. His influence however reached a smaller circle than Cecil's. It was Cecil's vacant positions that made confusion — Treasurer, Secretary of State, Master of Wards. "We are put into daily expectation of alterations and removes," wrote Chamberlain. "The *candidati* for every place ply their canvasse." Instead of a new Treasurer, a commission for treasury was named. Bacon was on it, with a dozen others. Strange choices, said Chamberlain, "seeing most of them are noted for not husbanding and well governing theyre own estate. God kepe them from base courses." Bacon and Sir Thomas Lake were rivals for the Secretaryship. The bets, said Chamberlain, ran ten to one for Lake, though he himself would rather place his money on Sir Francis. "The same rumors we have about the Lord Treasurer who alters almost every day, and now is lighted on the Lord Cooke as the most likelie and there hath rested alredy fowre dayes."

At long last, Bacon was in position to ask for place and power. His marriage to Alice Barnham had rescued him from debt. As matches for impoverished noblemen, the daughters of rich London aldermen were at a premium, Alice not the least of these prizes. The City had not forgotten Bacon's wedding . . . the splendid procession to church, the bridegroom almost staggering under a weight of gold lace, purple satin and brocade. Half his wife's fortune, said the gossips, had gone to the altar on Sir Francis's back. To King James, Bacon made himself useful in a hundred ways. The flexible brain turned and turned again, foreseeing the royal wish, anticipating royal desires. And if Bacon considered his mind to be the quickest, most resourceful in England, the world one day would confirm his estimate. Already, Sir Francis had taken all knowledge to be his province. No one in the realm had been as busy at diverse matters — or was better qualified to be. From time to time his boks appeared, piecemeal, in bits and chapters — the *Advancement of Learning*, dedicated to James; parts of the *Instauratio Magna*, limitless in scope, designed to render useless all previous systems of learning. (James, paging through, remarked that like the peace of God it passed all understanding.) In December of 1612 appeared a second edition of the *Essays*, containing thirty-eight discourses and opening with words destined to pass into common speech: "What is truth? said jesting Pilate; and would not stay for an answer."

The public seized upon the little volume. This was an age that cherished epigram, mordant wit, sayings that could be passed from mouth to mouth. Especially popular was a form of short satirical theme called *characters,* filled with puns and quips describing different types, as the courtier, the wife, the honest man. Robert Carr's old friend at court, Sir Thomas Overbury, had made "characters" fashionable; people liked to quote his *Mere Common Lawyer:* "No way to heaven he thinks so wise as through Westminster-Hall. In Astrology he is so far seen that he knows the Hall-days and finds by calculation that Michaelmas term will be long and dirty." Bacon's epigrams included few puns but they went deeper, seeming to touch Everyman. Sir Francis wrote *Of Travel, Of Followers and Friends, Of Vain Glory.* There was something almost frightening in his wit. Nothing escaped that hazel eye, "so like the eye of a viper." *The cat knows whose lips she licks. . . . Better be envied than pitied. . . . Always let losers have their words. . . . Why hath not God sent you my mind or me your means?*

One essay especially, struck spark. "In a chapter of deformitie," wrote Chamberlain, "the world takes notice that Sir Fraunces Bacon paints out his late little cousin to the life." Sharp and terrible, the words ran true. "Whosoever hath any thing fixed in his person that doth induce contempt, hath also a perpetual spur in himself to rescue and deliver himself from scorn. Therefore all deformed persons are extreme bold. First, as in their own defence, as being exposed to scorn; but in process of time by a general habit. Also it stirreth in them industry, and especially of this kind, to watch and observe the weakness of others, that they may have somewhat to repay. Again, in their superiors, it quencheth jealousy towards them, as persons that they think they may at pleasure despise: and it layeth their competitors and emulators asleep; as never believing they should be in possibility of advancement, till they see them in possession. So that in a great wit, deformity is an advantage to rising."

Coke saw the essay, how could he help but see it? *Deformity quencheth jealousy, it layeth competitors asleep. . . .* Months passed, and the offices of Treasurer and Secretary remained empty;

candidati continued to lose sleep. On August 7, 1613, Chief Justice Fleming of King's Bench died. The sun was scarcely set when Bacon had his letter ready:

It may please your excellent Majesty
Having understood of the death of the Lord Chief Justice, I do ground in all humbleness an assured hope, that your Majesty will not think of any other but your poor servants, your attorney [Hobart] and your solicitor [Bacon] for that place. Else we shall be like Noah's dove, not knowing where to rest our foot. . . . My Lord Coke is like to outlive us both. I have served your Majesty above a prenticehood, full seven years and more as your solicitor. . . . God hath brought mine own years to fifty-two, which I think is older than ever any solicitor continued unpreferred. . . .

The letter, as it unfolded, was plain enough. Should Hobart refuse the Chief Justiceship, Bacon himself would step into the place — a Chief Justice "sure to the prerogative." But Francis Bacon seldom was happy with a simple plan. The restless mind revolved. Would it not be more to the King's liking if Coke were made Chief Justice of King's Bench; Hobart, Chief Justice of Common Pleas and himself, Attorney General? Of all men in England, Bacon knew himself best fitted to be the King's watchdog; everything in his experience pointed to it. The place was enormously lucrative — "worth honestly," said Bacon, "£6,000 a year." Chief Justice of King's Bench meant Chief Justice of England — for Coke, a step upward in honor though not finance; clients' fees in King's Bench were not nearly so abundant. But the prestige of the office — together with a possible place as Privy Councilor — surely this would silence even Sir Edward Coke? Moreover, by its nature, King's Bench was closer to the royal interests than the court of Common Pleas.

Bacon wrote out his plan:

REASONS FOR THE REMOVE OF COKE

Reasons why it should be exceeding much for his Majesty's service to remove the Lord Coke from the place he now holdeth to be Chief Justice of England, and the Attorney [Hobart] *to succeed him, and the Solicitor* [Bacon] *to succeed the Attorney.*

"First, it will strengthen the King's causes greatly amongst the judges." As Chief Justice, Lord Coke would see the coveted position of Privy Councilor dangling "and thereupon turn obsequious." Hobart, the present Attorney General, was "timid and scrupulous both in Parliament and in other business," fit enough to follow the late Lord Treasurer's will — which, added Bacon, with a slap at Cecil's memory, "was to do little with much formality and protestation." Whereas Bacon himself, if advanced to Attorney General, "going more roundly to work and being of a quicker and more earnest temper and more effectual in that he dealeth in, is like to recover that strength due to the King's prerogative which it hath had in times past, and which is due it." And if, to crown all, there could be named as Solicitor General "some man of courage and speech and a grounded lawyer," his Majesty would "speedily find a marvelous change in his business." Even a bench "well disposed" is useless to government unless the King's Attorney be of a metal to prod the judges onward. "For in a weapon, what," added Bacon tersely, "is a back without an edge?"

A bench well-disposed was Baconian for a pliable bench. The sinuous mind wormed forward, exploring every crack. And the question went far beyond expediency or mere personal ambition on Bacon's part. In Parliament, the King was blocked; victory must be won on the judicial front — in High Commission, Star Chamber and, if possible, the great courts of common law. When Bacon spoke of the prerogative he was entirely sincere — if sincerity can inhabit an imagination so flexible. Of Bacon it is only fair to say that while he may have been against Coke, he was never, with the Howards, against Parliament and the Commons. Like Henry VIII, Bacon believed the English sovereign to be at his strongest in Parliament, not out of it: the government of England consisted of "the-King-in-Parliament." Bacon was no Robert Carr or Hay, no mere courtier willing to sacrifice the general welfare to his own advancement. Had he been of stuff so weak, Coke need not have fought him. Between these historic antagonists there lay a narrow difference: Bacon believed in the King's "absolute prerogative," intrinsic to the law yet above the law. Coke upheld only the King's "ordinary prerogative." "Prerogative absolute, prerogative ordinary" — the phrases were familiar to every barrister and Parliament man; they pepper the speeches in law court and Commons. That Coke's difference with Bacon was one of degree made it no less imperative; in politics as in religion, men have died for differences in degree.

Bacon's memorandum to James was skillful, unctuous, with its firstlies and secondlies. "Thirdly: the attorney's and solicitor's places are the champion's places for the King's rights and prerogative." Should these two officers not receive advancement from time to time, they would be disappointed. "Stripped of their expectations they will wax vile, and then his Majesty's prerogative goeth down the wind. Besides, the remove of my Lord Coke to a place of less profit (though it be with his will) yet will be thought abroad a kind of discipline to him for opposing himself in the King's causes, the example whereof will contain others in more awe."

"Lastly," wrote Bacon — and here the combination of Baconian and Elizabethan idiom almost defies translation, "Lastly," — rumor had it that government appointments were to be got not by merit but by "labour and canvass and money," awarded always to "great suitors" who could pay thousands of pounds for a Judgeship, an Attorney-Generalship. But should his Majesty take Bacon's advice, advancing Coke to be Chief Justice of King's Bench, Hobart to Common Pleas and Bacon as Attorney General, the whole would appear as "the King's own act, a course so natural and regular, as it is without all suspicion of those by-courses, to the King's infinite honour."

Coke heard of the plan and howled his protest, urged friends to help, sent his own letter to the King. Common Pleas was where he belonged, where he was fittest to be. In Common Pleas he hoped to end his days. "The choise of a new Lord Cheife," wrote Chamberlain, "hath bred great varietie and much canvassing. . . . And all to make way for Sir Fraunces Bacon to be atturny, whom the King hath promised to advance. The Lord Cooke doth so stickle and fence by all the meanes and frends he can make, not to remove, as beeing loth he sayes to be brought out of a court of law which is his element, and out of his profit, in regard whereof he values not the dignitie, that he hath written very earnestly to his Majestie about it, and the King is so gracious that he will not force him against his will, but saith if he will accept it he shall do it with as much honor as ever went to that place, which is a kind of promise of a baronie or councilor-ship at the least."

Bacon had his way. Coke was named Chief Justice of King's Bench — in common parlance, "Chief Justice of England." The ceremony was simple, so homely indeed that it hardly symbolized a change so great. On the twenty-fifth of October, 1613, Coke walked down the length of Westminster Hall from Common Pleas to the Court of King's Bench — parting "dolefully," wrote Chamberlain, "not only weeping himself but followed with the teares of all that bench and most of the officers of that court."

Beyond this brief description, no account remains. Yet it is good to read of tears shed by Coke's Brethren of Common Pleas. Clerks, beadles, tipstaffs, filacers, prothonotaries: there is a convincing note to Chamberlain's little qualifying phrase, "*most of the officers* of that court." Coke's Brethren loved him, it is plain. Now he was gone, banished to the northward by the length of some two hundred and fifty feet. But if at first he seemed out of touch, altogether out of reach in his new exalted place, Coke's Brethren of the common law were soon to hear his voice again, speaking in their behalf.

Sir Henry Hobart stepped into Common Pleas, Bacon was sworn Attorney General. For those in position to know, the shift was not propitious. Little good, wrote Chamberlain, was looked for from these changes. "There is a stronge apprehension that Bacon may prove a daungerous instrument." The new Chief Justice missed none of the implications of his new position. Meeting Bacon in the courts, Coke challenged him angrily. "Mr. Attorney, this is all your doing. It is you that have made this great stir!" Bacon's reply must instantly have gone the rounds, rejoicing Coke's enemies who had seen him wax rich in the law. "Ah, my lord!" said Bacon, "your Lordship all this while hath grown in breadth. You must needs now grow in height, or else you would be a monster!"

In such a retort, the smile, the bow ironic, are implicit. Bacon was master at the art. *The cat knows whose lips she licks. . . .*

CHAPTER TWENTY-SIX

1613-1615. Chief Justice of England. The Realm. Peacham's Case.

FOR the first years, Bacon's prophecy seemed justified. Coke made no attack on Chancery or the prerogative. All was harmonious; cases brought to King's Bench apparently did not lend themselves to jurisdictional dispute. Perhaps Coke was waiting, assaying his new position, trying the robe of new authority. Or perhaps this quiet state was accident, one of the lulls that come in times of public doubt and dispute.

On Sundays, Lord Coke went peaceably to church at St. Dunstan's and sat upon green cushions with his Brethren of the coif. His state was grander now; when the Lord Chief Justice of England walked into Westminster Hall, a Sergeant-at-Arms went before him with the mace. The face of London was changing. Sir Robert Cecil, before he died, had paved the Strand from the Savoy to his new house at Ivy Bridge. Beyond the City wall, Moorfields was filled in, leveled and set out with trees; Smithfield paved over, pleasant for promenade or market. Yet between London and Westminster there remained a mile of open country, dotted with the Netherlanders' gabled farms; at Charing Cross the King's falcons trailed their jesses above the royal Mews. In midsummer of 1613, the Globe Theatre burned down — ignited, wrote Stow the annalist, "by the negligent discharge of a peale of ordnance," sparks falling on dry thatch. By next season it was rebuilt, "the fayrest," said Chamberlain, "that ever was in England." Only the river did not change, with its single great bridge near Tower Hill, the high-bowed ocean ships below it and fleets of swans above, the salmon driving upstream in season, fat and sweet. London was chief seaport and metropolis not only of a nation now but of an empire. The word, so new for England, sounded with all its ringing implications.

In this time of extraordinary expansion, the problem for government was twofold: to keep order within the island and without. As Judge of Common Pleas, Coke had helped draw a treaty for union with Scotland, a scheme for the plantation of Ulster in Ireland. Elizabeth's great Captains, Drake and Hawkins, long were dead; Sir Walter Ralegh waited in the Tower. Yet England's needle still pointed west. Her mariners swept the ocean, brought home strange roots and fruits, new-drawn maps, less gold than James could wish, and now and again, for curiosity, an *American*, dressed in skins and feathers. The word "plantation" was much on English tongues and it meant the planting of people, not crops. Coke had earlier been called on to settle a charter "for a colony of our people into that part of America commonly called VIRGINIA, lying all along the sea-coasts from the 34th to the 45th parallel." It was old Popham's charter, dated April 1606; VIRGINIA covered a reach of coastline from what today is Cape Hatteras to Maine (enraging the Spanish King, who claimed a generous third for himself). Popham had put money in the venture; Prince Henry owned shares; Robert Cecil had sent "a number of stallions and other animals on his own account."

The settlers were to be ruled from England by a royal council appointed by the King. It would not have occurred to Coke or anyone else that a handful of settlers should form their own government. Wherever Englishmen were "planted," their roots took hold upon another England: there could be no question of loosened allegiance to the mother country. But in the year 1613, the Virginia adventure had fallen into bankruptcy. Lotteries were got up to raise money; large funds subscribed. But when no profit returned from this western El Dorado — when ships were lost and settlers vanished — speculators refused to part with their money. Chamberlain, himself a shareholder, showed delight when at last a ship brought good news — a princess captured, Pocohontas, "daughter of a king that was the planters' greatest enemie, taken as she was going a feasting upon a river to visit certain frends; for whose ransome the father offers whatsoever is in his power, and to become theyre frend and to bring them where they shall meet with gold mines."

The Virginia Company, the East India Company, the Russian Company, the powerful Merchant Adventurers — there was no limit to their enterprise. English vessels sailed home from the four corners of the world, their arrivals casually announced: "Our companie of Muscovie have found a new and rich trade of fishing for the whale; from the Bermudaes hath come great store of amber-greece this yeare. . . . There returned home the fleet from King James his Newland, commonly called Greenland." These great trading companies must be regulated by law, kept within bounds. Disputes among them came commonly to King's Bench. Coke's three Brethren were of higher caliber — certainly of more experience — than his colleagues in Common Pleas had been. Houghton, Croke, Doddridge, all within a year or two of Coke's age. Sir Robert Houghton, a Norfolkman, had represented the city of Norwich in the Parliament of '93 when Coke was Speaker. Sir John Croke, an Inner Templar, lived in Holborn, not far from Hatton House; he had served as Speaker in Elizabeth's last Parliament of 1601, and was editor of a volume of select cases known as *Keilway's Reports*. In the matter of prohibitions, Croke could be relied upon — yet somehow managed, unlike his Chief, to keep out of trouble with King and Privy Council.

The third Judge, Sir John Doddridge of Devonshire, was known as *the sleeping judge* because he closed his eyes while sitting — the better, he said, to hear the lawyers' arguments. He had written a manual for students, *The English Lawyer*, and a treatise on the prerogative. Complimented by a Commons member, "I have sat in this court many years," the old man replied, "and I should know something. Surely, if I had gone in a mill so long, some dust would cleave to my clothes!" But Doddridge's inclinations lay toward royalty and the prerogative absolute; Coke could not count on his support.

In the first year of his Chief-Justiceship, Coke published his tenth *Report*. The preface opened with a tranquil, happy note: "At my times of Leisure, after my publick Services (chearfully taking Industry my old Acquaintance for my Consort, and aiming at the Good of my dear Country for my Comfort) and beginning with this continual and fervent prayer, The glorious Majesty of the Lord our God be upon us, Oh prosper thou the Works of our Hands upon us, Oh prosper thou our handy Works, I have, by the most gracious direction and Assistance of the Almighty, brought forth and published this tenth Work to the View of the Learned and Benevolent Reader." Coke gave a copy to the Inner Temple; the librarian had the title pricked in gold and made careful record in his accounts: "to a stationer for setting the title of my Lord Cooke's Reports in golden letters, which he gave to the House, eighteen-pence."

It is pleasant to think of Coke's old society proudly placing his book, gold-titled, on its shelves. His "times of leisure" could only come between court terms, when Coke went out to Stoke to live. He still rode circuit, summer and spring; we have record of him at Cambridge Assizes and in Norfolk. London Assizes were held at the old Guildhall, a place long familiar to Coke. In a little room off the great dining hall were stored the giants Gogmagog and Corineus, used in Guild processions, figures fifteen feet high that moved and talked and smoked tobacco as they were drawn along the streets in chariots. Chief Justice Coke could not take a step in the City alone but must be followed by a dozen men in livery. When he attended church at St. Dunstan's, a clerk with a white wand preceded him. Officially the judges sat from eight to eleven in the morning and ate their dinner afterward. "For it is said in Exodus," wrote Sir Henry Spelman, "that Moses judged the Israelites from morning to evening. But the northern nations being more prone to distemper and excess of diet used the forenoon only, lest repletion should bring upon them drowsiness and oppression of spirit."

In June of 1614, Cambridge University by unanimous vote elected Coke High Steward, honorary office next below Chancellor of the University. Coke was immensely pleased. Setting it down in his private chronicle, "*Sit Deo gratias,*" he wrote beneath. Through Robert Cecil, Coke had procured for the University the right to send its own two representatives to Parliament, a matter of much practical benefit. At sixty-two, Coke still kept his chambers in the Temple, not only for business but for retreat. It was his custom, wrote his grandson, Roger Coke, to wake at three each morning, when "his little bell tinkled" and a servant prepared his breakfast.

Lady Hatton must have looked with horror on such habits; her husband went to bed at nine. Conjugal life was outwardly serene, perhaps because the two were seldom together. Lady Hatton spent much time at court, taking part in masques and bearing the Queen company. Frances, their daughter, was only twelve — sprightly and quick, with a promise of great beauty to come. Of Coke's children by Bridget Paston, five sons and two daughters survived. Clement, the fifth son, lived at the Inner Temple, ostensibly studying law; all five boys got through the parental allowance in short order and were forever in debt.

Lady Hatton in her middle thirties was handsome as ever, one of those women who never tire of fashionable life, bringing to each dinner party and ball a zest welcome to jaded court palates. When Coke was not available, his wife gave supper parties without him in the great dining hall of Hatton House. Her name flits through the news, often enough, it seems, in the act of getting what she wanted. "The *Dorcas* arrived within the river. My Lady Hatton laide claime to all the drincking glasses. Some litle difficultie there was about partition, by reason that the writing and superscriptions were worne off. . . ."

There was a great call of Serjeants-at-Law in 1614; eleven were created, with a splendid feast. Coke made a speech, then danced the solemn round dance hand in hand with benchers and ancients before the Temple fireplace. In the height of summer, 1614, Coke's eldest son, Sir Robert, was married in Gloucestershire. The bride, Lady Theophila Berkeley, had been bridesmaid for James's daughter, the Princess Elizabeth. For Robert Coke it was a brilliant marriage. Coke went down and stayed a week in the huge moated castle, hobnobbing with Lady Theophila's grandfather, the old Earl. (No mention is made of Lady Hatton; likely enough she stayed in London about her own business.) But Lord Berkeley's Steward has left a picture, felicitous and calm, considering the turmoil that was soon to come: "How contenting on Lord Berkeley's part this marriage of his grandchild was, by this may be collected, That when Henry Briggs his chaplin demaunded, Who giveth this woman to bee maryed to this man, Hee coming out of his seat in the Church (where he sate with Sir Edward Coke), taking her by the hand, *That doe I*, quoth hee, *with all my heart*. By which Sweet addition of the words (with all my heart) hee not only declared the Contentment of his own, but drew tears of joy from the eyes of the Bridegroome's Father, to both which mine eares and eyes were witnesses."

Afterward there was a great dinner, with mountains of food, wine in rivers and half a county fed at the gates, following which the guests retired to their chambers to take a nap. Coke, when he emerged, brought with him a sheaf of Latin verses composed for the occasion, replete with puns on the bridal morn — St. Clara's Day — and the heavy joviality which seems to mark new fathers-in-law:

Clara dies Clarae, conjunxit pignora Clara,
*Clarum Theophila et nomen et omen habet. . . .**

Coke and the old nobleman, aged eighty, rode toward London in one coach. The horses ran away, the coach overturned and dragged, the Steward wrote, a great distance on the ground "so that it moved Lord Coke presently to write from Stoke with comfort, that hee never heard that out of soe great danger there issued so little harme, especially to persons so farre stepped in years."

Coke was a Privy Councilor now. The King had disregarded Bacon's advice about reserving the place as bribe for good behavior. Determined to make the best of things, James welcomed his Chief Justice warmly to Council table. For Coke it meant a plunge headlong into politics — if indeed he had ever been out of them. Council was split with faction; and once again it was Spain-and-religion which made the division. Three of the great Catholic family Howard sat in Council: Henry, Earl of Northampton; Lord Treasurer Suffolk; Lord Admiral Nottingham. James, in Scotland, had kept close touch with Northampton; the Howards had befriended his mother and James seemed instinctively drawn to them. On his accession in 1603, all three Howards took the Oath of Allegiance without a qualm. Two were on the Spanish pension list; James did not discover it immediately, and when he did he simply swallowed it. He could not pay his servants what they deserved; let them, he intimated, accept what monies they could find.

* "The clear day of Clara conjoins a clear promise; Theophila has a clear omen."

While Robert Cecil lived, the Howard influence had been kept within bounds. But with Cecil's death the Howards took strength, joined forces with the favorite, Robert Carr, and managed to place their friends in key positions throughout the government. The family could not have attained such power but for the accident of a fresh and unexpected ally. Don Sarmiento de Acuña, Count Gondomar, arrived in London, Ambassador from Philip III. Handsome, suave, brilliantly experienced in diplomacy, "well skill'd in court holy-water," Gondomar in his single person was to prove a greater menace than the armadas which his royal master continued to threaten (but could no longer afford). At once, Gondomar gained the confidence of James and of Queen Anne, whose inclination to Catholicism made her friendly to Spain. At court the Ambassador's gaiety and wit rendered him indispensable; he "told a merry tale, read Shakespeare's plays, bought a first folio and liked English wines." Gondomar's portrait, at full length by Van Ceulen, hangs today at Hatfield House, perhaps the most compelling painting in that vast gallery. In padded breeches, cloak and ruff he stands, careless, arrogant, gold chain about his neck, plumed hat set at an angle just this side of raffish. The heavy nose and brows have a look Sephardic, high-bred; the dark shrewd eyes are merciless. From the first, the London populace hated Gondomar, nicknamed him *Fox Populi* and shouted curses after his coach in City streets. This was a man impossible to overestimate. From now on he will be met at every turn — his ambition, well-nigh attained before the end — to keep wide the breach between James and Parliament, arrange for a Spanish royal marriage and hope at length for an England come to her senses, no longer enemy to Mother Church.

During this same year of 1614, James, desperate for money, was persuaded to call a Parliament. Gondomar and the Howards fought hard against it. But the government was destitute. Roman Church lands — rich mine and depository of the Tudors — were long since distributed. Spanish carracks could no longer be despoiled of gold at sea; the City of London hesitated with crown loans that might never be repaid. A Parliamentary grant was James's last resort: Bacon, Coke, Winwood advised that with proper management, the Commons would give down milk. Writs went out for an election. In April, members took their seats. A Spaniard wrote home a description of the King's procession to Westminster on opening day. One of the Episcopal bishops fell from his horse, upon which a Puritan nobleman remarked that *at last they had got a Bishop down.* No sooner spoken than the Puritan himself tumbled off, whereupon a Catholic exclaimed triumphantly, "so would fall all the Protestants and Puritans of the kingdom." Francis Bacon had been returned member from Cambridge University. "Some in Parliament," added the Spaniard, "found fault with the election of the Attorney General, saying that he would repeat their speeches to the King; others praised his eloquence and capacity and yet said he would take away their courage." In the end, Bacon's seat was confirmed, but no Attorney General sat after him. (Coke, under like circumstances, had given up his seat.)

From the first day, this Parliament was rowdy. The *Addled Parliament,* it was to be called. "More like a cockpit than a grave council," wrote Chamberlain. Just before it met, James appointed Cecil's successor as Secretary of State: Sir Ralph Winwood, former Ambassador to Holland, totally without experience of Parliaments. The Howards had tried, during election, to pack the Commons with "undertakers": men who would *undertake* to control the Lower House by sheer numbers. The result was failure. The undertakers, young, inexperienced, were more fit to be among London's Roaring Boys than in such an assembly, wrote Sir James Whitelocke. Even Bacon, disgusted, told the Commons "the King were better call for a new pair of cards than play upon these if they be packed." James, ignoring the signs, addressed the Lower House as if all were well. This was to be "a Parliament of love," he said, "wherein the world would see his love to his subjects and their love to their King" — then remarked in the next breath that he would die a hundred deaths rather than make bargains or sacrifice a scrap of his prerogative. (King James was a man, the Venetian ambassador remarked, "with a wonderful capacity for doing himself harm.") As answer to James's overtures the Lower House outdid itself in Puritanism — suggested that recusants wear yellow caps and slippers for identification, brought up bills to restrain Morris dances and games on the Sabbath, thereby flaunting James's expressed predilection for the old-fashioned English Sunday, with games and pleasures after church. The Commons, shunning even the suspicion of High Church, refused to take Holy

Communion at Westminster Abbey, "for fear," they said, "of copes and wafer cakes." They went instead to St. Margaret's, the parish church across the road.

James, after a few weeks, dissolved Parliament, sent for Gondomar and told him he hoped Spain would hear the true reason for the dissolution, not "as told by gossips in London streets but as you hear it from me." Parliaments, James added, were a custom he found when he came to England and could not change. Could he, asked James wistfully, rely on the friendship of Spain in case he quarreled in future with his own subjects?

It was an extraordinary question from the mouth of an English King. Refusing to look on Parliament as truly representative, James was convinced that the late opposition stemmed merely from a small faction. Surely the country, appealed to at large, would respond with funds? English kings had more than once called on the people for a benevolence or "free gift"; Edward IV originated it. Parliament had no sooner risen than Archbishop Abbot came forward with a present of plate for the royal treasury, worth £200. Secretary Winwood gave £100, "the Lord Cooke £200 but the rest of the Judges came but slowly after, for I know," wrote Chamberlain, "where some presented but £20 and it was refused." Coke, though willing to give privately, protested that such a method of raising money was unconstitutional. Men would be afraid to decline, and a gift through fear was not "free." But Coke signed the begging letters from Privy Council, his name looking incongruous, somehow, between that of Ellesmere and Sir Julius Caesar.

County by county the realm protested. Of what use Parliaments, if money were raised in this way? And why had Archbishop Abbot and his London Churchmen taken it upon themselves to start the benevolence? A Wiltshire gentleman, Oliver St. John of Marlborough, wrote a violent letter to James—and got himself prosecuted in Star Chamber by Francis Bacon as a result. Whitelocke the lawyer "got the roll," he wrote, "into my hands in Michaelmas term and put myself 40 shillings which I did to avoyd the danger of giving more singlye. It is a great pitye that thear was occasion to seek for money this way."

Down in Somersetshire lived an elderly Church of England rector, named Edmund Peacham, frequently in trouble because of

Puritan sympathies. When collectors for the benevolence came round, Peacham balked. Having neither gold nor silver, he "would, like Saint Peter, give what he had, which was his prayers for the King." This pious announcement was made from the Gatehouse prison in London, where Peacham at the moment was locked up for insulting his diocesan Bishop of Bath and Wells. Pursuivants, searching Peacham's house, found some loose papers, thrown carelessly into an open casket in his study — rough notes for a sermon, apparently, and filled with threats and bluster. "The people might rise in rebellion against these new taxes . . . all the King's officers mought be put to the sword, and when Prince Charles assumed the throne, might not the people say, Come, this is the heir, let us kill him? King James had promised mercy and judgment, but we find neither. It is the duty of preachers to lay open the infirmities of princes and let them see their evil ways. . . ."

For James, one of the more irritating traits of Puritans was a self-righteous ambition to advertise the infirmities of princes. Like John Knox, every Puritan preacher assumed a tutorial duty over the sovereign. But Peacham was not content with moralisms. "On a sudden," he wrote, "the King might be strucken with death, *perhaps within eight days, as Ananias or Nabal.*"

James read the words and old fears enveloped him. Was this another Ravaillac, to let a King's blood in his coach? The royal bed was moved against the wall, barricaded with feather mattresses. Peacham's country neighbors had shared his reluctance about the benevolence. How many of the gentry stood behind these notes, how widespread was the conspiracy? Peacham must be transferred to the Tower and tried for high treason. James signed a warrant for his examination under the manacles, should he prove "obstinate and perverse." Before bringing Peacham to open trial it would be wise, the King told Bacon, to ascertain the opinion of the judges, especially the four judges of King's Bench. Peacham being no Jesuit but a Puritan with many friends in the late Parliament, it might be difficult to obtain a conviction. Let Bacon consult the judges, James said. And not together but singly, so their true minds would be revealed.

Sir Francis went first to Coke — and met with instant refusal. Such "particular and auricular taking of opinion" was not, said Coke, according to the custom of the realm; his Brethren would never consent to it. Bacon, at this, instructed two of the King's Serjeants and Yelverton, Solicitor General, to find out for themselves how Coke's Brethren felt on the subject. Report came back that Justice Doddridge was "very ready to give opinion in secret, every judge being bound expressly by his oath to counsel his Majesty when called." Justice Croke made "like answer." Justice Houghton, "who," Bacon told James, "is a soft man, seemed desirous first to confer [with his Brethren], alleging that the other three Judges had all served the Crown before they were Judges, but that he had not been much acquainted with business of this nature. . . . Howsoever," Bacon concluded, "I hope force of law and precedent will bind them to the truth; neither am I wholly out of hope that my Lord Coke himself, when I have in some dark manner put him in doubt that he shall be left alone, will not continue singular. . . ."

For Coke it was an almost hopeless dilemma. Though the judges indeed had sworn to "counsel the King in his need," in Coke's mind they were defended by a later clause of the oath saying that justice must not be delayed "for any letters of the King." Bacon and his Majesty found it convenient to interpret "counsel" as obligation to give out judgment before the case was heard. Coke's insistence that the King's request was a "delay of justice" comes under the heading of legal tricks; Coke himself had delayed many a case for lesser reason. Yet it was a trick used in the public interest: if cases were to be tried before they came to court, all semblance of justice would be gone. In his heart Coke must have known that of his three Brethren, not one could stand up to the ordeal of private consultation with Attorney General or King. As for precedents, Bacon could match them case for case, maxim for maxim.

Days passed and Sir Francis continued the assault; eloquent, learned, surely the most persuasive man in England. Cleverer than Coke, quicker with words, never at a loss, forever courteous. And after each attempt, reporting back to his royal master: 31 January, 1615: "For Peacham's case, I have since my last letter been with my Lord Coke twice. At the former time he fell upon the same allegation which he had begun at the council table; that Judges were not to give opinions by fractions, but entirely according to the vote whereupon they should settle upon conference; and that this auricular taking of opinions, single and apart, was new and dangerous; and other words more vehement than I repeat. I replied in civil and plain terms, that I wished his Lordship in my love to him to think better of it. . . ."

The Chief Justice asked for all the papers of the case: Peacham's answers under torture in the Tower, the notes seized in his parsonage chamber. Coke took them home and read them — angry words, scrawled in the familiar Puritan jargon. Never published nor delivered from the pulpit, never seen beyond Peacham's study chamber until the King's pursuivants had them in hand. To insult a Bishop and frighten a King: was this high treason? Ten years ago, Coke might have said it was. Since then he himself had insulted not merely Bishops but Archbishops and had defied King James in his Council Chamber. *Rex non debet esse sub homine, sed sub Deo et lege* . . . In his time, Coke had prosecuted many men for treason. It is to be doubted if he regretted a single prosecution, a single capital sentence passed at his incitement. The public knew Coke as a hard prosecutor and a just judge.

Peacham however was no Jesuit or Spaniard but an English country parson. Many in the last Parliament had talked with him when he came up from Somerset with his petition against the ecclesiastical courts. Coke, as a devout Church of England man, had little sympathy for Puritans. But if every Puritan parson in England were to be tried for his secret thoughts concerning bishops, ecclesiastical courts and the prerogative absolute, the realm would be wiped clear of all but High Churchmen in a year's time. . . . *Copes and wafer cakes, yellow shoes for recusants* . . . This infernal parson had thrust the Chief Justice of England into a position likely to lose him his place on the bench. Was it for such cases and such questions that Bacon had maneuvered him into King's Bench — to have a Chief Justice ready at command with a capital sentence in the King's cause? Even if Peacham were guilty as Judas, the Judges must not thus be forced by separate consultation. Coke did not think the parson guilty. Yet if, as Chief Justice, he refused this "consultation" with his Majesty, the act would be for Francis Bacon a very gift from heaven, a lever to lift Coke from the bench, be rid of him forever. Coke had no mind for a martyrdom which would leave his enemy in full possession of the field.

There was a third meeting between the antagonists, and a fourth. Bacon told Coke that his Brethren were prepared with their opinions; remained only his own. Reporting as usual to the palace, "Coming armed with divers precedents," wrote Bacon, "I thought to set in with the best strength I could. . . . My Lord Coke heard me in a grave fashion, more than accustomed, and took a pen and took notes of my divisions; and when he read the precedents and records, would say, *This you mean falleth within your first, or your second, &c. division. . . .*"

On the fourteenth of February, Coke came to Bacon with a judicial opinion in hand, written out and signed in what looked like capitulation. For the Attorney General it must have been a happy moment. He unrolled the paper. Coke's opinion was unfavorable; he declared that Peacham was not guilty! The parson's notes, scandalous though they were, did not constitute high treason because in them was no attempt "to disable the King's title."

Nothing in Bacon's letters and reports had indicated a suspicion that this might happen. He took the blow and doubled back. Sending Coke's opinion to the King, Bacon referred to it lightly as "my lord Cooke's *answers;* I will not call them rescripts, much less oracles." Should the people discover what Coke had said, harm might ensue. Let his Majesty be pleased, therefore, not to reveal what the Chief Justice had written but rather spread a rumor "as it were in secret and so a fame to slide" that the Chief Justice, by quibble and nicety, could find in Peacham's case no *act overt* — a different matter altogether from saying (as Coke actually had said) that Peacham had not committed treason at all.

Six months later, Peacham was arraigned in his home county. No judge of King's Bench sat at the trial. James sent down Chief Baron Tanfield of Exchequer Court (whose dislike of Coke was notorious) and King's Serjeant Montagu, brother to that same Bishop of Bath and Wells for whose slander Peacham had been imprisoned in the first place. The old parson received a traitor's sentence, but it was not carried out. Prison fever, almost as quick as hanging, from a monarch's point of view precluded the inconvenience of public martyrdom; Peacham lay in the foul cells of Taunton Jail and died. Coke's part in the affair was not forgotten. He had tricked Bacon at his own game. From the Chief Justice's hand, the King's Attorney had received as it were a closed box containing the precious gift of surrender. But when the lid was lifted, a spider lay within. "In Peacham's Case," said Bacon, "for as much as in him was, the Lord Coke prevailed."

CHAPTER TWENTY-SEVEN

1615-1616. Coke's fight with Chancery. The Overbury murder.

Sir Edward Coke at this time sate very loose and uneasy.
ROGER COKE

IF in Bacon's mind Coke carried his point, to Coke the matter must have tasted rather of defeat than victory. He had rendered opinion before trial in a capital case. And though by declaring Peacham innocent he had given the man a chance to live, in principle it was the King and Bacon who "prevailed." Three times, Coke had been called to conference and turned away, history cannot know with what agony of heart. Lacking his Brethren's full support, outright defiance was impossible. But in law, principles are seldom established in a day. The matter would come up again. James would demand "consultation" with his Judges and Coke must see to it that not one judge but twelve held firm. It would be necessary to visit his Brethren, sound them out severally as to future policy. In Peacham's Case they had plainly been intimidated. Yet timid men can be shamed into an appearance of courage; it would do no harm to try. Without support of Parliament and such men as Whitelocke, Fuller, Sandys, the common-law bench stood without a backing — a dozen pins to go down before those master bowlers, Bacon and Lord Ellesmere. On King's Bench sat the same three Judges: Houghton, that "soft man" and pliable; Doddridge the sleeping Judge; John Croke with his quick aptitude for playing two sides at once. Chief Baron Tanfield of Exchequer Court had no love for Coke.

Yet should a test case come up in his own court, Tanfield might rise to the challenge.

In this year of 1616, the forces and the factions showed their lines, clear and sharp. Small things revealed the wind's direction and the storm's approach. Coke's friends advised him to give ground in appearance at least; to placate the King in small ways would cost nothing of principle. Queen Anne was known as Coke's partisan, Prince Charles inclined toward him. More time spent at Whitehall Palace or Windsor, less time at Westminster and the Inns of Court — would not this benefit the matter at hand? Coke was a man who could make friends if he desired. A few drops of unction, a little incense spilled before the royal presence might easily sweeten the situation.

But Coke would not give ground. Sir James Whitelocke the barrister — Coke's friend and admirer — in this connection set down in his diary a significant brief episode. Sir James was young and fiery; after the last Parliament he had been summoned to Council Chamber and compelled to burn his speeches. He lived at Henley-on-Thames and liked to ride across country on Sundays for morning service at Windsor Royal Chapel. On one such occasion he spied Coke in the stalls above, sitting with Sir Ralph Winwood, Secretary of State. The sermon ended, Coke beckoned to the younger man. "Come, Mr. Whitelocke," he said. "I will make bold with you, one of my own coat. I pray thee let me have thy company out of church, for I am a stranger here."

"And so" (wrote Whitelocke), "I led him out of the churche by the arm and then went with him to his coach, into the upper court. And as I went with him, I asked why he stayed not at the court to dynner. He told me, that whilst he stood by the king at dynner, the king would be ever asking of him questions of that nature that he had as lief be out of the roome, and that made him be as far off as he might ever at such times. . . . I guess," finished Whitelocke, "it was concerning matters of his prerogative, whiche the king would take ill if he were not answered in them as he would have it."

In the spring of that same year occurred the affair of the stage play *Ignoramus*, written and performed by Cambridge students on the occasion of a royal visit to the campus. James and his court set up at Trinity, Coke's old college, with Prince Charles and a swarm of

Howard lords and ladies, come down for fun and festivities. Lord Treasurer Suffolk, their Howard host, put out a thousand pounds a day for wine and feasting. On the fourth night the visitors crowded Trinity Hall to see *Ignoramus*, which proved to be a potent satire on all practitioners of the common law. (The title came from legal procedure. When grand juries found a cause too weak for trial, they wrote on the indictment *Ignoramus** and returned the bill to the judges.) Dr. Cowell had taught Roman law at Cambridge for some thirty-seven years; in the matter of the dictionary the University took his side and the play gave perfect opportunity to let off spleen. The principal character was a pompous, silly old Inns of Court lawyer named Ignoramus — intended, actually, as caricature of the town recorder, Brackyn, with whom the University had long been at feud. But from the moment Ignoramus appeared, the audience saw him as Lord Coke to the life.

A more sympathetic audience could hardly have been found. James had suffered much at the hands of the common law; the Howards with their Catholic propensities were of course on Cowell's side. (Coke, incidentally, always referred to him as *Cow-heel.*) It was delicious to see Ignoramus stalk on stage, consumed with envy for all bishops and civilians, delicious to hear him spout pig-latin. "*Quota est clocka nunc?*" he asked when he wanted the time. There was a love story, complete with twin brothers and mistaken identity, opening the way for a ribald confusion of Anglo-Saxon bawdy words and Latin puns about horns. James held his sides with laughter, clapped his hands and called out "*Plaudite!*" Old Ignoramus composed verses to his pretty young love: "*Et dabo* FEE SIMPLE, *si monstras* love's pretty dimple. . . ."

The play as printed ran through seven editions. No one dared tire of it while the King was interested; James actually returned to Cambridge for a second performance. Coke was angry, his colleagues were angry. The other side, delighted, inquired if lawyers could not take a joke? "The Lord Cheife Justice," wrote Chamberlain, "both openly at the Kings Bench and divers other places hath galled and glaunced at schollers with much bitternes. They are too

* The word survived from a day when jurors were witnesses to fact, rather than judges of evidence. If a man were wrongfully indicted for stealing a sheep, his neighbors, called as jurors (witnesses), knowing the sheep was still in its owner's pasture, wrote on the bill of indictment, "*Ignoramus*" — we know of no such crime.

partiall to thinke themselves so *sacrosancti* that they may not be touched."

For Coke it was scarcely the moment to relish satire at his own expense or that of his profession. Matters were precarious, ridicule a potent weapon. The enemy increased, crown lawyers won their fights in court. Moreover, Coke's own Trinity College had done this thing, his Alma Mater, which last year had elected him to honorary office. When Sir Edward passed down Westminster steps in his robes or turned a corner in the labyrinth of corridors, the word "Ignoramus" seemed to follow down the hall. It was only an irritation, of course, no danger lay behind it. Yet in his long career, Coke had borne worse blows with better grace. There are times when a man feels beset, beleaguered.

East of King's Bench, across the width of Westminster Hall, Lord Chancellor Ellesmere presided in his marble chair. Chancery observed no seasonal terms but stood always open, crowded with suitors even in summer vacation when the rest of Westminster Hall lay deserted. This was the King's ancient court of equity, Star Chamber's sister, an extension of Privy Council authority. A *court of relief*, it was called. Coke himself indicated that equity is a just correction of law in some cases. The common law could punish but it could not prevent. If John Doe's neighbor began to build a spite wall that cut off view and sunlight, King's Bench could not stop him but Chancery might. Under common law, every wrong had (theoretically) its penalty. But human ingenuity is infinite in the construction of new sins, and when statute and custom failed, equity took hold to devise decent remedy. The common law was rigid. Suitors, appealing from a decision at common law, could obtain stay of judgment while Chancery reviewed the case. Ellesmere, especially vigorous in thus correcting the Common Bench, in twenty years of office had met with little or no resistance from the judges.

Toward the end of 1616, however, rumblings were heard from the southwest corner of Westminster Hall. "No appeal from the King's Bench," said Coke, "to any court except the High Court of Parliament." It was a reckless statement, born of desperation; among Coke's attacks against prerogative courts, the most daring by far.

The Lord Chancellor carried a prestige almost incalculable, taking precedence over all officers of the law, including both Chief Justices. All suits began in Chancery, every writ must have the Chancellor's seal. The Lord Chancellor presided over the House of Lords, the highest court in the land; on opening day he stood before the throne, the King's mouthpiece to instruct his Parliament. Coke's attack was not the first on record; common-lawyers had persistently resisted the growth of Chancery jurisdiction. One trouble was that Chancery, developing hit or miss down the centuries, had few rules to limit it. People liked to say the court was governed by the Lord Chancellor's conscience, the measure of which was the Chancellor's foot.* Ellesmere moreover was by nature a prerogative man; "the greatest enemye to the common law," wrote Whitelocke, "that ever did bear office of state in this kingdome."

A strong statement, no less significant because of Whitelocke's partisanship. Ellesmere's integrity was unquestioned. But by his side stood a very different figure: Sir Francis Bacon, ready to make use of Chancery in his great game of politics and prerogative. Ellesmere, seventy-five years old, had petitioned to be released from office. The marble chair would soon be empty — and Bacon's eye was fixed upon it. His father had sat there and why not he? "As your Majesty knoweth," Bacon wrote to James as the New Year (1616) opened, "your Chancellor is ever a principal counsellor and instrument of monarchy, of immediate dependence upon the King."

Through the courts of common law a tremor passed as the needle swung toward this new north. Coke and his colleagues stiffened. Resistance started with a small suit which rapidly became, at Bacon's own insistence, the famous *Case of the Rege Inconsulto.*

James, to please a gentleman of his palace, had granted to one John Michell the right to certain fees in Common Pleas, hitherto received by the prothonotary Brownlow. Brownlow brought action in King's Bench to restrain Michell; the case was heard and Brownlow won. Bacon declared such cancellation of a royal grant to be a slur on the prerogative. When his Majesty was a party to a suit, said Bacon, it could not be tried in the common-law courts. Casting

* "Equity," said John Selden, "is a roguish thing. For law we have a measure, know what to trust to. Equity is according to the conscience of him that is chancellor, and as that is larger or narrower, so is equity. 'Tis all one as if they should make the standard for the measure a chancellor's foot."

about, Sir Francis came up with an old writ, *De non procedendo ad assisam rege inconsulto:* no further proceeding without consulting the King [in Chancery]. Bacon appeared dazzled by his discovery. "Hampton Court or Windsor Castle is not so valuable to the King as this writ!" he said. "Yet the use of it hath bred a great buzz and a kind of amazement as if this were . . . a checking and shocking of justice." Planning to argue the case himself, he urged James to "remember and renew your former commandment which you gave my Lord Chief Justice in Michaelmas term; which was, after he had heard your Attorney, he should forbear furder proceeding until he had spoken with your Majesty. . . . The Lord Coke's *plerophoria* or over-confidence," Bacon added, "doth always subject things to a great deal of chance."

It was a wonderful word, not heard before or since. The case had its final argument in King's Bench toward the end of January, 1616. George Croke, brother of the Judge, argued against the Crown. Bacon, to everyone's surprise, threw aside his character of prerogative champion and argued wholly from law and precedent. "They little expected," he reported gleefully to James, "to have the matter so beaten down with book-law, upon which my argument wholly went. I lost not one auditor that was present in the beginning. . . . My Lord Cook was pleased to say that it was a famous argument."

Even against his convictions, Coke could appreciate good pleading. Over and above Bacon's "book-law," there played a bland quick wit, a quality of charm that could pass for sincerity. The bulk of his argument amounted to a skillful definition of Chancery's functions as complemented by the courts at Westminster. "The common law of England is an old servant of the crown. The twelve judges of the land may be compared to the twelve lions supporting Solomon's throne. . . ."

An author, surely, may borrow from his own *Essays.* The question, as the case progressed, resolved itself: Should the case be tried in King's Bench between party and party or between Brownlow and the King in Chancery? "So that all that troubles us," said Bacon finally, "is no more but this: That when Mr. Brownlow [the prothonotary] goes up Westminster Hall hereafter, he shall turn a little upon his right hand, and all shall be well!"

Upon the right hand was Chancery; upon the left, King's Bench.

Perhaps a man never lived more agreeably persuasive than Francis Bacon. The case ended in compromise. Prothonotary Brownlow relinquished his fees to Michell, the King's appointee; James agreed to forbear in future the creation of such new offices. The great writ *De Rege inconsulto* was not used, the case never went to Chancery. Yet once again Chancery had interfered, drawing on the King's support — entirely at Bacon's instigation. In Coke's long public service he had not experienced an adversary so potent.

Hilary term was not ended when King's Bench, in February of 1616, flung itself against Chancery once more. The selfsame principle was at issue: Chancery's right to stop judgment in the common-law courts. "A kind of sickness of my Lord Coke's," Bacon wrote to James, as if to question the prerogative were an aberration, fantasy of a diseased mind. And truly, Coke, to prove his point, seemed to choose cases unworthy of the principle involved, running head on against an adversary who never lost his coolness, his capacity for the shrewd quick double and turn. This time the Common Bench went far indeed, declaring interference by Chancery to be a legal offense against the ancient statute of premunire.

The cases in point revolved around two jewel merchants who by fraud had obtained judgment in King's Bench, forcing purchasers to pay many times the value of certain merchandise. The victims appealed to Chancery and obtained restitution. King's Bench Judges, angry at the reversal, struck back with a premunire. This was an old law from Edward III's time, useful in preventing appeal from English courts to Rome. In early days premunire had been looked on as a serious offense, entailing punishment equal to outlawry. But since the Reformation no one dreamed of appealing from English courts to the Pope, and the writ had lapsed. King's Bench, exhuming it now, interpreted premunire as forbidding not alone an appeal to Rome but to any other court except the last High Court of Parliament.* Let the jewel merchants — said King's Bench — bring indictments of premunire against the two purchasers who had appealed to Chancery and also against every officer in Chancery who had taken part in the proceedings.

It was highhanded and under the circumstances, egregiously ill-judged. Whether the plan originated with the Chief Justice or with his Brethren, in the end Coke bore full responsibility. When the

* Chapter Note.

two indictments for premunire came up before a grand jury, both were repudiated. Nineteen plain citizens, having reviewed the facts, decided the whole thing was a swindle, wrote on the bills that potent word, *Ignoramus*, and carried them to King's Bench. Coke rebuked the jurors sharply and sent them back to deliberate. If they did not find a true bill he would commit them, he said. "Some must be made an example, or the common law of England will be overthrown." Nineteen jurymen, after consultation, returned to King's Bench, their *Ignoramus* again in the foreman's hand. Only two men had changed to Coke's mind. "You have been tampered with!" Coke said angrily. He would give orders that the jewel merchants prepare their case anew for the coming Easter term of court, when he would expect a jury better qualified "and evidence given openly at the bar." If Chancery were not checked, the common-law judges, Coke finished, "would have little to do at next Assizes, by reason the light of the law was like to be obscured."

Danger to the common-law courts was real; Coke did not imagine it. He had struck in passion, using a wrong weapon, and the blow redoubled on himself. Francis Bacon, having bided his time, now stepped in. These premunires, he told James, had given public affront to Chancery, "the court of your Majesty's absolute power." The matter must not be permitted to pass over lightly. Let the puisne judges (Coke's Brethren) be admonished "upon their knees," and the two merchants come before Star Chamber. Such an affair had its good uses, "for the settling of your Majesty's authority and strengthening of your prerogative according to the true rules of monarchy." As for the Chief Justice, his public chastisement at this time seemed inconvenient. He was badly needed in the distressing business of the Overbury trials; he could ill be spared in Privy Council, "touching your Majesty's finances and matters of repair of your estate." If Coke must suffer dismissal from the bench, might it not come later, during summer recess? Concerning seventeen jurors who had returned an *Ignoramus*, "I think," added Bacon with that light humor so welcome to his royal master, "I think *Ignoramus* was wiser than those who knew too much." The legal point at issue — Chancery's right to receive appeals from King's Bench — could best be left, for determination, to his Majesty's Learned Counsel.

It was done. Without dissent, the King's Counsel Learned in the

Law* declared Chancery to be right and Coke wrong. James, not yet satisfied, planned to express his royal feelings next term in Star Chamber. It would benefit the realm to see their monarch seated as a judge, hear him expound the true meaning of prerogative and *the King's justice*. This matter of the premunires would provide most pertinent text.

Meanwhile there were, as Bacon had said, the Overbury trials to be got through — seven capital cases for murder, by all odds the worst public scandal of James's reign, skirting the edge of a dozen great names, not excluding the monarch's own. A full two years ago, in 1613, Sir Thomas Overbury had died, reputedly of natural causes. Sir Thomas, courtier and wit, for years had been close friend to James's favorite, the Earl of Somerset (once plain Robert Carr). Indeed, without Overbury's brains and management, young Carr would never, it was said, have reached such a plane of royal intimacy. But as Somerset's star rose, he grew impatient of Overbury's cautionary tactics, greatly desired to be rid of him yet at the same time feared to rouse the anger of so clever a man, who knew too much. Concocting a series of ruthless lies about Overbury, Somerset managed to have him shut up in the Tower, where after some months of ill health and misery, Sir Thomas died. For the Earl, things now sped smoothly until August of 1615, when an apothecary's boy, mortally ill and frightened of hell fire, made dying confession concerning poisons delivered to Overbury's jailer.

At once scandal burst, spreading, corrosive, never too fantastic to hold a grain of truth. The public did not wait for trial but made its own judgment: Somerset was the murderer, Somerset and his beautiful, sinful young wife, Lady Frances. Let a just King see to their punishment! For James the situation was perplexing in the extreme. The Earl and Countess, palpably, must face public trial, together with half a dozen accessories to the crime. Yet in Somerset James dealt with a dangerous, unscrupulous man with whom for more than a decade he had been extremely intimate. There was no telling what might be blurted out, and, true or false, the King would suffer for it. Nevertheless, Coke was commanded to make

* These comprised Attorney General Bacon, his Solicitor General, two King's Serjeants (Montague and Crew) and Prince Charles's attorney, young John Walter.

out a warrant for Somerset's arrest. "Search to the bottom of the conspiracy," said James. "God's curse be upon you if you spare any man, how great soever. And God's curse be upon me and mine if I pardon any of them." *

Seven trials ensued, conducted, by James's order, in full public light. London, as was to be expected, made a gala of it. The smaller fry were tried first, in the Guildhall with Coke presiding: Sir Gervase Helwys, Governor of the Tower (Lady Somerset's creature from the start); Weston, who had been Overbury's personal jailer; Mistress Ann Turner of the pretty figure and yellow starched ruff, adept equally at mixing poisons and love philters; Franklin, the apothecary who provided Mistress Turner with white arsenic, mercury, powder of diamonds and "great spiders" to bake in poor Overbury's home-cooked jelly tarts and sauces. By Christmas the four had been arraigned, convicted and hanged. (At Mistress Turner's execution the hangman made horrible farce by wearing huge cuffs, yellow starched, and a yellow collar.)

Remained the two principals to be tried, Somerset and his Lady. The entanglements were infinite. By this time, the whole unsavory tale of Lady Frances's first marriage had been revealed; how, at twelve, she had been married to the fourteen-year-old Earl of Essex and after seven years, fell in love with Somerset — a liaison in which Overbury acted as go-between and general adviser. Yet when Lady Frances suggested divorcing Essex and marrying Somerset, Sir Thomas Overbury, foreseeing danger, set obstacles in the way and thereby incurred the lovers' implacable anger and his own death. The trials spared no item; in bits and tatters it all came out. From a London astrologer, Lady Frances had procured aphrodisiacs for her lover, and for her husband something very different: a figure made of wax, "in the privity of which a thorn had been stuck from a tree that bare leaves but no fruit, and so their designs accomplished." On the grounds of impotence, Lady Frances's marriage was annulled and the wedding to Somerset followed, splendid as a prince's nuptials, with the King and Queen merrily present. (Bacon presented the happy pair with a masque that cost him two thou-

* See Chapter Note for Roger Coke's vivid story telling of Coke's notification by the King's messenger; of Coke's rising at three in the morning to go to James at Royston; Somerset's indignation and James's exclamation: "Nay, man — if Coke sends for me, I must go!"

sand pounds.) Lady Frances's recklessness knew no bounds; she even elected, as show of her virginity, to be married "in her hair," worn loose, flowing maidenlike to her feet. Her letters to the astrologer were quoted in court. "Sweet Father," she had written, imploringly. The little wax figure was produced, upon which, spectators, in one simultaneous eager movement, swayed forward. The scaffold emitted a thunderous crack; people jumped and fell, the hall was in turmoil. "As if the devil had been present," wrote a reporter, "and grown angry to have his workmanship shewed by such as were not of his own scholars."

Lady Frances was a Howard, daughter of Lord Treasurer Suffolk; scandal spread to high places. Dr. Forman, from whom Mistress Turner procured her love philters, had boasted a phenomenally successful following in palace circles, keeping a running list of every love affair incipient or realized. To the general disappointment, Coke refused to air this interesting information in court. But the prosecution possessed Forman's record of clients, known as the *Alphabetical Book*. Coke, one morning, commenced reading it aloud in court — and came to an abrupt stop. Instantly, news spread that he had met, on page two, the name of "Hatton, Lady Elizabeth." "And I well remember," wrote an eyewitness, "there was much mirth in the court." As the arraignments progressed, Coke slipped back into his old guise of advocate, remorseless, indefatigable, producing — Bacon said later — above three hundred examinations taken in his own handwriting. To Mrs. Turner he made a famous summing-up: "Thou hast the seven deadly sins, for thou art a whore, a bawd, a sorcerer, a witch, a papist, a felon and a murderer."

When at last the Somersets came to trial, Coke was if possible even more insulting — and more regardless of the consequences to himself. A pair so unscrupulous had seldom come before a judge; Coke seemed determined to lay bare every villainy. "This crime," he said, "slept two years, being shadowed with greatness, which cannot overcome the cry of the people." Three "loud-speaking relators," said Coke, stood against the defendants: the commonwealth, the voice of the oppressed and the cry of the laborer robbed of his hire. Something, Coke insisted, was being concealed. Why had neither Somerset's nor his Lady's Tower rooms been searched, according to usual procedure? Were the big fish to escape after the little fishes had been destroyed? To the four who were hanged, Coke had made promise that the great ones should not break through the net. But a long delay had intervened between trials. Lady Somerset was with child and remained in private custody until a daughter was born. Taken to the Tower in March of 1616 and told she was to occupy Sir Thomas Overbury's rooms, she grew hysterical, begged to be anywhere but there. Eight days earlier, Ralegh, without noise or fanfare, had been released. (He knew, he wrote James, where gold was to be found in Guiana; he would fit out his own expedition and promise to kill no Spaniards. "Sir Walter Ralegh," wrote Chamberlain, "goes up and downe, seeing sights and places built or bettered since his imprisonment.") Lady Somerset, locked in Ralegh's rooms, paced his Tower chamber in guilt and fear, walked where the old hero had walked on his wall above the Thames.

On the twenty-fourth of May, they took the Countess up the Thames for trial at Westminster. (Somerset was to be tried on the day following.) Seats were at a premium, bought weeks before: ten pounds for a pair, fifty pounds for a box. "Here is now such a hurrying to Westminster Hall," wrote a Londoner, "as it distracts everybody's mind from anything else." Trembling, her face hidden by a fan, Lady Somerset pleaded guilty and was sentenced to be hanged.

Next day her husband, with a bearing far from fearful, met trial before the same large commission of peers. To the prisoner's box he strode, "in a black sattin suit, hair curled, eyes sunk in his head," wearing his George and Garter, highest decoration in the King's gift. No guilty man may wear it. All day Somerset stood undaunted. Before trial, James and Bacon had agreed not to press too far, driving the prisoner to "desperation and flushes" — agreed also not to permit Coke's usual digressions into hints of treason and Spanish plots. The two might better have tried to dam the Thames. "Knowing as much as I know," said Coke, "if this plot had not been found out, neither the court, city nor any particular family had escaped the malice of this wicked cruelty. . . . I dare not discover secrets — yet such letters were produced, which makes our deliverance as great as any that happened to the children of Israel."

From all this, gossip assumed the worst: the family of Howard, with Somerset's help, had tried to poison Prince Henry — perhaps actually had killed him; Overbury died to keep the secret. A Popish plot! Even though Lady Somerset confessed the murder, surely one so young could not achieve, without assistance, a crime of such complexity, kept dark for twenty months? On the day of trial, James, at Greenwich, showed great anxiety, refused dinner and supper, dispatching messengers to meet every boat that came from Westminster to the Tower Wharf. After sundown, Somerset was found guilty and sentenced to death. Neither he nor Lady Somerset suffered the full penalty. Both lived for years under the King's pardon; the Lady at large, Somerset in the Tower hobnobbing with the Earl of Northumberland, sporting his George and ribbon, unrepentant, maintaining innocence until the end.

For Coke the thing was finished, he had done his part. He came out of it bearing the enmity of both factions: the Howards because he had threatened to expose them root and branch, the King and Bacon because he "marred" the trials by hinting at matters best left dark. Very likely the famous "secrets" concerned nothing more than James's scandalous intimacy with Somerset, intrigue among the Howards about Spanish pensions or a Spanish marriage for Prince Henry. Henry of course was dead, but Prince Charles at nearly sixteen had reached marriageable age. And though Coke's hints of Popish plot and gunpowder were palpably absurd, yet a Spanish marriage assumed full toleration for English Catholics — the mere whisper of which still had power to inflame.

In the history of nations, a private crime of passion, suddenly looming, can interrupt for weeks or months the course of events, throwing its long shadow over names, persons, causes with which logically it has no connection. The Overbury murder was such a crime. *The Great Oyer of Poisoning*, it came to be called — Coke's title. "I desire God," Coke had said at one of the trials, "that this precedent of Overbury might be an example and terror against this horrible crime, and therefore it might be called *The Great Oyer of Poisoning*."

For nearly ten months, the trials had held the city's attention. Hatred toward the Somersets did not diminish with conviction and imprisonment. Much later, Queen Anne, riding in her coach, was mistaken for Lady Frances. The mob pursued her, screaming; she feared for her life. Coke had played his part with harshness. Considering the rank and favor of those involved, he showed persistent, almost ferocious indiscretion, as if he hated everyone involved and did not care who knew it. Had he conducted himself more prudently, he might, like others in the drama, have used the trials to further his private fortune. Instead, he managed to antagonize nearly every Lord in Privy Council. Within a fortnight, he would feel on his shoulder the heavy hand of retribution.

CHAPTER TWENTY-EIGHT

June, 1616. Case of Commendams. King James in Star Chamber. "Pride, prohibitions, premunire and prerogative." Coke is dismissed from the bench.

The Lord Coke of late is fallen (I know not how) into disfavor. The whole course of his life is like to be ript up and look'd into . . . many men feare it may be his utter overthrow.

CHAMBERLAIN TO CARLETON, *8 June, 1616*

FOLLOWING Somerset's conviction, Francis Bacon was sworn a member of Privy Council, in his fifty-sixth year attaining a distinction for which he had yearned and plotted over three decades. From this new vantage point he at once renewed attack on Coke's position, using the still pending Chancery fight and an even more important jurisdictional battle, known to contemporaries as *Colt and Glover versus the Bishop of Coventry* and to history as the *Case of Commendams.*

The suit had opened in Exchequer Court several months earlier, when Serjeant Chibborne, for the plaintiffs, based his argument on a daring assumption that the King possessed no right to grant commendams at all. (James had given to Bishop Neile a benefice to be held *in commendam,* which meant that Neile received the revenues but the duties might be performed by deputy.) Actually, commendams had existed since the Church existed. On this occasion however, two gentlemen, Colt and Glover, claimed the presentation was theirs, not the King's, and sued the Bishop for deprivation.

When Chibborne's bold argument was reported to James, the King, through Bacon, commanded Coke to halt proceedings until after consultation with his royal self. Let Coke so inform the rest of the common-law judges, "whereof," finished Bacon's letter peremptorily, "your Lordship may not fail." Coke's answer was brief. If the judges were to receive such command, it would have to come from the King's Attorney, not the Chief Justice. Coke, in short, refused. Bacon then sat down and wrote eleven letters — three to King's Bench, four to Common Pleas and four to the Court of Exchequer — commanding the Judges in the King's name to stop procedure. "I was," he told James, "a little plain with my Lord Coke in these matters. I said he could never profit too much in knowing himself and his duty." In open defiance, the Case of Commendams was heard next day in the Exchequer chamber, following which twelve judges met at Serjeants' Inn and signed a letter, drafted by Coke:

> Most dread and most gracious Sovereign [it began]: . . . We, your Majesty's Justices of the courts of Westminster . . . hold it our duties to inform your Majesty that our oath is in these express words: *That in case any letters come unto us contrary to law, that we do nothing by such letters, but certify your Majesty thereof, and go forth to do the law, notwithstanding the same letters.* We have advisedly considered of the said letter of Mr. Attorney [Bacon] and with one consent do hold the same to be contrary to law, and such as we could not yield to the same by our oath. . . . And therefore knowing your Majesty's zeal to justice, we have, according to our oaths and duties (at the day openly prefixed the last term) proceeded, and thereof certified your Majesty; and shall ever pray to the Almighty for your Majesty in all honour, health and happiness long to reign over us.
>
> Your Majesty's most humble and faithful subjects and servants,
>
> Edw. Coke, Henry Hobart, Law. Tanfield,
> P. Warberton, Geo. Snigge, Ja. Altham,
> Ed. Bromley, Jo. Croke, Hump. Winche,
> Jo. Doddridge, Augustine Nicolls,
> Rob. Houghton.
>
> *Serjeant's-Inn*
> *27 April*

Once more the King had interfered, but this time the Judges stood firm. The bench not only "certified" that they were going ahead with trial despite royal orders, but when the Judges wrote their letter, trial had already been held. And instead of one judicial protest, James received twelve. His reply, from Theobalds, was peremptory and not a little sarcastic. The opening salutation addressed Coke as Privy Councilor, then the other Judges:

Trusty and well-beloved councillor, and trusty and well-beloved, we greet you well . . .

Ye might very well have spared your labour in informing us of the nature of your oath. For although we never studied the common law of England, yet are we not ignorant of any points which belong to a King to know. . . . But we cannot be contented to suffer the prerogative royal of our crown to be wounded through the sides of a private person: We have no care at all which of the parties shall win his process in this case, so that right prevail. . . . We are therefore to admonish you, that since the prerogative of our crown hath been more boldly dealt withal in Westminster-Hall during the time of our reign than ever it was before in the reigns of divers princes immediately preceding us, that we will no longer endure that popular and unlawful liberty. . . ."

As for a possible delay of justice, James continued ironically, he would be glad if no pleas at Westminster were of older date than this one.

Our pleasure therefore is, who are the head and fountain of justice under God in our dominions, and we out of our absolute power and authority royal do command you, that you forbear to meddle any further in this plea till our coming to town, and that out of our own mouth you may hear our pleasure in this business; which we do out of the care we have that our prerogative may not receive an unwitting and indirect blow. . . . So we heartily wish you well to fare.

On the sixth of June, the Judges were summoned to Whitehall. Around the long table sat Lord Chancellor Ellesmere and seventeen Lords of Privy Council, scarcely one of whom, beyond Secretary Winwood, could be called Coke's friend. Lord Treasurer Suffolk — Somerset's father-in-law — was hardly expected to love the Chief Justice; nor was Archbishop Abbot or the Bishop of Winchester, who had carried report of the Commendams argument to James. Sir Fulke Greville had long been Bacon's patron. Second Secretary Lake was pro-Spanish; Sir Julius Caesar, easily the best-natured man in high government circles, now was Master of the Rolls — Ellesmere's first assistant.

When all were settled in their places, the King entered, took his seat at the table's head. At his Majesty's request, the Bishop read aloud Serjeant Chibborne's bold arguments of the April hearing; next, Bacon's letter to Coke, with Coke's brief reply; then the letter signed by twelve Judges, and James's ironic answer. These preliminaries over, James broke out with angry queries: Why had not the Judges checked and bridled "impudent lawyers" who encroached not only on the prerogative but "on all other courts of justice?" The Judges' letter was itself "a new thing, very undecent and unfit for subjects to disobey the King's commandment, but most of all to proceed in the meantime and to return to him a bare certificate." With a violent gesture, James tore the letter across. Twelve Judges fell on their knees and craved humble pardon. Their letter, they confessed, had been wrong "in form."

But Coke, still on his knees, raised his face to the King. If the letter's form had been regrettable, he said — for the matter of it he must enter into a defense. "The stay required by your Majesty was a delay of justice and therefore contrary to law and the Judges' oath." "Mere sophistry!" James retorted. "Unto which," wrote the reporter, "the Lord Chief Justice in effect made no answer but only insisted upon the former opinion."

James appealed to Ellesmere, asked his opinion about the Judges' oath, and if the stay required had been contrary to law. Ellesmere hesitated. The King's Attorneys were better qualified to answer, he said discreetly. Bacon, hitherto in the background, was on his feet at once. Vigorously he expounded the meaning of the Judges' oath, then scolded the Judges for dereliction of duty "and so concluded his speech, and the rest of the learned counsel consented to his opinion."

Coke had not risen. But he turned, now, to his longtime enemy. "I take exception!" he said. "The King's counsel learned are to plead before the Judges, and not dispute with them." . . . "A strange exception!" Bacon retorted. "By oath and office, the King's learned counsel are to proceed against judge, peer or House of Parliament, should the King's prerogative be called in question." James agreed; such indeed was the duty of King's counsel. "I will not," Coke said, "dispute with your Majesty."

Ellesmere now delivered his opinion, "clearly and plainly:" the delay of trial which James had requested in the Commendams Case had not contravened the judges' oath. "And the Lord Chancellor," continued the reporter, "required that the oath itself might be read; which was done by the King's Solicitor [Yelverton] and all the words thereof weighed and considered. Thereupon his Majesty and the Lords thought good to ask the Judges severally their opinion; the question being put in this manner: Whether, if at any time, in a case depending before the Judges, which his Majesty conceived to concern him either in power or profit, and thereupon required to consult with them, and that they should stay proceedings in the meantime, they ought not to stay accordingly? . . . They all (the Lord Chief Justice only except) yielded that they would, and acknowledged it to be their duty to do so; only the Lord Chief Justice of the King's Bench said for answer, *That when the case should be, he would do that should be fit for a Judge to do.*"

It was a statement never to be forgotten, in simple dignity nullifying all that had gone before — and to the monarch, one last convincing proof that Coke must be humbled. On the final day of term before summer circuit — June 20, 1616 — James went to Star Chamber to sit in the emblazoned chair that had been so long (and wisely) left vacant by his forebears. The room was crowded, expectant, and where the common lawyers clustered in groups — barristers, Puritans, Parliament men — the air was charged with hostility. Since Henry VIII, no sovereign had presided in this ancient house of judgment beside the Thames. The breaking of so old a precedent presaged little good. Overhead against the painted ceiling, gilded constellations gleamed. As the official procession entered, Star Chamber fairly whirled with color; scarlet gowns and violet hoods, golden collars of SS; the mace, gold-tipped, the ushers' white wands held high. Bishops, Archbishops, Lords of Council walked in all the panoply of state. The King's coming was announced a long way off with trumpets, swelling as they advanced, clear, piercingly sweet against the summer air. The monarch wore his crown and kingly robes under a cloak of purple velvet, crimson lined; his sword hilt gleamed with jewels. The audience knelt, then rose at a signal as the sovereign prepared to speak.

"*Give thy judgments*," he began, "*to the King, O God, and thy righteousness to the King's son.* . . . Kings are properly Judges, and judgment properly belongs to them from God: for Kings sit in the throne of God, and thence all judgment is derived. It is atheism and blasphemy to dispute what God can do; so it is presumption and high contempt in a subject to dispute what a King can do, or say that a King cannot do this or that. . . . I remember Christ's saying, 'My sheep hear my voice,' and so I assure myself, my people will most willingly hear the voice of me, their own Shepherd and King."

No word that fell was new; James had said it before and often. Yet place and occasion lent it, today, an awful finality. Thirteen years of English residence had not, it was plain, changed this monarch one iota. An audience of lawyers knew it with dark foreboding. Only the times had changed. James remained the same Scottish absolutist who had crossed the border in 1603 and hanged a cutpurse without trial. "The absolute prerogative of the Crown," the royal voice continued, "is no subject for the tongue of a lawyer, nor is lawful to be disputed. In your pleas, presume not to meddle with things against the King's prerogative or honour. Some gentlemen of late have been too bold this ways; if the Judges suffer it, I must punish both them and you. Plead not upon new Puritanical strains that make all things popular; but keep you within the ancient limits of pleas. Judges! keep your selves within your own Benches, not to invade other jurisdictions, which is unfit and an unlawful thing. I thought it an odious and inept speech and it grieved me very much that it should be said in Westminster Hall, that a premunire lay against the Court of Chancery and officers there: How can the King grant a premunire against himself? The Chancery is called the dispenser of the King's conscience. And therefore, sitting here in a seat of judgment, I declare and command that no man hereafter presume to sue a premunire against the Chancery."

There was much more. And if James, as the foreign ambassador had said, possessed a talent for destroying himself, his talent extended to the destruction of those institutions which he most cherished. His coming to Star Chamber did much, it was afterward agreed, toward the eventual disappearance of that court.

Within a fortnight, James enforced his Star Chamber statement by published decree, bolstered with precedents dug out by Bacon: "We do will and command that our Chancellor or Keeper of the Great Seal shall . . . give unto our subjects upon their several complaints such relief in Equity (notwithstanding any former proceedings at the Common Law against them) as shall stand with the true merits and justice of their cases, and with the former ancient and continued practice and precedency of our Chancery."

From that day, Chancery's right to issue injunctions was not questioned. Coke never again contested the Lord Chancellor's subpoenas against the common-law courts. He expressed his bitterness in angry criticism, set down at random. Thirty years later, notes in his handwriting were discovered among his papers and incorporated in the *Third Institute:* "This decree was obtained by the importunity of the then Lord Chancellor being vehemently afraid: *sed judicandum est legibus* [judgment is by the laws], and no precedent can prevail against an act of Parliament. And besides, the supposed precedents (which we have seen) are not authenticall, being most of them in torn papers, and the rest of no credit."

It was a typical Cokeian statement. James's decree, published in July of 1616, was followed shortly by an extraordinary happening — nothing less, indeed, than murder in Fleet Street. One of the six Masters in Chancery, Sir John Tyndall, was killed by a pistol shot, three bullets being discharged (wrote Chamberlain) "by one Bertram, an aged gentleman," who declared that Tyndall had wronged him in the court of Chancery. Arrested, the murderer showed no remorse. If he had forfeited his life he had done it, he said, for the good of the commonwealth. "The cause," Chamberlain added, "breeds much discourse, the man beeing neare fowrescore yeares old that did it, and a comely grave man as is to be seene. . . . Sir William Walter sayes that the fellow mistooke his marke and should rather have shot hailshot at the whole court [of Chancery]: which indeed growes great and ingrosses all manner of cases, and breeds generally complaint for a decree passed there this terme (subscribed by all the Kinges learned counsel) wherby that court may review and call in question what judgements soever passe at the common law, wherby the jurisdiction of Chancery is inlarged out of measure, and so suits become as it were immortall.

"This successe," finished Chamberlain, "is come of my Lord Cooke and some of the judges oppugning the chauncerie so weakly and unseasonablie, that in stead of overthrowing the exoribitant authoritie thereof, they have more established and confirmed it."

But if the common lawyers were discouraged, Bacon found himself triumphant. "I do take comfort," he wrote to James, "that I was the first that advised you to come in person into Star Chamber." The next course was to summon Coke alone, without his Brethren, and let him be charged personally with offenses against the King. On the twenty-sixth of June, this was done. Ellesmere and Bacon were not present, but Lady Hatton was; the matter concerned her. The charges were three: (1) Sir Edward Coke, when Attorney General, had bound himself over to Sir Christopher Hatton* to withhold payment of a debt to the Crown owed by the late Lord Chancellor Hatton. (2) Last Hilary term in King's Bench, the Lord Chief Justice had given "too much heart and encouragement" to the cause of the premunires, and "too constantly directed the jury (turning them thrice from the bar) that if they set their hand to a bill after judgment, he would foreclose them the court. And farther, said that the common law of England would be overthrown and the light of the law would be obscured." (3) The Lord Coke showed indecent behavior before his Majesty, the Lords of Privy Council and Judges; taking exception to the King's Attorney [Bacon] in his Majesty's presence. Further, a question being put to "the rest of the Judges, *If his Majesty should send hereafter a like case*—the rest of the Judges submitting themselves, the Lord Coke only dissented from all the rest."

Invited to defend himself, Coke began with the business of Sir Christopher Hatton's bond and the debt, which he said were *elephanti libelli*, matters now twelve years past, incurred at a time when he was employed in the Powder Treason and Cobham's Treason. His memory therefore was dim. Nor had he any profit by the bond beyond one benefice in his presentation; the rest was all his wife's. Throughout the transaction, he had submitted himself to his Majesty and Council; the Crown had suffered no loss. Concerning disrespect to the Lord Chancellor, if he had erred he could only say *Erravimus cum patribus*, We erred with the fathers; he was

* Lady Hatton's first husband, adopted nephew of Lord Chancellor Hatton, had no son and his estates went to Christopher Hatton, son of the Chancellor's first cousin, John Hatton.

not the first to charge that Chancery had overreached, "to the subversion of the common law." In the matter of commendams, he had been wrong, Coke admitted, to check Mr. Attorney General in his Majesty's presence; but his answer to the sovereign, "When the time shall come, I shall do that which should become a Judge," had intended no disrespect.

That was all. Coke went home to await the King's conclusions. Weaker charges had never been brought against a judge. Coke knew it and knew by the same token that his enemies desired his blood. If they could find nothing more valid against him than they had today produced, they would gain their end by other means. The matter of Hatton's bond was nonsense and Ellesmere not likely to press it. What game was Bacon playing, and why did he thus hesitate? A dozen serious charges might be brought, turning on Coke's long fight against the prerogative: Coke's flat refusal, in the Commendams, to delay trial at the King's command; his denial of the royal "right to consultation" before a hearing; Peacham's Case, and Coke's failure to see treason where King and King's Counsel saw treason plainly; all the business against High Commission, Admiralty, Star Chamber, the Council of Wales and the Duchy of Lancaster, where Coke had openly ridiculed prerogative procedure. . . . Yet today, Solicitor General Yelverton could bring up nothing worse than "disrespect to the Chancellor and King's Counsel Learned." Were the crown forces fearful of engaging Coke in legal controversy, and were they taking a devious way round?

In this morning's performance had been something ominous; a man cannot fight shadows nor defend himself against a cloud. "I saw my Lord Coke and his Lady," noted a Londoner that evening, "come very heavily from Council Chamber." Chamberlain, too, missed nothing that could be seen with the naked eye, though remaining puzzled as to cause. "The truth is," he wrote, "that the Lord Coke's Lady hath stoode him in great steade both in sollicit-ing for him in privat and pleading for him at the Council table, wherin she hath don herself a great deale of honor, but specially in refusing to sever her state or cause from his (as she was moved to do) but resolving and publishing that she would run the same fortune with him." Coke's best hope, added Chamberlain, lay in the fact that should the King disgrace him now (following the Overbury trials) "and in such a cause, he would be accounted the martyr of the commonwealth."

Whatever Lady Hatton's motives, it was the last time she would win applause for supporting her husband; henceforth the race was to be run quite differently. Four days later, on June thirtieth, Coke was summoned again to Whitehall. The King, he heard, was not satisfied with his answers to Council last week. And though, taking into account his former services, his Majesty was not disposed to deal heavily, it was ordered (1) that the Lord Coke be suspended from his place in Privy Council; (2) that he forbear to ride his summer circuit as Justice of Assize; and (3) "that during the vacation, while he hath time to live privately, and dispose himself at home, he take into consideration and review his book of reports wherein, as his Majesty is informed, be many extravagant and exorbitant opinions set down and published for positive and good law. If, in reviewing and reading thereof, he find anything fit to be altered and amended, the correction is left to his discretion. Amongst other things the King is not well pleased with the title of the book wherein he entitled himself Lord Chief Justice of England, whereas he could challenge no more than Lord Chief Justice of the King's Bench. And having corrected what he find meet in these reports, his Majesty's pleasure is, that he should bring the same privately before himself, that he might consider thereof, as in his princely judgment should be found expedient."

There was nothing Coke could say. These were not charges to be refuted but royal commands. "Chief Justice of England"? In Coke's last volume of *Reports*, the words had followed his name as author — a title in common usage since the Conquest, modified from Chief Justiciar when the courts divided into King's Bench and Common Pleas. Coke himself had employed the words years before, in reporting Shelley's Case (1581). "Resolv'd by Sir Christopher Wray, Lord Chief Justice of England." No one hitherto had objected to such usage.*

Coke bowed. "I submit myself," he said, "to his Majesty's pleasure." He turned to go, but had not reached the door when Lord

* "And here it may be observed again," wrote Pettus in his *Constitution of Parliaments* (1680) "to prevent vulgar misunderstandings, That the Lord Chief Justice of England is Chief Justice of the King's Bench or upper Bench."

Treasurer Suffolk called him back. "His Majesty," said Suffolk abruptly, "hath been informed that the Lord Coke has suffered his coachman to ride bareheaded before him. This His Majesty desires may be foreborne in future."

The significance of bareheadedness in coachmen has been obscured by the passage of centuries; perhaps only royalty was entitled to servants with heads uncovered in the street. Whatever its meaning, the rebuke was extraordinary. To Coke it must have seemed sheer invention, Suffolk's last cut of the whip to show an arrogant barrister his place. "If my coachman," Coke replied, "hath rode before me bareheaded, he did it at his own ease and not by my order. This I beg your Lordships to take notice of and state to his Majesty from me with all humility."

Only one course remained. Coke must go home to Stoke and review, or make semblance of reviewing, five hundred-odd cases of the complete *Reports*, preparatory to making some kind of statement that might satisfy his Majesty. Meanwhile the news went round. "My Lord Cooke," wrote Philip Gawdy to a Norfolk kinsman, "is in great disgrace with his Majestie. He is suspended from the Council, put by his circuite and all the disgraces layde uppon him that his adversaryes can devise. Many are very sorry for him. The Quenes Majestie is his great frende. I pray God sende him many more." Chamberlain went deeply into it, rolling out every last piece of gossip for the benefit of Dudley Carleton at The Hague: "The King dined last weeke at Wimbleton, where the earl of Exeter [Lady Hatton's father] made great entertainment. The Lady Hatton was there and well graced, for the King kist her twice, but it seems it was but a lightning; for on Sonday last the Lord Cooke . . . was sequestered from the Council table, from riding his circuit and willed to review and correct his reports as many wayes faulty and full of novelties in point of law. Some that wish him well feare the matter will not end here, for he is wilfull and will take no council but . . . gives his enemies such advantage to worke upon the Kings indignation towards him that he is in great daunger. The world discourses diversly how he should run so far into the Kings displeasure, and will not take these alleaged causes for sound payment, but sticke not to say that he was too too busie in the late busines [the Somerset trials] and dived farther into secrets than there was need, and so perhaps might see Diana naked.* Howsoever it be he is not well advised that he doth not *cedere tempori* [give way to the times] and carrie himself more dutifully and submissely to his Majestie in his actions, though his wordes be now humble enough."

Humble words addressed to a sovereign were not difficult. Every man near the King had learned to use them extravagantly; it was a convention seldom overstepped unless by some arrogant favorite like Somerset, presuming upon intimacy. But as for submission, Coke had no intention of it. The eleven volumes of *Reports* represented his life's work. Moreover the *Reports* were standard usage in all the law courts, Star Chamber included, and had been since the first volume appeared in 1600. Even Bacon accepted them, though he had told James some years ago that they held "too much *de proprio* [of Coke himself]; great judges are unfit persons to be reporters, for they have either too little leisure or too much authority." Coke knew well where the offending passages lay, and not in errors of fact but of viewpoint: Bonham's Case, Peacham's Case, Owen's Case for treason in 1615, the case *De Rege Inconsulto* and a score of others. Ellesmere already had pointed out thirty such *errata*.

When summer was over, and the Long Vacation, Coke returned to London, ready, he said, with his amended *Reports*. On the second of October, he was summoned before Ellesmere, Bacon, Solicitor General Yelverton and King's Serjeant Montague. There were, Coke began, eleven books, covering about five hundred cases. Among so many, faults were to be expected. Even Plowden's Reports, "which he reverenced much," had been found to contain four errors. This brief preface concluded, Coke handed to the Lord Chancellor a single sheet on which were recorded five small, wholly trivial mistakes of fact or of Latin translation. Not a word concerning High Commission, Peacham's Case or the rest.

In dealing with James it was well to cover defeat by the light touch; here was a monarch who liked to laugh. "Your Majesty may perceive," wrote Bacon (enclosing Coke's single sheet), "that my Lord [Coke] is an happy man, that there should be no more errors in his five hundred cases than in a few cases of Plowden." James, having perused Coke's paper, sent word that whether the Chief

* Chamberlain used the Latin, "*nudam sine veste Dianam.*"

Justice were to be disgraced or pardoned, action must come quickly. Coke had asked for royal audience, having something of importance to impart. Yet as matters now stood, Coke's free admission to the presence would be impossible, implying, said James, "a grant of pardon before trial." The King's position was embarrassing. Coke had hinted at secrets of great urgency. "It would be dangerous and prejudicial," the King added, "to delay him too long."

What Coke had up his sleeve at the moment will never be known. But if Bacon could play games, Coke could at least try to match him. James looked on this stubborn Norfolkman with an apparent mixture of fear, respect and quite frantic frustration. The man was useful; he knew Parliament and how to raise money; he had friends everywhere except in high palace circles. Yet with such a Chief Justice, how could prerogative government proceed? For James the time had come to rid himself of this encumbrance. Ellesmere and Bacon however seemed not to take sudden alarm. Together, on October sixth, they wrote James a long letter, urging caution. Charges against Coke must be drawn into discernible bounds — "whether points of novelty which we collected, or only the faults of his books and the prohibitions and *habeas corpus* collected by my Lord of Canterbury [Archbishop Abbot]." To achieve this would require perhaps the whole of Michaelmas term. Meanwhile Coke must not sit as Judge in Westminster Hall, though he might be permitted to continue judicial business privately in chambers. His Brethren could dispatch suits in King's Bench. For Star Chamber the Lord Chancellor would supply a substitute and trials at *nisi prius* could be taken over by commission. "To give every man his due," Bacon further told the King, "had it not been for Sir Edward Coke's *Reports* (which though they may have errors and some peremptory and extrajudicial resolutions more than are warranted, yet they contain infinite good decisions and rulings over of cases) the law by this time had been almost like a ship without ballast."

On the seventeenth of October, Coke was again called up and told that his Majesty, "out of his gracious favor, was pleased that his memory should be refreshed [concerning] some passages in his books which his Majesty did yet distaste." Five special points were selected. Coke carried them home for study. A few days later he was back, bearing what was described as "an humble and direct answer to each point." Ellesmere looked sourly upon these answers. He had never thought well of Coke's *Reports*, which he said were inaccurate, purposely directed against ecclesiastical rights and the prerogative. Coke had a trick of writing, "Resolved by the court," then following it (said Ellesmere) with words that in truth were only passing remarks dropped by the judges, thus contriving to "scatter and sow his own conceits." Only a deep obedience to Majesty, wrote Ellesmere, kept him from humbly suing to be spared all future services concerning the Lord Coke.

The Lord Chancellor, weary, aged, desired to fight no more. But the King's Attorney General took hold with all the vigor that was in him. Bacon never expressed a doubt concerning Coke's eventual dismissal from the bench. Looking to be Lord Chancellor himself, he had no ambition to serve with a Chief Justice whose ideas of government so drastically opposed his own, even aside from the question of personal enmity. Not Coke's dismissal but the manner of it must be seriously considered. Privy Council should be told beforehand exactly the course his Majesty planned to take. And in that final meeting, when Coke must suffer public disgrace, method of procedure would be highly important. For the King's guidance, Bacon wrote out directions in his own hand:

> *His Majesty to declare* that on grounds of deceit, contempt and slander of his government, he might very justly not only have put the Lord Coke from his place of Chief Justice, but to have brought him in question in the Star Chamber (which would have been his utter overthrow).
>
> That his Majesty had noted in him a perpetual turbulent carriage, first towards the liberties of his church and the state ecclesiastical; then towards his prerogative royal and the branches thereof . . . in all which he hath raised troubles and new questions; and lastly, in that which might concern the safety of his royal person, by his exposition of the laws in cases of high treason.
>
> That besides the actions themselves, his Majesty in his princely wisdom hath made two special observations of him. The one, that he having in his nature not one part of those things which are popular in men, being neither liberal, nor affable, nor magnificent, he hath made himself popular by design only, pulling down government.

In Privy Council, too, Coke had been intractable, Bacon went on. And whereas his Majesty might have expected a change, considering the honor conveyed by such appointment — it had made "no change at all but to the worse, he holding on all his former behavior and running separate courses from the rest of the Council; and rather busying himself in casting fears before Council concerning what they could not do, than joining his advice what they should do." The matter of Coke's *Reports* must be given special consideration, and the public informed of "many dangerous conceits of his own uttered for law, to the prejudice of his Majesty's crown, parliament and subjects." His Majesty having graciously granted a summer's vacation to review these volumes, the Lord Coke "after three months time and consideration had offered his Majesty only five animadversions, being rather a scorn than a satisfaction to his Majesty; whereof one was that in the Prince's case he had found out the French statute, which was *filz aisné*, whereas the Latin was *primogenitus:* and so the Prince is Duke of Cornwall in French, and not Duke of Cornwall in Latin. And another was, that he had set Montague to be Chief Justice in Henry VIII's time, when it should have been in Edward VI's, and such other stuff; not falling upon any of those things which he could not but know were offensive."

It was now almost November. Coke's fate had hung fire a full five months. Twenty-eight objections to his *Reports*, being "either so weake in themselves or so well aunswered," were reduced to five, upon which the King's Counsel Learned had yet to pass. Not the least part of Coke's humiliation lay, said Chamberlain, in the King's choice of men to judge him: Bacon, Yelverton, Serjeants Montague, Crew and Finch, "whereof the greater part, excepting Yelverton, are held no great men of law. And withall to find so coarse usage, as not to be once offered to sit downe, and so unrespective and uncivill carriage from the Lord Chauncellors men, that not one of them did move a hat or make any other signe of regard towards him, wherof the Quene taking notice, his Majestie the King hath since sent word that he wold have him well used." Bacon, rather surprisingly, was thought by many to have changed over to Coke's side, "for that [Sir Francis] ever used him with more respect than the rest, as for divers speaches he gives out in his favor, as that a man of his learning and parts is not every day found, nor so soone made as marred." James was in the country; when next he came to town, resolution would be taken one way or the other. Coke's friends were hopeful, "for that the King hath saide that he doth this *ad correctionem*, not *ad destructionem*."

Perhaps Queen Anne's intercession had caused James to relent a little — or perhaps, in the fine fall hunting weather, he simply tired of the whole thing. At any rate, Bacon chose to jog the royal memory with a last statement of Coke's offenses. Entitled "Innovations into the Laws and Government," the paper contained, on a lefthand margin, seventeen charges, definite, pertinent, written out apparently by a secretary. Opposite each charge, Bacon set down comments in his own handwriting:

1. The Ecclesiastical Commission.	*In this he prevailed, and the commission was pared. . . .*
2. Against the Provincial Councils.	*In this he prevailed in such sort . . . as the jurisdictions grow into contempt, and more would, if the Lord Chancellor did not strengthen them by injunctions. . . .*
3. Against the Star-chamber for levying damages.	*In this he was overruled by the sentence of the court, but he bent all his strength and wits to have prevailed; and so did the other judges by long and laborious arguments: and if they had prevailed, the authority of the court had been overthrown. But the plurality of the court took more regard to their own precedents than to the Judges' opinions.*
4. Against the Admiralty.	*In this he prevaileth, for prohibitions fly continually and many times are cause of long suits, to the discontent of foreign ambassadors and to the King's dishonour and trouble by their remonstrances.*
5. Against the Court of the Duchy of Lancaster prohibitions go; and the like may do to the court of wards and exchequer-chamber.	*This is new, and would be forthwith restrained, and the others settled.*

6. Against the Court of Requests.	*In this he prevaileth; and this but lately brought in question.*
7. Against the Chancery for decrees after judgment.	*In this his Majesty hath made an establishment;* and he hath not prevailed but made a great noise and trouble.*
8. *Premunire* for suits in the chancery.	*This his Majesty hath also established,* being a strange attempt to make the Chancellor sit under a hatchet, instead of the King's arms.*
9. Disputed in the Common Pleas, whether that court may grant a prohibition to stay suits in the Chancery, and time given to search for precedents.	*This was but a bravery, and dieth of itself, especially the authority of the Chancery by his Majesty's late proceedings being so well established.**
10. Against the new boroughs of Ireland.	*This in good time was overruled by the voice of eight judges of ten, after they had heard your attorney* [Bacon]. *And had it prevailed, it had overthrown the parliament of Ireland, which would have been imputed to a fear in this state to have proceeded, and so his Majesty's authority and reputation lost in that kingdom.*
11. Against the writ *Dom. Rege inconsulto.*	*This is yet* sub judice: *but if it should prevail, it maketh the Judges absolute over all patents of the King's, be they of power or profit, contrary to the ancient and ever continued law of the crown; which doth call those causes before the King himself, as he is represented in Chancery.*
12. Against contribution,† that it was not lawful neither to levy it nor to move for it.	*In this he prevailed, and gave opinion, that the King by his great seal could not so much as move any of his subjects for benevolence. But this he retracted after*

* Referring to James's decree of July 18, 1616.
† Bacon here refers to the benevolence of 1614.

	in the Star-chamber, but it marred the benevolence in the meantime.
13. Peacham's Case.	*In this, for as much as in him was, and in the court of King's Bench, he prevailed, though it was holpen by the good service of others. But the opinion which he then held amounted in effect to this: That no words of scandal or defamation, importing that the King was utterly unable or unworthy to govern, were treason, except they disabled his title, etc.*
14. Owen's Case.*	*In this we prevailed with him to give opinion it was treason; but then it was upon a conceit of his own that was no less dangerous than if he had given his opinion against the King. . . .*
15. The value of benefices not to be according to the tax in the King's book of taxes.	*By this the intent of the statute of 21* HENRY VIII *is frustrated; for there is no benefice of so small an improved value as £8 by that kind of rating. For this the Judges may be assembled in the exchequer chamber for a conference.*
16. Suits for legacies ought to be in their proper dioceses, and not in the Prerogative Court. . . .	*The practice hath gone against this. And it is fit the suit be where the probate is. And this served but to put a pique between the Archbishops' courts and the Bishops' courts. This may be again propounded upon a conference of the Judges.*
17. Homicide beyond the seas may be tried and judged in England, by a new construction of the Statute *13, H.4.*	*This was a mere fancy of his own, by mistaking the construction of a statute never thought of before; and may be thought a device to bring in a constable of England. But this hath since reverted upon him.*

On November thirteenth, Bacon dispatched to James the note that sealed Coke's fate:

* Owen's Case, in 1615, grew out of the benevolence. Long and complex, it is one of many cases omitted in this book for want of space.

May it please your excellent Majesty,

I send your Majesty a form of discharge for my Lord Coke from his place of Chief Justice of your Bench.

I send also a warrant to the Lord Chancellor for making forth a writ for a new Chief Justice, leaving a blank for the name to be supplied by your Majesty.

And on the day following, Chamberlain in one superb sentence (which he said was common talk) summed up the whole of Coke's troubled fate: "Four Ps have overthrown and put him down, that is PRIDE, PROHIBITIONS, PREMUNIRE, and PREROGATIVE." Sir George Coppin brought the King's *supersedeas* to Coke in his chambers: "For certain causes now moving us, we will that you shall be no longer our Chief Justice to hold pleas before us, and we command you that you no longer interfere in that office, and by virtue of this presence, we at once remove and exonerate you from the same."

Taking the scroll in his hand, Coke read it, then bowed his head and wept.

On November eighteenth, Sir Henry Montague rode to Westminster to be sworn in Coke's place. Montague — King's Serjeant and Recorder of London — was a strong prerogative man; he had been chosen to sit as Judge at Peacham's trial in Taunton. The day before his swearing in, Montague sent a messenger, asking to buy Coke's collar of SS. Coke declined. "I will not part with it," he said, "but leave it to my posterity, that they may one day know they had a Chief Justice to their ancestor."

A *good answer*, Chamberlain remarked, recounting the scene. Montague made the journey from London to Westminster in much pomp, "accompanied with some earles, lords and others of great qualitie to the number of fifty horse, besides the whole fry of the Middle Temple and swarmes of other lawiers and officers. The Lord Chauncellor, though he were crazie* and had not come at Westminster five or sixe dayes before nor since, yet made shift to give him his oath, and withall many admonitions how to carrie himself in the place, wherin he glanced (not as they say obscurely, but in plaine termes) at his predecessor for many errors and vanities but specially for his ambitious popularitie."

Actually, Ellesmere had made a field day of it. Ill, tired, close to

* "Crazy" meant ill, in Elizabethan parlance.

death, the very name of Coke seemed to revivify him, "almost like a young duellist," Becan told the King, "who findeth himself behind-hand." Under the circumstances, open castigation, would have been impossible, lacking in dignity. Ellesmere spoke therefore in parables, thinly disguised to hold the rapt attention of his audience. One of Montague's ancestors, as it happened, had been Chief Justice under Edward VI, providing convenient text. "Set before your eyes your worthy grandfather!" Ellesmere told the new Chief Justice unctuously. "Remember his virtues! He never found in his learning to convict, upon the statute of Edward III, all the Commissioners of Sewers in a premunire, that whilst they were arguing a moot point, all the country might be drowned! Neither in his learning did he find upon the same Statute to convict the Chancery and those in it in a premunire (which, God be thanked, are proved but inept.) Neither would he have *Teste Edwardo Montague* to jostle with *Teste me ipso*,* and so oppose himself against the King that placed him here. Neither would he style himself *Chief Justice Totius Angliae*. . . . Neither did he ever dispute the King's prerogative writ when it came to him. Neither did he say that statutes were void because they were against common right and reason, but left the Parliament and King to judge what was common right and reason (and none fit to interpret of it but they).

"Remember also," finished Ellesmere with ponderous satisfaction and a shrewd working-in of the sovereign's new title, "the removing and putting down of your late predecessor, and by whom: the great *King of Great Britain*, whose wisdom and royal virtue and religious care . . ."

The remaining phrases might have been supplied by any courtier. But the incident had been telling; Ellesmere's device was witty enough to bear repeating over the evening's wine. Coke's friends, indignant and sorrowful, could do no more than bide their time. "A verye bitter invective," Whitelocke remarked of Ellesmere's speech. "What was the cawse of Sir Edward Coke's offence is not for subjects to meddle withe. But those that practised before him, or had cawses before him, found him the most just, honest and incorrupt judge that ever sate on benche."

* *Teste me ipso* — witness I myself: the form of attestation at the end of royal writs.

Chamberlain's version was as usual impartial: "If Sir Edward Coke could bear this misfortune constantly it were no great disgrace to him, for he goes away with a generall applause and goode opinion, and the King himself when he told his resolution at the Council table to remove him, yet gave him this testimonie that he thought him in no way corrupt, but a good justicer, with so many other goode words as if he meant to hang him with silken halter. Hitherto he beares himself well."

Coke's name had lent itself always to punning. A distich now went the rounds of Fleet Street and the Inns of Court. "A prettie epigram," Chamberlain called it, adding that "more no doubt will follow, for when men are downe the very drunkards make rimes and songes upon them. . . ."

Jus condere Cocus potuit, sed condere jure
Non potuit; potuit condere jura Cocis.

Coke could cook law books
But he couldn't cook by the books.
He could only cook books for Cokes.

Rhyme and distich, jibe and "pretty epigram"; Coke endured them all. When he walked the streets of Holborn no mace cleared the way from Old Palace Yard through the doors of Westminster Great Hall. In St. Dunstan's Church on Sunday mornings it was Montague who sat upon green cushions with the Brethren. Guildhall, and the judges' dais waiting at Assize week; Star Chamber beside the Thames . . . the Council Table at Whitehall laid out with papers; Lambeth Palace, where a Judge had stood before the High Commission . . . scenes of battle, glory or defeat. At Norwich Assizes, would countrymen ride in this summer from remote farms and hamlets, lacking news, thinking to see their friend?

Among many accounts of Coke's disgrace, perhaps the most expressive comes to us from a total stranger. Under date of November nineteenth, 1616, one John Castle writes to his friend (equally obscure):

"A thunderbolt hath fallen on the Lord Coke, which hath overthrown him from the very roots."

PART III

The Parliament Man

CHAPTER TWENTY-NINE

1617. Bacon, Coke and Lady Hatton.

Lord Coke is tossed up and down like a tennis ball. Lord Bacon is in slippery places, and self-interest prevails.

DR. GEORGE CARLETON TO SIR DUDLEY CARLETON,
October, 1617

GRIEVED, humiliated, Coke vanished into the countryside. Where service to the state was concerned, the best of life — though he could not know it now in his distress — still lay ahead. Coke was sixty-five, gray and lean, with a rugged, enduring look. In Hertfordshire his daughter Anne Sadleir welcomed him to the great house known as Standon Lordship — and for the first time in his life, Coke found himself idle by enforcement. As days passed, he responded with none of the resignation held proper to his years but with a restless anger, brooding, comfortless, ready to burst forth when opportunity presented. In London his name remained current; people could not believe the Lord Coke was gone from public life. During December — a month after his dismissal — rumor had it he was seen at Newmarket, begging royal audience to discuss a marriage between his daughter Frances and Sir John Villiers, brother of the King's new favorite.

If Bacon heard this startling bit, he gave, at the moment, no sign. For him all planets rode propitious. Lord Ellesmere was dying. Nothing but an old man's feeble breath lay now between Sir Francis and ultimate ambition. James paid a visit to York House, accepted Ellesmere's resignation and in appreciation for long service offered to create him Viscount Brackley. The Chancellor remained indifferent; the honor arrived too late, he said. On a table by his bed lay the Great Seal in its white leather bag, enclosed by a silk purse stamped with the royal arms in red and gold. Secretary Winwood and Sir George Villiers came and took it away.

On the seventh of March, before noon at Whitehall Palace, Bacon was named Lord Keeper. He carried the Great Seal home in his coach, and with overflowing heart sat down to write his gratitude. The letter began "My dearest Lord," and it was addressed to the Earl of Buckingham.

It was a name which already bore magic; no royal favorite of history had risen from obscurity so fast and stayed so long in power. In two years, George Villiers of Leicestershire became successively Cup Bearer to the King, Master of the Horse, Knight of the Garter, a Viscount and, in January of 1617, Privy Councilor and Earl of Buckingham, with the annual income of a prince. Not only James but James's son was to be ruled by him until in Europe they said that Buckingham was king of England. The royal eye had first been caught by Villiers at the play *Ignoramus* — "the handsomest bodied man of England, from head to foot not to be charged with any blemish." Gentle, sweet-tempered, generous, the young man seemed, after Somerset's arrogance and greed, a very angel come to court. Indeed, it was Archbishop Abbot who had introduced his name to Queen Anne as possible displacement for Somerset. (One of the oddest quirks of an extremely odd monarch was James's refusal to receive a favorite without the Queen's blessing.) Queen Anne accepted Villiers not without misgivings, though she was alone in these premonitions of evil. "This young man," she told the Archbishop, "will become more intolerable than any that were before him."

Already, at twenty-four, Buckingham had at his disposal "all the honours and all the offices of the three kingdoms, without a rival." No plan could be put through nor so much as a clerkship conferred without his nod. Even Coke's fall was attributed, as time passed, less to championship of the common law than to refusal of a certain lucrative clerkship for the Earl's patronage. The office (in Common Pleas) was worth £4000 a year; Coke had promised to divide it between Sir James Whitelocke and another. Coke's friends maintained that he refused a large sum of money for the place. "A judge must not pay a bribe nor take a bribe," he said.

Bacon, who took Buckingham's side, busied himself in the matter. Questioned point-blank one morning before a commission of lawyers, Coke told Bacon with some anger that his mind was set. "No, Mr. Attorney," he said; "I will not wrastle now in my latter times." Bacon repeated the scene to Villiers in the usual phonetic spelling. "A dialogue to make you merry," he called it. Before Coke's successor, Montague, was named as Chief Justice, Bacon made sure of him concerning the clerkship. Montague bestowed it as desired, himself receiving a pension of £500 a year, tacked on to the office as reward.

In March of 1617, about a week after Bacon received the Great Seal, James set out for Scotland, with Villiers of course in his train. It was the King's first visit to his old home. Moving northward in the cold spring weather, he saw ploughed hills and rolling seeded pastures give place to wild Scottish bogs and the crags he knew so well, rough meager country where in youth he had suffered hardship, terror and captivity. The royal chaplain preached, en route, on a text from Genesis; James appeared much affected: "And Abraham was very rich in cattle, in silver and gold. And he went on his journeys from the south even to Bethel, to the place where his tent had been at the beginning."

James was to be gone until September. Bacon, meantime, found himself to all intents and purposes in charge of government. Lord Treasurer Suffolk carried greater prestige of birth and blood, but the fall of Somerset had clipped the Howard wings and Suffolk himself was on the edge of danger. Secretary of State Sir Ralph Winwood, in whose hands policy would normally have rested (as in Cecil's day), disagreed sharply with Bacon's ideals of government, hated Spain, hated Ambassador Gondomar and the new secret plans for a royal Spanish marriage. "The boisterous Secretary," Bacon called him. The two began to show open friction. One morning, Winwood's shoulder pressed a little heavily against Bacon at the Council table; Bacon turned on him and bade him keep his distance. The Lord Keeper's dog lay sleeping on a chair. Winwood, to get him off, struck him. "Every gentleman," said Bacon with deadly emphasis, "loves a dog." Queen Anne, disturbed, inquired the cause of the quarrel. "Madam," Sir Francis told her, "I can say no more but he is proud and I am proud."

Having received the Great Seal during vacation, Bacon had not yet sat formally in Chancery. On the opening day of Easter term, he made triumphant journey from London to Westminster, gowned in purple satin, riding between Lord Treasurer Suffolk and the Keeper of the Privy Seal. Peers, Privy Councilors and Judges attended, besides the usual train from the Inns of Court. "There was," wrote Chamberlain, "a great deal more braverie and better shew of horse than was expected in the Kings absence, but both Quene and Prince sent all their followers and his other frends did their best to honor him. He made a speach in chancerie . . . pleased himself much in the flourishing of the lawe, and that great lawyers sons have the way to succeed their fathers, instancing in himself, the atturny generall [Yelverton] and solicitor [Coventry]. The greatest part of his traine dined with him that day, which cost him, as is generally reported, £700."

Tactfully, Bacon gave a dinner also to the judges — an old custom revived — making occasion to state that he would suffer no derogation of Chancery powers. If any man felt the wind in that direction he should, said Bacon, "freely and friendly acquaint me with it and we should soon agree." "At which speech of mine," Bacon wrote at once to James, "I did see cheer and comfort in their faces, as if it were a new world." Privately, to such judges as were well affected, Bacon proposed a scheme for extending the jurisdiction of High Commission. A new prison should be built especially for commission prisoners, with its own jailers and officials to guard against the former nuisance of High Commission prisoners being taken from jail by habeas corpus from the common-law courts.

The prison went up at once. Yet even in Bacon's hour of triumph, with old plans come to fruition and judges' faces showing such good cheer — even now, Sir Francis seemed plagued by the ghost of his fallen rival. The matter of Coke's *Reports* had not been settled and Bacon did not cease to press it. "I did call upon the committees," he wrote Buckingham, "for the proceeding in the purging of Sir Edward Coke's *Reports*, which I see they go on with seriously." There were other matters that Bacon could take hold of, left over from Coke's Justiceship, such as Coke's trouble with the Governor of Dieppe. Toward the end of last law term, Coke had released on bail one or more English sailors accused of piracy across the Channel. Piracy was perennial, ships preyed upon each other when they could. England, indeed, relied on her "gentlemen adventurers" to keep prowling warships from home shores and rejoiced when they brought home rich cargoes. "Did you ever hear of any that was counted a pirate for taking millions?" Ralegh once asked Bacon. "Tush, my Lord, they are poor mychers* that are called in question for piracy." It was a profitable little side-war, engaged in by all parties and protested periodically by authorities of the injured country. Englishmen of course must not prey on Englishmen; those earringed sailors who hung in chains above Thames tide water were the "poor mychers," caught robbing their own countrymen. But Coke had let his pirates out on bail. They fled, and the French Ambassador, spurred perhaps by Coke's enemies, asked reparation to the tune of five thousand pounds — a demand, said Chamberlain, "beyond all moderation." Coke acknowledged his responsibility and paid the Ambassador £4000 from his own pocket.

Added to all this, Coke and Lady Hatton were engaged in a noisy, prolonged battle over property. Large holdings being involved, husband and wife were summoned before Privy Council. Lady Hatton, expert at sustaining a role — had she not been masquer for Queen Anne these dozen years? — swept into Council Chamber, her titled relatives at her back: Lord and Lady Burghley, the Lords Danvers and Denny, Sir Thomas and Lady Howard. Rising after a graceful curtsy, she stood and told her wrongs. Sir Edward Coke had "menaced her and defeated her of her marriage jointure; he had kept property in her purchased lands. He and his fighting son, Clement, had threatened her servants so grievously that the men ran away to hide themselves. . . . He had broken into Hatton House and secured her coach and coach horses and even her apparel. His men had appeared on the Isle of Purbeck to seize and ship away all her goods from Corfe Castle; when the keeper refused, Sir Edward threatened to return with a warrant from Privy Council. . . .

As Lady Hatton gave it, the tale was brilliantly effective. "Divers saide," reported Chamberlain, "Burbage could not have acted better." (High praise, no actor on the stage surpassed Richard Burbage.) Coke stood to hear it out, and when the sweet troubled voice had ceased, countered with his own charges. His

* Petty thieves.

wife had "disfurnished his house at Holborn and at Stoke Poges, and carried away all the movables and plate she could come by. She had embezzled all his gilt and silver plate and vessels, and instead thereof foisted alchemy [brass] of the same sort, fashion and use, with the illusion to have cheated him of the other. And also she gave him to his face or by letter these unfit words of false treacherous villain. . . ."

On both sides the performance was lamentably undignified. Three months went by before the battle ended and the married pair, "after much animositie and wrangling" were made friends. London laughed, refusing to take the quarrel seriously. Yet Coke's reputation gained nothing thereby, and his good friend Secretary Winwood was anxious. If Sir Edward had remained quietly in Hertfordshire with his daughter and waited, his cause with the King might well have amended with time. Instead, he had come back to London and flung himself noisily in the public eye, as if even action ill advised were better than no action at all. In the matter of the proposed Villiers-Coke marriage, Sir Edward had proved intractable, balking at the dowry demanded by Lady Compton, mother of the intended bridegroom, who controlled the bargaining. (It was she who had proposed the match in the first place.) Herself thrice married, with little money and large ambition, Lady Compton saw the Coke-Hatton fortune as a rich vein of ore and set the dowry at ten thousand pounds outright, with a thousand a year additional while Coke lived. No! said Coke. Ten thousand marks (two-thirds the sum) was high enough, without yearly stipend. He "would not buy the King's favor too deare, being so uncertain and variable."

When this remark went round, it was the general opinion that Coke had taken leave of his senses. But Sir John Villiers, having seen the young lady, made known that he would take her penniless; "in her smock," as he phrased it. Of Frances Coke's beauty there was never disagreement. She seemed to possess a peculiar charm, a manner full of affection and warm spontaneity — later to lead her into much trouble. At the moment, she was not quite fifteen. "Sir Edward Coke," wrote a Londoner, "hath a daughter fit to be a wife of the greatest favorite's brother . . . but the strains in the handling breed storms." During the three-month battle over property, marriage negotiations had lapsed; in June of

1617, Winwood took upon himself to reopen bargaining. He sent a conciliatory letter to Buckingham, saying that Coke longed to be restored to royal favor, "without which he could no longer breathe. Sorry for his former respectless behavior, Sir Edward would be happy if the proposed marriage contract might be renewed. . . ." How much of this was Winwood's rhetoric and how much Coke's actual sentiment cannot be known. If Coke was stifled by neglect he had strange ways of showing it; from March to June his voice had shouted protest. But he agreed now to a dowry of £10,000, paid outright. Oddly enough, if Lady Hatton knew of the marriage negotiations, she had as yet said nothing. Coincident with Winwood's letter, she announced suddenly that she refused Sir John Villiers as son-in-law.

Perhaps it was not the choice of the bridegroom that Lady Hatton resented so much as Coke's highhandedness in going ahead without her. Actually, it would be a brilliant match, for Frances the best possible entrée into those very circles where Lady Hatton loved to move. Sir John Villiers — described in history as "elderly" — was not more than thirty. And though frail in body and subject to unexplained attacks of vagueness in the head, he was certainly no monster. (His good nature and devotion were later to be proved under most trying circumstances.) What Lady Hatton desired was full control of her daughter. The fashionable world expected Frances Coke to have a magnificent dowry. Yet here, in Lady Hatton's view, was Sir Edward Coke walking away with negotiations as if he were sole owner of the girl, quite obviously planning to benefit and mend thereby his own fortunes at court.

Lady Hatton, flashing into the role of outraged mother, did not stop to ask her daughter's wishes. Neither had Coke, for that matter. Why should the inclinations of a mere child enter in? Such a notion would have offended respectable parents, whose business it was to arrange matches for their children. "He that marries for love hath evil days and good nights." It was a favorite maxim. If young people were drawn to each other, so much the better; if not they could learn love in the school of marriage as others had done before them. Lady Hatton's ambition at the moment being to defeat her husband rather than to advance her child, she was willing to risk much. Mother, father and daughter were living at Hatton House in Holborn. One evening after Coke had gone early to bed, Frances and Lady Hatton threw on their cloaks, slipped through a garden gate to where the coach of a confederate waited, and made off westward to the country.

Twenty miles from London, near Hampton Court, Sir Edmund and Lady Withipole, Lady Hatton's cousins, had rented a house for the summer. Oatlands, the place was called; it belonged to the Duke of Argyle. Here the two women took refuge in secret. And here, to divert the tedium of seclusion, Lady Hatton conceived a strategy. Young Henry De Vere, eighteenth Earl of Oxford, a distant connection of Lady Hatton's, was in Venice on the grand tour that was part of every nobleman's education. He had never seen Frances Coke. But Lady Hatton wrote a letter, purporting to come from De Vere and proposing marriage. Forged signature and all, she showed it to Frances with every appearance of triumph. (Where in England could the name De Vere be matched for ancientry and glory?) Seeing her daughter receptive, Lady Hatton then composed what she called an *Obligation*, which the girl willingly wrote out and signed:

> I vow before God and take the Almyghtie to witnesse That I Frances Coke Yonger doughter to Sir Edward Coke late lord chiefe Justice of England doe gyve myselfe absolutely to Wyffe to Henry Vere Viscount Balboke Erl of Oxenford to whom I plyghte my trothe and inviolate vows to keepe myselfe till Death us do part: and if even I brake the leaste of these I pray God Damne mee Bodye and Soule in Hell fire in the world to come: and in theis world I humbly beseeche God the Erth maye open and swallowe mee up quicke to the Terror of all faythe brakers that remayne Alive. In witnesse whereof, I have written alle theis with my owne hande and seald it with my owne seale which I will weare till youre retourne mayke theis goode that I have sent You. And for further witnesses I here underneeth set to my Name,
>
> FRANCES COKE
>
> In the Presence of my deare Mother,
>
> ELIZA HATTON
>
> *10 July, 1617*

This passionate document — later to come as a great surprise to young De Vere — Coke did not see for some time. Waking at Hatton House to find his two birds flown, he set about at once to discover their hiding place. This accomplished, his next move was almost too strange for belief. From Sir Ralph Winwood he secured a warrant to search Sir Edmund Withipole's house. With ten or eleven retainers he then galloped off to Oatlands, "weaponed," said Privy Council afterward, "in violent manner." With him was his sixth son, Clement, known already for obvious reasons as *fighting Clem Coke*—a tall, strong young man of twenty-three who had spent some months at the Inner Temple and left when study interfered with pleasure. Arrived at Oatlands and refused admission, the little band roamed about noisily, examining doors and fastenings and parleying with the family at an upstairs window. At length Coke shouted that he was going to break in; he had a lawful warrant. Should those resisting be struck down, it would be justifiable homicide. But if any of his men were killed, "it would be MURDER!" With a heavy piece of timber, Coke's party drove against the doors until they fell, ran upstairs, found the two women and dragged them apart. "You will come home with me to Stoke," Sir Edward commanded his daughter.

Hardly had Frances disappeared into the night, riding pillion behind her stepbrother, Clem, when Lady Hatton ordered the horses harnessed. With various of her kinsmen she started in pursuit, but her coach wheels sank in the mire and the chase was abandoned. At once, Lady Hatton formed another plan. She would not go home but press on to London and seek help from Sir Francis Bacon. Surely, a man might be counted friend who once had asked one's hand in marriage? Lord Holles agreed to go along. He was a quarrelsome gentleman who recently had bought his title from the King for £10,000; as a friend of Somerset and the Howards, he was glad to do any disservice to Buckingham. Halfway to London, Lady Hatton's coach went too fast round a corner and fell on its side.

Bacon was living now at York House in the Strand. From here on we have the tale from a correspondent of Anne Sadleir's. "At last to my Lord Keeper's they come, but could not have instant access to him for that his people told them he was laid at rest, being not well. Then my La. Hatton desired she might be in the next room where my Lord lay, that she might be the first that [should] speak with him after he was stirring. The door-keeper fulfilled her desire and in the mean time gave her a chair to rest herself in, and there left her alone: but not long after, she rose up and bounced against my Lord Keeper's door, and waked him and affrighted him, that he called his men to him; and they opening the door, she thrust in with them, and desired his Lordship to pardon her boldness, but she was like a cow that had lost her calf, and so justified [herself] and pacified my Lord's anger, and got his warrant and my Lo. Treasurer's warrant and others of the Council to fetch her daughter from the father and bring them both to the Council."

Bacon, it seems, told Lady Hatton she must apply for warrant, not to him alone, but to Privy Conucil. On Sunday, July thirteenth, Lady Hatton duly repaired to Whitehall and delivered a petition, "complaining in somewhat a passionate and tragicall manner," Council reported, "that while by his Majesty's grace she was settlinge and securing her poore fortune, she was by violence dispossessed of her childe." After hearing her story — which lost nothing in the telling — Council appointed the following Tuesday to hear Coke's defense, then sent Lady Hatton away and turned to other business. A letter was written from the Board to Sir Edward Coke, acquainting him with his Lady's complaint and desire and requiring him to deliver his daughter to Mr. Edmondes, Clerk of the Council, to be brought by him to London and kept in his house until the hearing of the cause.

A messenger hurried out to Stoke. But when Coke read the order, he replied mildly that the evening was late and his daughter in no such extremity. He would, "upon his peril," deliver her next day to Mr. Edmondes. This was not quick enough for Lady Hatton. Hurrying back to Council, she procured a warrant "with a clause of assistance to bring her daughter to Mr. Edmondes' house accordingly." Actually, Frances at the moment was on the road, accompanied by her intended mother-in-law, Lady Compton, and sufficient horsemen. Lady Hatton set out from the opposite direction to meet the travelers head on. With her were fifty or sixty armed horsemen — described by a news writer as "three score men and pistolls," and by Lady Hatton afterward in Privy Council as "some tall fellows." Fortunately, the armies did not meet. "If they had," wrote a Londoner, "there had been a notable skirmish, for there was Clem Coke, my Lord's fighting son, and they all swore they would die in the place before they would part with her."

No sooner was Frances Coke delivered to Mr. Edmondes than friends and relatives of both sides came riding across country to see her. Privy Council, "doubting some disorder" from these eager partisans, arranged for the girl's removal "into some convenient place agreeable to her worth and quality." Coke and Lady Hatton, permitted a mutual choice of guardian, sent their daughter to Lord Knyvet, near Staines. "And wee likewise enjoyned Sir Edward and his Lady," Council reported, "to forbeare all occasion of violence or disturbance, whatsover, as well touching the person of their daughter as any other matter of pointe concerning that busines."

In the middle aisle of St. Paul's Church, the noonday gossips missed none of the fracas; fashionable London was delighted with it. Alone of Privy Council, Winwood knew the King's desires; from the first he had been aware that James and Buckingham together wished the marriage to go through. Francis Bacon's usual perception failed him; he remained strangely blind to the King's desires and to the hard fact that from now on James's wishes would follow Buckingham's. Perhaps Winwood had deliberately kept Sir Francis in the dark. At any rate, in Winwood's hands the Lord Keeper's ignorance was a rope to hang him with. Bacon's first move in the affair had been a letter to Buckingham, written the day before the Oatlands incident. With every word, one sees Bacon's head thrust deeper in the noose:

To the Earl of Buckingham

My very good Lord,

. . . It seemeth Secretary Winwood hath officiously busied himself to make a match between your brother and Sir Edward Coke's daughter: and as we hear, he doth it rather to make a faction than out of any great affection to your Lordship. . . . This match, out of my faith and freedom towards your Lordship, I hold very inconvenient both for your brother and yourself.

First, He shall marry into a disgraced house, which in reason of state is never held good.

Next, He shall marry into a troubled house of man and wife, which in religion and christian discretion is disliked.

Thirdly, Your lordship will go near to lose all such your friends as are adverse to Sir Edward Coke (myself only except, who out of a pure love and thankfulness shall ever be firm to you).

And lastly and chiefly (believe it), it will greatly weaken and distract the King's service. . . .

Your Lordship's true and most devoted friend and servant,
FR. BACON, C.S.

July 12, 1617

Lady Hatton's appearance before Council was on a Sunday; Coke was ordered to give his defense on the ensuing Tuesday. Accordingly, on Tuesday morning, July fifteenth, Sir Edward came to Council Chamber to answer a charge of "riot and force." Far from excusing himself, Coke affirmed that the law was on his side — a father whose daughter had been stolen from him — and brought countercharges against his wife, "(1) For conveying away her daughter *clam et secrete*. (2) For endeavoring to bind her to my Lord Oxford without her father's consent. (3) For counterfeiting a letter of my Lord of Oxford offering her marriage. (4) For plotting to surprise her daughter and take her away by force to the breach of the King's peace and for that purpose assembling a body of desperate fellows, whereof the consequences might have been dangerous."

The Lords of Council did not show themselves impressed. Coke was no longer Chief Justice. To his enemies he wore the guise of a disgraced man; his statement of the law, once looked on as oracular, need no longer be credited. The Lords, impatient and not a little rude, told Coke he must answer in Star Chamber "for the force and riot used by him upon the house of Sir Edmund Withipole, to be in that Court heard and sentenced as justice shall appertain." Coke wrote at once to Buckingham in Scotland:

Right Honourable,

After my wife, Sir Edmund Withipole and the lady his wife and their confederates, to prevent this match between Sir John Villiers and my daughter Frances, had conveyed away my dearest daughter out of my house, and in most secret manner to a house which Sir Edmund Withipole had taken for the summer . . . I, by God's wonderful providence finding where she was, together with my sons and ordinary attendants, did break open two doors and recovered my daughter, which I did for these causes:— First and principally, lest his Majesty should think I was of confederacy with my wife in conveying her away, or charge me with want of government in my household in suffering her to be carried away after I had engaged myself to his Majesty for the furtherance of this match. (2) For that I demanded my child of Sir Edmund and his wife and they denied to deliver to me. And yet for this, warrant is given to sue me in his Majesty's name in the Star Chamber with all expedition, which though I fear not well to defend, yet it will be a great vexation. But I have full cause to bring all the confederates into Star Chamber, for conveying away my child out of my house.

A few days later, Privy Council, meeting again, turned upon Secretary Winwood and advised that he was subject to a premunire for giving Coke a search warrant without consulting the other lords. They then sent for Lady Compton, declared they wished her well and were ready to serve her son the Earl of Buckingham "with all true affection, whereas others did it out of faction and ambition." For Winwood this was too much; he decided to show his cards. Snug in his pocket was a letter from King James, expressing approval of all that Winwood had done concerning the marriage. Producing it, Winwood passed it round the table and waited. Would the noble Lords, he asked politely when all had read, care to reconsider as to whose "faction and ambition" had inspired this trouble? "To which," Chamberlain reported succinctly, in Latin, "there was no reply." *

For Bacon it was a bad moment. He had refused a warrant to Coke and had given a warrant to Lady Hatton, had indeed helped Lady Hatton whenever he could. Memory of his own letter to Buckingham must have turned his stomach to water. In a day or two the King's own command came down from Falkland, addressed to Bacon and Archbishop Abbot. Lady Hatton must restore her daughter to Sir Edward Coke "and not again entice her away. And the Lady Frances shall not be contracted to anyone without the assent of Sir Edward Coke." In Bacon's mind there could be no further doubt. He had acted in opposition to the King's wishes; Winwood and Coke had outplayed him, kept him in the dark and dealt their cards. At once, Bacon sent letters north — a brief one for Buckingham ("God judge my sincerity," it said) and a long one for the King: "My suit is, that your Majesty would not think me so pusillanimous, as that I, who when I was but Mr. Bacon, had ever through your Majesty's favor good reason at Sir Edward Coke's hands when he was at the greatest, should now that your Majesty (by your great goodness) hath placed me so near your chair (being as I hope by God's grace and your instructions made a servant according to

* Chapter Note.

your heart and hand), fear him or take umbrage of him in respect of mine own particular."

On and on went the tormented pen; the phrases must be read twice to comprehend them — "That your Majesty would not think I fear him." Did the words, as Bacon wrote them, ring familiar, recalling a day long past and a letter to Edward Coke? *I write not this to shew my friends what a brave letter I have writ to Mr. Attorney; I have none of those humours. . . .* All his opposition to the match had stemmed, protested Bacon, from care lest his Majesty's prerogative suffer by Sir Edward Coke's return to government. Should another Parliament be called, it was of utmost importance to meet it with a Privy Council "united, not distracted," which could never be the case "if that man come in. He is by nature insociable and by habit popular, and too old now to take a new ply, and men begin already to conclude that he that raiseth such a smoke to get in, will set all on fire when he is in."

The words were prophetic; before long, Coke would raise a fire in Parliament itself. But James was not in the mood for warnings. Early in August, Sir Francis discovered the full extent of his mistake. A note came from Buckingham; it must have dropped like a stone into Bacon's breast:

My Lord,

. . . In this business of my brother's that you overtrouble yourself with, I understand from London by some of my friends that you have carried yourself with much scorn and neglect both toward myself and friends; which if it prove true I blame not you but myself, who ever was

Your Lordship's assured friend,

G. Buckingham.

There began now a correspondence which, even after the lapse of centuries, makes painful reading. The subtlest mind of England strains to twist upon itself, undo what is done, retreat from a cause where both retreat and victory are unworthy. "Your Majesty being satisfied [with the match] I do humbly acquiesce and anchor upon your Majesty's judgment. . . . I think Sir Edward Coke himself the last time he was before the Lords mought plainly perceive an alteration in my carriage. . . ." To Buckingham also, Bacon wrote humble apology, vowing to do all in his power in furtherance of the match. He had sent for Lady Hatton, told her she and her friends could no longer count on his support. As between Coke and Winwood, the latter, said Bacon, was worse to deal with: "for Sir Edward Coke I think is more modest and discreet. . . . God keep us from these long journeys and absence, which makes misunderstandings and gives advantage to untruth." Late in August came a letter from James himself; its tone made Bacon fear for his place of Lord Keeper: "You protest of your affection to Buckingham and thereafter confess that it is in some sort parent-like. . . . You say that you were afraid that the height of his fortune might make him too secure." Jealousy of Buckingham, his Majesty intimated, should ill become the King's Lord Keeper. "Whereas you excuse yourself of the oppositions you made against Sir Edward Coke, we never took upon us such a patrociny* of Sir Edward Coke, as if he were a man not to be meddled withal in any case. . . . But whereas you talk of the riot and violence committed by him, we wonder you make no mention of the riot and violence of them that stale away his daughter. . . . And except the father of a child might be proved to be either lunatic or idiot, we never read in any law that . . . it was matter of noise and streperous carriage for him to hunt for the recovery of his child again.

"We will not speak of obligation, for surely we think even in good manners you had reason not to have crossed anything . . . till you had heard from him [Buckingham]. For if you had willingly given your consent and hand to the recovery of the young gentlewoman, and then written both to us and to him what inconvenience appeared to you to be in such a match, that had been the part indeed of a true servant to us and a true friend to him; but first to make an opposition and then to give advice by way of friendship, is to make the plough to go before the horse."

The letter came from Cheshire; James was on his way home. Coke, meanwhile, had another trump card in his hand — his daughter's full consent to marry Villiers, and in writing, which to the legal mind made it doubly sure. No one could say again (as Coke's enemies were saying) that the Lady Frances had been forced against her will. Frances now was visiting at Kingston-on-Thames with her stepbrother, Sir Robert Coke, and his wife, Lady Theophila — the young couple whose wedding at Berkeley Castle had been so happy an event. The calm domestic atmosphere must

* Patronage, protection.

have given ease to Frances after months of strife, or perhaps her kind sister-in-law persuaded her. At any rate there is about the letter something touching, a loyalty to both parents, a child's desire to see them reconciled, a healthy yielding to the inevitable:

Madam,*

I must now humbly desire your patience in giving me leave to declare myself to you, which is, that without your allowance and liking, all the world shall never make me entangle or tie myself. But now, by my father's especial commandment, I obey him in presenting to you my humble duty in a tedious letter, which is to know your Ladyship's pleasure, not as a thing I desire; but I resolve to be wholly ruled by my father and yourself, knowing your judgments to be such that I may well rely upon, and hoping that conscience and the natural affection parents bear to children will let you do nothing but for my good, and that you may receive comfort, I being a mere child and not understanding the world nor what is good for myself. That which makes me a little give way to it is, that I hope it will be a means to procure a reconciliation between my father and your Ladyship. Also I think it will be a means of the King's favour to my father. Himself [Sir John Villiers] is not to be misliked; his fortune is very good, a gentleman well born.

So I humbly take my leave, praying that all things may be to every one's contentment.

Your Ladyship's most obedient
and humble daughter for ever,
FRANCES COKE

Dear Mother believe there has no violent means been used to me by word or deed.

Shortly after this, Lady Hatton and Coke were seen together in a coach on their way to Secretary Winwood's — though, wrote Chamberlain, "there is no great heed to be taken to their agreement, for of late they usually make peace and breake it twise in a fortnight." Coke and Winwood now went up to Coventry to meet the King. So did Attorney General Yelverton, who sent a hasty warning to Bacon, bidding him burn it when read. "My Lord, Sir Edward Coke, as if he were already upon his wings, triumphs exceedingly, hath much private conference with his Majesty and in public doth offer himself and thrust upon the King with as great boldness of speech as heretofore. . . . He hath not forborne by

* The original of this letter is unfortunately lost, with Frances Coke's expressive spelling.

any engine to heave both at your Honour and at myself, and he works by the weightiest instrument, the Earl of Buckingham, who as I see, sets him as close to him as his shirt. . . . With much audacity Sir Edward affirmeth his daughter to be most deeply in love with Sir John Villiers, that the contract pretended with the Earl [of Oxford] is counterfeit and the letter also, that is pretended to come from the Earl." It was "thought and much feared" that when the royal party reached Woodstock, Coke would be recalled to Privy Council. Buckingham reproached himself openly for having placed Sir Francis as Lord Keeper, "not forebearing in open speech to tax you," the letter continued, "as if it were an inveterate custom with you to be unfaithful to him as you were to the Earls of Essex and Somerset." Let Lord Bacon therefore hasten north at once. "Fail not, my noble Lord, to be with his Majesty at Woodstock. The sight of you will fright some. Seem not dismayed, but open yourself bravely and confidently, wherein you can excell all subjects; by which means I know you shall amaze some and daunt others."

Bacon apparently did not go to Woodstock. But he must have put every talent to use at home, for Lady Hatton agreed to double the dowry offered by her husband. ("It seemes," commented Chamberlain, "that the Lady Hatton would have all the honour and thanckes, and so defeat her husband's purposes.") The wedding plans were set for late September. Coke, however, did not trust his wife's word or her good will. There was no telling when she might change her mind, run off again with Frances or set the girl against him. Buckingham and the King must have been of Coke's mind, for when the royal party returned to London, Coke went straight to Bacon, asked a warrant for his wife's arrest, got it, and had her confined to the house of Alderman Bennet. It was by no means an uncomfortable prison; City aldermen lived extremely well. But it was humiliating. Lady Hatton heard that the marriage settlement had been drawn up under the King's own eye. The wedding was to be at Hampton Court Palace, a splendid affair with a great banquet following, and a masque in the evening. Lady Hatton could not even be certain of an invitation.

On the twenty-ninth of September, Michaelmas Day, Sir Edward called for his daughter at Kingston; a procession of nine coaches took the bridal party through the flat Thames country three miles to Hampton Court. "King, Queen and Prince," wrote a guest, "were present in the chappell to see them marryed. My Lord Coke gave his daughter to the King (with some words of complement at the givinge). The King gave her [to] Sir John Villers. The Prince sate with her to grand dinner and supper . . . many Lordes and Ladies, my Lord Canterbury, my Lord Treasurer, my Lord Chamberlayne, etc. The King dinner and supper drunk healthe to the bride, the bridegroom stood behind the bride, the dinner and supper. The bride and bridegroom lay next day a bedd till past 12 a clocke, for the King sent worde he would come to see them, therefore would they not rise. My Lord Coke looked with a merrie countenance and sate at the dinner and supper, but my Lady Hatton was not at the weddinge, but is still at Alderman Bennettes prisoner. The King sent for her to the weddinge, but [she] desired to be excused, sayinge she was sicke. My Lord of Buckingham, mother, brethren, there sons and his sisters were throughout day at Courte, my Lord Coke's sons and their sons, but I saw never a Cecill. The Sonday my Lord Coke was restored to his place of counsellor as befor."

Restored to his place . . . On the surface, a happy ending to this quarrel; actually, neither happy nor an ending. Coke again was Privy Councilor. Yet under James, the place did not imply (as under Elizabeth) security of tenure, the exercise of one's full capacities to serve the state. Buckingham ruled the Council table; a man's seat depended upon his pleasure — a position without honor and for Coke, a teetering on the edge of disaster. Not only did his ideas of policy clash with Buckingham's at nearly every point, but Sir Edward, no courtier, found himself in a courtier's world. Barely a month after the Coke-Villiers wedding, Secretary Winwood died — a blow to Coke, a boon to Lady Hatton, who now fought tooth and nail to regain her position at court and at the same time hold on to her money. It was a battle she would continue until Coke was in his grave, and after. Her forays and withdrawals, her alarums and excursions continued to embellish newsletters, annals, the records of Privy Council. She kept apart, lived in her own houses, strove for her own fortune and incidentally for Coke's defeat; once or twice it was thought she had achieved it. At a grand court audience for the Muscovian Ambassador, Coke was seen to stumble and fall before all the company; it was said that his wife had "driven him into a numbness of one side which is a fore runner of the dead palsy." Lady Hatton brought a bill against Coke in Star Chamber; when it was quashed, Coke retaliated with a bill (equally unsuccessful) against his wife's favorite protector, Lord Holles, known generally as her "prime privy councillor." News-letters describe a great banquet at Hatton House, "very magnifi-call," the King and Queen at table, the servants instructed to turn away Sir Edward, should he come to the door . . . tapers and flambeaux and a profusion of meat and drink, Lord Keeper Bacon (now fully restored to royal favor) rising to propose the first toast . . . twice, the King kissed Lady Hatton and from his place at table made "four of her creatures knights," including Withipole, who had sheltered mother and daughter at Oatlands. When his Majesty suggested a reconciliation with Sir Edward, "If he come in at one door," said Lady Hatton, "I will go out at the other."

Patently, the noise of quarrel at times exhausted Coke, a man not easily worn down. He missed several Council meetings; business was put off till his return, there being few present with his head for figures and finance. When he did arrive he wore his nightcap against the chill and declared with moody geniality that he was "ambulant and not current." It was endless and unhappy and people did not like it. Coke lived at chambers in the Temple (Serjeants' Inn), sent out for meals "to goodman Gibbes, a slovenly cook." In proportion as his lady triumphed, it was said that Sir Edward's chance of rising "was much abated. . . . It is verily thought she would not care to ruin herself to overthrow him."

CHAPTER THIRTY

Parliament of 1621. Pater patriae. *The impeachment of Bacon.*

Twas loudly exclaimed that there were sucking Horse-leeches in great places. Things not to be valued at money were saleable, and what could not Gold procure.

HACKET's life of Lord Keeper Williams

KING JAMES had not received a subsidy in ten years; "a very long time to live like a shellfish upon his own moisture." Money was needed, and not alone for domestic use. Spain and Bavaria had overrun the Palatinate; James's daughter Elizabeth, married to the Elector Frederick, was a Protestant besieged. Forced out of his country and driven from the Bohemian throne (where he had no business to be) Frederick looked to his father-in-law for help. James loathed war. Yet patently a rescue was in order; an armed expedition must be sent and expeditions cost money. England adored Elizabeth, raven-haired young mother of five children. *Queen of Hearts,* they called her; *fruitful nursery of the royal plants.* Protestants clamored for an army, Catholics deplored, though citizens were indefinite as to the whereabouts of Bohemia. "On the sea-coast," they said vaguely. James, seeking as always to avoid a Parliament, borrowed from the City of London, tried loan and levy on the counties. But the people held back. How could they be sure the money would be used to succor Elizabeth? If the Treasury could be filled by forced loans, Parliament might never meet again. Aside from the romantic rescue of a princess, the people had urgent reasons for desiring a Parliament. The monster *monopoly* was strangling trade, reaching its fingers to remote hamlets and affecting the lives of thousands. Nothing less than the concerted voice of the realm could remedy this evil.

Throughout the country the religious issue once more ran strong. Plans for a royal Spanish marriage had been openly announced: Prince Charles to wed the Infanta Maria, daughter of Philip III. English Protestants were fearful. Yet failing a Parliament, there was again no effectual way to reach the King. Preachers who spoke in their pulpits against the match were jailed for it. In government circles the Spanish faction had gained strength, though Buckingham had managed to oust the Howards (Somerset's old friends). Buckingham had recently married a beautiful heiress of the Catholic family of Manners. James liked his favorites to marry, and Lady Katherine, deeply in love, allowed herself to be "converted" for the purpose of an Anglican ceremony. No one believed the conversion would last. Sir George Calvert, Secretary of State, was a secret convert to Rome. Commons members called him "the King's popish Secretary and Hispaniolized papist." Coke hated Calvert; the two could scarcely meet without a clash.*

In three years the map of government had shifted drastically, and each shift bore its price. Lord Treasurer Suffolk — a Howard — went down in disgrace, accused of peculation; his wife was known as a great taker of bribes, particularly in Spanish coinage. Chief Justice Henry Montague (Coke's successor) bought the Treasurership for £20,000 and started for Newmarket to receive from James the white staff of office. Bacon, now fully restored to favor, met Montague's coach on the way. "Take care, my lord," said Bacon. "Wood is dearer at Newmarket than any place in the world." The only Howard henchman left was Sir Henry Yelverton, who had managed to obtain the Attorney-Generalship without buying it from Buckingham. After his swearing in, Yelverton went to the palace and handed James four thousand pounds in cash. Joyfully embracing him, James said that he would use the money for dishes. Sir James Ley at sixty-eight was Chief Justice of King's Bench. Known as a Buckingham ally, he had lately bought his baronetcy. The new Master of Wards, Sir Lionel Cranfield, had obtained his place by marrying one of Lady Buckingham's impecunious nieces.

* Later created Lord Baltimore, Calvert resigned from government and devoted himself to "the fruitful plantation of his Majesties colonies."

Cranfield was a rich City merchant of much ability who had begun life as a London apprentice — a lowly origin which the lords did not let him forget. Altogether in love with business, Cranfield wrote financial letters at one in the morning; later, as Lord Treasurer, he accomplished miracles of reform and retrenchment in James's household. But he was rough, overbearing and generally disliked; Parliament before long would take his measure cruelly.

The Howards had not gone down without a struggle. In hopes of superseding Villiers they introduced new young men at court and paraded them past the royal eye, notably Sir William Monson's handsome son, whose face was washed each day in curds for his complexion. The Howards might have saved their pains; to his friends the King had ever been loyal. Queen Anne was dead, carried off by dropsy in her great bed at Hampton Court, not before her fears of Buckingham were realized. Her husband's infatuation this time went deep beyond imagining. "I wish not to have it thought a defect," he told Privy Council earnestly. "Christ had his John, and I have my George." The favorite's wife came much to court, bringing, as time passed, her children. James liked to have them about; a courtier complained that corridors were noisy with little running feet. It was in brief a court fantastic as a palace in a dream. Its aging King, mild, pious, full of lore and oddments he called *learning*, remained as blind to the English temper as on the day he crossed the border; blind also to the implications of corruption in government and the national discontent therefrom. A long reign, scarred by ugly blots — and Ralegh's death was not the least of them.

"That great wise knight, being such an anti-Spaniard, was made a sacrifice to advance the matrimonial treaty." Condemned in 1603 for a supposed conniving with Spain, Sir Walter at the last was put to death for fighting Spain. Thirteen years in the Tower, freedom (but not pardon) from James, a two-year voyage to Guiana in search of gold, Sir Walter's solemn promise that no Spaniard would be harmed . . . The fight at San Tomas, four Spaniards killed, the town looted and burned, Ralegh's son dead of wounds, the faithful Captain Kemys a suicide . . . Landfall at Plymouth with no treasure in the hold, no royal profits from the fabled mine, the certainty of punishment ahead, a proclamation already posted against their coming: *Scandalous and enormous outrages committed at San Tomas, the peace with Spain maliciously broken. All persons having particular notice and understanding thereof required to repair at once to Privy Council. . . .*

Gondomar made plain that King Philip would no longer negotiate with a nation that "massacred" his subjects. The problem resolved into a choice of forms for the trial. By the common law, a man attainted could not be arraigned for a new fault. King James, said Gondomar, promised to send Sir Walter to be hanged "in the public square of Madrid." James denied it angrily. A commission of five was appointed, under Bacon's direction; Coke was among them. For eight weeks they examined witnesses — Ralegh's seamen, the French agents with whom Ralegh had made arrangements for possible refuge in France should the voyage fail. Evidence everywhere contradicted, Ralegh's included. The final word was Bacon's. Yet for Sir Edward it was a tormenting assignment. Fifteen years ago, as prosecutor, he had done what he could toward Ralegh's ruin. But times had changed. Next to Sir Walter, if any in the realm hated Spain, it was Edward Coke. And now this great Spaniard killer, this most celebrated of all King Philip's enemies was to be sacrificed to a loathsome peace, a royal match Coke hated from his soul. *Reasons of state* . . . Coke could not save Ralegh's life, nor is there evidence that he tried to save it. There is only the evidence of a letter in Coke's hand, written to James from the commission and advising public trial as against a private hearing. Let Sir Walter be heard in his own defense before the whole of Privy Council (forty-odd men), and certain of the judges. Let the chamber be free to such noblemen and gentlemen as might be witnesses. Attorney General Yelverton to open the case, examinations to be read aloud. At Winchester, Ralegh had asked in vain that Cobham — the one witness against him — be produced. This time, let all witnesses be brought to court, that none might say (as once they said) that proceedings were unfair. . . .

James read the letter and took fright. He refused the plan, reminded the commission how, at Winchester, Ralegh "by his wit had turned the hatred of men into compassion of him." Summoned privately before the commission, Sir Walter was severely censured by Bacon for the injuries he had done to Spain. "He had abused the permission to put to sea granted him by this King, when his professed object was to discover a gold mine, which he affirmed he knew where to find." Brought before the bar, Ralegh was formally sentenced by the Chief Justice. "You have lived like a star," they told him; "and like a star you must fall when it troubles the firmament."

On October twenty-ninth, Ralegh was taken to Westminster to die. A multitude had gathered in Old Palace Yard, they pushed at the barriers, friends and enemies that included two generations. The Earls of Northampton, Percy, Arundel, Oxford stood in windows above or sat their horses near the scaffold. Young John Eliot saw Ralegh die and was much moved; Oliver Cromwell heard of it and admired, as did John Hampden. Afterward the stories were endless, reverently repeated. Sir Walter's gentle jests on the way to Westminster that cold morning, his fearlessness before the awful panoply of execution: "What is death but an opinion and imagination? Though to others it might seem grievous, yet I had rather die so than of a burning fever." The sheriffs' offer to warm him by the fire . . . "Nay, good Sirs, let us dispatch. At this hour mine ague comes upon me. I would not have mine enemies to think I quaked from fear." With his thumb, Ralegh tested the axe edge while the crowd watched, still as midnight. "This is a fair sharp medicine to cure me of all diseases and miseries." Words that were to become legend, the pride and shame of England. . . . Sir Walter knelt by the block, the headsman bade him face east as he lay down. "What matter how the head lie," said Ralegh, "so the heart be right?"

Government put out a printed *Declaration*, explaining, extenuating, telling of the attack at San Tomas, the reasons for Ralegh's execution on the old charge of treason, aggravated by his breaking the peace with Spain. . . . Spaniard fighter, colonizer who brought home no gold, firebrand endangering the patient peaceful work of decades — his death was a necessity of state. The arguments were received indifferently; against the proven hour of Ralegh's death no word prevailed. Ralegh was not loved by the people as Essex had been loved. Sir Walter's was an old voice, calling from another day, another climate — the noontide of Queen Elizabeth, of Drake and Hawkins and the glory that was '88.

A far-off time, with policies outmoded. Yet Ralegh stood for *anti-Spain*, and every Protestant in England knew it.

"Great heart," wrote one that was anonymous:

> Great Heart, who taught thee so to die?
> Death yielding thee the victory . . .

The national hatred of Spain, irritation at the proposed Spanish match, turned full upon Gondomar. On public holidays he did not dare venture in the streets. It was his custom to ride about London in a litter. "There goes the devil in a dungcart!" an apprentice cried as he passed by. The youth and his friends were arrested, flogged through Fleet Street at a cart's tail. James put out a proclamation: *No man by look or countenance to show irreverance to strangers, especially such as are ambassadors.* For Coke it was ironic that Gondomar lived now at Ely House, behind the long wall of Lady Hatton's domain. The Bishop's old palace had been lavishly refurnished by James for the purpose: "more," wrote Chamberlain, "than I ever remember before afforded to any other ambassador. The chappell likewise trimmed up, with an altar (they say) and other implements." Gondomar, notable for success with the ladies, did his best to make friends with Lady Hatton. The door of her back wall gave on to the fields, where Gondomar liked to take the air. He asked Lady Hatton for a key but she would not give it — "not even," said Chamberlain, "upon a message from the King." A strange lady! Gondomar told James. "She will not suffer her husband, Sir Edward Coke, to come in at her fore doors, nor myself to go out at her back door."

To ease marriage negotiations at Madrid — Philip aimed at a toleration for English Catholics — James had let a hundred Catholic priests out of prison. From Hatton Gardens the bell rang openly for Mass. Sometimes the faithful were called by horn; the sound of it, long familiar from Temple Gardens, calling law students to dinner, made Holborn residents uneasy. Was there to be no end of this tempting to Rome? The ship *Mayflower* lay at Southampton docks. (There were more ways than one to foil persecution.) Yet when she sailed, few noted her departure. It was November, 1620, before Privy Council succeeded in persuading James that a Parliament must be called. Coke, Bacon and the two Chief Justices urged the King to be well prepared. Without doubt, monopolies would be first on the agenda. Coke had heard them complained of in his own county of Norfolk, especially Sir Giles Mompesson's monopoly of licenses for alehouses, which bore hard on the keepers of small inns. (Mompesson sent spies and agents into the country to close down houses that had not paid tribute.) Such licensing had hitherto been left to local justices of the peace; they greatly resented Londoners coming in to usurp their ancient jurisdiction. "This disheartheneth them," said Phelips; "for it maketh a justice of the peace to be buffeted by a base alehousekeeper." The King of course had power to cancel his royal gifts of patents and monopolies. Yet both Bacon and Coke thought it more politic and in the end more effectual if Parliament were permitted to take the matter in its own hands. The Commons would place monopolies first on their list of grievances, his Majesty would yield "of his grace." In return, a grateful Commons would vote large subsidies.

So it was settled and devised by Council, no one of whom — least of all Francis Bacon — dreamed that the plan would spring back upon him with lethal thrust. Council composed a proclamation, strong, reasonable, informing of the King's needs and why a Parliament must meet. James did not like it. The statement dealt, he said, with things above the people's capacity — foreign affairs, religion, "matters of state." James wrote his own proclamation: electors must not return "bankrupts or discontented persons that cannot fish but in troubled waters, nor yet curious and wrangling lawyers who may seek reputation by stirring needless questions." Nothing could induce him to leave out the last category, though Bacon pleaded.

It was important to seat as many Privy Councilors as possible. Placed near the Speaker they could control the House as in Elizabeth's time. Coke was returned from Liskeard in Cornwall, as royal nominee. In return for recent favors, especially his Privy Councilorship, Coke's full support was looked for — a point on which Bacon alone remained wary. But when elections opened in the counties, the people showed reluctance to vote for Privy Councilors. These great persons would not, they complained, be available to plain men, would not hear their petitions and requests. Secretary of State Calvert came in only on the shoulders of that popular Yorkshire landowner, Sir Thomas Wentworth. Prince Charles, now twenty-one, desired to sit with the Lords as voting member. Coke, Bacon and the two Chief Justices found precedents from Edward I to Henry VII. It would be strange to have his Highness seated, jeweled hat upon his fair head. But the august presence would serve to keep down disputes, especially when the Commons sent delegations with messages the Lords did not like. Moreover, with the royal intended bridegroom in their midst, it was thought that neither House could dare to mention adversely the Spanish match.

Few Parliaments of history have turned out so differently from plan. Coke in the Commons, the Earl of Southampton in the Lords led the opposition. The Crown endured an added hazard of public knowledgeableness beyond all experience. Speeches were printed and sold on the streets — pirated, ascribed to wrong names, often filled with error yet plainly revelatory of what Parliament men were saying and doing and voting. The first English newspaper, a weekly, was published this year in Amsterdam, and in London the year following. *Courants* or *corantos*, these were called.

Yet this Parliament, due to end disastrously, began in cheerfulness and mutual hope. The winter was very cold, the Thames frozen solid above the Bridge. Ice, thrown up by wind and tide, lay "like rockes and mountaines, with strange and hideous aspect. The watermen were quite undone to lose the benefit of [law] term and parlement both." On opening day — January thirtieth — James rode on horseback from Whitehall through the usual great throng. It was counted remarkable that he "spake often and lovingly to the people, standing thick and three-fold on all sides to behold him, 'God bless ye! God bless ye!' contrary to his former hasty and passionate custom which often in his sudden distemper would be a pox or a plague on such as flocked to see him." From the door of Westminster Hall, James was carried in a chair to the Lords' Chamber. His legs had lately grown much weaker. Strapped to the saddle, he continued his old pleasures of the chase and hopefully bathed legs and feet in the stag's warm belly after the kill — an excellent remedy to strengthen the sinews, it was said. Today he spoke for a full hour. He had not lost his peculiar eloquence, a homely frank warm manner of saying exactly what he meant to say. He reverted to the past, and for the general admiration reviewed not only parliamentary errors but his own mistakes.

"I have piped unto you," he said, "but you have not danced; I have often mourned but you have not lamented. . . . It may be it pleased God, seeing some vanity in me, to send back my words as wind spit into my own face. I know this Parliament hath been of great expectation—and so was that at my first coming, when I knew not the state of this land. I was then led by the old Councilors I found which the old Queen had left, and it may be there was a misleading and a misunderstanding between us which bred an abruption. And at the last Parliament [1614] there came up a strange kind of beasts called *Undertakers* which caused a dissolution. . . . I have brought mine expenses from £34,000 to £14,000: in my household abated £10,000 per annum, in the Navy £25,000 per annum, and shortly I hope to abate £10,000 more in mine ordnance. . . . Your supply will not fall into a bottomless purse. . . ."

It was wonderful; the pockets of burgesses loosened as they heard. What would not the Commons of England do for a King who stood before them in open manly acknowledgment of fault? Within a few weeks Parliament had voted two subsidies, making plain the money was to help the besieged Protestant Elizabeth and that no precedent should be taken of supply granted so early, before grievances. No fifteenths were voted; they fell too hard, members said, on the poorer sort. But James, delighted, told Parliament of his happiness to find himself, after eighteen years' enthronement, "enthronized now in his people's hearts."

And with that the love feast ended. Parliament sat four months and not a law was enacted. The Commons were vocal, busier than ever in their experience. Monopolies, patents, corruption in trade and in the courts of justice—these questions put a stop to ordinary business. "The monopolizer," Coke told the House, "engrosseth to himself what should be free for all men. The depopulator [encloser of land] turns all out of doors and keeps none but a shepherd and his dog." This was the High Court of Parliament, with power to judge and punish. "He that questions whether this House is a Court of Record,"* said Coke, "I would his tongue

* A *Court of Record* meant, in Coke's day, a court with power to fine and imprison. The High Commission (for instance) Coke had insisted was not a Court of Record. That technically he was probably wrong does not lessen the value of his position, which in the end would be confirmed by new laws.

might cleave to the roof of his mouth." Reviving the old impeachment process — unused three hundred and fifty years — Parliament brought to the bar for trial offenders from high places and low. It was an extraordinary, abrupt sweeping out, accomplished in perfect accommodation with the Lords — Commons as fact-finders, Lords as judges. "The House of Commons," said a member, "is like the grand jury for the whole commonwealth." And the makeup of this Commons was superbly suited to the program, "wrangling lawyers" being represented full strength. Coke, as chairman of the great Committee for Grievances, at once assumed a leading part — a strange position for a Privy Councilor; the King's Council traditionally was concerned with supply, not grievance. Coke moreover had been a judge; people still referred to him as *the Lord Coke*. He found himself in a position of extraordinary prestige. *Pater patriae*, father of his country, Parliament called him; *bellwether of the flock*. In the process of impeachment, those under attack were permitted to bring their own barristers to plead at the bar of Commons. But the best lawyers, it seemed, sat behind the bar — a whole brace of them in their thirties and forties; some, old Parliament men like Edward Alford; some, like John Pym, brand new, receiving now their training for rebellion.

There was a strong Puritan tinge to the Commons of '21. John Pym, round-faced, pink-cheeked as a farmer, could quote with equal facility the Hebrew Gospel and old Acts of Parliament from the Tower Rolls. Sir Thomas Crew was given to lashing out at "the Romish harlot" after a fashion that would be prevalent all too soon. William Noye, handsome of face and figure, a lawyer of much ability, carried a Bible in his pocket. One of "the biggest stars in the law" was Sir John Glanville, who sat for Plymouth. Of vast energies and many clients, he was known generally as "that pregnant western lawyer." William Hakewill, forty-seven, had served in three Parliaments and was compiling a book about parliamentary procedure. Sir Robert Phelips, whose father had been Speaker in 1604, was impetuous, eloquent, with a high sweet voice; people said his pronunciation was affected. Perhaps the most frequent debater, next to Coke and Phelips, was Sir Edwin Sandys of the Middle Temple, son of an Archbishop. Sandys had sat in Parliaments since 1586, outdating Coke, Bacon and Alford. Brave and tolerant, Sandys had suggested (in vain) that criminals be allowed the benefit of counsel in court. A great planter of foreign parts, Sir Edwin acted as treasurer of the joint-stock company which at the moment was busy devising a new charter for Virginia, providing for the first representative assembly in North America, with an elected House of Burgesses empowered to grant supply and originate laws. "A seminary for a seditious Parliament," James called the Virginia Company.

Sir Thomas Wentworth of Yorkshire, not yet thirty, bore a name that was to be forever associated with the terrible years that began in 1640. "A stern, down-looking man," * Carlyle said of him, dark-browed, with a deep anger and pride that were to bring him to a tragic end. A strange man, full of conscience and inconsistency, loving power, fearless, yet desiring always and uneasily an accommodation with the King. In the Commons, Wentworth had a claque of followers from his part of the country who voted after him. *The northern men,* they were called.

Besides these lawyers, Puritans, gentlemen farmers and men of business, the Commons boasted a half dozen blooded fashionables. Sir Edward Sackville, one of the handsomest gallants in London, had killed his rival in a duel over the beautiful Venetia Stanley; at thirty he was a sparkling, graceful speaker. Sir Benjamin Rudyerd, elegant man about town, wrote poetry and held the lucrative governmental post of Surveyor of Wards. Though he came in as spokesman for the Crown, Rudyerd could be savage over Romishness or threats to free speech. This was his first Parliament.

More brilliant perhaps than any — though not yet a member of the House — was John Selden, the Inner Templar who met with Coke's party for consultation at Sir Robert Cotton's house in Old Palace Yard next door. Selden wore his dark hair long, curling on his shoulders; to women he was irresistible. Given to epigram and pride of intellect, he was feared by minds less quick than his own, yet he was to play a large part in prerebellion Parliaments of the 1620's. Sir Robert Cotton, host to these knights and burgesses and lawyer-scholars, had been, with William Camden, a founder of the Society of Antiquaries, dissolved by James in 1604 as dangerous to the state. (Historians have an uncomfortable way of reviving a nation's legends

* Wentworth, (Earl of Strafford) later went over to the King's side. The Parliament of 1640 tried him for treason, with Pym as prime mover against him. He was beheaded on Tower Hill.

and putting them to new tunes.) Sir Robert Cotton knew the Tower records better than any man alive. For years he had collected books, old coins and medals. After his visits to the muniment rooms, Tower officials complained that valuable manuscripts were missing; Cotton walked London with papers stuffed beneath his coat. When he spoke of his treasures he grew excited and stuttered helplessly through his beard. He had a European reputation; Casaubon, Gondomar, the Earl of Southampton, James himself came to the famous library with its garden beside the Thames.

Coke, Sandys, Phelips, Pym, Wentworth, Alford, Rudyerd, Sackville, Noye — such were the leaders of the opposition. *Court* and *Country*, the two factions were called now — terms and titles that were to cross the Atlantic and find use in the mouths of rebellious New Englanders. The Parliament Journals of 1621 bore names long familiar: a Gawdy from Norfolk, a Knollys; two Nevilles, two Cecils, three Hastings, two Pophams; Sir Carew Ralegh, a Littleton from the old Judge's family. One name looks odd indeed among the lawyers and country gentlemen: Inigo Jones. In this memorable session a dozen diarists kept notes, yet none saw fit to quote the celebrated architect. Fighting Clem Coke sat in this Parliament, to be heard from later. More than four hundred elected members* of his Majesty's Commons House, active, powerful, for the most part noisy, hard to put down. Against them James and Buckingham could count but feeble support. Only a handful of Privy Councilors had won seats: Secretary Calvert, Sir Julius Caesar, Sir Richard Weston (Chancellor of the Exchequer); Sir Fulke Greville, a rich old courtier from Queen Elizabeth's day. The two of most ability were Lionel Cranfield, man of City business, and Sir Thomas Edmondes of the diplomatic service, whom Robert Cecil had much respected. Rudyerd, though eloquent, showed increasing sympathy with the opposition. None of these made headway for the King. Neither foreign service nor City experience, it seems, counted for much with the Commons of England.

"Bribery," Bishop Latimer the martyr had said, "is a princely kind of thieving, the noble theft of princes and magistrates. He

* Of elected members, it is estimated that about two hundred and fifty were on the floor at one time.

that took the silver basin and ewer for a bribe, thinketh it will never come out. O briber and bribery! It will never be merry in England till we have the skins of such."

When Parliament opened in January, 1621, Francis Bacon sat at the pinnacle of glory, the quarrel with Buckingham over Frances Coke's marriage forgotten and forgiven. No longer plain Keeper of the Seal (as his father had been), Bacon bore the splendid title of Lord Chancellor, Baron Verulam and Viscount St. Albans. The ceremony of his creation at Theobalds had been one of especial pomp and show, more than usually accorded to peers. Fortune showered her gifts. Bacon's *Novum Organum*, published in October, brought the plaudits of European scholars (and the gratitude of posterity). Bacon sent a copy to Coke, gold-tooled and stamped with the family crest, a golden boar. On the title page, Coke scrawled in inky Latin, "Gift from the author," and under it the angry couplet, destined to be quoted down the years:

> It deserveth not to be read in Schooles
> But to be freighted in the ship of Fooles.*

Below this, again in Latin, Coke's contemptuous advice: "You propose to reconstruct the teaching of wise men of old. Reconstruct first our laws and justice."

Sir Francis knew that he had enemies; no man could rise so high without envy from those less fortunate. Yet who could harm him, under the firm protection of King and favorite? Bacon harbored no suspicion that ruin lay ahead and very close. At St. Albans he lived magnificently among oak groves and gardens and stately walks of trees, using his father's mansion of Gorhambury for winter and Verulam House, his own creation, for summer. (A gentleman should have, he said, seats for summer and winter as well as clothes.) The two houses were a mile apart; between them Bacon built three parallel roads, running straight and wide so that seven coaches could roll abreast. Throngs of noblemen and knights came up these roads to ask for place or favor. "So nobly did he live it seemed as if the Court were there," said Aubrey. On the upper doors of Verulam House, above the balcony, were painted tall figures of Jupiter and Apollo, gilded and flashing in the sun. From the roof — "the leads" — where Bacon loved to walk and meditate,

* Chapter Note.

stretched a prospect of wide artificial ponds; if one went to the brink and looked down into the water, one saw fish traced in colored stones along the bottom.

When he was in town, Bacon occupied York House, his father's mansion on the river bank where he had been born. The week before Parliament opened, the Lord Chancellor had his sixtieth birthday and gave a feast for his friends. Music played from the balcony, wine flowed, tapers winked against dark paneling. Ben Jonson, genial before his host, declaimed verses made for the occasion:

> Son to the grave, wise Keeper of the Seal,
> Fame and foundation of the English weal;
> What then his father was, that since is he,
> Now with a title more to the degree:
> England's High Chancellor, the destin'd heir,
> In his soft cradle, to his father's chair;
> Whose even thread the Fates spin round and full,
> Out of their choicest and their whitest wool.

No mortal ever sat more fortunate or seemingly secure — his talents flowering in praise and fame; rich to magnificence, high in the counsels of state as man could go, adviser to a King, close friend to the King's favorite. In Parliament, Bacon presided on the Chancellor's woolsack, "prolocuter of the Lords," directing, manipulating, a little worried — but only a little — concerning fierce attacks the Commons were making upon monopolies and patents. For large or disputed monopolies, James, years ago, had appointed "referees" to examine if the grants were legal and fairly administered; Bacon had long been referee of the patent for inns. So far, however, the Commons had been wary of naming the referees as blamable. Bacon could expect enmity from Sir Edward. But criticism, strong in the wind, might carry to high places. "I woo no body," Bacon wrote to Buckingham. "I do but listen, and I have doubt only of Sir Edward Coke, who I wish had some round *caveat* given him from the King; for your lordship hath no great power with him, but I think a word from the King mates him."

A week later the dam burst. A flood of accusation rolled out. It began quietly, almost innocently, by Sir Robert Phelips rising in the Commons to report as chairman of a committee for inquiry "into some abuses in courts of justice." Certain practices in Chancery had already been questioned by Lionel Cranfield, who hated Bacon as only a practical man of affairs can hate a philosopher. Chancery clerks had been forging orders (pretending they came from barristers) and taking fees for it; creditors complained that Chancery sheltered debtors, making it difficult for businessmen to collect. Coke had seconded the complaint. Today, on March fourteenth, Phelips reported that two gentlemen, Aubrey and Egerton by name, had brought petitions to the House, alleging bribery and corruption on the part of the Lord Chancellor, "who is," added Phelips with troubled courtesy, "a man so endued with all parts both of nature and art as that I will say no more of him because I am not able to say enough."

Within a week, charges had piled up; all told, there would be twenty-eight articles of impeachment. From most of the complainants, Bacon had accepted money while their cases pended. Yet oddly enough he had decided against them. Whether as disappointed suitors the men brought charges out of pique, or whether they were inspired by Bacon's enemies in the Commons cannot be known. What we do know is that never was ruin accomplished with such politeness. Members outdid themselves in kindness, a seeming reluctance to spurn a great man stricken — something not often seen in large political assemblies. Bacon floated to his ruin on a flood of compliments. Heneage Finch was "sorry to see a man so noble born, who he had loved, to fall under an ungrateful accusation." Finch deplored that "so great a person, noble and of great worth, should fall under the censure of the gravest senate in the world." Coke, named on a committee to inquire further into the business, reported on four abuses that had long been prevalent in Chancery. ("A fifth he said he would retain in his heart.") Yet even Coke was strangely gentle. "I speak not because the Chancellor is in a cloud, but according to the liberty of a true subject. A corrupt judge is the grievance of grievances. I had rather speak this when he was in his greatness than now when he is suppressed."

The charges were extraordinary; Aubrey, through Sir George Hastings of Bacon's household (a member of the Commons), had sent a hundred pounds to the Lord Chancellor. Edward Egerton, embroiled in an endless lawsuit with a relative, had presented £400 in gold to one of Bacon's staff, who delivered it duly in the presence of Hastings, telling Bacon it was a "thankful remembrance from a client, designed to buy a new suit of hangings for York House." The Lord Chancellor, having already received plate worth fifty pounds from Egerton, was surprised. Weighing the purse in his hand, he said it was too much, "but presently put it behind a cushion. 'Mr. Egerton,' " he said, had not enriched him "but laid a tie upon him to do him justice in his right cause."

These charges were brought on Thursday morning, March fourteenth. Friday and Saturday were spent in further investigation of witnesses by a committee of four: Coke, Noye, Phelips, Sir Dudley Digges. It appeared that Egerton had also promised — should judgment be pronounced in his favor — six thousand pounds, to be divided between two of Bacon's retinue. (One of the two, Dr. Field, was a bishop, a fact which Puritan members used to advantage.) When the first petitioner — Aubrey — appeared at the bar of Commons, Bacon sat as usual on his woolsack in the House of Lords. Before nightfall he sent a note to Buckingham. He knew he had clean hands and a clean heart, and he hoped "a clean house for friends or servants." But if this was what it meant to be Lord Chancellor, "I think if the Great Seal lay upon Hounslow Heath, nobody would take it up." Above all things he was fearful that his health would break under the strain, and it would "be thought feigning or fainting. But I hope in God I shall hold out."

He did not hold out. The sensitive physique vibrated painfully to any reverse in fortune or reputation; all his life, Bacon had fallen sick under adverse circumstance. By Sunday, March eighteenth, he was prostrate in bed. "It is no feigning or fainting," he wrote the Lords, "but sickness both of my heart and of my back." He begged time to advise with counsel and make answer to the charges. "I shall not, by the grace of God, trick up an innocency with cavillations, but plainly and ingenuously (as your Lordships know my manner is) declare what I know and remember." A judge who makes "two thousand decrees and orders in a year" is hard put to recall each case, he said. If more petitions against him should appear, he begged the Lords that he might answer them "according to the rules of justice, severally and respectively."

The rules of justice. Coke, as a member of the committee,

already had conferred at some length with the Lords. Charges accumulated; it was said indeed that when suitors brought cases to Chancery, their lawyers' first question was, "How are you friended at York House?" From his sickbed, Bacon appealed to the King. "I fly unto your Majesty with the wings of a dove. . . . For the briberies and gifts wherewith I am charged, when the book of hearts shall be opened I hope I shall not be found to have the troubled fountain of a corrupt heart in a depraved habit of taking rewards to pervert justice; howsoever I may be frail and partake of the abuses of the times. I rest as clay in your Majesty's hands."

None knew better than King James the extent of bribery and corruption in government. "If," he once told the Venetian Ambassador, "I were to imitate the conduct of your republic and begin to punish those who take bribes, I should soon not have a single subject left." Lord Treasurer Montague,* when asked what his place was worth per annum, replied promptly, "Some thousand of pounds to him who after death would go instantly to heaven; twice as much to him who would go to Purgatory, and nobody knows how much to him who would adventure to a worse place." The system of fee taking had long been customary; salaries were far from a living wage. New Year's gifts, compliments of food at Christmas and Easter season — a fat buck or doe, a half-dozen brace of partridges were received by judges quite openly and entered in the account books of towns and boroughs where the Justices rode circuit: "Wine and sugar given to Judge Anderson. A bottle of wine and sugar given Mr. Gibbs (a lawyer)." Sir William Davenant described it in cheerful verse:

> Then reconcile the rich for gold-fring'd gloves,
> The poor for God's sake, or for sugar-loaves.

The difficulty was to distinguish between a bribe and a "compliment." Yet certain men made it their business so to distinguish. Sir Robert Cecil, the year that he became Lord Treasurer, refused New Year's gifts amounting to above £1800, "as supposing them to be some kind of bribes whereby he might wink at the corruption of officers." Sir George Croke, offered a Serjeant's coif,

* Sir Henry Montague, who, previous to buying the place of Lord Treasurer, had succeeded Coke as Chief Justice.

refused to pay the usual £600 to those in power and was much admired for it. Henry VIII's famous Chancellor turned off a compliment in classic manner. A gentleman who had a suit pending in Chancery, sent his servant to Sir Thomas More with a present of two handsome silver flagons. More, unwilling to accept the gift, made skillful pretense. The gentleman, he asked, desired to taste the Chancellor's wine? "Go to my cellar," said More. "Fill thy master's ewer with my best wine. Take it home, and let thy master know I do not grudge it."

With Bacon the fault seems not to have been conscious dishonesty but an almost criminal carelessness where money was concerned. He never stopped borrowing at interest, never knew how much he had nor where it came from. Some of his servants kept race horses. "In giving of rewards," wrote Fuller, "Lord Bacon knew no bounds but the bottom of his own purse. Wherefore, when King James heard that he had given ten pounds to an under-keeper by whom his Majesty had sent a buck, the King said merrily, 'I and he shall both die beggars.'" Bacon's money lay about in drawers, unlocked. A gentleman calling on him at Gorhambury was left alone for an hour in the Chancellor's study. In came a member of Bacon's retinue, opened a chest of drawers, took money by handfuls, stuffed it in his pockets and went out without a word. He was followed by a second man who repeated the performance. When the Lord Chancellor returned, the astonished visitor told what had occurred. Bacon only shook his head. "Sir," he said, "I cannot help myself."

James, when news broke about the Lord Chancellor's defalcation, showed a disposition to take the case in his own hands. "Those who strike at your Chancellor," Bacon had written, "it is much to be feared will strike at your crown. I wish that as I am the first, I may be the last of sacrifices." To make the matter move more quickly and perhaps more safely, James offered to name a special commission for trial, consisting of six Lords and twelve members of the Commons. Easter vacation was at hand; the commission could do its work during the week of Parliament's adjournment.

The offer was tempting — a commission on which the Commons outnumbered the Lords by six. Several members approved. But

Coke rose at once to object. Petitioners against Bacon had appealed not to the King but to the Commons; if the matter came to impeachment, prosecution should be the business of Parliament, not Crown. Coke had seen the work of many such commissions; they had a highhanded way of carrying things as they saw fit. "Let us take heed," he told the Lower House, "the King's Commission do not hinder our Parliamentary proceedings." The case gathered momentum as new petitioners appeared. It was testified that the Lady Wharton, with a decree pending in Chancery, drove to York House with a hundred pounds in a purse. "My Lord asked her," reported Phelips, "what she had in her hand. She replied, 'A purse of my own working,' and presented it to him; who took it and said, 'What lord could refuse a purse of so fair a lady's working?'" Later she sent two hundred pounds more, which Bacon received in the presence of several of his retinue. ("Strange to me," said Coke to the House, "that this money should be thus openly delivered. . . .") As witnesses piled up, the Commons were hard put to handle the affair. "They are fallen into a labirinth," wrote Chamberlain, "(whence they see no way out) of briberies and extortions in matters of justice, and the first tempest is fallen upon my Lord Chauncellor, against whom there come in daylie more petitions and accusations than they can overcome."

It was well into April before all witnesses were examined and the charges drawn up. The list of bribes is bewildering; there is something grotesque about the incidents: "A dozen of buttons in the cause of Hodie and Hodie, £50 . . . In the cause of Kenday and Valore, a cabinet worth £800 . . . Of Valore, borrowed at two times, £2000. In the Lord Mountaine's cause, £700 borrowed and more promised at the end of the cause . . . In a cause between Reynell and Peacock, £200 in money and a diamond ring worth £5 or £600 . . . In a business between the grocers and apothecaries, he had of the grocers £200, of the apothecaries £150 (besides a rich present of ambergris). . . . Of the French merchants, to constrain the vintners of London to take 1500 tuns of wine; received, £1000. . . . Lastly, that he gave way to great exactions by his servants, in respect of private seals and sealing injunctions."

Bacon remained sick in bed, "all swollen in his body and

suffering none to come at him. Some say he desired his gentlemen not to take any notice of him, but altogether to forget him and not hereafter to speak of him, or remember there was ever such a man in the world." Men of genius and fine sensibilities, when sickness comes with misfortune, are apt to think they are dying. Bacon wrote his will: "My soul to God above . . . my body to be buried obscurely . . . my name to the next ages and to foreign nations." In a solemn *Prayer* he made submission to God, unique and wholly Baconian: "I confess before thee that I am debtor to thee for the gracious talent of thy gifts and graces . . . which I have misspent in things for which I was least fit; so as I may truly say, my soul hath been a stranger in the course of my pilgrimage."

It is characteristic also of Bacon (perhaps of any writer extraordinarily talented) that no sooner was the *Prayer* on paper than he wrote buoyantly to James, bargaining for new literary compositions: "And because he that hath taken bribes is apt to give bribes, I will go furder and present your Majesty with a bribe. For if your Majesty will give me peace and leisure, and God give me life, I will present you with a good history of England, and a better digest of your laws."

Next day, Bacon composed his submission for the House of Lords. Though he had not yet seen the particular charges, he had been told enough to know there was no escape. "Without fig-leaves," he wrote, "I do ingenuously confess and acknowledge . . . that I find matter sufficient and full, both to move me to desert the defence, and to move your Lordships to condemn and censure me." He "professed gladness" that after this example, no judge or magistrate, however great, would find sanctuary in greatness but rather would fly from anything in the likeness of corruption, as from a serpent. "And therefore, my humble suit to your Lordships is, that my penitent submission may be my sentence and the loss of the seal my punishment; and that your Lordships will spare any further sentence, but recommend me to his Majesty's grace and pardon for all that is past."

Neither House was satisfied. The Lord Chancellor had created himself a judge to give his own sentence — that he was to lose the Seal and nothing more. Moreover, to the charges of bribery he replied only in general terms. The word "corruption" was not in his letter, only the phrase "likeness of corruption." The Lords sent a message to York House, expressing their discontent and enclosing the full bill of charges. On the last day of April they had their reply. A scroll, rolled and sealed, was delivered to the House of Lords. Breaking it open, the Clerk read the document aloud:

To the Right Honourable the Lords Spiritual and Temporal, in the High Court of Parliament assembled:

The Confession and humble Submission of me, the Lord Chancellor.

Upon advised consideration of the charge, descending into my own conscience, and calling my memory to account so far as I am able, I do plainly and ingenuously confess that I am guilty of corruption; and do renounce all defence, and put myself upon the grace and mercy of your Lordships.

The particulars I confess and declare to be as followeth. . . .

Twenty-eight charges were appended, each one copied out by the Lord Chancellor and confessed to. He begged mercy, prayed that the sentence might not "be heavy to his ruin, but gracious and mixt with mercy," and that the Lords would intercede with the King in his behalf.

A committee of twelve was sent to inquire if the confession were indeed the Lord Chancellor's hand, and if he would stand to it. From Bacon there issued now the cry that has come down in history as the very symbol of a ruined man: "My Lords, it is my act, my hand, my heart. I beseech your Lordships, be merciful to a broken reed." On the first of May, four Lords took away the Seal; Bacon saw them lift it from its place near the bed. "God gave it, by my own fault I have lost it," * he said sadly. Next day the Sergeant-at-Arms from the Upper House, mace in hand, gave Bacon a summons to appear in Parliament and hear sentence pronounced. He was too ill to come, said Bacon wearily. Were he well he would willingly comply.

On Thursday morning, May third, the Commons made their way through Westminster Palace to the House of Lords, crowding behind the bar as was their custom. Speaker Richardson, after three low congees, demanded, in the Commons' name, judgment against

* "*Deus dedit, culpa mea perdidit.*" Bacon said it in Latin.

"a corrupt Lord Chancellor, as the nature of his offences and demerits do require." Chief Justice Ley rose from his place to give sentence.

For Coke it was an extraordinary moment. With the other Privy Councilors he stood well to the front, in view of the Lords assembled. His enemy of thirty years was about to receive supreme humiliation, not at the King's hands or by any agency of Coke's but at the hands as it were of the whole realm. This was the man responsible for the bitterest hours of Coke's life. Bacon and none other had maneuvered him out of Common Pleas into King's Bench — a skillful, ruthless kick upstairs. *Your Lordship must needs now grow in height, else you would be a monster. . . .* The two had been rivals since the year '93 — for the Attorney's place, for Lady Hatton's hand. At the end it was Bacon's manipulation that had cost Coke his Judgeship, cast him from the bench to face what looked a life of idleness. Montague's offer for the golden collar of SS: had Bacon devised that too, and does a man sell his heart and the inheritance of his spirit?

The Lords sat fully robed, as for an occasion of state. Chief Justice Ley read out the sentence:

"The Lord Viscount St. Alban to pay a fine of £40,000. To be imprisoned in the Tower during the King's pleasure. To be for ever incapable to holding any public office, place or employment in the common wealth. Never to sit in Parliament nor come within the verge of the Court."

Five years of life remained to Francis Bacon. His fine was remitted, he spent but one day in the Tower; in 1624 the King granted him full pardon. Yet he never returned to public life and told his friends he lived in torment, especially during the first three years, when exiled to Gorhambury. Much has been written of Bacon's "poverty" after judgment. Actually, the government allowed him an annual pension of twelve hundred pounds; he had altogether about two thousand a year, a sum higher than most noblemen could count on. He refused to sell Gorhambury woods; he would not, he said, "be stripped of his feathers"; Buckingham had trouble persuading him to sell York House. Although deeply in debt (his invariable condition even at the height of greatness), Bacon lived with a fine show of outward elegance and was visited by savants and dignitaries of Europe. Prince Charles met his coach one day, complete with horsemen, footmen, outriders. "Do what we can," said the Prince, "this man scorns to go out like a snuff." Less than a year after his fall, Bacon published a *History of Henry VII*, followed by a Latin translation of the *Advancement of Learning*. He began a digest of the laws of England and a history of Henry VIII, added to his essays, dictated a book of *Apothegms* — long regarded as the best jest-book in England — translated Psalms into verse, drew up speeches for members of the Commons, addressed a treatise to the Prince *On Consideration of a War with Spain*, planned a new edition of his *Natural History* and never ceased his scientific experiments. It was one of these which brought him to his death at sixty-five. The ever curious, ever busy mind had wondered if cold as well as salt might serve as agency for preserving flesh. With a friend, Bacon went out in his coach one cold March day, bought a fowl of a farmer and stuffed it with snow he found lying behind a hedge. Re-entering his coach, he began to shiver and vomit. He did not go home but took refuge in Lord Arundel's house near Highgate. There, on the morning of Easter Sunday, Lord Bacon died.

"A rare man," said a contemporary, "a man of deep learning and I think the eloquentest that was born in this isle." A man whose life was in his mind, all warmth denied him. Cursed with a perpetual fever of restlessness, and bearing (as Dr. Harvey said) the serpent's eye. *Queen Elizabeth's watch-candle, which continually did burn.* He knew his failings and the knowledge was tragic to him: "My soul hath been a stranger in the course of my pilgrimage."

"None," said Fuller the historian, "can character him to the life, save himself."

CHAPTER THIRTY-ONE

Parliament of 1621, (continued). Declaration and Remonstrance. Coke in the Tower.

The times are daungerous and the world growes tender and jealous of free speach.

CHAMBERLAIN TO CARLETON, *February 16, 1622*

KING JAMES suffered not at all from Parliament's extraordinary zeal in searching out corruption of government and trade. Between March and June of 1621, "monopolies and briberies were beaten upon the anvil every day, almost every hour." President Judge Bennet of the High Commission was found guilty, Attorney General Yelverton, the Bishop of Llandaff, Fleet Warden Harris, Sir Giles Mompesson the monopolist and his attorney Sir Francis Michell (both members of Parliament), besides many lesser figures. "I am ashamed," James told Parliament, "and it makes my hair stand upright." His kingdom, he said, like some of his coppices that looked so thick and well grown from without, within was discovered bare and bitten, rotten at the heart. Buckingham also was quick to express surprise and shock. When his own brother's name came in question, he told the Lords that if found guilty, Sir Edward should be judged as severely as the rest. To run with the hounds is excellent tactics. Yet the Crown knew well that this was dangerous hunting; the spoor led close to home. "Make what law you will," Coke told the Commons; "inflict what punishment you will, little good will come of it if offices be bought and sold. He that buys must sell."

Coke's ear seemed tuned to catch any slightest infraction of the Commons' traditional privileges. Members, fearful under James's pre-Parliament proclamation, advised that his Majesty be "petitioned" concerning free speech. Coke at once saw the danger. As Speaker, he had in 1593 recited on opening day the traditional petition for the three great privileges of the Commons — freedom of speech, freedom from arrest and access to the sovereign "when the good of the Commonwealth shall require." But the House was now in session; to repeat the petition in any part would be a confession of weakness, uncertainty. "Take heed," Coke told the Commons, "that we lose not our liberties by petitioning for liberty to treat of grievances. The privileges of the House concern the whole kingdom. No proclamation can be in force against an act of Parliament." Sir James Perrot suggested petitioning the King to define his phrase "reason of state." Coke forestalled the move with a definition of his own: "Reason of state is often a trick to put us out of the right way; for when a man can give no reason for a thing, then he flieth to a higher strain and saith it is a *reason of state*."

If any in Parliament knew the phrase in all implications, it was Coke. Yet he did not speak in defiance of King James but rather in aid of the Commons, to clear up uncertainty and out of his experience to remind the House of its full powers. After one of Coke's early speeches, Alford rose to say in wonder that "this was the first Parliament wherein he ever saw Councilors of State so ready to do the Commonwealth service." Coke in the law courts had been accused of harshness at other men's expense. Now that he shared the risk he spoke with equal bluntness to the Commons, seeming not to count the cost. The duty of the House was "to preserve the innocent and punish the nocent. I was charged with bribery, but did I hang down my head? I was accused, but was I daunted? No! I hate bribery." Coke addressed the House in parables after his custom, cracked jokes and told stories, as perfectly at home as if he had never stretched his long legs under the King's Council table. "Commonly when you follow two hares you lose both," he told his colleagues jovially. "I would never take breviate of one side. I'll keep my ears open for both parties. I love to come even." Toward monopolies, Coke held to his old standpoint of 1604: "Best for a kingdom to have liberty of trade if it were well governed."

The Commons were breaking ground; uncertainty of procedure caused them to flounder, grow unruly. This again, Coke saw as danger; it was in the King's power to dissolve the session at any time he saw fit. And if in Coke's mind the King had no right to imprison members while Parliament was sitting, in James's mind the sovereign most certainly possessed this power and was prepared to use it. "Let us keep order in our proceedings," Coke urged his colleagues. "For Job, speaking of hell, sayeth, *Ubi nullus ordo* [where no order is]."

A House that laughs is a House softened to reason. During Mompesson's trial, when passions ran high, a female witness appeared at the door. Should she be admitted to the bar of Commons? There was no precedent, Coke said. Had the House read of St. Bernard? Entering a church in Germany and being on his knees at prayer, he heard our Lady's image before him cry out "in a small voice, *Welcome, Bernard, welcome!* 'Peace, Madam!' quoth Bernard. 'It is not lawful for a woman to speak in the congregation.' "

Members listened, were diverted, refreshed — and followed after. The Lords made evident they liked it too, though they did not show the Commons' respect for Coke's authority of scholarship and experience. There was, however, something reassuring, disarming about Coke's easy reference to the past. He brought in Lord Burghley's name, Popham's, Queen Elizabeth's — and more than once, Robert Cecil's, naming him affectionately as *the little great Lord Treasurer.* "When I was Speaker," he said. Or, "because I had served as the Queen's Attorney and so was conversant in every court. . . . It was resolved by Popham and all the judges, sole importation is a monopoly. And I, being Attorney General, brought *quo warrantes* against such and overthrew them all. . . . I sent prohibitions thick and threefold. . . . When I was the Queen's Attorney, she used to give this in charge many times, when any one was called to any office by her, that they should ever stand *pro veritate,* rather than *pro Regina.*" Coke's figures and similes came from the everyday life they all knew — the dance called Almagne, the tasteless spice, Herb-John, which cooks tossed in every pot. "Like *Herb-John,* neither good nor bad," he said of one proposal; and of the suggestion to postpone certain bills to autumn session — "It would be too great an Almagne leap betwixt this and Allhallowtide; the bills would take wind." Sent to the Lords with lengthy statistics on trade and coinage, Coke read his report aloud, then looked up. "Because I have tired their Lordships, I will refresh them with a tale: A friar, learned and devout, was sent to Rome to preach —"

The story was not very funny, but four diarists took it down painstakingly and when the House rose, Prince Charles came forward with congratulations, told Coke he "was never weary with hearing him, he mingled mirth with business to so good purpose." "If it please your Grace," Coke answered, "there is no danger in a merry man but only in a sullen and melancholy, as Caesar feared not Brutus, but pale and sad Cassius." Coke's good spirits knew no bounds. The pent-up energy of five restless years burst to overflowing. By turns jovial, indignant, triumphant, Coke worked and schemed with his colleagues, moving easily between the two Houses with messages, plans, reports. And always, he talked.* "Sir Edward Coke," wrote Chamberlain in mid-session, "hath won his spurres for ever, and they all confesse that they could not have missed him [done without him] for that he hath so ledd and directed them all this parlement, that they cannot be satisfied with applauding him both before and behinde his backe, and indeed he is a happie man if he can leave [stop] here, for he hath proceeded hitherto with a great deal of sinceritie, temper and discretion more than usuall in him."

But Coke, characteristically, could not "stop here." With success, his confidence returned threefold. The rough assurance of manner on which the Commons leaned commenced to ruffle their Lordships. For a man lately in disgrace, Sir Edward made himself overmuch at home with his betters. Would the Lords, Coke began pleasantly on one occasion, give him leave to say somewhat for the poor House of Commons? Their Lordships too were descended from gentlemen; they were indeed, gentlemen before they were noble. . . . Of the peers whom Coke addressed, nearly half had

* During this brief Parliament, separate diaries were kept by many members, some of which, printed, fill six large volumes. An index of nearly five pages is required for Coke's speeches alone — a record not approached by any other member.

bought the honor since the turn of the century and would have preferred to forget it. Coke did not blurt out his impudences but had a way of sliding into them, taking his hearers by surprise. Proclamation and royal speech had adjured the Commons to keep their hands from matters of prerogative and statecraft — war, foreign policy, the troubles of James's daughter in Bohemia, the Prince's Spanish marriage. His colleagues of the Lower House, Coke told the Lords, had indeed been *careful* in such things. The word dripped from his tongue with double implication, followed by a Latin rhyme which Coke rattled off and, for once, took pains to translate:

> When I would sing of mighty kings and eke of bloody war,
> Cinthius did pull me by the ear and said I went too far.

With his royal Highness seated in the front row, jeweled feather in his hat, this was treading the brink indeed. Coke's pleasantries were to the purpose, they had an edge. Here was no tyro but a man who knew all sides of government, a Privy Councilor, intimate with large secrets. "To bring the Lords in love with Parliaments," Coke said ingratiatingly one morning, "might he remind them of King Alfred's law?" Namely: there should be two Parliaments held each year "for avoiding injuries" to the realm.* Edward I had ordained a Parliament "for every two years at the least"; Edward III, "one Parliament every year for redressing mischiefs and grievances." Such a statement would have startled even the Commons; to the Lords it must have been stupefying. In proof, Coke quoted an old statute from the Parliament Rolls, entitled, he said, "*Brangwyn,* which in the British tongue signifies *White Crow.* . . . And he was called a crow," Coke went on confidently, "because he was oftentimes craving and acquiring. And white because he had *aulica et candida vestimenta* [princely and snow-white garments]."

This was too much for the Buckingham faction, which hated all Parliaments and had done their best to stop the calling of this one. Two Parliaments a year . . . King Alfred . . . White Crow? Coke, said the Lords, had invented it, and in law French too: "twice a year or oftener all the wise men called *pur parlementer pur guidance del Realme.*" Three days later, Coke met the challenge by bringing his precedents to the Lords "in a book, because," wrote a diarist, "he was suspected by some malevolent persons to have de-

* Chapter Note.

vised them of his own head. He read them and the Lords cleared him. But my Lord Marquis [Buckingham] told him that if the Lords did so charge him, they were like him that acted the play of *Ignoramus the Lawyer*, in Cambridge. This was taken to pass upon Sir Edward."

Coke received the thrust good-naturedly. "Now I know what Parliaments are," he said; "I will be a scholar and learn to do my King and country service." There was no questioning Sir Edward's loyalty to the Crown; Bacon had said correctly that "a word from the King mates him." But loyalty to James was not loyalty to monopolists and patentees, or to the great courtier who stood behind these grants. There came a day when Coke skirted near to open defiance. Who, he demanded of the Lords, in old days had received commission to inquire into the King's revenue? Only *ribaulds*, "such as always beg and never work. It's necessary that some law be made for time to come that no monopoly be granted, and they that procure any such may incur some great punishment. This will kill the serpent in the egg." Coke's words went out and were repeated. On that same day, his colleagues — Sandys, Glanville, Crew, Heneage Finch the Recorder — "came so short in theyre taske," wrote Chamberlain, "that they are generally decried and thought to prevaricat, not daring to touch matters to the quick concerning the referrees, which Sir Ed. Cooke who came next them perceving, spared not to lay open."

Coke had begun to manifest in this Parliament a kind of cold, hard self-forgetfulness that was new to him. Yet men brave in argument can be stubborn in small things, and Coke was no exception. A fervent Cantabrigian, when he had reason to mention the Universities, Coke had a habit of naming Cambridge first. "Cambridge and Oxford," he said blandly. Reminded on the floor that precedence belonged to Oxford "by vote of the House," Coke persisted, repeating the phrase at his convenience. A Privy Councilor — Sir Thomas Edmondes — interrupted with a rebuke. Whereupon, it was reported, Sir Edward "aunswered him somewhat short, that Sir Thomas needed not to trouble himself so much about it, for that he belonged to neither universitie."

James himself was becoming wary of the man he had restored to public life. Buckingham and the Prince ran to the palace with news of every happening. The Commons too had spies for the Crown.

"I am sorry," said Alford, "that his Majesty should be daily informed of our proceedings, which in time may prove very prejudicial to the House." For the moment, Coke skirted the smooth side of danger, using his courtroom skill to parry and defend. Challenged by the court party: Was it fitting that subjects should take upon themselves to prescribe how and upon whom his Majesty should bestow his favors and benefits (meaning monopolies) — "I hope," Coke answered, "every one that says, 'Our Father which art in heaven,' does not prescribe God Almighty what he shall do. So we speak of these things as petitioners to his Majesty, and not as prescribers." No Parliament of Coke's experience had worked so well and smoothly in conjunction with the Lords. It was of utmost importance that this continue. Coke watched for any infringement, any prearrangement by crown forces with the Commons. Once, during a conference in Star Chamber concerning a projected bill against informers, it came out that the Attorney General had already been taking soundings. "Ha, Mr. Attorney!" broke in Coke abruptly. "Do you talk with them aforehand? *So do not we!*"

The Commons could be cruel to their members when these were so hardy as to venture defiance, particularly in the touchy matter of religion. Pressure of events — the Spanish match, successes of the Catholic League on the Continent, James's leaning toward a toleration — combined to make this a Parliament fanatically anti-Catholic. There was angry talk concerning Masses said in Gondomar's Holborn chapel. New laws were proposed against recusants, together with a plan to exile Gondomar to Greenwich during the session. In the midst of it the member for Shaftesbury, one Thomas Shepherd, rose to his feet and with an air of merry innocence, inquired, "Shall we make these gins and snares for papists and not so much as a mouse-trap to catch a Puritan? King James allows of dancing on Sunday; he has so written in his book." * In short order, the House expelled Mr. Shepherd and ordered another elected in his place. Sir Giles Mompesson the monopolist, sentenced by the Lords to fine and imprisonment, fled his jailer and escaped to France. Parliament took prompt vengeance on Mompesson's attorney, Sir Francis Michell, of whom their

* James's *Declaration of Sports,* published in 1618, encouraged Sunday "dancing, archery, leaping, vaulting, May-games and morris-dances" and forbade bear- and bull-baiting.

treatment was little short of fantastic. Eight heralds in full armor came and broke Michell's sword above his head, cut his spurs from his heels and made proclamation in the City that "none hereafter should style him by the name of Sir Francis Michell, Knight, but *Francis Michell, arrant knave*." The Tower being "too worthy for him," he was thrown into Finsbury Gaol, "where he was wont to imprison others."

Worse still was the parliamentary censure upon poor Dr. Floyd, an elderly recusant in Fleet Prison who had done nothing more dangerous than cast a few jibes at Princess Elizabeth and her Protestant husband, the Palsgrave. Whip Floyd at the cart's tail! members cried. "Slit his tongue! Strip him, put him in the pillory clad only in prayer beads and friar's girdle. . . . Fling him in the dungeon called *Little Ease;* give him as many stripes as the Lady Elizabeth has years. And after the Spanish fashion, let hot bacon be dripped on him with every lash!"

Fortunately, none of this took place, owing to James's intervention. The Commons had no right to punish a man who was not a member of their House and James so informed them, though their leaders — Coke included — fought hard to establish that right. Ironically, it was only in the name of religion that the Commons of 1621 lost their heads and turned hysterical. Whenever Spain, popery, Puritanism were laid aside or momentarily forgotten, this same fanatic Commons could make humane and surprisingly prophetic suggestions. Under the common law, hundreds of persons were put to death each year for small offenses. Declaring now that capital sentence was no deterrent to crime, members proposed a bill changing death for small offenses to labor on the public works for a number of years, after which some trade be taught the prisoner and he be freed. The bill did not go through, yet the fact of its proposal showed enlightenment. Toward monopolists and judicial bribe takers, punishment was harsh, considering that those who received it were but a few among many guilty. Yet when corruption in government becomes habitual, when bribery and office selling are openly indulged, the situation can be remedied only by the sacrifice of some high offender. Call him victim or example, the result is the same, as Bacon himself acknowledged. One or two of the impeachments were purely political, like Attorney General Yelverton's, whose hearing and condemnation were conducted entirely by the

Lords; the Commons had nothing to do with it. As a Howard dependent, Yelverton had shown hostility to the Buckingham faction; concerning monopolies he seems to have given offense to both sides. During 1620 and 1621 he found himself consequently in and out of the Tower — released at the last — though not restored to office.*

But for the most part, the Parliament of 1621 aimed less at faction than at the public good — and achieved it, though the primary sinner went unscathed. At his second condemnation before the Lords (May, 1621) Yelverton made a reckless attack on Buckingham's honor, was punished — and Buckingham, at the palace, boasted openly that he was Parliament-proof.

Fighting Clem Coke, youngest of six brothers, in 1621 sat as Burgess for Dunwich. One April day on the Parliament stairs he struck Sir Charles Morison, member for Hertfordshire. Morison fell, recovered himself, ran for a sword, drew it and advanced toward Coke. Before harm could ensue, the two were parted. The House made much of it. By common law, the penalty for striking in Westminster Hall during court session was imprisonment for life and forfeit of all lands and goods. Westminster stairs was not Westminster Hall, yet such conduct in members was a serious breach. Should the House neglect to punish it, "some other court," said Pym, "might take hold of it to the hurt of our privileges." The two men, it came out under examination, had been conversing quietly in their places when the monopoly for glasses was mentioned. Morison said it reminded him of the old rhyme

> God made bees and bees made honey,
> God made men and men made money —

How did it run? he asked as they rose to go. "The King makes judges"? He had forgotten — somewhat of asses and glasses . . . judges riding upon asses? Judges, Clem Coke retorted hotly, had never ridden asses. It was mules they rode on. "Are you, Morison, for the asses?"

"Yes," said Morison, "if they have long ears."

Of such material are famous quarrels made. Clem was called sol-

* In 1625, King Charles named Sir Henry Yelverton as a fifth judge of Common Pleas.

emnly before the Speaker. "I struck Sir Charles with the back of my hand upon the stairs," he confessed, "and gave him a thrust withal." When Clem refused to apologize, the House grew rough. Bring him to the bar of Commons, said a member, and let Sir Charles be given a truncheon to beat him before the House! Sir Robert Phelips demurred, "for his father's sake," he said. Sir Edwin Sandys declared he loved Clem Coke "in his person and thrice for his father. But Mr. Coke took this rhyme ill, worse than it was meant." Pending judgment, both men must be taken into custody. Would Sir Edward, members asked, "undertake for his son, that he should be here in the morning?" Coke refused. "I have not seen my son," he said, "sithence the quarrel began." A Mr. Whitby, Recorder for Chester, offered to undertake for Clem; Sir Baptist Hicks did the same for Morison.

On the ninth of May, Fighting Clem was sent to the Tower, "during the pleasure of the Parliament." Two days later, chastened, he petitioned for release. But discussion continued. Had punishment been sufficient? Coke, who until now had said nothing, stood up in his place. A diarist records it: "Sir Edward begins to speak for his son but cannot for weeping." The House, compassionate, ordered Clem released into his father's custody; this time, Coke accepted. Clem returned to the House, made his apology at the bar and resumed his seat. For the Commons the incident was ended.

But Sir Edward cannot easily have put it from his mind. In his sixtieth year, a father thinks to lean upon his son, or at the least to show pride in him. Coke's life was solitary. His wife lived apart; of eight children, only a daughter, Anne Sadleir, remained close. The five sons were forever in debt, forever quarreling. Their father was aware, by now, which of his qualities they had inherited. Perhaps their defection could be laid at Coke's door; a powerful, ambitious father is not the happiest endowment for one son or for five. Yet consciousness of parental failure does not soften parental sadness, a disappointment irrevocable, irremediable.

On the twenty-eighth of May, James sent sudden word that Parliament must adjourn. The Commons were dismayed; their business was but half done. "We must not return home with trifles," Coke told the House. Adjournment was not prorogation. "Yet if we go to the country and tell them the difference they will not understand us. . . . *Non est discrimen intelligendum inter illiteratos.*" * The King consented to an additional ten days, and after adjournment, by proclamation swept away eighteen monopolies and listed another seventeen for examination by the courts. It was victory in fact but not in essence; Parliament had desired to cancel these grants through legislation, not by "the King's grace." The Earl of Southampton was arrested as he left the Council table and committed to close custody at Westminster, being "more curious in the powers and liberties of the Parliament than became any Privy Councilor." Southampton had led the country party in the Upper House as Coke led in the Lower, his adherents being the young Earl of Oxford (whom Lady Hatton once had desired as son-in-law), the Earls of Essex and Warwick, the Lords Saye and Spencer. Under examination it came out that meetings had been held in Southampton's Holborn house; the Earl was asked if he "had not practiced with some of the Lower House to cross the King." His worst offense was hatred of Buckingham; he had been heard to say he "liked not to come to the Council Board because there were so many boys and base Fellows."

Sir Edwin Sandys and John Selden were arrested and committed to the Sheriff's custody. (Selden, though not a Parliament man, had been active, giving much offense to the Crown.) Rumor said that Coke had been sent for. "Petitions," he had informed the Commons, "are either of grace or of right. Our grievances are of right, but the true physic is by bill in Parliament" — a stand which the sovereign could not countenance. In no sense fearful, merely indignant, James was determined to rule as a King by divine right and put down insolence where he found it. Sir Edward Cecil (Lady Hatton's brother) told the House that Coke had been misrepresented at Whitehall. " 'Tis dangerous when things go between the head and the heart. Those things that may be cavilled at in the Lord Coke's speeches are told the King with aggravation, but the good service he doth him is concealed."

Before Parliament reconvened, Sandys, Selden and Southampton were released. But their commitment — especially Sandys's — augured badly for the autumn session: were men to be silenced if they spoke their minds? James put out a second proclamation *against lavish and licentious talking in matters of state either at home or*

* Ignorant persons have not intelligence to make distinctions.

abroad, "which the common people," wrote Chamberlain, "know not how to understand, nor how far matter of state may stretch or extend; for they continue to take no notice of it but print every weeke (at least) corantas with all manner of newes." The Earl of Oxford next was taken into custody. One evening, slightly flown with wine, he had grumbled about the Spanish match and "popery"; some false friend reported him.

Coke's old opponent of the High Commission, Archbishop Abbot, fell into deep trouble of another kind, and Coke helped him out. On horseback in Lord Zouche's deer park, the Archbishop, shooting at a buck with his crossbow, wounded a keeper who had run forward among the herd. A coroner's jury returned a verdict of accidental death.* None, said James, but a fool or a knave would think worse of a man for such an accident; let his Lordship not discomfort himself. But Abbot's enemies — High Church clerics and friends of Buckingham — leaped to the attack. Bishops had no business hunting deer; the accident was a scandal. "What should a man of his place and profession be meddling with such edge-tools?" Abbot must be unfrocked, put down from his holy profession. An ecclesiastical commission was appointed, a day set for hearing. The matter, by now, turned not on homicide but wholly on whether a bishop had the right to hunt deer at all. Laws were searched, back to Richard II, back indeed to Exodus. Among other things it came out that Archbishop Whitgift, Coke's tutor at Cambridge, had killed twenty bucks at one hunting in Lord Cobham's park — "although he never shot well," the reporter added. The matter crossed the Channel; the Paris Sorbonne, debating three times, condemned Abbot out of hand. (He was, after all, fervently anti-Rome.) The Archbishop's friends scoured the courts for help. Sir Henry Savile rode out to Stoke, "to that oracle of the law, Sir Edward Coke," says Fuller, "whom he found a-bowling for his recreation." "My Lord," said Savile, "I come to be satisfied of you in a point of law: Whether a bishop may hunt in a park by the laws of the realm?"

"He may," Coke replied, "and by this very token: There is an old law that a bishop, when dying, is to leave his pack of dogs — called *muta canum* — to the King's free use and disposal."

That Coke's words got the Archbishop off would be too much to claim. Nevertheless they were often quoted, proof positive that

* *Per infortunium suae propriae culpae:* through an accident of his own fault.

bishops might have their sport. The commission barely absolved Abbot — by one vote. The keeper's wife, well pensioned, married again. But the incident was not forgotten. A decade later, Abbot's coach was blocked in the streets, and when he asked the crowd to let him through, "Ye had best shoot an arrow at us!" a woman screamed.

The summer and fall of 1621 saw important shifts in government and church. Lionel Cranfield, Master of the Court of Wards, became Baron Cranfield and married a cousin of Lady Buckingham's, thereby stabilizing his position, looking toward the Treasurership. John Donne was made Dean of St. Paul's Cathedral, an appointment offensive to many. Who was Donne after all but a poet and the disgraced secretary of Lord Chancellor Ellesmere? Chamberlain, announcing the appointment, remarked that if his Majesty would make Ben Jonson Dean of Westminster, "we should be furnished with three very pleasant poeticall Deans." * Dr. John Williams, Dean of Westminster Cathedral, was named Lord Keeper of the Seal, though the closest he had come to study of law was as Chancellor Ellesmere's chaplain. James, when there was objection, told Privy Council he was resolved to have no more lawyers — "men so bred and nousled in corruption that they could not leave it." Williams at once went to work at his law books and did well enough as Lord Keeper, though attorneys tried hard to trip him in court. (Once, when a barrister undertook to tangle him with obsolete legal words and phrases, Williams put him down nicely with terms out of logic and metaphysics — "categorematical," "syncategorimatical.")

Parliament reconvened on the twentieth of November. "Carry yourselves," the Lord Treasurer told them on opening day, "so as that the King may be in love with Parliaments." But the Commons were in fighting spirit. They could not forget their abrupt adjournment last June, nor Sandys's and Selden's arrest. Sandys had been ill since his release from custody. Nobody seemed to know where he was; even his brother, Sir Samuel, preferred to remain a little

* The third Dean, Richard Corbet of Christ Church, Oxford, later Bishop of Norwich, is remembered by his lines "Upon an Unhandsome Gentlewoman who made Love unto him." Donne's dismissal from Ellesmere's service had followed on his secret marriage to the Chancellor's niece, who lived in the household.

vague. James gave out that the arrest had been for matters said outside of Parliament. Let Sandys be sent for, members insisted, to give his own account. The first day of business, November twenty-sixth, opened with a fierce attack on popery and the Spanish match. "The passing bell tolls for religion," said Sackville solemnly. "Papists," said Phelips, "have grown so insolent they call us *the Protestant faction!*" "Papists breed with papists"; soon they would outnumber Protestants. The King of Spain aimed at a universal monarchy. "How," asked Wentworth, "to put a ring in the nose of this Leviathan?" A member remarked pacifically that Englishmen need not fear the Spanish match. He was "hemmed at," says a diarist, and sat down, silenced.

Next day, November twenty-seventh, Coke made the most savage anti-Spanish speech of his career. It must have lasted an hour; six diarists took it down. In all of England's history, had anything good, Coke demanded, come out of Spain? No! nought but traitors. Cullen, Annias, Yorke, Williams; he could name them tenfold. Squire, who would have poisoned Queen Elizabeth's saddle . . . He had met them, examined them in the Tower, prosecuted them as Queen's Attorney. And all, all sent on by Spain! "I myself have seen Parry walking with the Queen, his stiletto in his pocket (as he confessed afterwards). I have seen her sleep before her physician, Lopez, divers times, being one that used to read to her in the afternoons. And at that very time he had a weapon to have killed her, and a jewel from Spain as bribe. O, she was the flower of Queens as the rose is the Queen of flowers! There came the great Armado out of Spain, to make King Philip monarch of all Christendom — came while we were treating of peace with Spain. The first plague among our sheep was brought by a Spanish sheep to England. So also *morbus Gallicus* [syphilis] by Spaniards from Naples. Parson sent his treatise to set us all by the ears; as treasons have such prefaces. Cresswell, Tresswell, Holt, Archer, da Gama — all, traitors out of Spain! Then Father Garnet, Guy Fawkes, who said that they would blow up the place where so bloody laws were made against them! The Powder Treason . . . and now there is common access to the house of the Spanish ambassador. . . . In Troy, fifty men did more hurt in one night than thousands in a year. Remember the Armada!"

What Coke said was actually no harsher than Alford's words or

Phelips's, who spoke of "Spain's falsehood" and "the great Roman monster." Yet Coke's words carried the authority of long experience, an intimacy with the past that was evocative, stirring. When Sir Edward sat down, members vied in telling stories of recusants and papists. A minister in one of the shires had preached a Fifth of November sermon against the Powder Treason; three papists came to his door and beat him so that he barely escaped with his life. At Gondomar's house, people came "three hundred at a time" to Mass and christenings. ("The ladies," Coke broke in, "at Mass offer ten pieces, which will in time come to a good sum.") "They sound a horn in Holborn," a member added, "to draw a great number of Inns of Court gentlemen." Let Sir Edwin Sandys be sent for! said a voice; "Mr. Speaker, if we shall suffer the Council table to call in question such as sit here for Parliamentary business, then farewell England!" "See what England hath gotten by foreign matches!" Sir George Moore broke out: "Queen Mary was matched to Philip of Spain, which was the shortening of her days, the loss of Calais and exhausting of our treasure." Such things, asked Wentworth, were not to be spoken of within these walls? Yet in the third year of King James's reign there was a treason spoken of. "These walls, methinks, do yet shake at it. And I would know whether those thirty-six barrels of gunpowder under these walls do not require our speaking?"

"Every man's heart here concurreth," said Coke. "But the King not knowing our hearts, we must do it by words."

On the first of December, a Saturday, the House drew up a declaration and petition containing fourteen points of grievance. All of them concerned religion — Spain, rescue of the King's daughter in the Palatinate, the increase of papists at home. "And from these causes, as bitter roots, we humbly offer remedies unto your most excellent Majesty." Without apology, the Commons asked for war. "Let your Majesty take speedily and effectually your sword in your hand! And to frustrate [our enemies'] hopes for a future age, we beg that our most noble prince may be timely and happily married to one of our own religion."

There was more — though for James's resentment, no more was needed — ending with the promise of "one entire subsidy at the end of the season, *for the relief of the Palatinate only*." This was bargaining with a vengeance, and over points which Parliament had been forbidden to mention, let alone use as pressure against the Crown. The Commons knew their risk. "It's not enough to know what we ought to speak," a Privy Councilor had warned from the front row. "But we must also know what is fit for the King to hear."

James was at Newmarket, twelve miles from London. But Gondomar saw the declaration that same Saturday, before it was even formally adopted by the House. "I count on your Majesty's goodness," he wrote at once, "to punish the insolence of this Commons. Otherwise I should by now have left the country. To do so would have been my duty, as you would have ceased to be a King here and I have no army here at present to punish these people myself."

It was perhaps the most extraordinary message a monarch ever received from a foreign ambassador on home soil. Before the Commons' messengers could reach Newmarket with the petition, James already had a copy. Angrily, without admitting he had seen the document, James wrote to Speaker Richardson. "Fiery and popular spirits of the House" had debated matters "far above their reach and capacity." The Commons were commanded "not to meddle henceforth with any thing concerning our government or deep matters of state . . . not to deal with our dearest son's match with the daughter of Spain nor to touch the honour of that King or any other of our friends and confederates." He had heard, James continued, that Sir Edwin Sandys had been sent for, to give reasons for his imprisonment. "We think ourselves very free and able to punish any man's misdemeanors in Parliament, as well during their sitting as after: Which we mean not to spare hereafter, upon any occasion of any man's insolent behavior there." And if the Commons — the message ended — "have already touched any of these points which we have here forbidden, in any petition of theirs which is to be sent unto us, it is our pleasure that you [Mr. Speaker] shall tell them, That except they reform it before it come to our hands, we will not deign the hearing nor the answering of it."

The Commons had this message on Tuesday, December fourth. They were thrown into consternation; couriers were dispatched to overtake their messengers and bring back the petition. "The uncircumsized Philistines," Coke said grimly, "will rejoice at this letter." The House rose at once. Next morning the Speaker left the Chair and members met in Committee of the Whole, their mood one of grieved astonishment. Surely someone had carried lies to the

King — the original petition had been falsified? "There have been errors of relation," Coke said. His Majesty must be warned against false reporters. "I wish," a member declared passionately, "all false reporters to the King to be in the bottom of the sea with a millstone about their necks." "Evil spirits," said another, "by misinforming the King, put us upon these many rocks."

Actually, the House had sent a declaration calculated to enrage James I; to Elizabeth they would not have dared to send it. Their reaction however was characteristic. In English hearts, faith in the sovereign lay imbedded. King by blood and by anointing, surely his Majesty desired what his subjects desired? Unthinkable that he could be in league with the enemy! "The King is misled by some about him. Let us cast balm and heal the wound, not make it wider." Again and again the point came up, hopeless, childlike, a point insisted by prerevolutionary Parliaments and Congresses — to be urged in grief and bewilderment more than a century later by a Continental Congress across the sea: "King George, persuaded by wicked counsellors, has broken the covenant chain. . . . He has refused, he has forbidden, he has dissolved. . . . We hoped in vain, we bid a final adieu."

On the eleventh of December, 1621, a second petition was sent to King James. It had taken the Commons a week to hammer it out. Crown apologists, notably Secretary Calvert (the "Hispaniolized Englishman") declared they saw "no breach of our privileges in the King's letter." Coke turned on Calvert scornfully. There were things that must be said. What matter who spoke them, or if he then had leave to speak no more? Coke was no poet — few lawyers are. Yet as he answered Calvert, his words were charged with all the meaning of his sixty-nine years — a life in books and records, the written history of England translated, transcribed to the living assemblage before him. "Best to ask counsel of the dead!" he said. "For they will not flatter nor fawn to advance themselves, nor bribe, nor dissemble." The Parliament Rolls, Coke continued, showed that Henry IV refused to be informed by private persons of any matter debated, "but only by the whole House."

The Commons, much struck, moved to have the Roll copied out and every member given a copy. The second petition was virtually a repetition of the first — if anything, stronger, though it had an added paragraph begging his Majesty "hereafter not to give credit to private reports until you have been truly informed thereof from ourselves." But the same demands were made: "The voice of Bellona must be heard and not the voice of the turtle. Your Majesty must either abandon your children or engage yourself in a war. . . . Concerning the ancient liberty of Parliament for freedom of speech, jurisdiction, and just censure of the House and other proceedings there . . . a Liberty which, we assure ourselves, so wise and just a King will not infringe, the same being our ancient and undoubted rights and an inheritance from our ancestors, without which we cannot freely debate nor clearly discern of things in question before us. . . . We are therefore now again inforc'd, in all humbleness to pray your Majesty to allow the same and thereby to take away the doubts and scruples your Majesty's late letter to our Speaker hath wrought upon us."

There was much question as to choice of messengers. In the end twelve knights were selected, "all courtiers," wrote a diarist, "such persons as might win goodwill." It was very cold when the twelve rode out to Newmarket, the roads frozen in ruts. "A hard journey," noted Chamberlain. James received the knights favorably if a trifle ironically, bidding his servants "bring stools for the ambassadors." But after glancing at the petition he put it down, refused to read the points of remonstrance. Three days later the Commons had their reply. It opened with Queen Elizabeth's words, spoken on the famed occasion when she had replied in Latin to an insolent Polonian ambassador: "*Legatum expectabamus, heraldum accipimus* [We expected an ambassador, we are confronted by a herald]." Remember, James wrote, "that we are an old and experienced King, needing no such lessons." The Commons had better have listened to the Privy Councilors among them, rather than to certain "tribunitial orators." The Prince's match was no fit subject for Parliaments to discuss. As for freedom of speech and privileges, "we cannot allow of the style, calling it your *antient and undoubted right and inheritance;* but could rather have wished that ye had said, That your privileges were derived from the grace and permission of our ancestors and us, for most of them grow from precedents, which shows rather a toleration than inheritance."

This time there was no mistaking. No false messengers could be blamed; the King's words lay before them. "Sithence the beginning of this Parliament," said Coke, "I never spake but mine own conscience. The privileges of this House is the nurse and life of all our laws, the subject's best inheritance. If my sovereign will not allow me my inheritance, I must fly to Magna Charta and entreat explanation of his Majesty. Magna Charta is called *Charta libertatis quia liberos facit.* . . . The Charter of Liberty because it maketh freemen. When the King says he cannot allow our liberties of right, this strikes at the root. We serve here for thousands and ten thousands."

We serve for thousands. Twenty years ago or even ten, Coke could not have said it; the Commons had not been ready. The immediate question was what to do about the King's letter. One of the courtiers who had delivered the Commons' petition to Newmarket — Sir Richard Weston — revealed that it had been the Prince who sent the earlier copy to his Majesty, "complaining that his marriage was continually prostituted before the House." *Legatum expectabamus.* "I heard the Polonian Ambassador speak that speech to the Queen," Sir James Perrot broke in; "it was at Greenwich, spoken in a bold braving manner." Secretary Calvert, from the front row, moved to have the King's message entered in the *Commons Journals,* "to remain to posterity." There was loud objection. Coke urged a second protestation, "notwithstanding his Majesty's letter." Was this, he challenged, to be a *silent Parliament?* In the end it was decided to send no further petition — which might never be read — but to write out their grievances in the *Journal* of the House. "Let us set down wherein our privileges are impeached," Coke said. "Let us make a *Protestation,* enter it in the Journals and present the Journals to the King — but not as requiring an answer."

On Tuesday, December eighteenth, James adjourned Parliament. The Commons sat late, that day, and finished their *Protestation* by candlelight:

The Commons now assembled in Parliament . . . do make this Protestation following: That the liberties, franchises, privileges and jurisdictions of Parliament are the ancient and undoubted birthright and inheritance of the subjects of England; and that the arduous and urgent affairs concerning the King, state and defence of the realm, and of the Church of England, and the maintenance and making of laws and redress of mischiefs and grievances which daily happen within this realm, are proper subjects and matter of counsel and debate in Parliament; and that in the handling and proceeding of those businesses every member of the

House of Parliament hath and of right ought to have freedom of speech, to propound, treat, reason, and bring to conclusion the same: and that the Commons in Parliament have like liberty and freedom to treat of these matters in such order as in their judgments shall seem fittest: and that every member of the said House hath like freedom from all impeachment, imprisonment and molestation (other than by censure of the House itself) for or concerning any speaking, reasoning or declaring any matter or matters touching the Parliament or Parliament business; and that, if any of the said members be complained of and questioned for anything done or said in Parliament, the same is to be shewed to the King by the advice and assent of all the Commons assembled in Parliament, before the King give credence to any private information.

Almost immediately, Privy Council sent for Coke. "You have forgotten," they told him, "the duty of a servant, the duty of a Councilor of State and the duty of a subject." Kneeling, Coke was deprived of his place at Council table. "He aunswered little," reported Chamberlain; only "that he hoped he had fayled in none of these, but God's will and the King's be done." Eight guards escorted him to the Tower. He was locked in Lord Cobham's old quarters. One of the rooms had been used as a kitchen; as Coke approached with his guards he saw something scrawled on the door: "This room wants a cook."

The King came to Whitehall and sitting in Council Chamber, the Lords and Judges surrounding him, demanded the *Commons Journals.* The Clerk of the House laid the page open at the protestation. James read it and tore it from the book — as fit, he said, "to be razed out of all memorials and utterly to be annihilated." A proclamation was issued, dissolving the Parliament and explaining that "some particular members" had taken "inordinate liberties with our high prerogative." Gondomar wrote home jubilantly: "It is certain that the King will never summon another Parliament . . . or at least not another composed as this one was. It is the best thing that has happened in the interests of Spain and the Catholic religion since Luther began to preach heresy a hundred years ago. The King seems at times deeply distressed at the resolution which he has taken to leave all and attach himself to Spain. The Marquis of Buckingham has had a great part in this and deserves to be thanked."

Sir Robert Phelips was sent to the Tower, Pym was confined to his London house, Hakewill censured by Council. Three others were named on a commission for Ireland — a convenient way of getting them out of the country. Of them all, Coke had harshest treatment. Because he was a Privy Councilor, his offense had been the worst. Three gentlemen were ordered to search his chambers in the Temple. His books and papers were taken away, the doors locked and sealed. Privy Council debated how to exempt him from the King's General Pardon which accompanied a dissolution of Parliament. To strike his name from the list might rouse added resentment in the country. Best to accomplish the thing under cover of faults committed outside of Parliament. No man could be pardoned who had a bill against him in court. The Crown entered suit against Coke for thirty thousand pounds — the old debt due from Sir William Hatton to Queen Elizabeth, once more exhumed to serve its purpose. Sir Edward was put in close confinement, customary only for traitors or murderers. None of his family was permitted to see him, nor could he walk outside his rooms. "Many," reported Chamberlain, "lay his committment on Don Gondomar. Indeed I have not read nor heard of any ambassador so potent as he is saide to be."

Coke remained in the Tower nearly seven months. "Twenty-six weekes and five dayes," as he recorded it. Locked in Lord Cobham's rooms, on February second he had his seventieth birthday. The cold must have been nearly unendurable. Coke was allowed no books — perhaps the greatest deprivation of all — and like any poor forgotten prisoner, wrote verses with a piece of coal. Latin verses, they were, about the roaring of the Tower lions in their pit, the damp reeking walls so near the river, the smell (that prison stink of stone and old dried urine). "*Heu! horridus ille locus* — May God return me one day to my small house in Norfolk!" Stories circulated. How Prince Charles interceded, but the King said he knew no *Edward Coke*. "Mr. Coke, then," said the Prince. "I know none of that name neither," James retorted. "But by my saule there is one *Captain Cook*, leader of the faction in Parliament." The Earl of Arundel, President of Privy Council and Lord Marshal of England, examined Coke and declared that he had spoken in Parliament to stir up rebellion. "I charge you therefore with treason. I have heard you, Sir Edward, affirm that by law he is a traitor who goes about to withdraw subjects' hearts from their King."

"I hold such an one to be a traitor indeed," Coke answered. "But he that goes about to withdraw the King's heart from his subjects, him I hold to be an archtraitor." Coke's papers were searched in vain by Privy Council, "a whole standard of them." Sir Henry Guildford was sent out to Stoke to take inventory; the estate would be excellent pickings for courtiers. "I found little but underwood felled," Guildford reported to Council, "and no damage done to the deer. I have made inventory of the goods in Stoke House and sealed up the principal rooms and also made inventory of the goods at Bailie's Farm, but not sealed the rooms as Mr. Henry Coke* and his family live there. I have forbidden any felling of timber or removal of cattle."

This time, it looked indeed as though Coke's career were finished. "He has need to stand fast," wrote Chamberlain, "for if his footing faile never so litle he is in daunger to come downe headlong." Rumor had it that when Coke should be called to answer, it would be for his life. It was said also that the servant of a Gray's Inn lawyer, "Mr. Byng," had been racked for talking in defense of Sir Edward. The Earl of Arundel informed the prisoner that his Majesty, in spite of the order for close confinement, would permit eight of his most learned lawyers to confer with Sir Edward and advise him. Coke asked the Earl to thank the King for his favor. But knowing himself accounted of as much skill in the law as any in England, he needed no such help. Nor did he fear to be judged by law in the cause for which he was accused. "In such a one as I, if the King desire my head, he knows whereby he may have it."

Toward Easter, Coke's confinement was mitigated. He was permitted to walk in the Tower grounds; James gave order that his daughter, Anne Sadleir, might visit him, "she being a discreet woman and likely to endeavor to bring him to more conformity." Still later, Coke's eldest son, Sir Robert, was allowed to come and sit with him at dinner. Coke's case came up in the Court of Wards. "Much arguing there hath ben last terme and this," wrote Chamberlain on the first of July, "about Sir Ed. Cooke as having defrauded the King of greate summes in the extent he had together with his Lady of Sir Christofer Hattons lands. It shold have been decided on Saterday but the three Cheife Justices who

* Henry Coke was Sir Edward's fourth son, great-great-grandfather of Thomas Coke, first Earl of Leicester.

were present at all the hearings, have not digested the matter sufficiently to geve their sentence."

The three Justices were Sir James Ley, Sir Henry Hobart and Sir Lawrence Tanfield of Exchequer Court. Sir John Doddridge, "the sleeping Judge" and others conferred at Sergeants' Inn. The Attorney General pursued the case with all his powers. Yelverton had said openly in court that no sixpence should be abated of the fifty thousand pounds arrearages which Sir Edward owed the King. (Those in hopes of profiting had already, said Chamberlain, devoured their share, notably Sir Thomas Hatton and one Mr. Gibbe, who had followed the suit at great cost to themselves.) But Coke was cleared. Every Judge, those present in court and those who conferred, declared that Sir Edward "neither in law nor conscience was to be charged of any thing, either toward the King or toward Sir Christopher Hatton's heir." Sir John Walter, the Prince's attorney, even refused to help with the prosecution. "Let my tongue cleave to the roof of my mouth, whenever I open it against Sir Edward Coke." *

In August, Coke was released from the Tower and permitted to go home, confined however to within a compass of six miles from Stoke. Early in November he received full freedom and returned to his chambers at the Temple. The suit in Court of Wards had been merely an excuse; Coke's real offense was his conduct in Parliament. Other charges had been attempted — arrogant speeches made when Coke was Chief Justice, his comparing himself on one occasion to Samuel. But these had quickly collapsed. Nothing in Coke's papers showed even a suspicion of disloyalty. It was impossible to keep Sir Edward in bondage without cost to the Crown's prestige.

"Throw this man where you will," said James, "and he falls upon his legs."

* Chapter Note.

CHAPTER THIRTY-TWO

The Spanish journey and its result. King Charles I. The Parliament of 1625.

SINCE the year 1604, when Don Velasco in London signed the first treaty of friendship, James's dearest wish had been for peace with Spain. Through infinite difficulty he had achieved it. The road was long — Gondomar, the Spanish match proposed, Ralegh near to ruining it until himself ruined. . . . Two years before James's death, in February of 1623, Prince Charles and Buckingham embarked on a wild venture that forever broke James's plans, altered the foreign policy of England and by one of history's strange turns enabled Parliament to pass the most important legislation of the reign.

Prince Charles was twenty-two when Buckingham persuaded him. Marriage negotiations from afar would never succeed, said Buckingham; this waiting for the Infanta was not only tedious but ungallant. Let the pair of them set off alone, like heroes of a *romanza*, ride across Europe, storm the Madrid court and fetch the princess home. James consented reluctantly. At fifty-six he was older than his years; he could not withstand these fresh young spirits. Throwing himself on his bed in a fit of weeping, the King cried out that he was "undone, he should lose Baby Charles." Without advice or approval of Privy Council, the Prince and Buckingham departed secretly, as Jack and Tom Smith, their faces disguised by beards, only one attendant riding with them to the seacoast. "Such an adventure," wrote Roger Coke, "as Don Quixote never dreamed of in any of his."

The country took it in high distaste. Great lords declared outright that Buckingham had been treasonable in carrying the Prince from the realm; he must one day answer to Parliament for it. The people, angry, said it had been done "that the Prince might be married at a mass." News trickled back across the Channel. In Paris, the travelers had bought periwigs and attended incognito the rehearsal of a masque at the palace; among the dancers they saw the Princess Henrietta Maria, sister of the French King.

Aside from the religious and political implications, the venture showed a giddiness which alarmed. Signs and omens were unfavorable; the Thames in twelve hours ebbed and flowed three times, bespeaking calamity. King James remained scarcely less unhappy than his subjects. He sent off servants, courtiers and horses to the Prince, together with a silk pavilion for tilting and jewels from the Tower for court wear. Frequent letters passed across Europe, addressed to Baby Charles and Steenie — whose picture reposed, wrote the King, "in a blew ribben under my waistcoate, nexte my hairte." With Buckingham gone, no one stood now between the sovereign and the terrible importunacy of suitors, who followed begging through palace galleries. One day the King turned on them. "I would God you had first my doublet and then my shirt. Were I naked, I think you would give me leave to be quiet."

Summer approached and a fleet was fitted out to fetch home the Infanta, who was to bring, as reported, two dozen priests in attendance. It had been specified she would have control of her children's education until they reached the age of ten. Actually, negotiations in Madrid were at a standstill, broken on the question of an English toleration, refusal of the Pope's dispensation and above all, Philip's reluctance to promise aid to Elizabeth in the Palatinate. Buckingham had managed to offend the Spanish courtiers, who declared they "would rather put the Infanta headlong into a well than into his hands." The young woman begged to enter a convent. Prince Charles, impatient at Spanish etiquette that would not let him talk with his affianced, climbed a wall of the Infanta's garden; she ran off shrieking. From England, Buckingham was made a Duke; the title might enhance Spanish respect to the royal party. King Philip drew away.

By August the difficulties were insuperable. At Council table, Archbishop Abbot told James point-blank that a toleration could be achieved neither by law nor by grace. James swore bitterly and asked how he should get his son home again? "Sweet Boyes," he wrote despairingly, "come speedilie awaye, except ye never look to see your old Dade againe." The story went that Archie, the King's famous fool, advised his master that they two must change caps. Why? asked the King. "Why," said Archie, "*who sent the Prince into Spain?*" The King, said the Venetian ambassador, seemed "altogether stupefied" by the turn of events. Bursting into tears, James asked a courtier, "Do you think that I shall ever see the Prince again?" "My onlie sweete Sonne and my onlie best sweet Servant," he wrote in despair; "I care for Matche nor nothing so that I maye once have you in my armes againe. God grawnte it! God grawnte it! God grawnte it! Amen! Amen! Amen!"

In October, 1623, the Prince came home — without his bride. London went wild with joy. Bells pealed, drums beat; there were bonfires from Ludgate Hill to London Bridge, thanksgiving in the churches as if the nation had been delivered from a plague. St. Paul's choristers sang joyful anthems: "When Israel came out of Egypt, and the House of Jacob from among the barbarous people." Celebrations spread to Cambridge, Oxford and the countryside. Few asked why the match was broken; the nation cared only for the fact. Buckingham enjoyed sudden popularity. Spanish policy was reversed; the Duke called for war and the Prince echoed him. "I must go through with it one way or another," said James regretfully, "tho' I sell my jewels and all. War, like women, is *malum necessarium.*" It was agreed to hold a Parliament in the coming February (1624) and raise money to fit out a fleet.

No sooner had the Privy Council agreed to this step than they sent for Coke. The King, Sir Edward was told, had "special use of his service in a commission into Ireland"; he must sail within forty days. For Coke the blow was sharp and judging from his response, unexpected. Crown forces wished to keep him out of Parliament. Yet were there not ways less harsh than virtual banishment? Privy Council, it was plain, feared old Parliament men; Sir Edwin Sandys had been named Commissioner with Coke. Ireland! A wild, rough country, all bogs and water and half-clad peasants, speaking an outlandish tongue, cousins to the O'Neill and friends to the Spaniard. "Beeing surprised with this sodain alarme," wrote Chamberlain, "and pausing a while, the Council required [Sir Edward's] aunswer, which he gave in few wordes that he came not thether to aunswer but to obey: and within two dayes after went into Norfolke to settle his affaires. It was since saide that the Prince had laboured for his stay and to save him from so hard a journy in respect of his yeares. . . . The poore man sets a goode face on it and makes shew to go cherefully, but in secret tells his frends he never lookes to see them again. Indeed it is thought a hard journy for a man more then three-score and fowreteen yeare old and that never was at sea."

Coke was nearly seventy-two and it was true enough that he had never left England. On the last day of January, a newswriter reported that Sir Edward's journey had been "respited till May." Actually he never went to Ireland at all, nor did Sandys. Surprisingly enough, when Parliament opened, the two were in their seats, Coke for Coventry, Sandys for the county of Kent. Perhaps the Prince's intervention achieved it. Perhaps James wearied of the matter and, after his fashion, went off to Theobalds and let all slip. Perhaps indeed Coke pleaded the law. His *Second Institute* (which even then he must have been compiling) has trenchant reference:

> By the law of the land no man can be exiled or banished out of his native countrey but either by authority of parliament or in case of objuration for felony by the common law. Therefore the king cannot send any subject of England against his will to serve him out of this realme, for that should be an exile and he should *perdere patriam* [lose his country]. No, he cannot be sent against his will into Ireland to serve the king as his deputy there. . . . For if the king might send him out of this realme to any place under pretence of service, as ambassadour or the like, he might send him into the furthest part of the world, which being an exile is prohibited. . . .

The Parliament of 1624 opened in bright accord. Buckingham gave a vivid report on the Spanish journey, laying upon King Philip and his courtiers total blame for failure of negotiations. The Prince had stood fast to his religion, refusing every temptation to conversion. When it was found that Philip might imprison or at least restrain Prince Charles, the two had scorned to flee from Spain. Proudly the Duke told Count Olivares "that although they had stolen thither out of love, they would never steal from thence out of fear."

Parliament received all this with rapture. They were, in fact, completely taken in. Looking for a quick and easy war with Spain — entirely maritime, a second "glorious '88" — the Commons voted three subsidies and three fifteens, declared the Duke "deserved well of his country" and made a motion of giving thanks "to the Prince, the King and to God." So benign was the climate that James came down and asked Parliament's advice about his foreign policy. Between February and June, thirty-five laws were passed. Parliament in a bold gesture swept away monopolies forever, declared that "such royal grants" were to be illegal and left them to trial at common law. Coke's part in this was large. He had been on the original committee (1621) to draft the bill; he was on the final committee now in '24. Two diarists even credit him as author. "Penned by Cooke," writes John Symth of Gloucestershire. But Pym and the *Commons Journals* state that the bill was drawn by Noye and Crew. Very likely they all had a hand in it. "The greatest victory of the Commons," said Maitland, "during the reign of James."

Only one man in government suffered by this happy Parliament. Lionel Cranfield, Earl of Middlesex and Treasurer of England, was impeached on a charge of bribery and extortion in office. Buckingham stood behind it; during the Spanish journey, Cranfield had disputed the Duke's commands, balking at monies spent on the venture. James warned the favorite against launching this parliamentary attack. "By God, Steenie," he said, "you are a fool. You are making a rod with which you will be scourged yourself." To the Prince, James remarked that he would "live to have his bellyful of impeachments." The King did his best to intercede for Cranfield. "All Treasurers," he told the Lords, "if they do good service to their masters, must be generally hated. This party came in upon a reformation and he discovered the corruption of others." But Cranfield, like Bacon before him, was sentenced to loss of office, imprisonment in the Tower and heavy fines. (Sir Francis Bacon, congratulating the Treasurer on his advancement, had declared he had one rule for all great officers of the Crown: "Remember, a Parliament will come.")

Before the session ended, James's spirit seemed to sag. It was his last Parliament and somehow the King spoke as if he knew it. He had failed greatly while his son was in Spain, and though he seemingly had recovered, at fifty-seven he addressed the session in terms of an aged man. "I am old, but mine only son is young. . . . Give me leave, as an old King. . . . I wish to see, before God close up mine eyes . . ."

The summer was sickly. Two years of bad harvest had caused a near famine. In the northern shires the poor starved upon boiled nettles or ate cattle that had died by chance. The spotted fever made its appearance, looked on as cousin german to the plague and almost as quick. Coke's daughter Frances caught it and was very ill. Lady Hatton went off with her friends to Holland to visit James's daughter Elizabeth. Dr. John Donne, recovering from a fever, published his *Devotions* in verse, "wherein," noted Chamberlain, "are many curious and daintie conceits, not for common capacities, but surely full of pietie and true feeling. . . . Yet I could wish a man of his years and place to give over versifieng." A sad season showed but one bright hour — a play performed with Gondomar as subject. (Happily, the Count had not returned from Spain.) London flocked to the performance. A suit of Gondomar's old clothes had somehow been procured and the famous litter, which "the world sayes lack't nothing but a couple of asses to carry it. They counterfeited his person to the life, with all his graces and faces."

Prince Charles, after brief negotiation, became affianced to the Princess Henrietta Maria, sister of Louis XIII, the lady whom the Prince had seen dancing in Paris. The nation perforce accepted the arrangement. France was preferable to Spain, though the Princess was not a whit less Romish than the Infanta. Parliament had Charles's solemn promise that the marriage would bring no concessions to recusants; moreover, the French King would undertake, as English ally, assistance for recovery of the Palatinate. But in December, 1624, Charles broke his promise. Secret articles were agreed upon; an ambassador came from Paris to sign them and was received with ringing of bells, loud playing of Paul's Cathedral organ and salute of Tower guns. "God graunt," wrote a citizen, "it may prove worth all this noise."

At Christmas, King James fell sick at Theobalds and kept to his chamber during holiday season, only riding out in his litter when weather was fair to watch his hawks fly above the brook. Three months later he was seized with a quartain ague. But March brought rheums and ills galore and only the patient looked seriously on his indisposition. "An ague in the spring," quoted courtiers lightly, "is physic for a king." Buckingham's mother made a plaster and put it to his side; James complained it made him worse. The Duke gave a posset drink, applied plasters to wrists and belly — reckless acts which the Duke would hear of from Parliament. Royal physicians, angry, refused to minister further until the plasters were removed. James grew weaker, the fits of fever more severe. His tongue swelled; when he tried to speak he could not make himself understood. On Sunday morning, March twenty-seventh, the King appeared so ill that Prince Charles was sent for; he came running to the bedchamber in his nightshirt. James's mouth formed words; "*Veni, Domine Jesu.*" He did not speak again, and before noon he died.

James's son was chief mourner at the funeral, going on foot behind the bier as Kings of England had not been known to do for centuries. The hearse, magnificent, was designed by Inigo Jones, mourning black distributed to some nine thousand persons. James was buried in Westminster Abbey in the tomb of his great-great-grandfather, Henry VII. Bishop Williams — Lord Keeper — preached the funeral sermon and was at pains to prove the King had died a thorough Protestant, quoting words that James had spoken years ago to his son: "Marry where you will, but if she be the daughter of a Catholic king, marry her person but not her religion." Dr. John Donne preached beside the royal bier as it lay in state at Denmark House. Whether from affection or supreme art, his words were deathless and carried at least the sound of love: "This hand was not so hard a hand when we touched it last, nor so cold a hand when we kissed it last. . . ."

But the common run of citizens showed little grief. "It did not a little amaze me," wrote D'Ewes, "to see all men generally slight and disregard the loss of so mild and gentle a prince. For though he had his vices and deviations, we cannot but acknowledge that his death deserved more sorrow and condolement from his subjects than it found." Men tried to speak well of the dead and floundered, their praise emerging more grotesque than kind. When the King's body was opened, wrote one knight to another, the bones of his head were so strong they could hardly be broken with chisel and saw, and "so full of braynes as they could not upon the oppeninge, keep them from spillinge — a great mark of his infinite judgment."

Yet Anthony Weldon, as scurrilous a chronicler as ever set pen to paper, hater of all Stuarts and of the Roman Catholic religion, at James's death suddenly relented, finding softer words than many who were to write in later centuries: "He was (take him altogether and not in peeces) such a king, I wish this kingdome have never any worse. . . . For he lived in peace, dyed in peace and left all his kingdomes in a peaceable condition, with his own motto: *Beati pacifici* [Blessed are the peacemakers]."

King Charles was twenty-four, slight, hazel-eyed, with fair complexion. Parliament knew him well, or thought they did — knew the quick movements of a young man who "rather trotted than paced, he went so fast," the heavy, crippling stammer, the manner courteous and aloof. From the first, Charles showed extraordinary reserve; foreign ministers speculated if it were indifference or "a sign of consummate prudence." Sir Simonds D'Ewes, watching one day at the tiltyard when Charles was Prince of Wales, had remarked that "everything about him was full of delicacy and handsome features; his hands and face especially effeminate and curious." The nation had not yet time to know the mixture of courage and irresoluteness that made up their King — absolute bravery in the face of personal danger, weak failure to hold his course against such as Buckingham who would advise him. Royal portraiture is apt to be stilted. But Van Dyke has given us a living, breathing Charles, each feature characteristic: the pointed beard, large melancholy eyes and fine hair curling to the shoulders. In bright armor the young monarch curvets on horseback, in velvet and lace he sits among his family. The pale proud face remains forever tragic, the memory of Charles inseparable from his end.

Inheriting James's convictions as to the divinity of kingship, yet bred from birth to flattery and easy living, Charles, unlike his father, had no bitter childhood terrors to humble him — and none of his father's rough homely wit. Offended by the easy manners and hard drinking of James's entourage, this elegant young King had exquisite taste in the arts. "Of all princes living," said Rubens in 1625, "the most appreciative of good painting." The monarch's connubial faithfulness has been stressed in a phrase affected by contemporaries and posterity alike — "Charles I was free from vice." Comforting words, applied to a Stuart King. Ready to promise anything to Parliament, ready to break his promise when expediency demanded — and not to know it broken. "I must avow," Charles remarked, "that I owe the account of my actions to God alone." A regal debt yet all too comprehensive, allowing wide latitude for slippage and alteration; Charles, it has been said, possessed every grace save the grace of sincerity.

The nation manifested little joy at his accession. The son replaced the father — and Buckingham continued to direct England's policy. If any hoped to see the Duke put down, they were quickly disillusioned. Buckingham was favored as before. One day he rode to tennis in a litter; the King walked beside him. The wits took occasion to remark that "his Majesty was in very great favor with the Duke's grace."

Charles's French bride arrived in June; the couple had already been married by proxy. Queen Henrietta Maria came up the river from Greenwich by barge, with London church bells pealing and all the little boats on Thames set out with flags and streamers. Charles stood at her side, "both in suits of green," wrote an observer. "I never beheld the King to look so merrily." The Queen, barely fifteen, reached just to her husband's shoulder, though young enough, it was noted, to grow taller. The Tower ordnance went off with a glorious bang. Guns echoed from fifty ships; the heavens opened — as they have done and will do at English ceremonies — and rain poured down on river, barge and wherries and "all the people shouting amain. The Queen is nimble and quick, black-eyed, brown-haired and in a word, a brave lady, though perhaps a little touched with the green sickness."

For a few weeks — but not longer — there were hopes of the Queen's conversion. Was she not, after all, the daughter of Henry of Navarre? Asked if she disliked Huguenots, "Why?" she replied courteously. "Was not my father one?" But before a week was out, High Mass had been held at Denmark House and next at Whitehall Palace, with twenty-nine French priests officiating, and the Queen's own young Bishop. (Henrietta Maria was entirely within her rights; the marriage contract had specified that she bring clergy, attendants, ladies-in-waiting from France and exercise her religion as she saw fit.) In the palace, quarrels took place at dinner as to who should say grace, the Queen's confessor or the English court chaplain. Charles rose angrily and left the table, leading his young wife by the hand. Country comment turned acid. The Queen was skittish and frisky. She had brought with her such a set of ill-favored waiting-women, there was "not one worth the looking after save herself and the Duchess of Chevreuse, who though she be faire yet paints fowly." This same lady, one warm evening, swam across the Thames and got no praise for it. "A French trick, washing in Thames," said a newswriter, disgusted.

Actually, all merriment at court and in the city was dimmed by threat of universal sickness, the onset of plague which had showed itself as early as April. Though May was cold and frosty, the infection had gained pace. During June, heavy rains fell. The Thames overflowed, cellar beams rotted with damp. There was water in London lanes and alleys, water oozed in the Strand; the brown rats swarmed and scuttled. "We may well doubt," wrote a London physician, "that a deluge of destruction is coming upon us." The coronation was postponed indefinitely. A terrible omen, people said, that father and son should ascend the throne amidst such scenes.

Nevertheless, a Parliament was called — an act customary at the opening of a reign, to settle upon the new King such customary revenues as tonnage and poundage and serve as general introduction between sovereign and people. Ten months earlier, Buckingham had been the darling of Parliament, which had parted with all signs of amity and enthusiasm, to meet, by agreement, in November. They had not met but were prorogued again; Charles's French marriage was suspected as the reason. Terms of the contract had leaked out, making Protestants more than a little uneasy. And Louis XIII, far from aiding the cause of Elizabeth in the Palatinate, had refused to let English troops pass through France. Under a foreign commander — Count Mansfield — twelve thousand foot soldiers, sick and ill supplied, had perished in Holland of starvation and the plague. Mistrust of Buckingham returned tenfold.

Even before Parliament convened in April, hard-fought elections showed the temper of the country. Sir Edwin Sandys met defeat in Kent under a false rumor that he was to be made Secretary of State. Sir Henry Wotton, of the court faction, despite "all the frends he could make and though he spent almost fiftie pound in good drincke upon his followers," * lost the burgess-ship of Canterbury to a recruiting captain, one John Fisher. In the end it was a strong Lower House. Alford was there, and Sir Robert Cotton the antiquary; Pym, Phelips, Glanville the western lawyer, "Mr. Hampden of Great Hampden" (cousin to the Cromwells of Hinchinbrook) and that fiery member from Cornwall, Sir John Eliot, aged thirty-three. Coke sat for the county of Norfolk.

King Charles, before his opening speech, startled the assembly by doffing his crown and replacing it courteously as if it were a hat, repeating the gesture when he had done speaking. Parliament had drawn him into a war, he said; Parliament must find means to support it. Let the Commons vote supply without delay, that they might be adjourned in this sickly season. On the first day of business, the House responded with apparent goodwill. Coke moved that there might be no committee for grievance. This being the beginning of a new reign, there could be as yet no grievances. Sir Benjamin Rudyerd reminded the House that they had now a King "bred in Parliaments," who had traveled abroad and learned much therefrom. Let the Commons "take such course now to sweeten all things between King and people, that they may never afterwards disagree."

After these pacific motions all sweetness dissolved as at a signal. Parliament had been told that a large fleet was ready to sail. Yet against whom was it purposed? No war had been declared, his Majesty had not named the enemy. Who knew but the fleet might be used to the advantage of new Catholic allies? The Commons voted two subsidies — about £140,000 — hardly enough to pay Charles's obligations for a month. At the same time, they proposed a law limiting to one year the King's traditional lifetime receipts of tonnage and poundage. The voice of orators was accompanied by bells tolling for the dead. Members slipped out and went home; by July tenth, only sixty seats were filled. The Commons asked for adjournment, meaning to reconvene next winter when the sickness was gone. But Speaker Crewe, called to the Lords' Chamber, was told that while the King graciously accepted their two subsidies, the amount was not sufficient. Parliament must reassemble on the first of August, less than three weeks hence. They would meet at Oxford.

* Wotton, who was Provost of Eton, went to this Parliament after all as member for Sandwich.

The Commons were dismayed. Deaths from the plague had reached awful proportions; August was notoriously the month of most danger. The sickness was graver than in 1603, more severe indeed than any visitation since the Black Death three centuries ago. The town of Oxford had the infection, the influx of crowds would increase the risk. People were terrified. Meeting at evening, they bade each other not "Good night," but "God send us a joyful resurrection."

Nevertheless, Parliament reassembled on the first of August, the Commons sitting in the Oxford Divinity School, the Lords on the floor above. The King and court had moved to Woodstock nearby; at the palace gate a gibbet was set up to warn away intruders. (Actually, it was a peculiarity of the plague that only the poor succumbed. Except Orlando Gibbons, the King's chapel organist, not a man of note so far had died — and Gibbons's family gave out that he had smallpox.) During the brief recess, a political incident had occurred which grounded all hope of accommodation between Buckingham and the Commons. Eight ships of the Navy were lent to France; Louis used them to fight rebellious Huguenots in the maritime town of New Rochelle. Their English crews mutinied, swearing they would rather hang than be slaves to the French. Buckingham protested that Richelieu and Louis XIII, not the Commons of England, had paid for the expedition. Parliament did not believe it. The remainder of the session — twelve days — was no more than a protracted argument against granting further monies to the Crown. "It is not Parliamentary," Coke told the House, "to engraft subsidies upon subsidies." Trade, he said, was interrupted by reason of the pestilence, the nation could not afford such payments. Examples from ancient times taught what happened when the people were too far pressed. Such treatment brought rebellions; collectors had been slain. Since the Parliament of 1624, three subsidies and three fifteens had been collected.

Where had the money gone? demanded Coke. Where was the leakage in the ship of state? He would tell them where! In disorders of the royal household, frauds of the King's officers and servants, excess of pensions and annuities, the setting up of Spanish leagues and treaties. Above all, there was mismanagement in the Navy. "The office of Lord Admiral is the place of greatest trust and experience. The wisdom of ancient times was to put great men into places of great title, but men of parts into such places as require experience. Young and unskillful men are not to be trusted with such great offices, and besides, multiplicity of offices held by one man is a great prejudice. There were no dukes in England between the Conquest and Edward III's time. Were I to go to sea, I had rather go with a man that had been once on the seas, able to guide and manage a ship or fleets, than with him that had been times at the haven. It was never heard that Queen Elizabeth's navy did dance a pavane — so many men 'pressed, and to lie so long without doing anything."

Coke's speech, said Sir John Eliot, "for scope, gravity and weight had a prodigious effect." Sir Edward had not mentioned the Duke's name, there was no need to mention it. Coke probed into matters of commerce and finance, suggested remedies. The King's rents should be raised, waste grounds enclosed for tillage. His Majesty owned thirty-one forests — besides his parks — which yielded "nothing but a charge." Yet in the whole oration, the phrase that galled at court was the one about England's Navy dancing a pavane. Everybody knew the dance — grave, slow, with performers specially and elaborately costumed. A courtier member of the Commons jumped up and denied Coke's accusation; the Royal Navy was doing good service, he said. Edward Clarke was the member's name. The House quite literally howled him down, set him on his knees and made him beg forgiveness. A few days later, Coke offered to give a thousand pounds from his private purse rather than vote another subsidy, "and that willingly notwithstanding all my crosses, and I would hope that those of the King's Council would do as much."

There was an extraordinary spirit in the House, a contagious excitement that carried over from day to day. More was at stake than the mere voting of money. "We are the last monarchy in Christendom," said Phelips, "that retain our original rights and constitutions. Let us not perish now!" Sir John Eliot compared the early and latter days of James's reign. While Cecil lived and statesmen bred by Elizabeth were in his Majesty's service, honors were not for sale, the laws were executed, the Council table kept its ancient dignity, and no man held power such as "in himself to be master of all business."

On August eleventh, Speaker Crewe stepped down and the House went into Committee of the Whole to prepare a remonstrance, telling his Majesty plainly that whoever had put the kingdom into such hazard must be made to answer for it. The Chairman, next morning, was reading the clauses aloud when Glanville hurried into the room. There would be no time to finish the remonstrance, he said. Almost immediately, a knock sounded at the door. It was Black Rod, the royal messenger, with the word that meant dissolution. Speaker Crewe rose to resume his place but the House bade him stay. Black Rod waited outside. A new, brief protestation, put together by Glanville, was read and passed on. Veiled and ineffectual (Parliaments cannot move in haste), it merely reiterated "the true and hearty affections of his Majesty's poor Commons," and declared them ready "in a Parliamentary way," to "discover and reform the abuses and grievances of the realm and state."

Once more, the issue was postponed. Members from the shires, riding home, once more must meet "their countries" with negation, a tale of nothing done and the Duke's power undiminished.

CHAPTER THIRTY-THREE

The Five Knights' Case and habeas corpus. Coke's last Parliament (1628). The Petition of Right.

SIR EDWARD was banished from the Parliament of 1626 — "this great, warm and ruffling Parliament," Whitelocke called it. Charles achieved Coke's exclusion by the strategy of pricking him for High Sheriff of Buckinghamshire. A Sheriff's oath bound the incumbent to keep within his bailiwick for a year; Sir Edward must remain at Stoke House. Coke tried hard to escape. He could not take the Sheriff's oath, he said; it contained a clause against Lollardy. Was not Lollard but another name for Protestant? (Little Bilney, burned in Norwich Ditch, had been a Lollard.) But Privy Council, foiled once before in keeping Coke from Parliament, this time persisted. They consulted the judges, who declared that the offensive clause could be omitted from the oath.

There remained only acquiescence; such service to the King could not be refused. Coke was sworn and with him six powerful opposition men who had been pricked for Sheriff,* among them Wentworth, Phelips and Alford. "It is thought," wrote a cousin of the Duchess of Buckingham, "that the house is but weake for all the gloss they set of themselves, for ther is three score or fouer score culled out of the house, olde Parliament men with Sir Edward

* Sheriffs' names were "pricked" by the King's pen on the list presented to him — a word still in use. The offensive clause in the oath was as follows: "You shall do all your pain and diligence to destroy and make to cease all manner of heresies and errors commonly called Lollaries within your bayliwick from time to time, to all your powers."

Cooke. Me Lorde the Duke was never in so greate favor, never so confidant."

Sir Edward went home to Stoke and prepared for his duties as Sheriff — a position by no means inconsiderable. He must collect fines and fees for royal justice, preside over the county court and be responsible for the execution of royal writs. It was the Sheriff's part to entertain distinguished visitors passing through his county, foreign ambassadors and ministers, or the King himself if he came by on progress. Twice a year, the Sheriff rode out with his train to greet the Judges of Assize, betweentimes to meet such commissioners as might be sent down from the law courts. Only noblemen or gentlemen of means were pricked for Sheriff; a poor man could not support the retinue. The Sheriff of Lancashire, for instance, had seventy-six gentlemen and servants in livery, besides a household staff of fifty-six, counting watchmen and "twenty men to attend on the prisoners each day by turns." There is no reason to think that Coke kept lesser state.

Had it not been for the circumstances — an honorable but frustrating banishment — Coke might have enjoyed his duties. There was drama in it and irony. At seventy-four the old Judge rode out, white staff in hand, gold chain about his neck, to greet his one-time Brethren at the border and escort them to the shire court at Aylesbury, then home to Stoke House for hospitality. Up the long narrow lane from the highway they came, judges, lawyers, clerks — past Henry Coke's farm, where Sir Edward's grandchildren played each day among the trees, past servants bowing by tall wrought-iron gates that led to lawn and portico. Sir James Whitelocke was a Judge of King's Bench now; old Doddridge, "the sleeping Judge," remained in office. Whoever was chosen to ride the Buckinghamshire circuit knew Sir Edward well, knew why he was at Stoke rather than Westminster and brought him bulletins fresh from the House of Commons.

Parliament had determined to impeach the Duke of Buckingham. "The Cause of Causes," it was called in the *Commons Journals*. Thirteen articles were drawn up: The Duke had bought his great offices of Lord Admiral and Warden of the Cinque Ports; he had neglected to guard the Narrow Seas until shipping was ruined by pirates. Disaster at Cadiz was caused by his failure to appoint competent officers; he had lent English ships to the French King for use against Protestant Rochelle; he had sold places of judicature and titles of honor, and had enriched his kinsmen at the expense of the King's revenue; he had applied remedies to King James in his last illness, "an act of transcendant presumption and dangerous consequences."

When moderate members deplored and the timid viewed with alarm, Clem Coke rose in his place and exclaimed, "Better to die by an enemy than to suffer at home!" It was one of those remarks, neither very brilliant nor very telling, upon which men take hold in troubled times, repeating for their comfort. Sir Edward must have feared for his son's safety. A seditious speech! said Charles in a sharp message, implying that the Commons themselves would punish Clem. When the House did nothing, the Lord Keeper again rebuked them. Let the Commons "yield obedience to his Majesty's directions as formerly received, and cease this unparliamentary inquisition."

But the Commons would not let go. With the articles of impeachment ready in hand, they voted, 225 to 106, to have the Duke committed to prison, pending trial — a resolution altered, on second thoughts, to "safe custody." Eight Commons members, entitled Managers, reported the articles formally in the House of Lords: Eliot, Noye, Selden, Pym, Glanville, Sir Dudley Digges: an impressive group. Eliot and Digges especially were fearless, speaking their minds as they chose. Next day, sitting in their usual places in the Lower House, the two were called out of the room. In the hall they found an officer with a warrant from the King to carry them to the Tower.

So quietly were the two spirited away that it was some time before the Commons discovered they were gone. Tumult ensued, shouts of "Rise, rise!" That afternoon, members gathered informally in Westminster Hall to speak gravely of this new threat to their liberties. Thirty-six peers signed a paper, protesting that Digges had said nothing contrary to the King's honor. Charles thereupon released Sir Dudley; he could not do less. The Commons however refused to do further business until Eliot was restored to them. Charles, endeavoring to pin the imprisonment on to acts committed outside of Parliament, had Eliot's chambers searched and the prisoner closely examined in the Tower. Nothing treasonable could be found. Within the week, Eliot returned to his seat. Plainly, the King dared not risk the loss of subsidies; he was moreover in difficulties with the Lords concerning one of their members who had been committed.

On the eighth of June — Parliament had convened in February — Buckingham defended himself before the Upper House, answering each charge separately and with great skill. (His defense had been prepared by a Middle Temple barrister, Sir Nicholas Hyde.) "Who accused me?" the Duke demanded. "Common fame! Who gave me up to your Lordships? The House of Commons! The one is too subtle a body . . . the other too great for me to contest with. And I am confident, when my cause will be tried, neither the one nor the other will be found to be my enemy."

The Commons prepared a remonstrance begging for the Duke's dismissal, whom they believed "an enemy to both Church and State." To his Majesty and "the whole world," the House protested that any money they might give would, through "this great person," be turned to the hurt and prejudice of the kingdom, "as by lamentable experience we have found in those large supplies we have formerly and lately given."

At once the King replied that he would dissolve Parliament. The Lords begged for two days more. "Not a minute!" Charles said. On June fifteenth, before the Lords had time to pass upon the Duke's guilt or innocence, Parliament was dissolved. The King had saved Buckingham, but at vast expense to the Treasury; supply had not been granted. Like his father before him, Charles persisted in thinking the Commons merely fractious. A handful of ambitious demagogues — by no means representative of the nation — desired to usurp powers for which they were not fitted by birth. The people were incapable of governing. Profoundly, Charles believed it, he would never change. James too had believed it. Yet in James's time Parliament had not been ready; rather than acting, they had grieved. It was to be Charles's tragedy that he could not see the heightened stature of his Commons, could not recognize that Parliament had come of age. And it was the country's tragedy that they could not reach their King, nor would the death of Buckingham bring them nearer.

Charles's predecessors had not thought it necessary to answer to Parliament for acts done by the Crown. Should he consent so to answer, in Charles's mind he would fail the dignity and power of kingship. *The people were incapable of governing.* As sure of it as of his own divine right to rule, this second Stuart, "surprised and indignant to the last," would repeat his belief at that final hour on the scaffold: "For the people . . . I must tell you that their liberty and freedom consists in having of government those laws by which their life and their goods may be most of their own. It is not having share in government, sirs. That is nothing pertaining to them."

The present problem was how to raise funds without Parliament. Lacking trained forces and proper supply for men and ships, Charles had embroiled himself in leagues and martial alliances over half of Europe. A treaty with the Dutch against Spain had inspired the ill-fated Cadiz expedition of 1625. (Ralegh and Essex once had taken Cadiz, but Buckingham's crews were sick and starved, serving under ignorant captains in ships with tackle so old that some of it had been used against the Armada in '88.) Charles moreover had promised his uncle, Christian of Denmark, £30,000 a month for support in a German campaign. Parliamentary gentlemen, eager for the Protestant cause, yet better farmers than military strategists and naïvely ignorant of foreign policies, looked on Spain as Elizabeth's sole enemy against the Palatinate, forgetting Austria and the Emperor. Pirates were ruining the coastal fishing trade, a threat more immediate than anything that might occur in Austria. Why did not government spend its money to protect East Anglia from "Turks and Dunkirkers?" France, since the royal marriage, might have been expected to help in the Palatinate. Yet under Buckingham's influence, French goodwill was oozing rapidly away. Irritated by his wife's Gallic attendants, Charles sent them all home — contrary to the marriage contract — thereby deeply offending his father-in-law, who at best was reluctant to engage in war with Spain. Richelieu did what he could to keep the peace. But a French ship, carrying contraband to the Spanish Netherlands, was seized by English frigates. France retaliated and the two countries found themselves at war.

To raise money, Charles tried every device a distracted Treasury could think of. Two Parliaments had sat since his accession; neither had passed the customary act to grant him tonnage and poundage. Crown lawyers now assured the King that these receipts, being traditional, might be levied without parliamentary sanction. Let it be assumed that Parliament, had it sat longer, would have voted favorably. A like policy, even less plausible, was pursued with subsidies. The Parliament of '26 had "resolved" that the Crown needed five subsidies, a proportion larger than ever before considered. But the Commons had not voted; no bill went through. Charles now sent collectors through the country "with the same rigour," wrote Clarendon, "as if, in truth, an Act had passed to that purpose." To ensure success, the King cleared away all justices of the peace who might oppose collection: Eliot, Alford, Mansell, Digges, Wentworth. The last-named happened to be presiding in his Yorkshire court when the royal messenger arrived; Sir John Savile, a hated rival, had been given the place. For Middlesex County, collection was attempted in Westminster Hall. "There arose a great tumultuous shout," said a newswriter. "A Parliament! A Parliament! or else no subsidies."

In the past, individuals had more than once refused forced contributions. One nobleman — Lord Saye — in 1622 declared he "knew no law, besides Parliament, to compel men to give away their goods." Peacham and Oliver St. John in 1614 had done the same and gone to jail for it. But individuals could be easily dealt with. Now whole counties turned their backs on the collectors — Norfolk, Cumberland, Lincolnshire, Kent. Subsidies without Parliament, they said outright, were against the law of the realm. The Treasury tried the device of loans on the King's Privy Seal and failed again. "All such projects," noted Thomas Fuller, "to quench the thirst of the king's necessities proved no better than sucking bottles — soon emptied, and but cold the liquor they afforded. Nothing so natural as the milk of the breast; I mean, subsidies granted by Parliament." The religious issue swung again to the fore. Charles's favor to his anti-Calvinist Bishops and clergy offended Puritans until even the more lenient held back from giving.

In the autumn of 1626, two Knights — Sir Francis Barrington the Parliament man and his son-in-law, Sir William Massam — refused to serve as collectors in their county and were imprisoned. Westminster judges, though they had already contributed out of their pockets, now refused to sign the loan book. They would not set their names, they said, to a measure they considered contrary to law. The King sent for them. The Chief Justice of King's Bench, Sir Randolph Crewe, stood to his refusal. Angrily, Charles told him that he was deprived of office. The rest of the judges said they would sign if it were understood they did it out of courtesy to his Majesty, not as warrant of their approval. In Crewe's place, Charles at once appointed Sir Nicholas Hyde, the barrister who had written Buckingham's parliamentary defense against impeachment.

In the country, the effect was prodigious. Fifteen peers now joined the Refusers. Some, who had already signed the subscription, declared the judges' opinion absolved them from payment. In Northamptonshire, twenty-two of the leading gentry refused; in Gloucestershire, twelve out of twenty-five commissioners for collection. "Many are imprisoned daily," wrote a diarist (March, 1627), "for refusing to lend the king, and it's thought they shall be sent and imprisoned in divers gaols in the country, remote from their own dwelling." Nevertheless, money came into the Treasury. The price of refusal was too great for general rebellion; small, obscure refusers were impressed for the Navy, taken from their homes and sent to fight in France or Germany.

The Duke, forever sanguine, imagined that one dazzling military coup would remedy everything. From time to time he managed to seize a French merchant ship, obtaining money to pay at least a part of his troops. In June of 1627, embarking as Commander, he took a naval expedition against the Island of Rhé, was gone four months and returned in total defeat. At Plymouth, told of a plot to murder him, he shrugged it off, refused to protect himself on the journey to London. If his enemies thought him frightened, he would never be safe, he said. Charles welcomed him warmly and sent out a proclamation blaming the disaster at Rhé on delay in sending supplies to the ships. But the country found itself overrun with soldiers, hungry, unpaid, billeted on the people. Householders who would not take in the soldiers were punished. Sailors roamed London streets, crying out that the Duke had cheated them of their pay.

Shortly after Buckingham's return, there came to King's Bench the celebrated suit known to history as the *Case of the Five Knights*.* Formerly, the dozens of gentlemen who had been imprisoned as Refusers to the loan had sat in jail, writing letters to their wives and helplessly awaiting events. Five of them — Darnel,

* To contemporaries it was "Darnel's Case," or the "suit for the knights in their *habeas corpus*."

Corbet, Hampden (Sir Edmund), Heveningham and Earl — now sued out their habeas corpus in the court of King's Bench. On November twenty-second they were brought to the bar and their case argued by four lawyers of great ability, among them Selden and Noye. The King had a right to imprison subjects on suspicion; counsel could not argue against it. But cause of committal must be expressed, said Selden, so that when the matter came to court, the judges could either bail or remand (return) the accused to prison. In support of this doctrine, Magna Carta and other ancient statutes were quoted. Attorney General Heath, for the Crown, argued *reason of state:* men, even though innocent, could be dangerous enough so that custody was indicated. In other cases, persons charged with serious crimes must be imprisoned while the facts were being ascertained. Witness the dangerous plotters of Elizabeth's time. Elizabeth's judges, said Heath, had declared the Crown need not show cause for sending a man to prison.

Chief Justice Sir Nicholas Hyde was in a quandary. Tudor sovereigns since Henry VIII had issued forced loans and flung Refusers into jail when they chose — yet never before on such a scale, with the whole country roused. The Crown now pleaded legal precedent and practice; Selden pleaded fundamental law and the ancient charters of the land. England, urged Selden, was not Spain; men could not be kept in durance indefinitely without showing cause. The Five Knights moreover were considerable landowners, gentlemen of probity, property and Protestantism, who paid their debts, fed the poor of their parishes and had the support not only of their counties but — as the trial made obvious — of most of London as well. "Gentlemen recusants of the loan," the prisoners were called. Westminster Hall was crowded as if the hearings had been the play about Gondomar. Counsel for the prisoners, when their turn came, "pleaded with great applause," said a newswriter, "even of shouting and clapping of hands, which is unusual in that place."

Nevertheless, the Five Knights lost their case. (By the time it was over, there were only four knights. Darnel, terrified, withdrew his plea.) Judge Anderson's *Reports*, said Hyde, gave the deciding precedent which overrode all previous precedents of charter and ancient statute: In the 34th year of Elizabeth (1594) all twelve judges had declared that "a prisoner committed *per speciale mandatum* . . . at the King's command . . . was not bailable and cause for committal need not be shown." When a man is imprisoned by the King and cause given, he is bailable. But if the cause be not specified, the offense probably is too great for the general knowledge, dangerous for public discussion, perhaps not fit to be divulged for other reasons, or for the people to meddle with. "In brief," reported a newswriter, "the gentlemen are remanded to prison and there like to lie by it."

Nothing less than a Parliament could rescue the Five Knights; their lawyers needed the force of the realm behind them. Fortunately for the prisoners, the royal Treasury also needed a Parliament, though Charles demurred: "the very name was a bugbear unto him. Parliaments," he said, "are of the nature of cats. They ever grow cursed with age." Buckingham, sanguine as ever, proposed an attack on Calais in the spring — a hundred sail to be sent out, perhaps a standing army of eleven thousand established at home. £500,000 would be required. But with the jails full of Refusers, with principal gentry banished from their counties and popular feeling hot in their support, to call a Parliament would be awkward to say the least. In January, 1628, all prisoners for the loan were freed, including the Five Knights. Charles gave orders that writs be issued for a Parliament to assemble in March.

Elections went hard against the Crown. Every Refuser who ran was returned, including twenty-seven who had suffered imprisonment. The excluded sheriffs of the last Parliament were elected, some by double returns, as Alford for Colchester and Steyning, Coke as county member for Suffolk and Bucks. Coke's *Vade Mecum* bore a special note in Latin: "*Rara electus est* . . . It is rare when any knight is elected from two counties." Sir Thomas Wentworth defeated his court rival, Sir John Savile, who had been put in his place as Justice of the Peace. In London, excitement mounted. Recorders of the City traditionally were elected to Parliament. Yet Recorder Heneage Finch, though he had been Speaker in '26, lost because he had shown no sympathy with the Refusers. Buckingham desired his Steward, Sir Robert Pye, to be Burgess for Westminster. Neither money nor influence could achieve it, though election meetings, noisy, turbulent, lasted for three days. "When Sir Robert's party cried, 'A Pye! A Pye!' the adverse party would cry, 'A Pudding! A Pudding! A Pudding!' 'A lie! A lie! A lie!' " Sir Robert was defeated "by above a thousand voices."

It was to be an extraordinary Parliament, one of the two most celebrated in English history. The roster of names is glorious. Selden and Noye were there, who had argued for the Five Knights. Pym came in from Tavistock, Sir Dudley Digges from Kent, Sir John Eliot from the county of Cornwall. Mr. Oliver Cromwell, Esquire, aged thirty-three, sent up by the Puritans of Huntington as Burgess, took his place quietly among the steeple hats and short cloaks, his cousin Hampden not far off. On the right front benches were only three Privy Councilors. No more had been returned; the King was poorly represented. "The House of Commons," reported a news-writer on March twenty-first, "was both yesterday and to-day as full as one could sit by another. And they say it is the most noble, magnanimous assembly that ever those walls contained; and I heard a lord estimate that they were able to buy the upper house . . . thrice over, notwithstanding there be of lords temporal to the number of 118. And what lord in England would be followed by so many freeholders as some of those are?"

When the Upper House convened, five members were absent: Archbishop Abbot, Bishop Williams (no longer Lord Keeper), the Earls of Arundel, Bristol, Lincoln. Quickly the Peers made inquiry; in a few days the missing members appeared. All had been under restraint; the Lords, too, knew the taste of punishment. Charles's new-preferred Bishop, William Laud (no lover of Puritans), preached the opening sermon; his text, "Endeavor to keep the unity of the spirit in the bond of peace." The King's speech was short, his stammer would not let him dare orations. The common danger, he said, was the cause of this Parliament; supply, the chief end of it. If every man did not do his duty, then he as sovereign must use other means which God had put into his hands. "Take not this as a threatening, for I scorn to threaten any but my equals."

To Charles the common danger lay abroad, across the Channel — a definition which Parliament did not share. It was the enemy at home — Clem Coke had said it — from whom the people now suffered. Recent Parliaments had impeached and punished. After Cranfield's fall, an angry courtier had remarked that Sir Edward Coke "would die if he could not help to ruin a great man once in seven years." Actually, it had not been Cranfield, Bacon, Yelverton or even Buckingham that Coke and the Commons fought. Rather they struggled (if perhaps unconsciously) to force crown officers into a sense of responsibility toward Parliament. Quite palpably, they failed of their objective. Beyond the suppression of monopolies, impeachment had achieved little. Given fertile soil, one bad man grows up in another's place. Yelverton was back in office, raised by Charles to be a Judge of Common Pleas. Mompesson lived comfortably at home, Cranfield had been pardoned by the King. The great Duke remained *Parliament-proof*, as he had boasted.

In the past two years, Englishmen had suffered extraordinary attacks upon their personal liberties. Nothing comparable could be remembered — men imprisoned for refusing unlawful levies of money or the billeting of soldiers in their houses; the principal gentry summoned by hundreds to answer in Council Chamber, many kept from their homes and counties. Martial law was necessary, to keep troops under discipline. Yet martial law, if stretched too far, became a tyranny and must be checked. This Parliament might well be England's last, and the nation turn to arbitrary government, as every great nation on the Continent had turned. A plan of action was urgently necessary. Four days before the session opened, at a meeting in Sir Robert Cotton's house it was decided to avoid Buckingham's name for the moment, avoid even the question of "conscience and religion," which meant Protestantism versus Roman Catholicism, versus also the High Church doctrines of Bishop Laud, Charles and Buckingham. Coke, Phelips, Wentworth and Sir John Eliot were among those present. Liberty of person, they decided, must be the theme of this Parliament: the right of subjects against imprisonment without cause expressed, their right against banishment, against foreign service without consent.

How these matters were to be accomplished, the men in Cotton's library did not know, or whether they could be accomplished. The Five Knights' Case had shown where the judges stood — Chief Justice Hyde, at any rate. To prove the King's power to imprison without cause, crown lawyers could marshal legal opinions and actual practice under the Tudors. Parliament must fall back upon the fundamental law, upon Magna Carta and the famous Chapter 39: "No freeman shall be taken or imprisoned or disseised of any free tenement or of his liberties or free customs, or outlawed or exiled, or in any other way destroyed, nor will we go upon him nor send upon him, except by the lawful judgment of his peers or by the law of the land. To no one will we sell, to no one will we refuse or delay, right or justice." Against the exaction of forced loans, other statutes existed. The fact that kings had subverted them did not annul these ancient agreements. Bracton, said Coke, had declared an act against Magna Carta to be void. Parliament, in this emergency, must go above the statutes, appeal beyond the laws to The Law, to that universal right which Englishmen claimed as their inheritance. Scripture declared that it was against reason to send a man to prison without cause.*

The practical problem was whether to proceed by bill, petition, resolution or remonstrance. Petitions to his Majesty's grace and clemency were, after all, no more than a confession of weakness. Coke and Wentworth were for attempting a bill — a law confirming the ancient rights of the subject. If the King showed himself against it — which meant eventual veto — then other means must be found. Possible procedure would have to be thrashed out in committee and by conference with the Lords. Parliament must be educated to the problem and would be, unless the King prevented it by dissolution. Commons and Lords were well aware of their wrongs — but not of the remedies for wrong. In the end, failing passage of a bill, sheer weight of concerted conviction might do the trick and the King be touched at heart no matter in what form the protest was presented.

On Monday, March twenty-second, the Commons met for business. "This," Sir Benjamin Rudyerd told them, "is the crisis of Parliaments. We shall know by this if Parliaments live or die. . . . Men and brethren, what shall we do? Is there no balm in Gilead? If the King draw one way, the Parliament another, we must all sink." A magnificent orator, Rudyerd could portray gloom as only the silver-tongued can do. Coke rose next. At seventy-six, he stood up in his place with the sturdy confidence of an old man who has lived through trouble and danger and has seen bad days turn to better. "The estate is inclining to a consumption," he said, "yet not incurable. For this disease I will propound remedies. I will seek nothing out of mine own head, but from my heart and out of Acts of Parliament. . . . The King cannot tax any by way of loans. . . . I'll begin with a noble record, it cheers me to think of it. *25 Edward III;*

* For it seemeth to me unreasonable to send a prisoner, and not withal to signify the crimes laid against him." (Acts 25, 27). Coke did not quote this as Roman law but as Scripture.

it is worthy to be written in letters of gold: 'Loans against the will of the subject are against reason and the franchises of the land.' . . . What a word is that *franchise!* It is a French word, and in Latin it is *libertas*. In Magna Charta it is provided that *Nullus liber homo . . .*"

Coke quoted the clause in Latin: "*Nullus liber homo . . . imprisonetur . . . nisi . . . per . . . legem terrae.*" The Great Charter had been confirmed, Coke added, "by thirty good Kings and thirty good Parliaments." As debate proceeded, Coke and Selden explained that "*lex terrae,* the law of the land," meant process of law. Law never put a man in prison, but only process of law. When a man is committed on suspicion, his offense must be in himself, not merely in the King's mind. "For the gentlemen in their *habeas corpus,*" * said Selden earnestly, "I was of counsel, and then I spoke for my fee. Yet now I speak according to my knowledge and conscience. I think, confidently, it belongs to every subject that he ought to be bailed, or delivered."

None disputed the Englishman's right to his property, his goods, lands and inheritance. "*Meum* and *tuum,*" put in Sir Dudley Digges, "the law preserves as sacred, the nurse of industry, the mother of courage; for if a man hath no property, he has no care to defend it." Yet a man's person, it seemed, had become less secure than his goods. "Shall I," Coke demanded, "be made a tenant-at-will for my liberties, having property in my own house but not liberty in my person? There is no such tenure in all Littleton! . . . I leave it as bare as Aesop's crow. It is a maxim, *The common law hath admeasured the King's prerogative,* that in no case it can prejudice the inheritance of the subjects. It is against law that men should be committed and no cause shown. I would not speak this, but that I hope my gracious King will hear of it. Yet it is not I, Edward Coke, that speaks it but the records that speak it."

Debate hinged, actually, on the judges' decision in the Five Knights' Case. John Selden declared that judgment had never been enrolled, never entered in the records — which meant decision was not final and could not stand as precedent. On questioning various clerks of the court, Selden discovered further that Attorney General Heath had made his own draft of judgment and given it to a clerk for "special entry." The clerk had taken it to the judges, who

* The Five Knights.

refused to enter it. Witnesses of these proceedings being brought to the Commons, Coke interjected sourly that only one thing had prevented entry of judgment — fear of the coming Parliament. "A Parliament brings judges, officers and all men into good order." The four Justices of King's Bench, summoned now to the Upper House, defended their denial of bail but admitted that judgment had not been final. "We did remit them [to prison] only that we might better advise the matter. They might have renewed their *habeas corpus* next day had they pleased." Plainly, the court was pinched between Crown and Parliament. (No one had advised the prisoners to renew their writ; they had been returned to prison for a stay of ten weeks.) The court, Chief Justice Hyde told the Upper House, had only done as their predecessors on the bench had done in like case, who "sometimes bailed, sometimes remitted, sometimes discharged." The judges knew of no statute that could have delivered the prisoners.

There was danger the decision might still be enrolled, if his Majesty pressed the matter. "The draft of this judgment," said Coke, "should it be entered, will sting us all to death. What is this but to declare upon record that any subject, committed by such absolute command, may be detained in prison forever? What doth this tend to but the utter subversion of the choice liberty and right belonging to every freeborn subject of this kingdom?"

Attorney General Heath declared that the only way the Knights could have been bailed was by petition to the King. Selden, Coke, Littleton, Digges threw the words back in his teeth, setting their reliance on statutes cited, but mainly on Magna Carta and the writ of habeas corpus. With this last they must have known they were on thin ground. Actually, habeas corpus was a simple writ designed originally for nothing more than bringing into court those persons needed in proceedings. Its use by men claiming unjust imprisonment was only just emerging.* Coke's *Book of Entries* (1614) cited the writ in its more modern form: *Habeas cum causa* . . . "to have the body together with the cause of detention" — a striking change from older entries. The hazard of Coke's stand was dramatically illustrated by the fact that out of some hundred knights im-

* It would be 1679 bfeore a statute confirmed the power of Chancellor and judges to issue habeas corpus in term time or out, enabling subjects confidently to claim the writ against King and Council.

prisoned as Refusers, only five had dared to sue out their habeas corpus, and one of these retreated.

In the midst of debate on this vital subject, Coke, whose business was to cite precedents and explain them to the House, suffered a startling setback when the Solicitor General suddenly cited Sir Edward against himself. As Chief Justice, Coke had declared in a suit of 1616 (shortly before his dismissal) that the prisoners having been committed by order of Privy Council, the cause might be "*arcana regni*, or mystery of state, and need not be disclosed." Moreover, as Solicitor General in 1592, Coke had quoted the renowned Judge Stamford to the effect that "if Privy Council commit one, he is not bailable by any court of justice."

The Solicitor General, a lawyer of shrewd ability and energy, flourished the two statements triumphantly before the Commons. Taken aback, Coke floundered, blustering a little. Since the days of his Attorneyship under Elizabeth — since the time indeed of his Chief Justiceship — Sir Edward had changed his views more than he perhaps realized or had care to face. Attorney Generals do not think as Parliament men think, and a Privy Councilor may look east when a Commons man looks west. Coke believed that Stamford should be overruled. Two days after the Solicitor General's attack, Sir Edward rose in his place and without apology reversed himself, speaking with the rough simplicity of his years (at seventy-six, a man has no time left for flourishes): "I have not *veritatem ex cathedra*, or infallibility of spirit. I confess that when I read Stamford then [1616] and had it in my hands, I was of that opinion at the Council table. But when I perceived that some members of this House were taken away, even in the face of this House, and sent to prison, and when I was not far from that place myself, I went to my book and would not be quiet till I had satisfied myself. Stamford at the first was my guide, but my guide deceived me, therefore I swerved from it. I have now better guides. I have looked out precedents and Statutes of the Realm, whereby I am satisfied that such commitments are against the liberty of the subject. I desire to be free of the imputation that is cast upon me."

Phelips and Selden, in the meantime, had been busy on a legal committee to investigate the Commons' records and precedents as quoted. They rose now with their report. Judicial opinions, said Phelips (referring to Stamford), were but servants of the law; where anything was done against the statutes, it ought not to hold. "Sir Edward Coke is *Monarcha Juris*, King of the Law. And though it hath been the pleasure of the state to remove him from the King's Bench here, I hope he shall have a place in the King's Bench in heaven." With obvious affection, Selden echoed his colleague. "I shall be a little free," he said, "and vindicate that great *Monarcha Juris*, Sir Edward Coke, from the imputation that was cast upon him."

This pleasant small interlude took place on March thirty-first.* Several days later, the Commons drew up four resolutions, strong, comprehensive, plain: no freeman to be imprisoned without cause shown, even at the King's command; habeas corpus not to be denied; a prisoner brought to court on habeas corpus must be either bailed or freed; no "tax, taillage, loan, benevolence" to be commanded or levied without consent by act of Parliament.

Digges, Littleton,* Selden and Coke were deputed as Managers to carry these resolutions to the Upper House. The four men spoke in the order given and with great ability. Selden set out precedent and statute in impressive array. "Your lordships," said Coke when his turn came, "have heard seven acts of Parliament in point, and thirty-one precedents summarily collected and with great understanding delivered; which I have perused and understand them all thoroughly, and that there was not one of them against the Resolution of the House of Commons. Twelve of them are the very end of finality,† a whole jury of precedents, and to my understanding, they admit of no answer. . . . If these acts of Parliament cannot persuade you, my lords, nothing can. The arguments being so well pressed to your lordships by my colleagues, I think your lordships may wonder what my part may be. It is short but sweet: it is the reason of all those laws and precedents. I am very sorry I am so much straitened for want of time, for I am much delighted with these things."

Coke went on to explain the legal remedies for a freeman falsely imprisoned: the writs *De odio et atia* (Of malice and hatred), *De homine replegiando* (Concerning the replevying of men) and *Habeas corpus*, to which Coke referred as *Corpus cum causa* — produce the body together with the cause of detention. A freeman

* See Chapter Note.
† Coke said it in Latin: "*in terminis terminantibus.*"

imprisoned, Sir Edward told the Lords, was less than a bondsman or villein; he was civilly dead. "And a prison without a prefixed time is a kind of hell." Committal at will and pleasure of the sovereign was dangerous both for king and kingdom. Nor could the King impose a fine. Only the judges might fine a man — and never in chambers privately; it must be done in court, with the other judges sitting. "The greatest inheritance that a man hath is the liberty of his person, for all others are accessory to it." Everything that he had said and all his reasons given came, Coke added, not from his head but from the records; he had no law but what, by great pains and industry, he had learned at his book. "For at ten years of age I had no more law than other men of like age." As for reasons of state and the objection that to reveal cause of imprisonment might in certain cases be dangerous — was not treason or felony, couched in general terms, cause enough for imprisonment? What end could secrecy serve? "Does not all Cheapside know it as one is carried to the Tower?"

It had been objected, said Coke, that if the law were so clear, what need a declaration and remonstrance? Answer lay in the Five Knights' Case. "The subject hath sued for remedy in King's Bench by *habeas corpus* and hath found none. Therefore it is necessary to be cleared in Parliament." Lords and Commons shared this hazard. "*Commune periculum requirit commune auxilium:* common danger requires mutual help. And therefore the House of Commons asked that their Lordships make a like Declaration with their own."

The Lords, however, were not quick to respond. "The greater part," reported a newswriter, "stand for the King's prerogative against the subjects' Liberties." Before the peers were ready to join in such resolutions they must hear more on the other side. Attorney General Heath was called in and with one of his aides, Serjeant Ashley, argued for the King. Between the two Houses, feeling grew warm. On Heath's suggesting that the liberties claimed by the Commons "might be moderated," Coke quoted from the scriptural story of the two harlots who came before Solomon: "The true mother would never consent to the dividing of her child." Buckingham chose to take offense. Did Sir Edward intimate that "the King his master, was a whore?" "Your Grace," Coke replied blandly, "misinterprets me."

Heath again questioned the Commons' precedents as presented.

Vehemently, Selden defended them. He had, he told his colleagues, written "all the records with his own hand out of the Tower, the Exchequer and the King's Bench; they were truly and properly inferred." Littleton, too, swore he had examined "every one *syllabatim* by the records." Whoever declared them carelessly copied or mutilated, spoke falsely. Coke was scornful. "Upon my skill in law," he told the House, "it lieth not under Mr. Attorney's cap to answer to any one of our arguments."

While the Commons awaited the Lords' answer to their resolutions, they discussed the bill for supply and resolved on five full subsidies. Eliot suggested that the messenger who informed his Majesty should say that "not fear but love hath been the cause of this cheerfulness." It was done. King Charles, grateful, sent an affectionate note, marred by the Duke's adding his own thanks at the end. The arrogance of this assumption of regality was almost too much to bear. No date had been fixed for collection of the subsidies — a matter almost as important as the amount itself. "When we send down the time," said Sir Thomas Wentworth, "let us be sure the subjects' liberties go hand in hand together. Let us resolve the time, but not report it to the House until we have a bill for our liberties."

"Hereupon," says the reporter, "the Committee of the Whole resolved, That grievances and supply go hand in hand."

By April twenty-fifth, the Lords were ready with their Propositions. There were five; Archbishop Abbot brought them formally to the Lower House. To the Commons the document must have come as a desperate disappointment. All of their hard work, all that Coke, Selden, Digges, Littleton had labored for in the Upper House, resulted only in timorous paragraphs, each one opening with the phrase, "His Majesty would be graciously pleased to declare." The whole was sugared with assurance of "his Majesty's royal prerogative, intrinsical to his sovereignty, and entrusted him withal from God," and the Lords' conviction concerning the rightness of things done for reasons of state.

Coke attacked the Propositions with a kind of cold savagery. Was Magna Carta then to be accorded confirmation as a matter of grace? "When the King doth a thing 'of grace,' it implies that it is not our right. *Lex terrae* is the common law of the land." And what was this "intrinsical" prerogative? "It is a word we find not much in the law. Admit this intrinsic prerogative and all our laws are out." By the Lords' third proposal, his Majesty ratified to his subjects their "several just liberties, privileges and rights." What then were "just" liberties, and who might determine between liberties just and unjust? In the fourth proposal, the common law must yield to martial law. "The great question will be," said Coke, "When is time of peace and when of war?" A half-war was difficult to define. "It is certain that when the courts of justice are sitting, is time of peace." In the fifth proposition, if the King for "matter of state" commit a man, he will express the cause *at a convenient time.* "Who," demanded Coke, "shall judge of convenient time?" The Propositions had been written by a churchman, Bishop Harsnet of Norwich. "We see," finished Sir Edward, "what an advantage they have that are learned in the law, in penning articles, above them that are not, how wise soever. There was never yet any pillars or maxims of the common law shaken but infinite inconveniencies have followed."

"I think," said Selden, "there is not one of the five [Propositions] fit to be desired and asked. Ours were resolutions of law. Their Lordships propound what they would have to be law."

In toto, the Commons rejected the Lords' proposals. "Reason of state," said Coke, "lames Magna Carta."

On the twenty-eighth of April, King Charles came to the House of Lords and calling for the Commons to stand at the bar, spoke through his Lord Keeper. The affairs of Christendom would wait no longer upon this Parliament. Delay, he had heard, was due to a debate "touching the liberty of the subject." To shorten the business he therefore declared his heart and intention: "He holdeth Magna Charta and the other six statutes insisted upon to be all in force. He will maintain all his subjects in the just freedom of their person and safety of their estates. You shall find as much security in his Majesty's royal word and promise as in the strength of any law ye can make. And therefore his Majesty desires that no doubt of distrust may possess any man, but that ye will all proceed unanimously to his business."

The Commons returned to their chamber, where the King's first Secretary of State* pleaded with them to trust the royal word. Mod-

* Sir John Coke, no relation to Sir Edward.

erates of the House agreed, pointing out that dissolution had been hinted at. By overreaching, the Commons might lose all. Nevertheless the House stuck to its determination. A committee was appointed, a bill drawn up. Next morning, Coke presented it to the Commons: *An Act for the better securinge of every free man touching the proprietie of his goods and libertie of his person.* "In this law," said Coke, before he read it out, "we have made no preamble. We desired our pen might be in oil, not in vinegar." The bill was short, no more than twenty lines. "*Be it enacted,*" each brief section began, leaving no doubt as to the form of actual statute. There was provision against taxation without parliamentary consent, against imprisonment without cause given, against billeting of soldiers without private consent, and a declaration that any freeman, "returned upon a *habeas corpus,* ought to be delivered or bailed." *

Coke finished reading and debate broke out at once. The bill was not sufficient — a mere recital of old laws, with no penalties attached for infraction by the King's officers. To force the judges to give bail upon habeas corpus, something stronger was needed. For Coke an act of Parliament overrode judicial power. "What if the judges remand or remit a man?" he asked roughly. "What is that to acts of Parliament? I was committed to the Tower, and all my books and study searched, and thirty-seven manuscripts were taken away. Thirty-four were restored and I would give three hundred pounds for the other three." After the fashion of a scholar, Coke named them: "Lambard's abreviat of the Tower Records, his abreviat of the ancient orders of Chancery, and a treatise on the government and laws of Ireland. . . . After," continued Coke, "I was inquired what I had done. When a man is committed, it is easy to find causes against him. Cause found after commitment, this is fearful!"

A second royal message, brief and to the point, interrupted debate. His Majesty desired the House "clearly to let him know whether they would rest upon his royal word and promise, made at several times, and especially by my Lord Keeper's speech made in his own presence."

The House was struck dumb. "Upon this," says the reporter, "there was a silence for some time." The Secretary of State stepped

* See Chapter Note for the bill in full.

forward with conciliatory words. They fell on deaf ears. Phelips rose. "To speak in a plain language," he said, "we are now come to the end of our journey." Painfully the House twisted and turned, seeking a way out. Impossible that they should trust the King; impossible also to pronounce the word of distrust. His Majesty, Coke suggested, perhaps referred to some earlier message when he spoke of his "royal word?" Let the House propose a bill as coming not from the Commons but from the King himself: "We will and grant for Us and our successors, that we and our Successors will do thus and thus. . . ." Of course, Wentworth put in tactfully, the House trusted in the King's goodness. "But we are ambitious that his Majesty's goodness may remain to posterity. We are accountable to a public trust, and seeing there hath been a public violation of the laws by his ministers, nothing can satisfy them but a public amends . . . vindication of the subjects' rights by bill."

Next day — Friday, May second — a third message was delivered by the Speaker: his Majesty renewed his promises to maintain his subjects in liberty. But he would countenance no "encroachings upon that sovereignty or prerogative which God hath put into his hands for our good." Let the Commons contain themselves within the bounds and laws of their forefathers, "without straining or enlarging them by new explanations or additions in any sort." He could delay no longer. If the House were not done with their business by Tuesday week, then "it shall be their own faults."

The Commons returned answer next morning, begging that they might proceed by way of bill. They had no wish to "strain or enlarge the former laws in any sort" nor to encroach on the prerogative. They desired only to make "some necessary explanation" of the just sense and meaning of old laws, "with some moderate provision for execution and performance . . . as in times past, upon like occasion hath been used."

The King's reply came back in short order. He had expected "answer by action, not delay by discourse." Yet he would be content if Magna Carta be confirmed by bill, so long as the Commons did not add to it, paraphrase or "explain it." What need explanations, unless the Commons doubted their King's word? "It may well be said, What need a new law to confirm an old, if you repose confidence in the declaration made by his Majesty to both Houses?"

Blandly, King Charles ignored the Five Knights' Case, the Commons' assumption that committal without cause was against Magna Carta and a freeman's right to trial. Such matters were to be left to his Majesty's clemency and kingly justice. Should the Commons — the message ended — "seek to tie their King by new and indeed impossible bonds, they must be accountable to God and the Country for the ill success of this meeting."

The Secretary of State pressed the House not to proceed by bill, even with the royal sanction, but rather to rely on his Majesty's word. He hoped the Commons would debate this question in full session, and not in committee. "It is a new course, to go into a Committee of the whole House." (Mr. Secretary was shrewd, the Committee of the Whole was a dangerous weapon. With the mace laid aside, members spoke as they chose, knowing their words would not go into the records.) "Proceeding in a Committee," Eliot countered quickly, "is more noble and advantageous both to the King and the House. For that way leads most to truth, as it is a more open way, where every man may add his reasons and make answer upon the hearing of other men's reasons and arguments."

Immediately, the House went into Committee of the Whole. The key to the doors was given in charge, "and none were to go out without leave first asked." More moderate members spoke against proceeding by bill. Let some other way be found, they said. Coke referred to the royal promises. "Was it ever known," he asked, "that general words were a sufficient satisfaction to particular grievances? When grievances be, the Parliament is to redress them. Did ever Parliament rely on messages? The King's answer is very gracious; but what is the law of the realm, that is the question! I put no diffidence in his Majesty; but the King must speak by record and in particulars — not in general. Did you ever know the King's message come into a bill of subsidies? All succeeding Kings will say, 'Ye must trust me as well as ye did my predecessors, and trust my messages.' . . . But messages of love never came into a Parliament. Let us put up a Petition of Right! Not that I distrust the King; but that I cannot take his trust but in a Parliamentary way."

No one doubted Coke's meaning. Every member was familiar with petitions of right, which differed from petitions of grace as right differs from clemency and pardon. Carew Ralegh (for instance) had brought to the Commons a petition for restitution of blood, following his father's attaint — a petition of grace, asking pardon by act of Parliament. But if a man had been wronged, if his fundamental rights had been subverted, he petitioned not for grace and pardon but for restitution or restatement of his rights — a very different matter. The thing that would set this petition apart was its public nature. It must be voted by both Houses as a bill is voted. And it must have the King's assent, given publicly before Lords and Commons assembled. In substance it would reiterate an Englishman's right to personal liberty, his security from arbitrary imprisonment without cause. It would reaffirm and explain Magna Carta and the great statute of *28 Edward I* (*De tallagio non concedendo*), declaring unequivocally that these laws and charters had of late been subverted. It would protest the billeting of soldiers upon the people and the exercise of martial law in time of peace, the exaction of forced loans and taxes without consent by act of Parliament. In the end the petition would pray his Majesty to command his officers and ministers to serve him according to the laws and statutes of the realm as so laid down.

On Thursday, May eighth, the petition was ready. Coke had been chosen to present it to the Lords at a conference in the Painted Chamber. "My Lords," he said, "I am commanded from the House of Commons to express their singular care and affection they have of concurrence with your Lordships in these urgent affairs. . . . If we had hundreds of tongues, we were not able to express that desire. My Lords, it is evident what necessity there is, both in respect of yourselves and your posterities, to have good success in this business. We have received divers messages from our great sovereign the King. My Lords, when we had these messages (I deal plainly, for so I am commanded by the House of Commons) we did consider what way we might go for our more secure way — nay, yours! We did think it the safest way to go in a Parliamentary course. For we have a maxim in the House of Commons and written on the walls of our House, *That old ways are the safest and surest ways*. . . . Therefore, my Lords, we have drawn a form of a Petition, desiring your Lordships to concur with us therein. We come with a unanimous consent of all the House of Commons. Your Lordships are involved in the same condition, *commune periculum*. So now I shall be bold to read that which we have so agreed on, and I shall desire your Lordships leave that I may read it."

Coke read the document to the committee, then left it with the Lords for debate and consultation. Five days later, on Monday, Lord Keeper Coventry asked for another conference. The Lords, he said, most affectionately desired good concurrence with the House of Commons. They had considered the Petition of Right and assented to the substance of it. But they had also considered "whether, retaining the substance, there might not be some words altered, or put in to make it more sweet, to procure it a passable way to his Majesty?" Even while the Lords were so debating, a message had come to them from the King.

The Lord Keeper read it aloud. His Majesty refused to relinquish his royal right to imprison without cause shown. To do so would "soon dissolve the very foundation and frame of our monarchy. Wherefore, my lords, we have thought good to let you know, that without the overthrow of sovereignty we cannot suffer this power to be impeached." It was not in the royal heart to extend his power "beyond the just rule of moderation, nor would he or his Council commit a man in any cause wherein our judgment and conscience is not satisfied — which base thoughts, we hope, no man can imagine will fall into our royal breast."

Coke met the Lords in committee. A letter or message, he told them, "is no answer in a Parliamentary way." He trusted their Lordships might reply to the King by joining with the Commons in the Petition of Right. After three days' hesitation, the Lords concurred, sending down the petition to the Lower House unchanged save for an added paragraph: "We humbly present this petition to your Majesty, not only with a care of preserving our own Liberties, but with due regard to leave entire that sovereign Power, wherewith your Majesty is trusted, for the Protection, Safety, and Happiness of your People." This small alteration, the Lord Keeper assured the Lower House, was "no breach of the frame," but propounded only "that the Petition might have the easier passage with his Majesty."

As soon as the Commons were alone they broke into dismayed speech. *To leave entire that sovereign power* — The seemingly innocent, courteous little phrase could nullify their petition. Alford, Pym, Hakewill, Wentworth, Noye, Eliot spoke in turn: "What is this 'sovereign power'? Let us give that to the King the law gives him, and no more. . . . We cannot admit the words with safety. . . . If we do admit of this addition, we shall leave the subject worse than we found him, and we shall have little thanks when we come home."

"To speak plainly," Coke said, "this will overthrow all our Petition. It trenches to all parts of it; it flies at loans, and at the oath, at imprisonment and at the billeting of soldiers. This turns all about again. Look unto the petitions of former times! They never petitioned wherein there was a saving of the King's sovereignty. I know that prerogative is part of the law, but *sovereign power* is no Parliamentary word. Should we now add it, we shall weaken the foundation of law and then the building must needs fall. Take heed what we yield unto! Magna Charta is such a fellow that he will have no sovereign. I wonder this 'sovereign' was not in Magna Charta, or in the confirmation of it? If we grant this, by implication we give a sovereign power above all these laws. 'Power,' in law, is taken for a power with force: '*The Sheriff shall take the power of the county*.' What it means here, God only knows. It is repugnant to our Petition that is a *Petition of Right*, grounded on acts of Parliament. We must not admit of it, and to qualify it is impossible. Let us hold our privileges according to the law."

Sir John Eliot showed his anger. Were the Commons, then, to be "mere ciphers of nobility? No! I am confident that should the Lords desert us, we should yet continue flourishing and green." The Lords, however, would not give in but persisted, clinging to their "saving words." Five days passed. The King sent two brief messages, urging haste. He had need of it, the City had refused him a loan. When Buckingham, as punishment, threatened to billet six hundred soldiers upon London, the Lord Mayor replied that the City "would resist them to blood" — a stand which, said a newswriter, "made the next day, Friday, more happy in Parliament." To strengthen the Upper House, Charles created six peers, among them Lord Keeper Sir Thomas Coventry. A newswriter reported "the great business in Parliament" to be doubtful because the "court faction" in the Lords was "numerous and increasing." Charles sent for the judges, asked their opinion concerning his right to imprison without cause shown. They replied cautiously. "By the general rule of law, cause ought to be shown. Yet some cases might require such secrecy that the King may commit without showing the cause, for a convenient time."

The Commons, meanwhile, used all art and persuasion to bring the Lords around. Concerning "sovereign power," Glanville and Sir Henry Martin suggested tactfully that the words were unnecessary. Did not members acknowledge the King's power when they took their oath at the Parliament door? "I (A, B) do utterly testify and declare in my conscience, that the King's Highness is the supreme Governor of this Realm in all causes, &c." To this skillful argument the Lords capitulated, but not until they had composed a declaration — separate from the petition — assuring his Majesty that the Lords did not intend "to lessen or impeach any thing, which by the Oath of Supremacy, we have sworn to assist and defend."

Remained only to complete the proceedings in due form. The petition received its third reading, exactly like a bill, was voted unanimously by both Houses and engrossed. To the Upper House, the Commons sent "most hearty thanks," adding that their Lordships "had not only dealt nobly with them in words but also in deeds." A deputation carried the document to Whitehall for Charles's initial perusal, the spokesman being rigorously instructed to say nothing more than that he acted on unanimous command of Parliament, then beg that "in respect of the great weight of the business, and for the more comfort of his loving people, his Majesty would be pleased to give his assent [to the Petition] in full Parliament."

On the second of June, the King came down to Parliament and took his seat on the throne. "Gentlemen," he said, "I am come hither to perform my promise. I think no man can think it long, since I have not taken so many days in answering the Petition as ye have spent weeks in framing it. And I am come hither to show you that, as well in formal things as essential, I desire to give you as much content as in me lies."

The Petition of Right was now read aloud: "Humbly shew unto our Sovereign Lord the King, the Lords Spiritual and Temporal and Commons in Parliament assembled: That whereas it is declared and enacted by a statute made in the time of the reign of King Edward the First, commonly called *Statutum de Tallagio non concedendo*, that no tallage or aid shall be laid or levied by the King or his heirs in this realm, without the goodwill and assent of the

Archbishops, Bishops, Earls, Barons, Knights, Burgesses and other the freemen of the commonalty of this realm . . . Yet nevertheless, of late, your people . . . have been required to lend certain sums of money unto your Majesty, and many of them upon their refusal, have been imprisoned, confined and sundry other ways molested and disquieted. . . . And where also by the statute called 'The Great Charter of the Liberties of England,' it is declared and enacted, that no freeman may be taken or imprisoned or be disseised of his freeholds or liberties . . . Nevertheless . . . divers of your subjects have of late been imprisoned without any cause shewed, and when for their deliverance they were brought before your justices by your Majesty's writs of *habeas corpus* . . . and their keepers commanded to certify the causes of their detainer; no cause was certified, but that they were detained by your Majesty's special command, signified by the Lords of your Privy Council, and yet were returned back to several prisons, without being charged with any thing to which they might make answer according to law. . . ."

On and on it went, the great roll and roster confirming the rights of Englishmen. Nothing was slurred over, nothing extenuated. About this petition was no fine language, no conscious "poetry" or philosophical argument concerning freedom and the soul of man. Penned by lawyers, it spoke the plain language of the common law: a practical instrument to keep innocent men out of prison, to relieve them if put there arbitrarily and to give each subject, whether innocent or guilty, his chance at trial. The petition could not be called a law; it did not include the law's penalty for infraction. (That would come later, in the year 1679.) Nevertheless it carried authority. The judges, Coke had said, must abide by it if the King gave consent in the traditional words: "*Soit droit fait comme il est desiré* . . . Let right be done as is desired."

Charles sat on his throne and listened, until the voice ceased with the words "that your Majesty would be graciously pleased . . . to declare your royal will and pleasure, That in the things aforesaid, all your ministers shall serve you according to the laws and statutes of this realm, as they tender the honour of your Majesty, and the prosperity of this kingdom."

Lords and Commons waited for the King's reply. It came through the Lord Keeper: "The King willeth that right be done according to the laws and customs of the realm and that the statutes be put in due execution, that his subjects may have no cause to complain of any wrong or oppressions, contrary to their just right and liberties: to the preservation whereof, he holds himself in conscience as well obliged, as of his prerogative."

The Commons had failed. The traditional word had not been spoken, *Soit droit fait.* The King had not so much as mentioned the petition, let alone answered it. His words were soothing but meaningless, as to children who must be comforted. He had conceded nothing. When the Commons met next day, Eliot rose and without once mentioning the Duke's name poured out a passionate catalogue of governmental mismanagement — the disasters at Cadiz, at Rhé and at Rochelle . . . an empty Treasury, crown lands sold, even the royal jewels pawned. . . . A Privy Councilor — Sir Humphrey May — cried out, bidding him halt. "Go on, go on!" the House shouted. "If he goes on," said May, "I hope that I may myself go out." "Begone! Begone!" was the reply. Coke suggested a remonstrance, telling the King direct of these great grievances. The House agreed, fixing tomorrow for discussion. The weapon of supply was still in their hands. The Commons, though they had "resolved" upon five subsidies, had not yet voted the amount.

Next day, however, the King sent a message: The session must end within a week; the Commons were to "proceed to business" (the subsidy) and "entertain no new matters." As though the royal message had not come, the House next morning went into committee for the remonstrance. They were interrupted by a second message: His Majesty willed the Commons to remember his word of yesterday, by which he had set a day to end the session. He would "certainly hold that day without alteration." Therefore he required "that they enter not into, or proceed with any new business . . . which may lay any scandal or aspersion upon the state-government, or ministers thereof."

Sitting in their ancient chapel of St. Stephen's, the Commons mourned as the exiled mourn, or those who have lost their country. Phelips was first to rise, his voice broken with emotion. "If ever my passions were wrought upon," he said, "it is now. I hear this with grief as the saddest message of the greatest loss in the world. I perceive that towards God and man there is little hope, after our humble and careful endeavors. We came hither full of wounds, and we have cured what we could. Yet what is the return of all but misery and desolation?"

Perhaps, Eliot suggested, there had been misrepresentation to the King? His Majesty had spoken of "some aspersion" cast on his ministers. "I am confident no minister, how dear soever, can —"

Before Buckingham's name could be pronounced, Speaker Finch started from his chair. Tears stood in his eyes and the House saw it. He had a command upon him, said the Speaker, "to interrupt any that should go about to lay an aspersion on the ministers of state."

Whereupon, says the reporter, *Sir John Eliot sat down.*

"Unless we may speak of these things in Parliament," Sir Dudley Digges began, "let us arise and be gone, or sit in silence. We are miserable, we know not what to do." *Hereupon there was a deep silence in the House for a while.* Sir Nathaniel Rich was first to break it. "We must speak now or forever hold our peace. Shall we now sit still and do nothing and so be scattered? Let us go to the Lords and show our dangers." Subdued, uneasy, members talked together. Eliot's speech must have given offense to the King. Timid members blamed him; others, more resolute, recalled the fact of Bacon's impeachment. Pym rose, tried to speak and wept outright; Coke followed with a like dramatic result. "Overcome with passion, and seeing the desolation likely to ensue, Sir Edward Coke was forced to sit down when he began to speak, through the abundance of tears. Yea, the Speaker in his speech could not refrain from weeping and shedding of tears, besides a great many whose great griefs made them dumb and silent. Yet some bore up in that storm and encouraged others."

"That black and doleful Thursday," a newswriter called it. "Such a spectacle of passions, as the like had seldom been seen in such an assembly, some weeping, some expostulating, some prophecying the fatal ruin of our kingdom; some playing the divines in confessing their own and country's sins, which drew those judgements upon us; some finding, as it were, fault with those that wept. I have been told by a parliament man that there were above an hundred weeping eyes."

It was an extraordinary scene. These men who wept outright

before their fellows were not the timid spirits of Parliament but members whose courage already had been tested, some of whom had suffered imprisonment for the cause. They wept from helplessness, frustration, a temporary loss of hope. By the King's message it would seem he stood against his subjects altogether and could not be separated from that man of evil who was at the root of all the kingdom's wrongs. At last it was decided to go into Committee of the Whole and discuss freely some plan of action. The doors were locked, order given that no man go out "upon pain of going to the Tower." Only Speaker Finch, "with tears flowing in his eyes," asked permission to leave the House "for half an hour." It was granted, though the Commons knew he must go straight to the King, perhaps return with orders for a dissolution. But the fact of his departure — perhaps the very desperateness of their situation — seemed to renew the courage of the House. Coke rose, speaking this time with his accustomed resoluteness. "We have dealt," he said, "with that duty and moderation that never was the like, after such violation of the liberties of the subject. Let us take this to heart."

What Coke said now was to be his last recorded speech on the liberty of the subject. He told of precedents in history where men had spoken out. A Parliament of Edward III had dared to name John of Gaunt — the King's own son — and members had gone to the Tower for it. Under Henry IV, two Parliaments had complained of the Privy Council. "Now, when there is such a downfall of the state, shall we hold our tongues? How shall we answer our duties to God and men? Why may we not name those that are the cause of all our evils? In the fourth year of Henry III and the twenty-seventh of Edward III and in the thirteenth of Richard II, the Parliament moderated the King's prerogative. Nothing grows to abuse but this House hath power to treat of it. What shall we do? Let us palliate no longer! If we do, God will not prosper us. And therefore, not knowing if I shall ever speak in this House again, I shall now speak freely. I think the Duke of Buckingham is the cause of all our miseries. And till the King be informed thereof, we shall never go out with honour or sit with honour here. That man is the grievance of grievances! Let us set down the causes of all our disasters and they will all reflect on him. Our liberties are now impeached, we are deeply concerned. As for going to the Lords, that is not *Via Regia*,* for the Lords are not participant with our liberties. It is not the King but the Duke that saith, '*We require you not to meddle with state government or the ministers thereof.*' . . ."

At the word "Duke," Sir Edward was interrupted by cries from all quarters of the House. "The Duke! The Duke! 'Tis he! 'Tis he!" "As when one good hound" (wrote a country member) "recovers the scent, the rest come in with a full cry, so we pursued it, and every one came on home, and laid the blame where he thought the fault was." The great name had been spoken at last; the block that held them back was shattered. "Let the charge [against Buckingham] be renewed!" said Selden.

As the clock in the tower struck eleven, Speaker Finch hurried into the chamber. "Had he not returned at that very moment," wrote Mead, "I hear it from a Parliament knight they had voted the Duke a traitor and arch enemy to the king and kingdom, with a worse appendix thereto." His Majesty, said Finch, adjourned the House until tomorrow, "all committees to cease in the meantime." A like message went to the Lords. But the Peers, this time, stood out. After brief conference with the Commons they dispatched a joint deputation to ask his Majesty for "a clear and satisfactory answer," given in full Parliament, to their Petition of Right.

Long ago, Coke had told the Commons that no sovereign could resist a request if it came from both Houses. The prophecy was correct. King and Lords of Privy Council sat all afternoon "on the question whether the Parliament should be dissolved." Next morning, Speaker Finch brought word that his Majesty wished to meet again with Parliament, "that all Christendom might take notice of a sweet parting between him and his people." The words were winning and full of charm. The Commons however were not yet sure if they spelled dissolution or something better, nor had a time been set for the King's coming. Two days later, on Saturday at four in the afternoon, Black Rod knocked with his staff upon the Commons' door.

Members trooped upstairs, through the long corridors into the Lords' Chamber. When they were gathered behind the bar, as

* The common road, the King's highway.

many as could find place, Lord Keeper Coventry addressed the sovereign in the Parliament's name. "Taking into considerations," he said, "that the good intelligence between your Majesty and your people doth much depend upon your Majesty's answer to their Petition of Right formerly presented; the Lords Spiritual and Temporal and the Commons in Parliament assembled, with unanimous consent do now become most humble suitors unto your Majesty, that you would be graciously pleased to give a clear and satisfactory answer thereunto."

He could not have imagined, Charles replied, but that his former answer should have given full satisfaction — it had been approved "by the judgments of so many wise men." But to show there was no doubleness in his meaning, he was willing to please "as well in words as in substance." Let the petition once more be read, and both Houses would have an answer that he was sure would satisfy.

Once more, the scroll appeared. Once more, the Commons heard their words as they had set them down, the confirmation of their ancient rights and liberties. Over and over, the ancient phrases repeated, after the legal fashion which leaves no loophole for misinterpretation. The Clerk's voice ceased and the Commons broke into applause, quickly subdued as the Clerk once more stepped forward, about to read aloud the royal answer.

"*Soit droit fait*," he said, "*comme il est desiré.*"

As the words were pronounced, a great shout rang, and was repeated again and again. News spread to the street — "broke out," wrote a Privy Councilor, "into ringing of bells and bonfires miraculously." From steeple to steeple the joyous sound was echoed. The City heard, three miles away, and as the June dusk began to fall there were bonfires "at every door, such as were never seen but upon his Majesty's return from Spain." "But, which was strange if not ominous," wrote Mead, "a great part of them were made upon a misprision that the Duke either was or should be sent to the Tower . . . in so much (as some say) the old scaffold on Tower Hill was pulled down and burned by certain unhappy boys, who said they would have a new one built for the Duke of Bucks. This misapprehension prevailed so far that it went down westward and other parts of the country, as to Ware and other places, where bonfires were likewise made upon the like apprehension."

The Commons had triumphed. For the moment, King and country were one. Above the City, night came down as bonfires flared, prophetic indeed of violence to come.

CHAPTER THIRTY-FOUR

1628-1632. Coke's Reports. *His* Institutes of the Laws of England. *Farewell to Parliament.*

PARLIAMENT rose in June. Sir Edward went home to Stoke House. Much work lay ahead; at seventy-six there was question if heaven would spare him to do it. The First Part of his *Institutes — A Commentary upon Littleton* — had just been published. The edition was faulty; a new one must be prepared. The Second and Third Parts lay in manuscript, awaiting correction. The Fourth Part was yet unwritten — altogether a tremendous task for any one man. In addition, Coke's study held notes for two volumes of law *Reports*, to follow the eleven parts already published.

The *Reports*, covering forty years of court cases, had been issued serially from 1600 to 1616. While yet a student at the Temple, Coke had begun to write them, by no means limiting himself to suits which he had himself witnessed. Anything that could be gleaned in Westminster, London Guildhall or the circuit courts in the counties he set down in his own form and fashion, adding comment, aside, comparison. No law reports had hitherto been half so comprehensive; Coke must have lived and walked and sat and talked with notebook in hand. At once the books became — as Blackstone indicated in 1765 — an intrinsic authority in the courts of justice. For two centuries and more, a citation from "the Lord Coke" was to be the final word.

After the custom of the times, Coke wrote his *Reports* in Norman French, with pleadings entered in Latin. But the several

Prefaces were, happily, in English, though tradition was served by printing the Latin beside it. Coke had early told Sir Robert Cecil that he wished "the cases could be as well understood as the Prefaces, and then they would both teach and delight." In his long life, Coke composed nothing more charming than these eleven Prefaces. Addressed to the student, they are at once learned, easy and warm — touched throughout with the fire of conviction. "There is no jewel in the world," writes Coke, "comparable to learning; no learning so excellent both for Prince and subject, as knowledge of laws; and no knowledge of any laws (I speak of human) so necessary for all estates and for all causes, concerning goods, lands or life, as the common laws of England." Therefore, Coke begs, let not cases be committed "to slippery memory, which seldom yieldeth a certain reckoning. In troth, reading, hearing, conference, meditation, and recordation are necessary."

Sir Edward looked on his writings as a "measure of quitment" for a lifetime debt he owed the law. "And do acknowledge my self," says the Ninth Preface, "to owe much more to my profession, than all my true and faithful labours can satisfy." Certain of the *Reports* are little histories in themselves. "For that I fear," says Coke, "that many of my dear countrymen, for want of understanding of their own evidence, do want the true knowledge of their ancient birthright in some points of greatest importance." Sometimes Coke finds himself straying too far afield. "But here," he says genially, "I will stay my foot and fix my staff awhile." Sir Edward cautions the student against elaborate diction. "Certainly the fair outsides of enamel'd words and sentences, do sometimes so bedazzle the eye of the reader's mind with their glittering shew, as they cause them not to see or not to pierce into the inside of the matter; and he that busily hunteth after affected words, and followeth the strong scent of great swelling phrases, is many times (in winding of them in, to shew a little verbal pride) at a dead loss of the matter of itself. To speak effectually, plainly, and shortly, it becometh the gravity of this profession. Truth takes small delight with varnish of words and garnish of flowers."

Coke's *Reports* are the most famous ever written in the law. They went into many printings, abridgments, translations, the last (1826) being a reprint of the final edition of 1777. Tiny pocket editions appeared (1742, 1825), with arguments and pleadings omitted and the judges' decisions summarized in couplets — designed, says the editor's preface, "to refresh the memory and afford a pleasing recreation to gentlemen of the law" —

> CALVIN, Scotch ante nati aliens were,
> But post nati in England subjects are.
>
> CAWDRY, 'Gainst common prayer if parson say
> In sermon aught, bishop deprive him may.
>
> MONOPOLIES, Granted by king are void,
> They spoil the trade in which the youth's employ'd.

Coke's *Reports* are not hard to come by; most legal booksellers today can produce a set. The books have not the bulk of modern law reports. Leatherbound, light to the hand, each of the seven volumes contains two books or Parts.* The *Reports* are old, their cases obsolete. Yet about them hovers something immediate and telling, the stark hard language of the courtroom. In Coke's day they were a landmark, superseding the ancient Year Books. Even Francis Bacon acknowledged it. "Had it not been for Sir Edward Coke's *Reports* . . . the law by this time had been almost like a ship without ballast, for that the cases of modern experience are fled from those that are adjudged and ruled in former time."

Sir Edward was no Puritan. Yet he had the Puritan's sense of mission; these books were half his life on earth. In the year 1628, taking leave forever of Parliament, of Westminster Hall and the courts that had known him so long, Coke set himself to finish the work he had begun. For more than fifty years he had lived in the law; the law was inseparable from his life. To write it down, all that he knew of it, all that he had learned in mind and spirit, was not only imperative but intrinsic. In his head the English law lay outlined, a vast and intricate map: the land law first (a man's propriety in his house and acres); second, the ancient charters, background and authority of laws present and future — Magna Carta, Westminster I and II, Merton, Gloucester; third, the criminal law of England, each crime with its definition, whether *high treason*, *simony*, *premunire*, or *the stealing of hawks*, and judg-

* The final volume, containing Parts Twelve and Thirteen, was published posthumously.

ments recorded with their legal reasons; fourth and last, the system of court procedure in all its ramifications, limits, boundaries, from the High Court of Parliament down to the lowly Courts of the Clerks of Market.

Each category would make up a volume, an *Institute;* together they should represent the whole law of England, spread upon paper for students to read and see. This and no less comprised Coke's aim. It was a double vision; *Reports* and *Institutes* complementary one to the other: the *Institutes* as authority, the *Reports* as illustration by actual practice in the law courts — what today we call *case law.* Coke's title took its meaning from the Latin: *instituo* — I instruct, I arrange and make order. "I have termed them *Institutes,*" he wrote, "because my desire is, that they should institute and instruct the studious, and guide him in a ready way to the knowledge of the national laws of England." Justinian's *Institutes* had long ago presented the Roman law; Coke's would define the native law — and for the first time in its entirety, with past related to present, the old adapted to the new.

No one had attempted a picture so comprehensive, legal exposition on so grand a scale. Separate books of law existed, classics in their field. The Preface to Coke's Eighth *Report* (1601) had listed them, giving honor to each author: Ranulf de Glanvil — dead four hundred years — the fruit of whose writing, said Coke, he himself had reaped; the great Justice Bracton, who in the thirteenth century had written *Of the Laws and Customs of England;* Chief Justice Sir John Fortescue, author of *De Laudibus Legum Angliae;* Judge Littleton of the *Tenures,* the subject of Coke's *First Institute;* Fitzherbert of the *Natura Brevium;* Judge Stamford, whose *Pleas of the Crown* had been quoted against Coke in Parliament.

Yet these great books were fractional and some were ancient; they could not give the quality of continuity. Coke's scheme, despite its grandeur (or because of it) was simple and wholly practical. Sir Edward was no doctrinaire, no Bodin or Hobbes, with a "theory of sovereignty" to present. Coke had his bias, it is true — a conviction, deep and strong, in favor of the common law. But he did not urge it as Bacon, for instance, would have urged a concept, with brilliant introductory passages of persuasion. Coke defined the English law as simply as he could, then praised it with an equal simplicity: "The common law is the best and most common birth-right that the subject hath for the safeguard and defence, not onely of his goods, lands and revenues, but of his wife and children, his body, fame and life also."

Each *Institute* made up its own volume, entitled by Coke as a *Part:*

I. *The First Part of the Institutes of the Laws of England; or, A Commentary upon Littleton.*

II. *The Second Part of the Institutes of the Laws of England, Containing the Exposition of Many Ancient and Other Statutes.*

III. *The Third Part of the Institutes of the Laws of England, Concerning High Treason and Other Pleas of the Crown, and Criminal Causes.*

IV. *The Fourth Part of the Institutes of the Laws of England, Concerning the Jurisdiction of Courts.*

Part One, *A Commentary upon Littleton,* is the best known of the four. *Coke on Littleton,* as the *Commentary* soon was called, carried Sir Edward's name across the ocean. Throughout three centuries the book was issued and reissued, corrected, amended, abridged, edited with commentaries upon Coke's commentary. The first American printing, in 1812, was taken from the sixteenth London edition and comprised three heavy volumes, with Hargrave and Butler's famous notes, and "also the notes of Lord Chief Justice Hale and Lord Chief Justice Nottingham, and an Analysis of Littleton written by an unknown Hand." Of all Coke's works, the *Commentary on Littleton* is most original, though the word sounds strange applied to subjects so aged and dry as land tenure, real property and copyhold. Coke's edition of 1629 — the second — is a handsome folio of 395 pages, printed in black-letter, with Judge Littleton's portrait engraved as frontispiece. Reproduced from a window of Frankley Chapel, the picture shows the old Judge kneeling on a cushion in his robes and coif; from his mouth come the words, *Ung Dieu et ung Roy.*

Coke's generation was used to commentaries — a form much used by legal and Biblical scholars, with the text at the head of a page, followed by the author's criticism and commentary. "Tenant in fee simple," says the opening sentence, "is he which hath lands or tenements to hold to him and his heires for ever." From this classic text of Littleton's, Coke spins eleven long sections, each section explanatory of a clause — and so on with one text after another: fee tail and villenage, rents, dower, claims, releases, confirmations. The book which Coke chose for commentary already was famous; Sir Thomas Littleton had written it some time in the 1470's, for the instruction of his son Richard. It was a brief, black-letter treatise on the land law, describing the customs and legality that had surrounded, since time out of mind, the ownership and inheritance of English real property. Coke regarded it with deepest admiration. "The ornament of the common law," he said; "the most perfect and absolute work that ever was written in any human science, and as free from error as any book that I have known to be written of any humane learning."

Coke's praise has been ridiculed as extravagant, especially by those whose pride is in their modernity and who forget that their longer view is gained by standing on other men's shoulders — forget also that an irrational and passionate enthusiasm is necessary to carry a man through any great work. Coke wrote the *Commentary on Littleton* — and the other three *Institutes* — in English, a novelty he was at pains to justify. Legal works had hitherto been written (like Coke's own *Reports*) in Latin or law French. "I cannot conjecture," says the Preface, "that the general communicating of these laws in the English tongue can work any inconvenience, but introduce great profit. No man ought to be wiser than the law. . . . Our English language is as copious and significant, and as able to expresse any thing in as few and apt words, as any other native language that is spoken at this day. And (to speake what we think), we would derive from the Conqueror as little as we could."

One of the delights of all four *Institutes* is that Coke does speak what he thinks. "In the Eleven Books of our Reports," he confesses, "we have related the opinions and judgments of others; but herein we have set down our own." The reader is cautioned therefore not to take all that is said for law. The books should serve rather "to open some windowes of the law, and to let in more light to the student, or to move him to doubt." Repeatedly, Coke begs for skepticism. Let the scholar not take authority on faith but go to the records, discover truth for himself. Early editions of the *Commentary* were swelled in size by inclusion of Littleton's

Tenures in French as well as English. Coke's preface therefore is a little anxious, speaks of "this pain-full and large volume" and pleads with the reader not to "conceive any opinion against it" until he has read it all and tested each statement by "diligently searching out the several authorities which we have cited."

The plea was well taken; seldom has the student been confronted with a text more awesome. On these crowded pages Coke flung, it would seem, everything that he knew from books and from life, pell-mell and helter-skelter — his only fear being that he might leave something out. "There is no knowledge, case or point in law, seeme it of never so little account, but will stand our student in stead at one time or other, and therefore in reading, nothing to be pretermitted." Judge Littleton's every phrase is deemed worthy of comment and exposition. "Certain it is," says Coke, "that there is never a period, nor (for the most part) a word, nor an *&c* but affordeth excellent matter of learning." When Littleton states that in certain cases the defendant "shall go quit without day," Coke makes a long and fascinating excursion into the legal meaning of the word "day," tells about the English term times: Michaelmas, Hilary, Easter, Trinity — quotes Britton, Plowden, the Parliament Rolls and the Year Books. "Divers nations begin the day at divers times. The Jewes, the Chaldeans and Babylonians, begin the day at the rising of the sun; the Athenians at the fall; the Aegyptians and Romanes from midnight; and so doth the law of England in many cases. . . . Of all of which," Coke appends, "you shall read plentifull matter in our bookes, and in my *Reports*, which by this short instruction you shall the better understand."

For Sir Edward Coke, every facet of the land law was a joy to study. What, for instance, did the word "tenant" mean; from whence derived? And "fee simple" — whether absolute, conditional, or qualified? For want of proper definitions, a lawyer could lose a suit and a defendant his house and goods! The French for "fee," Coke explains, is *fief;* in Domesday Book it was *feudum.* "It is a maxime in law," Littleton had written, in Section 3. Coke seized upon the phrase. "Maxim," he wrote; "i.e., a sure foundation or ground of art, a principle, all one with a rule, a common ground, postulatum or an axiome, which it were too much curiositie to make nice distinctions betweene them." The two words "in law" set Coke off upon a zestful frolic into laws of the Crown, statute law, law canon and civil, *lex naturae* (the law of nature) and *communis Lex Angliae*, the common law of England.

Certain of Coke's etymologies, like certain of his historical facts, went very wide of the mark. Yet they were shared by scholars of the day, nor was Coke always the first man responsible. William Lambarde the antiquary, in his *Archion*,* had given (before Coke gave it in the *Second Institute*) the famous derivation for *parliament:* "From two French words, *parler*, to speak; and *ment*, the mind. . . . Because," added Coke, "every member of that court should sincerely and discreetly *parler la ment* for the general good of the common wealth." Coke's bland statement that the Druids talked Greek did not upset his contemporaries, nor does it detract from the overall value of his work. A scholar builds from the sources available: Shakespeare wrote of King John as a virtuous, unfortunate king, badly influenced.

One of Coke's more famous definitions concerned the word *hotspot.* (After the *Commentary* appeared, attorneys in court would sometimes bring up the word slyly, as if to start a laugh.) Littleton had spoken of "lands given in frankmarriage in hotchpot." Coke pounced upon it, rolled in it, a pedant in his particular catnip. "*Hutspot* or *hotspot* is an old Saxon word. The French use hotchpot for a commixion of divers things together. It signifieth here metaphorically in *partem positio*. In English we use to say hodge-podge, in Latin *farrago* or *miscellaneum.*"

To Coke it was impossible that every scholar, if he but persisted, would not share his appetite for such excursions. "We have armed our student," says Coke brightly, "with the signification of ancient bookes, charters, deeds and records, to the end he may proceed in his reading with alacrity, and set upon, and know how to worke into with delight these rough mines of hidden treasure." Yet on finishing the *Commentary*, Coke looked back, troubled by "the multitude of conclusions in law, the manifold diversities between cases and points of learning." Would it not be expedient to abridge the book, make an alphabetical table for the student? Coke decided against it. "Tables and abridgments are most profitable to them that make them; I have left that worke to everie

* *Archion,* or *A Commentary upon the High Courts* (1591). To his definition Lambarde, apparently troubled, adds, "But Laurence Valla misliketh that manner of Etymology, and therefore I will not stand upon it."

studious reader. . . . And for a farewell to our jurisprudent," says Sir Edward's epilogue, "I wish unto him the gladsome light of jurisprudence, the lovelinesse of temperance, the stabilitie of fortitude, and the soliditie of justice."

Of these handsome qualities, the stability of fortitude was most urgent. Generations of students were to wrestle grimly with *Coke-Littleton.* Lord Keeper North, fifty years later, declared that the volume should not be given to a young student; "it breeds more disorder in the brains than any other book can." Lord Justice Reeves in 1787 spoke of "venturing" upon it. After outlining a course in preparatory reading, "then venture," he wrote, "upon Coke's Comment. After the first reading (for it will require many more than one) abridge it throughout, or compare it with some authentic abridgement, sentence by sentence and by your additions and corrections, make it your own." Then, said Reeves, read Serjeant Hawkins to throw light on Coke, and Wood to throw light on Hawkins. Lord Chancellor Eldon in 1800 advised the student to read Coke's *Institutes* "again and again, as he who toils up that hill will have the world before him." Present-day students, Eldon added, acquired their law too cheaply, "by learning it from Blackstone and less elegant compilers. Depend upon it, men so bred will never be lawyers (though they may be barristers), whatever they call themselves."

American students were to voice loud complaint. Daniel Webster said he never understood a quarter of *Coke-Littleton;* "no boy of twenty could understand Coke." Study of the book caused him to "despair and almost to give up law for school teaching." Mr. Justice Story of Massachusetts as a young man tried "day after day" to read *Coke-Littleton,* then "set himself down and wept bitterly." Yet he persisted — "went on and on," he says, "and began at last to see daylight, ay, and to feel that I could comprehend and reason upon the text and comments. When I had completed the reading of this most formidable work, I felt that I breathed a purer air and that I had acquired a new power." When Colonel Otis, father of James Otis the Revolutionary patriot, studied law in Barnstable, Massachusetts, the only books available were Coke's *Institutes,* Brownlow's *Entries* and Plowden's *Commentaries* and *Reports.* The earliest catalogue of the Harvard College Library (1723) lists the *First* and *Second Institutes.* Rhode Island law students before 1770 were brought up on *Coke-Littleton*, Cowell's *Interpreter* and the same fifteenth-century *Doctor and Student* that Coke himself had studied. Patrick Henry as a young man was admitted to the bar after six weeks' study of nothing but *Coke-Littleton* and the *Virginia Statutes*. (George Wythe refused to sign his license but the Randolph brothers, after confessing Henry to be "very ignorant of the law," declared that he had a genius "and would soon qualify himself.") Nine years later, John Rutledge of South Carolina wrote to his brother in London, who was studying at the Inns of Court: "In regard to particular law books — Coke's *Institutes* seem to be almost the foundation of our law. . . . Blackstone I think useful."

There is no end to the roster. Chief Justices John Jay of New York and Theophilus Parsons of Massachusetts were brought up on *Coke-Littleton*. John Adams as a law student (1760-1765) was urged by Jeremiah Gridley to make himself master of Coke's *Institutes*. "You must conquer the *Institutes*. The road of science is much easier now [said Gridley] than it was when I set out; I began with Coke-Littleton, and broke through." Adams's *Diary* reflects his anxiety: "I have read a multitude of law books — mastered but few. Wood's *Institutes of Common Law* I never read but once and my Lord Coke's *Commentary on Littleton* I never read but once. These two authors I must get and read over and over again. And I will get them and break through, as Mr. Gridley expressed it, all obstructions."

John Adams's son, John Quincy, struggled valiantly with the "folio of Lord Coke which has been hanging heavily upon me these ten weeks." Thomas Jefferson read the *First Institute* in the early 1760's and later wrote of it not as a lawyer but (characteristically) as a politician. "Coke Lyttleton was the universal elementary book of law students and a sounder Whig never wrote nor profounder learning in the orthodox doctrines of British liberties. . . . But when his black letter text and uncouth but cunning learning got out of fashion, and the honeyed Mansfieldism of Blackstone became the student's book, from that moment that profession (the nursery of our Congress) began to slide into Toryism."

In England, Coke's contemporary, the great Thomas Hobbes, attacked the *Institutes* on grounds of the same principles that

Jefferson had found so satisfying — Hobbes being one who, like Francis Bacon, saw all law as proceeding from the sovereign. (*Let the judges be lions, but lions under the throne.*) "I wonder," Hobbes asked, "why Sir Edward Coke should cite a statute above two hundred years before expired and other two petitions, as if they were statutes, when they were not passed by the King; unless he did it on purpose to diminish, as he endeavors to do throughout his *Institutes*, the King's authority."

Coke's works have been attacked, throughout the centuries, from many angles: his pedantry as repulsive, his assertions overbearing. Some of his citations are incorrect. When he desires to mystify he slides off into Latin; he credits works that later were discredited, as *The Mirrour of Justices*. He uses the Bible as legal authority, digresses into fancy quotations from the poets — Virgil to Chaucer. His knowledge in science is called lamentable; "he asserts that the metals are six: sulphur and quicksilver are their father and mother." Yet Francis Bacon, too, believed firmly in the transmutation of metals; Sir Thomas Browne encouraged the alchemists and shared Coke's respect for witches. As for Sir Edward's "inaccuracy," Holdsworth, the great legal historian, reminds us that neither Bacon nor Lord Chancellor Ellesmere found serious errors in the *Reports* except in political or semipolitical cases, and they knew the law of their own day more intimately than we know it. In all of Coke's works, states Holdsworth, it is only in political cases that he can be accused of inaccuracy.

Many of Coke's critics ended by acknowledging his extraordinary influence. His works, wrote Judge Stephen — next to Macaulay, Coke's harshest detractor — "may be regarded as having coloured English law for more than two centuries; the *Institutes* have had a greater influence on the law of England than any work written between the days of Bracton and those of Blackstone."

"What Shakespeare has been to literature," says Holdsworth, "what Bacon has been to philosophy, what the translators of the authorized version of the Bible have been to religion, Coke has been to the public and private law of England."

Sir Edward, struggling at Stoke with the last of his four *Institutes*, looked on himself in no such glorious terms. Merely, he had a task to do, an old man's failing strength and spirit to bring to it. The four Parts of the *Institutes* have a common dedication: "To my much honoured and beloved allies and friends of the county of Norfolk, my dear and native country; and to Suffolk, where I passed my middle age; and of Buckinghamshire, where in my old age I live." The several prefaces reveal the author's doubts and fears; his awe at the magnitude of the endeavor, his prayers sent up to God; and in separate, brief epilogues, his joy at the finished creation. "A work arduous," says the Proeme to the *Third Institute*, "and full of such difficultie, as none can either feele or believe, but he onely which maketh tryall of it. And albeit it did often terrifie me, yet could it not in the end make me desist from my purpose; so farre hath the love and honour of my countrey, to passe through all labours, doubts and difficulties, prevailed with me."

Immediate publication of the *Commentary on Littleton* was safe enough and politic; the book contained little that was controversial. The same could be said of Coke's *Book of Entries* (1614), a collection of pleadings for professional use, and his *Compleat Copyholder*, published in 1630 . . . "Being," says the subtitle, "a learned discourse of the antiquity and nature of manors and copyholds with all things thereto incident." The last three Parts of the *Institutes* must wait. King Charles, hearing that Coke was about to produce another book, ordered his Lord Keeper to halt publication. "The King fears," wrote Lord Holland to Secretary Dorchester, "somewhat may be to the prejudice of his prerogative, for Sir Edward is held too great an oracle amongst the people, and they may be misled by anything that carries such an authority as all things do that he either speaks or writes; for the prevention of which the King thinks it should not come forth."

Charles had good reason to fear the appearance of Coke's *Second Institute*. This was the commentary on Magna Carta and some thirty-eight other charters and statutes. Coke on Magna Carta was meat for Parliament, not for Crown. All that he urged in the House of Commons was here set down with peculiar eloquence and authority—*Capitus* 39: *Nullus liber homo capiatur, vel imprisonetur* . . . "Upon this chapter, as out of a roote," says Coke, "many fruitfull branches of the law of England have sprung. . . . As the goldfiner will not out of the dust, threds or shreds or gold, let pass the least crum, in respect of the excellency of the metall; so ought not the learned reader to let passe any syllable of this law, in respect of the excellency of the matter." *Nisi per legem terrae* to Coke meant "without due process of the *common* law" — not merely of the law. "Generally all monopolies are against this great charter, because they are against the liberty and freedome of the subject, and against the law of the land."

Sir Edward on *Capitus 39* reads like the Petition of Right itself. Habeas corpus is here defined — and not in prerogative terms — as also delay of justice and *rectum*, right, "whereby justice distributive is guided." It is here, too, that Coke declares a man "cannot be sent against his will into Ireland, to serve the King; which being an exile is prohibited by this Act." . . . "*De tallagio non concedendo*. . . . No tallage or aid shall be taken or levied . . . without the goodwill and consent of . . . barons, knights, burgesses and other freemen of the land." Coke quotes this great statute of 1263 and after his fashion brings it up to date, including taxes that Edward I never heard of: "all subsidies, tenths, fifteens, impositions and other burthens or charge put or set upon any man." In this second Part of the *Institutes*, Coke on ecclesiastical jurisdiction and prohibitions would have made Archbishop Whitgift turn in his grave: "The interpretation of all statutes concerning the clergy, being parcell of the lawes of the realme, doe belong to the judges of the common law."

The Second Part of the *Institutes*, defining the great charters, was published in 1642, the Third and Fourth Parts in 1644. The Long Parliament achieved it at a time when Parliament had power and the King must yield.* Charles had not destroyed Coke's manuscripts; English kings, whatever their faults, have not been known as book burners. The Commons dug Coke's *Institutes* from hiding, the initial motion being made by one of Coke's sons, "as supposing [the books] contain many monuments of the subject's liberties." Actually, the Third Part, *High Treason, Pleas of the Crown and Criminal Causes*, in certain sections gave strong support to the Crown; Coke's views on high treason had not changed since his early days as prosecutor. (Roger Coke declared that in the first years of the Rebellion, writers for the King's side "chiefly maintained his cause out of Sir Edward's *Pleas of the Crown*.") Murder and homicide, robbery and rape — all these were clear; their history and provenance did not touch on politics, though Coke criticized

* Chapter Note.

in strong terms the cruelty of current penalties. "Lawes justly made for the preservation of the common-wealth without extreame punishment, are more often obeyed and kept, than lawes and statutes made with great and extreame punishments. Those offences are often committed that are often punished, for the frequency of the punishment makes it so familiar as it is not feared."

Coke's *Third Institute* is the most readable of the four. The headings, as in certain of Coke's *Reports*, are wonderfully revelatory of contemporary life: *Stealing of Hawks; Hunters in the Night; Imbesiling the King's Armour; Of Felony for having a Plague sore upon him, contrary to Commandment, goeth abroad; Piracy; Of Brothel-Houses and Bordellos; Against Monopolists; Against Forestallers and Vexatious Informers; Roberdsmen; Of not pursuing upon the Hue and Cry*. Coke defines each crime, gives the laws with their history and lists the penalties. Often enough, he illustrates from a case within his experience and says what he thinks of the statute involved — "Being a dangerous act, as some had felt in *anno 23 Eliz.* [1581]." . . . "God blessed and prospered this act with happy and desired success." Coke shows much interest in the rules for fairs and markets; as a countryman he knew the tricks by which a farmer could cheat his neighbor. It is forestalling, he says, to sell your wheat in the sheaf, unthreshed. His definition of "Roberdsmen" makes short shrift of a popular hero: "It is an English proverb That many men talk of Robin Hood that never shot in his bow. This Robert Hood lived in the reigne of king R. I, in woods and deserts, with vagabonds, idle wanderers, nightwalkers and draw-latches. . . ."

Coke never misses a chance to sing his country's praise: "And we have observed, that God hath blessed this realme with things for the defence of the same, and maintenance of trade and traffick, that no other part of the Christian world hath the like: viz. Iron to make gunnes, &c. more serviceable and perdurable than any other. Secondly, timber for the making and repairing of our navie, and especially for the knees of the ships, better than any other. Thirdly, our fullers earth is better for the fulling of our cloth, then any other. Fourthly, our wooll makes better cloth, and more lasting and defensible against winde and weather, than the wooll in any nation out of the kings dominions; and many other speciall gifts of God."

Sometimes Coke stops to recite a case that interests him, as of one William Hain, who in 1613 "digged up the graves of divers severall men," stole the winding sheets and reburied the bodies. The problem was, Who owned these sheets? They must belong to someone, for — said the judges — "the dead body is not capable of any property." The court awarded the sheets to the dead man's executors and a jury found the defendant guilty of petty larceny, "for which," Coke adds, "he was whipped, as he well deserved." The book tells of the Overbury murder, adding curious facts not brought out at the trial. In the section on High Treason, Coke refers to the trials of Lords Cobham and Grey, Watson and Clarke, "seminary priests" — but contrives not once to mention the name of Ralegh. Let judges take care, Coke admonishes in another place, "that they in case of life judge not too hastily upon bare presumption" — and illustrates with a case in Warwickshire where an innocent man was hanged for murder.

On certain subjects, Sir Edward could not resist a general preachment. Drunkenness, he says, was brought to England "by the Danes," though King Edgar tried to limit his men by marking their cups with nails. As for gluttony and overrich attire, it became gentlemen of quality to show good example, eat no flesh on fish days and wear cloth "wrought within the realm." These asides, amid the catalogue of crimes, are reassuring; they carry the accents of the author: "Sordid bribery, which we hate, as in the proper chapter thereof before appeareth." Flattery in high places Coke regarded dangerous to the state. "The Holy Ghost hath styled flattery *oleum peccatoris*, the oile of the sinner. Parliaments, palaces of princes and pulpits should be free from adulation and flattery." Sir Edward had seen its effects, under James and Charles I; flattery could undermine even the courts of justice. See — he admonishes — what fell out with King Canutus! "He set his feet on the sea strond, as the sea was flowing, and commanded the sea not to rise and wet his lordly and majestick feet nor clothes: the sea keeping on his accustomed course, both wet his feet and thighs also: whereat being sore amazed repented his presumption (which he had undertaken by wicked flattery)."

Coke's tales are characteristic, like his parables and fables to the grand juries when he was Judge. To emphasize the need of statutes against corrupt judges, he tells the incident — so dramatically used by Shakespeare — of Henry V, when a youth, striking Chief Justice Gascoigne while he sat in court. The Judge committed him and the King, approving, thanked God who had given him a fearless judge. Occasionally, Sir Edward's emotions overmaster him and he stops short in his tale. "And what heavy event ensued thereupon," he says, "let historians inform you, for it is grievous to me to remember it." These brief personal touches have their poignancy; the proofs and cases seem to come alive on the page. "And I heard Wray, chief justice in the King's bench, *anno 23 Eliz.* report. . . . In King James his reign, when I was a commissioner of the treasury. . . . For I reade in an ancient and authenticall manuscript . . . And God forbid that in cases so penall, the law should not be certaine. . . . Queen Elizabeth, *Angliae amor.*"

King Charles did well to suppress so dramatic and essentially contemporary a treatise. Coke on premunire in the *Third Institute,* Coke on the High Court of Parliament in the *Fourth* — these could serve as torch to kindling. "The power and jurisdiction of the parliament for making of laws in proceeding by bill, is so transcendent and absolute, as it cannot be confined either for causes or persons within any bounds. . . . The Commons being the generall inquisitors of the realm, have principall care in the beginning of the parliament to appoint days of committees, viz. of grievances (both in the church and common-wealth) of courts of justice, or priviledges and of advancement of trade." It was Coke the Parliament man all over again; his voice speaks from the page, flat and sure. "No subsidy before the end of the parliament, because it is to accompany the pardon."

Courts of equity and Exchequer, the Court of Chancery, Star Chamber, Admiralty: in the *Fourth Institute,* Coke describes them all. "And our desired end is," he says, "that all these high and honourable tribunals . . . may prosper and flourish in distribution of justice, which assuredly they shall doe, if they derive all their power and strength from their proper roots." *Their proper roots,* to Edward Coke, lay in the common law — and in Parliament, servant and handmaid of the common law. "These things being understood," says Coke in a phrase that has been quoted for centuries, "let us now peruse our ancient authors, for out of the old fields must come the new corne." * Throughout his *Fourth* (and

* Chapter Note.

last) *Institute*, on the "Jurisdiction of Courts," there runs a serene assurance which to royalists must have been more disturbing than the loudest rantings of the House of Commons. "The parliament holden *anno 21* of king James [1624]," writes Coke, "was called *felix parliamentum*, the happy parliament." This was well enough; no royalist objected to reminders of the break with Spain and subsidies willingly rendered. "And the parliament holden in the third yeare of our soveraigne lord king Charles [1628]," Coke goes on blandly, "was *benedictum parliamentum*, the blessed parliament. The severall reasons . . . are yet fresh in memory."

During June of 1628, before Sir Edward left Westminster, the Petition of Right had been enrolled in the courts of justice, printed among the Acts of Parliament, its validity ensured. (Actually it was not a statute, as King Charles had every intention of proving.) The session by no means ended with the King's blessing. The Commons had voted a strong remonstrance against the Duke of Buckingham, asking his removal from "great offices or his place of nearness and counsel" about the King's person. Charles rejected it; the Commons retaliated by declaring tonnage and poundage to be illegal. Charles prorogued the session and distributed throughout the country thousands of copies of the Petition of Right, signed not with the *Soit droit fait* but with his earlier, inconclusive answer.

The London populace was in ugly mood; the Duke must surely be author of these evils. Searching an outlet for their anger, the people fixed on old Dr. Lambe, one of Buckingham's retainers, well known about town as a conjurer and astrologer — a kind of masculine Mistress Turner. One night, coming from the theater, Lambe was set upon and stoned to death. The savagery of it, even in a savage time, was awful; the old man was literally torn to pieces. Libels were found in the streets or written on the walls:

> Let Charles and George do what they can,
> The Duke will die like Doctor Lambe.

"Who rules the kingdom? — the King. Who rules the King? — the Duke. Who rules the Duke? — the Devil."

Buckingham refused to be frightened. Urged to wear chain mail under his shirt, he replied that against any popular fury it would be useless, and as to single assault, he did not feel in danger. "There are no Roman spirits left," he said. On the twenty-third of August, a Saturday, the Duke was at Portsmouth, preparing to sail with the fleet. In a crowded hallway, a man — John Felton by name — walked up and stabbed Buckingham with a tenpenny knife. In fifteen minutes he was dead. Felton made no attempt to escape and swore he had no confederate; his "only setter-on was the remonstrance of the parliament, which he then thought verily in his soul and conscience to be a sufficient warrant for what he did."

Everywhere, the people showed their joy. Poems poured out upon the town; in city taverns, in the wine cellars of Oxford and Cambridge, Felton's health was drunk. Men lost their ears in the pillory for what they said and did. On Felton's journey to London, crowds gathered to see him. "Lord comfort thee!" they cried out. "Lord be merciful unto thee!" As he passed through Kingston-on-Thames, an old woman saluted him. "Now God bless thee, little David!" she said. Threatened by the Earl of Dorset with torture to make him disclose his accomplices, "If I be put upon the rack," said Felton, "I will name you, my Lord of Dorset, and none but yourself." Spared the rack, on November twenty-eighth Felton was hanged at Tyburn.

At Stoke House, Coke heard of these things; he did not live in seclusion. Parliament reconvened in January, 1629; the Speaker sent a message, asking Coke's presence. He did not come; the *Commons Journals* has no explanation. Oliver Cromwell gave his maiden speech, brief and quite dull, a few words against popery. Clem Coke spoke boldly: "He that shall pay tonnage and poundage is an enemy to the law and liberties of the subject and kingdom." In March, after only five weeks of sitting, Charles dissolved the session and proclaimed that no further Parliaments would be held "until the people have come to a better understanding of Us themselves." Six Commons members were arrested — Eliot, Selden, Holles, Long, Valentine, Strode — charged with seditious speeches, contempt against the King in resisting adjournment, and conspiracy to keep the Speaker forcibly in the chair when Black Rod knocked. At their trial, all six refused to plead, claiming parliamentary privilege against arrest. They were remitted to the Tower. Three made their submission and were freed — among them, John Selden. But Valentine and Strode remained in prison for eleven years. Sir John Eliot, who could have won his freedom with a word, died in the Tower of consumption.

There is no record of the year and day when Coke set down the last word of his *Institutes*. But the epilogue to the Fourth Part confesses again the hardship that Sir Edward felt in composition: "Whilst we were in hand with these foure parts of the Institutes, we often having occasion to go into the city, and from thence into the country, did in some sort envy the state of the honest plowman, and other mechanics; for the one when he was at his work would merrily sing, and the plowman whistle some self-pleasing tune, and yet their work both proceeded and succeeded: but he that takes upon him to write, doth captivate all the faculties and powers both of his minde and body, and must be only intentive to that which he collecteth, without any expression of joy or cheerfulnesse, whilest he is in his work."

In the concluding paragraphs there is humility and a high seriousness, as of a man who knows that his life, like his work, is near its end. "Thus have we, by the great goodnesse of the Almighty brought this painfull Work to a conclusion. . . . Honourable and reverend judges and justices, that do or shall sit in the high tribunals and courts or seats of justice as aforesaid, fear not to do right to all, and to deliver your opinions justly according to the laws; for feare is nothing but a betraying of the succours that reason should afford. And if you shall sincerely execute justice, be assured of three things; first, though some may maligne you, yet God will give you his blessing. Secondly, that though thereby you may offend great men and favourites, yet you shall have the favourable kindnesse of the Almighty, and be his favourites. And lastly, that in so doing, against all scandalous complaints and pragmaticall devices against you, God will defend you as with a shield."

After this solemn adjuration there must have occurred to Coke — and for the thousandth time — the doubts and fears experienced by the author of any large work. The *Institutes* by their very bulk were bound to harbor mistakes in scores, perhaps in hundreds. Every crown lawyer and civilian in England would be ready to pounce, happy to see the giant stumble. To beg mercy beforehand would be useless. Coke braved it out. His final paragraph asks, not leniency or forgiveness, but posterity's revising pen:

"And for that we have broken the ice, and out of our owne industry and observation framed this high and honourable building of the jurisdiction of courts, without the help or furtherance of any that hath written of this argument before, I shall heartily desire the wise hearted and expert builders (justice being *architectonica virtus*) to amend both the method or uniformity, and the structure it selfe, wherein they shall finde either want of windowes, or sufficient lights, or other deficiency in the architecture whatsoever. And we will conclude with the aphorisme of the great lawyer* and sage of the law (which we have heard him often say) *Blessed be the amending hand.*"

* Edmund Plowden.

CHAPTER THIRTY-FIVE

Stoke House, the last years. Death of Sir Edward Coke.

STOKE HOUSE was built of stone, three-storied, with high slim brick chimneys clustered behind steep roof and straggling wings — a cheerful, handsome pile with many windows to let in the light. Above the leads a tower, with egress at the top, was railed so one could walk and view the country round. The estate comprised a thousand acres, much of it ancient forest of the original manor, oaks and giant beeches, old almost as Domesday Book.* Coke had bought the house in 1599 from one Serjeant-at-Law Branthwaite, who held a heavy mortgage from the owner, Henry, Earl of Huntingdon. Lord Chancellor Sir Christopher Hatton once had lived here, though the records do not tell us when.

Sir Edward loved the place. The approach was through a long narrow lane, blocked twice by tall wrought-iron gates that bore Coke's crest, an "ostrich argent, holding in its beak a horseshoe." Near the house, a stream was dammed to make a little lake, after the fashion when a man improved his country place. "Build a new dove-house, pave the court, bring a spring or conduit of excellent water, make fayre and large pondes, plant a great orchard, make a reasonable spacious garden with delicat arboures and fence it with a fayre bricke wall." So, on another estate, wrote friend to owner as work progressed. Here at Stoke, some twenty miles from London, Sir Edward had rich Thames soil to work with — a far cry

* The records of Stoke Poges go back to 1086. Huntingdon lost the place, rumor has it, as a gambling debt.

from the harsh salt marshes and killing winds of his Norfolk birthplace. Spring rains came gently to these fertile lowlands. All summer, turf and meadows flourished emerald green under the kind English sun, while overhead sea clouds drifted, fat with mist. The ponds were stocked, the fields and woods abounded in game — pheasant and grouse and lark and thrush; in springtime that favorite dish of squires, "partridges with egges," came often to the table.

In the great hall, Lord Chancellor Hatton's arms presided in stone above the fireplace, guarded on each side by a prancing stone lion. Above and below the scutcheon figures were carved in walnut, gay and fanciful — a musician blowing his recorder, a woman with a harp upon her lap. Tapestries covered the walls; in nine wide panels Pharaoh and the children of Israel marched round the chamber. A Persian carpet lay over a table; high-backed chairs were upholstered in leather, window seats bore long cushions "all of branched silver wrought with tawny." Upstairs in the best chamber the bedstead was gilded, the tester of white embroidered satin with a top of "stript cloth of silver" and "five curtains of clouded taffita, fringed with gould and silke." There were parlors carpeted in red, windows hung with scarlet velvet and on the walls, "eight faire pictures whereof foure are of the elements and foure of the 4 seasons of the yeare. In the Gallery the pictures of Sir Thomas More, Bishopp Fox and Bishopp Fisher."

It is all set down in inventory: "*Household Stuffe at Stoke which never was Sir Xtofer Hatton's. . . .* A mappe of the world, a Mappe of the Colledge of Cambridge. Five cupps of wood, painted suitable. A Great Yron chestt, one little white Cabinett of ivory." Everywhere, bright color and carven wood, silks and velvets, spaciousness and stone over against a discomfort ancient and customary — cold corridors and scorching open hearths; servants with stiff round brooms sweeping dust merrily from one place to another. Green sweet rushes laid for guests and in forgotten corners, stale rushes that harbored fleas in hordes. Coke was no easy master in any department. Yet his domestic accounts spell pleasant country living — sheep to crop the turf, cows grazing near the house, the stables within sight and sound, cattle sheds for winter, henhouses, a hawk shelter with a falcon or two. In letters to his tenants, Coke discusses the felling of trees or the spiteful blocking of a meadow path. "I will see you recyve no wrong. . . . I pray you let me know, and you shall be in peace." Sir James Whitelocke, Coke's friend and neighbor, sat one morning in Stoke manorial court to settle some disputes concerning deeds and boundaries. Coke had sent for him, asked him to search the copy rolls and to "order all things," wrote Whitelocke, "as I sholde see cawse in justice and that he wold be contented withe what I determined with him or against him. And accordinglye I did keepe his court upon Tuesday after Michaelmas day, and gave good satisfaction to those that made clamor against him — the most religious and orderlye man in his house that ever lived in our state."

Coke owned, throughout England, upwards of sixty manors. At Holkham the records show ninety-six separate purchases of "manors, lands, tenements and advowsons" — holdings that exceed £100,000 in value.* Huntingfield Hall in Suffolk, bought from Lord Hunsdon; Cokeley, with the parish church where Sir Edward had married Bridget Paston; Elmham in Norfolk, that had been Lord Cromwell's — the same irascible peer whose suit against his vicar had long ago been lost at young Coke's hands. (*Scandalum Magnatum.* "Thou art a false varlet and I like not of thee.") Coke had bought Donyatt House in Somersetshire from the Earl of Pembroke and the handsome manor of Longford in Derbyshire, which he gave to his son Clem. There was Minster Lovell, once the Earl of Bedford's; Lord Burghley's former property in Bucks, called Cippenham. Grand estates, tenanted and farmed, self-sufficient as little cities. Largest was Castle Acre in Norfolk, purchased from Lady Hatton's father, the Earl of Exeter. The towering stone gates still stood in Coke's day; the moats gaped deep. A cloistered priory was part of the estate, with green lawns and meadows, a rectory, a lovely church on a hill. Coke had bought Castle Acre in 1616. The story goes that King James, fearful of these spreading lands and holdings (should any one subject command such wealth?) ordered Sir Edward to buy no more. Coke petitioned that he might purchase "one more acre" — conquered Majesty by a pun and thus acquired Castle Acre.

A large part of these rents and properties went to pay the already notorious debts of Coke's sons. Ambitious to see them well settled and seated, Sir Edward turned over various manors as each child married or when the first grandchildren were born. From Sir Robert to Fighting Clem, Coke's sons managed to run through

* Chapter Note.

money as if spending were a duty. Yet they had married heiresses, begot children, lived respectably on their country estates and except for Clem — who had a propensity for dueling — they fell into no serious troubles. What they did with the money is a mystery; Sir Robert's debts alone amounted to nearly twenty-eight thousand pounds. Taken all together it was a king's ransom. His sons, remarked Sir Edward, could not have enjoyed the spending of his money more than he enjoyed the getting of it. He paid without complaint — though Chamberlain said that he had once been half insane by reason of these obligations. "There goes a doubtfull speach abrode that Sir Ed. Cooke shod be crackt, his braines being overburthened with a surcharge of his childrens debts that arise to £26000 besides £10000 of his owne, but this is only whispered as yet, and I hope may prove false."

Beyond their debts and the names of their wives, children and estates, little is known of Coke's sons. His two daughters by Bridget Paston were to survive him. But of the sons, only four were living in 1629: Sir Robert, John, Henry and Clement. Like good squires they sat for their boroughs occasionally in Parliament, but only Fighting Clem was quoted memorably for what he said or did there. Sir Robert, with his wife, Lady Theophila, lived in the old family place of Huntingfield, where most of Bridget Coke's children had been born. John Coke had married a Norfolk girl with a good property at Holkham on the North Sea. John's portrait hangs today at Holkham, full length, in armor — a towering, strong countryman, known to his neighbors as a great shouter and brawler at conferences and meetings. "Faith!" wrote a contemporary, "any man that ever saw him — a great fellow in large folio — would sweare that he should rather be written *oo* than *o*." The fifth son, Henry, is notable for leaving no debts; he had lately married a Kentish heiress and moved away from Stoke.

Fighting Clem was Coke's youngest and perhaps his favorite son. In the spring of 1629, Coke lost him; Clem died at thirty-five. His father had him buried in the ancient Round Church within the Temple gates. For a brief time, after Clem left Cambridge, he had been entered as a law student — "by special admission," the records have it. His Temple career had been anything but distinguished; he seems to have drifted away as ingloriously as he came. There is a note almost of desperation in Sir Edward's strange choice of burial place, as if a tomb, so placed, repaired all sad omissions and commissions in his son. "Being a Fellow of the Inner Temple," said Clem's monument, "Christianly and Comfortably in his flourishing Age yielded up his Soul to the Almighty."

It would seem that Coke's daughters afforded him more comfort than all his sons together. Anne Coke Sadleir loved her father deeply; long after his death she remembered him and wrote of him with fervent affection and loyalty. Meriel, wife of John Coke, sent small domestic presents from Holkham. "Thank my good daughter," the old man wrote back, "for her excellent cakes and honey, which came in good time." Bridget Coke Skynner lived with her second husband amidst great magnificence in an ancient Lincolnshire priory, big enough to house an order of monks. It was to Bridget's son that John Milton wrote a labored sonnet — Coke might have called it *pain-full:*

> Syriack, whose grandsire on the royal bench
> Of British Themis, with no mean applause,
> Pronounced, and in his volumes taught, our laws,
> Which others at their bar so often wrench. . . .

Of Coke's many children, the one who came at the last to manage his house and watch over him was, ironically enough, his daughter by Lady Hatton. Frances Villiers, Lady Purbeck, had grown into a willful, passionate young woman, ravishingly lovely to look at. "A lady of transcending beauty," said a contemporary, "but accused for wantonness." Her career, since her marriage to Buckingham's elder brother, now Lord Purbeck, had been stormy — some fifteen years of hot and doubtful adventure, all in the highest circles and most of it known and relished throughout London. Her husband adored her. Poor Lord Purbeck, gentle and kind when in health, was subject to fits of mad melancholy, in the course of which he smashed windows with his fists until the blood ran. Buckingham and his mother took violent dislike to Frances, declared she had bewitched her husband and must leave him. "There is an imputation laide on her," wrote Chamberlain, "that with powders and potions she did intoxicate her husbands braines, and practised somwhat in that kind upon the D. of Buckingham."

Torn from her husband, Frances lived sometimes with her mother, sometimes with friends. Beautiful and distracted, she fell in love with young Sir Robert Howard, fifth son of the Earl of Suffolk — Buckingham's old enemy. A boy was born. Frances hid him and had him christened secretly as Robert Wright. He was discovered, and scandal burst upon London like a summer storm. Frances stood her ground. Robert was Lord Purbeck's child, she said; she had been "forced to meet her husband secretly, for fear of the Duke," and for fear of the Duke she had hidden the boy.

Buckingham, at this, swore the child could not be his brother's; Purbeck was "insufficient" — current euphemism for impotent. The lover's mother, the old Countess of Suffolk, with more expediency than kindness at once declared that her son also was insufficient, "and so not liable to such a scandal." Buckingham appealed to the Attorney General and Lord Chief Justice. Young Howard was put in Fleet prison. Frances, caught between two powerful factions, found herself in the custody of Alderman Barkham. It was impossible to put her down. Carried to Serjeants' Inn to be examined by the Lord Chief Justice and others, she remarked — as the Alderman's coach rattled over the cobbles — that she "marvelled what these poor old cuckolds had to say to her."

There were two trials before the High Commission — one at Lambeth, the second at the Bishop of London's palace. Frances and her lover were accused of adultery. (Somewhere along the way, Buckingham had decided not to press the charge of witchcraft.) No Southwark theater could offer better entertainment; everyone came who could squeeze in. Sir Robert refused to take the oath *ex officio.* The Commission, wishing to fine him for his obstinacy, referred to their letters patent to make sure of their powers. "We found," the Lord Keeper wrote to Buckingham, "that Sir Edward Coke (far-seeing, out of a prophetical spirit how near it might concern a grand-child of his one day) hath expunged this clause . . . out of the Commission, and left us nothing but the rustie sword of the Church, Excommunication to vindicate the authority of this Court."

Gossips declared that all "he and she goodfellows of the town commend Sir Robert who is sure to dye a martyr, and most of the ladies in town will offer at his shrine." Whether or no Coke had coached his daughter in her part, her answers were worthy of him. Frances confessed that her reputation had been damaged, but laid it to the malice of Buckingham's family. No one, she said stoutly, was obliged to accuse himself in court; "the burden of proof lies with the accusers." Witnesses had seen the Lady Frances come to Sir Robert's chamber "in the habit of a maid servant with a basket on her arm and provision in it for their suppers." Sir Robert, when his turn came, refused point-blank to take the oath *ex officio*, claiming privilege of Parliament. (He sat as a burgess from Shropshire.) The Archbishop, at his wit's end, sentenced both parties to public excommunication. At the second trial, Frances again maintained her ground and swore the boy was Purbeck's. The court judged her guilty, fined her five hundred pounds and declared she must do public penance — walk barefoot, draped in a white sheet, from Paul's Cross to the Savoy and stand before the church for all to see.

But on the Sunday appointed, Frances Purbeck was not to be found. With her son she had taken refuge in a little house behind the garden of the Ambassador from Savoy. It was some weeks before the Constable, discovering her whereabouts, came with his men to take her. The Ambassador refused to let them through his grounds; the officers stood in the crowded street and waited. At dinner-time — full midday — a coach pulled up at the door. A young woman emerged, hurried, furtive, ran to the coach and was driven off before the Constable could make up his mind to seize her. Immediately he gave chase with his men.

No sooner were the officers out of sight than a second coach drew up next door to the Ambassador's. Frances Purbeck, her small son in her arms, stepped in and drove away. The pursuivants, overtaking the first coach, found in it one of the Ambassador's pages — a handsome, fair-haired youth — disguised as a lady and wearing his silks with an air.

Such was the tempestuous and beautiful young woman who at length took refuge in her father's house. It is pleasant to think of them at Stoke together: the old man writing his law books and riding out each day on horseback for his pleasure; the erring, spirited daughter whose adventures were by no means ended. Lady Hatton lived in London, busy with battles over her property. (She had rented Hatton House to the Duchess of Richmond, whom she disliked and soon tried to evict.) Only when she needed Coke's help in court did Lady Hatton venture to Stoke. "Would you thincke," wrote Chamberlain, "the Lady Hattons stomacke could stoupe to go to seeke her Lord Cooke at Stoke for his counsaile and assistance?"

In January of 1631, King Charles heard that Sir Edward had been ill and was "not likely to last long." Charles instructed his Secretary to choose some person whom he might trust to inquire after Coke's health. Should Sir Edward be near death, let care be taken to seal up his study, "where such papers are, as use may be made of them (having passed through so many great places in the state) for his Majesty's service, and some suppressed that may dis-serve him. For he is held too great an oracle amongst the people, and they may be misled by any thing that carries such an authority as all things do that he either speaks or writes."

To Coke, nothing lay in his study which might "dis-serve" him. He was proud of his library and asked in his will that his books might be preserved for posterity. He had three years of life before him and no desire to be coddled. Friends sent physicians to inquire after his health. Sir Edward told them "he had never taken physic since he was born and would not now begin; and that he had now upon him a disease which all the drugs of Asia, the gold of Africa, the silver of America, nor all the doctors of Europe could cure — old age. He therefore both thanked them and his friend that sent them, and dismissed them nobly with a reward of twenty pieces to each man." Among Sir Edward's books was Thomas Paynell's *Regimen of Health.* In the margin, Coke scribbled out the Latin prescriptions, rhymed into English:

> If physicke fayle
> For thy advayle,
> Three Doctors you shall find,
> Doctor due diet,
> And Doctor Quiet,
> And Doctor merry-mynde.

When Coke was three months past his eightieth birthday, he met with an accident. Sir Edward made light of it. "The 3rd May, *Anno Domini* 1632," he writes, "riding in the morning in Stoke, between 8 and 9 of the clocke to take the air, my horse under me had a strange stumble backward, fell upon me. . . . And yet, by the Providence of Almighty God, thoughe I was in the greatest danger, yet I had not the least hurt — nay, no hurt at all. For Almighty God saith by his prophet David, 'the Aungels of the Lord tarieth round about them that feare him, and delivereth them,' *et nomen Domini benedictum*, for it was his doinge."

A year later, rumor reached London that Coke was dead. In Westminster Hall they talked of it, "all one morning," wrote a Londoner, "insomuch that Sir Edward's wife got her brother, Lord Wimbledon, to post with her to Stoke to take possession of that place; but beyond Colebrook they met with one of his physicians coming from him, who told her of his much amendment, which made them return also to London; some distemper he had fallen into for want of sleep, but is now well again."

Coke rallied, yet the thread of life was thin. On the ninth of June, 1634, he called for pen and paper, desiring to set down the testament of his faith. That Sir Edward was a man sincerely devout, friends and family have borne witness. Yet now in his weakness, faith seemed to falter, sink with the sinking of his heart, the uncertain course of blood along his veins. Old Lord Burghley, in his last sickness, had prayed in words that are much like Coke's, revealing fear, not of death but of ebbing faith, the Christian's last ingratitude. "All my long life," wrote Coke, "I have had the seale of the blessed Sacrament of his bodye and blood so often conferred to mee, to persuade mee of his Grace and favour to mee. The God of all consolation and comforte give mee in myne olde and weake age a strong faith, and patience, together with the testimony of a Good Conscience to the end, against the temptations and fyery dartes of the enemye. Soe, deare God, I believe, O merciful God, of thy Grace and mercie, help the weakness of my faith, Amen, Amen."

All summer Coke lingered. September approached and it was seen that he would not recover. A warrant was issued to search Stoke House, bearing the date of 1 September, 1634, "by order of his Majesty's Privy Council." The King's men rode out to Stoke, and they were thorough. As Coke lay dying in the great curtained bed, they ransacked study and library, took away the manuscripts of all four Parts of the *Institutes*, the manuscript notes for two additional books of *Reports* — "and I think," wrote Roger Coke, "51 other manuscripts, with the last will of Sir Edward, wherein he had for several years been making provisions for his younger grandchildren."

Sir Edward did not hear the King's men or know that they were near. Charles was very careful in this business. Coke's chambers at the Temple too were searched. After six years of quiet and retirement in the country, Sir Edward, dying, still was dangerous. His chambers in the Temple yielded a considerable cache, brought solemnly to Whitehall: "A black buckrom bagg, containing the business of the late Earl of Essex. A black buckrom bagg of the Powder Treason. A bundle of draughts, acts and petitions touching the late Parliament. . . ." Coke's confidential secretary, John Pepys (cousin to the diarist), surrendered a trunk, which the King himself opened at Bagshot. The date of search is gravely rendered, together with a catalogue of contents: "A table book, embroidered with gold and silke. Six keys tied together. Three silver and gilte clasps of a book and one clasp of silver. One lidde of an old painted box. One paper of poetry to his children. . . ."

His Majesty poked and stirred in the dusty relics of a life — and fished up "one great iron key; one silver seal with his arms, set in white bone; an old crown piece, seventy pieces of 10 s. 6d., all put in an old purse." Nothing seditious, nothing that might discredit.

On the third of September, Coke died. His work was done, he met his end with patience. Beyond his chamber window the scene bespoke its country symbolism. Summer was gone, the land awaited harvest. Fruit dropped from the vine, the meadow grass was ready for a second mowing. The old heart slowed and ceased to beat. "Died at his house at Stoke," wrote Sir Julius Caesar, Master of the Rolls, "mine old friend and fellow Bencher, Sir Edward Coke, Knt., being Wednesday between eleven and twelve of the clock at night, in his bed quietly, like a lambe, without any groans or outward signs of sickness, but only spent by age."

Stoke had its church and churchyard at the gates. Coke's father was buried in St. Andrew's, Holborn; Clem Coke in Temple Church. Yet Sir Edward had chosen none of these. "That my body," said his will, "may be inclosed in lead and carried to Tittleshall Church and bee laid in the vault there where my first good wife lyeth. A convenient monument to bee made for me there by the discretion of myne executors. But I will noe funeral pompe to be made for mee." Coke's body was carried home to Norfolk, up the north road that he had ridden so often in his prime. Past Cambridge, Thetford, Swaffham, skirting the fen country, where wind blew from the cold Wash and sea birds screamed above the farms. It was the country Coke knew best — harsh, grudging its fruits. The small brown cows were spare and meager; sheep grazed on downs of chalk. Windmills and round Norman towers . . . the mournful long flat marshes between Holkham and the sea . . .

After the strange fashion of the time, Coke's body was kept a full month between death and burial. Likely enough, the coffin lay at Sir Edward's own house of Godwick, so that friends and relatives might gather. Pastons from Oxmead, Gawdys from Norwich, Yelvertons and Knyvets and Hobarts and Pernes, riding across country to pay their last respects. On October fourth, the funeral was held at St. Mary's, the parish church of Tittleshall, a mile across the fields from Godwick.

Even today, St. Mary's seems remote. It lies in a checkerboard of barley fields; the road that runs to it is narrow. The church is very old. Its square tower, built of Norfolk flint stone, dates from the fourteenth century. Across the road, cows graze. Coke's tomb is in the chancel, below the altar to the south. Made of polished marble, large and handsome, it is a work of the celebrated statuary Nicholas Stone. Sir Edward's effigy lies full length upon the tomb, in judge's robes with ruff and coif, the SS collar across his breast. Eight shields hold armorial bearings, some in color, reds and blues and faded argent. A Latin inscription, long and elaborate, is reckless with facts and words not seen before in any language: Primi-condus, madidoculus. "*Duodecem Liberorum*," *it reads*, "*Tredecim Librorum Pater*" . . . Father of twelve children and thirteen books. Perhaps John of Holkham wrote it, adding a child or two, a book or two; perhaps the sculptor was responsible. There is a second inscription, in English:

> In his younger yeares Recorder of the Cities
> of Norwich & London, next Sollicitor Generall
> to Quene Eliza. and Speaker of the Parliament
> in ye XXXV yeare of her Raigne. Afterwards
> Attornye Generall to the same Queene, as also
> to her Successor Kinge James. To both a
> Faithfull Servant, for their Majesties for theire
> Safetyes. By King James constituted Chief Justice

> of both Benches successively. In both a just, in
> both an exemplary Judge. One of his Majesties
> most honorable Privie Counsell, as also of Counsell
> to Queen Anne, & Chief Justice in Eire
> of all hir Forrests, Chases and Parkes. Recorder
> of ye Cittie of Coventrye and High Steward of
> the University of Cambridge, whereof he was some
> time a Member in Trinitye Colledge. A chast husband,
> a provident father. He crowned his pious life with a
> pious and Christian departure at Stoke Poges in the
> county of Buckingham. His laste wordes, Thy kingdome
> come, thye will be done.
> Learne, reader to live so
> That thou may'st so dye.

Bridget Coke's monument is set in the wall above. In effigy she prays, hands pointed, her children kneel behind her in a row. Sir Edward rests beneath his marble sepulture. Men who knew him or whose fathers had known him set down his name in their chronicles with Burghley, Sandys, Sir Robert Cecil, Bacon, Selden — men who had left their mark upon the times. These chroniclers wrote stiffly, with all the dignity of elegy, as became men of their profession. William Camden, the annalist, declared that Coke had "greatly obliged both his own age and posterity." Sir Henry Spelman, the antiquary, knew well the feuds and factions of a scholar's world. Coke, he wrote, "was the founder of our legal storehouse, and, which his rivals must confess though their spleen doth burst by reason of it, the head of our jurisprudence." Sir Julius Caesar, having battled Coke through the law courts for some thirty years, like a stout adversary rendered due tribute. "Of the most famous memorie," wrote Caesar; "a generall good scholar and most skilfull in the common lawe of England of any man in his time, or before him for the space of three hundred yeares at least." Thomas Fuller, clergyman and historian, roamed the counties for his *Worthies of England*, characterizing friend and foe alike with a witty pen; but when he came to Coke the Norfolkman, Fuller softened and the words flowed out in praise: "The jewel of his mind was put into a fair case, a beautiful body with a comely countenance. His works will last to be admired whilst Fame hath a trumpet left her, and any breath to blow therein."

CHAPTER NOTES

CHAPTER ONE

Page 5. In 1882, the law courts were moved to London and given their own building in the Strand. Concerning the royal tennis, in 1949, workmen, repairing the roof beams of Westminster Hall, found a tennis ball of Henry VIII's time.

Page 11. The Privy Council was a small, powerful ruling body whose members were chosen by the Queen, as opposed to the traditional Great Council, or Parliament, which sat for seven or eight weeks every three years (on an average). The number of Privy Councilors varied. Elizabeth's predecessor and half-sister, Mary Tudor, had fifty; Elizabeth, in 1593, had eighteen, five of whom sat with the Commons, the others with the Lords. A seat in Privy Council was the ambition of every man in public life.

CHAPTER TWO

Page 16. The woolsacks were supplied to Parliament by the great guild of wool merchants, "to mind the state-officers," says Pettus, "of the Staple Commodity of the Kingdom." [*The Constitution of Parliaments in England* (ed. 1680) p. 58.] Even today, the Lord Chancellor presides on his woolsack in the House of Lords, and people refer symbolically to "the woolsack," as to "Downing Street."

Page 20. Coke's recitation of the petitions being much garbled in D'Ewes and Townshend, I have taken them partly from Coke's own printed version of customary procedure, "Presentment of the Speaker," [4 *Institute* (ed. 1797) p. 8] where, significantly, Coke is careful to call the first petition (free speech), a *protestation* rather than a petition and defines it as Commons' right, in debate, not to be confined merely to the matters urged by the Lord Chancellor on opening day. Sir Thomas More had petitioned for freedom of speech as Speaker of the Commons in the Parliament of 1523, but it is clear that he did not consider his petition as a matter of right according to ancient form. Such a petition was presented in 1542 and again in 1554. From the first year of Elizabeth the petition is regularly included in the Speaker's protestation to the Crown. [J. E. NEALE "The Commons' Privilege of Free Speech in Parliament," in *Tudor Studies* (ed. Seton-Watson, 1924).]

CHAPTER THREE

Page 32. De Republica Anglorum. The Commons sat on in St. Stephen's until it burned down in the great fire of 1834. Barry then rebuilt it with the same dimensions, the same seating arrangement. Bombed out by the Germans in 1941, the Commons Chamber was rebuilt. And though the House had now six hundred members, at Winston Churchill's suggestion the chapel dimensions were preserved, a building committee declaring that the "sense of intimacy and almost conversational form of debate encouraged by the dimensions of the old Chamber . . . firmly established in the affections of the nation . . . should be maintained." The House of Lords is nearly thirty feet longer than the Commons; the committee was impressed by a "noticeable diminution of the sense of intimacy produced by this slight difference in length." [MAURICE HASTINGS *Parliament House* (ed. 1950) pp. 185-186.]

American visitors, accustomed to the spacious semicircular form of our halls of Congress, are struck with the dramatic intimacy of this crowded choirstall arrangement and the fact that the Chamber never looks empty during a speech, even when half the members are absent in committee.

CHAPTER FOUR

Page 33. "A Fifteene and a Tenth (that I may note it for forrainers sakes,) is a certaine taxation upon every City, Burrough, and Towne, not upon every particular man, but in generall, in respect of the fifteenth part of the wealth of the places. A Subsidy we call that, which is imposed upon every man, being cessed by the powle [poll], man by man, according to the valuation of their goods and lands. But neither is this nor the other taxation ever imposed, but by the consent of the Estates in Parliament." [WILLIAM CAMDEN *Ann. Eliz.* (ed. 1635) pp. 49-50.]

CHAPTER SIX

Page 62. Much ink has been spilled over the origin of this phrase. Holdsworth [*History of English Law* (ed. 1923) II, 504] say that "Utter Barrister" had no reference to an actual bar of wood and derives from the fact that those who were to argue in moot court sat on forms or benches. Utter Barristers sat "uttermost (outermost) on the formes which they call the Barre." In *Acts of the Privy Council*, XIX (1590) p. 388, "Owtward Barrister" is used. After 1700, the hierarchy shifted. The Utter Barrister was called within the bar and became an Inner Barrister — and still later, "a silk," from the gown, the junior barrister taking the name Utter Barrister or "stuff (woolen) gownsmen." [HUGH BELLOT *The Inner and Middle Temple* (1902) pp. 38-39.] As the Inns declined, degrees became contingent upon the official "eating of dinners" in legal term time. When a man had eaten so many dinners, he was ready for the bar. In the eighteenth century, a surprising number of American-born students attended the Inns of Court — 236 of them before 1815 — most of whom were admitted between 1750 and 1775. Of these, 74 were from South Carolina, 49 from Virginia, 19 from Massachusetts and so on in decreasing numbers. Peyton Randolph of Virginia, first President of the Continental Congress, was a Middle Temple man, as was Thomas McKean, Chief Justice of Pennsylvania.

Page 64. After 1688 the number of death penalties increased. In 1810 Sir Samuel Romilly said, "There is probably no other country in the world in which so many and so great a variety of human actions are punishable with loss of life as in England." In 1819, Sir T. F. Buxton put the number of capital offenses at 223. A statute of 1823 (Sir Robert Peel) reformed the criminal code and cut down drastically the number of capital offenses. [L. RADZINOWICZ *A History of English Criminal Law* (1948) pp. 3, 4, 584.]

Page 65. The Inns of Court had done much to save the common law for England at a time when Henry VIII found the Roman law more useful to his purpose. In the sixteenth century, all Europe (including Scotland) embraced the civil law of Rome. Henry VIII suggested that the Inns of Court be "reformed" on lines convenient to authority. The Year Books ceased (1535) and there was danger that the common law might cease with them. Mary Tudor, a Catholic, turned instinctively to Roman law and the Papal Decretals. Litigants flocked to Chancery, which was influenced by the Roman system. Stow, the annalist, complained that in Westminster Hall the Serjeants and common-law judges had "naught to do but look about them." Through it all, the Inns and Temple never ceased their teaching, and gentlemen's sons continued to frequent them — perhaps for no better reason than that it was the customary thing to do. The influence, strong and continuous, prevailed.

Page 70. The declaration or formal pleading is the first statement a lawyer hands to the court in explanation of why his client brings suit. Today a case cannot be thrown out of court because of technical errors in pleading. In Coke's day, formality still ruled the courts. There were scores of formulae and rules, almost like magic passwords, which a lawyer must know if he wished to keep his case in court — inheritance of a time when God was looked on as final arbiter of every suit, and the judges, God's spokesmen. In Saxon or Norman days, trials were by "ordeal" — the ordeal by fire, water or the dry crust offered before witnesses. An innocent man swallowed his crust, a guilty man choked because God, seeing his perfidy, closed his throat; a guilty man, carrying the requisite number of hot coals on his bare hand the requisite number of paces, acquired burns that would heal in the requisite number of days. Accompanying the ordeals were prayers and formulae. Even the smallest mistake of recitation manifested guilt. (God had twisted the perfidious tongue.)

It has been the business of courts to weed out the superstition of the ancient formulae, yet retain the strict procedure which is the defendant's protection.

Page 75. The legend is not forgotten. In 1951 I saw the oak — shattered but huge of base — and heard from the tenant farmer how Queen Elizabeth, perched in the broad branches, shot her deer. A

Suffolk clergyman, Mr. C. Davy, as a boy saw Huntingfield Hall before it was demolished, and in 1836 wrote a description to his son. [C. W. Johnson *Life of Sir Edward Coke* (ed. 1837) I, p. 121.]

CHAPTER EIGHT

Page 102. 20 April, 1597. *Atty-Gen. v. Wades and others.* (Forgery):

"He pleaded 'Not Guilty', and on interrogatories he made answer, 'I can say nothing.' Whereupon it was ruled by the Court that, by the course of the Court, it is held as a confession, and the cause may be judged immediately without other examinations." [John Hawarde *Les Reportes del Cases in Camera Stellata, 1593-1609* (ed. 1894) p. 72.]

22 April. "If a man plead in his answer Not Guilty, and will not answer the articles [interrogatories] it shall be held as a confession." [*Ibid.* p. 74.]

CHAPTER NINE

Page 113. In 1603 the ceiling was repainted, doors and doorsills replaced with new ones.

CHAPTER TWELVE

Page 143. 3 *Institute*, p. 79. In spite of this law of 1606, the old practice held. Acts of 1547 and 1552 had provided that in treason trials, the accused should be confronted by two witnesses. These statutes were repealed under Mary (1 & 2 *P.* & *M.* c. 10) and written depositions substituted. Elizabeth's Parliaments restored the older statutory rule (1 *Eliz.* c. 5; 13 *Eliz.* c. 1), but in the excited state of opinion prevailing after Elizabeth's excommunication of 1570, the courts had largely evaded it. Coke himself, as advocate and judge, defended the older, less generous ruling by saying that "the court [the judges] should stand as counsel for the prisoner," and that "evidence against him should be so manifest that it cannot be contradicted." Yet, by the time he wrote the *Third Institute* (posthumously published) he seems to have come around to a less harsh point of view. [See 3 *Inst.*, pp. 79, 138; also THAYER *Treatise on Evidence* (ed. 1898) p. 159 n.] Actually it was 1853 before felons were given full statutory authority to call witnesses and have counsel.

Concerning prisoners speaking in their own defense, an experienced English judge has this to say: "I am by no means sure that the practice of examining the prisoner pointedly and minutely at his trial was not an advantage to him if he was innocent; and I doubt whether the absence of all rules of evidence, and the habit of reading depositions instead of having the witnesses produced in court, made so much difference as our modern notions would lead us to believe." [SIR J. FITZJAMES STEPHEN *History of the Criminal Law of England* (ed. 1882) I, 356-357.]

CHAPTER THIRTEEN

Page 162. Ovid's *Metamorphosis* contains the story of Actaeon, turned into a stag by the fleeing Diana and hunted to death by his own hounds. Stags have horns, and to Elizabethans a man "horned" was a man cuckolded. A favorite device for annoying a hated neighbor was to set a pair of stag horns at his gate. The raising of two fingers (in what today is the V sign) was a fighting gesture. Cuffe on this occasion turned a superb phrase. On Coke's shouting at him, "*Dominum cognoscite vestrum!*" [Know your own master!] (Actaeon's words when his hounds attacked him), Cuffe replied smoothly, "Mr. Attorney, you leave out the former part of the verse, which you should have repeated, '*Actaeon ego sum*'—I am Actaeon (the stag)." It was an allusion easily recognized by any Englishman who had been to grammar school—which meant, certainly, all the judges and commissioners for trial and, very likely, the jury of merchants and City aldermen. [JOHN AUBREY *Aubrey's Brief Lives* (ed. 1950) p. 68.]

Page 165. Ralegh's words from the scaffold 29 October, 1618: "I will now only borrow a little time of Mr. Sheriff to speak of one thing not appertaining to this matter, but which doth make my heart bleed to hear that such an imputation should be laid upon me; for it is said that I was a prosecutor of the death of the Earl of Essex, and that I stood in a window over against him when he suffered in the Tower, and puffed out tobacco in disdain of him. I take God to witness that I had no hand in his blood and was none of those that procured his death. I shed tears for him when he died; and as I hope to look God in the face hereafter, my Lord of Essex did not see my face when he suffered; for I was afar off in the Armoury, where I saw him but he saw not me. I was heartily sorry for him, though I confess I was of a contrary faction and helped to pluck him down; but in respect of his worth I loved him, and I knew that it would be worse with me when he was gone; for I got the hate of those that wished me well before; and those that set me against him afterwards set themselves against me and were my greatest enemies. My soul hath many times since been grieved that I was not nearer to him when he died, because, as I understood afterwards, he asked for me at his death, to have been reconciled unto me. . . . I am now at this instant to render up my account to God; and I protest, as I shall appear before him, this that I have spoken is true — I hope I shall be believed." [David Jardine *Criminal Trials* (ed. 1832) I, p. 507. Jardine takes the account from Cayley, adding details from "a letter by an eye-witness, from the Ralegh collection of papers in the P.R.O."]

CHAPTER FIFTEEN

Page 192. As late as 1794, Edmund Burke, referring in Parliament to the trial of Warren Hastings, ridiculed the notion of laws or rules of evidence. He hardly knew, he said, what was meant by the phrase, and though something had been written on such rules, it was "very general, very abstract, and comprised in so small a compass that a parrot he had known might get them by rote in one half hour and repeat them in five minutes." [J. H. Wigmore "A General Survey of the History of the Rules of Evidence," in *Selected Essays in Anglo-American Legal History* (ed. 1908) II, p. 695.]

Page 195. Coke referred here to the old law of approvers, whereby the statements of an accomplice who, in accusing another, thereby accuses himself, carries the same weight as a grand jury indictment. "An approver is one that, confessing a felony, accuses others to be guilty of the crime with him. He is called Approver because he must prove his allegation, and that proof was in former ages by battle or the country. By the common law the Approver is sworn to discover all felonies, and his confession and oath makes his accusation of another of the same crime to amount to an indictment. And if his partners are convicted, the King is to pardon him, as to his life, but he ought not to be suffered to continue in the Kingdom." [GILES JACOB *New Law Dictionary* (ed. 1729).]

Page 195. Ralegh's trial opens Volume II of Cobbett's famous *Collection of State Trials*, published in London from 1809 to 1898 — forty-two volumes in all, beginning with the trial of Thomas à Becket in 1163 and ending with the conviction of four English traitors at the Old Bailey in 1820. It is unknown who wrote down Ralegh's trial. The account is obviously garbled, sometimes unintelligible, not only because of Elizabethan sentence structure with its galloping prepositions, but because sentences and whole sections are apparently left out. Jardine, in his two volumes, *Criminal Trials* (1832), has supplied some of these omissions from letters and other contemporary sources.

Page 201. See *Cramer v. United States* [321 U. S. 1 (1945)], where the decision of the Supreme Court was five to four for acquittal. Justice Jackson's majority opinion and Justice Douglas's dissent contain full discussion of this point of the overt act, tracing it historically to the colonial statutes of New York, Massachusetts, etc., and still further to the statute of 1351 [25 *Ed.* C. 3]. See also *Haupt v. U. S.* [330 U. S. 631, (1947)], and Willard Hurst's article, "Treason in the United States down to the Constitution." [*Harvard Law Review*, LVIII, no. 226, 1944.]

CHAPTER SIXTEEN

Page 217. This judicial afterthought of Popham's brought bitter criticism from a Solicitor General three generations later. "Judges ought to be bound up by the reasons given in public, and not satisfy or make good their judgment by afterthought of reasons. How very ill did it become the chief justice Popham, a person of learning and parts, in the attainting sir Walter Raleigh, of which trial all since that time have complained — when he gave his opinion, that the affidavit of the lord Cobham, taken in the abscence of sir Walter, might be given in evidence against him, without producing the lord Cobham face to face to sir Walter. . . . When he summed up the evidence, he said, '*Just then it came into his mind*, why the accuser should not come face to face to the prisoner, because he might retract his evidence.' Did it become a just man," wrote Sir John Hawles, "to give his opinion and bethink himself of a reason afterwards?

"And I think," (added Hawles), "this may be justly called the first mute judgment given in Westminster Hall." [SIR JOHN HAWLES "Remarks on the Trial of Fitzherbert" (1689), published later in COBBETT *State Trials* (ed. 1809-1898) VIII, pp. 434-435.]

CHAPTER TWENTY

Page 259. In his *Third Institute* [(ed. 1797) p. 222] under "Judgments and Executions," Coke goes on to give the symbolic meaning of *attaint of blood* in high treason, with authority from the Old Testament for each clause: "Implied in this judgment is, first the forfeiture of all his manors, lands, tenements, and hereditaments in fee-simple, or fee-tail of whomsoever they be holden. Secondly, his wife to lose her dower. Thirdly, he shall lose his children (for they become base ignoble.) Fourthly, he shall lose his posterity, for his blood is stained and corrupted, and they cannot inherit to him or any other auncestor. Fifthly, all his goods and chattels, &c. And reason is, that his body, lands, goods, posterity, &c. shall be torn, pulled asunder, and destroyed, that intended to tear, and destroy the majesty of government. And all these severall punishments are found for treason in holy scripture." [*Op. cit.* p. 210.] Not long after the trial, all the conspirators were attainted by Act of Parliament, including those already dead, and Hugh Owen in Flanders, whom Coke had been instructed to "lay as foul" as he could.

Page 266. Signed declaration of Henry Garnett in the Tower, 13 March, 1606.

Only the italicized passages were read at the trial. The marginal letters ABDF are in Coke's handwriting, indicating to the Clerk the sentences to be read aloud.

A
B
D
F

13° Martii.

A *I have remembered some things, which, because they were long before my knowledge of the Powder acts, I had forgotten.*

B *About Michaelmas after the King came in, Mr. Catesby told me that there would be some stirring, seeing the King kept not promise.*

C And I greatly misliked it, saying it was against the Pope's express commandment; for I had a letter from our General thereof, dated in July before, wherein was earnestly, by Clement, commanded the very same, which this Pope commanded the last summer. Therefore I earnestly desired him that he and Mr. Thomas Winter would not join with any in such tumults; for in respect of their often conversation with us, we should be thought accessory. He assured me he would not. But neither he told, nor I asked, any particulars.

D *Long after this, about Midsummer was twelve-month, either Mr. Catesby alone, or he and Thomas Winter together, insinuated that they had somewhat in hand, and that they would sure prevail.*

E I still reproved them; but they entered into no particulars.

F *Soon after came Mr. Greenwell* (Greenway) *to me, and told me as much.*

G I greatly misliked any stirring, and said, "Good Lord! how is it possible that God work any good effect by these men? These are not God's knights, but the devil's knights." Mr. Greenwell told this to Thomas Winter, who, about a month after Michaelmas, came to me and expostulated that I had so hard a conceit of him, and would never tell him of it. As for their intermeddling in matters of tumults, since I misliked it, he promised they would give over; and I never heard more of it until the question propounded by Mr. Catesby. As for his asking me of the lawfulness of killing the King, I am sure it was never asked me in my life; and I was always resolute that it was not lawful; but he was so resolved in conscience, that it was lawful in itself to take arms for religion that no man could dissuade it, but by the Pope's prohibition, which afterwards I inculcated, as I have said before. The ground of this his resolute opinion I will think of.

Henry Garnett.

[JARDINE *Criminal Trials*, II, pp. 357-358.]

CHAPTER TWENTY-ONE

Page 277. Shortly after Coke gave this speech and charge, a man named Robert Pricket calmly pirated it and published it with a dedication to Lady Hatton's father, the Earl of Exeter. In the preface to his Seventh *Report*, Coke showed himself much annoyed. "An erroneous and ill-spelled pamphlet," he calls it, "under the name *Pricket*, published without my privity and dedicated to my singular good Lord and Father-in-Law, the Earl of Exeter . . . the whole context in that rude and ragged stile, wholly dissonant from a lawyer's dialect." Posterity is indebted to Mr. Pricket. Coke's spontaneous delivery and absence of "lawyer's dialect" constitutes the charm of this plainly heartfelt little talk to his Norfolk countrymen.

CHAPTER TWENTY-TWO

Page 295. Prohibitions were by no means new. The writ had long been used by the common-law courts to assert their jurisdiction against Admiralty and ecclesiastical courts. Medieval church authorities had countered with a statutory confirmation of their power to proceed, the prohibition notwithstanding, under a writ of consultation (24 *Ed.* I). The common-law courts had continued to assert their jurisdiction, and the conflict had continued into the Reformation period. [WILLIAM S. HOLDSWORTH *A History of English Law* (ed. 1924) I, pp. 202-203.]

CHAPTER TWENTY-SEVEN

Page 362. Technically this was a permissible construction, seeing the writ itself said only, in law French, "*no appeal d'autrui court* [to another court]." The writ took its name from the first words of the statute, *Premunire facias.* Dictionarists are hard put to translate the garbled Latin of medieval statutes. The first word of this one may have been, originally, *Premonere* — to forewarn — and drifted into *Pre* (or *Prae*) *munire* — to forearm — which makes no sense. The subject is forewarned that to remove a suit from the King's court is prohibited, etc.

Page 365. "I speak this with confidence for I had it from one of Sir Edward's sons. Sir Edward lay then at the Temple and measured out his time at regular hours, two whereof were to go to bed at Nine a clock, and in the morning to rise at three: At this time Sir Edward's son and some others were in Sir Edward's lodgings, but not in bed, when the Messenger about one in the morning knockt at the door, where the Son met him and knew him. Says he, *I come from the King and must immediately speak with your Father.* 'If you come from ten Kings,' he answer'd, you shall not, for I know my Father's disposition to be such, that if he be disturbed in his sleep, he will not be fit for any Business. But if you will do as we do, you shall be welcome, and about two hours hence my Father will rise, and you then may do as you please.' To which he assented.

"At three Sir Edward rung a little Bell, to give notice to his Servant to come to him, and then the Messenger went to him and gave him the King's letter, and Sir Edward immediately made a warrant to apprehend Somerset, and sent to the King that he would wait upon him that day. The Messenger went back post to Royston, and arrived there about Ten in the Morning. The King had a loathsome Way of Lolling his Arms about his Favourites necks, and kissing them, and in this posture the Messenger found the King with Somerset, saying, *When shall I see thee again?* When he was arrested by Sir Edward's Warrant, Somerset exclaimed that never such an Affront was offered to a Peer of England in the presence of the King. 'Nay, Man!' said the King. 'If Coke sends for me I must go'; and when he was gone, 'Now the Devil go with thee,' said the King, 'for I will never see thy Face more.'

"About three in the Afternoon the Chief Justice came to Royston, and so soon as he had seen the King, the King told him, that he was acquainted with the most wicked murder by Somerset and his wife, that was ever perpetrated, upon Sir Thomas Overbury, and that they made him a Pimp to carry on their Bawdry and Murder: and therefore commanded the Chief Justice with all the Scrutiny possible, to search into the bottom of the Conspiracy, and to spare no Man how great soever, concluding, 'God's curse be upon you and yours, if you spare any of them; and God's curse be upon me and mine if I pardon any one of them.'" [ROGER COKE *Detection* (ed. 1719) I, pp. 86-87.]

CHAPTER TWENTY-NINE

Page 405. The chronology of these meetings and letters is difficult to match. A letter from James to Winwood, dated July 16 from Falkland, cannot be the one that Winwood produced at Council table, seeing that Chamberlain reports the incident on the seventeenth and the journey from Edinburgh took four or five days. James's July sixteenth letter must however be substantially a repetition of earlier ones. It strongly disapproves Lady Hatton's behavior, inquires why, if she had objections, she did not voice them earlier? She must be "commanded" to yield. Should she refuse, "we will leave her to the course of law and suffer her husband to take such order with his children and estate as in ordinary course of justice he may, without taking any consideration of her therein."

The letter of James to Winwood, 16 July 1617, and the one to Bacon and Archbishop Abbot are in the *Buccleuch Papers* (H.M.C. 1899) I, pp. 205-206.

CHAPTER THIRTY

Page 424. Coke referred to Sebastian Brand's old *Shyp of Folys*, published in London in 1509 and enormously popular. Coke's copy of the *Novum Organum* still exists at Holkham. The author saw it — dramatic by virtue of binding and print, let alone association. The title page is beautifully engraved with a ship at full sail, flanked by stylized columns; the long horizon rolls beyond. The author's name appears as *Francisci de Verulamio, Summi Angliae Cancellar'*. Under that is the maxim, *Multi pertransibunt et augebitur scientia.* Scrawled beside all this glory, Coke's rhyme looks impudent indeed.

CHAPTER THIRTY-ONE

Page 439. Coke refers perhaps to some tradition about Alfred current in his time. Alfred often did summon the witenagemot to meet twice during the year, but his laws refer only to frequent meetings.

Page 457. Roger Coke, often incorrect, says Coke's case was decided in King's Bench. Chamberlain's letter of July 1, 1622, says Court of Wards, as does Walter Yonge's *Diary*, p. 62. Chamberlain is usually correct. [ROGER COKE *Detection* (ed. 1719) I, p. 122.]

CHAPTER THIRTY-THREE

Page 487. This date is according to Nicholas's notes. In the various reports of this Parliament, dates are confused; it is possible that Selden and Phelips made their justification of Coke later, on April 10, after the long conference with the Lords.

Page 487. Sir Edward Littleton was chairman of the Committee for Grievances. An Inner Templar and legal scholar, he had sat in Charles's first two Parliaments and had been active in Buckingham's impeachment of 1626. There is a telling contemporary description of this conference:

"The Lord President, who reported the Conference to the house, begun thus: 'The Conference upon Monday last with the lower house, was about the Liberty of the Subject; to set forth, they employed four Speakers: The first was sir Dudley Diggs, a man of a voluble and eloquent speech, his part was the introduction; the second was Mr. Littleton, a grave and learned lawyer, whose part was to represent the Resolution of the House and their grounds whereupon they went. The third was Mr. Selden, a great antiquary and a pregnant man; his part was to shew the law and the precedents in point. The fourth was the lord Coke, that famous reporter of the law, whose part was to shew the reason of all that the others had said, and all that which was said was but an affirmance of the common law." [From a MS belonging to Peter le Neve. Quoted in *State Trials*, III, p. 126.]

Page 491. "An Act for the better securinge of every free man touching proprietie of his goods and libertie of his person.

"Whereas it is declared and enacted by Magna Charta that noe free man is to bee convicted, destroyed, etc., and whereas by a statute made in E: 1 called *de tallagio non concedendo:* And whereas by the Parliament 5 E: 3 and 14 E: 3 and 29 E: 3 etc., And whereas the said great Charter was confirmed and that the other laws etc. Be it enacted that Magna Charta and the same acts of explanation and other the Acts bee putt in due execution and that all judgments, awards, and rules given are [or] to be given to the contrarie shall bee voyd. And whereas by the common laws and statutes it appears that noe free man ought to bee committed by Command of the King, etc.; and if anie free man bee soe committed and the same returned uppon an habeas Corpus, hee ought to bee delivered or bailed. Bee it now enacted that noe free man shall bee committed by the command of the King or the privie counsell but the cause ought to bee expressed and the same beeing returned uppon an habeas Corpus, hee shall bee delivered or bailed; and whereas by the common lawe and statutes every free man hath a proprietie in his goods and estate as no taxe, tallage, etc., Bee it now enacted that noe taxe, tallage, loane, shall be levied, etc. by the King or anie minister without act of parliament and that none bee compelled to receive anie soldier into his house against his will," etc. [From F. H. RELF *The Petition of Right* (1917) App. B, p. 63. Miss Relf's sources are *Harl. MSS.* 2313 and 5324; Sir Richard Grosvenor's *Notes of Proceedings*, Library of Trinity College, Dublin.]

CHAPTER THIRTY-FOUR

Page 517. Sir Simonds D'Ewes, antiquarian and member of the Long Parliament, says in his *Journal* that on December 5, 1640, "a motion was made to recover Sir Edward Coke's written books or other bookes being 19 in number which were taken from him during his last sicknes: etc. and a Committee appointed to search for them, of which I was one." On December 21, D'Ewes records that "Sir Thomas Roe brought a message from the King touching Sir

Edward Cookes bookes which were in Secretarie Windebankes hande should bee delivered before Christmas Eve into the hands of Sir Thomas Crew one of his executors: which message gave the Howse great content." On May 12, 1641, the *Commons Journals* noted that "The House doth desire and hold it fit that the heir of Sir Edward Cooke do publish in Print his Commentary upon Magna Charta [*Second Institute*], The Pleas of the Crown [*Third Institute*] and the Jurisdiction of Courts [*Fourth Institute*] according to the Intention of the said Edward Cooke."

Page 520. Coke, as in his first Report, was paraphrasing Chaucer, *The Parlement of Foules.* Chaucer said: "Out of the old fields, as men saith, cometh al this new corne fro yere to yere." For this information I am indebted to Mr. Putnam of the Harvard Law School Library. He in turn had it from a Japanese gentleman who was showing some Japanese judges around the Treasure Room and spotted the quotation above the mantel, attributed to Coke.

CHAPTER THIRTY-FIVE

Page 527.

1576. Tittleshall Austens. £5. Robert Austen, *alias* Reeve, yeoman.
1580. Godwick. £3,600. John and Robert Drewry.
1585. Thorington Hall. £1,100. Edmund Moulton. (Bridget Paston's mother was a Moulton.)
1585. House in Bevis Marks. £340. Sir Robert Wingfield.
1587. Pitsey. £1,260. Earl of Arundel.
1592. Thorington Wimples, etc. £2,500. Anthony Wingfield.
1592. Wellingham Weasenham, Toftrees. £1,900. Edward Stanupe.
1596. Cippenham (Bucks). £4,200. Lord Burghley.
1598. Elmham. £6,200. Edward, Lord Cromwell.
1599. Stoke Poges. £4,000. Katherine, Countess of Huntingdon.
1600. Wherstead Hall. £1,400. William Barrow.
1602. Minster Lovell. £5,000. Earl of Bedford.
1606. Okeford and Shillingston (Dorset). £3,300. Sir William Ross.
1606. Beck and Beck Hall. £3,200. Thomas Curzon, of Belaugh.

1607. Baylies, near Stoke. £900. Edmund Fitton.
1609. Bournehall (Wherstead). £1,600. Thomas Hall.
1609. Manor and Rectory, Wood Ditton (Cambs). £2,350. Earl of Suffolk.
1609. Bishops Cleave Advowson, "for a competent some of money." Sir Christofer Hatton.
1609. Aldham Hall (Suffolk). £3,800. Thomas Tylney.
1610. Knightleys (Staffs). £5,300. Sir Francis Lacon, of Kinlet, Co. Salop.
1610. Holkham Neales, Lucas, etc. £3,400. William Armiger.
1610. Longham Priors. Watlington (Norfolk). £2,800. Arthur Futter.
1611. Thorington. £1,100. Sir Edward Clere, of Ormsby.
1611. Huntingfield Hall and Park. £4,500. Lord Hunsdon.
1612. Sparham, Stivekey Hall. £2,820. Charles Blakeney.
1613. Paston House. Conisforth Street, Norwich. £800. Sir William Cope of Hardwick, Oxon.
1615. Donyatt (Somerset). £4,200. William, Earl of Pembroke.
1616. Castle Acre. £8,000. Thomas, Earl of Exeter (Lady Hatton's father).
1616. Longford (Derby). £5,000. Trustees of Mrs. Longford of Longford.
1618. Cokeley (Suffolk). £1,000. Christopher Hayward.

[C. W. JAMES *Chief Justice Coke* (1929) pp. 305-306.]

ACKNOWLEDGMENTS

THE farther back in time a biographer ventures, the more difficult becomes the search and the writing that follows the search. As the notes and records pile up, a writer's great need is someone to talk with who knows intimately the names, people, scenes she is describing. The distinguished Elizabethan scholar, my neighbor, Conyers Read, not only gave my manuscript careful scrutiny but showed himself ready night and noon to talk Elizabethan shop, discuss the families Cecil, Bacon, Hatton, Coke. When my story reached the Stuart era, Professor Caroline Robbins of Bryn Mawr College talked (and let me talk) about the emergent men of Privy Council, their duties and their changing function in the seventeenth century. Margaret Hastings, medievalist, author of *The Court of Common Pleas in Fifteenth Century England*, read my manuscript with the keen yet sympathetic eye which means so much to a writer. Elizabeth Read Foster discussed the Parliaments of the 1620's and showed me her then unpublished monograph, "Procedure of the House of Commons . . . 1621-1624." Judge Joseph Sloane brought me books from city law libraries and with gentle enthusiasm took note of a sameness between law courts and litigants, 1600 to 1957. Professors C. H. McIlwain of Harvard and Samuel Thorne, when I went to them with queries, answered by asking me searching questions about Coke; I am grateful for the challenge. I want to thank John H. Powell, historian and bibliographer, for generosity in the giving of time and counsel; Judge Herbert F. Goodrich for reading the manuscript and bringing me reassurance; McKean Downs for patience beyond the limits of husbandly duty.

I cannot take leave without a word of gratitude to friends in England. Sir Evelyn Wrench helped me to find and enter Stoke House — Coke's Buckinghamshire mansion — and shared with me his eager enthusiasm for Anglo-American history. Mr. Hart, librarian at the Inner Temple, showed me his treasures. Mr. Wheeler of George Harding's Bookshop shipped me, during five years, many boxes of books, always with a courteous word slipped beside the invoice. I want to thank certain working members of Parliament and the Inns of Court — Geoffrey de Freitas, Lord Milner of Leeds, Lord Jowett, Sir Godfrey Russell Vick. To a biographer, many things are valuable that cannot be got from books: the sight of the Great Seal of England in its velvet-lined box, lying on a chair in the Lord Chancellor's office, barristers' wigs on their hooks in chambers, an opportunity to sit in the High Court of Justice, the Old Bailey in session, where at first hand one sees the very illustration of Chief Justice Coke's daily work. Sir Albert Richardson of Ampthill showed me treasures that had nothing to do with Coke but much to do with English history and manners. I want to thank Chief Warder Cook of the Tower of London; Katharine Boyd, who drove with me through Norfolk; Mr. Rupert Evans, Lecturer in History at University College, Leicester, who later read my manuscript and made many valuable suggestions; Mr. Penny, a complete stranger encountered in Fetter Lane who lent me (in an emergency) his *Dod's Parliamentary Companion* and let me carry it off to the House of Commons.

For the biographer, local history and customs are of utmost importance. In my search after Coke through Norfolk and the shires, I asked help of local historians and antiquarians — Mr. Ketton-Cremer of Felbrigge Hall; Mr. Stephenson, Headmaster of Norwich Grammar School, where Coke had his primary education; the Reverend Mr. Squire of Mileham Rectory, who one summer day casually opened a desk drawer and drew out Coke's baptismal certificate, written on parchment and inscribed as of February, 1552. John Booth, Mary Wellesley, Antoinette and Oliver Esher, Lady Dent; the young Creasys of Huntingfield Hall, built on the site of Bridget Coke's Suffolk mansion — all these in their several ways helped me to find Coke's England. Your true scholar on either side of the ocean is generous. Sir John Neale of London University and Professor Radzinowicz of Cambridge gave me words of encouragement at the start.

In the past thirty years, a large part of my life has been spent in research libraries. No biography has put me so much in the librarians' debt as Sir Edward Coke's. I want to thank Dr. Louis Wright, Virginia Freund and staff of the Folger Library in Washington; Lois Schwrorer; Mr. Hassall, librarian at Holkham House in

Norfolk, where Coke's own books are kept; the gentlemen in the print room on the top floor of the British Museum; Mr. Putnam of the Harvard Law School Library; Miss Shaffer and Mr. Heaney, in charge of the Carson Law Collection at the Philadelphia Free Library; also the staff of that unique organization, the Union Catalogue, which supplied me by telephone with the location of many books; Dr. Setton's office at the University of Pennsylvania Library; the staff at Haverford and Bryn Mawr College libraries and the girls behind the desk at the Biddle Law Library; Mrs. Sellers, my resourceful and never-daunted secretary; Mary Ellen Morris for expert aid in the arrangement of source references and bibliography. Lastly, I want to thank my editorial consultant, Barbara Rex, for the skillful reading she has given me through not one but three biographies — Holmes, Adams, Sir Edward Coke.

SOURCES AND METHOD

THE family correspondence, diaries and domestic records upon which biographers rely are in Coke's case conspicuously lacking. Sir Edward left almost no personal letters. A few, to Lord Burghley and Sir Robert Cecil, are calendared among the *Salisbury Papers*, the *Buccleuch Papers* and elsewhere in the Historical Manuscript Commission Reports. Coke's famous copy of Littleton's *Tenures* is at Holkham House, with Sir Edward's comments written marginally or interleaved in his own crabbed hand. (I saw it when it was on loan at the British Museum.) Here and there among the legal matters, Coke inserted lines recording principal events of his life; he referred to it as his *Vade Mecum.* Fortunately for posterity, however, Coke's law *Reports* and his *Institutes of the Laws of England* are brilliantly revealing of their writer. Sir Edward did not compose the conventional legal report, dry, impersonal. On the contrary he said what he thought about the judge, the barrister, the clients on both sides and the prisoner in the dock. Each of the eleven Parts of the *Reports* (the Twelfth and Thirteenth were posthumously published) has a preface worthy of being printed separately; I could wish some enterprising publisher would attempt all eleven in one volume. Sir Francis Bacon's stricture, "the Lord Coke's Reports hold too much *de proprio*," is the biographer's great good fortune. The same holds for the *Institutes.* Coke talks with the reader — "*candide Lector*" — or with the student as a father and friend would talk, eager to share his love for scholarship, his love for the common law and for England.

It is a little strange that so few biographies of Coke have been attempted — only Serjeant Woolrych (1826), Cuthbert William Johnson (1837), and Lyon and Block (1929). For brief lives we have those of Lord Campbell in his *Chief Justices of England*, Edward Foss in *Judges of England*, McDonnell's excellent article in the *Dictionary of National Biography*, and a few others. Charles

Warburton James, in *Chief Justice Coke, His Family and Descendants* (1929) tells more of the descendants than of Coke. Mr. Hassall, the Earl of Leicester's librarian, compiled a most interesting catalogue (1950) of Sir Edward's library at Holkham. Laura Norsworthy's life of Lady Hatton, *The Lady of Bleeding Heart Yard*, appeared in 1935; Thomas Longueville's *Curious Case of Lady Purbeck* was published in 1909.

The political scene derives from abundant contemporary sources: the State Papers Domestic and Venetian, Historical Manuscript Commission Reports, D'Ewes's *Journals*, Townshend's *Collections* for the last four Parliaments of Elizabeth; printed diaries such as those of Whitelocke, Wilbraham, Manningham, Yonge, Bowyer; Sir John Harington's *Letters and Epigrams;* the familiar collections known as *Nugae Antiquae*, *Cabala*, *Fragmenta Regalia*, *Harleian Miscellany*, *Somers Tracts;* Nichols's *Progresses* of Elizabeth and of James. For Coke in the Star Chamber, we have John Hawarde's *Reportes del Cases in Camera Stellata.* Written from January, 1593 to March, 1608, and privately printed, it is one of the most entertaining compilations ever set down in any courtroom. Cobbett's *State Trials* and Jardine's *Criminal Trials* tell of the Essex treason and Ralegh's arraignment at Winchester. The Parliaments of James I and Charles I are much more fully documented than those of Elizabeth, the *Commons Journals* more detailed. Rushworth's *Collections*, Notestein and Relf's *Commons Debates, 1621*, and the volumes known as *Old Parliamentary History* are full and excellently arranged. Nobody knows the Parliaments of Elizabeth as does Professor J. E. Neale of London University; every student of the period is indebted to his scholarly and lively articles in the learned journals, his *Elizabethan House of Commons* (1949) and *Elizabeth and Her Parliaments* (1953).

Descriptions of people and personalities came largely from newswriters, notably the eagle-eyed Chamberlain, and from letters in the Calendars of State Papers, Winwood's *Memorials*, the collections of Ellis and Lodge, the Mead to Stuteville series. Hacket's life of Lord Keeper Williams was useful, and Fuller's wonderful *Worthies of England* and Lloyd's *State-Worthies* (plagiarisms and all); Bishop Goodman's *Court and Times*, the *Annals* of Camden and Stow; Birch's *Memoirs of the Reign of Elizabeth*, containing the Bacon letters; and the so-called gossip writers — Anthony Welden, Sanderson, Osborne, Roger Coke, William Harris. Contemporary writers such as Strype, Arthur Wilson, Thomas Fuller in his *Church History* showed all the passion of bias; their willful distortion brings back the scene.

I make no claim to the discovery of new material. My aim is introduction, evocation; I hope that my book will recall a great man long forgotten. This biography is written as narrative, not as exposition; I have always found the narrative method more persuasive. But no phrase or sentence, taken from diary or letter, has been transposed into conversation. For matter quoted directly, source references will be found, pages 609 to 637. Many of the printed references that I used were unavailable fifty, even thirty years ago; today they are reliably calendared and so extensive as to threaten the biographer with a deluge rather than a dearth. But though Coke left few personal letters, his handwriting can be seen in abundance at the London Public Record Office — page on page of depositions taken from prisoners in the Tower, examinations, notes to counsel before trial. In that extraordinary temple of scholars known as the Round Room, so quiet one hears the crackling of dried parchment unrolled beneath the readers' hands, I sat before bound sheaves of manuscript called the Ralegh Book, the Gunpowder Book. Here I saw Sir Walter's handwriting, Guy Fawkes's signature before and after torture — John Johnson, he called himself. And in one margin, Coke's sudden scrawl, addressed to Secretary Winwood: "From the Tower, at 3 o'clock in the morning." There is no minimizing the value, for the biographer, of the sight and handling of such documents. My book was written three thousand miles from Chancery Lane and the Round Room. Yet I never forgot those scribbled words. They told me Coke was more than a scholar's legend; he had lived.

With the spelling of quoted matter I have chosen to be inconsistent. When the original draft was available I reproduced the seventeenth-century spelling, not for quaintness or "authenticity" but because there is something wonderfully characteristic about it. Few letter writers have surpassed John Chamberlain. In an age before English dictionaries, he spells as only a cultivated man of imagination could spell; his orthography makes lively passages livelier. But I have not reproduced the long *s*'s, the *y* for *i;* when an occasional word was incomprehensible I modernized it. Unfortunately I could not always procure original letters and diaries; the reader may feel discomfort at finding a letter in Elizabethan spelling followed closely by one (perhaps from the same writer) in modern dress. Seventeenth-century state trials were garbled in report, as every scholar knows. What the prosecution said and what the defendant said differ as the persons differed who recorded them. My method was to study such reports as I could find, compare them and take from each what seemed pertinent and credible. I did the same with the many parliamentary diaries of 1621, edited with such distinction by Notestein and Relf. Coke's easy Latin, medieval or diluted with law French, stands as he wrote it.

Concerning the physical scene, Coke's biographer is fortunate. Sir Edward's house in Norwich exists and is lived in — the Paston half, medieval; Coke's "new-built" portion, Elizabethan. I saw the house inside and out, a charming old mansion on a quiet street, with the river Wensum flowing past the garden. The grammar school that Coke attended stands in Norwich Cathedral Close; boys still say their lessons in that cold bleak upstairs chapel. In Buckinghamshire a wing of Stoke House sits grandly by its little lake; I drove through the wrought-iron gates bearing Coke's crest and in the great hall viewed the Hatton arms above the fireplace. Inner Temple Hall was destroyed by a German bomb in 1941, but Middle Temple has been restored and the ancient Round Church rises from its ruins. The Temple today is busy. Lawyers keep their chambers in Brick Court; below the garden, river barges move downstream; the bargeman's horn calls hoarse and short as it did when Coke was a student. Westminster Hall, Greenwich Palace on the Thames, Windsor Castle, where Coke was often summoned by the Queen, the hall at Winchester beneath which Ralegh was imprisoned — all exist and are in use, lived in or worked in. Winchester Great Hall, when I saw it, was divided by plywood partitions so one law court would not conflict with another. In the nearby museum is a horn like the one that Ralegh heard at dawn on the morning of his trial. Holkham House in Norfolk, seat of the present-day Cokes, is what the British call "new" — built in 1760 by Sir Thomas Coke, first Earl of Leicester. In Sir Edward's day no stone of it existed. But the North Sea is there, unchanged, the cold wind that turns the Norfolk mill-wheels — and Sir Edward's books in the white and gold Palladian library of Holkham House. Mileham Church still stands, where Edward Coke was baptized, and St. Mary's at Tittleshall, where Coke and Bridget, his "first good wife," are buried.

A list of books follows. Its purpose is twofold: to identify sources from which material has been quoted, and to indicate the scope of research, answering for the general reader a question which meets me frequently: "How did you find the road back (to Coke or Holmes or Adams or Peter Tchaikovsky)?" It has always seemed to me that readers of a biography are entitled to see the author's sources, just as the audience at an explorer's lecture expects the chairman's introduction, a preliminary reassurance that the speaker really did travel to the North Pole and live among the Eskimos. What to include presents a real problem; much that was not immediately relevant to Coke was valuable in giving life and color to the scene. My own bibliographies usually include a half-dozen rather questionable treatises, as (from the present list) a paperback called *Our Old Nobility*, published in 1913 by the London *Daily News*, a lively, sly genealogy of the great English families, revealing much by innuendo, whether or not one credits it. "The Cecils," one chapter begins, "assert that they come from an ancient Hertfordshire family, though some have maintained that one of their ancestors was an innkeeper at Stamford." The statement, bland, impudent, makes the Cecils suddenly human and besides, it brightens the biographer's day, after copying out heavily encrusted elegiac paragraphs written by relatives of the deceased. To a biographer, not the facts of history alone are valuable but what people thought (or think) about the facts.

The English Renaissance is particularly rich in literature, whether of poetry, geography and exploration, philosophy or the beginnings of modern law and science. The road back is a familiar one, but no less an adventure for that. Books which today are classics, in Coke's time were new; the biographer learns to look on them with a fresh eye. I was tempted to include in my bibliography the King James translation of the Bible, undertaken when Coke was in his fifties, matter for conversation and intense local interest during the eight years that scholars worked on it. Contrariwise, Coke — to my knowledge at least — never mentioned

William Shakespeare. The only time I could bring Shakespeare into the scene was in 1604, when Sir Edward walked in King James's coronation procession and the records told of four and a half yards of scarlet cloth issued to Shakespeare and his players for suits to wear *en marche*. Coke's critics have said that his lack of interest in Shakespeare was a sign of ignorance, or at best, disregard for art and literature, though Coke's legal writings quote the poets from Virgil to Chaucer. What one forgets is that Shakespeare, to most of Coke's contemporaries, was one clever playwright among many. By that same token I have been wary of certain working terms of the professional historian: *medievalism, the feudal system, the Renaissance*. Coke never heard of these words, they were invented later. He lived within their framework (or at the edge of it); their use would obscure the scene, lower a curtain between us and Coke's England.

The great books which influenced Coke, such as Fortescue's *De Laudibus*, Bracton's *De Legibus*, Judge Littleton's *Tenures*, Sir Thomas Smith's *De Republica:* these belong in my bibliography rather than the celebrated social philosophers — as for instance Jean Bodin, whose name was on many lips in Coke's time and later. Sir Edward was a working judge; his passionate concern with English government and English liberties was a daily, practical matter, to be proven in law court and Parliament, untried by legislation and judicial decision rather than by the word of contemporary theorists. To limit this bibliography to books that Coke knew would be absurd; what I have said is indicative of a list which includes many general political and constitutional histories but does not follow the conventional pattern. New evidence alters historical judgments. Yet the classic historians keep their place upon the shelf; the biographer, if he is wise, will turn to them often. Froude's account of the Armada fight in '88, Bagehot's witty strictures on the men who should or should not rule the nation, Judge Stephen's blunt personal reminiscences from the bench — these carry the foreigner, the American, into that strange island, so close yet so remote, so like any country yet so unlike — called England. Trevelyan, Gardiner, Holdsworth, Dicey, Stubbs: their books, during the five years of writing, became as much part of this biography as the maps that covered my study walls — Norfolk, London, Westminster, the Thames, the British Isles.

BIBLIOGRAPHY

Sir Edward Coke

Coke's Writings

The list below indicates Coke's most important writings and those of his works which were helpful in drawing his character. No attempt has been made to enumerate or evaluate the many editions of the *Institutes* and *Reports,* both English and foreign; the reader is referred to George P. McDonnell's excellent article on Coke in the *Dictionary of National Biography.* The student who wishes to see and handle early editions of Coke's works can do so at the Carson Collection (Free Library of Philadelphia) or in one of the great university law libraries.

Institutes of the Laws of England

For Coke's *Commentary on Littleton,* the best editions begin with the 13th (1788), containing notes from the manuscripts of Hall, Sir W. Jones and Lord Nottingham, edited by F. Hargrave and continued by C. Butler. I have used the 1817 editions, and, for the other three parts, the edition of 1797.

The First Part of the Institutes of the Laws of England; or, *A Commentary upon Littleton.* 2 vols. 17th ed. London, 1817. 1st ed. 1628; 2d to 12th ed. 1629-1738; 13th and best ed. 1788; 15th to 19th 1789-1832.

The Second Part of the Institutes of the Laws of England, Containing the Exposition of Many Ancient and Other Statutes. 2 vols. London, 1797. Finished by Coke in 1628, 1st ed. posthumously published by order of the House of Commons, 1642; other eds. 1662-1681, all folio; published with 3rd and 4th *Parts* 1797-1817.

The Third Part of the Institutes of the Laws of England, Concerning High Treason, and Other Pleas of the Crown and Criminal Causes. London, 1797. Finished by Coke in 1628, 1st ed. posthumously published by order of the House of Commons, 1644; other eds. 1648-1680, all in folio; published with 2d and 4th *Parts* 1797-1817.

The Fourth Part of the Institutes of the Laws of England, Concerning the Jurisdiction of Courts. London, 1797. Materials collected by Coke, 1st ed. posthumously published by order of the House of Commons, 1644; other eds. 1648-1681; published with 2d and 3rd *Parts* 1797-1817.

The Reports

For Coke's *Reports*, the edition of 1738 is here listed, simply because I own it and used it for quotation and reference. I have not heard one special edition of the *Reports* named as superior, though, as mentioned earlier, scholars are suspicious of Parts Twelve and Thirteen, edited and published posthumously. Coke's *Reports* have had numerous editions, with notes from distinguished judges and legal scholars; they have been issued in neat abridgments and condensed into rhyming couplets — mine bears the date 1742. Wallace and McDonnell contain interesting discussions of the different editions. For the reader's interest we have listed below the first edition of *The First Part of the Reports* as given by Johnson in his life of Coke. Also given is the usual entry covering publication of the thirteen Parts.

The First Part of the Reports of Sir Edward Coke Knt., her Majesty's Attorney-General, of Divers Resolutions and Judgments, Given with Great Deliberation by the Reverend Judges . . . during the Most Happy Reign of . . . Queen Elizabeth. . . . St. Omer, 1600. In law French with a Latin preface, the 1st ed.

Les Reports de Edward Coke. By Sir E. Coke. 13 vols. folio. London, 1600-1615, 1656, 1659. In law French, the first eleven parts published at different times between 1600 and 1615; the last two edited and published posthumously in 1656 and 1659.

The Reports of Sir Edward Coke Kt. in English in Thirteen Parts Compleat. . . . 7 vols. The Savoy (London), 1738.

The Reports of Sir Edward Coke, Kt., in Verse. Ed. John Worrall. London, 1742.

Other Writings

Autograph MS., *Reports in the King's Bench, 15th-19th Years of the Reign of James I.* Carson Collection on Growth of the Common Law, Philadelphia Free Library. Folio, 97 leaves, in the handwriting of Sir Edward Coke.

A Booke of Entries. London, 1614. Latin and law French.

Compleat Copy-Holder . . . Whereunto is newly added the Relation between the Lord of a Mannor and the Copy-Holder his Tenant. London, 1650.

Historical Manuscript Commission *Holkham Papers; the MSS. of the Right Honourable the Earl of Leicester, Holkham Hall, Norfolk.* London, 1884, 9th Rept. Pt. II, 357-375; Bridget Coke's Household Book, calendared; Biographical Notebook of Sir Edward Coke.

A Little Treatise of Bail and Mainprize, written at the request of Sir William Hayden. B. M. 1635, 1637, 1715.

The Lord Coke, His Speech and Charge; With a Discoverie of the Abuses and Corruption of Officers. London, 1607. Speech at Norwich charging the jury; epistle dedicatory signed R. P. (Robert Pricket). In Folger Shakespeare Library, Washington, D.C.

"*Vade Mecum*," Coke's annotations in his copy of *Littleton's Tenures*, 1592. Printed in *Collectanea Topographica et Genealogica*, VI. Ed. John G. Nichols. London, 1840. Original is in British Museum, Harleian MS. 1572.

Appraisals of Coke's Writings

Gest, John Marshall "The Writings of Sir Edward Coke." *Yale Law Journal*, XVII (1909).

Holdsworth, William S. "Coke's Writings." *History of English Law.* London, 1924. Vol. V, 456-490.

Johnson, Cuthbert William *The Life of Sir Edward Coke.* London, 1837. Vol. II, 404-434; 443-490.

McDonnell, George Paul "Sir Edward Coke." *Dictionary of National Biography.* Vol. IV, 685-700.

Parsons, Robert *An Ansuuere to the Fifth Part of Reportes, Lately Set Forth by Sir Edward Cooke . . . the King's Attorney Generall.* Imprinted with Licence by a Catholicke Deuyne. 1606.

"A Vindication of the Judgment given by King James in the Case of the Jurisdiction of the Court of Chancery, that the Lord Chancellor should not Desist to give Relief in Equity, notwithstanding any Proceedings at the Common Law, Contrary to an Opinion lately Published after the Supposed Author's, Lord Coke's, Death . . . (With Reference to notes printed in the Third and Fourth Institutes)." *Collectanea Juridica*, I. London, 1791.

Wallace, John William Coke's *Reports.* "The Common Law Reporters." In *The Reporters.* Boston, 1882.

Winfield, Percy H. An appraisal of Coke's *Institutes* and *Reports* in *Chief Sources of English Legal History.* Cambridge, 1925, *passim.*

Books and Articles about Coke

Considering Coke's reputation, very few books have been written about him; for the biographer it is a question of gleaning here and there. Some of the titles below were especially helpful: Carthew, Holdsworth, Spedding, Foss, James, Johnson. Lord Campbell, who is always referred to as "full of errors," has collected more information about Coke and his colleagues than has anyone else. Actually, bearing in mind the bulk of Campbell's ten volumes on the Lord Chancellors and four volumes on the Chief Justices, his errors are few. His articles about Bacon, Ellesmere and Coke together form an excellent account of the enmity and friendship, the give and take between three extraordinary men. Among the more doubtful titles listed below, *The Curious Case of Lady Purbeck* is not, properly speaking, a book about Coke but about his daughter Frances. Yet it contains documents not printed elsewhere. In my experience such works — especially those published before 1900 — are not to be scorned by the biographer; often they contain excerpts from letters or diaries not listed elsewhere, or later lost, or not immediately available in manuscript.

AUBREY, JOHN *Aubrey's Brief Lives.* Ed. Oliver Lawson Dick. London, 1950.

BIRKENHEAD, EARL OF *Fourteen English Judges.* New York, 1926.

BURKE, EDWARD P. *Sir Edward Coke.* [Lives of Eminent Persons.] London, 1833.

Calendar of State Papers Domestic for the period of Coke's life, 1552-1634.

CAMPBELL, LORD JOHN *The Lives of the Chief Justices of England.* New York, 1874. Vol. I.

CARTHEW, G. A. *The Hundred of Launditch and Deanery of Brisley.* 3 vols. Norwich, 1877-1879. Contains fullest genealogy of the Coke family.

CHALMERS, ALEXANDER, ed. *General Biographical Dictionary . . .* New ed. 32 vols. London, 1812-1817. Art. "Edward Coke," X, 1-14.

Chambers's Biographical Dictionary; the Great of All Nations and All Times. New ed. London, 1938.

CLARK, WALTER *Coke, Blackstone and the Common Law.* Reprint from *Case and Comment*, XXIV, no. 11. Rochester, N.Y., 1918.

COKE, ROGER *A Detection of the Court and State of England during the Reigns of K. James I, Charles I, Charles II, and James II. . . .* 3 vols. London, 1719.

CUNNINGHAM, GEORGE G. *A History of England in the Lives of Englishmen.* London, 1853. Vol. II, no. 228. Art. "Sir Edward Coke." 387-391.

FOSS, EDWARD *The Judges of England.* London, 1857-1864. Vol. VI.

FULLER, THOMAS *The History of the Worthies of England.* 3 vols. London, 1840.

GARDINER, SAMUEL R. *History of England.* London, 1894-1896. Vols. I-VII *passim.*

HASSALL, W. O., Ed. *A Catalogue of the Library of Sir Edward Coke.* With a preface by Samuel E. Thorne. New Haven, 1950.

HISTORICAL MANUSCRIPT COMMISSION *Cowper Papers; the MSS. of Earl Cowper, Preserved at Melbourne Hall, Derbyshire.* London, 1888-1889.

—— *Charters, Early Conveyances, Court Rolls, &c . . . of the Earl of Leicester, Preserved at Holkham Hall, Norfolk.* In *Various Collections*, IV. Dublin, 1907.

HOLDSWORTH, WILLIAM S. "The Influence of Coke on the Development of English Law." In *Essays in Legal History.* Ed. Paul Vinogradoff. Oxford, 1914.

JAMES, CHARLES W. *Chief Justice Coke, His Family and Descendants at Holkham.* London, 1929.

JOHNSON, CUTHBERT WILLIAM *The Life of Sir Edward Coke.* 2 vols. London, 1837.

"Letter of the Council to Sir Thomas Lake, Relating to the Proceedings of Sir Edward Coke at Oatlands." Council Register, [21] July 1617. *Camden Miscellany*, V. Camden Society, 1864.

LLOYD, DAVID *State-Worthies or the Statesmen and Favourites of England Since the Reformation.* 2d ed. London, 1670.

LONGUEVILLE, THOMAS *The Curious Case of Lady Purbeck.* London, 1909.

LYON, HASTINGS and BLOCK, HERMAN *Edward Coke, Oracle of the Law.* Boston, 1929.

McDONNELL, GEORGE P. "Sir Edward Coke." *Dictionary of National Biography.* Vol. IV, 685-700.

MACKAY, R. A. "Coke — Parliamentary Sovereignty or the Supremacy of the Law." *Michigan Law Review*, XXII, 215-247.

MULLETT, CHARLES F. "Coke and the American Revolution." *Economica*, XII (1932), 457-471.

NAUNTON, SIR ROBERT *Fragmenta Regalia; or Observations on the Late Queen Elizabeth, Her Times and Favourites.* Ed. Edward Arber. London, 1870.

NORSWORTHY, LAURA *The Lady of Bleeding Heart Yard.* London, 1935.

Penny Cyclopedia of the Society for the Diffusion of Useful Knowledge. London, 1833-1842. Art. "Sir Edward Coke," VII, 332-335.

PLUCKNETT, THEODORE F. T. "Bonham's Case and Judicial Review." *Harvard Law Review*, XL (1926-1927), 30.

Record of a Tercentenary Commemoration of Sir Edward Coke (1551-1634), 17 Dec. Text by F. D. MacKinnon. London, 1934.

"Sir Edward Coke." *Encyclopaedia Britannica.* 11th ed., New Form. Vol. VI, 654-655. Contains some inaccuracies.

SPEDDING, JAMES *The Letters and the Life of Francis Bacon.* 14 vols. London, 1890. Vols. I-VII have a great deal about Coke.

STIRLING, A. M. W. *Coke of Norfolk and His Friends; the Life of Thomas William Coke.* London, 1912.

Students Admitted to Inner Temple; 1547-1660. Printed for the Inner Temple, 1883.

THORNE, SAMUEL E. "Courts of Record and Sir Edward Coke." *Toronto Law Journal*, II, no. 1 (1937).

—— "Dr. Bonham's Case." *Law Quarterly Review*, LIV, no. 216 (1938), 543.

USHER, ROLAND G. "James I and Sir Edward Coke." *English Historical Review*, XVIII (1903), 664-675.

WAGNER, DONALD O. "Coke and the Rise of Economic Liberalism." *Economic History Review*, VI, no. 1 (1935).

WOOLRYCH, HUMPHRY W. *The Life of the Right Honourable Sir Edward Coke Knt.* London, 1826.

Portraits

Lists of Coke's portraits are old and incomplete. I have named the pictures that were most useful in finding how Sir Edward looked; for the reader's convenience I have added the titles of available books which reproduce them. There is considerable controversy as to the authenticity of certain portraits. But they all have features in common — the piercing eye and level brow, the tall figure, robust at first and growing more spare with the years.

The Paintings

Portrait of Sir Edward Coke, Recorder of Norwich, 1587. In council chamber of Guildhall, Norwich, Norfolk. Coke holds a glove in one hand and rests the other on a death's head. Three-quarter length, oil.

Portrait of Edward Coke, Attorney-General to Queen Elizabeth (aged 41). Holkham House, Holkham, Norfolk. Dated 1593. Oil, three-quarter length. Reproduced as frontispiece of this book. Coke is holding a scroll in his right hand. Portrait itself, dated 1593, bears label, apparently added later, "Lord Chief Justice Coke. Cornelius Jansens pinxit." As Jansen was born in 1593, he could not have painted it; also Coke was Attorney-General at this time.

Portrait of Sir Edward Coke as Chief Justice, by unknown artist. Formerly owned by Clement's Inn, now in Parliament Chamber of Inner Temple. Dated 1613, but probably done earlier. Reproduced in A. M. W. Stirling *Coke of Norfolk* opp. p. 4.

Portrait of Sir Edward Coke as Chief Justice, purportedly by Cornelius Van Ceulen Jansen. Painted 1608 (?). Formerly in Hall of Serjeants' Inn, Chancery Lane, now in National Portrait Gallery. Reproduced in *Shakespeare's England,* I, 399.

Portrait of Chief Justice Coke, by Paul Van Somer; said by some to have been painted by Cornelius Jansen, by others to have been the work of Michael Wright. Dated 1616. Given to Inner Temple by Mrs. Anne Sadleir, Coke's daughter. Reproduced in *Record of Tercentenary Commemoration of Sir Edward Coke,* frontispiece.

Engravings

Engraving of Sir Edward Coke, signed W. Read, Sc. Reproduced in *Westminster Hall,* III, opp. p. 108. Coke as young man, no head covering, nonofficial garb.

Engraving of Sir Edward Coke, Lord Chief Justice, by J. Houbraken. In ruff and plain fusted gown, probably as Attorney General. In Birch *Heads of Illustrious Persons,* opp. p. 65.

Engraving of Sir Edward Coke, by Simon Van de Pass (S. Passoeus),

British Museum. Shows the golden collar of SS with the portcullis and Tudor rose, and the ring supposed to have been the gift of Elizabeth. Reproduced in INDERWICK *The King's Peace*, opp. p. 181.

Engraving of Sir Edward Coke, "Prudens qui patiens," 1629, by J. Payne. Has whistle hanging on cord around Coke's neck. In several editions of Coke's works, for example 1648 ed. of 3 *Institute.*

SCULPTURE

Bust of Sir Edward Coke, Library of Trinity College, Cambridge. Gift of Sir Thomas Coke, 1st Earl of Leicester. Work of Sculptor Roubiliac.

Effigy of Sir Edward Coke in white marble, on black sarcophagus of monument at Tittleshall Church, Norfolk, by Nicholas Stone. Closely resembles Van Somer portrait of Coke as Chief Justice. Photograph in *Record of Tercentenary Commemoration of Sir Edward Coke,* between pp. 17 and 18. It is possible that the effigy itself was the work of Stone's assistant, Hargrave.

REFERENCE WORKS

The following books were useful in finding Coke's portraits and in checking their authenticity.

BIRCH, THOMAS, ed. *The Heads of Illustrious Persons of Great Britain. . . .* London, 1747.

Bryan's Dictionary of Painters and Engravers. Ed. George C. Williamson. 5 vols. London, 1918. Art. "Cornelius Janssens." Vol. III.

Catalogue of the Paintings, Serjeants, Rugs, Plate, Stained Glass, Sculpture, etc. . . . belonging to the Honourable Society of the Inner Temple. London, 1915.

FINBERG, ALEXANDER J., ed. *The Tenth Volume of the Walpole Society, 1921-22.* Oxford, 1922. For Cornelius Jansen.

GRANGER, JAMES *Biographical History of England . . . Adapted to a Methodical Catalogue of Engraved British Heads.* 4th ed. London, 1804. Gives list of engravings and paintings of Coke. 5th ed., 6 vols., London, 1824, has three additional entries.

INDERWICK, F. A. and FIELD, LEONARD *Report on the Inner Temple Pictures of Judge Littleton and Sir Edward Coke.* London, 1894.

JOHNSON, CUTHBERT WILLIAM *The Life of Sir Edward Coke.* London, 1837. Gives list of thirteen engravings and six portraits, pp. 483-485.

LODGE, EDMUND *Portraits of Illustrious Personages of Great Britain.* 12 vols. in 6. London, 1835.

MACKINNON, F. D. *Record of a Tercentenary Commemoration of Sir Edward Coke (1551-1634).* Description of Inner Temple and Gray's Inn portraits of Coke, p. 13.

THIEME, CONRAD ULRICH and BECKER, FELIX *Allgemeines Lexicon der bildenden Künstler von der Antike bis zur Gegenwart.* . . . Leipzig, 1926. Vol. XIX. Art. "Cornelius Jansen."

Coke's Contemporaries

The Principal Characters of This Book

QUEEN ELIZABETH (1558-1603)

BIRCH, THOMAS *Memoirs of the Reign of Queen Elizabeth from 1581 Till Her Death.* 2 vols. London, 1754. From the original papers of Anthony Bacon.

CAREY, ROBERT *Memoirs of the Life of Robert Cary, Earl of Monmouth.* Ed. H. Powell. London, 1905. Over three quarters of these memoirs devoted to Queen Elizabeth, including Carey's observations on her death.

CHAMBERLIN, FREDERICK *The Private Character of Queen Elizabeth.* London, 1921.

CREIGHTON, MANDELL *Queen Elizabeth.* London, 1899.

England's Mourning Garment . . . in memory . . . of Elisabeth. . . . Harleian MS. 15, in *A Selection from the Harleian Miscellany of Tracts. . . .* London, 1793.

JESSOPP, AUGUSTUS "Elizabeth, Queen of England." *Dictionary of National Biography.* Vol. VI, 621-649.

NEALE, JOHN E. *Queen Elizabeth.* London, 1934.

—— "The Sayings of Queen Elizabeth." *History,* X (1925), 212-233.

NICHOLS, JOHN *The Progresses and Public Processions of Queen Elizabeth. . . .* 3 vols. London, 1823.

OSBORNE, FRANCIS *Traditional Memoirs of the Reign of Queen Elizabeth. . . .* In *Secret History of the Court of James the First.* Ed. Sir Walter Scott.

POLLARD, ALBERT F. "Elizabeth, Queen of England." *Encyclopaedia Britannica.* 11th ed. Vol. IX, 282-283.

Queen Elizabeth and Her Times. . . . 2 vols. Ed. Thomas Wright. London, 1838.

READ, CONYERS "Good Queen Bess." *Amer. Hist. R.,* XXXI (1926), 647-661.

—— *Mr. Secretary Walsingham and the Policy of Queen Elizabeth.* 3 vols. Oxford, 1925.

STRACHEY, LYTTON *Elizabeth and Essex.* London, 1928.

JAMES I (1566-1623)

DAVIES, GODFREY "The Character of James VI and I." *Huntington Library Quarterly,* V, no. 1 (1941).

D'ISRAELI, ISAAC "Character of James the First." *The Literary Character.* New Ed. London, 1859.

DONNE, JOHN "At the Bier of a King." *Seventeenth Century Prose and Poetry*. Ed. R. P. Coffin and Alexander Witherspoon. N.Y., 1946.
Encyclopaedia Britannica, 11th ed., New Form. Art. "James I." Vol. V, 136-138.
GARDINER, SAMUEL RAWSON "James VI of Scotland (James I of England)." *Dictionary of National Biography*. Vol. X, 598-618.
JAMES I. *Daemonologie* (1597); *Newes From Scotland* (1591). Ed. G. B. Harrison. London, 1924.
—— *The Essay of a Prentise in the Divine Art of Poesie* (1585); *A Counterblaste to Tobacco* (1604). Ed. Edward Arber. London, 1869.
—— *New Poems by James I of England*. Ed. Allan F. Westcott. N.Y., 1911.
—— *The Political Works of James I*. Ed. Charles H. McIlwain. Cambridge (Mass.), 1918.
Letters of Queen Elizabeth and King James VI of Scotland. Ed. John Bruce. Camden Society, 1849.
NICHOLS, JOHN *The Progresses, Progressions and Magnificent Festivities of King James* . . . 4 vols. London, 1928.
Message from James I to the Earl of Somerset, 29 Dec. 1615 Through Sir George More, Lieutenant of the Tower. Loseley MSS. Printed in *Archaeologia*, XLI (1847).
SCOTT, SIR WALTER *The Fortunes of Nigel*. Boston, 1822.
SPEDDING, JAMES "Review of the Evidence Respecting the Conduct of King James I in the Case of Sir Thomas Overbury." *Archaeologia*, XLI (1847).
STAFFORD, HELEN GEORGIA *James VI of Scotland and the Throne of England*. New York, 1940.
WILLSON, DAVID HARRIS *King James VI and I*. London, 1956.

THE CECILS

WILLIAM CECIL, LORD BURGHLEY (1520-1598)
ROBERT CECIL, BARON OF ESSINGDON, VISCOUNT CRANBORNE, 1ST EARL OF SALISBURY (1563-1612)

ANTROBUS, JOCELYN *Hatfield; Some Memories of its Past*. Pub. at Bishop's Hatfield in the County of Hertford, 1930. Pamphlet, 103 pp., 7th ed.
CECIL, ALGERNON *A Life of Robert Cecil*. London, 1915.
CECIL, ROBERT *Correspondence of King James VI of Scotland with Sir Robert Cecil and Others in England During the Reign of Queen Elizabeth*. Ed. John Bruce. Camden Society, LXXVIII, 1861.
—— *The Secret Correspondence of Sir Robert Cecil with James I*. Ed. Lord Hailes. Edinburgh, 1766.
"The Cecils." *Encyclopaedia Britannica*. 11th ed., New Form. Vol. V, 593.

"Contemporary Life of Lord Burghley." In *Desiderata Curiosa*. Ed. Francis Peck. London, 1779.

Historical Manuscript Commission *Salisbury Papers*, I-XVIII. London, 1883-1938.

Hume, Martin A. S. *The Great Lord Burghley; a Study in Elizabethan Statecraft*. London, 1898.

Jessopp, Augustus *Historical Monograph, William Cecil, Lord Burghley*. London, 1904.

—— "Robert Cecil, First Earl of Salisbury." *Dictionary of National Biography*. Vol. III, 1309-1313.

—— "William Cecil, Lord Burghley." *Dictionary of National Biography*. Vol. III, 1315-1321.

Macauley, Thomas B. "Burleigh and His Times." *Critical, Historical and Miscellaneous Essays*. Vol. III. New York, 1860.

Read, Conyers *Mr. Secretary Cecil and Queen Elizabeth*. New York, 1955.

SIR FRANCIS BACON, Baron Verulam, Viscount St. Albans (1561-1626)

Abbott, Edwin A. *Bacon and Essex, a Sketch of Bacon's Earlier Life*. London, 1877.

—— *Francis Bacon; an Account of His Life and Works*. London, 1885.

Bacon, Sir Francis *The Essays; Colours of Good and Evil; Advancement of Learning*. Bibliographical note by A. W. Pollard. London, 1925.

—— *The Works of Francis Bacon. . . .* Ed. James Spedding, Robert L. Ellis and Douglas D. Heath. 15 vols. Boston, 1861-1864.

—— *The Works of Francis Bacon*. New Ed. Spedding, Ellis and Heath. London, 1872.

Benson, George Vere "Francis Bacon." *Dictionary of National Biography*. Vol. I, 800-833.

Campbell, John *Lives of the Lord Chancellors*. London, 1856. Vol. III, 1-147.

Historical Manuscript Commission *Bacon Papers, MSS. of the Earl of Verulam*. London, 1906.

Macaulay, Thomas B. "Lord Bacon." *Critical, Historical and Miscellaneous Essays*. Vol. III, 336-495.

Mitchell, Robert Adamson "Francis Bacon." *Encyclopaedia Britannica*. 11th ed., New Form. Vol. III, 135-152.

Napier, MacVey *Lord Bacon and Sir Walter Raleigh*. Cambridge, 1853.

Spedding, James *The Letters and the Life of Francis Bacon*. 14 vols. London, 1857-1874.

—— *An Account of the Life and Times of Francis Bacon*. 2 vols. London, 1878.

THOMAS EGERTON, BARON ELLESMERE AND VISCOUNT BRACKLEY (1540-1617)

CAMPBELL, JOHN *Lives of the Lord Chancellors of England.* London, 1856. Vol. II, 3008-3038.
COLLIER, JOHN PAYNE *A Catalogue of Early English History, forming a Portion of the Library at Bridgewater House, the Property of L[d] Egerton, M.P.* Privately printed, 1873.
"The Earl of Oxford's Case, 13 Jac. 1," in *Leading Cases in Equity.* London, 1910.
EGERTON, F. H. *A Compilation of Various Authentic Evidences and Historical Authorities Tending to Illustrate the Life and Character of Thomas Egerton.* In Kippis's *Biographia Britannica.* London, 1778-1793.
—— *The Egerton Papers; a Collection of Public and Private Documents, Chiefly Illustrative of the Times of Elizabeth and James I.* From the original MSS. Ed. J. Payne Collier. London, Camden Soc., 1840.
EGERTON, THOMAS *Certaine Observations Concerning the Office of Lord Chancellor.* London, 1651.
—— *The Lord Chancellor Egerton's Observations on the Lord Coke's Reports. . . .* Ed. G. Paul. London, 1710. Egerton's authorship of this MS. in the Inner Temple has been questioned.
LEE, SIDNEY "Sir Thomas Egerton." *Dictionary of National Biography.* Vol. VI, 579-581.

ROBERT DEVEREUX, 2ND EARL OF ESSEX (1566-1601)

ABBOTT, E. A. *Bacon and Essex, a Sketch of Bacon's Earlier Life.* London, 1877.
CADWALLADER, LAURA HANES *The Career of the Earl of Essex from 1597-1601.* A Thesis in History, University of Pennsylvania, 1923.
CODRINGTON, ROBERT *The Life and Death of the Illustrious Robert, Earl of Essex. . . .* In *A Selection from the Harleian Miscellany of Tracts.* London, 1793.
DEVEREUX, WALTER B. *Lives and Letters of the Devereux, Earls of Essex, 1540-1646.* 2 vols. London, 1853.
HISTORICAL MANUSCRIPT COMMISSION *Earl of Essex Papers.* In *Various Collections,* VII. London, 1914.
HYDE, HENRY (Earl of Clarendon) "The Difference and Disparity Between the Estates of George, Duke of Buckingham, and Robert, Earl of Essex." In SIR HENRY WOTTON *Reliquiae Wottonianae.* London, 1651.
"Robert Devereux, 2d Earl of Essex." *Encyclopaedia Britannica.* 11th ed., New Form. Vol. IX, 782-783.
STRACHEY, LYTTON *Elizabeth and Essex.* London, 1928.

SIR WALTER RALEGH (1552?-1618)

ANTHONY, IRVIN *Ralegh and His World.* New York, 1934.

BIRCH, THOMAS *The Life of Sir Walter Ralegh.* In *The Works of Sir Walter Ralegh.* Oxford, 1829. Vol. I, 571-648.

—— *The Trial of Sir Walter Ralegh, Knight, for High Treason.* In *The Works of Sir Walter Ralegh.* Oxford, 1829. Vol. I, 649-696.

"A Brief Relation of Sir Walter Raleigh's Troubles: With the Taking Away the Lands and Castle of Sherburn in Dorset from Him, and his Heirs, Being His Indubitable Inheritance." Petition of Carew Ralegh to the House of Commons. In *A Selection from the Harleian Miscellany.* London, 1793, 225-227.

BROOKE, C. F. TUCKER "Ralegh as Poet and Philosopher." *Journal of English Literary History,* V. no. 2 (1938).

BRUSHFIELD, T. N. "The History of Durham House." *Trans. of Devonshire Assoc.* XXVI (1903), 539-580.

CAYLEY, ARTHUR *The Life of Sir Walter Ralegh, Knt.* 2d ed. 2 vols. London, 1806.

CREIGHTON, LOUISE *Life of Sir Walter Ralegh.* London, 1882.

"Demeanor and Carriage of Sir Walter Raleigh." In *A Selection from the Harleian Miscellany.* London, 1793, 214-225.

EDWARDS, EDWARD *The Life of Sir Walter Ralegh . . . Together with His Letters.* 2 vols. London, 1868.

EWEN, C. L'ESTRANGE "Sir Walter Ralegh's Interpretation of the *Lex Mercatoria.*" Printed for the author. 1938.

—— "Ralegh's Last Adventure." Printed for the author. 1938.

HANNAY, DAVID "Sir Walter Raleigh." *Encyclopaedia Britannica.* 11th ed., New Form. Vol. XXII, 869-870.

HARLOW, VINCENT T., ed. *The Discoverie of the Large and Beautiful Empire of Guiana.* London, 1928.

—— *Ralegh's Last Voyage.* London, 1932.

A History of Hampshire and the Isle of Wight. The *Victoria History of the Counties of England.* Ed. William Page. Westminster, 1901-1906. Vol. V. Good for Ralegh trial.

HUME, MARTIN A. S. *Sir Walter Raleigh.* London, 1847.

LATHAM, AGNES M. C. "Sir Walter Ralegh's Gold Mine; New Light on the Last Guiana Voyage." In *Essays and Studies.* New Series. Ed. Geoffrey Tillotson. London, 1951. Vol. IV, 94-111.

LEE, SIDNEY and LAUGHTON, JOHN KNOX "Sir Walter Ralegh." *Dictionary of National Biography.* Vol. XVI, 629-649.

NAPIER, MACVEY *Lord Bacon and Sir Walter Raleigh.* Cambridge, 1853.

—— "The Works of Sir Walter Raleigh, Kt." *Edinburgh Review or Critical Journal,* LXXI, no. 143 (1849), 1-98.

Newes of Sr Walter Rauleigh with a True Description of Guiana Sent from a Gentleman of His Fleet from . . . the Coast of Guiana. (Nov. 17, 1617.) London, 1618. Forces Collection.

OLDYS, WILLIAM *The Life of Sir Walter Ralegh.* In *The Works of Sir Walter Ralegh.* Oxford, 1829. Vol. I, 2-568.

POWELL, WILLIAM S. "John Pory on the Death of Sir Walter Raleigh." *William and Mary Quarterly*, Oct. 1952.

RALEGH, SIR WALTER *The Historie of the World.* London, 1652.

—— *Poems of Sir Walter Ralegh.* Ed. Agnes M. C. Latham. London, 1929.

—— *The Prerogative of Parliaments in England; proved in a Dialogue Between a Counsellor of State, and a Justice of Peace.* Harl. MS. 287, in *A Selection from the Harleian Miscellany.* London, 1793.

—— *The Works of Sir Walter Raleigh.* Ed. Thomas Birch. 8 vols. Oxford, 1829.

STEBBING, WILLIAM *Sir Walter Ralegh.* London, 1899.

STEPHEN, SIR HARRY L. "The Trial of Sir Walter Raleigh." In *Trans. Royal Historical Society*, 4th Series, II (1919), 172-187.

STRATHMANN, ERNEST A. "The History of the World and Ralegh's Skepticism." *Huntington Library Quarterly*, April, 1940.

—— *Sir Walter Ralegh; A Study in Elizabethan Skepticism.* New York, 1951.

—— "Sir Walter Ralegh on Natural Philosophy." *Modern Language Quarterly*, I (1940).

TYTLER, PATRICK F. *Life of Sir Walter Raleigh.* . . . 5th ed. Edinburgh, 1844.

WALDMAN, MILTON *Sir Walter Raleigh.* London, 1928.

WHITEHEAD, CHARLES *The Life and Times of Sir Walter Raleigh.* London, 1854.

WILLIAMS, ARNOLD LEDGERWOOD *Christopher Marlowe and the Ralegh Circle.* Chapel Hill, 1930.

WILLIAMSON, JAMES A. *The English Colonies in Guiana and on the Amazon, 1604-1668.* Oxford, 1923.

CHARLES I (1600-1649)

BIGHAM, CLIVE *The Kings of England.* London, 1929.

[CHARLES I] *Eikon Basilike; The Pourtraicture of His Sacred Majestie in His Solitudes and Sufferings.* A reprint of the ed. of 1648. London, 1880. Sometimes ascribed to (John? Gauden?).

DAVIES, GODFREY *The Early Stuarts, 1603-1660.* Ed. G. N. Clark. Oxford, 1937.

GARDINER, SAMUEL RAWSON "Charles I." *Dictionary of National Biography.* Vol. IV, 67-84.

—— *Prince Charles and the Spanish Marriage; 1613-1623.* London, 1869.

HIGHAM, F. M. G. *Charles I; a Study.* London, 1932.

HISTORICAL MANUSCRIPT COMMISSION *Beaufort Papers; Letters of Charles I to the Marquis of Worcester, 1639-1645,* . . . London, 1891.

PETRIE, SIR CHARLES *The Stuarts.* London, 1937.

—— *The Letters, Speeches and Proclamations of King Charles I.* London, 1935.

WILLIAMS, ROBERT FOLKSTONE, ed. *The Court and Times of Charles the First.* Thomas Birch transcriptions. 2 vols. London, 1848.

WYNNE, SIR RICHARD *Prince Charles; an Account of the Journey of the Prince's Servants into Spain, A.D. 1623.* In D'EWES *Autobiography*, vol. II.

YORKE, PHILIP CHESNEY "Charles I." *Encyclopaedia Britannica.* 11th ed., New Form. Vol. IV, 906-912.

Other Contemporary Figures

These names of men and books are included because they were either liberally mentioned, quoted or otherwise used. With some, like Anne Clifford, Dr. John Dee the astrologer or the malevolent charlatan Simon Forman, necromancer, their diaries were helpful, yet the writers themselves never appear on our scene. Others, such as Gondomar or Father John Gerard, were very active in Coke's story.

SIR JULIUS CAESAR (1558-1636)

FOSS, EDWARD *The Judges of England.* London, 1857. Vol. VI, 266-272.

LODGE, EDMUND *Life of Sir Julius Caesar, Knt.* London, 1827.

RIGG, JAMES M. "Sir Julius Caesar." *Dictionary of National Biography.* Vol. III, 656-659.

ANNE CLIFFORD, COUNTESS OF PEMBROKE, DORSET AND MONTGOMERY (1590-1676)

BARKER, GEORGE FISHER RUSSELL "Anne Clifford." *Dictionary of National Biography.* Vol. IV, 512-513.

CLIFFORD, ANNE *The Diary of Lady Anne Clifford, 1590-1676.* New York, n.d.

SIR JOHN COKE (1563-1644)

COKE, DOROTHEA *The Last Elizabethan; Sir John Coke, 1563-1644.* London, 1937.

FIRTH, CHARLES HARDING "Sir John Coke." *Dictionary of National Biography.* Vol. IV, 700-702.

DR. JOHN DEE (1527-1608)

COOPER, THOMPSON "John Dee." *Dictionary of National Biography.* Vol. V, 721-729.

DEE, JOHN *The Private Diary of Dr. John Dee, 1554-1601.* Ed. J. A. Halliwell. London, Camden Society, 1842.

Sir John Eliot (1592-1632)

"Eliot, Sir John." *Encyclopaedia Britannica.* 11th ed., New Form. Vol. IX, 277-278.

Forster, John *Sir John Eliot, 1592-1632.* 2 vols. London, 1864.

Gardiner, Samuel Rawson "Sir John Eliot." *Dictionary of National Biography.* Vol. VI, 604-607.

—— *History of England.* London, 1894-1896. Vols. V-VII *passim.*

Higham, F. M. G. *Charles I; a Study.* London, 1932. Chap. IV, 62-90.

Dr. Simon Forman (1552-1611)

Forman, Dr. Simon *The Autobiography and Personal Diary of Dr. Simon Forman, the Celebrated Astrologer.* Ed. J. A. Halliwell. London, 1849.

Lee, Sidney "Simon Forman." *Dictionary of National Biography.* Vol. VII, 438-441.

Father John Gerard (1564-1637)

Cooper, Thompson "John Gerard." *Dictionary of National Biography.* Vol. VII, 1100-1101.

Gerard, John *The Autobiography of an Elizabethan.* Trans. from the Latin by Philip Caraman. London, 1951.

Diego Sarmiento de Acuña, Count of Gondomar (1567-1626)

"Diego de Sarmiento Acuña, Count of Gondomar." *Encyclopaedia Britannica.* 11th ed., New Form. Vol. XII, 232-233.

Gardiner, Samuel Rawson *History of England.* London, 1894-1896. Vols. IX-X *passim.*

Gondomar, Ct. Diego Sarmiento de Acuña *Letters of Gondomar.* Ed. S. R. Gardiner. *Archaeologia,* XLI (1867).

Sir Christopher Hatton, Lord Chancellor (1540-1591)

Brooks, Eric St. John *Sir Christopher Hatton, Queen Elizabeth's Favourite.* London, 1946.

Correspondence of the Family of Hatton, being Chiefly Letters Addressed to Christopher Hatton, First Viscount Hatton, A.D. 1601-1704. Ed. Edward M. Thompson, 2 vols. London, Camden Society, 1878.

Nicolas, Sir Harris *Memoirs of the Life and Times of Sir Christopher Hatton.* London, 1847.

Riggs, James M. "Christopher Hatton." *Dictionary of National Biography.* Vol. IX, 159-162.

Henry, Prince of Wales (1594-1612)

Birch, Thomas *The Life of Henry, Prince of Wales.* London, 1760.
Cornwallis, Sir Charles *An Account of the Baptism, Life and Death of Henry, Prince of Wales.* Reprinted 1751.
—— *A Discourse of the Most Illustrious Prince Henry, late Prince of Wales.* In *A Selection from the Harleian Miscellany.* London, 1793. Also in *Somers Tracts.* London, 1809. Vol. II.

Father Robert Parsons (1546-1610)

Doleman, Robert (Robert Parsons) *A Conference about the Next Succession to the Crowne of England. . . .* (Antwerp?), 1594.
Law, Thomas Graves "Robert Parsons." *Dictionary of National Biography.* Vol. XV, 411-418.

The Pastons

The Correspondence of Lady Katherine Paston, 1603-1627. Ed. Ruth Hughey. Norfolk Record Society, 1941.
The Paston Letters, 1422-1509 A.D. Ed. James Gairdner of P.R.O. 3 vols. London, 1904.

John Selden (1584-1654)

Fry, Edward "John Selden." *Dictionary of National Biography.* Vol. XVII, 1150-1162.
Johnson, George *Memoirs of John Selden.* London, 1835.
Selden, John *The Table Talk of John Selden.* Ed. Sir Frederick Pollock, with account of Selden and his work by Sir Edward Fry. London, 1927.

Arabella Stuart (1575-1615)

Hardy, B. C. *Arbella Stuart.* London, 1913.
Gardiner, Samuel Rawson "Arabella Stuart." *Dictionary of National Biography.* Vol. I, 525.
Riggs, James M. "William Seymour." *Dictionary of National Biography.* Vol. XVII, 1271-1273. Arabella's husband.

Peter Wentworth (1530?-1596)

Dilkes, Charles Wentworth "Peter Wentworth." *Dictionary of National Biography.* Vol. XX, 1172-1174.
Neale, J. E. "Peter Wentworth." *Engl. Hist. R.* XXXIX (1924).

George Villiers, 1st Duke of Buckingham (1592-1628)

Gardiner, Samuel Rawson "George Villiers." *Dictionary of National Biography*. Vol. XX, 327-337.

Wotton, Sir Henry "A Short View of the Life and Death of George Villiers, Duke of Buckingham." In *A Selection from the Harleian Miscellany*. London, 1793, 278-286.

Sir Henry Wotton (1568-1639)

Lee, Sidney "Sir Henry Wotton." *Dictionary of National Biography*. Vol. XXI, 966-972.

Smith, Logan Pearsall *The Life and Letters of Sir Henry Wotton*. 2 vols. London, 1907.

Wotton, Sir Henry *Reliquiae Wottonianae*. London, 1851.

Minutiae Historicae

Letters, Autobiographies, Diaries, Collections

Aubrey, John *Aubrey's Brief Lives*. Ed. Oliver L. Dick. London, 1950.

Birch, Thomas *The Court and Times of Charles the First*. Ed. Robert Folkestone Williams. 2 vols. London, 1848.

—— *The Court and Times of James the First*. 2 vols. London, 1849.

Cabala Sine Scrinia Sacra; Mysteries of State and Government in Letters of Illustrious Persons . . . in the Reigns of King Henry the Eighth, Queen Elizabeth, King James, and King Charles. . . . London, 1663.

Calendar of State Papers, Domestic, 1581-1635; Domestic Addenda, 1580-1625.

Calendar of State Papers, Venetian, 1592-1635.

Carlyle, Thomas *Historical Sketches of Notable Persons and Events in the Reigns of James I and Charles I*. Posth. ed. Alexander Carlyle. London, 1898.

Chamberlain, John *The Letters of John Chamberlain*. Ed. Norman McClure. 2 vols. Philadelphia, 1939.

Cornwallis, Jane Lady *The Private Correspondence of Jane Lady Cornwallis, 1613-1644*. London, 1842. Wife of Nathaniel Bacon.

DeMaisse, André Hierault, Sieur *A Journal of All that was Accomplished by Monsieur De Maisse, Ambassador in England from King Henri IV to Queen Elizabeth, anno Domini 1597*. Trans. and ed. G. B. Harrison and R. A. Jones. London, 1931.

D'Ewes, Sir Simonds *The Autobiography and Correspondence During the Reigns of James I and Charles I*. Ed. James O. Halliwell. London, 1845.

D'Israeli, Isaac *Amenities of Literature*. 3 vols. London, 1842.

EARLE, JOHN Bishop of Worcester and Salisbury. *Micro-Cosmographie or, a Piece of the World Discovered; in Essays and Characters.* 6th ed. London, 1904.

ELLIS, SIR HENRY, ed. *Original Letters Illustrative of English History . . . from Autographs in the British Museum.* 11 vols. London, 1824-1846. 1st, 2d and 3rd Series.

FULLER, THOMAS *The History of the Worthies of England.* 3 vols. London, 1840.

GAWDY, PHILIP *Letters of Philip Gawdy of West Harling, Norfolk, and of London to Various Members of His Family, 1579-1616.* Ed. I. H. Jeayes. London, 1906.

GOODMAN, DR. GODFREY *The Court of King James the First.* 2 vols. London, 1839.

HACKET, JOHN *Scrinia Reserata; a Memorial Offer'd to the Great Deservings of John Williams, D.D.* . . . London, 1693. Lord Keeper Williams.

HALLIWELL, JAMES ORCHARD, ed. *Letters of the Kings of England.* 2 vols. London, 1846.

HARINGTON, SIR JOHN *The Letters and Epigrams of Sir John Harington.* Ed. Norman E. McClure. Philadelphia, 1930.

—— *Nugae Antiquae; being a Miscellaneous Collection of Original Papers Written During the Reigns of Henry VIII, Mary, Elizabeth, King James.* 2 vols. London, 1804.

HARDWICKE, PHILIP YORKE, 2D EARL OF. *Miscellaneous State Papers from 1501-1726.* 2 vols. London, 1778.

HERBERT, EDWARD, LORD *The Autobiography of Edward, Lord Herbert of Cherbury.* Ed. Sidney L. Lee. New York, 1886.

HISTORICAL MANUSCRIPT COMMISSION *Braye Papers; Report on the MSS. of the Marquess of Abergavenny.* London, 1887.

—— *Buccleuch Papers; Report on the MSS. of the Duke of Buccleuch and Queensberry.* London, 1899.

—— *Miss Buxton Papers,* in *Various Collections,* II. London, 1903.

—— *De L'Isle and Dudley Papers; Report on the MSS. of Lord De L'Isle and Dudley, Preserved at Penshurst Place.* 4 vols. London, 1925.

—— *G. M. Fortescue Papers; 2d Report,* xiii, and app. 49-63. London, 1874.

—— *Gawdy Papers; Report on the MSS. of the Family of Gawdy . . . Formerly of Norfolk.* London, 1885.

—— *Records of the Dissolved Corporation of Dunwich.* In *Various Collections,* VII. London, 1914.

—— *Rutland Papers; Report on the MSS. of the Duke of Rutland.* London, 1888.

—— *Salisbury Papers; the MSS. of the Marquess of Salisbury.* 18 vols. London, 1883-1938.

—— *Shrewsbury Papers; the MSS. of Lord Edmund Talbot,* in *Various Collections,* II. London, 1903.

—— *Trumbull Papers; Report on the MSS. of the Marquess of Downshire.* 3 vols. London, 1938.

HOWELL, JAMES *Epistolae Ho-Elianae; the Familiar Letters of James Howell.* London, 1890.

HYDE, EDWARD, EARL OF CLARENDON *The Life of Edward Earl of Clarendon.* 3 vols. London, 1759.

LODGE, EDMUND *Illustrations of British History, Biography and Manners in the Reigns of Henry VIII, Edward VI, Mary, Elizabeth and James I.* 3 vols. London, 1891.

—— *Portraits of Illustrious Personages of Great Britain. . . .* 12 vols. in 6. London, 1825.

MANNINGHAM, JOHN *Diary of John Manningham of the Middle Temple.* Ed. John Bruce. Westminster, 1868.

MILWARD, JOHN *The Diary of John Milward, Esq.* Ed. Caroline Robbins. Cambridge, 1938.

MORYSON, FYNES *Itinerary.* London, 1903.

NAUNTON, SIR ROBERT *Fragmenta Regalia, or Observations on the Late Queen Elizabeth, Her Times and Favourites.* Ed. Edward Arber. London, 1870.

NICHOLS, JOHN *Progresses* (of Queen Elizabeth and James I). London, 1928 and 1923. The footnotes are a mine of biographical information.

OVERBURY, SIR THOMAS *The Overburian Characters. . . .* Oxford, 1936.

PECK, FRANCIS, ed. *Desiderata Curiosa.* 2 vols. in one. London, 1779.

PENRY, JOHN *The Notebook of John Penry, 1593.* Ed. Albert Peel. London, 1944.

The Phenix; a Collection of Choice, Scarce and Valuable Tracts . . . by a Gentleman who has Search'd After Them for Above Twenty Years. London, 1721.

PYM, JOHN *The Diary of John Pym.* Ed. Charles Edward Wade. London, 1912.

SADLER, SIR RALPH *The State Papers and Letters of Sir Ralph Sadler.* Ed. Arthur Clifford. 3 vols. Edinburgh, 1809.

A Selection from the Harleian Miscellany of Tracts, which Principally Regard the English History. . . . London, 1793.

SIDNEY, SIRS HENRY, PHILIP and ROBERT *Letters and Memorials of State, Written and Collected by Sir Henry Sidney . . . , Sir Philip Sidney and his Brother Sir Robert Sidney. . . .* Transcr. from originals at Penshurst Place in Kent, and the Office of Papers and Records, by Arthur Collins. 2 vols. London, 1746.

SOMERS, LORD JOHN *A Collection of Scarce and Valuable Tracts of the most Interesting and Entertaining Subjects . . . of the Late Lord Somers.* 2d ed., Sir Walter Scott. London, 1809.

STRAFFORD, THOMAS WENTWORTH, EARL OF *The Earle of Strafforde's Letters and Despatches with an Essay Towards his Life by Sir George Radcliffe. . . .* Ed. William Knowler. Dublin, 1740.

STRYPE, JOHN *Ecclesiastical Memorials . . . Under the Reigns of King Henry VIII, King Edward IV and Queen Mary I.* 7 vols. London, 1806.

Stuart Tracts, 1603-1693. Reprinted from *English Garner* (ed. Arber, 1877-1890). Ed. G. H. Firth. New York, n.d.

WHITELOCKE, SIR JAMES *Liber Famelicus of Sir James Whitelocke*. Ed. John Bruce. Camden Society, 1858.
WILBRAHAM, SIR ROGER *The Journal of Sir Roger Wilbraham for the Years 1593-1616*. Ed. H. S. Scott; *Camden Miscellany*, X. London, 1902.
WINSTANLEY, WILLIAM *England's Worthies*. London, 1684.
WINWOOD, SIR RALPH *Memorials of State*. 3 vols. London, 1725.
YONGE, WALTER *The Diary of Walter Yonge*. Camden Society, 1848.

The Physical Scene

General

CAMDEN, WILLIAM *Britannia, or a Chorographical Description of Great Britain and Ireland*. Ed. Edmund Gibson. 3 vols. London, 1789.
CHAUNCY, SIR HENRY *Historical Antiquities of Hertfordshire*. 2 vols. London, 1826.
DARBY, H. C. *An Historical Geography of England Before A.D. 1800*. Cambridge, 1951.
EBERLEIN, HAROLD DONALDSON *Little Known England; Rambles in the Welsh Borderland, the Cotswolds, the Chalk Hills and the Eastern Counties*. London, 1930.
HARRISON, WILLIAM *An Historicall Description of the Iland of Britaine . . .* 4 vols. London, 1908.
—— *Harrison's Description of England in Shakespere's Youth, . . .* Ed. Frederick J. Furnivall, from first two eds. of Holinshed's *Chronicles*. London, 1877.
MUIRHEAD, L. RUSSELL, ed. *England*. 5th ed. London, 1950.
NICHOLS, JOHN G., ed. *Collectanea Topographica et Genealogica*. 8 vols. London, 1834-1843.
PAGE, WILLIAM, ed. *Victoria History of the Counties of Hampshire and the Isle of Wight*. Westminster, 1901-1906.
SMITH, WILLIAM *The Particular Description of England (1588)*. London, 1879.
TAYLOR, E. G. R. *Tudor Geography, 1485-1583*. London, 1932.

London

BELL, WALTER GEORGE *Fleet Street in Seven Centuries*. London, 1912.
BENHAM, WILLIAM *The Tower of London*. London, 1906.
BERESFORD, EDWIN *The Annals of Fleet Street, its Traditions and Associations*. New York, 1912.
BESANT, WALTER *London*. London, 1894.
—— *London in the Time of the Stuarts*. London, 1903.
—— *London in the Time of the Tudors*. London, 1904.
—— *London North of the Thames*. London, 1911.
BRAYLEY, EDWARD W. *Londiniana*. 4 vols. London, 1829.

—— and BRITTON, JOHN *The History of the Ancient Palace and Late House of Parliament at Westminster.* London, 1936.
CARKEET-JONES, COL. E. H. *His Majesty's Tower of London.* London, 1950.
CHAMBERLAIN, HENRY, ed. *A Compleat History and Survey of the Cities of London and Westminster.* London, 1770.
CHUTE, MARCHETTE *Shakespeare of London.* New York, 1949.
CUNNINGHAM, PETER *A Handbook for London, Past and Present.* 2 vols. London, 1844.
DIXON, WILLIAM HEPWORTH *Her Majesty's Tower.* Popular ed. 2 vols. London, 1901.
DUCAREL, DR. *The History and Antiquities of the Archiepiscopal Palace of Lambeth.* London, 1785.
FOSS, EDWARD *Memories of Westminster Hall.* 2 vols. London, n.d.
GOMME, SIR LAURENCE *The Making of London.* Oxford, 1912.
HARRISON, WALTER *History, Description and Survey of the Cities of London and Westminster. . . .* London, 1776.
HERBERT, W. and BRAYLEY, EDWARD W. *Concise Account, Historical and Descriptive, of Lambeth Palace.* London, 1806.
LINDSAY, MARTIN *The House of Commons.* London, 1947.
LUCAS, E. V. *A Wanderer in London.* New York, 1910.
MEE, ARTHUR *London; Heart of the Empire and Wonder of the World.* London, 1951.
MOYES, A. J. *Debating Chambers of the House of Commons.* London, n.d.
MUIRHEAD, FINDLAY *London and Its Environs.* London, 1918.
O'DONNELL, BERNARD *The Old Bailey and Its Trials.* London, 1951.
SHEPPARD, EDGAR *Memorials of St. James's Palace.* 2 vols. London, 1894.
SMITH, JOHN THOMAS *Antiquities of Westminster; the Old Palace; St. Stephen's Chapel (Now the House of Commons), &c. &c.* 2 vols. London, 1807.
STEPHENSON, HENRY THEW *Shakespeare's London.* New York, 1905.
STOW, JOHN *A Survey of London; reprinted from the Text of 1603.* Ed. C. L. Kingsford. 2 vols. Oxford, 1908.

Norfolk

ASTLEY, H. J. D. *Memorials of Old Norfolk.* London, 1908.
BACON, SIR NATHANIEL *The Official Papers of Sir Nathaniel Bacon of Stiffkey, Norfolk, as Justice of the Peace, 1580-1620.* Ed. H. W. Saunders; *Camden Miscellany*, XXVI. London, 1915.
BLOMEFIELD, FRANCES and PARKIN, C. *Topographical History of . . . the County of Norfolk.* 11 vols. London, 1805-1810.
A Brief History of the Manor and Parish of Stoke-Poges, Bucks. London, n.d. To be seen in the Gate-house to the Manor, or Garden of Remembrance, Stoke-Poges.

CARTHEW, G. A. *The Hundred of Launditch and Deanery of Brisley. . . .* 3 vols. Norwich, 1877-1879.

CHAMBERS, JOHN *A General History of the County of Norfolk. . . .* 3 vols. Norwich, 1829.

COZENS-HARDY, BASIL and KENT, ERNEST A. *The Mayors of Norwich, 1403-1835.* Norwich, 1938.

DAVENPORT, FRANCES GARDINER *The Economic Development of a Norfolk Manor, 1086-1565.* Cambridge, 1906.

DUTT, W. A. *Norfolk.* London, 1949.

GLYDE, JOHN, JR., ed. *The Norfolk Garland; a collection of the superstitious beliefs and practices, proverbs, curious customs, ballads and songs, of the people of Norfolk, as well as anecdotes, illustrative of the genius or peculiarities of Norfolk celebrities. . . .* London, 1872.

JESSOPP, AUGUSTUS *One Generation of a Norfolk House; a Contribution to Elizabethan History.* Norwich, 1878.

KENT, ARNOLD and STEPHENSON, ANDREW *Norwich Inheritance.* Norwich, n.d.

KETTON-CREMER, R. WYNDHAM *Norfolk Portraits.* London, 1944.

—— *A Norfolk Gallery.* London, 1948.

MOTTRAM, R. H. *Norfolk.* London, 1948.

NORDEN, JOHN *The Chorography of Norfolk.* Ed. Christobel M. Hood. Norwich, 1938.

Notices and Illustrations of the Costumes, Processions, Pageantry . . . Formerly Displayed by the Corporation of Norwich. Norwich, 1850.

RUSSELL, FREDERICK WILLIAM *Kett's Rebellion in Norfolk.* London, 1859.

RYE, WALTER *A History of Norfolk.* London, 1885.

—— *Norwich Houses before 1600.* Norwich, 1916.

—— *The Recreations of a Norfolk Antiquary.* Norwich, 1920.

—— *Tourist's Guide to Norfolk.* London, 1892.

SPELMAN, HENRY "*Icenia sive Norfolciae. . . .*" In *Reliquiae Spelmannianae.* London, 1698.

Victoria History of the County of Norfolk. 2 vols. Westminster, 1901-1906.

WILLINS, EDWARD PRESTON *Quaint Old Norwich.* Norwich, 1884.

Constitutional and Legal History

General

Acts of the Privy Council of England, 1542-1628. Ed. J. R. Dasent and others. 43 vols. London, 1890-1940 (1949).

ADAIR, EDWARD R. *The Sources for the History of the Council in the Sixteenth and Seventeenth Centuries.* London, 1924.

ADAMS, GEORGE BURTON *An Outline Sketch of English Constitutional History.* New Haven, 1918.

ALLEN, JOHN W. *A History of Political Thought in the Sixteenth Century.* London, 1928.

AMES, JAMES BARR *Lectures on Legal History.* Cambridge (Mass.), 1913.

AMOS, ANDREW *The Great Oyer of Poisoning.* London, 1846. The trial of the Earl of Somerset for the poisoning of Sir Thomas Overbury.

ANSON, SIR WILLIAM R. *The Law and Custom of the Constitution.* 2 vols. Oxford, 1892.

BAGEHOT, WALTER *The English Constitution.* London, 1913.

BEARD, CHARLES *The Supreme Court and the Constitution.* New York, 1916.

BELL, H. E. *An Introduction to the History and Records of the Court of Wards and Liveries.* Cambridge, 1953.

BLACKSTONE, SIR WILLIAM *Commentaries on the Laws of England.* 4 vols. 11th ed. London, 1791.

The Book of Oaths and the Several Forms thereof, both Antient and Modern, faithfully Collected out of Sundry Authentike Books and Records. . . . London, 1649.

BOUDIN, LEONARD B. "The Constitutional Privilege in Operation," in *Lawyers Guild Review,* XII, no. 3 (Summer, 1952).

BRIDGMAN, RICHARD WHALLEY *A Short View of Legal Bibliography: Containing Critical Observations on the Authority of the Reporters and Other Law Writers. . . .* London, 1807.

BRODIE, GEORGE *A Constitutional History of the British Empire.* 3 vols. London, 1866.

CAIRNS, HUNTINGTON *Legal Philosophy from Plato to Hegel.* Baltimore, 1949.

CAMPBELL, LORD JOHN *Lives of the Lord Chancellors and Keepers of the Great Seal of England.* 10 vols. 4th ed. London, 1856.

CARLYLE, ALEXANDER J. *A History of Medieval Political Theory in the West.* 6 vols. New York, 1936.

CARRIGHAN, TERENTIUS *The Chancery Students Guide in the Form of a Didactic Poem.* London, 1850.

CHAFEE, ZECHARIAH *How Human Rights Got into the Constitution.* Boston, 1952.

CHEYNEY, EDWARD P. "The Court of Star Chamber," in *American Historical Review,* XVIII (July 1913) 727-750.

COBBETT, WILLIAM, HOWELL, T. B. *et al. A Complete Collection of State Trials and Proceedings for High Treason. . . .* 42 vols. London, 1809-1898.

Collectanea Juridica; Consisting of Tracts Relative to the Law and Constitution of England. Ed. Francis Hargrave. 2 vols. London, 1791.

The Constitution Reconsidered. Ed. Conyers Read. New York, 1938.

CORWIN, EDWARD S. *The Doctrine of Judicial Supremacy.* Princeton, 1914.

—— "The Higher Law, Background of American Constitutional Law." *Harvard Law Review,* XLII (1928) no. 2, 149-185; XLII (1929) no. 3, 365-409.

—— *Liberty Against Government.* Baton Rouge (La.), 1948.

COSIN, RICHARD *An Apologie for Sundrie Proceedings by Jurisdiction Ecclesiastical.* London, 1593.
COWELL, JOHN *The Interpreter: or Booke Containing the Signification of Words. . . .* Cambridge, 1607.
CROKE, SIR GEORGE *Reports of Sir G. Croke, Knight, of such Select Cases as were Adjudged in the Said Courts During the Reign of James I.* 4th ed. London, 1791.
DANIELL, EDMUND ROBERT *Pleading and Practice of the High Court of Chancery.* 6th American ed. 3 vols. Boston, 1894.
DICEY, ALBERT V. *Introduction to the Study of the Law of the Constitution.* London, 1902.
—— *The Privy Council.* London, 1887.
DOBB, MAURICE *Political Economy and Capitalism.* New York, 1940.
DODDRIDGE, SIR JOHN *The English Lawyer.* London, 1631.
DUNNING, WILLIAM ARCHIBALD *A History of Political Theories from Luther to Montesquieu.* New York, 1943.
The English Philosophers from Bacon to Mill. Ed. Edwin A. Burtt. New York, 1939.
ESMEIN, ADHÉMAR *A History of Continental Criminal Procedure.* Boston, 1913.
Essays in Legal History. Ed. Paul Vinogradoff. Oxford, 1914.
FIGGIS, JOHN NEVILLE *The Divine Right of Kings.* 2d ed. Cambridge, 1922.
—— *Studies of Political Thought from Gerson to Grotius, 1414-1625.*
FORTESCUE, SIR JOHN *De Laudibus Angliae; a Treatise in Commendation of the Laws of England.* Cincinnati, 1874.
FOSS, EDWARD *A Biographical Dictionary of the Judges of England, 1066-1870.* 9 vols. London, 1870.
—— *The Judges of England, 1066-1870.* 6 vols. London, 1857-1864.
—— *Tabulae Curiae: or Tables of the Superior Courts of Westminster Hall, Showing the Judges Who Sat in Them from 1066 to 1864; with the Attorney- and Solicitor-generals of Each Reign. . . .* London, 1865.
FOSTER, SIR MICHAEL *Report of Some Proceedings on the Commission for the Trial of the Rebels in the Year 1746 and of other Crown Cases.* 3rd ed. London, 1792.
GARDINER, SAMUEL RAWSON, ed. *The Constitutional Documents of the Puritan Revolution 1625-1660.* Oxford, 1899.
GEST, JOHN *The Lawyer, a Literary Man.* Boston, 1913.
GIERKE, DR. OTTO F. VON *Political Theories of the Middle Ages.* Cambridge, 1900.
GILBERT, SIR GEOFFREY *The History and Practice of the High Court of Chancery.* London, 1758.
GOOCH, GEORGE PEABODY *English Democratic Ideas in the Seventeenth Century.* Ed. Harold J. Laski. Cambridge, 1927.
—— *Political Thought in England from Bacon to Halifax.* London, 1929.
GRISWOLD, DEAN ERWIN N. *The 5th Amendment Today; Three Speeches.* Cambridge (Mass.), 1955.
HADLEY, JAMES *Introduction to Roman Law.* New York, 1873.

HALE, SIR MATTHEW *The History of the Common Law of England.* 3rd ed. The Savoy (London), 1739.
HALLAM, HENRY *Constitutional History of England from the Accession of Henry VII to the Death of George II.* London, 1870.
HALLIFAX, SAMUEL *An Analysis of the Roman Civil Law. . . .* Cambridge, 1775.
HAMILTON, ALEXANDER H. A. *Quarter Sessions from Queen Elizabeth to Queen Anne.* London, 1878.
HARCOURT, L. W. VERNON *His Grace the Steward and the Trial of Peers.* London, 1907.
HARRINGTON, JAMES *Oceana.* Ed. with notes by S. B. Liljegren. Heidelberg, 1924.
HASTINGS, MARGARET *The Court of Common Pleas in Fifteenth Century England.* Ithaca (N.Y.), 1947.
HAWARDE, JOHN *Les Reportes del Cases in Camera Stellata, 1593-1609.* Ed. W. P. Baildon. London, 1894.
HEARNE, THOMAS *A Collection of Curious Discourses on our English Antiquities.* 2 vols. London, 1775.
HEARNSHAW, FOSSEY J. C. *The Social and Political Ideas of Some Great Thinkers of the Sixteenth and Seventeenth Centuries.* New York, 1949.
HIGHAM, MRS. C. S. S. (Florence M. Greir Evans) *The Principal Secretary of State; A Survey of the Office, 1558-1680.* Manchester, 1923.
HOBBES, THOMAS "A Dialogue Between a Philosopher and a Student of the Common Laws of England," in *The English Works of Thomas Hobbes.* Ed. Sir William Molesworth. London, 1840. Vol. VI.
HOLDSWORTH, WILLIAM S. "Defamation in the Sixteenth and Seventeenth Centuries," in *Law Quarterly Review,* XL (July 1924), 302.
—— *Essays in Law and History.* Oxford, 1946.
—— *A History of English Law.* 12 vols. London, 1903-1938.
—— *Some Lessons from Our Legal History.* New York, 1928.
—— *Some Makers of English Law.* The Tagore Lectures. Cambridge, 1938.
—— *Sources and Literature of English Law.* London, 1925.
HOLMES, OLIVER WENDELL, JR. *The Common Law.* Boston, 1938.
HORNE, ANDREW *The Mirrour of Justices.* Trans. by W. Hughes. London, 1840.
HUDSON, WILLIAM *A Treatise of the Star Chamber.* Pub. in *Collectanea Juridica,* vol. II. London, 1792.
HURST, WILLARD "Treason in the United States," Part I, in *Harvard Law Review,* LVIII, no. 226 (1944).
INDERWICK, F. A. *The King's Peace; a Historical Sketch of the English Law Courts.* London, 1895.
JACOB, GILES *The New Law Dictionary . . . carefully Abridged. . . .* London, 1743.
JARDINE, DAVID *Criminal Trials.* 2 vols. London, 1882.
—— *A Reading on the Use of Torture in the Criminal Law of England.* London, 1837.

JENKS, EDWARD *A Short History of English Law*. Boston, 1922.
—— "The Story of the Habeas Corpus," in *Law Quarterly Review*, XVIII (Jan. 1902).
JUDSON, MARGARET ATWOOD *The Crisis of the Constitution; an Essay in Constitutional and Political Thought in England, 1603-1645*. New Brunswick (N.J.), 1949.
KEETON, GEORGE W. *Shakespeare and His Legal Problems*. London, 1930.
KEIR, SIR DAVID LINDSAY *The Constitutional History of Modern Britain, 1485-1937*. London, 1938.
KOENIGSBERG, SAMUEL M. and STAVIS, MORTON "Test Oaths: Henry VIII to the American Bar Association." *Lawyers Guild Review*, XI, no. 3 (Summer 1951).
LAMBARDE, WILLIAM *Archion, or, a Commentary Upon the High Courts of Justice in England*. Completed, but not published, in 1591. London, 1635.
—— *Eirenarcha, or Of the Office of the Justices of Peace*. London, 1610.
—— "William Lambarde's *Collections on Chancery*." Ed. Paul L. Ward. In *Harvard Library Bulletin*, VII (Autumn 1953).
—— "William Lambarde's *Ephemeris*, 1580-1588." Ed. Conyers Read. *Huntington Library Quarterly*, XV, no. 2 (Feb. 1952).
Law Quibbles, or, a Treatise of the Evasions, Tricks, Turns and Quibbles, Commonly Used in the Profession of the Law, to the Prejudice of Clients, and others. . . . The Savoy (London), 1724.
LEA, HENRY C. *Superstition and Force; Essays on the Wager of Law, the Wager of Battle, the Ordeal, Torture*. Philadelphia, 1870.
Leading Cases in Equity. Ed. by F. H. White and O. D. Tudor. 2 vols. London, 1910.
Littleton's Tenures. Ed. E. Wambaugh. Washington, 1903.
LODGE, ELEANOR C. and THORNTON, GLADYS A. *English Constitutional Documents, 1307-1485*. Cambridge, 1935.
LOVEJOY, ARTHUR O. *The Great Chain of Being*. Cambridge (Mass.), 1936.
LOWELL, ABBOTT L. *Government of England*. 2 vols. New York, 1908.
McILWAIN, CHARLES HOWARD *The American Revolution; a Constitutional Interpretation*. New York, 1923.
—— *Constitutionalism, Ancient and Modern*. Ithaca (N.Y.), 1947.
—— *Constitutionalism and the Changing World*. New York, 1939.
—— *The Growth of Political Thought in the West*. New York, 1932.
McKECHNIE, WILLIAM SHARP *Magna Carta, a Commentary on the Great Charter of King John*. 2d rev. ed. Glasgow, 1914.
MAINE, SIR HENRY SUMNER *Ancient Law. . . .* World's Classics ed. London, 1950.
MAITLAND, FREDERIC W. *The Collected Works of Frederic William Maitland*. Ed. H. A. L. Fisher. 3 vols. Cambridge, 1911.
—— *The Constitutional History of England*. Cambridge, 1926.
—— *English Law and the Renaissance*. Rede Lecture for 1901. Cambridge, 1901.

—— and MONTAGUE, FRANCIS C. *A Sketch of English Legal History.* Ed. James F. Colby. Dartmouth (N.H.), 1915.

MARTIN, J. E., ed. *Masters of the Bench.* London, 1883.

MAYNARD, JOHN *Les Reports de Cases en Ley (Edward IV).* London, 1680.

MORE, SIR THOMAS *Utopia.* Trans. by Ralph Robinson; ed. Edward Arber. London, 1859.

MOSSE, GEORGE L. *The Struggle for Sovereignty in England, from the Reign of Queen Elizabeth to the Petition of Right.* East Lansing (Michigan), 1950.

NEILSON, GEORGE *Trial by Combat.* New York, 1891.

Nicholas Faunt's Discourse Touching the Office of Principal Secretary of Estate. . . . Engl. Hist. R., XX (1905), 499-508.

PETIT-DUTAILLIS, CHARLES *Studies and Notes Supplementary to Stubb's Constitutional History. . . .* Ed. James Tait. 2 vols. Oxford, 1908.

PLUCKNETT, THEODORE F. T. *A Concise History of the Common Law.* 4th ed. London, 1948.

POLLARD, ALBERT F. "Council, Star Chamber and Privy Council Under the Tudors," in *Engl. Hist. R.*, XXXVII (1922); XXXVIII (1923).

POLLOCK, SIR FREDERICK *The Expansion of the Common Law.* London, 1904.

—— *An Introduction to the Science of Politics.* London, 1935.

—— "The Transformation of Equity," in *Essays in Legal History.* Oxford, 1914.

POUND, ROSCOE *An Introduction to the Philosophy of Law.* New Haven, 1922.

—— *Justice According to Law.* New Haven, 1951.

—— *The Spirit of the Common Law.* Francestown (N.H.), 1947.

PROTHERO, GEORGE W. *Select Statutes and Other Constitutional Documents Illustrative of the Reigns of Elizabeth and James I.* Oxford, 1934.

PUTNAM, BERTHA H. "Early Treatises on the Practice of the Justices of the Peace in the Fifteenth and Sixteenth Centuries." *Oxford Studies in Social and Legal History*, VII, no. 13. Oxford, 1924.

QUINCY, JOSIAH, JR. *Reports of Cases in the Superior Court of Judicature of the Province of Massachusetts Bay.* Boston, 1865.

RADZINOWICZ, LEON *A History of English Criminal Law and Its Administration from 1750.* New York, 1948.

READ, CONYERS *Factions in the English Privy Council under Elizabeth.* Amer. Hist. Assoc. Rept. (1911), I, 109-119.

REEVES, JOHN *A History of English Law from the Time of the Saxons to the End of the Reign of Elizabeth.* 3rd ed. 5 vols. London, 1814-1829.

RYMER, THOMAS, comp. *Foedera, Conventiones, Litterae, et Cujuscunque Generis Acta Publica. . . .* 17 vols. London, 1704-1717.

SAINT GERMAIN, CHRISTOPHER *Doctor and Student, or Dialogues Between a Doctor of Divinity and a Student in the Laws of England.* 16th ed. London, 1761.

SALMOND, SIR JOHN W. *Jurisprudence, or, The Theory of Law.* London, 1902. Ralegh trial.

Select Essays in Anglo-American Legal History. Ed. E. Freund, E. W. Mikell, J. H. Wigmore. 3 vols. Boston, 1908.

SMITH, SIR THOMAS *De Republica Anglorum; a Discourse on the Commonwealth of England.* Ed. L. Alston. Cambridge, 1906.

SPELMAN, SIR HENRY *Reliquiae Spelmannianae; Relating to Laws and Antiquities of England.* London, 1723.

Statutes of the Realm. Ed. A. Luders, T. R. Tomlins, J. Raithby *et al.* 4 vols. London, 1810-1828.

STEELE, ROBERT, ed. *Tudor and Stuart Proclamations, 1485-1714.* 2 vols. Oxford, 1910.

STEPHEN, SIR JAMES FITZJAMES *A History of the Criminal Law of England.* 3 vols. London, 1883.

STEPHEN, SIR HERBERT L. *State Trials, Political and Social.* 2 vols. London, 1899.

STEPHENSON, CARL and MARCHAM, FREDERICK *Sources of English Constitutional History. . . . from A.D. 600 to the Present.* New York, 1937.

STRYKER, LLOYD PAUL *The Art of Advocacy.* New York, 1954.

STUBBS, WILLIAM *The Constitutional History of England.* 5th ed. 3 vols. Oxford, 1891.

TANNER, JOSEPH R. *Constitutional Documents of the Reign of James I, 1603-1625.* Cambridge, 1930.

—— *English Constitutional Conflicts of the Seventeenth Century, 1603-1689.* Cambridge, 1947.

—— *Tudor Constitutional Documents, A.D. 1485-1603; with an Historical Commentary.* Cambridge, 1948.

THAYER, JAMES BRADLEY *A Preliminary Treatise on Evidence at the Common Law.* Boston, 1898.

THOMPSON, FAITH *Magna Carta; Its Role in the Making of the English Constitution, 1300-1629.* Minneapolis, 1948.

THORNE, SAMUEL E. *A Discourse upon the Exposicion & Understandinge of Statutes with Sir Thomas Egerton's Additions.* San Marino, Huntington Library, 1942.

TURNER, EDWARD R. "The Lords Justices of England." *Engl. Hist. R.,* XXIX (July 1914).

—— "The Secrecy of the Past." *Engl. Hist. R.,* XXXIII (1918).

USHER, ROLAND G. *The Rise and Fall of the High Commission.* Oxford, 1913.

VON MOSCHZISKER, ROBERT *Trial by Jury.* Philadelphia, 1930.

WALLACE, JOHN WILLIAM *The Reporters Arranged and Characterized. . . .* Ed. F. F. Heard. 4th ed. Boston, 1882.

WARREN, CHARLES *History of the Harvard Law School and of Early Legal Conditions in America.* 2 vols. New York, 1908.

WEBB, SIDNEY and BEATRICE *English Local Government.* 3 vols. London, 1927.

Westminster Hall, or Professional Relics and Anecdotes of the Bar,

Bench and Woolsack. Ed. Henry T. Roscoe. 3 vols. London, 1825. Legal gossip.

WHITELOCKE, SIR JAMES *Liber Famelicus of a Judge of the Court of King's Bench, James I and Charles I*. Camden Society, 1858. Legal gossip.

WIGMORE, JOHN H. "A General Survey of the History of the Rules of Evidence," in *Select Essays in Anglo-American Legal History*, II. Boston, 1908.

—— "The Privilege Against Self-Crimination; Its History." *Harvard Law Review*, XV (1901-1902), 610.

—— *A Treatise on the Anglo-American System of Evidence in Trials at Common Law*. 3rd ed. 10 vols. Boston, 1940.

WINFIELD, PERCY H. *The Chief Sources of English Legal History*. Cambridge (Mass.), 1925.

—— *The History of Conspiracy and Abuse of Legal Procedure*. Cambridge, 1921.

WOOLRYCH, HUMPHRY W. *Lives of Eminent Serjeants-at-Law of the English Bar*. 2 vols. London, 1826.

WRIGHT, RT. HON. LORD "The Study of Law," in *Law Quarterly Review*, LIV, no. 214 (1938).

Year Books of Edward IV, 1461-1483. Ed. Miss Neilson. London, Selden Society, 1931.

Inns of Court

BELLOT, HUGH H. L. "The Exclusion of Attorneys from the Inns of Court," in *Law Quarterly Review*, XXVI (1920), 137.

—— *The Inner and Middle Temple Legal, Literary and Historic Associations*. London, 1902.

—— "The Jurisdiction of the Inns of Court Over the Inns of Chancery," in *Law Quarterly Review*, XXVI (1910), 384.

BUC, GEORGE *The Third University of England, or a Treatise of the Foundation of All the Colleges, Within and About London*. Pub. at the end of John Stow's *Annales*. London, 1615.

FOSS, EDWARD *The Judges of England*. London, 1857. Vol. VI, 236-248.

FOSTER, JOSEPH *Men at the Bar; a Biographical Hand List of the Members of the Various Inns of Court. . . .* 2d ed. London, 1885.

HAWKES, CHARLES P. *Chambers in the Temple*. London, 1930.

HERBERT, WILLIAM *Antiquities of the Inns of Court and Chancery, with a History of the English Law*. London, 1804.

INDERWICK, F. A. *A Calendar of the Inner Temple Records*. 3 vols. London, 1896-1901.

JONES, E. ALFRED *American Members of the Inns of Court*. London, 1924.

MACKINNON, SIR FRANK DOUGLAS *Inner Temple Papers*. London, 1948.

ODGERS, W. B. "A Sketch of the History of the Four Inns of Court," in *Essays in Legal History*. Ed. Paul Vinogradoff. Oxford, 1914.

PAGE, WILLIAM *Clifford's Inn*. London, 1920.

PULLING, ALEXANDER *The Order of the Coif*. London, 1884.

SMITH, PHILIP ANSTIE *A History of Education for the English Bar*. London, 1860.

Table of Fees of All the Courts at Westminster. London, 1594.

WARREN, EDWARD H. "Serjeants-at-Law, the Order of the Coif," in *Virginia Law Review* (May 1942).

WILLIAMSON, J. BRUCE *The History of the Temple*. London, 1924.

Parliament

Parliamentary Debates, Diaries and Journals

Second only to Coke's *Institutes* and *Reports*, these parliamentary diaries and recorded debates were my most fertile (and vital) source for Coke's biography. To read D'Ewes's *Journal* for the first time is an extraordinary experience. Speaker Coke's eager teaching, in 1593, when he tells the Commons how to vote a new law, whether to sit still for *No* or leave the Chamber for *Aye*, and his reasons . . . Cecil's angry exchanges with Ralegh, the suave knowledgeableness of Privy Councilors, the wisdom of old Lord Burghley, the strong partisanship of James Morrice or Peter Wentworth . . . on those old folio pages the words and scenes come alive, quick with the magnificent idiom of the day. Half of Coke's character — the Parliament half — remained closed to me until I studied D'Ewes's *Journal* of Elizabeth's Parliaments, the *Commons Debates* for 1621, Rushworth's *Collections* for the great Parliaments of the 1620's.

ARCHBOLD, W. A. J. "A Diary of the Parliament of 1626." *Engl. Hist. R.*, XVII (1902). Diarist possibly Bulstrode Whitelocke.

BOWYER, ROBERT *The Parliamentary Diary of Robert Bowyer, 1606-1607*. Ed. David Harris Willson. Minneapolis, 1931.

COBBETT, WILLIAM, ed. *The Parliamentary History of England from the Earliest Period to the Year 1803*. 36 vols. London, 1806-1820.

D'EWES, SIR SIMONDS *A Complete Journal of . . . the House of Lords and the House of Commons . . . During the Reign of Queen Elizabeth*. London, 1693.

—— *The Journal of Sir Simonds D'Ewes from the Beginning of the Long Parliament to the Opening of the Trial of the Earl of Strafford*. Ed. Wallace Notestein. New Haven, 1923.

Documents Illustrating the Impeachment of the Duke of Buckingham in 1626. Ed. S. R. Gardiner. Camden Society, 1889.

The Commons Debates for 1629. . . . Ed. Wallace Notestein, Helen Relf. Minneapolis, 1921.

Commons Debates 1621. Ed. Notestein, Relf, Hartley Simpson. 7 vols. New Haven, 1935.

Debates in the House of Commons in 1625. Ed. S. R. Gardiner. Camden Society, 1873.

Journals of the House of Commons, 1547-1714. 17 vols. London, 1803.

Journals of the House of Lords, 1578-1714. 19 vols. London, 1846.

NICHOLAS, SIR EDWARD *A Critical Edition of Nicholas' Notes on the Parliament of 1627-8.* Ed. Louise Sumner. MS. of a thesis submitted to the faculty of the Graduate School of the University of Minnesota, June 1913.

Parliamentary Debates in 1610 from the Notes of a Member of the House of Commons. Ed. S. R. Gardiner. Camden Society, 1862.

The Parliamentary or Constitutional History of England . . . (1066-1660). 24 vols. London, 1751-1761. Known as the *Old Parliamentary History.*

RUSHWORTH, JOHN *Historical Collections of Private Passages of State . . . Beginning the Sixteenth Year of King James Anno 1618 and Ending the Fifth Year of King Charles, 1629.* 8 vols. London, 1721.

TOWNSHEND, HEYWOOD *Historical Collections: or, An Exact Account of the Four Last Parliaments of Queen Elizabeth. . . .* London, 1680. Contains complete Journals of Lords and Commons taken from the original records of their houses.

Parliamentary History, Descriptive and Critical

ADAIR, E. R. "The Petition of Right." *History,* V (1921), 99-103.

COTTON, SIR ROBERT *Cottoni Posthuma.* Ed. J. Howell. London, 1651. Studies on the relation of Crown and Parliament.

DASENT, ARTHUR IRWIN *The Speakers of the House of Commons.* London, 1911.

Dod's Parliamentary Companion for 1951. London, 1951.

GORDON, STRATHEARN *Our Parliament.* London, 1945.

HAKEWILL, WILLIAM *The Libertie of the Subject Against the Pretended Power of Impositions Maintained by an Argument in Parliament An. 7 Jacobi Regis.* London, 1641.

—— *The Manner How Statutes are Enacted in Parliament by Passing of Bills.* London, 1641. Later enlarged into *Modus Tenendi Parliamentum.*

—— *Modus Tenendi Parliamentum: or, the Old Manner of Holding Parliaments in England.* London, 1671. Includes *The Manner How Statutes Are Enacted.*

HASKINS, GEORGE L. *The Growth of English Representative Government.* Philadelphia, 1948.

HULME, H. "Opinion in the House of Commons on the Proposal for a Petition of Right, 6 May, 1628." *Engl. Hist. R.,* vol. L (1935), 302-306.

MCILWAIN, CHARLES HOWARD *The High Court of Parliament and its Supremacy. . . .* New Haven, 1934.

MANNING, JAMES ALEXANDER *The Lives of the Speakers of the House of Commons, Edward III to Queen Victoria.* London, 1851.

MAY, THOMAS ERSKINE *A Practical Treatise on the Law, Privileges, Proceedings and Usage of Parliament.* 4th ed. London, 1859.

NEALE, JOHN E. "The Authorship of Townshend's *Historical Collections.*" *Engl. Hist. R.*, XXXIV (1921); XXXVI (1921), 96-99.

—— "The Commons Journals of the Tudor Period." *Trans. Royal Hist. Soc.*, 4th ser., III, 136-170.

—— "Commons Privilege of Free Speech in Parliament." In *Tudor Studies.* Ed. R. W. Seton-Watson. London, 1924.

—— *Elizabeth I and Her Parliaments, 1559-1581.* London, 1953.

—— *The Elizabethan House of Commons.* London, 1949.

—— "The Lord Keeper's Speech to the Parliament of 1592/3." *Engl. Hist. R.*, XXXI (1916), 128-137.

—— "Parliament and the Succession Question in 1563 and 1566." *Engl. Hist. R.*, XXXVI (1921), 497-520.

—— "Queen Elizabeth's Quashing of Bills in 1597/8." *Engl. Hist. R.*, XXXIV (1919), 586-588; XXXVI (1921), 480.

NOTESTEIN, WALLACE "The Winning of the Initiative by the House of Commons." Repr. from *Proc. Brit. Acad.* London, 1926.

PARRY, C. H. *The Parliaments and Councils of England . . . to 1688.* London, 1839.

PETTUS, SIR JOHN *The Constitution of Parliaments in England. . . .* London, 1680.

PETYT, WILLIAM *The Antient Right of the Commons of England Asserted. . . .* London, 1680.

PIKE, LUKE OWEN *A Constitutional History of the House of Lords.* London, 1894.

POLLARD, ALBERT F. *The Evolution of Parliament.* 2d ed. rev. London, 1926.

PRICE, WILLIAM HYDE *The English Patents of Monopoly.* Cambridge (Mass.), 1913.

READ, ELIZABETH *The Procedure of the House of Commons Against Patents and Monopolies, 1621-1624.* Unpub'd MS., 1938, in Stirling Mem. Library, Yale University.

REDLICH, J. *Procedure of the House of Commons, 1547-1641.* Trans. by A. E. Steinthal. 3 vols. London, 1908.

RELF, FRANCES HELEN *The Petition of Right.* Minneapolis, 1917.

Return of the Name of Every Member of the Lower House of the Parliaments of England, Scotland, and Ireland . . . 1213-1874. 3 vols. London, 1878.

SAUNDER, NICHOLAS "Letter to Sir William More, 1593, About the Parliament." *London Times*, Dec. 12, 1929. Sent by Miss M. De Havilland.

SPELMAN, HENRY "Of Parliaments." In *Reliquiae Spelmannianae.* London, 1698.

(SIMS), CATHERINE STRATEMAN, ed. *The Liverpool Tractate; an Eighteenth Century Manual on the Procedure of the House of Commons.* New York, 1937.

—— "Policies in Parliaments; and Early Seventeenth Century Tractate on House of Commons Procedure." *Huntington Library Quarterly*, XV, no. 1 (1951).

—— "The Speaker of the House of Commons; an Early Seventeenth Century Tractate." *Amer. Hist. R.*, XLV (1939).
"Two Lists Showing Alterations in the House of Commons, 1509-1625." *Somers Tracts*, XIII. London, 1809-1815.
WILLSON, DAVID HARRIS *The Privy Councillors in the House of Commons, 1604-1629.* Minneapolis, 1940.
—— "Summoning and Dissolving Parliament, 1603-25: the Council's Advice to James I." *Amer. Hist. R.*, XLV (1940), 281-284.

Economic and Social Scene

General

Again, the biographer of Coke must range from books on palace manners, such as Castiglione's *Courtier*, to homely treatises on farming like Tusser's, or Ascham's touching and justly famous *Scholemaster*. Contemporary ballads were a great help in determining popular feeling at such times as the Essex riot, the Ralegh trial. John Aubrey on *Knockings and Dreams Invisible*, Clowes's *Maister in Chirurgery* show the widespread superstition and fearful surgical and medicinal remedies which in Coke's time killed more than they cured. The Duke of Buckingham's genuine fear of Frances Purbeck's witchcraft is more easily understood when one reads Hole's *Witchcraft in England* or William Carlisle on *Evil Spirits, or, Reasons to Prove their Existence*, written as late as 1825. *The Book of the Craft of Dying* mentions neither Coke nor the law, yet, as with the other books listed, it would be hard to write Coke's life without some knowledge of how men looked on death and life, on devils, witches and man's immortal soul.

ARMSTRONG, ARCHIBALD *A Banquet of Jeasts, or Change of Cheare*, Pt. I. London, 1630.
AUBREY, JOHN *Miscellanies, Upon Dreams, Knockings, Blows Invisible. . . .* London, 1721.
—— *The Scandal and Credulities of John Aubrey.* Ed. John Collier. New York, 1931.
AULT, NORMAN *Seventeenth Century Lyrics from the Original Texts.* 2d ed. London, 1950.
BARKER, R. and PERCEVAL, A. P. *The Original Sources for the State Holidays.* London, 1838.
Bishop Percy's Folio Manuscript; Ballads and Romances. Ed. John W. Hales, Frederick J. Furnivall. 3 vols. London, 1867-1868.
The Book of Common Prayer. Oxford, 1662. Ed. of Charles II.
BRADLEY, ROSE M. *The English Housewife in the Seventeenth and Eighteenth Centuries.* London, 1912.
BUTTERFIELD, HERBERT *The Origins of Modern Science, 1300-1800.* New York, 1951.

CALTHROP, DION CLAYTON *English Costume*. London, 1923.

CARLISLE, WILLIAM *An Essay on Evil Spirits, or, Reasons to Prove Their Existence*. Bradford (Eng.), 1825.

CASTIGLIONE, BALDASSARE *The Courtyer of Count Baldessar Castilo, Divided into Foure Bookes. Very Necessary and Profitable for Yonge Gentilmen & Gentilwomen Abiding in Court, Palaice or Place, Done into Englyshe by Thomas Hoby*. Ed. Janet E. Ashbee and C. R. Ashbee. London, 1900.

CLARK, ANDREW, ed. *The Shirburn Ballads, 1585-1616*. Oxford, 1907.

CLARKE, G. N. *Science and Social Welfare in the Age of Newton*. Oxford, 1949.

CLINCH, GEORGE *English Costume from Prehistoric Times to the End of the Eighteenth Century*. London, 1909.

CLOWES, WILLIAM *Maister in Chirurgery* and *A Treatise of the French or Spanish Pocks, by John Almena, a Spanish Phisition*. London, 1588.

COATE, MARY *Social Life in Stuart England*. New York, 1925.

COGAN, THOMAS *The Haven of Health*. London, 1605.

COLLMANN, H. L., ed. *Ballads and Broadsides*. Roxburgh Club, 1912.

COMPER, FRANCES M. M., ed. *The Book of the Craft of Dying (De Arte Moriendi), and Other Early English Tracts Concerning Death*. London, 1917.

DEKKER, THOMAS *The Seven Deadly Sinnes of London*. Ed. H. F. B. Brett-Smith, Oxford, 1922.

—— *The Wonderfull Yeare (1603)*. In *The Non-Dramatic Works of Thomas Dekker*. London, 1884.

EDEN, RICHARD *The Arte of Navigation*. London, 1584.

ELYOT, SIR THOMAS *The Castell of Health*. London, 1595.

FAIRHOLT, F. W. *Costume in England*. . . . London, 1846.

FIRTH, SIR CHARLES *Essays Historical and Literary*. Oxford, 1938.

FITZHERBERT, SIR ANTHONY *The Boke of Husbandry, Surveyenge*. London, 1539. (Actually by John Fitzherbert.) Reprinted in *Certain Ancient Tracts Concerning the Management of Landed Property*. Ed. Vansittart. London, 1757.

FRIIS, ASTRID *Alderman Cockayne's Project and the Cloth Trade, 1603-1625*. London, 1927.

FURNIVALL, FREDERICK J., ed. *Manners and Meals in Olden Time*. London, 1868.

GREEN, MRS. J. R. *Town Life in the Fifteenth Century*. New York, 1894.

HARINGTON, SIR JOHN *A New Discourse of a Stale Subject, called The Metamorphosis of Ajax*. By Misacmos, to his friend Philostilpnos. 1596.

HOLE, CHRISTINA *Witchcraft in England*. London, 1945.

INDERWICK, F. A. *Side-Lights on the Stuarts*. London, 1891.

JOHNSON, FRANCIS R. *Astronomical Thought in Renaissance England*. Baltimore, 1937.

JONSON, BEN *The Works of Ben Jonson*. Ed. F. Cunningham. 9 vols. London, 1875.

JUDGES, A. V., ed. *The Elizabethan Underworld.* London, 1930.

KELSO, RUTH *The Doctrine of the English Gentleman in the Sixteenth Century.* Urbana, 1929. Univ. of Illinois Studies in Language and Literature, XIV.

LEWIS, GEORGE RANDALL *The Stanneries; a Study of the English Tin Mines.* Cambridge (Mass.), 1908.

LILLY, JOSEPH *A Collection of Black-Letter Ballads.* London, 1870.

LIPSON, EPHRAIM *The Growth of English Society; a Short Economic History.* London, 1949.

LLOYD, NATHANIEL *A History of the English House from Primitive Times to the Victorian Period.* London, 1951.

MACHIAVELLI, NICCOLÒ *The Prince.* Trans. by Luigi Ricci. London, 1903.

MACKENZIE, SIR JAMES D. *Castles of England.* 2 vols. New York, 1896.

MAYERNE, SIR THEODORE TURQUET DE *Opera Medica.* Ed. Joseph Browne. London, 1701.

MILLER, PERRY "The End of the World." *William and Mary Quarterly,* April, 1954.

MORSE, H. K. *Elizabethan Pageantry; a Pictorial Survey of Costume, 1560-1620.* London, 1934.

NICHOLS, JOHN *The Progresses and Public Processions of Queen Elizabeth.* 3 vols. London, 1823.

The Oeconomy of the Fleete or an Apologiticall Answere of Alexander Harris (late Warden) Unto XIX Articles Sett Forth Against Him by the Prisoners. Camden Society, 1879.

Old English Ballads, 1553-1625. Ed. Hyder E. Rollins. Cambridge, 1920.

ORR, JOHN *A Short History of British Agriculture.* London, 1922.

ORWIN, C. S. *The Open Fields.* Oxford, 1938.

PAUL, HENRY N. *The Royal Play of Macbeth; When, Why and How it was Written by Shakespeare.* New York, 1950. Interesting about ghosts, witches, treason and time of James I.

PEACHAM, HENRY *Peacham's Compleat Gentleman.* Ed. G. S. Gordon. London, 1906.

PETTIGREW, THOMAS JOSEPH *On Superstitions Connected with the History and Practice of Medicine and Surgery.* Philadelphia, 1844.

The Pilgrimage to Parnassus, with the Two Parts of The Return from Parnassus. Ed. W. D. Macray. Oxford, 1886.

Practical Wisdom; a Manual of Life. 2d impression. London, 1907. Contains advice of Francis Osborne, Lord Burghley, and Sir Walter Ralegh to their sons.

PROTHERO, ROWLAND EDMUND (Baron Ernle) *English Farming Past and Present.* London, 1912.

READ, CONYERS "Tudor Economic Policy." In SCHUYLER *The Making of English History.* Oxford, 1952, 175-201.

RECORDE, ROBERT *The Castle of Knowledge, a Treatise on Astronomy and the Sphere.* 1551.

RICH, E. E. "The Population of Elizabethan England." *Econ. Hist. R.* 2nd Series, II, no. 3 (1950), 247-265.

RICHARDSON, A. E. and EBERLEIN, H. DONALDSON *The English Inn, Past and Present.* London, 1925.

ROLLINS, H. H. *The Pepys Ballads.* Cambridge (Mass.), 1929.

ROWSE, A. L. *The England of Elizabeth.* London, 1951.

RYE, WILLIAM BRENCHLEY *England as Seen by Foreigners in the Days of Elizabeth and James the First.* London, 1865.

Shakespeare's England; an Account of the Life & Manners of his Age. 2 vols. Ed. C. T. Onions. Oxford, 1950.

STONE, LAWRENCE "The Anatomy of Elizabethan Aristocracy." *Econ. Hist. R.*, XVIII, nos. 1 & 2 (1948), 1-53.

—— "The Elizabethan Aristocracy — a Restatement." *Econ. Hist. R.* 2nd Series, IV, no. 3 (1952), pp. 302-321.

STRATTON, ARTHUR *The Styles of English Architecture.* London, 1949.

STRUTT, JOSEPH *Glig-gamena angel-ðeod, Or, The Sports and Pastimes of the People of England.* London, 1833.

TAWNEY, R. H. *The Agrarian Problem in the Sixteenth Century.* London, 1912.

—— "The Rise of the Gentry, 1558-1640." *Econ. Hist. R.*, XI (1941), 1-38.

—— "The Rise of the Gentry: A Postscript." *Econ. Hist. R.*, 2nd Series, VII, no. 1 (1954).

TAYLOR, F. SHERWOOD *The Alchemists.* New York, 1949.

—— *A Short History of Science and Scientific Thought.* New York, 1949.

THISTLETON-DYER, T. F. *English Folk-Lore.* London, 1880.

THOMS, WILLIAM J., ed. *Anecdotes and Traditions Derived from MS. Sources.* London, 1839.

TRAILL, HENRY DUFF *Social England, a Record of the Progress of the People in Religion, Laws, Learning, Arts, Industry, Commerce, Science, Literature and Manners from the Earliest Times to the Present Day.* 6 vols. London, 1893-1897.

TREVELYAN, G. M. *English Social History; a Survey of Six Centuries, Chaucer to Queen Victoria.* London, 1946.

TREVOR-ROPER, H. R. "The Elizabethan Aristocracy: an Anatomy Anatomized." *Econ. Hist. R.* 2nd Ser., III, no. 3 (1951), 279-298.

TURNER, EDWARD R. "The Secrecy of the Post." *Engl. Hist. R.* XXXIII (1918), 320-327.

TUSSER, THOMAS *Five Hundred Points of Good Husbandrie . . . with Huswiferie. . . .* Ed. W. F. Manor. London, 1812.

WENDELL, BARRETT *The Temper of the XVIIth Century in English Literature.* New York, 1904.

WILSON, F. P. *The Plague in Shakespeare's London.* Oxford, 1927.

WILSON, JOHN DOVER, ed. *Life in Shakespeare's England.* Cambridge, 1949.

WINSTANLEY, WILLIAM *Historical Rareties and Curious Observations.* London, 1684.

WRIGHT, LOUIS B. *Middle Class Culture in Elizabethan England.* Chapel Hill (N.C.), 1935.

WRIGHT, THOMAS *The Political Songs of England from the Reign of John to Edward II.* London, 1839.

Education

ASCHAM, ROGER *The Scholemaster.* Ed. Edward Arber. London, 1869.

BRINSLEY, JOHN *Ludus Literarius: or, the Grammar Schoole.* London, 1612.

BUTTERWORTH, CHARLES C. *The English Primers, 1529-1545.* Philadelphia, 1953.

CLARK, JOHN WILLIS *Brief Historical and Descriptive Notes.* London, 1890.

COOPER, CHARLES HENRY *Memorials of Cambridge.* Enlarged from the work of J. Le Keux. 3 vols. Cambridge, 1858-1866.

—— and COOPER, THOMPSON *Athenae Cantabrigienses.* 2 vols. Cambridge, 1858-1861.

ELYOT, SIR THOMAS *The Boke Named The Governour.* Ed. A. T. Eliot. London, 1834.

ERASMUS, DESIDERIUS *The Education of a Christian Prince, Written for Young Charles V.* Ed. Lester K. Born. New York, 1936.

FURNIVALL, FREDERICK J. *Education in Early England.* London, 1867.

GRAY, ARTHUR *Cambridge and its Colleges.* Boston, 1899.

—— *Cambridge and Its Story.* London, 1912.

HAZLITT, W. C. *Schools, School-books and Schoolmasters.* London, 1888.

LEACH, ARTHUR F. *English Schools at the Reformation, 1546-48.* Westminster, 1896.

—— *A History of Winchester College.* London, 1899.

MAUSBRIDGE, ALBERT *The Older Universities of England; Oxford and Cambridge.* Boston, 1923.

MULLINGER, JAMES BASS *The University of Cambridge from the Royal Injunctions of 1535 to the Accession of Charles I.* 3 vols. Cambridge, 1884.

PEACOCK, GEORGE *Observations on the Statutes of the University of Cambridge.* London, 1841.

RASHDALL, H. *The Universities of Europe in the Middle Ages.* Ed. F. M. Powicke and A. B. Emden. 3 vols. Oxford, 1936.

SAUNDERS, H. W. *A History of the Norwich Grammar School.* Norwich, 1932.

SMITH, PHILIP ANSTIE *A History of Education for the English Bar; with Suggestions as to Subjects and Methods of Study.* London, 1860.

STOWE, A. R. M. *The English Grammar Schools in the Reign of Queen Elizabeth.* New York, 1908.

The Student's Handbook to the University and Colleges of Cambridge. Cambridge, 1929.

THOMPSON, A. HAMILTON *Cambridge and Its Colleges.* Boston, 1899.

TREVELYAN, G. M. *Trinity College Cambridge; a History and Guide.* Cambridge, n.d.

—— *Trinity College; an Historical Sketch.* Cambridge, 1946.

WATSON, FOSTER "The Curriculum and Text Books of English Schools in the First Half of the Seventeenth Century." *Bibliographical Society Transactions.* London, 1900, 159-267.

—— *The Old Grammar Schools.* New York, 1916.

WOOD, ANTHONY À. *Athenae Oxonienses. . . .* 2 vols. London, 1721.

WRIGHT, THOMAS and JONES, H. LONGUEVILLE *Memorials of Cambridge.* The work of J. Le Keux. 2 vols. London, 1841.

General Historical, Political and Religious Works

Annals and chronicles speak for themselves: if the biographer's first task is to find the subject's whereabouts at given times, his second concerns the placing of the supporting cast, their groupings, their comings and goings at times of national crisis and importance. For biographies and general histories, my rule for inclusion was simply whether or not the books were useful. John Adams's *Works*, for instance, gave the letter quoted in Chapter 23; Becker's *Declaration of Independence*, like Butterfield's *Englishman and his History*, is included because of extraordinary perception concerning the shape of things to come. No biographer of Coke dares be limited to the round dates of the subject's life.

Gossip Writers

The gossip writers of James I's time are for the biographer a joy and a treat. Francis Osborne, for instance, was a witty, quite wise gentleman, except when bitter distrust of the Stuart kings smeared his pen with slightly obscuring mud. *Les on dit*, old Isaac D'Israeli called the gossip writers; *les on dit* who gave us the *pourquoi* of the *pourquoi.*

GREVILLE, SIR CHARLES CAVENDISH FULKE (Foullk Grevill). *The Five Years of King James; or, the Condition of the State of England and the Relation it Had to Other Provinces.* In *A Selection from the Harleian Miscellany.* London, 1793, 286-314.

HARRIS, WILLIAM *An Historical and Critical Account of the Life and Writings of James I.* London, 1772.

LILLY, WILLIAM *History of His Life and Times.* London, 1774.

—— *Mr. William Lilly's True History of King James the First and King Charles the First.* London, 1715.

Observations Upon Some Particular Persons and Passages, in a Book Lately Made Publick. London, 1656. Issued anonymously, but generally attributed to Carew Ralegh.

OSBORNE, FRANCIS *Traditional Memoirs of the Reigns of Queen Elizabeth and King James I* (1658). In *Secret History of James I*, vol. I.

PEYTON, SIR EDWARD *The Divine Catastrophe of the Kingly Family of the House of Stuart* (1652). In *Secret History of James I*, vol. II.

SANDERSON, SIR WILLIAM *A Compleat History of the Lives and Reigns of Mary Queen of Scotland, and of her Son . . . James the Sixth . . . in Vindication of Him Against the Scandalous Authors* [Sir Anthony Weldon and Arthur Wilson]. London, 1656.

——*Aulicus Coquinariae* (1650). In *Secret History of James I*, vol. II.

SCOTT, SIR WALTER, ed. *Secret History of the Court of James the First. . . . with Notes and Introduction.* 2 vols. Edinburgh, 1811.

WELDON, SIR ANTHONY *The Court and Character of James I* (1650). In *Secret History of James I*, vols. I-II.

WILSON, ARTHUR *The History of Great Britain, being the Life and Reign of James the First, King of Great Britain.* In *A Complete History of England.* Ed. W. Kennett and J. Hughes. London, 1706. Vol. II.

—— *The Secret History of the Reign of King James I.* In D'Ewes, *Autobiography*, vol. II.

Chronicles

CAMDEN, WILLIAM *Annales or, the History of the Most Renowned and Victorious Princesse Elizabeth, Late Queen of England* . . . 3rd ed. London, 1635.

—— *The Annals of Mr. William Camden in the Reign of King James I, 1603-1623.* In *A Complete History of England*, vol. II.

HAYWARD, SIR JOHN *Annals of the First Four Years of the Reign of Queen Elizabeth.* London, 1840.

STOW, JOHN *Three Fifteenth Century Chronicles with Historical Memoranda by John Stow. . . .* Ed. James Gairdner. Camden Society, 1880.

—— *Annales or, a Generall Chronicle of England.* Begun by John Stow and finished by Edmond Howes. London, 1631.

STRYPE, JOHN *Annals of the Reformation . . . during the First Twelve Years of Queen Elizabeth.* 3 vols. London, 1709.

Biographies, General Histories

ADAMS, JOHN *The Works of John Adams. . . .* 10 vols. Boston, 1851-1856.

BECKER, CARL *The Declaration of Independence; a Study in the History of Political Ideas.* New York, 1922.

—— *The Eve of Revolution.* Yale Chronicle Series. New Haven, 1920.

BIGHAM, CLIVE *The Kings of England.* London, 1929.

BINDOFF, STANLEY T. *Tudor England.* Middlesex, 1951.

BLACK, J. B. *The Reign of Queen Elizabeth, 1558-1603.* Oxford, 1949.

BOWEN, CATHERINE DRINKER *John Adams and the American Revolution.* Boston, 1951.

BRIGHTMAN, F. E. *The English Rite, being a Synopsis of the Sources and Revisions of the Book of Common Prayer.* London, 1915.

BURNET, BISHOP *Bishop Burnet's History of His Own Time. . . .* London, 1838.

BUTTERFIELD, HERBERT *The Englishman and His History*. Cambridge, 1944.

The Cambridge History of the British Empire. Cambridge, 1929.

The Cambridge Modern History. Ed. A. W. Ward, G. W. Prothero, Stanley. New York, 1934.

CARTE, THOMAS *A General History of England from the Earliest Times (to 1654)*. 4 vols. London, 1747-1755.

CHEYNEY, EDWARD P. *A History of England from the Defeat of the Armada to the Death of Elizabeth*. 2 vols. New York, 1914.

CLAPHAM, JOHN *Historie (1608)*. Ed. by E. P. and Conyers Read. Philadelphia, 1951.

CLARK, G. N. *The Later Stuarts*. Oxford, 1934.

—— *The Seventeenth Century*. 2d ed. Oxford, 1937.

COMMAGER, HENRY STEELE, ed. *Documents of American History*, 3rd ed. New York, 1944.

COULTON, G. G. *Medieval Panorama; the English Scene from Conquest to Reformation*. Cambridge, 1949.

DAVIES, GODFREY *The Early Stuarts; 1603-1660*. Oxford, 1937.

D'ISRAELI, ISAAC *Commentaries on the Life and Reign of Charles the First, King of England*. 5 vols. London, 1828-1831.

—— *The Literary Character, or, The History of Men of Genius*. New York, 1881.

DODD, C. *History of England*. 5 vols. Ed. M. A. Tierney. London, 1839-1843.

ECHARD, LAURENCE *The History of England from the First Entrance of Julius Caesar and the Romans to the Conclusion of the Reign of King James the Second . . . to the Year 1688*. 3rd ed. London, 1720.

EVANS, HOWARD *Our Old Nobility*. 9th ed. London, 1913.

FROUDE, ANTHONY *The Reign of Elizabeth*. 5 vols. London, 1930.

FULLER, THOMAS *Church History of Britain . . . to 1648*. 3 vols. London, 1868.

GARDINER, SAMUEL RAWSON *History of England from the Accession of James I to the Outbreak of the Civil War, 1603-1642*. New Impression. 10 vols. London, 1894-1896.

—— *What Gunpowder Plot Was*. London, 1897.

GERARD, FATHER JOHN *Narrative of the Gunpowder Plot*. From Gerard's MS. of 1606. In *The Condition of Catholics Under James I*. Ed. John Morris. London, 1871.

GODWIN, WILLIAM *History of the Commonwealth of England from its Commencement to the Restoration of Charles the Second*. 4 vols. London, 1824-1828.

GOODMAN, DR. GODFREY *The Court of King James the First*. 2 vols. London, 1839.

GREEN, JOHN RICHARD *A Short History of the English People*. 2 vols. New York, 1900.

HARRISON, GEORGE B. *An Elizabethan Journal, 1591-1594*. Reprint, New York, 1929.

—— *A Second Elizabethan Journal, 1595-1598.* London, 1931.
—— *A Last Elizabethan Journal, 1599-1603.* London, 1933.
—— *A Jacobean Journal, 1603-1606.* New York, 1941.
HUME, MARTIN A. S. *Treason and Plot; Struggles for Catholic Supremacy in the Last Years of Queen Elizabeth.* New York, 1908.
HYDE, EDWARD, EARL OF CLARENDON *The History of the Rebellion and Civil Wars in England.* 6 vols. Oxford, 1888.
JARDINE, DAVID *A Narrative of the Gunpowder Plot.* London, 1857.
JORDAN, WILBUR K. *The Development of Religious Toleration in England from the Beginning of the Reformation to the Death of Queen Elizabeth.* Cambridge, 1932.
—— *The Development of Religious Toleration in England from the Accession of James I to the Convention of the Long Parliament.* Cambridge, 1936.
KENNETT, W., ed. *A Complete History of England: with the Lives of all the Kings and Queens thereof; from the Earliest Account of Time to the Death of His Late Majesty King William III.* 3 vols. London, 1706.
LATIMER, HUGH *Sermon on the Ploughers.* 18 January, 1549. Ed. E. Arber. King's College, London, 1869.
—— *Seven Sermons Before Edward VI.* Ed. E. Arber. Birmingham, 1869.
—— *The Works of Hugh Latimer, Sometime Bishop of Worcester, Martyr, 1555.* 2 vols. Ed. George E. Corrie. Cambridge, 1844-1845.
LAUD, WILLIAM *The Works of William Laud. . . .* Ed. W. Scott and J. Bliss. 9 vols. Oxford, 1847-1860.
LINGARD, JOHN *The History of England, from the First Invasion by the Romans to the Accession of William and Mary in 1688.* 10 vols. London, 1855.
LUPTON, J. H. *A Life of John Colet.* London, 1909.
MACAULAY, LORD THOMAS BABINGTON *Critical, Historial and Miscellaneous Essays.* New York, 1860. 6 vols. in 3. Essay on Bacon.
—— *The History of England from the Accession of James II.* 2 vols. London, 1877.
MATHEW, DAVID *The Celtic Peoples and Renaissance Europe.* London, 1933.
—— *The Jacobean Age.* London, 1938.
MERRIMAN, R. B. *Rise of the Spanish Empire.* 4 vols. New York, 1934.
MEYER, ARNOLD OSCAR *England and the Catholic Church under Queen Elizabeth.* Eng. trans. by J. R. McKee. London, 1916.
MILTON, JOHN Poem to Cyriack Skinner, Coke's grandson. *The Poetical Works of John Milton.* London, 1911.
MONTAGUE, F. C. *The History of England, 1603-1660.* 12 vols. London, 1907.
MORE, THOMAS *The Life of Sir Thomas More.* By his great grandson, Thomas More, Esq. London, 1726.
NORTH, ROGER *Lives of the Right Hon. Francis North, Baron Guilford,*

the Hon. Sir Dudley North; and the Hon. and Rev. Dr. John North. 3 vols. London, 1826.

NOTESTEIN, WALLACE *The English People on the Eve of Colonization.* New York, 1954.

PETRIE, SIR CHARLES *The Stuarts.* London, 1937.

POWELL, ANTHONY *John Aubrey and His Friends.* London, 1948.

PRESCOTT, H. F. M. *Mary Tudor.* New York, 1953.

READ, CONYERS *Social and Political Forces in the English Reformation.* Houston, 1953.

—— *The Tudors; Personalities and Practical Politics in Sixteenth Century England.* New York, 1936.

ROPER, WILLIAM *The Life, Arraignement and Death of . . . Thomas More.* Ed. S. W. Singer. Chiswick (Eng.), 1817.

ROWSE, A. L. *The Expansion of Elizabethan England.* New York, 1955.

SCHUYLER, ROBERT LIVINGSTON and AUSUBEL, HERMAN, eds. *The Making of English History.* Dryden History Series. Oxford, 1952.

STRYPE, JOHN *Life and Acts of John Whitgift D. D.* 4 vols. Oxford, 1822.

—— *The Life of the Learned Sir T. Smith. . . .* Oxford, 1821.

TAUNTON, ETHELRED L. *The History of the Jesuits in England, 1580-1773.* London, 1901.

TAWNEY, R. H. *Religion and the Rise of Capitalism.* London, 1929.

THOU, JACQUE AUGUSTUS [THUANUS] *The History of the Gunpowder-Treasons; Collected from Approved Authors, as well Popish as Protestant.* Based on narrative of Thuanus and Jo. Barclay, 1606. In *A Selection from the Harleian Miscellany.* London, 1793.

—— *A True Narrative of . . . the Gunpowder Treason.* Edinburgh, 1885.

TOUT, T. F. *An Advanced History of Great Britain from the Earliest Times to 1923.* 3 vols. London, 1925.

TREVELYAN, GEORGE MACAULAY *England Under the Stuarts.* New York, 1949.

—— *History of England.* 2d ed. London, 1926.

TREVOR-ROPER, H. R. *Archbishop Laud.* London, 1940.

USHER, ROLAND G. "Nicholas Fuller, a Forgotten Exponent of English Liberty." in *Engl. Hist. R.*, XII, 743-760.

—— *The Reconstruction of the English Church.* 2 vols. New York, 1910.

WILLEY, BASIL *The Seventeenth Century Background; Studies in the Thought of the Age in Relation to Poetry and Religion.* London, 1934.

WILLIAMS, C. H. *England Under the Early Tudors, 1485-1529.* London, 1925.

—— *The Making of the Tudor Despotism.* London, 1935.

WILSON, THOMAS *The State of England Anno Dom. 1600.* Ed. F. J. Fisher, *Camden Miscellany*, XVI. Camden Society, 1936.

WRENCH, JOHN EVELYN *Transatlantic London; Three Centuries of Association Between England and America.* London, 1948.

General Reference Works

BATESON, F. W., ed. *The Cambridge Bibliography of English Literature.* 4 vols. New York, 1941.

BRUSHFIELD, THOMAS N. *A Bibliography of Sir Walter Ralegh, Knt.* 2d ed. Exeter, 1908.

BUTTERFIELD, HERBERT *The Whig Interpretation of History.* London, 1951.

CHALMERS, ALEXANDER *General Biographical Dictionary* . . . New ed. 32 vols. London, 1812-1817.

Chambers's Biographical Dictionary; the Great of all Nations and all Times. New ed., W. and J. L. Geddie. London, 1938.

COKAYNE, GEORGE EDWARD *The Complete Peerage, or a History of the House of Lords and its Members from the Earliest Times.* Ed. H. A. Doubleday and Lord Howard de Walden; new ed., rev., 12 vols. London, 1910-1953.

DARLOW, T. H. and MOULE, H. F. *Historical Catalogue of the Printed Editions of the Holy Scripture in the Library of the British and Foreign Bible Society.* 3 vols. London, 1903.

DAVIES, GODFREY *Bibliography of British History; Stuart Period, 1603-1714.* Oxford, 1928.

The Dictionary of National Biography. Ed. Leslie Stephen and Sidney Lee. London, 1949-1950.

EKWALL, EILERT *The Concise Oxford Dictionary of English Place-Names.* Oxford, 1951.

Encyclopaedia Britannica. 11th ed., New Form. New York, 1910.

ESDAILE, ARUNDELL *The British Museum Library.* London, 1946.

GARDINER, SAMUEL RAWSON *A School Atlas of English History.* New Impression. London, 1907.

GOOCH, GEORGE P. *History and Historians in the Nineteenth Century.* New York, 1949.

JENKINSON, HILARY *The Later Court Hands in England from the Fifteenth to the Seventeenth Century.* 2 folio vols. Cambridge, 1927.

KIPPIS, ANDREW, D. D. *Biographia Britannica.* 2d ed. 5 vols. London, 1778-1793.

McKERROW, RONALD B. *An Introduction to Bibliography for Literary Students.* Oxford, 1927.

MATTHEWS, WILLIAM, ed. *British Diaries; An Annotated Bibliography of British Diaries Written between 1442 and 1942.* Berkeley, 1950.

PARTRIDGE, ERIC *A Dictionary of Slang and Unconventional English.* London, 1951.

Penny Cyclopedia of the Society for the Diffusion of Useful Knowledge. 27 vols. London, 1833-1842.

POLLARD, A. W. and REDGRAVE, G. R. *A Short-Title Catalogue of Books Printed in England, Scotland and Ireland; and of English Books Printed Abroad, 1475-1640.* London, 1950.

READ, CONYERS, ed. *Bibliography of British History; Tudor Period, 1485-1603*. Oxford, 1933.

SHEPHERD, WILLIAM R. *Historical Atlas.* New York, 1629.

The Shorter Oxford English Dictionary on Historical Principles. 2 vols. Ed. C. T. Onions. Oxford, 1947.

THOMSON, THEODORE RADFORD *Catalogue of British Family Histories.* London, 1928.

SOURCE REFERENCES

In order to minimize interruptions of the text, the source references have been reduced and grouped, where possible, by paragraph or by general subject. Isolated quotations are indicated where they appear. The references indicate the source from which information has been directly drawn. The usual practice has been followed of giving full name and date of publication of any book the first time cited and citing it thereafter by abbreviated title or the name of the author. The page and line of text ("P." and "l.") on which each passage to be identified appears is given at the beginning of each source reference.

CHAPTER ONE

P. 3, opening quotation. T. FULLER *Worthies* (ed. 1840) II, 333.
P. 7, l. 28. SIR E. COKE *Vade Mecum*, in *Collectanea Topographica* (ed. 1840) VI, 115.
P. 11, l. 13. J. STRYPE *Life of Sir Thomas Smith* (ed. 1821) 192.
P. 12, l. 28. SIR F. BACON "Apophthegms," in *Works* (ed. 1641-1644) XIII, 341-342.

CHAPTER TWO

P. 13, title. SIR S. D'EWES *Journal* (ed. 1693) 468 gives Monday the 19th as the first day of the House of Commons of Parliament, and Thursday the 22nd as the day the Queen came to open it. H. TOWNSHEND *Historical Collections* (ed. 1680) 51 gives same date.
P. 13, opening quotation. COKE, 4 *Institute* (ed. 1797) 1-2.
P. 13, l. 3. This and following Coke citations from D'EWES 458-460.
P. 16, l. 28. D. LLOYD *State-Worthies* (ed. 1670) 485; L. ECHARD *History of England* (ed. 1720) 369.
P. 17, l. 34. Speaker Henry Yelverton, D'EWES 549; Puckering, J. CAMPBELL *Lives of the Lord Chancellors* (ed. 1856) II, 297.
P. 21, l. 31. JAMES R. HARRINGTON *Oceana* (ed. 1924) 49.
P. 22, l. 12. J. E. NEALE "The Lord Keeper's Speech to the Parliament of 1592-1593," in *English Historical Review* XXXI (1916), 128.

CHAPTER THREE

P. 24, opening quotation. COKE, 4 *Inst.* 8.
P. 25, l. 32. D'EWES *Journal* 470.
P. 27, l. 9. NEALE *Elizabethan House of Commons* (1949) 402.
P. 27, l. 38. D'EWES 500; NEALE *op. cit.* 397.
P. 28, l. 29. W. NOTESTEIN *Winning of the Initiative by the House of Commons* (1918) 20; D'EWES 477, 475; NEALE *op. cit.* 407; TOWNSHEND *Collections* 282.
P. 29, l. 10. TOWNSHEND 321-322; anonymous, quoted in M. WALDMAN *Sir Walter Raleigh* (1950) 73.
P. 29, l. 18. SIR R. NAUNTON *Fragmenta Regalia* (ed. 1870) 60.
P. 30, l. 2. Robert Cecil to Lord Burghley, 16 Feb. 1588, in A. CECIL *Life of Robert Cecil* (1915) 24; C. READ *Mr. Secretary Cecil* (1955) 215.
P. 30, l. 12. Sir Francis Bacon to Elizabeth, written 1584-1585, in J. SPEDDING *Letters and Life of Francis Bacon* (ed. 1857-1874) I, 49.
P. 32, l. 11. A. JESSOPP *One Generation of a Norfolk House* (ed. 1878) notes, 14.

CHAPTER FOUR

P. 33, opening quotation. Brome Whorwood, member for Oxford, in J. MILWARD *Diary* (ed. 1938) 40-41.
P. 33, l. 3. All citations from debate in House of Commons on the subsidy bill and parliamentary procedures, 22 Feb. to 3 Mar., from D'EWES *Journal* 478-515.
P. 38, l. 24. *Statutes of the Realm, 1592-1593* (ed. 1819) IV, 867.
P. 39, l. 3. D'EWES 500.
P. 40, l. 16. *Statutes of the Realm* IV, 843.
P. 40, l. 33. H. Barrow, "Third Examination before Archbishop of Whitgift," in J. R. TANNER *Tudor Constitutional Documents* (1948) 188.
P. 41, l. 3. Martin Marprelate, "The Epistle," and "The Act against Seditious Sectaries, 1593," in TANNER *Tudor Const. Docs.* 195-199.
P. 41, l. 30. Sir Nicholas Saunder to Sir William More, 9 April 1593. As printed in *The Times*, 12 Dec. 1929, by Miss De Haviland, who quotes from the *Loseley Papers.*
P. 42, l. 8. All citations on Coke's presentation of the subsidy bill to the Queen, 10 April 1593, from D'EWES 465-467.
P. 44, l. 17. *Ibid.* 515.
P. 44, l. 32. COKE, 4 *Inst.* 3.

CHAPTER FIVE

P. 45, opening quotation. W. CAMDEN *Britannia* (ed. 1789) II, 93.
P. 46, l. 8. H. SPELMAN "*Icenia sive Norfolciae . . .*" in *Reliquiae Spelmannianae* (ed. 1723) 150.

P. 48, l. 9. H. W. SAUNDERS *History of Norwich Grammar School* (1932) 136.
P. 48, l. 30. J. H. LUPTON *Life of Dean Colet* (1909) 289.
P. 49, l. 33. Mrs. Anne Coke Sadleir to Roger Williams, 1648, in C. W. JAMES *Chief Justice Coke, His Family and Descendants* (London, 1929) 62; COKE, 4 *Report* (ed. 1738) pref., xvi; 2 *Rep.* (ed. 1738) pref., vii; 4 *Inst.* pref., iv.
P. 50, l. 15. COKE, 4 *Inst.* 258, 256.
P. 54, l. 2. COKE *Commentary on Littleton* (or 1 *Inst.*, ed. 1817) pref., xxxiii.
P. 54, l. 19. J. B. MULLINGER *The University of Cambridge* (ed. 1888) 35.
P. 55, l. 25. *Ibid.* ch. 5; J. GERARD *Autobiography of an Elizabethan* (1951) notes, 219.
P. 56, l. 37. T. COGAN *The Haven of Health* (ed. 1605) 63.
P. 58, footnote. COKE *Co. Litt.* 235.
P. 58, l. 26. *Ibid.* pref., xxxiii.

CHAPTER SIX

P. 59, opening quotation. COKE, 2 *Inst.* (ed. 1797) pref., v.
P. 60, l. 9. H. H. L. BELLOT *The Inner and Middle Temple* (1902) 282.
P. 61, l. 29. COKE, 4 *Inst.* pref., iii.
P. 63, l. 2. *Co. Litt.* pref., xl, 45a, 86a; 3 *Inst.* (ed. 1797) pref., i.
P. 63, l. 17. *Co. Litt.* 40; 3 *Inst.* pref., i-ii; *Co. Litt.* pref., xliv.
P. 63, l. 28. 9 *Rep.* (ed. 1738) 15; 1 *Rep.* (ed. 1738) pref., v; *Co. Litt.* 71a.
P. 64, l. 19. 3 *Inst.* epilogue, 244.
P. 65, l. 7. 2 *Inst.* 45.
P. 65, l. 21. 2 *Rep.* (ed. 1738) pref., x.
P. 66, l. 17. 3 *Rep.* (ed. 1738) pref., iv; 10 *Rep.* pref., xixb.
P. 67, l. 15. 8 *Rep.* (ed. 1738) pref., xiv; W. ROPER *Life of Sir Thomas More* (ed. Singer, 1817) pref., xi.
P. 68, l. 24. LLOYD *State-Worthies* 820.
P. 68, l. 39. *Book of Oaths* (ed. 1649) 29.
P. 69, l. 25. JOHN HARINGTON *Nugae Antiquae* (ed. 1804) I, 167.
P. 70, l. 7. COKE, 4 *Rep.* 13.
P. 71, l. 18. *Ibid.* 14.
P. 72, l. 5. *Co. Litt.* 62a.
P. 73, l. 13. J. AUBREY *Brief Lives* (ed. 1950) 68; COKE, 9 *Rep.* 14b; 5 *Rep.* (ed. 1738) 3b; 4 *Rep.* 39; 1 *Rep.* 93.
P. 74, l. 26. FULLER *Worthies* II, 462; G. A. CARTHEW *The Hundred of Launditch and Deanery of Brisley* (Norwich, 1877-1879).
P. 75, l. 24. Coke to Burghley, 15 Oct. 1587, from Osterly in Essex, *Lansdowne MSS.* LIII, 63. For this reference I am indebted to Conyers Read.

CHAPTER SEVEN

P. 76, opening quotation. SPEDDING *Letters and Life* I, 254.
P. 77, l. 7. D'EWES *Journal* 472; SPEDDING I, 254.
P. 77, l. 12. Anthony Standen to Anthony Bacon, Feb. 1594, in T. BIRCH *Memoirs of the Reign of Queen Elizabeth* (ed. 1754) I, 154.
P. 77, l. 33. A. WILSON *Life and Reign of James I*, in W. KENNETT *The Complete History of England* (ed. 1706) II, 736; AUBREY *Lives* 11.
P. 78, l. 3. "Sir Francis Bacon, his Apologie in Certaine Imputations concerning the Late Earl of Essex," in SPEDDING III, 143.
P. 79, l. 2. Essex to Bacon, in *ibid.* I, 258-298 *passim.*
P. 79, l. 18. Henry Goswold to A. Bacon in *ibid.* 268.
P. 80, l. 4. Bacon to Essex, in *ibid.* 262.
P. 80, l. 12. *Ibid.* 245.
P. 80, l. 19. R. ASCHAM *The Scholemaster* (ed. 1869) 54.
P. 80, l. 31. BIRCH *Mem. Eliz.*, I, 120.
P. 81, l. 9. SPEDDING I, 289.
P. 81, l. 30. *Ibid.* 290-291, 359; to A. Bacon in *ibid.* 348; Lady Bacon to A. Bacon, 30 June 1595, in *ibid.* 364.
P. 82, l. 6. *Ibid.* 371.
P. 82, l. 13. *Ibid.* II, 61.
P. 82, l. 26. COKE, 3 *Inst.* 79.
P. 82, l. 32. FULLER *Worthies* II, 453.
P. 83, l. 4. De Maisse, Ambassador in 1597 from Henry IV; A. H. DE MAISSE *Journal* (ed. 1931) 38.
P. 83, l. 15. H. Walpole to Crisswell, 17 Oct. 1591, in JESSOPP *Norfolk House* 159.
P. 84, l. 19. STRYPE *Annals of the Reformation* (ed. 1709) III, 628; FULLER *Church History of Britain* (3rd ed.) III, 68.
P. 85, l. 13. J. MENDHAM *Important Considerations* 65, quoted in C. H. MCILWAIN *Political Works of James I* (ed. 1918) app., dxcii; Parsons to d'Idiaquez, April 1591, in *D.N.B.*, XV, 415-416, art. "Robert Parsons."
P. 86, l. 27. J. LINGARD *History of England* (ed. 1855) VI, 259.
P. 86, l. 34. Accounts of this and the following Star Chamber cases in: J. HAWARDE *Reportes del Cases in Camera Stellata* (ed. 1894) 34-48.
P. 88, l. 28. R. G. USHER *Rise and Fall of the High Commission* (ed. 1913) 133-134.
P. 88, l. 35. *D.N.B.*, I, 217, art. "Henry Barron."
P. 89, l 11. *Statutes of the Realm* IV, 659.

CHAPTER EIGHT

P. 90, opening quotation. CAMDEN *Annales of Elizabeth* (ed. 1635) 429.
P. 90, l. 11. *D.N.B.*, XII, 133, art. "Roderigo Lopez"; SPEDDING *Letters and Life* I, 278.

P. 91, l. 24. BIRCH *Mem. Eliz.*, I, 150; Essex to A. Bacon, 1594, in *ibid.* 152.
P. 92, l. 9. COKE, 3 *Inst.* 35.
P. 92, l. 18. SIR T. SMITH *De Republica Anglorum* (ed. 1906) lib. 2, ch. 24.
P. 93, l. 31. Standen to A. Bacon, 2 Mar. 1594, in BIRCH *Mem. Eliz.*, I, 160.
P. 94, l. 7. Account of trial of Lopez in *Cal. State Papers Domestic, 1591-1594*, 444-446, unless otherwise indicated.
P. 94, l. 28. SPEDDING I, 313.
P. 95, l. 5. CAMDEN *op. cit.* 430-431.
P. 95, l. 32. This and following citations about conspiracies of the 1590's from *C.S.P.D., 1591-1594*, 66-585 *passim.*
P. 98, l. 8. J. GERARD *Autobiography* 82.
P. 98, l. 19. COKE, 10 *Rep.* (ed. 1738) 34.
P. 98, l. 29. Account of examination of J. Gerard in GERARD *op. cit.* 99-269, unless otherwise indicated.
P. 101, l. 14. STRYPE *Annals* IV, 429.
P. 102, l. 4. *Ibid.* 427-429.
P. 102, l. 37. In USHER *Rise and Fall* 127.
P. 103, l. 19. COKE, 3 *Inst.* epilogue; 4 *Inst.* 57.

CHAPTER NINE

P. 105, l. 31. C. JAMES *Coke and Descendants* 16-25.
P. 107, l. 8. E. P. CHEYNEY *History of England* (1914) II, 25.
P. 107, l. 30. *Ibid.; De L'Isle and Dudley Papers* (H.M.C. 1925) II, 319, 299; HAWARDE *Rep. del Cases* 71.
P. 108, footnote. F. POLLOCK *Expansion of the Common Law* (1904) 85.
P. 108, l. 14. *Ibid.* lxi; COKE, 4 *Inst.* 65b; W. LAMBARDE *Archion* (ed. 1635) 215; 29 Apr. 1607, in HAWARDE 320.
P. 108, l. 28. J. HACKET *Scrinia Reserata: a Memorial to John Williams* [Lord Keeper] (ed. 1693) I, 82; HAWARDE 40, 114.
P. 109, l. 7. *Ibid.* 35.
P. 109, l. 30. COKE, 4 *Inst.* 65b.
P. 110, l. 2. RUSHWORTH *Historical Collections* (ed. 1721) II, 473.
P. 110, l. 26. CAMPBELL *Lord Chancellors* II, 319.
P. 110, l. 32. This and following citations about Star Chamber proceedings from HAWARDE *op. cit.* 13-250 *passim.*
P. 114, l. 6. Account of Coke's domestic life in Norfolk and London from C. JAMES *op. cit.* 20-25, unless otherwise indicated.
P. 114, l. 19. Clement Paston to Robert Buxton, 4 Sept. 1596, in *Miss Buxton Papers, Various Collections* (H.M.C. 1903) II, 248.
P. 115, l. 16. Information on borough business from "Records of the Dissolved Corp. of Dunwich," in *ibid.* VII (H.M.C. 1914) 84-85.
P. 116, l. 11. HAWARDE *op. cit.* 99. The records say that Bridget Coke died 27 June 1598.

CHAPTER TEN

P. 117, opening quotation. From "Ten Precepts" addressed by William Cecil to Robert Cecil, in A. CECIL *Life of Robert Cecil* 49.
P. 118, l. 27. SHAKESPEARE *Richard III* Act. III, Sc. 4.
P. 119, l. 8. *Cal. Salisbury MSS.* I (H.M.C. 1883) 33.
P. 119, l. 27. COKE, 7 *Rep.* (ed. 1738) 20.
P. 120, l. 13. Bacon to Essex, 1597, in SPEDDING *Letters and Life* II, 55; "Epistle Dedicatory to 1625 Ed.," in BACON *Essays* (ed. 1825).
P. 120, l. 28. Essex to Lady Cecil and Sir T. Cecil, 24 June 1597, in BIRCH *Mem. Eliz.*, II, 347-348.
P. 122, l. 20. NEALE *Queen Elizabeth* (1934) 349, 228.
P. 122, l. 29. FULLER *Worthies* II, 279; *C.S.P.D., 1598-1601*, 29 Aug. 1598, 84; Chamberlain to Carleton, 30 Aug. 1598, in *Letters of John Chamberlain* (ed. McClure, 1939) I, 41.
P. 122, l. 39. *C.S.P.D., 1634-1635*, 405-406.
P. 123, l. 9. *Letters of Chamberlain* I, 53.
P. 123, l. 27. 11 June 1617, Council Register, as quoted in GARDINER *Hist. of Eng.* (ed. 1894-1896) III, 86n.
P. 124, l. 39. STRYPE *Life of Whitgift* (ed. 1822) II, 376, 401.
P. 125, l. 14. AUBREY *Lives* 67-68.
P. 126, l. 5. *C.S.P.D., 1598-1601*, 189-190.
P. 126, l. 13. *Letters of Chamberlain* I, 84-85.

CHAPTER ELEVEN

P. 127, opening quotation. COKE, 3 *Inst.* 35.
P. 128, l. 14. BIRCH *Mem. Eliz.*, II, 386; DE MAISSE *Journal* 33.
P. 128, l. 33. F. MORYSON *Itinerary* (ed. 1907) II, 242.
P. 129, l. 24. Sir J. Harington to Markham in HARINGTON *Letters and Epigrams* (ed. 1930) 122; MORYSON II, 221.
P. 130, l. 5. CAMDEN *Ann. Eliz.* 530.
P. 130, l. 17. *De Lisle and Dudley Papers* II, 468.
P. 130, l. 29. *Sidney Papers* (ed. Collins, 1746) II, 200-201; Rowland White to Sir Robert Sidney, 11 June 1600, in *De L'Isle and Dudley Papers* II, 468.
P. 131, l. 6. CAMDEN *op. cit.* 533; Essex letters to Queen, *C.S.P.D., 1598-1601*, 393-479 *passim;* HARINGTON *Nugae* I, 179-180.
P. 131, l. 12. CAMDEN *op. cit.* 535.
P. 131, l. 34. NICHOLS *Progresses and Processions of Queen Elizabeth* (ed. 1823) III, 552; BACON "Apophthegms," in *Works* (ed. 1861-1864) XIII, 341.
P. 132, l. 28. *C.S.P.D., 1598-1601*, 552; D. JARDINE *Criminal Trials* (ed. 1882) I, 345.
P. 133, l. 16. Declaration of William Masham before Lord Treasurer, 10 Feb.(?) 1601, in *C.S.P.D., 1598-1601*, 547.

P. 133, l. 38. CAMDEN *op. cit.*, 540; SPEDDING *Letters and Life* II, 271; *C.S.P.D., 1598-1601*, 574.
P. 134, l. 4. H. ELLIS *Original Letters*, 2d Series (ed. 1827) III, 192.
P. 134, l. 18. Account of Essex Rebellion and preparation for his trial in: letters of Vincent Hussey, 11 and 18 Feb. 1601, in *C.S.P.D., 1598-1601*, 549-551, 582-585; in *ibid.* 546, 555-556, 569, 579; in WILLIAM COBBETT *State Trials* (ed. Howell, 1809-1898) I, 1339-1359; and in CAMDEN *op. cit.* 536-542.
P. 136, l. 4. *C.S.P.D., 1598-1601*, 556.

CHAPTER TWELVE

P. 139, l. 8. All accounts and citations from trial of Essex in: JARDINE *Criminal Trials* I, 313-359; *State Trials* I, 1334-1358; CAMDEN *Ann. Eliz.* 543-550, unless otherwise indicated.
P. 140, l. 14. A. M. C. LATHAM *Poems of Sir Walter Ralegh* (ed. London, 1929) 4, as quoted from letter of Ralegh to Cecil.
P. 141, l. 19. Chamberlain to Carleton, 24 Feb. 1601, in *Letters of Ch.*, I, 120.
P. 145, l. 20. *Year Book* 17 ed. IV.
P. 150, l. 36. SPEDDING *Letters and Life* II, 223n.
P. 153, l. 2. *Ibid.* I, 338.
P. 153, l. 6. D. MATHEW *Celtic Peoples and Renaissance Europe* (1933) 390.
P. 155, l. 20. Bacon's testimony vs. Essex in SPEDDING II, 225-230; JARDINE I, 352-353.
P. 157, l. 28. The French Ambassador, in SIR R. WINWOOD *Memorials of State* (ed. 1725) I, 299.

CHAPTER THIRTEEN

P. 160, opening quotation. A. CECIL *Robert Cecil* 11.
P. 160, l. 3. Account of Essex confession and execution in *C.S.P.D., 1598-1601*, 590-598; CAMDEN *Ann. Eliz.* 352-552 *passim;* JARDINE *Criminal Trials* I, 376-380; SPEDDING *Letters and Life* II, 233-237n.
P. 162, l. 14. NEALE *Queen Eliz.* 378.
P. 162, l. 20. Account of trial and sentencing of other Essex conspirators in: CAMDEN *Ann. Eliz.* 553-556; *State Trials* I, 1410-1451.
P. 163, l. 22. Mountjoy to the Earl of Nottingham, in MORYSON *Itinerary* II, 89.
P. 163, l. 31. Winwood to Cecil, 20 Apr. 1602, in WINWOOD *Memorials* I, 316.
P. 164, l. 12. Bacon to Michael Hicks, Aug. 1601, in SPEDDING III, 14.
P. 164, l. 17. See his long letter to Mountjoy, 1604, in SPEDDING III, 141-160.
P. 165, l. 20. *State Trials* I, 1422; CAMDEN *Ann. Eliz.* 551; WALDMAN *Raleigh* 51; *D.N.B.*, XVI, 635-636, art. "Sir Walter Ralegh"; E. A. STRATHMANN *Sir Walter Ralegh* (1951) *passim;* and STRATHMANN, quot-

ing Robert Gray, *An Alarum to England* (1609) in *Modern Language Quarterly* I (1940) 53, n. 16.

P. 165, l. 26. CAMDEN *Ann. Eliz.* 551.

P. 166, l. 35. NEALE *op. cit.* 378.

P. 167, l. 10. Chamberlain to Carleton, 19 Sept. 1601, in *Letters of Ch.*, I, 131.

P. 167, l. 33. 10 Aug. 1601, *Cal. Salisbury MSS.* XI (H.M.C. 1906) 332; *ibid.* 373.

P. 168, l. 19. Chamberlain to Carleton, 17 Sept. 1601, *op. cit.* I, 13.

P. 169, l. 15. SPEDDING III, 4-5.

P. 169, l. 31. *C.S.P.D., 1634-1635,* 405; L. NORSWORTHY *Lady of Bleeding Heart Yard* (1935) app., 277.

P. 170, l. 11. Coke to Cecil, 14 Oct. and 27 July 1599, in *Cal. Salisbury MSS.* IX (H.M.C. 1902) 371, 250.

P. 171, l. 9. 18 Feb. and 8 Mar. 1599 in *Cal. Salisbury MSS.* IX, 74, 95; *ibid.* XI, 572; 29 Mar. 1602 in *ibid.* XII (H.M.C. 1910) 90; Coke to Cecil, 1605, in *ibid.* XVII, (H.M.C. 1938) 583; Lady Hatton to Cecil 1602, *ibid.* XII, 546.

P. 171, l. 20. Greville to Cecil, 12 July (1603), in *ibid.* XV (H.M.C. 1930) 182; 29 Aug. 1602, in *ibid.* XII, 330.

P. 171, l. 34. Lord Howard to Earl of Marr, in *Secret Correspondence of Sir Robert Cecil with James I* (ed. Hailes) 26; D'EWES *Journal* 602; apology concerning Essex in SPEDDING III, 145.

P. 172, footnote. In R. B. MERRIMAN *Rise of the Spanish Empire* (1934) IV, 666.

P. 173, l. 3. D'EWES 653.

P. 174, l. 13. *Correspondence of King James VI of Scotland with Sir Robert Cecil and Others in England* (ed. Bruce, 1861) 31, 62.

P. 174, l. 29. NICHOLS *Progr. Eliz.*, II, 553; HARINGTON *Nugae* I, 326; CAMDEN *Ann. Eliz.* 585.

P. 175, l. 3. HARINGTON *op. cit.* 318; De Beaumont to the French Ambassador in Spain, 3 Apr. 1603, in *C.S.P. Venetian* X, 15-16; J. CLAPHAM *Elizabeth of England* (ed. Read, 1951) 99; 13 Apr. 1603, in J. MANNINGHAM *Diary* (ed. 1868) 170.

P. 175, l. 22. 23 Mar. 1603, in MANNINGHAM *op. cit.* 146.

P. 175, l. 26. 24 Mar. 1603, in *ibid.* 146. Manningham had his information from Dr. Parry, one of the Queen's chaplains, who was present at her death.

P. 175, l. 35. Scaramelli to the Doge, 7 Apr. 1603, in *C.S.P.V.*, IX, 1169; Cecil to J. Harington, 29 May 1603, in HARINGTON *op cit.* 345; NEALE *op. cit.* 386.

P. 175, l. 38. SIR J. HAYWARD *Annals, Elizabeth* (ed. 1840) 6.

CHAPTER FOURTEEN

P. 176, opening quotation. T. DEKKER "The Wonderfull Yeare (1603)," in *Non-Dramatic Works of Thomas Dekker* (ed. 1884) I, 97.

P. 176, l. 17. NICHOLS *Prog. James I* (ed. 1828) I, 27; MANNINGHAM *Diary* 147.
P. 177, l. 12. MANNINGHAM *op. cit.* 148.
P. 177, l. 26. Degli Effetti, *C.S.P.V.*, X, pref., ix.
P. 178, l. 3. A. WILSON in *Complete Hist. of Eng.* I, 662.
P. 178, l. 15. HARINGTON *Nugae* I, 188.
P. 178, l. 28. Scaramelli to the Doge, 24 Apr. 1603, in *C.S.P.V.*, X, 9; CLAPHAM *Historie* (ed. Read, 1951) 112.
P. 179, l. 17. *Ibid.*
P. 179, l. 28. AUBREY *Lives* 257.
P. 180, l. 9. JARDINE *Criminal Trials* I, 319.
P. 180, l. 19. D'ISRAELI *Amenities of Literature* (ed. 1842) III, 167.
P. 180, l. 39. JAMES I, *A Counterblaste to Tobacco* (ed. 1869) 101.
P. 181, l. 9. Chamberlain to Carleton, 30 Mar. 1603, in *Letters of Ch.*, I, 189.
P. 181, l. 25. NICHOLS *op. cit.* I, 113.
P. 182, l. 6. *Cal. Salisbury MSS.* XV, 72; *ibid.* 388.
P. 182, l. 27. Michael Stanhope to Cecil, undated (1603), in *ibid.* 388; Scaramelli to the Doge, 10 July 1603, in *C.S.P.V.*, X, 64; NICHOLS *op. cit.* I, 174, 195.
P. 183, l. 20. Scaramelli to the Doge, 26 June 1603, in *C.S.P.V.*, X, 54; W. HARRIS *Life of James I* (ed. 1772) 175n., 177-178n.; ECHARD *Hist. Eng.* 378; letter to Cecil, 30 July 1603, in SPEDDING *Letters and Life* III, 80-81.
P. 183, l. 33. AUBREY 254.
P. 184, l. 17. F. EGERTON *Egerton Papers* (ed. 1840) 380.
P. 185, l. 5. AUBREY 255; 4 Dec. 1601, in *Secret Corres.* 29.
P. 186, l. 9. HARINGTON *op. cit.* I, 180.
P. 187, l. 13. BIRCH *Mem. Eliz.*, II, 516.
P. 188, l. 2. M. Hicks to Earl of Shrewsbury, in E. LODGE *Illustrations of British History* (ed. 1838) III, 217.

CHAPTER FIFTEEN

P. 190, opening quotation. RUSHWORTH *Collections* I, 4.
P. 190, opening quotation. Harington, Elizabeth's godson, to Dr. John Still, Bishop of Bath and Wells, in HARINGTON *Letters and Epigrams* 108-109.
P. 190, l. 12. Cobham to Cecil, in EDWARDS *Life of Ralegh* (ed. 1868) I, 354.
P. 191, l. 29. The account and citations of trial of Ralegh from JARDINE *Criminal Trials* I, 401-420, and *State Trials* (ed. Howell) II, 2-35, unless otherwise indicated.
P. 195, l. 32. Cecil to Winwood, 3 Oct. 1603, in WINWOOD *Memorials* II, 8.
P. 199, l. 36. Roger Ashton to James I, quoted in letter of Carleton to Chamberlain, 27 Nov. 1603, in JARDINE I, 466.

P. 200, l. 11. CAMDEN *Ann. Eliz.* 540.
P. 201, l. 20. TANNER *Tudor Const. Docs.* 374.

CHAPTER SIXTEEN

P. 204, opening quotation. JARDINE *Criminal Trials* I, 466.
P. 204, l. 13. The account and citations of the trial of Ralegh from: JARDINE I, 421-466 and *State Trials* II, 2-35, unless otherwise indicated.
P. 207, l. 8. From *Miscellaneous Letters*, ed. by Sir Toby Matthew, quoted in JARDINE I, 461. The writer has not been identified. In W. STEBBING *Sir Walter Raleigh* 299, the saying is attributed to Sir Toby himself.
P. 216, l. 33. From a letter quoted in BISHOP GOODMAN *Court of King James the First* II, 93-97, transcribed from Serj. Yelverton's Collection in All Soul's College Library.

CHAPTER SEVENTEEN

P. 218, title. ECHARD *Hist. Eng.* 379.
P. 218, l. 16. Unless otherwise indicated, this and other reactions to the Ralegh trial, and the description of the trials and execution of the other alleged conspirators in JARDINE *Criminal Trials* I, 447, 449n., 462, 464-476.
P. 219, l. 4. SIR J. PETTUS *The Constitution of Parliament in England* (ed. 1680) 368; M. Hicks to the Earl of Shrewsbury, 6 Dec. 1603, in LODGE *Illustrations* III, 217.
P. 219, l. 22. COKE, 3 *Inst.* 36.
P. 221, l. 5. R. Hobart to Sir J. Hobart, 5 Dec. 1603, in GOODMAN *Court of James*, II, 88; J. STOW *Annales of England* (ed. Howes, 1631) 831.
P. 222, l. 21. EDWARDS *Life of Ralegh* II, 286.
P. 223, l. 5. AUBREY *Lives* 257; "The Difference and Disparity Between the Estates of George, Duke of Buckingham, and Robert, Earl of Essex," in SIR H. WOTTON *Reliquiae Wottonianae* (ed. 1651) 43.
P. 223, l. 16. F. OSBORNE *Traditional Memoirs* (1698), in SIR W. SCOTT *Secret History of James I* (ed. 1811) II, 118; SPEDDING *Letters and Life*, VI, 366.
P. 224, l. 4. Latimer to Ridley at the stake, in *D.N.B.*, XVI, 1174, art. "Nicholas Ridley."
P. 224, l. 28. *Cal. Salisbury MSS.* XVII, 372-379, 444; Waad to Cecil, 9 Dec. 1608, in *ibid.* XVII, 548; STEBBING *Sir W. Ralegh* 240.

CHAPTER EIGHTEEN

P. 225, opening quotation. *Shirburn Ballads, 1518-1616* (ed. Clark, 1907) 320.
P. 226, l. 3. *Hentzner's Journal*, in W. B. RYE *England as Seen by Foreigners* (ed. 1865) 283.
P. 226, l. 26. F. P. WILSON *The Plague in Shakespeare's London* (1927) 37.

P. 227, l. 10. A. WELDON *Court and Character of King James*, in *Secret History* II, 2.

P. 228, l. 6. ROGER COKE *A Detection of the Court and State of England* (ed. 1719) 78; WELDON in *Secret Hist.* II, 3; HARRIS *Life of James* 66-67; SIR R. WILBRAHAM *Journal* (*Camden Misc.* X) 60; 29 Mar. 1603 in MANNINGHAM *Diary* 155.

P. 228, l. 35. WELDON in *Secret Hist.* II, 2; JAMES I, *Basilikon Doron*, in *Political Works of James I* (ed. McIlwain, 1918) 38; JAMES I, *Counter-blaste* 100-108.

P. 229, l. 5. JAMES I, *The Trew Law of Free Monarchies*, in *Pol. Works* 70.

P. 229, l. 18. JAMES I, *Bas. Doron* in *ibid.* 12; *Trew Law* in *ibid.* 61.

P. 229, l. 39. Cecil to Shrewsbury, in LODGE *Illustrations* III, 182, 187; Worcester to Shrewsbury, 4 Dec. 1604, in *ibid.* 247.

P. 230, l. 19. (4 Dec. 1604) in *ibid.* 245.

P. 230, l. 31. OSBORNE in *Secret Hist.* I, 71; F. BLOMEFIELD *County of Norfolk* (1806) III, 324.

P. 231, l. 21. WELDON in *Secret Hist.* I, 369-370.

P. 231, l. 38. Gawdy to his brother (early Aug. 1603) in *Letters of Philip Gawdy* (ed. 1906) 136.

P. 232, l. 15. OSBORNE in *Secret Hist.* I, 79; to the Earl of Shrewsbury, Sept. 1603, in LODGE III, 187; Worcester to Shrewsbury, 24 Sept. 1603, in *ibid.* 188.

P. 232, l. 25. 18 Dec. 1604, in *ibid.* 252; 1 Feb. 1604, in *ibid.* 262; Worcester to Cecil, 25 Feb. 1604, in *ibid.* 263.

P. 232, l. 39. Cecil to Shrewsbury, 17 Sept. 1603, in *ibid.* 182; HARINGTON *Nugae* I, 245.

P. 233, l. 26. W. Bird to Cecil, Jan. 1604, in *Cal Salisbury MSS.* XVI H.M.C., 1933) 15; A. CECIL *Robert Cecil* 222.

P. 234, l. 21. HARINGTON *op. cit.* 181-182.

P. 234, l. 31. FULLER *Church Hist.* III, 253-254.

P. 235, l. 12. NICHOLS *Prog. James*, I, 320-321.

P. 235, l. 38. Account of procession through City of London, 1604, in *ibid.* 325-376.

CHAPTER NINETEEN

P. 237, opening quotation. *State Trials* II, 166.

P. 237, opening quotation. FULLER *Church Hist.* III, 238.

P. 238, l. 14. Scaramelli to the Doge and Senate, 1 May 1603, in *C.S.P.V.*, X, 218.

P. 239, l. 9. Memoirs of Maximilian de Bethune, Duke of Sully, quoted in LODGE *Illustrations* I, 113.

P. 239, l. 17. Sir Everard Digby to Cecil, May 1605, as quoted in GARDINER *What Gunpowder Plot Was* (1897) 171.

P. 240, l. 9. *Correspondence of James VI with Robert Cecil* 56; GARDINER *Hist. of Eng.* I, 100.

P. 242, l. 38. Examination of A. Rookwood, 2 Dec. 1605, JARDINE *Criminal Trials* II, 160.

P. 243, l. 19. Examination of R. Keyes, 30 Nov. 1605, in *C.S.P.D., 1603-1610,* 264.

P. 244, l. 10. JARDINE II, 61-62.

P. 244, l. 15. Molin to the Doge, 16 Nov. 1605, in *C.S.P.V.*, X, 442.

P. 245, l. 25. Description in Molin's letters to the Doge, 16, 17, 21, 23 Nov. 1605, in *C.S.P.V.*, X, 288; Sir Edward Hoby to Sir Thomas Edmondes, 19 Nov. 1605, in NICHOLS *Prog. James,* I, 585.

P. 246, l. 30. Examination of J. Johnson, 6 Nov. 1605, in *C.S.P.D., 1603-1610,* 241; A. WILSON in *Complete Hist. of Eng.* I, 675; Waad to Cecil, 8 Nov. 1605, in *C.S.P.D., 1603-1610,* 246-247.

P. 247, footnote. FULLER *Church Hist.* III, 259.

P. 248, l. 14. Chamberlain to Carleton, 2 Apr. 1606, in *Letters of Ch.*, I, 219.

P. 248, l. 29. 16 Nov. 1605, in *C.S.P.D., 1603-1610,* 258; Carleton to Chamberlain, 13 Nov. 1605, in *ibid.* 255; OSBORNE in *Secret Hist.* I, 177.

P. 249, l. 2. Ben Jonson to Cecil, 8 Nov. 1605, in *C.S.P.D., 1063-1610,* 245.

P. 249, footnote. JAMES I, *Pol. Works* 269.

P. 249, l. 28. HAWARDE *Rep. del Cases* 289.

P. 249, footnote. (1605) in *Cal. Salisbury MSS.* XVII, 569.

P. 250, l. 15. Molin to the Doge, 21 Nov. 1605, in *C.S.P.V.*, X, 293.

P. 250, l. 26. Elizabeth Vaux to Sir J. Roger, 10 Nov. 1605, in *C.S.P.D., 1603-1610,* 249.

P. 257, l. 14. GARDINER *Hist. of Eng.* I, 177, 191.

P. 251, l. 26. JAMES I, *Pol. Works* 282-284.

P. 251, l. 35. 12 Feb. 1606, in BIRCH *Court and Times of James I* (ed. 1849) I, 52.

P. 252, l. 13. Sir T. Hoby to Edmondes, 10 Feb. 1606, in *ibid.* 46.

CHAPTER TWENTY

P. 253, title. HAWARDE *Rep. del Cases* 298.

P. 254, footnote. *C.S.P.D., 1603-1610,* 6 Nov. 1605, 240.

P. 255, l. 2. Account and citations of first trial of conspirators and trial of Garnett from: *State Trials* II, 159-184, 234; JARDINE *Criminal Trials* II, 116-355 *passim,* unless otherwise indicated.

P. 257, l. 9. HAWARDE 255-266; *State Trials* II, 182.

P. 258, l. 33. Thomas Elliott to Richard Percival, Burgess from Yorkshire, 1605, in *Cal. Salisbury MSS.* XVII, 592.

P. 259, l. 29. HAWARDE 256.

P. 260, l. 29. Account of death of conspirators from *Somers Tracts* (ed. 1809) II, 112-117.

P. 262, l. 10. GOODMAN *Court of James I,* I, 103-104.

P. 263, l. 10. Chamberlain to Carleton, 2 Apr. 1606, in *Letters of Ch.*, II, 221.

P. 263, l. 29. 28 Mar. 1606, in *C.S.P.D., 1603-1610,* 306.

P. 268, l. 18. 20 Apr. 1606, in *C.S.P.V.*, X, 510.
P. 268, l. 22. Carleton to Chamberlain, 2 May 1606, in JARDINE II, 334.
P. 269, l. 20. OSBORNE in *Secret Hist.* I, 179n.
P. 269, l. 31. FULLER *Church Hist.* III, 249.
P. 270, l. 9. HAWARDE 297-299 for account of Percy's trial.
P. 271, l. 13. FULLER *op. cit.* III, 247-248.
P. 272, l. 39. *Book of Common Prayer* (ed. 1662), known as the *Restoration Prayer Book.*
P. 273, footnote. FULLER *op. cit.* III, 244.
P. 273, l. 28. *Old English Ballads* (ed. Rollins, 1920) 361-362.

CHAPTER TWENTY-ONE

P. 277, opening quotation. COKE *Co. Litt.* 293b.
P. 277, l. 9. A. CECIL *Robert Cecil* 329.
P. 278, l. 20. FORTESCUE *De Laudibus Legum Angliae* (ed. 1874) 201.
P. 279, l. 12. J. COWELL *The Interpreter* (ed. 1672), art. "Serjeant-at-law"; COKE, 10 *Rep.* pref., xxiii; JARDINE *Criminal Trials* II, 295.
P. 279, l. 21. 2 Feb. 1606, *Cal. Salisbury MSS.* XVIII (H.M.C. 1940) 42.
P. 280, l. 6. SIR G. CROKE *Reports Jac.* (4th ed., 1791) 125; COKE, 2 *Inst.* 55.
P. 280, l. 11. W. LAMBARDE *Eirenarcha* (ed. 1610) 52.
P. 280, l. 20. *Book of Oaths.*
P. 280, l. 25. SPEDDING *Letters and Life* V, 359-360.
P. 280, l. 36. Coke to Cecil, 10 Dec. 1600, in *Cal. Salisbury MSS.* X, 415.
P. 281, l. 11. CHEYNEY *Hist. Eng.* II, 381-382.
P. 281, l. 23. SMITH *De Rep. Ang.* 88; Archbishop Warham, writing to Cardinal Wolsey, 5 Apr. 1525, advising against collecting certain monies in summer, in TANNER *Tudor Const. Docs.* 623.
P. 282, l. 16. COKE, 3 *Inst.* 190b; *ibid.* 219.
P. 282, l. 34. R. BOWYER *Parliamentary Diary* (ed. 1931) 41.
P. 283, l. 11. COKE *Co. Litt.* 293b.
P. 284, l. 1. 3 *Inst.* 197; *C.S.P.D., 1598-1601*, 519; COKE, 8 *Rep.* 416.
P. 284, l. 9. LORD CLARENDON *Autobiography* (ed. 1759) I, 28.
P. 286, l. 12. All citations from Coke's Norwich charge to the jury in COKE *The Lord Coke his Speech and Charge* (ed. 1607).
P. 288, l. 27. RYE *Norfolk*, in *Victoria History of the Counties of England* (ed. Page, 1900) 95; Coke to Cecil, 27 Aug. 1602, in *Cal. Salisbury MSS.* XII, 322.
P. 290, footnote. COKE, 3 *Inst.* 194.

CHAPTER TWENTY-TWO

P. 292, l. 2. SPEDDING *Letters and Life* IV, 379; RUSHWORTH *Collections* I, 509; *State Trials* III, 132; J. FORSTER *Sir John Eliot* (ed. 1864) II, 150; COKE, 12 *Rep.* (ed. 1738) 64; 2 *Inst.* 658.
P. 292, l. 31. COKE, 5 Rep. (ed. 1738) 1; for the material on judges' salaries

I am indebted to M. HASTINGS *The Court of Common Pleas in the Fifteenth Century* (1947).

P. 292, l. 35. *Cal. Salisbury MSS.* III (H.M.C. 1889) 5.

P. 293, l. 26. *State Trials* IX, 763, Sir Bartholomew Shower.

P. 294, l. 28. JAMES I, *Trew Law,* in *Pol. Works* 62; Calvin's Case, *State Trials* II, 693; COKE, 12 *Rep.* 64; BACON, "Of Judicature," in *Essays,* 136.

P. 296, l. 24. JAMES I, *Bas. Doron,* in *Pol. Works* 12; *Trew Law,* in *ibid.* 63; COWELL *Interpreter,* art. "King."

P. 297, l. 18. WIGMORE, "The Privilege against Self-Crimination," in *Harvard Law Review* XV 617; Burghley to Whitgift, 1 July 1584, in STRYPE *Life of John Whitgift* III, 105-106.

P. 298, l. 12. GARDINER *Hist. Eng.* I, 319; Hampton Court Conference, 1604, in FULLER *Church Hist.* III, 211.

P. 298, l. 24. COKE, 12 *Rep.* 26.

P. 299, l. 6. Account of Fuller Case in T. FULLER, *op. cit.* III, 270; USHER *Reconstruction of the English Church* (ed. 1910) II, 143. Thomas Fuller was no relative of Nicholas Fuller.

P. 300, l. 29. Account of Lord Ellesmere's speech in the Exchequer Chamber in Postnati Case from *State Trials* II, 659-695 *passim.*

P. 301, l. 11. Ellesmere's opinion was printed separately, in *State Trials* II, *loc. cit.* Coke was the only lawyer present who reported Calvin's Case, in 7 *Rep.* 11.

P. 301, l. 23. FORTESCUE *De Laud. Leg. Ang.* 22.

P. 301, l. 36. Chamberlain to Carleton, 5 and 8 Jan. 1608, in *Letters of Ch.*, I, 251, 253.

P. 302, l. 12. *Ibid.* 269.

P. 303, l. 13. Account of final interpretation of High Commission controversy in USHER *Reconstr.* II, 213-215; USHER "James I and Sir Edward Coke," in *Engl. Hist. R.* (Oct. 1903) 668-675; COKE, 12 *Rep.* 64-65.

P. 306, l. 5. LODGE *Illustrations* III, 364-365.

CHAPTER TWENTY-THREE

P. 307, opening quotation. 7 Feb. 1607, in *The Journal of Sir Roger Wilbraham,* in *Camden Miscellany* X (ed. 1902) 96.

P. 308, l. 3. J. SELDEN *Table Talk* (ed. Pollock, 1927) 61; *Old Parliamentary History* (ed. 1751) VIII, 59; FORSTER *Sir John Eliot* I, 137-138.

P. 308, l. 37. Foss *The Judges of England* VI, 135; FULLER *Worthies* 512.

P. 309, l. 9. Lochner *v.* New York (1905) U.S., 76.

P. 309, l. 37. COKE, 13 *Rep.* (ed. 1738) 10.

P. 310, l. 8. Account of Edwards Case in *ibid.* 9-12.

P. 310, l. 15. COKE *Co. Litt.* 48a, 48b.

P. 311, l. 4. ECHARD *Hist. Eng.* 388; OSBORNE in *Secret Hist.* I, 270-272.

P. 312, l. 3. Thomas Wentworth, in letter of J. More to Sir R. Winwood, 1 Dec. 1610, in WINWOOD *Memorials* III, 155; *Parliamentary Debates in 1610* (ed. 1862) 11; GARDINER *Hist. Eng.* II, 66; 25 Mar. 1610, in *Tudor and Stuart Proclamations* (ed. Steele, 1910) I, 128.

P. 312, l. 14. Citations of JAMES I, in *Pol. Works* 307-316 *passim*.

P. 313, l. 18. Petition of grievances from *Jus Parliamentarium* 321, in *State Trials* II, 519-531 *passim*.

P. 314, l. 23. F. A. INDERWICK *The King's Peace* (ed. 1894) 111.

P. 314, l. 36. Report of judges to Ellesmere, USHER *Rise and Fall* 191; COKE, 13 *Rep.* 11.

P. 315, l. 4. This treatise, called by Usher "a noble monument," has never been published. USHER *Reconstr.* II, 241-242.

P. 315, l. 10. Account of Bonham's Case from COKE, 8 *Rep.* 116-121.

P. 316, l. 6. J. QUINCY, JR. *Reports of Cases in the Superior Court . . . of Mass. Bay, 1761-1762* (ed. 1865) app. I; C. BECKER *The Eve of Revolution* (Y.C.S. 1920) 70; J. Adams to Wm. Cushing, 9 June 1776, in JOHN ADAMS *Works* (ed. 1854) IX, 390-391.

P. 316, l. 22. CAMPBELL *Lives of the Chief Justices* (ed. 1874) I, 341; C. MCILWAIN *The High Court of Parliament* (1910) 307 and T. PLUCKNETT "Bonham's Case and Judicial Review," in *Harvard Law Review* XL (1926-1927) 69-70. See Earl of Oxford's Case in *Leading Cases in Equity* (ed. White & Tudor, 1910) 779.

CHAPTER TWENTY-FOUR

P. 318, opening quotation. F. W. MAITLAND *English Law and the Renaissance* (ed. 1901) 29.

P. 318, l. 9. W. YONGE *Diary* (ed. 1848) May 1610, 20; La Boderie, 24 May 1610, in RYE *England Seen by Foreigners* 250.

P. 319, l. 8. *Parl. Deb. in 1610*, 53.

P. 319, l. 12. John More to R. Winwood, 8 June 1611, in WINWOOD *Memorials* III, 281; More to Trumbull, 5 June 1611, in *Trumbull Papers* III (*Downshire MSS.*, H.M.C. 1938) 85.

P. 319, l. 28. TANNER *Const. Docs. of the Reign of James I* (1930) 154.

P. 320, l. 18. Dudley Carleton to Sir T. Edmondes, 13 July 1610, in BIRCH *Ct. and Times, James*, I, 122; SPEDDING *Letters and Life* IV, 203.

P. 321, l. 8. More to Winwood, 1 Dec. 1610, in WINWOOD *Memorials* III, 235; Correr to the Doge and Senate, 16 Jan. 1610, in *C.S.P.V.*, XI, 509; Carleton to Edmondes, 13 July 1610, in BIRCH *op. cit.* 121-122; 23 Nov. 1610, in *Parl. Deb. in 1610*, 144; G. D. to A. W., 28 July 1610, in *ibid.* app. B, 154.

P. 321, l. 18. Coke's account of Privy Council meeting on proclamations in COKE, 12 *Rep.* 74-76.

P. 323, l. 9. SIR W. ANSON *Law and Custom of the Constitution* (ed. 1892) I, 323; Lake to Cecil, 25 Nov. 1610 and James to Salisbury, 6 Dec. 1610, in D. H. WILLSON, "The Summoning and Dissolving Parliament, 1603-1625," in *Amer. Hist. R.* (Jan. 1940), 281-284.

P. 323, l. 24. James to Council, 7 Dec. 1610, and Lake to Salisbury, 4 Dec. 1610, in *ibid.* 282-284.

P. 324, l. 5. Account of criticism of Coke's opposition to royal prerogative in USHER *Rise and Fall* 210-216.

P. 325, l. 14. *Ibid.* 215-216; Coke's defense in 12 *Rep.* 86-89.
P. 326, l. 13. See Coke, 4 *Inst.* 330b for *enormous* crimes.
P. 328, l. 22. W. Laud *Works* (ed. 1847-1860) IV, 138.

CHAPTER TWENTY-FIVE

P. 329, l. 7. Dr. Mayerne *Opera Medica* (ed. Browne, 1701) 78-90; letter of John Beaulieu to Trumbull, 6 May 1612, in Winwood *Memorials* III, 363.
P. 329, l. 23. Chamberlain to Carleton, 11 Mar. 1612, in *Letters of Ch.*, I, 338; Wilbraham *Journal*, 24 May 1612, 106; Molin to the Doge, "Report on England," 1607, in *C.S.P.V.*, X, 516.
P. 330, l. 15. Chamberlain to Carleton, 29 Apr. 1612, *op. cit.* I, 346-347.
P. 330, l. 20. Coke to Cecil, 17 Apr. 1594, in *Cal. Salisbury MSS.* IV (H.M.C. 1892) 511.
P. 330, l. 36. C. James *Coke and Descendants* 21.
P. 331, l. 15. 1604, *Cal. Salisbury MSS.* XVI, 395.
P. 331, l. 29. Chamberlain to Carleton, 27 May 1612, *op. cit.* I, 351.
P. 332, l. 5. A. Cecil *Robert Cecil* 355; D'Ewes *Autobiography* (ed. 1845) I, 50-51; Chamberlain to Carleton, *loc. cit.;* Osborne in *Secret Hist.* I, 235.
P. 332, l. 17. First eight lines in D'Ewes *op cit.* I, 51 n.; last two lines in Osborne, *Secret Hist.* I, 235-236.
P. 332, l. 27. D'Ewes *op. cit.* 51.
P. 333, l. 15. *Trumbull Papers* III, 289.
P. 333, l. 22. Spedding *Letters and Life* IV, 282.
P. 333, l. 36. Fuller *Ch. Hist.* III, 289; Birch *Life of Henry, Prince of Wales* (ed. 1760) 347; R. Coke *Detection* 71; Birch *op. cit.* 392.
P. 334, l. 8. *Ibid.* 330; Chamberlain to Carleton, 12 Nov. 1612, *op. cit.* I, 388.
P. 334, l. 22. Birch *op. cit.* 329, 348; Chamberlain to Carleton, *loc. cit.;* Birch *op. cit.* 354.
P. 335, l. 6. *Cal. Salisbury MSS.* XVII, 378; Chamberlain to Carleton, 11 Aug. 1612, *op. cit.* I, 374; A. Wilson in *Complete Hist. of Eng.* II, 714n; Chamberlain to Carleton, 12 Nov. 1612, *op. cit.* I, 389.
P. 335, l. 25. Correr to the Doge, 23 June 1610, in *C.S.P.V.*, XI, 516; Molin to the Doge, 1607, in *ibid.* X, 513-514; R. Coke *Detection* I, 71; Birch *op. cit.* 399; Goodman *Court of James I*, I, 252.
P. 335, l. 39. Sir W. Ralegh *The Historie of the World* (ed. 1652) pref., p. A; Chamberlain to Carleton, 12 Nov. 1612, *loc. cit.*
P. 336, l. 18. Chamberlain to Carleton, 19 Nov. 1612, *op. cit.* I, 391; 11 Aug. and 26 Nov. 1612, *ibid.* 377, 394.
P. 336, l. 38. E. Abbott *Francis Bacon* (ed. 1885) 284.
P. 337, l. 20. Sir T. Overbury *Overburian Characters* (ed. 1936) 32; Aubrey *Lives* 11; Bacon *Works* (ed. 1872) VII, 202, 201, 199.
P. 337, l. 36. Chamberlain to Carleton, 17 Dec. 1612, *op. cit.* I, 397; Bacon *Essays* 108.

P. 338, l. 13. All citations from Bacon's memorandum and his letter to James, 12 Feb. 1615, in: SPEDDING IV, 378-382 *passim; ibid.* V, 242.

P. 340, l. 36. Reaction to Coke's appointment as Chief Justice in: Chamberlain to Carleton, 14 and 27 Oct. 1613, *op. cit.* I, 479, 481-482.

P. 341, l. 28. Bacon himself has given us the story in BACON "Apophthegms," in *Works* (ed. 1861-1864) XIII, 392.

CHAPTER TWENTY-SIX

P. 343, l. 5. STOW *Annales* 1003; Chamberlain to Carleton, 30 June 1614, in *Letters of Ch.*, I, 544.

P. 343, l. 25. First Charter of Virginia, 10 Apr. 1606, in *Docs. of American History* (ed. Commager, 1944) 8; Correr to the Doge, 27 Feb. 1609, in *C.S.P.V.*, XI, 237.

P. 344, l. 3. News from the New World in Chamberlain to Carleton, 1 Aug. and 27 Oct. 1613, *op. cit.* I, 470, 482; STOW *op. cit.* 1017.

P. 344, l. 32. RUSHWORTH *Collections* I, 511.

P. 345, l. 10. COKE, 10 *Rep.* pref., ii; SIR F. D. MACKINNON *Inner Temple Papers* (1948) 61.

P. 345, l. 29. SPELMAN *Reliquiae*, p. B89.

P. 346, l. 20. Chamberlain to Carleton, 4 Dec. 1611, in *Letters of Ch.*, I, 320.

P. 347, l. 3. Account of wedding from J. Smyth (Steward of the Berkeley Hundred), "Lives of the Berkeleys," in JAMES *Coke and Descendants*, app. VII, 325.

P. 348, l. 29. A. WILSON in *Complete Hist. of Eng.* I, 727; LORD HERBERT OF CHERBURY *Autobiography* (ed. 1886) 236n.

P. 349, l. 13. 14 April 1614, in *C.S.P.D. Add. 1580-1620*, 539-540.

P. 350, l. 3. Chamberlain to Carleton, 9 June 1614, *op. cit.* I 538; SPEDDING *Letters and Life* V, 45; *O.P.H.*, V, 279; *Commons Debates, 1621* (ed. Notestein *et al.*) VII, app. B, 632; *C.S.P.V.*, XI, 78; *C.D. 1621*, VII, app. B, 636; Chamberlain to Carleton, 14 Apr. 1614, *op. cit.* I, 525.

P. 350, l. 10. Gondomar to Philip III, 20 June 1614, in D. WILLSON, *Amer. Hist. R.* (Jan. 1940), 289n.

P. 350, l. 27. Chamberlain to Carleton, 30 June 1614, *op. cit.* I, 542; G. H. A. HAMILTON *Quarter Sessions from Queen Elizabeth to Queen Anne* (ed. 1878) 44.

P. 350, l. 37. SIR J. WHITELOCKE *Liber Famelicus* (ed. 1858) 45.

P. 351, l. 15. *D.N.B.*, XV, art. "Edward Peacham"; *State Trials* II, 869-870.

P. 351, l. 21. This and following citations from proceedings attendant to Peacham's Case from SPEDDING V, 92-124 *passim.*

CHAPTER TWENTY-SEVEN

P. 356, opening quotation. R. COKE *Detection* I, 91.

P. 357, l. 35. WHITELOCKE *Lib. Fam.* 48.

P. 358, l. 28. MULLINGER *The Univ. of Cambridge* 529-538; R. COKE *op. cit.* 81-82.

P. 359, l. 2. Chamberlain to Carleton, 20 May 1615, in *Letters of Ch.*, I, 598.

P. 359, l. 21. COKE, 4 *Inst.* 79b.

P. 360, l. 14. *Ibid.* 71; WHITELOCKE *op. cit.* 53.

P. 360, footnote. SELDEN *Table Talk* 43.

P. 360, l. 24. Bacon to James, 27 Jan. 1616, in SPEDDING *Letters and Life* V, 236.

P. 360, l. 28. All citations from cases of *Rege Inconsulto* and jewel merchants (Glanville and Allen) from SPEDDING V, 223-253 and *Collectanea Juridica* (ed. 1791) I, 168-181, unless otherwise indicated.

P. 361, l. 5. Bacon, in *Works* (ed. 1861-1864) XV, 260, 263.

P. 363, l. 16. MS. in *Egerton Papers* as cited in CAMPBELL *Chief Justices* II, 363-364.

P. 365, l. 4. R. COKE *op. cit.* I, 49-51.

P. 365, l. 14. Bacon's charge in case Lady Somerset pleaded not guilty, in *State Trials* II, 962; and BACON *Works* (*ed. cit.*) III, 493.

P. 365, l. 32. A. WILSON *Secret History of James I*, in D'EWES *Autobiography* II, 345.

P. 366, l. 3. Chamberlain to Carleton, 30 Dec. 1613, *op. cit.* I, 495.

P. 366, l. 10. This and subsequent citations from Overbury trial in *State Trials* II, 928-967, unless otherwise indicated.

P. 366, l. 22. WELDON in *Secret Hist.* I, 418; D'EWES *op. cit.* II, 79.

P. 367, l. 14. Sir John Finet to second Earl of Salisbury, 14 Nov. 1619, in D. MATHEW *The Jacobean Age* (ed. 1938) 175n; Chamberlain to Carleton, 27 Mar. 1616, *op. cit.* I, 617.

P. 367, l. 20. Sir Charles Montague to Sir Edward Montague, 15 May 1616, in *Buccleuch Papers* (H.M.C. 1889) I, 248.

CHAPTER TWENTY-EIGHT

P. 370, opening quotation. *Letters of Ch.*, II, 6.

P. 371, l. 13. The citations above and following relating to the Commendams Case from: SPEDDING *Letters and Life* V, 275-395 *passim*, unless otherwise indicated.

P. 374, l. 35. Excerpts following from James's Star Chamber speech, not always in their order, from *Pol. Works* 326-355 *passim.*

P. 376, l. 7. SPEDDING V, 395.

P. 376, l. 10. W. HOLDSWORTH *History of English Law* (ed. 1922-1926) I 465.

P. 376, l. 18. COKE, 3 *Inst.* 124b. The *Third Institute* was published in 1644, ten years after Coke's death. See also "Jurisdiction of Chancery," in 3 *Inst.* and *Collectanea Jur.* I, 23-78 for an interesting anonymous article, "A Vindication, etc. . . . ," written before 1650.

P. 377, l. 2. Chamberlain to Carleton, 14 Nov. 1616, *op. cit.* II, 36.

P. 377, l. 6. Undated letter of Bacon to James, probably written 1 Jan.

1620. This and following citations relating to Coke's censure and suspension from office in: SPEDDING V, 381-399, and W. C. JOHNSON *Life of Coke* (ed. 1837) 304-398 *passim*, unless otherwise indicated.

P. 377, l. 19. *Encycl. Brit.* (11th ed.) V-VI, 655, art. "Sir Edward Coke."

P. 379, l. 3. Sir Charles Montague to Edward Montague 26 June 1616, in *Buccleuch Papers* I, 248; Chamberlain to Carleton, 22 June 1616, *op. cit.* II, 11.

P. 379, footnote. PETTUS *Const. of Parls.* 330.

P. 380, l. 4. Account of this incident in CAMPBELL *Chief Justices* I, 339.

P. 381, l. 5. Philip Gawdy, son of the Judge, "to his Nephew Framlingham," 10 Aug. 1616 in *Letters of Philip Gawdy* 183; Chamberlain to Carleton, 6 July 1616, from London, *op. cit.* II, 14.

P. 381, l. 17. Further account of quarrel over Coke including letter of Villiers to Bacon, 3 Oct. 1616; the observations of Lord Chancellor Egerton (Ellesmere); "Remembrance of his Majesty's declarative touching the Lord Coke"; and Bacon's charges and note, in: SPEDDING VI, 76-97.

P. 385, l. 3. Chamberlain to Carleton, 26 Oct. 1616, *op. cit.* II, 29.

P. 388, l. 15. CAMPBELL *op. cit.* 343; Chamberlain to Carleton, 14 Nov. 1616, *op. cit.* II, 34.

P. 388, l. 17. "He received it with dejection and tears." J. Castle to J. Miller, 19 Nov. 1616, in BIRCH *Ct. and Times, James*, I, 440.

P. 388, l. 19. Account of Montague's installation as Chief Justice from: Chamberlain to Carleton, 23 Nov. 1616, *op. cit.* II, 38; SPEDDING V, 249; *Buccleuch Papers* III, 196. Three versions of Ellesmere's speech exist. One is in the P.R.O.; one in *Moor's Reports* as quoted in CAMPBELL *op. cit.* 344-346; and one in *Buccleuch Papers, loc. cit.* The last has been used except for the final paragraph, which comes from Moor.

P. 389, l. 37. WHITELOCKE *Lib. Fam.* 51.

P. 390, l. 8. Chamberlain to Carleton, 23 Nov. 1616, *op. cit.* II, 40.

P. 390, l. 18. *Ibid.* 40; Castle to Miller, 19 Nov. 1621, as transcribed in I. D'ISRAELI *The Literary Character* (ed. 1881) 424n.

P. 390, l. 35. Castle to Miller, in *ibid.* 423.

CHAPTER TWENTY-NINE

P. 393, opening quotation. Carleton to Chamberlain, 22 Oct. 1617, in *C.S.P.D., 1611-1618*, 489.

P. 394, l. 29. GOODMAN *Court of James I*, I, 225; and W. WINSTANLEY *England's Worthies* (ed. 1684) 397; R. COKE *Detection* I, 83.

P. 395, l. 10. CLARENDON *Hist. of the Rebellion* I, 12; R. COKE *op. cit.* 92; Bacon to Villiers, 22 Jan. 1615 in SPEDDING *Letters and Life* V, 228.

P. 395, l. 21. Gen. xiii, 2, 3; FULLER *Ch. Hist.* III, 297.

P. 395, l. 38. Chamberlain to Carleton, 11 Oct. 1617, *Letters of Ch.*, II, 92; GOODMAN I, 2, 3; Chamberlain to Carleton, *op. cit.* II, 102.

P. 396, l. 14. Account of Bacon's progress to and first speech in Chancery from: Camden *Ann. James* in *Complete Hist. Eng.* II, 647; and Chamberlain to Carleton, 10 May 1617, *op. cit.* II, 72-73.

P. 396, l. 21. Spedding VI, 198.

P. 397, l. 16. *Ibid.* 199, 347; Winwood to Lake, 2 June 1617, in *C.S.P.D., 1611-1618*, 471; Chamberlain to Carleton, 4 June 1617, in *ibid.* and in *Letters of Ch.*, II, 80.

P. 397, l. 33. Norsworthy *Lady* 31-32.

P. 398, l. 7. Chamberlain to Carleton, 24 May 1617 and 23 Nov. 1616, *op. cit.* II, 77, 38; Norsworthy 31; and Geo. Gerrard to Carleton, 4 June 1617, in *C.S.P.D., 1611-1618*, 471.

P. 398, l. 28. Chamberlain to Carleton, 4 June and 15 Mar. 1617, *op cit.* II, 80, 64.

P. 399, l. 13. Thomas Coke to Sir John Coke, 1 Mar. 1617, in *Cowper Papers* (H.M.C. 1888) I, 94; Spedding VI, 221.

P. 400, l. 34. Enclosed in a letter from Geo. Gerrard to Carleton, 18 Aug. 1617, in *C.S.P.D., 1611-1618*, 482; Norsworthy 43.

P. 401, l. 4. Letter of Council to Lake, July 1617, *Lake's Council Register*, in *Camden Miscellany* V (ed. 1864). The following account of the quarrel between Coke and Lady Hatton over Frances Coke's marriage taken from: *ibid.*; Campbell *Chief Justices* I, 348-355; Spedding VI, 220-231; Gerrard to Carleton, 22 July 1617, in T. Longueville *The Curious Case of Lady Purbeck* (1909) 39-40; and Chamberlain to Carleton, 19 July 1617, *op. cit.* II, 88-89.

P. 405, l. 19. Chamberlain to Carleton, 19 July 1617, in Birch *Court and Times, James*, II, 20-21.

P. 405, l. 20. The account of the differences between Bacon, Buckingham and Coke and the conclusion of the Coke family quarrel from: Spedding VI, 232-267; Longueville *op. cit.* 39-40; Chamberlain to Carleton, 9 and 27 Aug. 1617, *op. cit.* II, 91-98; *Buccleuch Papers* I, 205-206.

P. 410, l. 1. The account of the marriage of Frances Coke and John Villiers from letter of Sir Gerrard Herbert to Carleton, 6 Oct. 1617, in *C.S.P.D., 1611-1618*, 487; Norsworthy, ch. 7; Longueville, ch. 6.

P. 411, l. 17. Nathaniel Brent to Carleton, 30 Mar. 1618, in *C.S.P.D., 1611-1618*, 531; Chamberlain to Carleton, 15 Nov. 1617, *op. cit.* II, 116-117; Sir John Peyton to (Carleton), Nov. 1617, in *C.S.P.D., 1611-1618*, 495.

P. 411, l. 28. Bacon to Buckingham, 20 November 1619, in Spedding VI, 61; Brent to Carleton, 14 Nov. 1617, in *C.S.P.D., 1611-1618*, 497; Sir Thomas Wentworth to Sir H. Wotton, 8 Nov. 1617, in *Strafford Letters* (ed. 1740) I, 5; Chamberlain to Carleton, 11 Oct. 1617, *op. cit.* II, 101.

CHAPTER THIRTY

P. 412, opening quotation. Hacket *Scrinia Reserata* 54.

P. 413, l. 3. *Ibid.* 48; J. Bourgrave to Sir T. Wentworth, 26 May 1620, in *Strafford Letters* I, 7.

P. 413, l. 19. D. WILLSON *Privy Councillors in the House of Commons* (1940) 88.
P. 413, l. 28. BACON "Some Additional Apophthegms" in *Works* (ed. 1861-1864) XIII, 406.
P. 414, l. 18. GARDINER *Hist. Eng.* III, 98.
P. 415, l. 4. James Howell to Carew Ralegh, undated, in *State Trials* II, 59; *Somers Tracts* II, 456-457; SPEDDING *Letters and Life* VI, 353-354.
P. 415, l. 10. GARDINER III, 132-134; King of Spain to J. S. de Alloa, 26 Sept. 1618, in *C.S.P.D., 1611-1618*, 577.
P. 415, l. 14. From RALEGH "Apology," written shortly after his arrest at Plymouth, in *Works* (ed. Birch, 1829) VIII, 479.
P. 416, l. 5. SPEDDING VI, 363; letter from Julian Sanchez de Alloa, Spanish agent in London, to Philip III, dated 6 Nov. 1618, in ibid. 368n; *State Trials* II, 34.
P. 416, l. 26. SPEDDING VI, 342; John Pory to Carleton, 31 Oct. 1618, in *C.S.P.D., 1611-1618*, 588; Chamberlain to Carleton, 31 Oct. 1618, *Letters of Chamberlain* II, 177.
P. 417, l. 5. WALDMAN *Sir Walter Raleigh* 238.
P. 417, l. 26. Mead to Stuteville, 9 Apr. 1621, in BIRCH *Ct. and Times, James*, II, 247-248; Chamberlain to Carleton, 11 and 20 Mar. 1620, *op. cit.* II 293, 296; Howell to Sir Jas. Croft, 22 Mar. 1622, in J. HOWELL *Familiar Letters* (ed. 1890) 148.
P. 418, l. 9. *C.D. 1621*, II, 109-110. For this citation I am indebted to Elizabeth Read Foster.
P. 418, l. 27. *O.P.H.*, V, 311; Chamberlain to Carleton, 9 Nov. 1621, *op. cit.* II, 328.
P. 419, l. 3. SPEDDING VII, 142-144.
P. 420, l. 15. Chamberlain to Carleton, 3 Feb. 1621 and 26 June 1619, *op. cit.* II, 337, 249; D'EWES *Autobiog.* I, 170; *O.P.H.*, V, 312-319.
P. 420, l. 25. Mead to Stuteville, 31 Mar. 1621, in BIRCH *op. cit.* 245.
P. 421, l. 21. W. COBBETT *Parliamentary History of England* (ed. Hansard, 1806) I, 1198; *C.D. 1621*, V, 133; Christopher Brooke, 16 Mar. 1621, *Holland's Diary*, in *ibid.* VI, 70; Chamberlain to Carleton, 17 Feb. 1621, *op. cit.* II, 345.
P. 422, l. 7. D. WILLSON *Privy Councillors* 345. Hakewill's book was called *The Manner how Statutes are enacted in Parliament . . .* (1641), afterwards enlarged as *Modus Tenendi Parliamentum*. *D.N.B.*, XVII, 777, art. "Sir Edwin Sandys."
P. 422, l. 16. T. CARLYLE *Historical Sketches* (ed. 1898) 324; FORSTER *Sir John Eliot* I, 128.
P. 424, l. 3. BISHOP LATIMER *Works* (ed. 1844-1845) I, 250-261.
P. 424, l. 34. AUBREY *Lives* 9.
P. 425, l. 18. BEN JONSON "Lord Bacon's Birthday," 1621, in *The Works of Ben Jonson* (ed. 1875) VIII, 424.
P. 425, l. 35. 7 Mar. 1620, in SPEDDING VII, 192.
P. 426, l. 13. *C.D. 1621*, II, 224.

P. 426, l. 34. *Ibid.* VI, 67, 433; *ibid.* V, 79; Chamberlain to Carleton, 24 Mar. 1621, *op. cit.* II, 356; *C.D. 1621,* III, 98.
P. 427, l. 7. GARDINER IV, 63; *C.D. 1621,* VI, 74.
P. 427, l. 24. Bacon's letters to Buckingham, the Lords, and the King, in SPEDDING VII, 213-216.
P. 428, l. 11. *State Trials* II, 1096; SPEDDING VII, 225-226.
P. 429, l. 9. GARDINER III, 75; LLOYD *State-Worthies* 1028; YONGE *Diary* 37n.; GOODMAN *Court of James I,* I, 36; BACON "Apophthegms," in *Works* (ed. 1861-1864) XIII, 334.
P. 429, l. 26. FULLER *Ch. Hist.* III, 325; SPEDDING VII, 564.
P. 429, l. 31. *Ibid.* 199; GARDINER IV, 53.
P. 430, l. 23. *C.D. 1621,* II, 245; *ibid.* VI, 73; *ibid.* II, 247-248; *State Trials* II, 1096; Chamberlain to Carleton, 24 Mar. 1621, *op. cit.* II 354.
P. 340, l. 38. *State Trials* II, 1101-1102.
P. 431, l. 13. Mead to Stuteville, from Cambridge, 24 Mar. 1621, in BIRCH *op. cit.* 241; Bacon's will and last prayer, in SPEDDING VII, 228-230.
P. 431, l. 21. Bacon's letter to James, his message to Lords answering charges and verifying his confession, and his comment when Seal was removed, in: *ibid.* 241-262; letter to Mead, 4 May 1621, in BIRCH *op. cit.* 252.
P. 433, l. 3. Account of the judgment of Bacon from: SPEDDING VII, 270; *C.D. 1621,* II, 342; *State Trials* II, 1113.
P. 434, l. 5. SIR W. SANDERSON (?) *Aulicus Coquinariae,* in *Secret History* II, 268.
P. 434, l. 32. James Howell to Dr. Pritchard, 6 Jan. 1626, in HOWELL *Fam. Letters* 219; letter to the King, 31 May 1612, in SPEDDING IV, 93; *ibid.* VII, 230-231; FULLER *Ch. Hist.* III, 325.

CHAPTER THIRTY-ONE

P. 435, opening quotation. *Letters of Chamberlain* II, 423.
P. 435, l. 20. HACKET *Scrinia Reserata* 49; *O.P.H.,* V, 380, 390; *C.D. 1621,* V, 95.
P. 436, l. 19. *C.D. 1621,* II, 22; *Parl. Hist.* 1187; CAMPBELL *Chief Justices* I, 368.
P. 437, l. 2. *C.D. 1621,* VI, 251; *Journals of the House of Commons* (ed. 1852) I, 595; *C.D. 1621,* V, 91; II, 313, 202; V, 67, 88; *Alderman Cockayne's Project and the Cloth Trade* (ed. Friis) 407.
P. 437, l. 11. *C.D. 1621,* III, 2.
P. 437, l. 19. *Ibid.* V, 8, 254.
P. 438, l. 7. *Ibid.* VI, 286, 127; II, 307; V, 38, 152; F. THOMPSON *Magna Carta* (1948) 299; *C.D. 1621,* III, 85; V, 184, 42; II, 230.
P. 438, l. 26. *C.D. 1621,* V, 43; Chamberlain to Carleton, 10 Mar. 1621, *Letters of Chamberlain* II, 352.
P. 439, l. 29. *C.D. 1621,* III, 181; figure of new-made peers given as 42 out of 91 in GARDINER *Hist. Eng.* IV, 37; *C.D. 1621,* V, 42; IV, 136; V, 36 and n.; COKE, 10 *Rep.* 113.

P. 440, l. 5. *C.D. 1621*, V, 36; COKE, 9 *Rep.* pref., vi; *C.D. 1621*, V, 36; VI, 381.
P. 440, l. 24. *Ibid.* II, 212, 194; Chamberlain to Carleton, *op. cit.* II, 351.
P. 440, l. 36. 2 May 1621, in *ibid.* 369-370.
P. 441, l. 18. *C.D. 1621*, VI, 116; Mead to Stuteville, 3 Mar. 1621, in BIRCH *Ct. and Times, James*, II, 234; *C.D. 1621*, III, 86.
P. 442, l. 7. *Ibid.* II, 82; Mead to Stuteville, 23 June 1621, in BIRCH *op. cit.* II, 262; *C.D. 1621*, III, 171.
P. 442, l. 16. 1 May 1621, *C.J.*, I, 601-602; *C.D. 1621*, III, 123-128.
P. 442, l. 39. 6 Feb. 1621, *C.S.P.D., 1619-1623*, 221.
P. 443, l. 12. Chamberlain to Carleton, 19 May 1621, *op. cit.* II, 374.
P. 443, l. 34. Account of Clem Coke's quarrel, parliamentary censure and apology in: COKE, 3 *Inst.* 217; *C.D. 1621*, IV, 316; III, 202-203, 215-219, 230; VI, 144-145; II, 395.
P. 444, l. 35. Following account of Parliament's forced adjournment, and arrest and release of Privy Councillor Southampton and Commons Members Sandys and Selden from: *C.D. 1621*, III, 339; V, 189-191, 390; VII, 616; D. WILLSON *Privy Councillors* 46, 154; Chamberlain to Carleton, 4 Aug. 1621, *op. cit.* II, 396.
P. 446, l. 9. Account of Archbishop Abbot's difficulties in: Chamberlain to Carleton, *op. cit.* II, 395; *State Trials* II, 1165-1169; FULLER *Ch. Hist.* III, 322; *D.N.B.* I, 19, art. "George Abbot, Archbishop of Canterbury."
P. 447, l. 27. Chamberlain to Carleton, 17 Nov. and 23 June 1621, *op. cit.* II, 407-408, 383; HACKET *op. cit.* 76.
P. 448, l. 12. *C.D. 1621*, III, 425; V, 211; III, 450; II, 448; 26 Nov. 1621, *C.J.*, I, 646; Wentworth to Wandesford, 17 June 1624, in *Strafford Letters* I, 22; *C.D. 1621*, VI, 220.
P. 448, l. 14. Coke's anti-Spanish speech of 27 Nov. 1621 is a composite of the accounts of several diarists in *C.D. 1621*, II, III, IV, V, VI, unless otherwise indicated.
P. 448, l. 31. FATHER PARSONS (Robert Doleman) *Conference on the Succession to the Crown of England* (ed. 1594) 17.
P. 449, l. 2. Continued discussion of recusants and papists by House of Commons members and declaration of grievances in: *C.D. 1621*, II, 475-492; III, 468-469; *C.J.*, I, 657; *O.P.H.*, V, 490.
P. 450, l. 32. Protest of Gondomar and James's message to House of Commons in: GARDINER IV, 249; *O.P.H.*, V, 492.
P. 450, l. 33. Unless otherwise indicated, continuation of argument in House of Commons, 4-18 Dec. 1621, over grievances, and resulting Protestation from: *C.D. 1621*, II, 509; V, 237-241, 414; VI, 225-240; *C.J.*, I, 659-665; *O.P.H.*, V, 494-506; RUSHWORTH *Collections* I, 53.
P. 451, l. 20. American attitude toward George III: "Appeal to the Six Nations," quoted in C. D. BOWEN *John Adams and the American Revolution* (1951) 537; "Declaration of Independence," 4 July 1776, *Docs. of Amer. Hist.* 101; "Instructions, Town of Malden, Mass. for a Declaration of Independence," 27 May 1776, in *ibid.* 97.
P. 452, l. 19. Chamberlain to Carleton, 15 Dec. 1621, *op. cit.* II, 414.

P. 454, l. 13. Unless otherwise indicated, account of Coke's censure by Privy Council, imprisonment in Tower, and clearing by Court of Wards from: *C.S.P.D., 1619-1623*, 335 and 347; *O.P.H.*, V, 514, 521; C. JAMES *Coke and Descendants* 40-41; letters of Chamberlain to Carleton, 4 Jan. and 1, 13 July 1622, *op. cit.* II, 418-419, 444-445; letters of Mead to Stuteville, 10 and 22 Jan. and 2 Feb. 1622, in BIRCH *Ct. and Times, James*, II, 281, 287-289.

P. 454, l. 8. Gondomar to the Infanta, 22 and 23 Dec. 1622, in GARDINER IV, 266; last sentence from D. WILLSON *op. cit.* 149.

P. 457, l. 18. R. COKE *Detection* I, 122.

P. 457, l. 31. LLOYD *State-Worthies* 826.

CHAPTER THIRTY-TWO

P. 458, l. 24. CLARENDON *Hist. of the Rebellion* I, 21; Sir Henry Wotton, quoted in NICHOLS *Prog. James*, IV, 807; R. COKE *Detection* I, 126.

P. 459, l. 5. Chamberlain to Carleton, 22 Feb. 1623, in *Letters of Ch.*, II, 481.

P. 459, l. 22. 10 Feb. 1623, in *ibid.* 477; NICHOLS IV, 811; Tobie Matthew (son of the Archbishop of York) to Buckingham in Spain, undated, in GOODMAN *Court of James I*, II, 268.

P. 459, l. 37. Chamberlain to Carleton, 26 July 1623, *op. cit.* II, 510; G. M. TREVELYAN *England Under the Stuarts* (1949) 105.

P. 460, l. 13. Mead to Stuteville, 11 July 1623, in BIRCH *Ct. and Times, James*, II, 409; NICHOLS *op. cit.* IV, 874; R. COKE *op. cit.* I, 131; GARDINER *Prince Charles and the Spanish Marriage, 1617-1623* (ed. 1869) II, 352; NICHOLS *op. cit.* IV, 874.

P. 460, l. 27. Chamberlain to Carleton, 11 Oct. 1623, *op. cit.* II, 516; *O.P.H.*, VI, 119; *ibid.* 93.

P. 460, l. 30. Chamberlain to Carleton, 3 Jan. 1624, *op. cit.* II, 536; 17 Jan. 1624, in *ibid.* 540; 31 Jan. 1624, in *ibid.* 543; COKE, 2 *Inst.* 47.

P. 461, l. 30. Account of the auspicious opening of 1624 Parliament and background of monopoly bill from: *O.P.H.*, VI, 28-35; GARDINER *Hist. of Eng.* V, 188; *C.J.*, I, 538-539, 549, 690; *C.D. 1621*, II, 167-168 (*Anon. Diary*); IV, 160 (*Pym's Diary*); V, 272-290 (*Smyth's Diary*); F. W. MAITLAND *Constitutional History of England* (1926) 261.

P. 462, l. 36. CLARENDON *op. cit.* I, 28; *O.P.H.*, VI, 193-195; JOHNSON *Life of Coke* II, 139, quoting Petyt's *Miscellanea Parliamentaria.*

P. 463, l. 4. *O.P.H.*, VI, 118, 92, 378.

P. 463, l. 21. Chamberlain to Carleton, 21 Feb. and 21 Aug. 1624, and 23 Apr. 1625, *op. cit.* II, 545, 578, 613.

P. 463, l. 34. Chamberlain to Carleton, 4 Dec. 1624, in *ibid.* 588.

P. 463, l. 37. Citations about King's illness, death and funeral from: GARDINER *Hist. Eng.* V, 313; NICHOLS *op. cit.* IV, 1032n.; D'EWES *Autobiog.*, I, 264; Sir W. Neve to Sir T. Holland, 6 Apr. 1625, in NICHOLS *op. cit.* IV, 1037n.; WELDON in *Secret Hist.* II, 11-12.

P. 465, l. 28. Account of Charles I, his Queen and his court from: W.

LILLY *Life and Death of Charles I* (ed. 1774) 186; *D.N.B.*, IV, 71, art. "Charles I"; D'EWES *op. cit.* I, 166; *Encycl. Brit.* V, 912, art. "Charles I"; *O.P.H.*, VIII, 241; letters of Mead to Stuteville, 8 Oct. and 17 Dec. 1625, 11 Nov. 1626, 3 Feb. 1627, in BIRCH *Ct. and Times, Charles I* (ed. Wms., 1848) I, 52, 68, 169, 191; letters of Dr. Meddus to Mead, 17 June 1626, in *ibid.* 30-31; Chamberlain to Carleton, 25 June 1625, *op. cit.* II, 625.

P. 467, l. 16. S. Bradwell *A Watch Man for the Pest* (1625) 5, as quoted in WILSON *The Plague in Shakespeare's London* 133.

P. 468, l. 7. FORSTER *Sir John Eliot* I, 221-227; Chamberlain to Carleton, 6 May 1625, *op. cit.* II, 615.

P. 468, l. 20. *O.P.H.*, VI, 351-352.

P. 469, l. 27. Coke's speech of 5 Aug. 1625 is taken from: GARDINER *Commons Debates in 1625* (ed. 1873) 85-87; FORSTER *op. cit.* I, 373-380; *C.J.*, I, 811.

P. 470, l. 11. Citations from debate over matters of finance, royal favorites and commerce 5 Aug. until dissolution of Parliament in: FORSTER *op. cit.* I, 379-409 *passim;* GARDINER *op. cit.* V, 110-115; *O.P.H.*, VI, 404.

CHAPTER THIRTY-THREE

P. 472, l. 2. J. WHITELOCKE *Memorials of the English Affairs* 7, as quoted in TANNER *English Parliamentary Conflicts* (1947) 59.

P. 472, footnote. RUSHWORTH *Collections* I, 197.

P. 473, l. 2. Henry Manners to Sir G. Manners, June 1625, in *Rutland Papers* (H.M.C. 1888) I, 478.

P. 473, l. 17. CHEYNEY *Hist. Eng.* II, 345.

P. 473, l. 33. Unless otherwise indicated, the account of the attempted impeachment of Buckingham in the House of Commons in: *C.J.*, I, 853-857; *O.P.H.*, VI, 425-467 and VII, 1-20; RUSHWORTH I, 218-223, 304-353, 375, 405.

P. 475, l. 20. Meddus to Mead, 15 June 1626, in BIRCH *Court and Times, Charles*, I, 112.

P. 476, l. 7. TREVELYAN *Eng. Under Stuarts* 112, 239.

P. 477, l. 15. CLARENDON *Hist. of Rebellion* I, 6; Mead to Stuteville, 22 July 1626, in BIRCH *op. cit.* I, 130-131.

P. 477, l. 31. Letter to Mead, 31 May 1622, in BIRCH *Ct. and Times, James*, II, 312; FULLER *Ch. Hist.* III, 395.

P. 478, l. 14. YONGE *Diary* 105.

P. 478, l. 35. Unless otherwise indicated, the account of the trial of the Five Knights and the ensuing debates on habeas corpus from: *State Trials* III, 1-169 *passim; O.P.H.*, VI and VII *passim;* F. RELF *The Petition of Right* (1917); E. NICHOLAS *Notes* (MS. ed., L. Sumners); RUSHWORTH I, 304-539 *passim;* GARDINER *Hist. Eng.* VI, 261; letters from Beaulieu and Mead, to Mead, Puckering or Stuteville, of 16, 23, 28, 30 Nov. 1627 and 19, 28 April 1628, in BIRCH *Ct. and Times, Charles*, I,

285-347 *passim;* W. LILLY *Life and Times* (ed. 1774) 196 and TANNER *Eng. Const. Conflicts* 70.

P. 480, l. 22. See *Coll. Topogr.* 120; Mead to Stuteville, Pory to Mead, 8 and 21 Mar. 1628, in BIRCH *op. cit.* I, 327, 331; GARDINER VI, 230; RUSHWORTH I, 476-477 for citations about elections and opening of Parliament by Charles.

P. 481, l. 37. Sir Edward Conway, Jr. to Sir D. Carleton, 18 Apr. 1624, in *C.S.P.D., 1623-1625,* 216.

P. 485, l. 35. E. JENKS "The Story of Habeas Corpus" in *Law Quarterly Review* XVIII, 69.

P. 486, l. 12. See HOLDSWORTH *History of Eng. Law* V, app., 495-496 for the judges' opinion of 1591 concerning imprisonment by order of Privy Council.

P. 486, l. 35. This speech by Coke is taken from: BUTTERFIELD *The Englishman and his History* (1944) 61; *State Trials* III, 82; and NICHOLAS *Notes* 18-19.

P. 490, l. 25. Unless otherwise indicated, the account of the continued debates on liberty of the subject preceding Charles's final acceptance of the Petition of Right in this chapter is from: *State Trials* III, 189-194; *O.P.H.*, VIII, 94-202 *passim;* RELF *op. cit.;* NICHOLAS *op. cit.;* RUSHWORTH I, 549-613 *passim.*

P. 491, l. 25. THOMPSON *Magna Carta* 311; GARDINER IV, 267.

P. 496, l. 25. GARDINER VI, 284.

P. 496, l. 39. Mead to Stuteville, 3 May 1628, in BIRCH *Ct. and Times, Chas.*, I, 350-351.

P. 500, l. 10. Citations and account of this scene from letter of Sir Thomas Allured, a Yorkshire Burgess, to Mr. Chamberlain of the Court of Wards, 6 June 1628, in RUSHWORTH I, 609-610; and letter of Mead to Stuteville, 15 June 1628, in BIRCH *op. cit.* 359-360.

P. 502, l. 10. Allured to Chamberlain, RUSHWORTH *loc. cit.*

P. 502, l. 17. Mead to Stuteville, 15 June 1628, BIRCH *loc. cit.*

P. 502, l. 27. Sir Francis Nethersole to Elizabeth, Queen of Bohemia, describing "this aguish Parliament," 7 June 1628, in *C.S.P.D., 1628-1629,* 153.

P. 503, l. 28. Sec. Conway to Sec. Sir John Coke, 9 June 1628, in *ibid.* 156.

P. 504, l. 2. Nethersole to Queen of Bohemia, *loc. cit.;* Mead to Stuteville, *loc. cit.*

CHAPTER THIRTY-FOUR

P. 505, l. 20. SIR W. BLACKSTONE *Commentaries on the Laws of England* (ed. 1791) I, 72.

P. 506, l. 15. Coke to Cecil, 1604, in *Cal. Salisbury MSS.* XVI, 236; COKE, 2 *Rep.* pref., viii; 1 *Rep.* pref., i-ii, iv.

P. 506, l. 35. 9 *Rep.* pref., xv; 5 *Rep.* pref., iii; 9 *Rep.* pref., v; 3 *Rep.* pref., xxxii(b)-xxxiii(a); 10 *Rep.* pref., ii.

P. 507, l. 9. *The Reports of Sir Edward Coke, Knt., in Verse* (ed. 1742) Pt. V, Case I; Pt. VII, Case I; Pt. XI, Case XX.
P. 507, l. 20. SPEDDING *Letters and Life* VI, 65.
P. 508, l. 15. COKE *Co. Litt.* pref., xl.
P. 509, l. 4. *Ibid.* 142a.
P. 510, l. 14. *Ibid.* pref., xxxviii.
P. 510, l. 29. *Ibid.* xl-xli; 3 *Inst.*, proeme, iii.
P. 511, l. 11. *Co. Litt.* pref., xlii; *ibid.*, epilogue, 395a; *ibid.* pref., xliii.
P. 511, l. 27. *Ibid.* 9a; *ibid.* pref., xxxix; *ibid.* 134a; *ibid.* 135b.
P. 512, l. 2. *Ibid.* 10b, 11a.
P. 512, l. 15. *Ibid.* 110a; 3 *Rep.* pref., ix.
P. 512, l. 24. *Co. Litt.* 177a.
P. 512, footnote. LAMBARDE *Archion* 236.
P. 513, l. 4. *Ibid.* 6a; *ibid.* epilogue, 395a.
P. 513, l. 23. R. NORTH *Lives of the Norths* (ed. 1826) I, 21n.; Chief Justice Reeves to his nephew, in *Coll. Jurid.* I, 79-81; Twiss, *Life of Lord Eldon,* as quoted in WARREN *History of the Harvard Law School* (1908) I, 139-140.
P. 514, l. 12. Daniel Webster, *Autobiography* (1829); letter of Judge Story to his son, 9 Feb. 1841; William Wirt, *Life of Patrick Henry;* all as quoted in *ibid.* 132-152 *passim.*
P. 514, l. 25. JOHN ADAMS *Diary,* in *Life and Works* (ed. 1850) II, 46-47; *ibid.* 103-104.
P. 514, l. 37. John Q. Adams *Diary,* quoted in WARREN *op. cit.* 141; Jefferson, quoted in *ibid.* 139.
P. 515, l. 8. T. HOBBES, "Dialogue between a Philosopher and a Student of the Common Laws of England," in *The English Works* (ed. 1840) VI, 62.
P. 515, l. 25. CAMPBELL *Chief Justices* I, 396; HOLDSWORTH *Some Makers of English Law* (1938) 125.
P. 515, l. 31. SIR J. F. STEPHEN *History of the Criminal Law of England* (1883) II, 205.
P. 515, l. 35. HOLDSWORTH *op. cit.* 132.
P. 516, l. 13. COKE *Co. Litt.* pref., xxxiii; 3 *Inst.* proeme, ii.
P. 516, l. 28. Henry, Earl of Holland to Sec. Dorchester, 24 Jan. 1631, in *C.S.P.D., 1629-1631,* 490.
P. 517, l. 5. COKE, 2 *Inst.* 45, 46.
P. 517, l. 22. *Ibid.* 56, 47, 530, 532, 617a.
P. 518, l. 6. Sir John Coke, son of Sec. Coke, to his father, 15 Dec. 1640, in *Cowper Papers* II (H.M.C. 1888) 266, 270; R. COKE *Detection* I, 342; E. COKE, 3 *Inst.* 14 and epilogue.
P. 518, l. 27. *Ibid.* 218, 226, 197.
P. 518, l. 39. *Ibid.* 96.
P. 519, l. 16. *Ibid.* 110, 48a-50, 11a, 231a.
P. 519, l. 36. *Ibid.* 200a, 198a, 224, 204-208.
P. 520, l. 13. *Ibid.* 224-225, 226; 4 *Inst.* 323, 32, 57; 3 *Inst.* 4, 577.
P. 520, l. 27. 4 *Inst.* 36, 11, 34.

P. 521, l. 10. *Ibid.* epilogue, 109; 2 *Inst.* 21a; 1 *Rep.* pref., vii; 3 *Inst.* 2a.
P. 521, l. 18. RUSHWORTH *Collections* I, 626.
P. 521, l. 24. Account of general hostility toward the Duke and his assassination, and Felton's execution from: *D.N.B.*, XX, art. "George Villiers"; RUSHWORTH I, 618; letters of Mead to Stuteville (29 June, 13 and 19 Sept. 1628) in BIRCH *Ct. and Times, Chas.*, I, 368, 394, 401; letters of Mead to Stuteville (19, 20 and 27 Sept. 1628) in ELLIS *Orig. Letters* III (1st series) 261-267.
P. 522, l. 30. Account of brief Parliament of 1629 from: *C.J.*, I, 921; *Commons Debates for 1629* (ed. Notestein and Relf, 1921) 58, 170, 191; RUSHWORTH II, 3.
P. 523, l. 5. Remaining Coke citations from COKE, 4 *Inst.* epilogue.

CHAPTER THIRTY-FIVE

P. 526, l. 7. Descriptions of Stoke House from: Chamberlain to Carleton, 9 Aug. 1617 and 11 Oct. 1623, in *Letters of Ch.*, II, 90-91, 515; C. JAMES *Coke and Descendants* 310, 320-322; WHITELOCKE *Lib. Fam.* 50.
P. 527, l. 33. Foss *Judges of England* VI, 127.
P. 528, l. 14. Chamberlain to Carleton, 8 Mar. 1623, *op. cit.* II, 484.
P. 528, l. 29. L'Estrange, in *Anecdotes and Traditions* (ed. Thoms, 1839) 61.
P. 529, l. 4. C. JAMES *op. cit.* 123.
P. 529, l. 11. *Ibid.* 95.
P. 529, l. 19. J. MILTON *Poetical Works* (ed. 1911) 552.
P. 529, l. 36. Account of difficulties and two trials of Frances Coke from: A. WILSON in *Complete Hist. of Eng.* II, 727; letters of Chamberlain to Carleton, 8 June 1622, 12 and 26 Feb. 1625, *op. cit.* II, 43, 594, 601; NORSWORTHY *Lady* 187 and app. III, 281; letters of Lord Keeper Williams to the Duke, 11 and 13 Mar. 1624, in *Cabala Sine Scrinia Sacra* (ed. 1663) I, 306-307; letter to Mead, 30 Nov. 1627, in BIRCH *Ct. and Times, Chas.*, I, 296.
P. 532, l. 4. Chamberlain to Carleton, 26 Feb. 1625, *op. cit.* II, 601.
P. 532, l. 14. Henry, Earl of Holland to Lord Dorchester, 24 Jan. 1631, in *C.S.P.D., 1629-1631*, 490.
P. 532, l. 16. Coke's will, dated 10 Nov. 1623, in *C.S.P.D., 1623-1625*, 119.
P. 532, l. 25. Mead to Stuteville, 30 Jan. 1631, in ELLIS *Orig. Letters* (2d series) III, 263.
P. 532, l. 33. C. JAMES *op. cit.* 46. The book is at Holkham.
P. 533, l. 5. COKE, *Vade Mecum*, in *Coll. Topogr.* VI, 120.
P. 533, l. 13. Mr. Garrard to Sir T. Wentworth, 20 June 1634, in *Strafford Letters* I, 265-266.
P. 533, l. 29. "The Foundation of Ye Faith of Sir Edward Coke, all written with his Owne hands in the extremity of his last sickness," June 1634, quoted in C. JAMES *op. cit.* 47-48.
P. 534, l. 1. Notes preceding Coke's *Vade Mecum* in *Coll. Topogr.* VI, 108; R. COKE *Detection* I, 300.

P. 534, l. 20. JOHNSON *Life of Coke* II, 323-328.
P. 534, l. 30. LODGE *Life of Sir Julius Caesar, Knt.* (ed. 1827) 32.
P. 534, l. 38. MACKINNON *Inner Temple Papers* 63-64.
P. 536, l. 39. CAMDEN *Britannia* 351; SPELMAN *Reliquiae*, quoted in CAMPBELL *Chief Justices* I, 404; LODGE *op. cit.* 33; FULLER *Worthies* II, 452.

INDEX

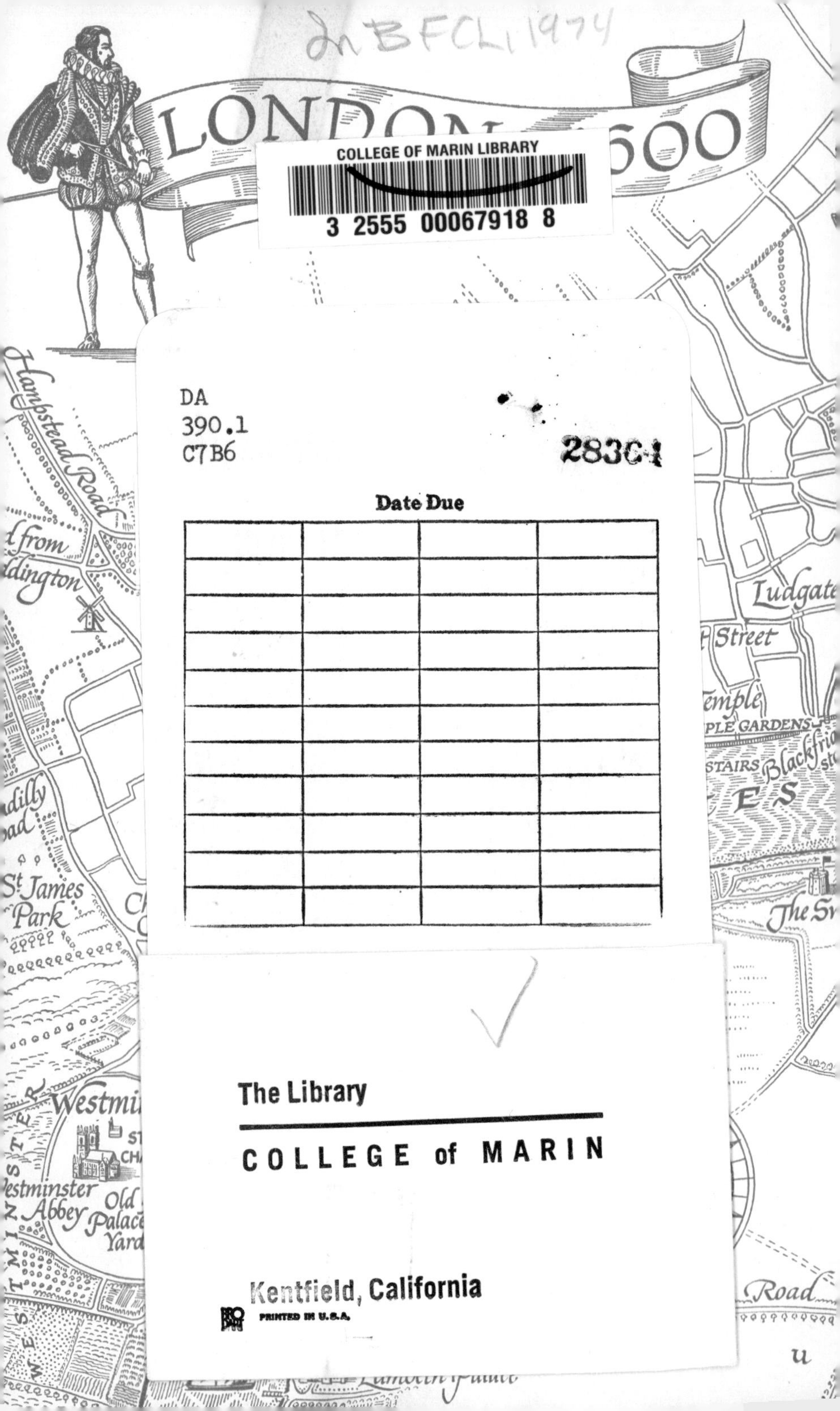
LONDON 1600
Hampstead Road
from
Paddington
Ludgate
Street
Temple
PLE GARDENS
STAIRS
Blackfri
Piccadilly
Road
St. James
Park
Westminster Abbey
Old Palace Yard
WESTMINSTER
The Strand
Road
Lambeth Palace

